MILITARY STRATEGY

PRINCIPLES, PRACTICES, AND HISTORICAL PERSPECTIVES

Also by John M. Collins

Military Geography: For Professionals and the Public

Special Operations Forces

America's Small Wars

Military Space Forces

Green Berets, SEALs, and Spetsnaz

U.S.-Soviet Military Balance, 1980–1985

U.S. Defense Planning: A Critique

U.S.-Soviet Military Balance, 1960–1980

American and Soviet Military Trends

Imbalance of Power (with Anthony Cordesman)

Grand Strategy: Principles and Practices

MILITARY STRATEGY

PRINCIPLES, PRACTICES, AND HISTORICAL PERSPECTIVES

John M. Collins

With a Foreword by
General Robert C. Kingston, USA (Ret.)

Potomac Books, Inc.
Washington, D.C.

Maps by Jay Karamales

Library of Congress Cataloging-in-Publication Data
Collins, John M., 1921–
    Military Strategy: Principles, Practices, and Historical Perspectives / John M. Collins; with a foreword by Robert C. Kingston.—1st ed.
        p. cm.
Includes Index
ISBN 978-1-57488-430-2
1. Strategy. I. Title.
U162.c643 2002
335'.03—dc21

Printed in the United States of America on acid-free paper that meets the American National Standards Institute Z39–48 Standard.

Potomac Books, Inc.
22841 Quicksilver Drive
Dulles, Virginia 20166

First Edition

10 9 8 7 6 5 4 3

To

Successive Commandants of the National War College

1968–73

Lieutenant General John E. Kelly, United States Army,
who changed all my life goals as I neared age fifty,
when he made me Director of Military Strategy Studies,

and

Lieutenant General John B. McPherson, United States Air Force,
who thereafter directed me to organize and serve as
Chief of a politico-military Strategic Research Group.

Contents

List of Figures   x

List of Tables   x

List of Maps   xi

Foreword   xiii

Acknowledgments   xv

Prospectus   1

1. **Overview**   3
   Strategic Hierarchy   3
   Strategic Processes   5
   Strategic Summation   8

Part I
The Framework of Military Strategy

2. **National Security Interests**   13
   Basic Attributes   13
   Universally Valuable Interests   14
   Variably Valuable Interests   16
   Conflicts of Interest   18
   Key Points   18

3. **Foreign and Domestic Threats**   21
   The Conflict Spectrum   21
   Strategic Guidance   22
   Enemy Military Power   23
   Intelligence Estimates   25
   Net Assessments   28
   Threat Assessments   30
   Key Points   31

4. **Basic Security Objectives**   35
   National Security Objectives   35
   National Military Aims   36
   Military Roles and Missions   39
   Strategic Centers of Gravity   41
   Key Points   44

5. **The Primacy of Policy**   47
   Basic Policy Attributes   47
   Civil-Military Policies   49
   Foreign vs. Domestic Policies   51
   Military vs. Nonmilitary Power   52
   Strategic Bead-Stringing   53
   Key Points   53

Part II
Fundamentals of Military Strategy

6. **Strategic Starting Points**   59
   Strategic Building Blocks   59
   Strategic Schools of Thought   61
   Elemental Alternatives   62
   Politico-Military Assumptions   64
   Strategic Paths and Pitfalls   65
   Key Points   67

7. **Fundamentals of Deterrence**   71
   The Dynamics of Deterrence   71
   Causes of Conflict   72
   Principles of Deterrence   73
   Deterrent Theories and Concepts   75
   Key Points   77

8. **War-Fighting Fundamentals**   81
   Principles of War   81
   Premier War-Fighting Policies   85
   War-Fighting Theories and Concepts   88
   Conflict Termination   91
   Key Points   93

9. **Fundamentals of Military Preparedness**   99
   Readiness vs. Sustainability   99
   Principles of Preparedness   99

CONTENTS

Present Preparedness   102
Future Preparedness   106
Key Points   106

10. **Fundamentals of Arms Control**   109
Arms Control Aims   109
Quantitative Restrictions   109
Qualitative Limitations   113
Negotiating Techniques   115
Compliance Problems   116
Key Points   117

Part III
Specialized Military Strategies

11. **Counterproliferation Strategies**   123
Causes of Proliferation   123
Intelligence Indicators   126
Counterproliferation   127
Current Outlook   130
Key Points   130

12. **Nuclear Warfare Strategies**   133
The Nature of Nuclear Warfare   133
Nuclear Arms Control   135
Nuclear Deterrent Strategies   136
Nuclear War-Fighting Strategies   140
Nuclear War Termination Strategies   142
Key Points   143

13. **Biological and Chemical Warfare Strategies**   145
Biological and Chemical Weapons   145
Biological and Chemical Arms Control   147
Biological Warfare Strategies   148
Chemical Warfare Strategies   149
Needs for Creative Concepts   151
Key Points   151

14. **Traditional Forces and Strategies**   155
Complementary Force Contributions   155
Comparative Force Postures   156

Traditional Deterrence   157
Traditional War Fighting   159
Nuclear Warfare Nexus   161
Traditional Warfare Fulcrum   162
Key Points   162

15. **Insurgency Strategies**   167
The Nature of Insurgencies   167
Revolutionary Warfare   168
Counterrevolutions   173
Resistance Movements   174
Traditional Warfare Nexus   175
Key Points   177

16. **Counterinsurgency Strategies**   181
The Nature of Counterinsurgency   181
Anti-Underground Strategies   182
Counterguerrilla Strategies   186
Pacification Programs   189
Prescriptions for Success   190
Key Points   190

17. **Sociopolitical Terrorism**   193
The Nature of Sociopolitical Terrorism   193
Atypical Terrorists   193
Typical Terrorist Organizations   194
Terrorist Tools   194
Terrorist Targets and Tactics   196
Sponsorship and Support   200
Key Points   200

18. **Counterterrorism Strategies**   205
The Nature of Counterterrorism   205
Participants and Control   205
Overarching Issues   206
Deterrent Dilemmas   207
Defensive Counterterrorism   208
Offensive Counterterrorism   211
Democratic Constraints   213
Key Points   215

19. **Nonlethal Warfare Strategies** 219

   The Nature of Nonlethal Warfare   219

   Political Warfare   220

   Economic Warfare   222

   Technological Warfare   224

   Psychological Warfare   227

   Cybernetic Warfare   230

   Key Points   232

20. **Coalition Warfare Strategies**   237

   Collective Security Incentives   237

   Collective Security Choices   238

   Compatibility Prospects   239

   Formal and Informal Coalitions   240

   Command and Control   242

   Respective Contributions   243

   Requirements for Review   244

   Key Points   245

Part IV
Keys to Strategic Superiority

21. **Strategic Trailblazers**   251

   Illustrative Role Models   251

   Coveted Characteristics   253

   Composite Requirements   254

   Key Points   254

22. **Strategic Stepping-Stones**   257

   Creative Environments   257

   Strategic Education   258

   Strategic Research   260

   Key Points   263

Part V
Applied Strategies

23. **Balkan Tar-Babies**   267

   Politico-Military Backdrop   267

   Peacekeeping in Bosnia   268

   Peacemaking in Kosovo   275

   Strategic Critiques   282

   Intervention Checklist   285

   Key Points   287

24. **Final Reflections**   291

Appendix A. Strategic Terminology   293

Appendix B. Abbreviations   309

Appendix C. A Bookshelf for Military Strategists   311

Index   319

About the Author   333

Figures

1. Six-Step Strategic Planning Process 6
2. The Conflict Spectrum 22
3. Deterrent Effects of Homeland Defense 137
4. Cellular Underground Organizations 171
5. Sample Clearinghouse Advertisement 262

Tables

1. Strategic and Tactical Hierarchy 4
2. Typical Security Interests 14
3. Typical Elements of Military Power 23
4. Typical Statistical Summaries 24
5. Net Assessment Types and Topics 29
6. National Security Interests and Complementary Objectives 36
7. National Security Objectives and Basic Military Aims 37
8. Typical Military Functions 40
9. Polarized Politico-Military Policy Options 48
10. Strategic Building Blocks 60
11. Deterrent Techniques Connected to Causes of Conflict 76
12. Typical War-Fighting Options 88
13. Conflict Termination Related to Postwar Prospects 92
14. NBC Weapon Possession and Programs 124
15. Factors That Affect Nuclear Weapon Effectiveness 134
16. Biological Warfare Agents 146
17. Chemical Warfare Agents 147
18. Characteristics of Classical Insurgency 168
19. Typical Resistance Movements in the Twentieth Century 175
20. Counterinsurgencies Compared with Traditional Conflicts 182
21. Counterinsurgencies Compared with Classical Insurgencies 183
22. Typical PSYWAR Techniques 229
23. Diversified Coalition Characteristics 237
24. Comparative Purposes in Bosnia 271
25. Comparative Purposes in Kosovo 278

Maps

1. The Former Yugoslavia and Neighboring Countries   268
2. Bosnia and Herzegovina   270
3. Bosnian Boundaries Prescribed by the Dayton Peace Agreement, 1995   274
4. IFOR-SFOR Areas of Responsibility   276
5. Kosovo and Vicinity   277
6. KFOR Areas of Responsibility   281

Foreword

Stars fell on the National War College Class of 1969, of which I was a member; John Collins was my faculty adviser. Five out of seventy-four lieutenant colonels and naval commanders eventually reached four-star rank. Two became combatant commanders in chief, another was SHAPE's Chief of Staff, then Deputy Commander. Four military students and one faculty member became lieutenant generals or vice admirals. Nearly twenty more graduates wore one or two stars before they retired.

All were experienced tacticians and most knew a lot about operational art in 1968, but military strategy formulation generally was a foreign field. The National War College unfortunately did little to correct that deficiency, despite a mission statement that promised to prepare students "for the exercise of joint and combined high-level policy, command and staff functions and for the planning of national strategy." The brief strategy course lacked a text. The only book that every student was obligated to read from cover to cover was Bernard Brodie's 1959 treatise, *Strategy in the Missile Age,* which investigated a small sliver of the conflict spectrum. Supplemental readings barely scratched the surface of other important subjects, and few stressed fundamentals.

What the Class of 1969 needed most was a comprehensive textbook like *Military Strategy.* The chapter on coalition warfare strategies would have helped me immensely before I took charge of the Rapid Deployment Joint Task Force in 1981 and subsequently became the first Commander in Chief of U.S. Central Command, which included nineteen Southwest Asian and Northeast African countries within its Area of Responsibility. Distinctions between net assessments and threat assessments, the value of strategic centers of gravity, tradeoffs between military and nonmilitary power, and principles of military preparedness are just a few of the many topics that could have provided everybody with a better education than we actually received. I particularly like the intervention checklist that concludes Chapter 23. Armed with such insights, I could have participated more effectively in the JCS "tank" during debates about strategic courses of action and explained complex matters more easily in testimony before Congress.

This compendium, which I read in draft, reached print three decades too late to benefit the National War College Class of 1969, but twenty-first century students of military strategy in the United States and abroad should benefit immensely from the vast array of intellectual tools between its covers. Politico-military problem solvers who use the following pages as litmus papers to test options before they reach decisions should make fewer strategic mistakes than predecessors who, by and large, lacked ready references for such purposes.

General Robert C. Kingston
United States Army (Retired)

Acknowledgments

The thirty-two-year gestation of this document began in 1969, when Lieutenant General John E. Kelly, then-Commandant of the National War College (NWC), told me, "You are now Director of Military Strategy Studies." My response was, "Sir, I can't even spell strategy," to which he replied, "Neither can anyone else. Go make a name for yourself."

The 1969 NWC military strategy syllabus was my first stab, followed by a primer entitled *Strategy for Beginners,* which received nine rejection slips before the Naval Institute Press published it in 1973 as *Grand Strategy: Principles and Practices.* That book has been out of print for more than two decades but, with the publisher's permission, I have clipped, reshuffled, and repasted many snippets herein, along with extracts from some of my other writings that first saw light as Congressional Research Service (CRS) issue briefs and reports.

My appreciation for military strategy has improved somewhat since 1973, but not nearly enough to write a book on that subject without professional help from assorted authorities who could, without compassion, critique the table of contents and every draft chapter before publication. I therefore sought and received invaluable insights from many knowledgeable individuals whose relevant experience ranged from no less than fifteen to more than thirty years. Each received the following guidance: "Please tell me what is wrong, what you would add, and what you would subtract. Did you easily find your way from Point A to Points B, C, and D, or does the sequence require adjustment? Is the writing clear? Are there too many endnotes or not enough? Can you recommend better sources to cite? Be brutally frank, because I'd rather hear bad news *before* rather than *after* publication."

Correspondence from five four-star U.S. officers expressed strong support for the project at its onset in the summer of 1998: General Henry H. Shelton, Chairman of the Joint Chiefs of Staff; General Dennis J. Reimer, Army Chief of Staff; Admiral Jay L. Johnson, Chief of Naval Operations; General Michael E. Ryan, Air Force Chief of Staff; and General Charles C. Krulak, Commandant of the Marine Corps. Each designated a contact to represent his interests.

Nine highly valued advisors dissected the entire first draft, or most of it, page-by-page. Colonel Jim Kurtz, a politico-military purist who formerly directed the J-5 Policy Division for the Joint Chiefs of Staff, kept me honest every foot of the way. So did Army Lieutenant General Dick Trefry and Air Force Brigadier General Walter Jajko, along with Army Colonels Scot Crerar, Bob Killebrew, Glenn Harned, and Ed Bruner, all of whom possess extensive high-level joint service policy, plans, and operational experience that they have embellished since retirement. Steve Bowman and Bob Goldich specialize in foreign affairs and national defense at CRS. Their individual and collective input, which covered the full spectrum of strategic subjects in depth, improved the final product by several orders of magnitude.

General Wayne Downing, a savvy past Commander in Chief of U.S. Special Operations Command (USSOCOM), was my sounding board concerning counterterrorism and military infrastructure protection. Lieutenant General Bill Yarborough, who sold President John F. Kennedy on special operations in 1961, was a peerless source of information about insurgencies, counterinsurgencies, and psychological warfare. Army Colonels Ed Phillips and "Taffy" Carlin, with Air Force Colonel Greg Tribon, dissected such topics for USSOCOM. Colonel Jim Kraus, who accumulated a wealth of first-hand knowledge about military operations in Bosnia and Kosovo, sanded the Tar-Baby case study.

I shamelessly solicited input from former colleagues at CRS, who furnished otherwise unobtainable facts and invaluable advice, as countless endnotes indicate: Richard Best, intelligence; Steve Bowman, biological and chemical warfare, Bosnia and Kosovo; Marjorie Browne, United Nations; Ray Copson and Carl Ek, Africa; Steve Daggett, military budgets; Zack Davis and Bob Shuey, proliferation and counterproliferation; Karen Donfried, Ireland; Charlie Doyle, *Posse Comitatus;* Susan Fletcher, Kyoto Treaty; Bob Goldich, military manpower; Stuart Goldman, USSR and Russia; Paul Gallis, Western Europe; Dick Grimmett, military assistance; Steve Hildreth, national and theater missile defense; Shirley Kan, China; Julie Kim and Steve Woehrel, Bosnia and Kosovo; Jon Medalia and Amy Woof, strategic nuclear topics; Lois McHugh, humanitarian matters; Clyde Mark and Al Prados, Middle East; Larry Niksch, East Asia; Rinn Sup Shinn, Korea; Nina Serafino, counterinsurgency; Stan Sloan, NATO; Marsha Smith, space; and Maureen Taft-Morales, Latin America. Dianne Rennack, my junior partner in a previous incarnation, furnished information about economic sanctions and was a multipurpose fact finder par excellence.

Lieutenant General Richard Chilcoat, in his capacity as President of National Defense University (NDU), conferred on me the honorary title of Distinguished Visiting Research Fellow and provided a pass with which to invade the premises during non-duty hours. The NDU Library staff provided flawless assistance, as they previously did when I was struggling to write *Military Geography.*

Major General Tom Wilkerson (USMC, Ret.) gave great aid and comfort while I sought a publisher. Don McKeon, my long-term contact at Brassey's, convinced his bosses that the product was worthwhile. Senior Assistant Editor Don Jacobs gave the draft a keen going over, then passed it to Julie Wrinn, who managed copyediting, typesetting, proofreading, printing, and binding. Jane Graf and Allyson Bolin took the book to market. I am eternally grateful to Brassey's entire crew, which was a pleasure to work with.

Finally, if it were within my power, I would award my bride Swift the world's highest decoration, because she has kept the Collins family afloat for more than fifty years while I stared at blank sheets of paper wondering what words to write. I salute her, along with all the rest.

JOHN M. COLLINS
Distinguished Visiting Research Fellow
National Defense University

Prospectus

*It doesn't make any difference how well chickens
are cooked if they aren't worth cooking to begin with.*

Frank Perdue
Television Ad
Late 1980s

Major General Samuel Koster, while serving as Superintendent of the United States Military Academy at West Point in 1970, was asked why, after nearly 200 years of nationhood, U.S. Armed Services seldom sired strategic thinkers comparable to Prussian Major General Carl von Clausewitz, whose intellectual breadth and depth enabled him to write his incomparable tome entitled *On War* early in the nineteenth century.[1] "We're more interested in the 'doer' than the thinker" was that two-star educator's reply.[2]

Armed forces ashore, aloft, and afloat, however, seldom do as well as they should unless skilled strategists think. Men of action who are organized and trained to employ technologically superlative weapon systems under adverse conditions may win every battle but nonetheless lose wars unless the overarching schemes they support are sound. That happened to U.S. Armed Forces in Vietnam (1965–73) where, to paraphrase Frank Perdue, "the tactical chickens they cooked perfectly weren't worth cooking from strategic standpoints." Similar shortcomings have been commonplace around the world throughout recorded history.

Present strategists and their successors thus might benefit from a comprehensive document that consolidates, synthesizes, and discusses inputs, options, and outputs, then provides historical perspectives. This smörgåsbord of interrelated topics accordingly seeks to fulfill a threefold purpose:

- To provide a textbook for use by students of military strategy
- To provide a handbook for use by politico-military policy-makers, strategists, and planners
- To enhance public appreciation of military strategy

Military Strategy, unlike its companion piece *Military Geography,*[3] deals primarily with arguable theses, antitheses, and syntheses rather than physical science and facts. Part I focuses on national security interests, threats, objectives, and policies that form the framework of military strategy. Part II concentrates on strategic building blocks, schools of thought, theories, concepts, principles, and other fundamentals. Part III spotlights assorted military strategies across the conflict spectrum from warfare with weapons of mass destruction to nonlethal combat. Part IV suggests ways to develop talented individuals and produce a ceaseless supply of innovative ideas with which to solve strategic problems. Part V puts principles into practice with a case study that critiques competing strategies in Bosnia-Herzegovina and Kosovo. Each chapter terminates with key points, which final reflections reinforce. Historical precedents threaded throughout illuminate options that worked well or poorly in the past, together with reasons why. Appendix C, a bookshelf for military strategists, recommends supplemental readings.

The resultant compendium could have been entitled *Politico-Military Strategy,* because foreign and domestic policies strongly influence or decisively shape military strategies in principle and practice from start to finish. Experience amassed over several millennia suggests that "school solutions" appropriate for every occasion are nearly nonexistent. Presentations therefore encapsulate many options but champion none. Each reader must maintain an open mind and ascertain for himself or herself what makes sense in given situations.

* * * * * * * * * *

This treatise already had been typeset when transnational terrorists toppled both towers of the World Trade Center in Manhattan and collapsed part of the Pentagon on September 11, 2001, with devastating political, military, economic, and psychological effects around the world as well as within the United States, where perpetrators succeeded beyond their wildest dreams:

- Round-the-clock television and radio broadcasts, coupled with banner headlines in all major newspapers and periodicals, trumpeted terrorist "triumphs"
- More dead littered landscapes than at Antietam after the bloodiest one-day battle of the U.S. Civil War
- The Dow Jones Industrial Average plummeted 685 points when the U.S. Stock Exchange reopened on September 17, 2001
- Major U.S. airlines and commercial aircraft industries faced bankruptcy unless they received enormous bailouts

- Countless wage earners in the aircraft business alone lost jobs or faced extensive layoffs
- Dire straits afflicted hotels, restaurants, shops, and other activities that depend on tourist trade
- Anti-Islamic "hate crimes" that assailed innocent Muslims and their mosques helped terrorist recruiters make a case for holy war (Jihad)
- President George W. Bush, in response, sought to put Osama bin Laden out of business "dead or alive," successfully solicited large-scale global support for his campaign against terrorism, announced objectives that "are not open to negotiation or discussion," and launched operations to achieve those aims.

Neither those events nor subsequent developments invalidate chapters in this book that concern sociopolitical terrorism, counterterrorism, and associated topics. On the contrary, *Military Strategy* provides contexts that should help readers better understand events as they unfold and simultaneously clarifies relationships with all other forms of national security.

NOTES

1. Carl von Clausewitz, *On War,* ed. and trans. by Michael Howard and Peter Paret (Princeton, NJ: Princeton University Press, 1976).
2. Ward Just, *Military Men* (New York: Alfred A. Knopf, 1970), 24.
3. John M. Collins, *Military Geography: For Professionals and the Public* (Washington, DC: Brassey's, 1998).

1. Overview

I keep six honest serving men,
(they taught me all I knew);
their names are What and Why and When
and How and Where and Who.

Rudyard Kipling
Just-So Stories
"The Elephant's Child"

No nation can flourish long in competitive environments without satisfactory ways to promote and protect bedrock interests and prerequisites that flow therefrom. Strategists who strive to ensure sufficient security at acceptable costs knowingly or not employ Kipling's six honest serving men in their quest to match meaningful ends with measured means while minimizing risks:

- "What" and "Why" correspond to perceived requirements (**ends**)
- "How, When, and Where" indicate optional courses of action (**ways**)
- "Who" concerns available forces and resources (**means**)

The rapid pace of political, economic, demographic, social, scientific, and technological changes imposes unprecedented challenges. Needs for innovative deterrent, war-fighting, and conflict termination concepts followed the first use of nuclear weapons in August 1945. Politico-military policy-makers and strategists have barely scratched perplexing problems associated with military operations in space, a medium quite unlike land, sea, and air. Rogue states and nongovernmental groups armed with biological and cybernetic warfare weapons are beginning to expand the conflict spectrum far beyond past confines. Needs for competent military strategists will multiply if trends toward complexity continue to accelerate.[1]

STRATEGIC HIERARCHY

Strategies and tactics influence almost every field of human endeavor, whether it be football, lovemaking, or bank robberies. Those that nation states and coalitions customarily employ occupy a complex hierarchy, with national strategies at the pinnacle and military tactics at the base. Table 1 depicts, and accompanying texts describe, elementary relationships.

National Strategies

Governmental officials at the apex develop, and Chiefs of State approve, national strategies and plans designed to achieve national objectives. Key considerations include such diversified subjects as agriculture, armed forces, commerce, economics, crime prevention, ecology, education, energy, finance, governmental operations, health, housing, information, international relations, justice, labor, public welfare, and transportation. Policy guidelines in each case commonly take national purposes, life styles, ethics, laws, and values into account.

Table 1

Strategic and Tactical Hierarchy

	Primary Focus	Primary Participants	Primary Policies	Primary Input	Primary Output
National Strategies	National Objectives	Chief of State; Governmental Advisers	National Policies	National Power	National Plans
National Security Strategies	National Security Objectives	Chief of State; Security Advisers	National Security Policies	Suitable National Power	National Security Plans
National Military Strategies	National Military Objectives	Chief of State; Military Advisers	National Military Policies	Military Power	National Military Plans
Regional Strategies	Regional Objectives	Foreign Ministers; Ambassadors	Foreign Policies	Diplomacy; Economic Levers	International Accords
Theater Military Strategies	Regional Military Missions	Defense Ministers; CINCs	Unilateral or Coalition Policies	Unilateral or Coalition Forces	Unilateral or Coalition Plans and Ops
Operational Art and Tactics	Subordinate Military Missions	Subordinate Military Commanders	Joint or Uniservice Policies	Joint or Uniservice Forces	Joint or Uniservice Plans and Ops

National Security Strategies

Politico-military specialists at the highest levels develop, and Chiefs of State approve, national security or grand strategies and plans that apply suitable forms of national power during peacetime as well as war to achieve national security objectives despite foreign and domestic threats. Such strategies employ diplomatic, economic, psychological, cybernetic, technological, and other implements, of which armed forces may be the most or least useful.

National Military Strategies

Defense ministers (who may be civilians), together with senior generals and admirals, develop strategies that employ armed forces to achieve national military objectives, given guidance from and subsequent approval by Chiefs of State. Attendant procedures occupy two distinctive but interrelated planes, one abstract, the other concrete. The former is peopled with strategic philosophers ad theoreticians, the latter with policy-makers and planners who assess situations, weigh alternative courses of action, and recommend implementing resources.

Regional Strategies

Chiefs of State appoint, and direct the activities of, foreign ministers and ambassadors, who galvanize multipurpose strategies within given geographic regions abroad. Those emissaries use all instruments to promote their nation's interests, support friends, favorably influence neutrals, and undermine perceived enemies. Diplomacy, often accompanied by economic incentives or sanctions, normally takes precedence. Primary outputs comprise treaties and other international accords, which may be explicit or tacit, with short-, medium-, or long-term implications.

Theater Military Strategies

Defense ministers and regional commanders in chief (CINCs), frequently in concert with allied counterparts, develop theater military strategies (sometimes called "grand tactics") to accomplish military missions that underpin regional objectives during armed combat or under conditions other than war. National military and theater military strategies are identical in nations that deploy no armed forces beyond their borders.

Joint policies and plans unilaterally orchestrate military operations by all land, sea, air, and space forces within given theaters when no partners are present. Coalition strategies, which are infinitely more complex, coordinate forces from two or more countries, given guidance from and approval by contributors who may or may not be equally influential.

Operational Art and Tactics

Generals and admirals who command major formations (such as divisions, carrier battle groups, and expeditionary air wings) practice operational art, which implements theater military strategies. Campaigns predominate if armed combat occurs. Tacticians at lower levels arrange and maneuver smaller units in relation to each other and the enemy. Battles and engagements predominate, if armed combat occurs.[2]

Joint task force (JTF) commanders and their staffs prepare plans for, and employ armed forces from, more than one military service to accomplish operational and tactical missions. Combined joint task forces (CJTFs) perform analogous functions for coalitions. Uniservice organizations, in contrast, deal exclusively with land, sea, air, amphibious, or space forces.

The Primacy of Strategy Over Tactics

Strategies, operational art, and tactics constitute interdependent links. Weaknesses anywhere could be ruinous, but requirements for sound strategies come first, because members of armed forces that function impeccably bleed and die for naught if the overarching concepts they support are defective. British theoretician Basil H. Liddell Hart, in *Thoughts on War*, announced that after-action reports as a rule "should deal kindly with mistakes of execution natural to anyone in the fog and tension of war, and reserve caustic criticism for errors of conception . . . in the [strategist's] plan, which is based on his appreciation of the problem."[3]

STRATEGIC PROCESSES

There would be no need for strategies or tactics of any kind if national interests were self-satisfying, which seldom is the case. Policy-making and planning therefore should ideally proceed through a six-step process, much of which is nonmilitary (Figure 1). Step 1 specifies national interests. Step 2 appraises opposition. Step 3 concentrates on politico-military objectives, the attainment of which would safeguard interests despite all obstacles. Step 4 devises strategies designed to achieve those objectives in concert with policy guidelines. Step 5 allocates resources to cover requirements without incurring intolerable risks. Step 6 ascertains whether allotted assets are sufficient to support preferred concepts and, if not, identifies alternatives.

Few strategists quibble about the sequence of Steps 1–3 (**ends** and threats thereto), but whether Step 4 (**ways**) should precede Step 5 (**means**) incites disputes. One school, which asserts that impoverished strategies are impotent, allocates resources first, formulates plans to fit, then assesses risks that result from insufficient forces or budgetary shortfalls. Members of a second school prefer to put strategy formulation first, then request implementing forces and funds, because plans predicated on insufficient resources cannot achieve essential objectives. Both views are correct, but this survey, mindful that the six-step process is iterative instead of linear, emphasizes connections between **ways and ends** rather than **ways and means**.

Step 1: Specify National Interests

When Alice in Wonderland plaintively asked the Cheshire Cat, "Would you tell me, please, which way I ought to go from here?" she received the following response: "That depends a good deal on where you want to get to." A clear sense of national purposes predicated on specific interests in order of importance similarly must underlie meaningful strategies, plans, programs, and operations. National security interests, which are highly generalized ex-

Figure 1

Six-Step Strategic Planning Process

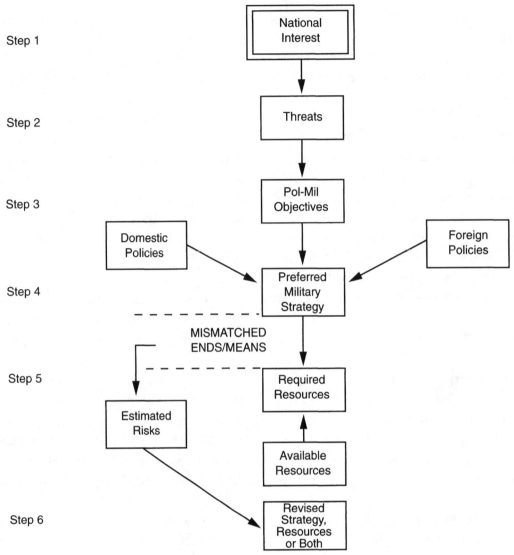

pressions of wants and needs, may seek to expand a State's jurisdictions, maintain the status quo, or merely preserve independence and territorial integrity with traditional lifestyles, fundamental institutions, values, and honor acceptably intact.[4]

Step 2: Appraise Opposition

Military strategists who lack accurate, timely intelligence are like blindfolded boxers, who can neither foresee impending disaster nor win except by accident. The nature, imminence, and intensity of appar-

ent perils indeed determine what, if anything, should and could be done in order of priority to safeguard security interests against present and projected threats, both foreign and domestic.

Intelligence communities first estimate enemy *capabilities* (what opponents could do, if so inclined), then try to divine *intentions* (what course of action enemies seem most likely to elect). Assessments that compare friendly with enemy situations thereafter enable senior politico-military officials to prioritize perceived threats.[5] Margins for error usually are slim at every stage, because some pieces of each puzzle almost always fit imprecisely while others are missing. Policy-makers and strategists consequently work with factual fabrics that at best are full of holes, and at worst are holes around which intelligence analysts have woven bits of fabric.

Step 3: Identify Key Objectives

National security decision-makers who don't know what needs to be done can't sensibly plan how to do it. Properly prioritized short-, mid-, and long-range objectives that last from a few weeks to a decade or more thus are indispensable.

Goals that concentrate on primary pressure points called "strategic centers of gravity" are preferable to aims that lack a sharp focus.[6] Contrast the overriding U.S. purpose throughout the Civil War, which was to preserve the Union, with vacillating objectives in Vietnam (1955–75), and it becomes clear that the former provided an infinitely superior platform for strategic planning.

Step 4: Formulate Strategies

Strategy formulation is the art and science of options. Selections that suit one leader or nation may be faulty under different conditions. National security strategists, within policy guidelines, consequently pick theories and concepts they believe would best apply national power to satisfy objectives. The most successful practitioners tailor every plan to meet specialized needs, for strategies cannot be transferred from one time period to another without precise appreciation for changes that transpire in the interim. French and British strategists, oblivious to that fact, tried to refight World War I from static defensive positions in May–June 1940, and thereby enabled Hitler's highly mobile forces to overrun all of West Central Europe in six weeks. Neither can strategies be transplanted from place to place unless situations are similar. Heavy-handed Soviet forces, for example, quickly crushed urban rebellions in East Berlin (1953), Budapest (1956),

and Prague (1968), but failed to prevail during a decade of guerrilla warfare in rural Afghanistan (1979–89).

Assumptions, which are presumed to be true in the absence of contrary proof, fill informational chasms when facts are unavailable. Wishful thinkers try to assume problems away, whereas pessimists cause costs to skyrocket. Well-schooled policy-makers and planners, who shun those polarized approaches to strategic problem solving, consciously articulate assumptions and subject them to constant scrutiny, so conjectures will correspond with facts as closely as possible when operations begin.

Step 5: Allocate Resources

National security and military strategists, in collaboration with logisticians and budget specialists, compare resource requirements with present and projected capabilities to confirm or deny the feasibility of strategic and tactical plans. Trade-offs between ends and means are not always obvious, because costs, risks, and other imponderables commonly cloud crucial issues.

Budgetary costs associated with any military strategy are easy to calculate compared with political, psychological, and opportunity costs, which may be equally or more important. U.S. strategies that emphasized attrition in Vietnam created progressively greater involvement than President Lyndon B. Johnson could justify to the American people or Congress, but costs already incurred encouraged continuation until public support collapsed. Repercussions undercut U.S. interests in military power and curtailed national military options for more than a decade, beginning about 1968.[7]

Assessors with access to the same intelligence frequently perceive different risks, because they have different personalities, temperaments, inclinations, social backgrounds, and experience. Proclivities for risk taking additionally differ markedly. A 60 percent chance of success might tempt professional poker players to plunge ahead, but prudent strategists who deal with weapons of mass destruction would find those odds unattractive, because the stakes are sky-high.

Step 6: Reconciliations

Step 5 terminates strategy formulation and firms up force requirements if aspirations and assets seem consistent. Step 6 offers alternatives, singly or in some combination, if unacceptable risks occupy the breach between ends and means:[8]

- **Reduce Waste** caused by institutional, organizational, procedural, or cultural inefficiencies
- **Compress or Discard Objectives,** as the United Nations did in Korea after Chinese "volunteers" intervened en masse
- **Reshape Strategies,** as Japan did when it switched from offense to defense after Allied power in the Pacific basin surged during World War II
- **Mobilize More Assets,** as President Franklin D. Roosevelt did in 1942 after Japanese raiders hit Pearl Harbor
- **Decrease Reliance on Military Power,** which Stalin did when he insidiously swallowed nine countries in Central Europe during the 1940s
- **Bluff,** as Hitler did in 1936 when he marched into and annexed the Rhineland with embryonic armed forces that the Treaty of Versailles prohibited
- **Produce a Miracle,** which U.S. magicians pulled out of a hat in 1945 when they unveiled *Little Boy* and *Fat Man,* the first atom bombs
- **Withdraw,** because the cause isn't worth the cost, as French decision-makers did in Vietnam (1954) and Algeria (1962)
- **Practice Self-Delusion,** which U.S. defense decision-makers habitually do in peacetime

when they pretend that gaps between ends and means don't exist

Military strategists in any case should be cautious, lest corrective actions boomerang. Security interests seldom disappear just because strategists adjust their goals. Telescoping objectives and tinkering with strategies is less likely to stir up political storms than requesting more resources, but the Law of Diminishing Returns strictly limits benefits. Trimming "fat" can curtail current and future capabilities if careless surgeons cut into "muscle." Political, economic, and psychological power are poor substitutes for firepower when quick results are essential, while habitual bluffing is bound to be a loser. Finally, overoptimization stifles flexibility, as demonstrated during early stages of the Cold War, when the U.S. strategy of Massive Retaliation failed to solve the full range of national security problems.[9]

STRATEGIC SUMMATION

Former French Prime Minister Georges Clemenceau once proclaimed that "War is much too serious to leave to generals." A corollary pronouncement might read, "National security is much too serious to leave entirely to civilians," because politico-military affairs are intertwined in peacetime as well as war.

Military strategy indeed is a game that anyone in uniform or mufti can play, but only gifted participants win prizes. There are games within games, and all are related. Every game is played simultaneously on a global or regional board. There is no limit to the number of players, who may participate singly or form teams, but who is on which side often is ambiguous. No two players start with pieces of the same quantities and qualities. Every player places different values on his own pieces compared with those of opponents, partners, and neutrals. Whole piles of pieces, not just one at a time, shift suddenly in any direction at anyone's whim, without regard for mutually agreeable rules. Players, pieces, values, and rules moreover are subject to unannounced change, and such games, of course, never end.

National security interests, threats, and objectives, in summation, form the framework within which policies, strategies, operational art, and tactics fit like pieces in a jigsaw puzzle. The main aim of the game is to match realistic ends with measured means, minimizing risks in the process but, as Carl von Clausewitz explained in his classic, *On War,* "We should admit that scientific formulas and problems are not under discussion. . . . Everything in strategy," he concluded, "is very simple, but that does not mean that everything is very easy."[10]

Well said. Modern military strategists ply their trade in volatile environments that are fraught with more uncertainties, complexities, and ambiguities than Clausewitz imagined. Cultural restrictions, bureaucratically constrained resources, and demands for disquieting compromises are commonplace. Chapters that follow expand every notion in this overview to furnish aspiring strategists with the intellectual tools they need to start fast and compete proficiently.

NOTES

1. A compilation of views is contained in George Edward Thibault, ed., *The Art and Practice of Military Strategy* (Washington: National Defense University, 1984).

2. FM 100-7, *Decisive Force: The Army in Theater Operations* (Washington: Headquarters U.S. Army, May 1995); ST 3-0, *Operations* (Fort Leavenworth, KS: U.S. Army Command and General Staff College, October 2000); Milan N. Vego, *Operational Warfare,* NWC 1004 (Newport, RI: Naval War College, 2000).

3. Basil H. Liddell Hart, *Thoughts on War* (London: Faber and Faber, 1944), 136.

4. *Strategy and National Interests: Reflections for the Future* (Washington: National Strategy Information Center, 1971).

5. Sherman Kent, *Strategic Intelligence* (Princeton, NJ: Princeton University Press, 1965); John M. Collins, "Essentials of Net Assessment," in *U.S.-Soviet Military Balance: Concepts and Capabilities, 1960-1980* (Washington: McGraw-Hill Publications, 1980), 3-14.

6. Basil H. Liddell Hart, *Strategy,* 2d rev. ed. (New York: Praeger, 1967), Chapter XXI, "National Object and Military Aim"; Carl von Clausewitz, *On War,* ed. and trans. Michael Howard and Peter Paret (Princeton, NJ: Princeton University Press, 1976), 595-97, 617-19.

7. Neil Sheehan et al., *The Pentagon Papers* (New York: Quadrangle Books, 1971); Tom Wells, *The War Within: America's Battle Over Vietnam* (Berkeley: University of California Press, 1994).

8. Général d'Armée André Beaufre, *An Introduction to Strategy* (New York: Praeger, 1965), 28-29; Charles F. Bunnell, Jr., *Ends and Means—The Military Component* (Washington: Strategic Research Group, National War College, 1972), 12-16.

9. General Maxwell D. Taylor, *The Uncertain Trumpet* (New York: Harper and Brothers, 1959).

10. Clausewitz, *On War,* 178.

PART I

THE FRAMEWORK OF MILITARY STRATEGY

2. National Security Interests

Some men see things as they are and say, why;
I see things that never were and say, why not.

Senator Robert F. Kennedy
Campaign speech, 1968

Presidential candidate Robert Kennedy, a dreamer who took pity on the underprivileged, believed he was honor-bound to combat injustice and defend the defenseless wherever found. Counterparts early in the twenty-first century similarly see a surplus of causes that make stoics weep. Population explosions greater than Malthus imagined in his pessimistic estimates 200 years ago plague already impoverished countries. Politically-induced famines that starve infants, nursing mothers, and the infirm along with sturdy opponents are commonplace in many African and Asian countries. Ethnic, religious, and cultural conflicts butcher innocent bystanders. Mass emigrations to escape resultant miseries frequently engulf luckless neighbors.

Chiefs of State and their politico-military advisers nevertheless must root national security interests firmly in reality or ends and means fail to match. No nation, not even the United States of America, possesses sufficient assets to feed, clothe, house, and police the whole world. Sensible priorities thus are imperative.

BASIC ATTRIBUTES

National security interests are highly generalized expressions of a nation's wants and needs, especially those that concern protection for its people, territory, traditional lifestyle, institutions, and values. Whoever compiles the list for any given country makes monumentally important decisions, because interests form the foundation for national security objectives, policies, strategies, and programs.[1]

Superpower interests cover all seven continents, every ocean, and an overarching envelope loosely called aerospace. Lesser states and subnational groups usually concentrate on local or regional interests. Political, economic, military, social, ideological, religious, moral, and emotional motivations commonly are evident. "Nuclear winter," which emerged as a strategic issue in the 1980s, and the December 1997 Kyoto Treaty on global warming involved environmental interests.[2]

Dictatorial vs. Democratic Interests

Not many nations formally enunciate security interests, but senior officials certify them implicitly or explicitly, by actions and in public or private pronouncements. Autocrats and cabals generally are able to do as they see fit with scant concern for popular support, whereas democratic governments generally require communal approval. Irreconcilable differences of opinion otherwise may cause disastrous rifts, which happened in the United States after Vietnamese General Vo Nguyen Giap launched his psychologically successful Tet Offensive in February 1968. Johnson and Nixon Administrations thereafter found it impossible to defend perceived interests that were at odds with those of a majority in Congress and across the country.[3]

Permanence Versus Perishability

A few elemental interests are timeless, but British Foreign Secretary Henry John Temple Palmerston didn't have it quite right in 1848 when, in a speech before the House of Commons, he implied that *all* "interests are eternal and perpetual."[4] History in fact repeatedly records substantial change on short notice.

Countries dissatisfied with existing power relationships tend to abandon the status quo. Apathetic "have not" nations that come under the influence of charismatic leaders may suddenly aspire to affluence. "Have" nations under similar spells may suddenly want more, as President Saddam Hussein confirmed when he redefined Iraq's regional interests in the early 1980s, soon after he came to power.[5] The Soviet Union's collapse caused U.S. security interests to shift so sharply that the 1991 *National Security Strategy of the United States* flatly stated, "We have entered a new era, one whose outline would have been unimaginable only three years ago. . . . We face new challenges not only to our security, but to our ways of thinking about security."[6]

Prioritization

Responsible citizens everywhere are willing to spill blood, spend billions, and accept high risks when crucial interests clearly are at stake. Few Americans, for example, complained when President John F. Kennedy publicly ordered Nikita Khrushchev to remove Soviet nuclear-capable ballistic missiles from Cuba in October 1962 or face dire consequences that could have led to mass casualties on both sides. Popular support for combat in Korea during the previous decade conversely was muted in the United States, because the cause was poorly articulated and many military men as well as civilians questioned whether that unpopular "police action" was worth the cost in lives and money.

Humanitarian and other less compelling interests may merit the use of armed forces, but not of armed force. National security policy-makers consequently need to put interests in priority before they decide whether military power is the most appropriate instrument.

UNIVERSALLY VALUABLE INTERESTS

Every country has intrinsic interests in survival and security against all enemies, foreign and domestic (Table 2). Most also entertain enduring interests in military power, credibility, and freedom of action. Other interests of variable importance only occasionally receive high priorities.

Table 2
Typical Security Interests

Universally Important	Variably Important
Survival	Peace
Homeland Defense	Stability
Domestic Tranquility	Prosperity
Military Power	Ideology
National Credibility	Geostrategic Position
Freedom of Action	Morality

National Survival

Nations routinely risk war to ensure interests in survival, which are invariably vital in every sense of that word. Victors nowadays normally offer more lenient terms to the vanquished than Assyria, Babylonia, and Carthage received in ancient times, but Sir Winston Churchill didn't count on humane treatment from Nazi Germany when he addressed the House of Commons on May 13, 1940, soon after his appointment as Britain's wartime Prime Minister. "You ask, What is our aim? I can answer in one word: Victory—victory at all costs, victory in spite of all terror, victory however long and hard the road may be; for without victory there is no survival."[7]

"Victory at all costs" unfortunately may be too high a price to pay in the Age of Nuclear and Biological Warfare (BW) Weapons, because liberal employment of such munitions could decimate populations and inflict uncontrollable, long-lasting effects. "Winners" would be so difficult to differentiate from "losers" that survivors of large-scale nuclear attacks on key cities indeed might envy the dead, as Herman Kahn predicted.[8] Unprecedented casualties also would accompany cataclysmic BW assaults.

Nations nearing defeat occasionally may survive by capitulating before recuperation becomes impossible, whereas resistance that culminates in national suicide guarantees irrevocable ruin. The United States, Britain, France, and the Soviet Union, for example, divided Hitler's Third Reich after that shattered country surrendered unconditionally at the end of World War II, but West Germany recovered quickly, became NATO's strongest European member, and reunited with East Germany after the Iron Curtain came down in 1990. Japan involuntarily underwent tremendous political and cultural transformations after its defeat in 1945, yet emerged as an economic superpower within a few decades.

Homeland Defense

Concern for security against external aggression that seriously threatens homelands depends to great degrees on geographic circumstances. Russian Tsars, their Soviet successors, and current occupants of the Kremlin, exposed to real and imagined pressures from powerful adversaries along lengthy frontiers, have put a premium on defense of Mother Russia for several centuries, whereas the Continental United States, isolated by oceans and flanked by friendly countries, has been free from invasion since January 8, 1815, when British troops lost the Battle of New Orleans. No adversary yet possesses sufficient airborne and amphibious assault, naval air power, and transoceanic logistical capabilities to seize, secure, expand, and sustain sizable lodgments on U.S. shores.

Soviet long-range Tu-95 Bear bombers and nuclear-tipped missiles that could strike urban targets anywhere in the United States greatly intensified U.S. interests in homeland defense from the mid-1950s until Cold War confrontations ceased thirty-five years later. President George W. Bush subsequently pursued a trustworthy shield to counter increasingly potent ballistic missiles in the hands of present and potential enemies, although success remains elusive and opposition at home and abroad remains strong.[9]

Domestic Tranquility

U.S. Founding Fathers established a Constitution in 1789, partly to "insure domestic Tranquility." That universal interest becomes vital if severe internal turmoil makes effective governmental and military operations impossible until reconciliation, accommodation, or oppressive countermeasures control dissent. President Lincoln in Springfield, Illinois on July 17, 1858 put domestic tranquility requirements in bold relief when he told attendees at the Republican State Convention that "A house divided against itself cannot stand." Abe's observation remains sound today. Nations that fail to dampen dissidence effectively indeed invite civil disobedience that may range from demonstrations to secessionist movements, incipient insurgencies, even full-scale civil wars. Adverse consequences are costly at best, and at worst tear countries apart.

Military Power

Impressive deterrent and combat capabilities often enable possessors to impose their will on rivals without fighting and improve prospects for favorable outcomes if armed conflicts erupt. The psychological impact of obvious military superiority not only comforts friends, but enhances opportunities to influence their conduct and the demeanor of neutrals as well.[10]

Nations that lack sufficiently strong armed forces on the contrary can neither fulfill interests in survival and homeland defense nor support foreign policies to best advantage. Those that rely heavily on allies cannot perpetually assume that assistance will be assured during crises. Japan, for example, has counted on U.S. military power since World War II, but can safely continue to do so only as long as basic security interests of both countries coincide.

National Credibility

Credibility often requires clearly evident military capabilities and the will to employ them wherever and whenever necessary. That quality is indispensable for any nation that seeks respect from friends and neutrals as well as foes. Support for every other security interest is a by-product.

U.S. interests in credibility increased by orders of magnitude immediately after World War II, when American military power became a Free World bulwark against the spread of Communism. Quests for credibility motivated President Lyndon B. Johnson in 1965 to assert that "If we are driven from the field in Vietnam, then no nation can ever have the same confidence in American promises, or in American protection."[11] See-sawing, however, soon cast doubts about U.S. resolve, which plummeted after the United States abandoned its Vietnamese ally early in 1973.

Credibility rebounded with scintillating performances during Operations Just Cause (Panama, December 1989–January 1990)[12] and Desert Storm (Iraq, January–February 1991),[13] then sagged badly after bloody battles with warlord Mohammed Farah Aideed's motley mobs made President Clinton withdraw all U.S. forces from Somalia in March 1994.[14] Political restraints rather than requisite military power have shaped a spotty record ever since.

Freedom of Action

Armed forces that lack strategic initiative must react rather than act. "The battle of wills," in the words of French Général d'Armée André Beaufre, "comes down to a struggle for freedom of action."[15] Freedom of the seas, for example, was at stake when U.S. leathernecks and blue jackets defeated Barbary pirates off the coast of Tripolitania (now Libya) nearly two centuries ago. Freedom of action in space became a crucial U.S. interest as soon as the Soviet Union launched *Sputnik I* into a low Earth orbit on October 4, 1957.

VARIABLY VALUABLE INTERESTS

Variable security interests that supplement the universal core may be strategic or tactical, active or passive, positive or negative, immediate or deferred,

regional or worldwide. Values depend on the proclivities of national leaders who, if they are wise, recurrently review lists to ascertain which entries remain valid and which are obsolete. Samples displayed on Table 2 (p. 14) and summarized below are illustrative.

Peace

Fewer armed conflicts would infect this world if true peace devoid of hostile intent in international relations were a universal interest, but not every nation or subnational group shares that aspiration. Soviet leaders from Lenin at least through Yuri Andropov saw no prospect of such benign relations until socialism triumphed. "Peaceful coexistence," as they practiced it, "exclude[d] war, and primarily world war, as a means of settling interstate disputes," but politico-military struggles with non-Communist countries otherwise were constant.[16]

Altruistic nations generally espouse interests in peace as a matter of principle, whereas aggressive governments take advantage of peace while they prepare for war. Peace becomes particularly important when adversaries perceive a lot to lose and little or nothing to gain from war. General of the Army Omar N. Bradley, when he was Chairman of the Joint Chiefs of Staff, identified peace as a salient U.S. interest for that reason shortly after the Soviet Union detonated its first nuclear device in 1949, because even limited strife between rivals armed with weapons of mass destruction might unexpectedly escalate out of control to the detriment of neutrals as well as combatants.[17]

Stability

Countries satisfied with current power relationships profess interest in stability (the status quo), primarily to preserve existing balances at acceptable costs.[18] That condition is most easily achievable if Parties A and B find it mutually acceptable, Party A is so superior that Party B deems accommodation more attractive than competition, or Party B is too passive or impoverished to alter equations significantly.

Adversarial states may maintain the same relative position at ever higher levels throughout prolonged arms races, but that process incurs increased costs, international tensions, and risks. U.S. strategists, for example, strained unsuccessfully to assure a stable U.S.-Soviet nuclear balance predicated on policies variously dubbed "parity," "sufficiency," and "essential equivalence" because, as Secretary of Defense Harold Brown ruefully observed, "When we build they build; when we cut they build."[19] The practical value of resultant Soviet quantitative superiority was questionable, but the psychological value was incalculable.

Prosperity

The prosperity of every developed nation on this increasingly interdependent planet depends to some degree on foreign raw materials and markets. Persian Gulf petroleum, for example, is so important to many countries that U.S. leaders in 1974–75 openly contemplated military action if manipulations by the Organization of Petroleum Exporting Countries (OPEC) threatened to "strangle" the industrialized world.[20] A multinational coalition defeated Iraq in 1991, mainly to maintain free-flowing Middle East oil supplies. The uneven distribution of key metals and minerals similarly stimulates contentious interests that likely will magnify as soon as scientists devise cost-effective ways to tap such resources in Antarctica, on ocean floors, and in space.[21]

Prosperity as a rule contributes to domestic tranquility in democratic countries, but not necessarily in dictatorships, where kingpins commonly line their own pockets and pay bully boys a comparative pittance to keep poverty-stricken common people under control. President Mobutu Sese Seko, who fleeced Zaire (now the Congo) of riches worth several billion U.S. dollars during a corrupt thirty-three-year reign (1965–98), may hold the world's record in that regard, despite fierce competition from other famous despots.[22]

Ideology

Ideological interests frequently lead to political, cultural, even military collisions.[23] The United States, which helped defeat the Central Powers during World War I to "keep the world safe for democracy," currently focuses on democratic reforms throughout the world.[24] Communism sprouted in Europe during the 1840s, started to expand after the Russian Revolution in 1917, then spread worldwide before all countries save China, North Korea, Cuba, and Vietnam chose other forms of government. Militant fascism, which reached its zenith under Adolf Hitler and Benito Mussolini, still has scattered adherents. Theocracies, presently typified by regimes in Iran, Afghanistan, and Algeria, are closely akin to ideologies and serve similar purposes, which are primarily to perpetuate control over indigenous populations.

Totalitarianism or authoritarianism, differentiated by a greater degree of autocracy in the former, may accompany almost any ideological interest except democracy. Absolute monarchies and "benevolent dictatorships" occasionally enjoy foreign and domestic support, but most despots are unpopular at home, abroad, or both.[25]

Geostrategic Position

World powers attach particular importance to geostrategic position when they deploy armed forces abroad for offensive, defensive, or deterrent purposes. Three examples that span widely separated time periods are representative.

Access to open water became a consuming Russian aspiration late in the seventeenth century when Peter the Great was Tsar because, as Admiral of the Fleet of the Soviet Union Sergei G. Gorshkov explained much later, "History patently confirmed that without a strong fleet Russia could not take its place among the great powers."[26] Security for lifelines of empire prompted Britain to establish a strong presence at naval choke points from Gibraltar through Suez to Singapore in the nineteenth century. U.S. interests in strategic position centered on sites from which to contain Soviet expansion throughout the Cold War (1946–1989). More than 1,700 American military installations, picked primarily to ensure early warning of impending Soviet attack and block the most likely land, sea, and aerospace avenues of advance, eventually speckled the Canadian arctic, NATO Europe, and the eastern edge of Asia.[27]

Morality

Humanitarianism led numerous nations to sign several Hague and Geneva conventions that outlaw barbaric practices in combat and prescribe how prisoners of war should be treated.[28] A Geneva Protocol subsequently forbade the employment of chemical and biological warfare weapons and many signatories further approved a convention that prohibits the development, production, and stockpiling of BW and toxin munitions.[29]

Moral and emotional interests, however, may be admirable or evil, depending on perspectives. Religious interests, perhaps the epitome of morality, have motivated many of the most vicious wars on record. Niccolò Machiavelli, who believed that ends justify almost any means, advised Cesare Borgia that "A wise leader cannot and should not keep his word when keeping it is not to his advantage or when

the reasons that made him give it are no longer valid."[30] The Khmer Rouge in Cambodia cared little for human rights,[31] which have been an explicit aspect of U.S. foreign policy since President Jimmy Carter's Administration.[32] Serbs and Croatians in Bosnia-Herzegovina as well as Serbs and Albanians in Kosovo practiced "ethnic cleansing" in the 1990s, a course of action that the International Criminal Tribunal for the Former Yugoslavia considered felonious[33] (see Chapter 23 for details).

CONFLICTS OF INTEREST

Many of the world's politico-military problems can be traced to international and intranational conflicts of interest that need not be rational. Status quo and change are incompatible. Overemphasis on prosperity can sabotage interests in military power. Freedom of action may collide with peace and stability. U.S. economic interests in Persian Gulf petroleum have conflicted sharply with moral and emotional interests in Israel since 1948. Similar inconsistencies seem almost endless. Nations pay penalties whenever foreign policy specialists and military strategists fail to put interests in proper priority; security objectives, concepts, plans, programs, and operations otherwise are like castles built on sand.

KEY POINTS

- National security interests are logical starting points for all politico-military strategies.
- Political, military, economic, social, ideological, moral, and emotional motivations all are important.
- Despots determine security interests and assign priorities with far greater independence than democratic leaders, who must pay greater attention to legal and ethical constraints, as well as public opinion.
- Most elemental interests are subject to reinterpretations when circumstances change.
- Survival is the only invariably vital interest.
- The value of other interests varies from time to time and place to place.
- Conflicts of interest cause most of the world's politico-military problems.
- Nations pay penalties whenever foreign policy specialists and military strategists fail to reconcile or successfully override conflicting interests.

NOTES

1. Bernard Brodie, "Vital Interests: By Whom and How Determined?," *Strategy and National Interests: Reflections for the Future* (Washington: National Strategy Information Center, 1971), 11-24.

2. Susan R. Fletcher, *Global Climate Change: Summary of the Kyoto Protocol,* Rpt. No. RL 30692 (Washington: Congressional Research Service, April 11, 2001, updated routinely); Jonathan Schell, "The Fate of the Earth," *New Yorker,* February 1, 1982, 47-113; February 8, 48-109; and February 15, 45-107; Carl Sagan, "Nuclear War and Climatic Catastrophe: Some Policy Implications," *Foreign Affairs,* Winter 1983/84, 257-92, 293-317.

3. Literature devoted to divergent interpretations of U.S. interests during the Vietnam War is voluminous. See, for example, P. Edward Haley, *Congress and the Fall of South Vietnam and Cambodia* (Rutherford, NJ: Fairleigh Dickinson University Press, 1982); Melvin Small, *Johnson, Nixon, and the Doves* (New Brunswick, NJ: Rutgers University Press, 1988).

4. Charles W. Freeman, Jr., *The Diplomat's Dictionary* (Washington: National Defense University Press, 1994), 186.

5. Kanan Makiya, *Republic of Fear* (Berkeley: University of California Press, 1998); Elaine Sciolino, *The Outlaw State* (New York: John Wiley & Sons, 1991).

6. *National Security Strategy of the United States* (Washington: The White House, August 1991), 1. See also *National Military Strategy* (Washington: Chairman of the Joint Chiefs of Staff, January 1992), 1; General Colin L. Powell with Joseph E. Persico, *My American Journey* (New York: Random House, 1995), Chapter 17.

7. Sir Winston S. Churchill, *Blood, Sweat, and Tears* (New York: G. P. Putnam's Sons, 1941), 276.

8. Herman Kahn, *On Thermonuclear War* (Princeton, NJ: Princeton University Press, 1960), Chapter 2.

9. President Richard M. Nixon, *U.S. Foreign Policy for the 1970s: A New Strategy for Peace* (Washington: U.S. Government Printing Office, February 18, 1970), 125-26; *Report of the Commission to Assess the Ballistic Missile Threat to the United States* (the Rumsfeld Commission), July 15, 1998; Stephen Hildreth and Amy Woolf, *National Missile Defense,* Issue Brief 10034 (Washington: Congressional Research Service, June 2001, updated periodically).

10. For distinctions between force and military power, see Edward N. Luttwak, "Perceptions of Military Force and U.S. Defense Policy," *Survival,* January/February 1977, 2-8.

11. President Lyndon B. Johnson, "The President's News Conference on July 28, 1965; Why We are in Vietnam," *Public Papers of the Presidents of the United States,* Book II (Washington: U.S. Government Printing Office, 1966), 794.

12. "An Auspicious Comeback in Panama," Chapter 4 in *Commando Operations* (Alexandria, VA: Time-Life Books, 1991).

13. General H. Norman Schwarzkopf, *It Doesn't Take Hero* (New York: Bantam Books, 1992); HRH General Khlid bin Sultan, *Desert Warrior* (New York: Harper Collins, 1995).

14. Mark Bowden, *Blackhawk Down* (New York: Atlantic Monthly Press, 1999); *Military Operations in Somalia: A Message from the President of the United States Transmitting a Report on the Military Operations in Somalia* (Washington: U.S. Government Printing Office, 1993).

15. Général d'Armée André Beaufre, *An Introduction to Strategy* (New York: Praeger, 1965), 35.

16. V. I. Lenin, *Collected Works,* Vol. I (Moscow: Progress Publishers, 1970), 771; Leo Gruliow, ed., *Current Soviet Policies: III. The Documentary Record of the 20th Communist Party Congress and Its Aftermath* (New York: Praeger, 1957), 36-37; article by Observer, "For the Liquidation of Colonialism and The Triumph of Peace," *Pravda,* October 24, 1964.

17. Congress, House, *Unification and Strategy,* Armed Services Committee, Doc. No. 600, 81st Cong., 2d sess. (Washington: U.S. Government Printing Office, March 1, 1950), 14.

18. For various perspectives concerning status quo, see Hans J. Morgenthau, *Politics Among Nations,* 5th ed. (New York: Alfred A. Knopf, 1972), 40-44, 92-94.

19. Fred Charles Iklé, "The Idol of Stability," *The National Interest* (Winter 1986-1987), 75-79; Suzy Platt, ed., *Respectfully Quoted: A Dictionary of Quotations Requested from the Congressional Research Service* (Washington: Library of Congress, 1989), 80.

20. Congress, House, *Oil Fields As Military Objectives: A Feasibility Study,* prepared for the Special Subcommittee on Investigations of the Committee on International Relations by the Congressional Research Service, 94th Cong., 1st sess. (Washington: U.S. Government Printing Office, August 21, 1975).

21. Ben Bova, "Moonbase Orientation Manual I: Transport and Manufacturing," *Analog* (June 1987), 65-70, 77, 80-87; Gregg E. Maryniak, "Living Off the Land: The Use of Resources in Space," in *America Plans for Space* (Washington: National Defense University Press, 1986), 53-80.

22. Sean Kelly, *America's Tyrant: The CIA and Mobutu of Zaire* (Washington: American University Press, 1993).

23. Insights concerning ideologies are contained in James H. Billington, *Fire in the Minds of Men* (New York: Basic Books, 1980); Eric Hofer, *The True Believer* (New York: Harper, 1951).

24. *A National Security Strategy for a New Century* (Washington: The White House, December, 1999), 2, 3, 25-27, 34, 38-39, 41, 44-45, 47.

25. Hannah Arendt, *Origins of Totalitarianism* (New York: Harcourt, Brace and Jovanovich, 1973); Jeanne Kirkpatrick, "Dictatorships and Double Standards," *Commentary,* November 1979, 34-45; Michael Levin, "How to Tell Bad from Worse," *Newsweek,* July 20, 1981, 7.

26. Admiral of the Fleet of the Soviet Union Sergei G. Gorshkov, *The Sea Power of the State* (Annapolis, MD: Naval Institute Press, 1976), 66-83, 124-26, 133-55; the quotation is on 66.

27. *United States Foreign Policy Objectives and Overseas Military Installations,* prepared for the Senate Committee on Foreign Relations by the Congressional Research Service, 96th Cong., 1st sess. (Washington: U.S. Government Printing Office, April 1979).

28. *Treaties in Force: A List of Treaties and Other International Agreements of the United States in Force on January 1, 1990* (Washington: U.S. Government Printing Office, 1990), 369-75.

29. *Arms Control and Disarmament Agreements* (Washington: U.S. Arms Control and Disarmament Agency, 1982): 9-18, 120-31.

30. Niccolò Machiavelli, *The Prince* (Chicago: University of Chicago Press, 1985).

31. Chanrithy Him, *When Broken Glass Floats: Growing Up Under the Khmer Rouge* (New York: W. W. Norton, 2000).

32. Dilys M, Hill, ed., *Human Rights and Foreign Policy: Principles and Practices* (New York: St. Martin's Press, 1988); Louis Cingranelli, ed., *Human Rights: Theory and Measurement* (New York: St. Martin's Press, 1988).

33. *Bosnia War Crimes: The International Criminal Tribunal for the Former Yugoslavia and U.S. Policy,* Rpt. 96-404F, coordinated by Steven Woehel (Washington: Congressional Research Service, April 23, 1998, updated regularly).

3. Foreign and Domestic Threats

"The Duke is seven feet, nine inches tall, and . . . in his prime," a tosspot gurgled. "His hand is cold enough to stop a clock, and strong enough to choke a bull, and swift enough to catch the wind. He breaks up minstrels in his soup, like crackers."

James Thurber
The Thirteen Clocks

National security interests would be self-satisfying if human relations were eternally serene, but military strategists must constantly consider foreign and domestic opposition. Intelligence estimates, net assessments, and threat assessments that objectively evaluate and prioritize challenges are preferable to inflated, one-sided findings like those of the drunkard cited above. Accurate answers to five questions are required:

- How much military power of what kinds does each adversary possess and where is it deployed?
- What courses of action are open to each adversary, given its current and projected posture?
- What course(s) of action is each adversary likely to adopt, given apparent motives, opportunities, vulnerabilities, inhibitions, and historical precedents?
- What are enemy prospects for success, given the assets and liabilities of friendly armed forces?
- What enemy threats seem most important, given the comparative value of security interests involved?

Intelligence communities grapple with Questions 1, 2, and 3. Net assessors ponder Question 4. Chiefs of State and their politico-military advisers, who deal with Question 5, appraise the imminence, intensity, and seriousness of short-, mid-, and long-range threats, then assign priorities.

THE CONFLICT SPECTRUM

Threats span a conflict spectrum that begins with bickering just above normal peacetime competition and culminates in the most violent wars conceivable (Figure 2).[1] Intranational and international enemy options of low, mid, or high intensity range from nonlethal political, economic, technological, cybernetic, and psychological warfare (PSYWAR) through insurgencies, counterinsurgencies, and terrorism to traditional military, nuclear, biological, chemical, and radiological conflicts. Overlaps and interlocks are commonplace. Guerrilla warfare behind the lines, for example, greatly assisted Soviet traditional operations against Nazi Germany and might accompany a general nuclear conflagration with equal effectiveness. Propaganda, disinformation, other forms of PSYWAR, and deception have utility, regardless of conflict types and intensities.[2]

The spectrum of conflict creates a spectrum of

Figure 2
The Conflict Spectrum

Relative Conflict Intensities		
Low[1]	**Mid**	**High**
		Unrestrained Global Wars Unrestrained Regional Wars Endemic NBCR Terrorism[3]
	Limited Global Wars Limited Regional Wars Unrestrained Local Wars Insurgencies (Phases III)[2] Local NBCR Terrorism[3]	

Violent Conflicts
   Limited Local Wars
   Insurgencies (Phases I and II)[2]
   Traditional Warfare
   Terrorism
   Narco Conflicts
   Some Coups d'État
 	
Nonviolent Conflicts
   Political Warfare
   Economic Warfare
   Technological Warfare
   Psychological Warfare
   Cybernetic Warfare
   Some Coups d'État
 	
Crises
Subcrises		

[1] Biological, chemical, radiological, political, economic, technological, psychological, and cybernetic warfare, plus terrorism and insurgencies, may augment nuclear and/or traditional conflicts of any intensity.
[2] Phase I and II insurgencies generally feature undergrounds and guerrillas, whereas large military or paramilitary formations normally dominate during Phase III.
[3] NBCR is the acronym for nuclear, biological, chemical, and radiological warfare.

strategic problems that are increasingly difficult to categorize. Most professional observers considered unrestrained nuclear warfare unlikely when the United States and the Soviet Union were the only antagonists so armed, but uncertainties soared in 1998 when India and Pakistan backed volatile claims to Kashmir with newly acquired nuclear weapons.[3] Osama bin Laden, a multimillionaire Saudi Arabian expatriate who for several years formulated and funded transnational terrorist activities from a protected perch in Afghanistan, gave new meanings to the term "strategic unpredictability."[4] Risks will skyrocket if, as many pundits predict, nuclear and biological weapons vest small groups with powers to cripple large urban centers or hold them hostage until negotiators meet their demands. Cybernetic assaults began to cause consternation before the twentieth century closed.[5] Threat assessments thus are immeasurably more complex than those in the relatively recent past.

STRATEGIC GUIDANCE

Lieutenant General (later General) Robert C. Kingston, in his capacity as the first Commander in Chief of U.S. Central Command in 1984, was concerned about Soviet intentions toward Persian Gulf oil-producing states. When asked, "Are you getting enough intelligence?" he answered, "I don't know. I only know what I'm getting. What's going on that I don't know?" General Howell Estes III, Kingston's counterpart at U.S. Space Command 14 years later, expressed similar sentiments when queried about the possible proliferation of intercontinental ballistic missiles among unfriendly nations: "You get the feeling that there's more going on than we know about."[6]

Intelligence specialists, whose task is to determine what's going on, patrol the pre-conflict and conflict spectrum in search of pertinent information, but do so most effectively only if military strategists furnish sharp requirements and keep them constantly informed about ongoing plans. Otherwise, they must assume what lines of inquiry are most important and establish priorities without fully understanding the problems they seek to solve.[7]

ENEMY MILITARY POWER

Military intelligence communities estimate how much manpower, firepower, mobility, and staying power of what quality is readily available to rival military, paramilitary, and irregular forces and how tightly each possessor ties them together (Table 3). Similar assessments concern friends and fence-straddlers who could reinforce either side.

Quantitative Considerations

Statistical snapshots taken at particular points in time are soon overtaken by events. Summaries that cover several consecutive years are preferable, because they reveal which currents are strong, which are weak, which are shifting, and which are steady. Experienced strategists request assorted displays that aggregate foreign armed forces organizationally, functionally, and regionally, since each presentation affords uniquely useful insights (Table 4).[8]

Intercontinental ballistic missiles (ICBMs), armored vehicles, combat aircraft, and surface ships are easier to count than biological and chemical warfare (BW, CW) dispensers. Guerrillas, who wear no uniforms, shun fixed bases, and conduct surreptitious operations, are far harder to quantify than orthodox armed forces. Underground organizations that furnish them with administrative and logistical support are even less conspicuous, because members are local civilians who occupy small cells that seldom if ever make direct contact with each other.[9] High and low calculations, based on conflicting and often inaccurate information, thus may differ markedly (U.S. estimates of North Vietnamese and Viet Cong personnel strengths varied by as much as 300,000).[10]

Qualitative Considerations

Raw strength figures can be dangerously deceptive, as evidenced during World War II, when vastly out-

Table 3
Typical Elements of Military Power

Manpower	Firepower	Mobility	Integrating Factors
Manpower Pools	Quantities	Vehicles	Roles & Missions
Active Forces	Performance	Airlift	Organizations
Ready Reserves	Production Rates	Sealift	
	R&D Programs	Spacecraft	Policies
Traditions			Strategies
Temperament	of	**Staying Power**	Tactics
Intellect		Supply	Doctrines
Education	Small Arms	Maintenance	
Training	Crewed Weapons	Transportation	Command/Control
Experience	Armor	Construction	Communications
Vigor	Artillery	Storage	Intelligence
Hardiness	Missiles	Distribution	
Attitudes	Munitions	Evacuation	**Overarching**
Adaptability	Armed Aircraft	Medical Care	**Imperatives**
Discipline	Surface Combatants	Services	Political Will
Morale	Submarines		Leadership
Loyalty			

Table 4
Typical Statistical Summaries

Organizational Summaries	Functional Summaries	Regional Summaries
Armies	Deep strike	Europe
Navies	Ballistic missile defense	Southeast Asia
Air Forces	Air defense	Southwest Asia
Amphibious forces	Ground combat	Northern Africa
Military space forces	Aerial combat	Subsaharan Africa
Merchant Marines	Aerial reconnaissance	Latin America
Special operations forces	Naval surface warfare	
Paramilitary forces	Submarine warfare	Atlantic Ocean
Terrorist groups	Antisubmarine warfare	Pacific Ocean
	Amphibious warfare	Indian Ocean
	Special operations	
	Border security	Space
	Internal security	
	Space operations	
	Airlift	
	Sealift	

numbered Japanese Armed Forces fought with a ferocity that ANZAC (Australia and New Zealand), British, Burmese, Chinese, Dutch, Indian, Filipino, and U.S. antagonists did not initially anticipate. Iraq's huge military machine, which boasted half a million men at the onset of Operation Desert Storm in January 1991, conversely folded so fast that one wag quipped, "It was like being in the Super Bowl, but one team was bush league!"

Military strategists consequently seek intelligence concerning qualitative as well as quantitative characteristics of foreign armed forces. Key indicators include:

- Basic attributes of military manpower pools, especially attitudes toward military service and amenability to discipline
- Recruiting standards, which determine the intellectual and physical characteristics of volunteers and conscripts
- Progressive education and training programs that convert junior officers and enlisted personnel into military professionals
- Present and projected technological characteristics of weapon systems, munitions, equipment, and supplies

- Logistical abilities to deploy, maintain, sustain, and otherwise serve armed forces wherever they may be located
- Recent relevant experience, especially confrontations with or armed combat against worthy opponents

Criteria listed above raise legitimate questions about China's military behemoth, which is the world's largest. Practical experience since 1953, when combat ceased in Korea, has been confined to artillery bombardments of Nationalist Chinese–held Quemoy and Matsu islands (1950s), the subjugation of primitive Tibet (1959), altercations along borders with the former Soviet Union and India (1960s), and a bigger brouhaha with Vietnam that ended in embarrassment (1970s). Nuclear-tipped Chinese ballistic missiles can reach the United States, but Beijing's ground forces early in the twenty-first century still lack sufficient air support, mobility, and logistical capabilities to project and sustain military power far inside neighboring Russia or India. The Chinese Navy ousted Vietnamese forces from the Paracel Islands in 1973 but, despite recent improvements, is poorly prepared to conduct large-scale amphibious operations against Taiwan.

Quantitative and qualitative assets, in short, are not yet well matched.[11]

Military strategists generally should question all-inclusive assessments, because the quality of large armed forces rarely is uniform. Iraq and Iran, for example, respectively prize Republican and Revolutionary Guards that are several cuts above average compared with run-of-the-mill formations in those countries. It seems unlikely that all former Soviet Spetsnaz (estimated active strength between 12,000 and 30,000) were equally proficient, because "cream of the cream" cannot be mass-produced. The same could be said about North Korean Special Operations Forces, which reportedly number about 100,000.[12]

It always is wise to put qualitative findings in perspective. A drumbeat of complaints, beginning about 1998, contended that insufficient funds for training and logistical support, coupled with multiple humanitarian missions, peacekeeping, and other nontraditional duties, had dulled the cutting edge of U.S. Armed Forces since their brilliant performance against Iraq less than a decade earlier. Such allegations remain correct, but U.S. quality nevertheless outclasses potential opponents and America's military machine hardly deserves a "hollow" label like the one that Army Chief of Staff General Edward C. (Shy) Meyer pinned on its post–Vietnam War predecessor in May 1980 before Presidents Carter and Reagan began to rebuild all military services.[13]

Integrating Factors

Modern military power depends primarily on teamwork rather than individual prowess or impressive inventories. Strategists therefore need to know whether foreign armed forces are equal to, exceed, or are less than the quantitative and qualitative sum of their parts. Roles, functions, missions, organizational structures, policies, strategies, tactics, doctrines, command/control lash-ups, and interoperable communications typify many topics that demand exploration.

All armed forces must keep pace with events or become outmoded, but budgetary and bureaucratic stumbling blocks are common. Basil H. Liddell Hart was right when he wrote, "the only thing harder than getting a new idea into the military mind is to get an old one out."[14] The U.S. Army fought tenaciously to retain horse cavalry in 1940. The last large "blue water" surface naval battle took place off Kyushu on April 6–7, 1945, yet fifty years elapsed before U.S. naval policies, doctrines, plans, and programs officially began to emphasize littoral warfare as well as open ocean combat.[15] The United States Air Force (USAF) for many years insisted that airplane pilots must command ICBM wings and still resists unmanned aerial vehicles, partly because large inventories would drastically reduce the number of USAF officers.

Leadership and Political Will

Nearly every politico-military confrontation ultimately becomes a contest between opposing wills, in which one side or the other bends or breaks. Military power thus demands strong leadership at every command level and the political determination to employ armed forces in support of national security interests whenever authentic requirements arise. Carl von Clausewitz claimed that physical and psychological factors constitute "an organic whole which, unlike a metal alloy, is inseparable. . . . One might say that the physical seems little more than the wooden hilt, while the moral factors are the precious metal, the real weapon, the finely honed blade."[16]

INTELLIGENCE ESTIMATES

Intelligence analysts everywhere interpret available facts about all aspects of national power that foes, friends, and neutrals possess, fill in blanks with assumptions, then put findings in context with past, present, and portending situations. Short-, mid-, and long-range estimates thereafter indicate what options seem open to particular countries, coalitions, or subnational groups at particular times and places and which courses of action each seems most likely to elect. Margins for error are considerable, because pieces of such puzzles almost always are missing or incomprehensible, even under best-case conditions.

Foreign Military Capabilities

Intelligence communities produce capability estimates that focus attention on what foreign armed forces could do if so desired (deter, attack, defend, deceive, reinforce, withdraw) without regard for intentions or probabilities of success. Offensive options that the Soviet-led Warsaw Pact might have elected late in the Cold War are illustrative:[17]

- Assault the United States with strategic nuclear weapons
- Invade Western Europe with little warning, using air and ground forces in East Germany, Czechoslovakia, and Poland
- Support traditional military operations with theater nuclear and chemical weapons targeted against NATO's armed forces, airfields, ports, command/control centers, and logistical installations
- Challenge NATO for air supremacy over contested areas
- Challenge NATO's navies in the North Atlantic and approaches thereto
- Reinforce initial efforts with active forces in the Soviet Union and Central European satellite states
- Mobilize additional combat power

Elemental capabilities like those outlined above rarely change rapidly for better or worse, but intelligence analysts must remain alert, because cataclysmic exceptions occasionally occur. Causes include political upheavals (especially coups); public opinions that flip-flop from "hawkish" to "dovish" or vice versa; traumatic defeats typified by the French disaster at Dien Bien Phu; prodigious mobilization, such as accelerated U.S. rearmament after the Japanese attack on Pearl Harbor; and precipitous demobilization, such as hasty U.S. retrenchment after most American wars.

The proliferation of nuclear, biological, chemical, and radiological programs made it immensely more difficult to estimate foreign military capabilities than in decades past, when only a few nations were so armed and their identities were well known. Several scoundrels now possess "probable" or "suspected" holdings that are matters for conjecture.[18] Estimative problems will increase by orders of magnitude if, as widely predicted, transnational terrorists, religious extremists, disgruntled ethnic groups, drug cartels, and criminal syndicates beg, borrow, steal, or buy even a few NBCR weapons.

Inexpensive cybernetic tools and tactics that became widely available during the 1990s enable nations, subnational groups, even freelance individuals to shut down poorly protected computers that belong to adversaries or, if they wish, steal, erase, corrupt, or manipulate codes and data. Nonlethal but potentially crippling options include abilities to deny military commanders crucial information during crises, misdirect missiles in flight, and alter electronically transmitted orders.[19]

Foreign Military Intentions

Estimates that identify probable courses of enemy action must precede the formulation of meaningful military plans, because the most dangerous military capabilities imaginable constitute dangerous threats only if accompanied by determination to employ them. Russia and the United States, for example, retained more than enough nuclear weapons to atomize each other many times over after the Cold War ended, but rational employment appears improbable as long as each retains strong retaliatory capabilities.

Perplexities

Intentions, which are subjective states of mind, generally are difficult to divine. Most intelligence communities therefore monitor numerous indicators (NATO's catalogue once contained more than 700 items[20]) and assign weights, because values vary considerably. On-site intelligence agents who watched Iraqi Armed Forces cross the Kuwaiti border in August 1990, for example, were clueless about their ultimate objective, which might have been Saudi Arabian oil fields.[21] Analysts at distant assessment centers could only speculate whether Iran massed troops and aircraft near the Afghan frontier to do battle with or merely intimidate Taliban forces that reportedly had massacred Shiite civilians at Mazar-e Sharif early in September 1998.[22]

Even documents purloined from opponents' closely guarded, limited access files may be suspect because, as Sherman Kent sagely observed in his classic textbook *Strategic Intelligence,* none ever proclaim:

"I am *not* the offbeat thoughts and recommendations of a highly placed but erratic adviser; I am *not* a draft from high headquarters intended solely as a basis for discussion; I am *not* one of those records of decisions which will be rescinded orally the next day, or pushed under the rug and forgotten, or nibbled to death by disapproving implementers. . . . *I am authoritative and firm; I represent an approved intention and I am in effect.*"[23]

Relevant documents indeed may not exist. A September 1947 memorandum from the Joint Chiefs of Staff to Secretary of State George C. Marshall concluded that, "from the standpoint of military security, the United States has little strategic interest in maintaining the present troops and bases in Korea." President Harry Truman in April 1948 announced that warfare in Korea would not constitute a U.S. casus belli and, in a January 1950 speech before the National Press Club, Dean Acheson (Marshall's successor as Secretary of State) outlined a defense perimeter that excluded Korea. Key leaders in Congress concurred.[24] Kim Il Sung, Stalin, and

Mao thus were surprised when President Truman, backed by the United Nations, decided to defend South Korea one day after North Korean forces swarmed across the 38th Parallel in June 1950.

Opportunities

The search for enemy intentions even so is by no means hopeless. Political demagogues and dictators, who are secretive in most respects, paradoxically are prone to propagandize. Lenin let the world know where Communism was headed when he wrote *What Is to Be Done?* before the Russian Revolution erupted in 1917.[25] Hitler outlined his aims in *Mein Kampf* (1925).[26] Mao's collected works were equally revealing.[27]

Behavior patterns help intelligence analysts identify enemy intentions, provided they interpret trends correctly. Ultranationalistic radicals like those who ran amok in pre-World War II Japan should have warned observers to expect the worst.[28] Soviet leaders called themselves revolutionaries, but their proclivity for risk-taking was low throughout the Cold War, except for altercations over Berlin in 1961 and the Cuban missile crisis of 1962.[29] Kim Il Sung, who was President of North Korea from 1948 until his death in 1994, hoped to reunify that divided nation under Communist rule,[30] but avoided a full-scale war after 1953 despite strident rhetoric and intimidating military capabilities. He declined to re-invade the Republic of Korea when most U.S. long-haul airlift and sealift forces were needed to deploy and sustain military operations in Southeast Asia (1965–72) and again during U.S. operations to eject Iraq from Kuwait (1990–91), probably because obvious risks seemed to outweigh obtainable gains.

Cautionary Notes

Strategic intelligence specialists enjoy greater advantages than tactical counterparts, because they generally have more time to study situations and reach conclusions concerning foreign military capabilities, limitations, intentions, and vulnerabilities, plus insights concerning personal idiosyncrasies of parties in power. A labyrinth of special security classifications nevertheless may keep left hands from knowing what right hands are doing. Every estimator is opinionated to some degree, efforts at objectivity notwithstanding. Best-case estimates assume problems away, worst-case estimates magnify them, both warp reality, and built-in biases tend to create blind spots. "Lowest common denominator" approaches to intelligence production can cause genuine disagreements to disappear in clouds of collective wisdom, compromise, and politically expedient consensus.

Savvy politico-military policy-makers and strategists seek second and third opinions when hard evidence is tenuous or open to divergent interpretations. That process is cost-effective, despite redundant efforts and extra expense, because it helps them determine which rationales make the most common sense before they make decisions. Assistance by outsiders also can help keep intelligence estimates "honest." Team A versus Team B debates in 1976 did a lot to sharpen official U.S. insights concerning Soviet strategic nuclear capabilities and intentions. Teams C, D, and E in some instances might be beneficial.[31] Military strategists in any case should remain acutely aware that the best available intelligence estimates may be fallible, and fashion alternative plans for immediate use if prognostications prove wrong. So doing preserves operational flexibility and, if armed combat occurs, can save precious lives.

NET ASSESSMENTS

Twenty-five centuries ago, Sun Tzu advised, "Know your enemy, know yourself; in a hundred battles, you will never be in peril."[32] He overstated his case, but net assessments that dispassionately compare Blue sides with Red (friends with foes) nonetheless are needed to conclude which is better able to promote its interests despite opposition by the other.[33]

It often is useful to compare third parties as well. War between India and Pakistan or Arabs and Israelis, for example, could involve other nations.

Purposes and Products

Net assessors juxtapose Blue side data from friendly files with matching information about the Red side from intelligence estimates to calculate balances of power,[34] or what the Soviet Union and its associates called the "correlation of forces."[35] Comprehensive assessments contend with the full range of relevant military and nonmilitary factors. Cogent economic considerations, for example, include natural resources, raw materials, and defense industries. Compartmentalized appraisals concentrate on organizations, functions, demographics, and other specialized topics (Table 5). Scientific and technological assessments seek to ascertain how well Blue weapon and support systems compare with Red counterparts. The ultimate purpose in every instance is to rate relative strengths, weaknesses, problems, and opportunities.

Assessments that trace trends are preferable to snapshots. Those that forecast outcomes give some feel for probabilities, but prudent strategists treat them cautiously, because predicting winners and losers is a tricky proposition based on abilities to devise plausible scenarios (what if one country or coalition did this, at this time and place, with these aims in mind, using these forces and tactics to execute this strategy, and this was the response?). Even if input on both sides were precise, the frictions and fog of war—fear, fatigue, confusion, unforeseen events—could confuse cause-effect relationships and cast doubt on judgments buttressed by computerized war games.[36]

Assessing Statistical Asymmetries

Military net assessments, like intelligence estimates, commonly start with statistics, because historical records confirm that armed forces rarely win wars

Table 5

Net Assessment Types and Topics

Typical Focus	Typical Topics	
Diagnostic Assessments	**Diagnostic Assessments**	
Countries	North Korea vs. South Korea	
Coalitions	NATO vs. Warsaw Pact	
Regions	Southeast Asia; Persian Gulf	
Time Periods	Present; Future	
Organizational	Land, Sea, Air, and Space Forces	
Functional	General & Special Purpose Forces	
Side-by-Side	*Blue Side*	*Red Side*
	Aircraft	Aircraft
	Submarines	Submarines
	Tanks	Tanks
Head-to-Head	*Blue Side*	*Red Side*
	Aircraft	Air Defense
	Submarines	ASW Forces
	Tanks	Antitank Weapons
Demographic	Military Manpower	
Scientific/Technological	Research and Development	
Military-Industrial Complex	Production Potential	
Dynamic Assessments	**Dynamic Assessments**	
Portray Trends	U.S.-Soviet Balance, 1946–1989	
Predict Outcomes	War Games; Computer Simulations	

against much larger opponents who are comparably or more proficient. Quantitative superiority, equality, and inferiority, however, may have positive, negative or neutral effects, depending on circumstances. Adding ICBMs and SLBMs to swollen inventories, for example, *might* enhance deterrence, but reliable Blue defenses would better offset Red superiority in ballistic missiles if deterrence failed.[37]

Active Forces

Numbers nonetheless *do* count. Soviet military strategists, who sanctified V. I. Lenin's contention that "quantity has a quality all its own," therefore retained obsolescent weapon systems that U.S. counterparts would have slated for early retirement. Two well matched football teams illuminate the Kremlin's rationale: Paramedics cart star players off the field early in the first quarter. Referees cannot enforce the rules, so the Red side reinforces with its second string,

which has twenty-two players, not eleven as authorized. The Blue side has no second string. The Red team's coach then piles on his third string, which has thirty-three players, not twenty-two. Guess who gets steamrolled?[38] Substitute U.S. Armed Forces for the Blue team and Soviet adversaries for the Red, and it becomes clear why 1,000 MiG-21 fighter aircraft, first deployed in 1956, remained active as late as 1982. The same could be said for nearly 20,000 Soviet T-54 and T-55 tanks, the first of which saw service in 1947.

Reserve Components

Relatively small active armed forces as a rule lack much operational flexibility if they face numerically superior foes on even one broad front (much less two or more), and cannot tolerate lengthy wars of attrition. Many nations therefore rely extensively on reserve components to save money and conserve manpower in peacetime.

"Bean counters" consequently scrutinize enemy mobilization machinery to ascertain how quickly units and individual replacements might reinforce active-duty components and how long they could remain mobilized without seriously disrupting civilian routines. Israeli Armed Forces earned high marks for abilities to man ramparts in record time with large numbers of skilled reserves during wars in 1956, 1967, and 1973, the most lengthy of which lasted one month, but chaos could ensue if future call-ups deprived the economy of essential civilian workers for lengthy periods. Pluses thus might outweigh minuses on some occasions and vice versa.

Assessing Qualitative Asymmetries

Qualitative asymmetries are more difficult to assess than quantitative equivalents, whether analysts compare Blue and Red components "side-by-side" or offensive and defensive forces "head-to-head," as shown on Table 5 (page 29). Enemy aircraft speeds, service ceilings, combat radii, payload capacities, reliability, and readiness, for example, often are subjects for speculation. Indeed, technical specialists cannot always reach a consensus even after they inspect captured material.

Composite Assessments

Net assessments, which customarily are shot full of assumptions, seldom tell the truth, the whole truth, and nothing but the truth, no matter how hard their architects try. Systems analysis "Whiz Kids" who worked for Secretary of Defense Robert McNamara in the 1960s consequently postulated "various sets of assumptions, ranging from optimistic to pessimistic," then, in the absence of facts, assigned "a range of capabilities" regarding Soviet pluses and minuses. Their motto was, "It is Better to Be Roughly Right Than Precisely Wrong," for "all the facts will never be in, and in the meantime decisions have to be made on the best information available."[39]

The best net assessments, like intelligence estimates, frequently seem fallible when seen in that light. Fortunate strategists consequently consult more than one oracle before finalizing security plans, implementing costly programs, and initiating operations that might prove imprudent.

THREAT ASSESSMENTS

Military threats occupy at least eight categories: global and regional; short-, mid-, and long-range; low-, mid-, and high-intensity; receding, expanding, and steady; national, multinational, and subnational; military and nonmilitary; lethal and nonlethal; nuclear, biological, chemical, radiological, traditional, and unconventional. When perceived threats are hydraheaded, wise Chiefs of State and their advisers couple comparative capabilities with probable courses of enemy action, establish priorities according to imminence and intensities, then concentrate on the greatest hazards.[40]

Some such choices might stump Solomon. The most demanding mission of U.S. Armed Forces at the onset of the twenty-first century was to "deter and, if deterrence fails, defeat large-scale, cross-border aggression in two distant theaters in overlapping time frames."[41] President Clinton's national security team concluded early on that major regional contingencies of that magnitude most likely might erupt in Korea and the Middle East. The key question in such event was: Which requirement should take precedence if U.S. and allied assets prove insufficient to cope with both concurrently?

Complexities of that sort make threat assessments at the national level more an art than a science. Policy-makers and strategists must do the best they can with imprecise intelligence estimates and net assessments, solicit advice from voices of experience, elect the option that seems most appropriate, and adjust when situations change.

KEY POINTS

- The conflict spectrum spans the full range of potential national security threats
- Intelligence communities perform most effectively only if customers furnish strategic guidance
- Military power available to friends and neutrals as well as foes strongly influences military intelligence estimates, net assessments, and threat assessments
- Military power depends on quantitative and qualitative characteristics of armed forces, together with integrating factors such as roles, functions, organizational structures, policies, strategies, tactics, doctrines, and command/control procedures
- The most dangerous enemy capabilities imaginable constitute dangerous threats only if accompanied by intentions to implement them
- The purpose of intelligence estimates is to identify what courses of action are open to foreign armed forces and which option(s) they likely will elect
- Net assessments compare the capabilities and intentions of friendly, enemy, and neutral armed forces to reveal relative strengths, weaknesses, vulnerabilities, and opportunities
- The best intelligence estimates and net assessments are fallible, because the data upon which they predicate findings are incomplete
- Savvy Chiefs of State and their politico-military advisers habitually prioritize threat assessments

NOTES

1. Julian Lider, *Military Theory: Concept, Structure, Problems* (Aldershot, UK: Gower, 1983), 170–85.

2. Herman Kahn, *On Escalation: Metaphors and Scenarios* (New York: Praeger, 1965), 37–195, 218.

3. Robert G. Wirsing, *India, Pakistan, and the Kashmir Dispute* (New York: St. Martin's Press, 1994).

4. Vernon Loeb, "A Global, Pan-Islamic Network," *Washington Post*, August 23, 1998, A1, A24–A25.

5. *Critical Foundations: Protecting America's Infrastructures,* Report of the President's Commission on Critical Infrastructure Protection, October 1997, 15–20, 23, 27–31, and Appendix A; *Report of the Defense Science Board Task Force on Information Warfare-Defense (IW-D)* (Washington: Office of the Under Secretary of Defense for Acquisition and Technology, November 1997).

6. "Interview With Lt. Gen. Robert C. Kingston," *Armed Forces Journal,* July 1984, 72; "Washington Whispers," *U.S. News & World Report,* August 10, 1998, 10.

7. Sherman Kent, *Strategic Intelligence* (Princeton, NJ: Princeton University Press, 1965), 3–65, 180–84, 209–20.

8. For quantitative trends over twenty consecutive years, see John M. Collins with Bernard Victory, *U.S./Soviet Military Balance, Statistical Trends, 1970–1979,* Rpt. 87-839 S (Washington: Congressional Research Service, September 18, 1987) and *Statistical Trends, 1980–1989,* with Dianne Rennack, Rpt. 90-401 RCO 9 (August 6, 1990).

9. Andrew R. Molnar et al., DA Pamphlet 550-104, *Human Factors Considerations of Undergrounds in Insurgencies* (Washington: Headquarters, Department of the Army, September 1966), 17–35, 101–07.

10. Benjamin Burton, *Fair Play: CBS, General Westmoreland, and How a Television Documentary Went Wrong* (New York: Harper & Row, 1988); T. L. Cubbage, "Westmoreland vs. CBS: Was Intelligence Corrupted by Policy Demands?" *Intelligence and National Security,* March 3, 1988, 118–80.

11. *Selected Military Capabilities of the People's Republic of China,* Report to Congress Pursuant to Section 1305 of the FY 97 National Defense Authorization Act from the Secretary of Defense (April 1997).

12. Major William H. Burgess, III, ed., *Inside Spetsnaz: Soviet Special Operations, A Critical Analysis* (Novato, CA: Presidio Press, 1990); *Defense White Paper, 1997–1998* (Seoul: Ministry of National Defense, Republic of Korea, 1998), 50.

13. General Frederick J. Kroesen, "What Is Hollow?" *Army,* February 1999, 9. General Edward C. Meyer discussed "hollowness" during hearings before the Investigations Subcommittee of the House Armed Services Committee. See *National Defense Funding*

Levels for Fiscal Year 1981, 96th Cong., 2d sess., May 29, 1980, 18.

14. Basil H. Liddell Hart, *Thoughts on War* (London: Faber and Faber, 1944), 115.

15. *The Maritime Strategy,* supplement to *U.S. Naval Institute Proceedings,* January 1986. Superseded by *From the Sea: Preparing the Naval Service for the 21st Century,* a White Paper (Washington: Department of the Navy, September 1992); *Forward . . . From the Sea* (Washington: Department of the Navy, 1994).

16. Carl von Clausewitz, *On War,* ed. and trans. Michael Howard and Peter Paret (Princeton, NJ: Princeton University Press, 1976), 184–85.

17. *NATO-WARSAW Pact: Conventional Force Balance: Papers for U.S. and Soviet Perspectives Workshops,* Supplement B (Washington: General Accounting Office, 1988), 87–88.

18. Robert D. Shuey, *Nuclear, Biological, and Chemical Weapons and Missiles: The Current Situation and Trends,* Rpt. RC 30699 (Washington: Congressional Research Service, January 5, 2001).

19. *Critical Foundations: Protecting America's Infrastructures,* 7, 14; James Adams, *The Next World War* (New York: Simon & Schuster, 1998).

20. The U.S. European Command furnished watchlist statistics on November 18, 1977. For related indicators, see Field Manual (FM) 30-102, *Opposing Forces Europe* (Washington: Department of the Army, November 8, 1977), 2-26 through 2-32.

21. General Colin L. Powell with Joseph E. Persico, *My American Journey* (New York: Random House, 1995), 459–71.

22. Dana Priest, "Iran Poises Its Forces on Afghan Border," *Washington Post,* September 5, 1998, A1, A22.

23. Kent, *Strategic Intelligence,* xxii.

24. William Manchester, *American Caesar: Douglas MacArthur, 1880-1964* (Boston: Little, Brown, 1978), 538-42; General Matthew B. Ridgway, *The Korean War* (Garden City, NY: Doubleday & Co., 1967), 10-13.

25. Vladimir I. Lenin, *What Is to Be Done?,* trans. S. V. and Patricia Utechin, ed. S. V. Utechin (Oxford, UK: Clarendon Press, 1963).

26. Adolf Hitler, *Mein Kampf,* trans. Ralph Mannheim (Boston: Houghton Mifflin, 1943).

27. *Selected Works of Mao Tse-Tung,* 4 vols. (Beijing: Foreign Languages Press, 1965).

28. Nobutaka Ike, *Japanese Politics* (London: Eyre & Spottiswoode, 1958), 251-62; Harold S. Quigley and John E. Turner, *The New Japan: Government and Politics* (Minneapolis: University of Minnesota Press, 1956), 29-43.

29. Raymond L. Garthoff, *Détente and Confrontation: American-Soviet Relations from Nixon to Reagan* (Washington: Brookings Institution, 1985).

30. Rinn-Sup Shinn, *North Korea: Policy Determinants, Alternative Outcomes, U.S. Policy Approaches,* Rpt. 93-612F (Washington: Congressional Research Service, June 24, 1993); Robert G. Sutter, *Korea-U.S. Relations: Issues for Congress,* Issue Brief 92068 (Washington: Congressional Research Service, March 21, 1994).

31. *National Intelligence Estimates A-B Team Episode Concerning Soviet Strategic Capability and Objectives.* Report of the Senate Select Committee on Intelligence, Subcommittee on Selection, Production, and Quality, 95th Cong., 2d sess. (Washington, U.S. Government Printing Office, February 16, 1968); Richard Pipes, "Team B: The Reality Behind the Myth," *Commentary,* October 1986, 25–40; Alexander George, "The Case for Multiple Advocacy in Making Foreign Policy," *American Political Science Review,* September 1972, 751–85.

32. Sun Tzu, *The Art of War,* trans. Samuel B. Griffith (New York: Oxford University Press, 1963), 84.

33. John M. Collins, "Essentials of Net Assessment," in *U.S.-Soviet Military Balance, Concepts and Capabilities, 1960-1980* (Washington: McGraw-Hill Publications, 1980), 3–14.

34. Hans J. Morgenthau, *Politics Among Nations,* 5th ed. (New York: Alfred A. Knopf, 1972), 167–223, 327–50.

35. G. Shakhazarov, "On Problems of Correlation of Forces in the World," *Strategic Review,* Fall 1974, 109–14; Ellen Jones, *Correlation of Forces in Soviet Military Decisionmaking* (a paper delivered at the Bicentennial Conference, Section on Military Studies, International Studies Association, Charleston, SC, November 10, 1978).

36. Clausewitz, *On War,* 119-23; John Keegan portrays the effects of friction in *The Face of Battle* (New York: Viking Press, 1976).

37. *United States/Soviet Military Balance: A Frame of Reference for Congress,* Senate Committee on Armed Services, 94th Cong., 2d sess. (Washington: U.S. Government Printing Office, January 1976), 21–26.

38. "Bean Counting," correspondence from the author to Hon. Patricia Schroeder, Chairperson, Defense Burden Sharing Panel, House Armed Services Committee, March 4, 1988.

39. Robert S. McNamara, *Statement before the Senate Armed Services Committee on the FY 1969-73 Defense Program and 1969 Defense Budget* (January 22, 1968), 43; Alain C. Enthoven and K. Wayne Smith, *How Much Is Enough? Shaping the Defense*

Program, 1961–1969 (New York: Harper & Row, 1971), 68.

40. *Global Trends 2015: Dialogue About the Future with Nongovernment Experts,* NIC 2000-02 (Washington: paper prepared under the direction of the National Intelligence Council for publication by the National Intelligence Board, December 2000).

41. *A National Security Strategy for a New Century* (Washington: The White House, December 1999), 19.

4. Basic Security Objectives

Purpose is the central ingredient of power. Powerful people and organizations have a strong . . . sense of purpose, [which] is worth 80 IQ points.

Michael Eisner
Strategy and Business

Michael Eisner hit the nail on the head. Basic security objectives, which indicate what must be done to safeguard essential interests despite foreign and domestic threats, underpin the formulation of policies, strategies, plans, and programs that indicate how to do it. National security policy-makers and military strategists consequently must keep crucial goals in sight day and night. Failure to do so can needlessly intensify perils, waste lives, squander resources, and perhaps court defeat.

Prewar, intrawar, and postwar objectives, like the interests they seek to assure, may be global, regional, or functional, major or minor, positive or negative, immediate or deferred. Optimum results consistently ensue only if political purposes, military aims, and implementing missions mesh well and focus appropriate power on strategic centers of gravity.

NATIONAL SECURITY OBJECTIVES

Chiefs of State, assisted by trusted lieutenants, promote objectives they believe would serve national security interests best, bearing in mind that strong institutions, economies, and social systems often are more important than military power.[1] Aims that seek to balance budgets, reduce tax burdens, curb inflation, and promote other domestic programs thus bump into those that demand strong armed forces.

Prerequisites for Approval

Autocrats commonly determine national purposes independently, whereas democratic governments must pay more attention to the wants, needs, and aspirations of people they serve. Chief executives who hope to avoid acrimonious disputes take public opinion into account before rather than after crises occur.

Solid approval even so may evaporate if situations turn sour, as President Lyndon B. Johnson discovered during the Vietnam War. Congress and most concerned citizens approved when his announced purpose was to contain the spread of Communism in Southeast Asia, but the Tonkin Gulf Resolution of August 7, 1964, which passed by a vote of 88–2 in the Senate and 416–0 in the House, was fast forgotten after U.S. body bags began to accumulate. Widespread dissent continued until U.S. ground forces completed their withdrawal in 1972.[2]

Typical Objectives at the Top

Samples from the rich menu of broad, enduring national security objectives appear on Table 6. Each entry opens with a verb that denotes necessary action. Every such list should be realistic and internally consistent, which Table 6 in some respects is not. "Avoid Confrontations" and "Oppose Oppressors," for example, are mutually exclusive ways to protect interests in peace. "Encourage Capitalism,"

Table 6
National Security Interests and Complementary Objectives

Selected Security Interests	Sample Security Objectives
Homeland Defense	Deter or Defeat Invasions Protect People and Production Base Retrieve Lost Territory Improve Recuperative Powers
Peace	Avoid Confrontations Oppose Oppressors Promote Peacekeeping Promote Democracy Promote Human Rights
Stability	Neutralize Imperialistic Regimes Depose Rogue Leaders Prevent NBC Proliferation Isolate Transnational Terrorists Minimize Refugee Problems
Prosperity	Eliminate Poverty Encourage Capitalism Encourage Free Trade Conserve Natural Resources Preserve Global Environments Prevent Inflation or Recession
Domestic Tranquility	Eliminate Causes of Insurgency Suppress Crime Eliminate Illicit Drug Traffic Improve Education Raise Living Standards
Military Power	Modernize Armed Forces Maintain Force Sufficiency Create Strong Coalitions Foster Technological Innovation Promote Arms Control

a companion of security objectives that promote democracy and free trade, contributes to economic chaos instead of prosperity in post-Soviet Russia.[3]

High-level objectives seldom exist in vacuums. Soviet divisions, for example, could have crushed Poland in the 1980s, when Lech Walesa and his "counterrevolutionary" labor union *Solidarity* were pains in the Kremlin's posterior, but the Politburo spurned that objective because brutal suppression almost certainly would have alarmed NATO, deprived the USSR of much needed hard currency, prevented completion of a Soviet pipeline into Western Europe, risked a lengthy conflict like the one

then raging in Afghanistan, encouraged domestic agitation, and precluded potentially beneficial arms control accords with the United States.[4]

NATIONAL MILITARY AIMS

Well-crafted national military aims complement national political objectives, which they support (Table 7). Each should be unambiguous, consistent, attainable with available armed forces, and flexible enough to accommodate change when circumstances require. Two topics merit particular attention: standards of success and the value of military victory.

Table 7
National Security Objectives and Basic Military Aims

Selected Security Objectives	Sample Military Aims
Deter Aggressors	Avoid Provocations Deploy Superior Power Instill Fear of Reprisal Deceive Opponents Demoralize Opponents
Defeat Aggressors	Destroy Enemy Armed Forces Confine Collateral Damage Occupy Enemy Territory Pacify Insurgents Eradicate Terrorist Sanctuaries
Ensure Force Sufficiency	Improve Land Force Mobility Improve Littoral Warfare Posture Perpetuate Superior Air Power Improve Missile Defense Capabilities Improve CW and BW Defenses Strengthen Information Dominance
Create Strong Coalitions	Promote Compatible Doctrines Improve Joint/Combined Training Promote Interoperable Materiel Strengthen Security Assistance Obtain or Retain Base Rights Abroad
Foster Technological Progress	Improve Requirement Forecasting Improve Program Management Shorten Acquisition Times Improve Cross-Service Applicability Decrease Costs
Improve Recuperative Powers	Strengthen Reserve Components Improve Mobilization Procedures Improve Mass Casualty Care Invigorate Civil Defense Tighten Military-Industrial Ties

Standards of Success

Clearly stated military aims not only tell recipients precisely what to do, but constitute achievement standards with which to measure success. Problems arise in both regards when goals are too vague for strategic concept formulation and planning.

U.S. and British Combined Chiefs of Staff on February 12, 1944 left no room for anything less than unconditional surrender when they directed General Dwight D. Eisenhower to "enter the continent of Europe and . . . undertake operations aimed at the heart of Germany and the destruction of her

Armed Forces." When that task was complete, Ike wrote, "The mission of this Allied force was fulfilled at 0241 local time, May 7, 1945."[5]

The Reagan Doctrine, in contrast, simply sought to assist anti-Communist insurgents and resistance movements around the world.[6] Its basic aim in the 1980s was to help friends help themselves, but help them do what was seldom transparent. Help them overthrow oppressive governments? Achieve military victory? Avoid defeat? Compel reforms? Promote negotiated settlements? All of the above? Such imprecision eventually caused Congress to curtail covert activities and invoke stringent restrictions on funds for counterrevolutionary Contras, who struggled to unseat the Communist Sandinista Government in Nicaragua.[7]

Values of Military Victory

Basil H. Liddell Hart, whose writings on strategy are renowned, was wont to remind readers that one must make sharp distinctions between national security objectives and military aims, because "history shows that gaining military victory is not in itself equivalent to gaining the objective of policy." When armed combat occurs, "policy has too often been governed by the military aim—and [victory] has been regarded as an end in itself, instead of merely a means to an end."[8] Those insightful words apply to cold and lukewarm as well as heated conflicts.

Victory Without Peace

U.S. statesmen and military strategists demonstrated Liddell Hart's points conclusively during World War II, when their preoccupation with military victory largely ignored political implications. General Eisenhower, reminiscing about his experiences as Supreme Commander of Allied Expeditionary Forces in Europe, revealed that the "future division of Germany did not influence our military plans for the final conquest of [that] country." Berlin, he acknowledged, "was politically and psychologically important as the symbol of remaining German power" in April 1945, but he decided that "it was not the logical or the most desirable objective for the forces of the Western Allies."[9]

Short-sighted (mainly U.S.) concessions at the Teheran, Yalta, and Potsdam conferences meanwhile redrew political maps in ways that helped the Soviet Union acquire superpower status, settled Stalin in Central Europe, and ushered in the Cold War on the Kremlin's terms. The Iron Curtain that separated East from West in 1946 remained firmly in place and prevented true peace for more than forty years.[10]

Victory Without War

Sun Tzu, in his essays on *The Art of War* circa 500 B.C., asserted that "to subdue the enemy without fighting is the acme of skill. . . . Thus a victorious army wins its victories before seeking battle." Liddell Hart said essentially the same thing more than two millennia later: "The true aim is not so much to seek battle as to seek a strategic situation so advantageous that if it does not of itself produce the decision, its continuation by a battle is sure to achieve [that objective.]"[11]

The United States to those ends amassed overwhelming land, sea, air, and amphibious forces near the most likely battleground during the Cuban missile crisis of October 1962 and prepared to support them along sea lines of communication that reached only ninety miles across the Florida Strait. Soviet adversaries on the other hand were poorly disposed to mass (much less sustain) traditional combat power several thousand miles from home bases. Nikita Khrushchev blustered, but backed down without firing a shot.[12] NATO's armed forces, being geographically disadvantaged and configured primarily for deterrence and defense rather than offensive combat, similarly found discretion to be the better part of valor when Soviet troops well behind the Iron Curtain savaged anti-Communist recalcitrants in East Berlin (1953), Budapest (1956), and Prague (1968).[13]

War Without Victory

War without victory, the precise opposite of victory without war, involves armed conflicts that Chiefs of State, by mutual consent, terminate on compromise terms before either side emerges a clear winner.[14] Overly ambitious military aims are unacceptable under such conditions.

General of the Army Douglas MacArthur, an old centurion who saw "no substitute for victory," discovered that fact of life the hard way in 1950–51 during wintry combat with Chinese "volunteers" in frozen Chosin. He surreptitiously petitioned Congress after the Joint Chiefs of Staff repeatedly rejected his recommendations to bomb sanctuaries in Manchuria, blockade the Chinese coast, and unleash Chiang Kai-shek's Nationalist Chinese forces on Taiwan to fight on the Chinese mainland. President Harry Truman on April 9, 1951 finally fired his five-star commander for insubordination because, as he put it, "I was left with one simple conclusion: General MacArthur was willing to risk general war. I was not."[15]

Victory at Excessive Cost

Pyrrhus of Epirus, a kinsman of Alexander the Great, reportedly lamented, "One more such victory and we are undone," after he defeated Roman adversaries at Heraclea and Asculum in 297 B.C.[16] Substitutes for victory ever since then have been attractive unless crucial interests were at stake and cost-benefit ratios were favorable.

U.S. military involvement in Vietnam (1965–73) dramatically demonstrated the penalties for pursuing military aims despite exorbitant expenditures of political capital, time, money, materiel, and young lives. Ho Chi Minh, his successors, and Viet Cong insurgents steadfastly aimed to unite that nation under Communist rule. All *really were* willing to "pay any price, bear any burden, meet any hardship, support any friend, oppose any foe"[17] to safeguard their vital interests. U.S. leaders, whose security interests and supporting objectives paled by comparison, *really were not.*

General William C. Westmoreland, who headed U.S. Military Assistance Command Vietnam from June 1964 until June 1968, later observed that, "A lack of determination to stay the course, to react with meaningful moves to the enemy's flagrant violations of solemn international agreements demonstrated in Cambodia, South Vietnam, and Laos that the alternative to victory is defeat."[18] President Richard M. Nixon and Congress, however, found defeat preferable to mounting casualties, open-ended monetary costs, and domestic disorders that were ripping the United States asunder.

MILITARY ROLES AND MISSIONS

Armed forces everywhere organize, equip, and train to perform broad, enduring *roles.*[19] Senior military commanders employ forces to accomplish strategically significant *missions* and perform *functions* that support national security objectives and national military aims.[20] Resultant responsibilities generate distinctive force posture objectives.

Military Roles and Functions

Each military service is optimized to function most effectively on land, at sea, in the air, in space, or in some combination of geographic environments (Table 8). Important responsibilities occasionally interlock and overlap, but well-crafted roles nevertheless determine which Service should be authorized to employ personnel and materiel for given purposes:

- The primary role of every army is to conduct prompt and sustained operations on land. All organize, equip, and train forces to deter or defeat enemy ground forces and, if necessary, seize, secure, occupy, and govern hostile territory.
- The primary role of all naval forces is to conduct prompt and sustained operations at sea and along littorals. All organize, equip, and train forces to deter or defeat enemy navies, control essential sea lines of communication, and furnish sealift.
- The primary role of all land-based and naval air forces is to achieve air superiority. All additionally organize, equip, and train forces to conduct reconnaissance missions and interdict enemy landlines of communication. Some furnish land forces with air transportation as well as close air support.
- The primary role of military space forces early in the twenty-first century is to provide reconnaissance, surveillance, early warning, communications, navigation, and

weather forecasting support for armed forces on Earth. Future roles almost certainly will include offensive and defensive combat.

Some land forces occasionally participate in amphibious operations, some air forces assist in sea control, some naval forces conduct inflight refueling, but not every nation assigns every function that Table 8 depicts. Only a few nations for example possess enough economic and technological wherewithal to deploy military space capabilities. Soviet Border Guards and Internal Security Troops, which together totaled more than 800,000 in the mid-1980s, were larger than most armies, whereas assorted restrictions prohibit direct participation

by U.S. military personnel (other than the Coast Guard) in "search, seizure, arrest or other similar activities. . .unless otherwise authorized by law."[21]

Military Missions

Implementing missions, unlike national security objectives and military aims, direct armed forces to undertake particular tasks at particular times and places. Properly composed instructions that tell commanders what to do, but not how to do it, preserve initiative.

Strategic Missions

Military missions of strategic significance generally cover large regions or blanket the globe. President Truman's *Outline Command Plan* in the aftermath

Table 8
Typical Military Functions

	Land Forces	Naval Forces	Air Forces	Space Forces
Combat Functions				
Offensive Combat	X	X	X	
Air Defense	X	X	X	
Missile Defense	X	X	X	X
Airborne Operations	X		X	
Amphibious Operations		X		
Antisubmarine Warfare		X		
Unconventional Warfare	X	X	X	
Counterinsurgency	X	X	X	
Counterterrorism	X	X		
Coastal Security		X		
Internal Security	X			
Combat Support Functions				
Intelligence	X	X	X	X
Communications	X	X	X	X
Psychological Operations	X		X	
Electronic Warfare	X	X	X	
Inflight Refueling			X	
Search and Rescue		X	X	
Service Support Functions				
Airlift (Long Haul)			X	
Sealift (Long Haul)		X		
Spacecraft Launch/Recovery				X
Logistics	X	X	X	
Civil Affairs	X			
Meteorological		X	X	X
Navigation		X	X	X
Nonmilitary Functions				
Humanitarian Assistance	X		X	
Disaster Relief	X		X	
Civic Works	X			

of World War II instructed newly activated U.S. European Command to occupy Germany, support U.S. national policy for Europe, and plan for a general emergency. He concurrently told U.S. Pacific Command to secure sea and air lines of communication across the Pacific Ocean and protect the United States against attacks from that quarter. Six other commanders in chief received equally specific assignments.[22]

The Kremlin during the Cold War issued analogous missions to the commanders of five continental and two oceanic theaters. Four Groups of Forces headquartered in East Germany, Poland, Czechoslovakia, and Hungary shared responsibilities for Central Europe. Comparable missions went to Border Guards and Internal Security Troops, plus sixteen Military Districts that, on call, were scheduled to become army groups called "fronts" inside the Soviet Union.[23]

Operational and Tactical Missions

Missions at successively lower levels focus ever more sharply, are mainly operational or tactical rather than strategic in nature, and areas of responsibility range from regional to local. Military space forces, for example, might be told to verify the presence or absence of nuclear weapon facilities at Site C in Iraq or help forecasters predict weather conditions over the Strait of Hormuz next Wednesday.

Mission Creep

Statesmen and strategists consistently need to guard against "mission creep" which, if uncontrolled, may incrementally create unreasonable requirements.[24] U.S. policy-makers in Somalia belatedly rediscovered that the road to hell can be paved with best intentions when they switched from humanitarian assistance to peacemaking and nation building in the summer of 1993. Subsequent shootouts between U.S./UN Armed Forces and enraged mobs beholden to fugitive warlord Mohammad Farah Aideed made the new mission so dubious that President Clinton,

sensitive to adverse public opinion at home and abroad, withdrew all U.S. troops before they fully accomplished *any* mission.[25]

STRATEGIC CENTERS OF GRAVITY

Strategic centers of gravity, according to Clausewitz, are "the hub of all power and movement, on which everything depends. That is the point against which all energies should be directed." The fundamental task as he saw it is "to identify the enemy's centers of gravity, and if possible trace them back to a single [decisive objective]."[26] National and regional centers of gravity may be animate or inanimate, tangible or intangible, permanent, semipermanent, or transitory.

National Centers of Gravity

Capital cities, key individuals, and collective esprit typify national strategic centers of gravity. Crucial economic elements of military power also qualify. Allied armed forces to wit repeatedly attacked Nazi German ball bearing plants, hydroelectric dams, and petroleum production installations during World War II.[27]

Metropoli

Metropoli that house political, administrative, industrial, commercial, financial, cultural, and telecommunication facilities frequently constitute strategic centers of gravity. Small countries and city-states like Singapore are especially vulnerable. Cuba could hardly function if Havana fell. Panama capitulated quickly after U.S. Armed Forces seized control of its capital in January 1990 during Operation Just Cause. Resistance likewise crumbled the following August when Iraqi armored columns overran Kuwait City, an oasis in otherwise desolate territory.

Capital cities often are centers of gravity, even in countries that disperse vital assets over large areas. France and Germany both put Paris in that category during both World Wars. The Soviet Union might have collapsed if Nazi invaders had invested Moscow in 1941, but not in 1942, because many governmental offices, crucial defense industries, and perhaps 2,000,000 people by then had dispersed to the Ural Mountains, Western Siberia, and Central Asia.[28] Seoul changed hands four times in 1950–51, because North and South Korea both saw that war-torn city as a center of gravity.[29]

"Kingpins"

"Kill the head and the body will die," an ancient axiom, applied perfectly when Chiefs of State personally led troops into battle, because those "kingpins" were rallying points for friends and prime targets for foes. Wars often ceased when they fell; William the Conqueror, for example, won the Battle of Hastings in 1066 after King Harold of Wessex took an arrow in the eye.

Key individuals still can constitute strategic centers of gravity. Direct, discriminating, and economical operations to eliminate rival leaders are the essence of every coup d'état.[30] The U.S.-Soviet military balance might have developed quite differently if the project manager, chief scientists, and other prime movers of Project Manhattan had met untimely ends before they perfected the first atom bomb[31] or if Admiral Hyman Rickover had disappeared in the early 1950s, when he alone was pressing the development of U.S. nuclear-powered submarines.[32]

Great gains, however, normally entail great risks. Historical records include many ill-considered assassinations, such as those of Julius Caesar, Abraham Lincoln, and Austro-Hungarian Archduke Franz Ferdinand. A U.S. decision to hit the "God Emperor" Hirohito in the midst of World War II might have provoked a fight to the finish with Japan. Strategists therefore would be well advised to think problems through before they pick "kingpins" as centers of gravity.

Hearts and Minds

Lenin once wrote that "the soundest strategy is to postpone [military] operations until the moral disintegration of the enemy renders . . . a mortal blow both possible and easy."[33] Strategists may encourage affection or foment disaffection among adversaries to perform that feat. The hearts and minds of common people generally are the center of gravity in either case.

Hitler, who had scant concern for hearts and minds, perhaps lost World War II because he brutalized rather than embraced anti-Soviet Ukrainians who initially welcomed his panzer spearheads with flowers and open arms.[34] The Kremlin needed repressive internal security measures throughout the Cold War to keep minorities under control in most Soviet Socialist Republics, which were geographically, linguistically, and culturally separate from the Slavic core. Inhabitants therein expressed preference for freedom as soon as President Mikhail Gorbachev relaxed restraints.[35] North Vietnamese and Viet Cong forces lost the battle for hearts and minds in South Vietnam and took a terrible drubbing during the Tet offensive of February 1968, but mounting casualties that intensified domestic discontent throughout the United States gave them a great psychological victory.[36] Problem solvers in Hanoi thereafter tailored campaigns to tighten screws on the true center of gravity, which was U.S. national will, until they emerged victorious.[37]

Regional Centers of Gravity

Regional centers of gravity may lie within friendly or enemy boundaries. Centers also may migrate, which happened during the Second Punic War when legions led by the great Roman general Scipio Africanus sailed across the Mediterranean Sea to Carthage. Hannibal followed to defend his homeland, which had become key terrain. His defeat at Zama and destruction of the Carthaginian power base in 202 B.C. eliminated Roman fears that he or any successor might reinvade *Italia*.[38]

Continents as Centers of Gravity

Whole continents sometimes constitute regional centers of gravity. The Monroe Doctrine on December 2, 1823 proclaimed that lands in the Western

Hemisphere "are not henceforth to be considered as subjects for future colonization by any European powers."[39] U.S. strategists, who saw Europe as the overarching center of gravity during World War II, accorded that continent top priority until Nazi Germany capitulated,[40] then prolonged that precedence throughout the Cold War, because the Free World would have experienced serious trouble if the Soviet Union had added Western Europe's immense power base to its own.

Coalitions as Centers of Gravity

Clausewitz claimed that "as a principle . . . if you can vanquish all your enemies by defeating one of them. . .that must be the main objective."[41] Liddell Hart disagreed when he asserted that "it is more fruitful to concentrate first against the weaker partner[s,]" and thereby turned Clausewitzian center of gravity theories inside out.[42] Both theses bear close inspection, because neither seems to be invariably applicable.

The United States and the Soviet Union assuredly were strategic centers of gravity as Cold War leaders of NATO and the Warsaw Pact. Each alliance would have retained incredible military power if all lesser members had capitulated, whereas neither alliance could have lasted long without superpower participation. The coalition that ejected Iraqi Armed Forces from Kuwait in 1991 conversely balked in 1998, because only the United States (by far its most powerful member) favored the use of force when Saddam Hussein refused to let UN teams inspect suspected biological and chemical weapon facilities. Lack of political rather than military support from Arab allies left U.S. policy-makers and strategists with two unattractive options: take action alone and risk condemnation or rely entirely on sanctions to change Saddam's mind.[43]

Centers of Gravity in Space

Centers of gravity in space someday may outrank terrestrial counterparts. The most commanding locations in the entire Earth-Moon System may be lunar libration points L4 and L5, which respectively inscribe circles 60 degrees ahead of and 60 degrees behind the Moon in its orbit. Military space forces theoretically could loiter indefinitely at either location without expending precious fuel if, as computer calculations indicate, the gravitational pull of Earth and Moon actually cancel each other. Abilities to linger would confer unprecedented advantages, because armed forces positioned so favorably could easily launch offensive operations in any direction and, being atop the "gravity wells" of Earth as well as Moon, could defend effectively against adversaries on the bottom.[44]

Opposing Opinions

Most commentators believe that national security objectives, complementary military aims, and implementing missions should focus on centers of gravity.[45] At least one well published analyst, however, believes that "critical vulnerabilities and centers of gravity . . . rarely exist." He further contends that "by looking for a silver bullet . . . planners may ignore other, more modest but more realistic, objectives, or may oversell their plans as being potentially more effective than is the case. Arguably this is what happened in Desert Storm, where [the U.S.-led coalition] flawlessly executed plans aimed at critical vulnerabilities and centers of gravity, yet still had no decisive outcome." Allied ground forces concentrated on Iraq's Republican Guard, Allied air forces on Iraqi infrastructure, and Allied navies kept Iraq from exporting petroleum, but "nothing [they] did forced Saddam Hussein out of power or made him change his basic attitudes."[46]

Even so, there seems to be a valid explanation (if not an excuse) for that outcome. Coalition leaders fully understood that "kingpin" Saddam Hussein was a genuine center of gravity but, as JCS Chairman General Colin L. Powell later recalled, "his elimination was not a stated objective," mainly for political reasons.[47] Lesser centers that were primarily of operational or tactical rather than strategic importance accordingly had to suffice.

KEY POINTS

- National security objectives, subordinate military aims, and implementing missions underpin the formulation of politico-military policies, strategies, plans, and programs
- Properly crafted national military aims should be precise, clearly expressed, and consistent with security interests and objectives as well as available military power
- Properly crafted national security objectives take political, economic, geographic, cultural, legal, and moral as well as military matters into account
- Precisely stated military aims not only tell commanders what to do, but constitute achievement standards with which to measure success
- Military victories that nullify political objectives rarely are beneficial
- Land, sea, air, and space forces organize, equip, and train to perform broad, enduring roles and functions
- Strategically significant military missions at the highest levels generally cover large regions or blanket the globe
- Military missions at lower levels are mainly operational or tactical rather than strategic in nature, and areas of operation are regional or local
- Strategic centers of gravity afford a sharp focus for national security objectives, complementary military aims, and implementing missions

NOTES

1. George C. McGhee, ed., *National Interests and Global Goals* (Lanham, MD: University Press of America, 1989).
2. Neil Sheehan et al., *The Pentagon Papers* (New York: Quadrangle Books, 1971), 242-78; Tom Wells, *The War Within: America's Battle Over Vietnam* (Berkeley: University of California Press, 1994).
3. Robert J. Samuelson, "Global Capitalism, R.I.P.?," *Newsweek*, September 14, 1998, 40-42.
4. Nicholas G. Andrews, *Poland 1980-81: Solidarity Versus the Party* (Washington: National Defense University Press, 1985); Karen Dawisha, *Eastern Europe, Gorbachev, and Reform* (New York: Cambridge University Press, 1990).
5. General of the Army Dwight D. Eisenhower, *Crusade in Europe* (New York: Doubleday & Co., 1948), 138, 225, 397; General Walter Bedell Smith, *Eisenhower's Six Great Decisions* (New York: Longmans, Green, and Co., 1956), 229.
6. William R. Bodie, "The Reagan Doctrine," *Strategic Review*, Winter 1986, 21-29; George Liska, "The Reagan Doctrine: Monroe and Dulles Reincarnate," *SAIS Review*, Summer-Fall 1986, 83-98.
7. Nina M. Serafino and Maureen Taft-Morales, *Contra Aid: Summary and Chronology of Major Congressional Action, 1981-1989*, Rpt. Nr. 89-611F (Washington: Congressional Research Service, November 1, 1989).
8. Basil H. Liddell Hart, *Strategy*, 2d rev. ed. (New York: Praeger, 1967), Chapter XXI, "National Object and Military Aim," quotations on 351.
9. Eisenhower, *Crusade in Europe*, 396.
10. John Lewis Gaddis, *The United States and the Origins of the Cold War, 1941-1947* (Princeton, NJ: Princeton University Press, 1972); Fraser Harbut, *The Iron Curtain: Churchill, America, and the Origins of the Cold War* (New York: Oxford University Press, 1987).
11. Sun Tzu, *The Art of War*, trans. Samuel B. Griffith (New York: Oxford University Press, 1963), 77, 87; Liddell Hart, *Strategy*, 365.
12. James A. Nathan, ed., *The Cuban Missile Crisis Revisited* (New York: St. Martin's Press, 1993); Robert Smith Thompson, *The Missiles of October: The Unclassified Story of John F. Kennedy and the Cuban Missile Crisis* (New York: Simon and Schuster, 1992).
13. Wolfgang H. Kraus, "East Germany (June 1953)" and Leonard Bushkoff, "Hungary (October-November 1956)," both in *Challenge and Response in International Conflicts*, ed. Doris M. Condit and Bert H. Cooper, Jr., et al., vol. II, The Experience in Europe and the Middle East (Washington: Center for Research

in Social Systems, American University, March 1967), 457–96, 529–78; Harry Schwartz, *Prague's 200 Days: The Struggle for Democracy in Czechoslovakia* (New York: Praeger, 1969).

14. Lieutenant General Raymond B. Furlong, "On War, Political Objectives, and Military Strategy," *Parameters,* December 1983, 2–10.

15. T. R. Fehrenbach, *This Kind of War* (New York: Macmillan Co., 1963), Chapter 24, "Vae Caesar." The quotation is on 397.

16. R. Ernest and Trevor N. Dupuy, *The Harper Encyclopedia of Military History: From 3,500 B.C. to the Present,* 4th ed. (New York: HarperCollins, 1993), 66.

17. President John F. Kennedy, Inaugural Address, January 20, 1961.

18. General William C. Westmoreland, *A Soldier Reports* (Garden City, NY: Doubleday & Co., 1976), 490.

19. The broad roles and general functions of U.S. military services are contained in Title 10, United States Code: Section 167, Special Operations Forces; Section 3062, Army; Section 5062, Navy; Section 5063, Marine Corps; Section 8062, Air Force; and Title 14, Coast Guard. For amplifications, see *Department of Defense Directive 5100.1: Functions of the Department of Defense and Its Major Components* (Washington, September 25, 1987), 10–21.

20. Responsibilities of the nine U.S. unified combatant commands are contained in *Unified Command Plan,* Memorandum for the Secretary of Defense (Washington: The White House, September 29, 1999).

21. Title 10, United States Code, Sections 375 and 379; Title 18, Section 1385, "Use of Army and Air Force As *Posse Comitatus.*" See also, Charles Doyle, *Use of the Military to Enforce Civilian Law: Posse Comitatus Act and Other Considerations,* Rpt. 95-964S (Washington: Congressional Research Service, September 12, 1995).

22. Walter S. Poole, *The History of the Unified Command Plan, 1946–1993* (Washington: Joint History Office, Office of the Chairman of the Joint Chiefs of Staff, February 1995), 12–13, 127–29.

23. Harriet Fast Scott and William F. Scott, *The Armed Forces of the USSR* (Boulder, CO: Westview Press, 1979), 173–226; *Soviet Military Power* (Washington: U.S. Government Printing Office, March 1987), 63–70.

24. Adam B. Siegel, "Mission Creep or Mission Misunderstood?" *Joint Force Quarterly,* Summer 2000, 112–15.

25. Robert B. Oakley, "An Envoy's Perspective," *Joint Force Quarterly,* Autumn 1993, 44–55.

26. Carl von Clausewitz, *On War,* ed. and trans. Michael Howard and Peter Paret (Princeton, NJ: Princeton University Press, 1976), 595–97, 617–19.

27. *U.S. Strategic Bombing Survey: European War* (Washington: U.S. Government Printing Office, 1945–1947), especially No. 2, "Overall Report," No. 3, "The Effects of Strategic Bombing on the German War Economy," and No. 64A, "The Impact of Allied Air Effort on German Logistics."

28. Alexander Werth, *Russia At War, 1941–1945* (New York: E. P. Dutton, 1964), 213–24, 235, 241.

29. Fehrenbach, *This Kind of War,* 71–76, 237–53, 384, 443.

30. Edward Luttwak, *Coup d'État* (New York: Alfred A. Knopf, 1969).

31. Richard Rhodes, *The Making of the Atomic Bomb* (New York: Simon and Schuster, 1986).

32. Francis Duncan, *Rickover and the Nuclear Navy: The Discipline of Technology* (Annapolis, MD: Naval Institute Press, 1989).

33. Robert D. Heinl, Jr., *Dictionary of Military and Naval Quotations* (Annapolis, MD: Naval Institute Press, 1966), 311.

34. Werth, *Russia at War,* 599–618, 790–800.

35. Gary L. Guertner, "Competitive Strategies and Soviet Vulnerabilities," *Parameters,* March 1988, 26–36; Steven J. Woehrel, *Soviet Union: An Assessment of Recent Republic and Local Elections,* Rpt. No. 90-355F (Washington: Congressional Research Service, July 20, 1990).

36. Don Oberdorfer, *Tet!* (New York: Doubleday and Co., 1971).

37. General Bruce Palmer, Jr., *The 25-Year War: America's Role in Vietnam* (Lexington: University Press of Kentucky, 1984); Harry Summers, *On Strategy: A Critical Analysis of the Vietnam War* (Novato, CA: Presidio Press, 1982).

38. Basil H. Liddell Hart, *Scipio Africanus: Greater Than Napoleon* (New York: Biblo and Tannen, 1971), 123–203.

39. Samuel Flagg Bemis, *A Diplomatic History of the United States,* 5th ed. (New York: Holt, Rinehart and Winston, 1965), 210–11.

40. Louis Morton, "Germany First: The Basic Concept of Allied Strategy in World War II," in *Command Decisions,* ed. by Kent Roberts Greenfield (New York: Harcourt, Brace and Co., 1959), 11–47.

41. Clausewitz, *On War,* 596–97, 617.

42. Basil H. Liddell Hart, *Thoughts on War* (London: Faber and Faber, 1943), 60.

43. John M. Goshko, "U.S. Stands Alone in Seeking Force Against Iraq," *Washington Post,* September 21, 1998, A16.

44. G. Harry Stine, *Confrontation in Space* (Englewood Cliffs, NJ: Prentice-Hall, 1981), 57, 58, 60–61, 86–87.

45. Steven Metz and Frederick M. Downey, "Centers of Gravity and Strategic Planning," *Military Review,* April 1988, 27-33.

46. Mark Cancian, "Centers of Gravity Are a Myth," *U.S. Naval Institute Proceedings,* September 1998, 30-34.

47. General Colin L. Powell and Joseph R. Persico, *My American Journey* (New York: Random House, 1995), quotation on 490. See also 491, 524, 526-27.

5. The Primacy of Policy

*There is an eternal dispute between those who
imagine the world to suit their policy, and those who
correct their policy to suit the realities of the world.*

Attributed to
Albert Sorel
Respectfully Quoted

Illinois Governor Adlai E. Stevenson, speaking to the Los Angeles Town Club on September 11, 1952, asserted that "The really basic thing in government is policy. Bad administration, to be sure, can destroy good policy, but good administration can never save bad policy." His sage observation has major national security implications, because national security policies not only govern objectives (ends) and resource allocations (means), but constrain acceptable courses of action (ways) and otherwise shape politico-military strategies, whether instigators freewheel or take real world conditions into account.

This chapter describes basic policy attributes, then concentrates on three of the pivotal options that Table 9 depicts: civil-military control (who calls the shots), relationships between foreign and domestic policy (which receives most resources); and relative ranks of military and nonmilitary power (which options take precedence).

BASIC POLICY ATTRIBUTES

National security policies, which reflect cultural contexts, vary from time to time and place to place. Unlike commitments, they incur no obligations. Policies also differ from military doctrines, which standardize offensive and defensive procedures under various conditions on land (in the arctic, jungles,

mountains, deserts, cities), at sea (surface, subsurface), along littorals, in Earth's atmosphere, and in space.[1]

Policies Compared with Commitments

Policies differ essentially from commitments, which make governments take action in response to specified conditions. Collective security policies, for example, loosely link communities of nations that have common wants and needs, whereas Article 5 of the North Atlantic Treaty stipulates that "an armed attack against one or more [members] . . . shall be considered an attack against them all," and thereby obliges each signatory to take "such action as it deems necessary, including the use of armed force." The United States, which has no security contract with Israel, supports that nation's independence and territorial integrity as a matter of policy, but incurs no commitment.

Stability vs. Change

National security policies are relatively stable as a rule, but reversals occasionally occur on short notice without any alteration in national interests, as previously militaristic Japanese policy-makers confirmed when they embraced a pacifist constitution shortly after atom bombs devastated Hiroshima and

Table 9
Polarized Politico-Military Policy Options

Polarized Control Options	Civilian Control or Military Control Central Control or Diffuse Control
Polarized Foreign Policy Options	Foreign Policy or Domestic Policy Military Power or Nonmilitary Power Global Influence or Regional Influence Lead or Follow Risk Management or Risk Avoidance Collective Security or Unilateral Action Security Assistance or Laissez Faire Arms Race or Arms Control
Polarized Force Development Options	Unified Services or Separate Services Quantity or Quality Balanced Forces or Dominant Service Conscripts or Volunteers Active Forces or Reserve Forces Revolutionary or Evolutionary Basic Research or Applied Technology Innovative or Proven Systems
Polarized Resource Allocation Options	Forward Presence or Power Projection Guns or Butter Cyclical Cutbacks or Continuity Plentiful Funding or Skimpy Funding Early Acquisition or Deferred Acquisition
Polarized Force Employment Options	No Time Limits or Tight Time Limits Strike First or Retaliate Decisive Force or Gradual Escalation Firepower or Maneuver Destruction or Dislocation Deep Strike or Close Combat Overt or Covert Few Civic Duties or Many Civic Duties

Nagasaki.[2] President Lyndon B. Johnson and his successor Richard M. Nixon both believed that U.S. security would suffer if Communists won the Vietnam War, but the former Americanized that conflict from 1965 through 1968 as a matter of policy, whereas the latter adopted a policy called Vietnamization immediately after he entered office on January 20, 1969.[3]

Cultural Contexts

Politiciomilitary cultures strongly influence predispositions to accept or reject particular policies. Geopolitical settings, attitudes toward armed forces and their employment, bureaucratic institutions,

technological competence, budgetary priorities, traditions, ideologies, habit patterns, beliefs, laws, ethics, and cherished values are a few among many cogent considerations. Intelligence estimators, net assessors, and strategists who endeavor to determine which among many options opponents most likely will pick thus try to worm their way inside enemy minds.[4]

History confirms that cultural influences on security policies are deeply rooted phenomena. Autocratic Assyria fathered bloodthirsty guidelines that democratic Athens found anathema. Imperial Rome adopted prescriptions that commercially inclined Phoenicia rejected, and ancient China took an entirely different tack.[5] Subnational and nongovernmental organizations as well as nation-states still elect idiosyncratic policy guidelines in response to ever-evolving cultural circumstances.

CIVIL-MILITARY POLICIES

The most elemental of all national security policies specifies whether civilian or military leaders at the highest levels exert centralized or decentralized control over armed forces. Excessive political control can undermine military effectiveness. Insufficient political control invites coups d'état and leaves military leaders free to pursue objectives that may conflict with important national interests.

Military Control

Armed forces that function as autonomous power centers rather than as servants of the State endanger dictatorships as well as democracies, because all too often they determine what roles military power should play in society, decide where and when to employ it, topple governments with which they disagree, then repress political opponents to retain control.[6] Military regimes installed without benefit of free elections dominated Latin America until democracies began to blossom late in the twentieth century[7] and continue to speckle Africa, where weak or repressive regimes beg to be replaced.[8]

Disaffected factions that favor military control sometimes instigate insurgencies and coups, even in nations that traditionally transfer political power by peaceful means. French Generals Maurice Challe, Raoul Salan, Edmond Jouhaud, and André Zeller in the spring of 1961, for example, demanded that President Charles de Gaulle renege on his offer to grant Algeria independence. The *Organisation de l'Armée Sécrète* (OAS), perhaps 40,000 strong with 18,000 paratroopers and legionnaires at the core, seized Algiers on April 22d without firing a shot, but the coup quickly collapsed because all four leaders lost heart when few other military formations rallied round their flag. Algeria gained independence

the following July; Challe and Zeller were jailed for fifteen years; Salan and Jouhaud received death sentences in absentia; senior subordinates were cashiered without pensions; and many less culpable participants suffered early retirements.[9]

Civilian Control in Autocracies

The Soviet system of supercentralized control over its military machine has served as a model for many autocratic Chiefs of State. Occupants of the Kremlin preserved that policy for seven decades, because they remembered that the Russian Revolution erupted when much of the Baltic Fleet mutinied and the cruiser *Aurora* opened fire on the Tsar's Winter Palace in Petrograd.[10] Policies and programs designed to obviate "counterrevolutionary" uprisings thus enjoyed consistently high priorities.

Preemptive Purges

Stalin preemptively squelched any possible rebellion in 1937–38 when he arrested, convicted, and executed, or imprisoned nearly 43,000 commissioned officers who conceivably might have challenged his rule, including close friends of long-standing. Axed combatant commanders reportedly included three out of five marshals, fourteen of sixteen military district commanders, eight out of nine fleet admirals and admirals in the next lower grade, fifty of fifty-seven corps commanders, 154 of 186 division commanders, and a slew of brigade commanders. Barely half of all colonels and above remained unscathed after the bloodletting ceased, some simply because they were far removed from Moscow.[11]

Those merciless purges, which shook the Soviet military establishment to its foundation, eliminated the officer corps as a possible source of competition for Stalin's political crown, but combat capabilities plummeted. Heavily outnumbered Finnish defenders outclassed substandard Soviet adversaries from November 1939 until March 1940, when sheer mass finally overwhelmed them.[12] The Generalissimo's counterproductive policy nevertheless persisted until Nazi invaders put Soviet survival at stake in June 1941. Stalin soon thereafter released and rehabilitated perhaps one fourth of all officers that kangaroo courts had incarcerated, because he desperately needed professional help to save Mother Russia.

Intrusive Control

Increasingly restrictive organizational arrangements that might have inspired Big Brother in George Orwell's horror story entitled *1984* prevented military meddling in Soviet political affairs. Communist Party control mechanisms subjected all ranks to continuous scrutiny, rewarded informants, punished miscreants, and thereby ensured strict compliance with stringent rules. Political officers at every echelon after February 1956 overrode military commanders in many regards that included responsibilities for combat readiness.[13]

Not even Marshal Georgy K. Zhukov, a charismatic Hero of the Soviet Union several times over, was immune from punitive action. Nikita Khrushchev, in his capacity as First Secretary of the Communist Party, made him Minister of Defense in 1955 and a full-fledged member of the ruling Presidium in June 1957, then sacked him four months later, partly because Zhukov's resistance to political control allegedly violated "Leninist principles concerning the administration of the armed forces" and partly because Khrushchev's cronies complained that Zhukov was "heading for a military coup d'état."[14]

Autocratic Control Appraised

Political strangleholds just described virtually obviated military rebellions, but liabilities otherwise outweighed assets. Soviet-style political controls disrupted military chains of command; insidious surveillance fostered paranoia, because friends and informers were indistinguishable; quests for conformity inhibited innovation; and subordinates hesitated to take initiative without prior permission.[15]

Civilian Control in Democracies

Most democratic countries prefer decentralized control over their armed forces. The U.S. model, which has served reasonably well for more than two centuries, reflects the Constitution, subsequent legislation, implementing directives, and long-standing traditions that segregate political from military authority. Executive and Legislative Branches of the Federal Government share national security responsibilities so no "man on horseback" might easily amass enough military power to conduct a successful coup.[16]

Key Restrictions

George Washington, Andrew Jackson, Zachary Taylor, Ulysses S. Grant, and Dwight D. Eisenhower were professional soldiers before they became President of the United States. President Jimmy Carter was a Navy careerist. Several others wore uniforms for a few years,[17] but no military person of any rank has ever occupied the Oval Office while on active duty (President Eisenhower resigned his lifetime five-star commission to avoid possible accusations of impropriety).

Authoritarian German regimes attacked neighbors twice in the twentieth century (1914, 1939) using strategies that an elite General Staff with operational as well as planning powers produced.[18] Those performances fostered phobias in the United States, which framed the *National Security Act of 1947* to safeguard the nation against all foes, including U.S. Armed Forces, which perchance could threaten cherished freedoms if unfettered. That document, revised, updated, and codified in *Title 10, U.S. Code,* prohibits the appointment of any individual as Secretary of Defense (SECDEF), Deputy SECDEF, or Under Secretary "within 10 years after relief from active duty as a commissioned officer of a regular component of an armed force." Second lieutenants and ensigns are just as ineligible as generals and admirals.[19] Congress granted General of the Army George C. Marshall a special dispensation in

September 1950, but expressly stipulated that "after [he] leaves office . . . no additional appointments of military men shall be made."[20]

Diversified Power Centers

The Chief Executive exercises high-level politico-military functions in most democratic as well as totalitarian countries, but the U.S. Constitution deliberately separates those responsibilities. Article II, Section 2 designates the President as "Commander in Chief of the Army and Navy . . . and of the Militia of the several States, when called into the actual Service of the United States." Article I, Section 8 empowers Congress to declare wars and "provide for the common Defense" by raising and supporting regular armed forces plus a militia. Section 8 also prescribes rules.[21] Cabinet officers who share national security responsibilities report directly to the President. Members of the National Security Council (NSC) since 1947 have been duty bound to "assess and appraise [U.S.] objectives, commitments, and risks . . . in relation to . . . actual and potential military power," then advise him "with respect to the integration of domestic, foreign, and military policies."[22]

Congress, cast in the role of resource allocator and critic, does not prepare national security policies and plans per se, but its budgetary powers and oversight authorities strongly influence the size, shape, characteristics, and capabilities of U.S. Armed Forces, together with concepts for their employment.[23] Subcommittees concentrate on regional interests around the world. International operations, human rights, narcotics, and terrorism attract continuing attention. Military concerns include readiness, personnel, strategic nuclear and air-land forces, seapower, research, development, installations, and facilities. Statutes that restrict presidential war powers,[24] covert operations,[25] and security assistance to countries that violate human rights[26] additionally constrain national security policies and military strategies.

Democratic Control Appraised

Decentralized civilian control of armed forces complicates national security planning. Elected officials and appointees, many of whom lack military experience, span a political spectrum from far left to far right. Resultant inefficiencies sometimes spill blood and waste money unnecessarily, but the system works reasonably well on balance and military megalomaniacs rarely threaten democracy.

FOREIGN VS. DOMESTIC POLICIES

International and intranational policies compete for top priority, but a reasonable balance is mandatory, because excessive attention to domestic matters may jeopardize objectives abroad, while excessive attention to foreign affairs may invite trouble on the home front. Heavy investments in military power that deprive the domestic sector of resources seldom are sustainable over long hauls, except in police states that brutally discourage dissent and in countries that receive substantial subsidies from outsiders. U.S. and Soviet stances are instructive in such respects.

U.S. Priorities

Obligations to "provide for the common defense [and] promote the general welfare," as stipulated in the Preamble to the U.S. Constitution, are as valid today as they were when signatories put pen to paper on September 17, 1787. Most Presidents and Congress in peacetime, however, have reversed that sequence with public approval.

Pre–World War II

President Theodore Roosevelt devoted serious attention to international as well as internal affairs from 1901 to 1909 but, with time out for World War I and its immediate aftermath, domestic matters dominated for the next thirty years during six consecutive Administrations (William H. Taft, Woodrow Wilson, Warren Harding, Calvin Coolidge, Herbert Hoover, and Franklin D. Roosevelt well into his second term). Strategically significant military activities throughout those three decades, all small-scale and low-profile, were confined to pacification programs in the Philippines, gunboat diplomacy in China, and punitive expeditions against Mexico's Pancho Villa, plus peace enforcement duties in Colombia/Panama, the Dominican Republic, Haiti, and Nicaragua.[27] Financially (but not intellectually) impoverished U.S. military strategists nevertheless more than earned their pay between 1919 and 1938 by exploring problems that U.S. and Allied Armed Forces soon would face in real-life theaters of operation throughout the world.[28]

Cold War

Foreign policy overshadowed U.S. domestic policy during most of the Cold War (1946–1989). The United States, in its capacity as leader of what was widely known as the "Free World," sought to contain the spread of Communism wherever it encroached in whatever guise. Deterrence and defense against Soviet aggression retained high priorities even after opposition to the Vietnam War generated acrimonious debates about the proper balance between international and domestic needs.[29]

Early Post–Cold War

U.S. foreign policies remained assertive early in the twenty-first century, despite the Soviet demise. President George Bush visualized a "New World Order," established in concert with a community of allied nations that shared U.S. interests.[30] President Bill Clinton, his successor, early on admitted that the United States "cannot solve every problem, [but] will serve as a fulcrum for change and a pivot point for peace."[31] His commitment to that course was steadfast despite close attention to economic interests, as noted in the 1998 version of *A National Security Strategy for a New Century:* "At this moment in history, the United States is called upon to lead—to organize the forces of freedom and progress; to channel the unruly energies of the global economy into positive avenues; and to advance our

prosperity, reinforce our democratic ideals and values, and enhance our security."[32]

Soviet Priorities

President Nixon during U.S. involvement in Vietnam warned protesters and congressional budget cutters not to "pose a false choice between meeting [U.S.] responsibilities abroad and meeting the needs of our people at home. We shall meet both or we shall meet neither."[33] Soviet leaders from Joseph Stalin through Konstantin Chernenko, oblivious to that reality, largely ignored their nation's domestic needs until 1985, with devastating effects.

The Kremlin's Cold War claim to superpower status depended mainly on mammoth armed forces that demanded immense resources, but troubles brewed in the 1980s, because the economy stagnated while military costs soared. Mikhail Gorbachev, newly installed at the peak of the Soviet politico-military pyramid, thus found himself in a "no-win" position: the U.S.-Soviet military balance would gradually favor the United States and its allies unless reforms strengthened the civilian economy; diverting funds from Soviet Armed Forces risked a military rebellion and might lead to social upheavals by a populace with appetites for better living standards. Gorbachev gambled on Glasnost (openness) and Perestroika (restructuring) programs that included economic conversions, unilateral force reductions, unprecedented arms control agreements, and withdrawal from Afghanistan after a decade of inconclusive combat. Intolerable strains consequently caused the Soviet Union to collapse.[34]

MILITARY VS. NONMILITARY POWER

Foreign policies, which specify national roles within international communities, help shape military strategies. Military capabilities contribute abundantly to each country's political clout. Close connections thus are indispensable.

Military Power Predominates

Military power has figured prominently in foreign relations since ancient Egyptian, Hyksos, Hittite, and Assyrian leaders relied on armed forces to amass the world's first empires.[35] Persian monarchs, Alexander the Great, and Roman caesars, followed by analogues in Arabia, Central Asia, and the Orient, did likewise.[36] Britain, France, and Spain relied less on coercion to accumulate huge holdings in the Americas, Asia, and Africa, but employed "muscle" liberally to defend their colonies.[37] Force or threats of force in this day and age remain valid alternatives if other measures fail to achieve foreign policy objectives. Past and present despots like Joseph Stalin and Iraqi President Saddam Hussein seem to understand no other language ("The Pope! How many divisions does *he* have?" is the former's widely quoted quip, delivered during French Premier Pierre Laval's visit to Moscow in May 1937).

Nonmilitary Power Predominates

Nonaggressive nations normally employ military power to further foreign policy objectives only when diplomatic and economic leverage fail to achieve required results. Crucial considerations even then concern cost-benefit ratios. JCS Chairman General Colin L. Powell in February 1993, for example, publicly opposed the commitment of U.S. Armed Forces in Bosnia-Herzegovina until the President and his advisers produced "a clear political policy." Unjustifiable gaps otherwise might open between ends and means. Madeleine Albright, who then was U.S. Ambassador to the United Nations and subsequently served as Secretary of State, asked in frustration, "What's the point of having this superb military that you're always talking about if we can't use it?" His response restated his original requirement: "Set tough policy goals first."[38]

STRATEGIC BEAD-STRINGING

The full significance of national security policies emerges when politico-military strategists string them together like beads. High-quality concepts and plans, however, ensue only if implementing forces receive harmonious guidelines. NATO's deterrent strategy, which denied Warsaw Pact opponents any hope of quick victory at acceptable cost during the Cold War, successfully knitted together nonprovocation, containment (rather than rollback), collective security, economy of force, forward defense, controlled escalation, nuclear second strike, and an option to use nuclear weapons first if the Kremlin triggered a traditional war.[39] U.S. bead-stringing throughout the Vietnam War conversely featured stringent policy constraints and repeated flip-flops, which made it impossible to sustain any strategy that might have preserved South Vietnam as an independent nation.[40]

KEY POINTS

- Politico-military policies are basic ingredients of strategy.
- National security policy-makers, who establish objectives, allocate resources, and limit military courses of action, provide the focus for strategic concepts and plans.
- Policy options contain many alternatives between polarized extremes.
- National security policies normally are stable, but occasionally change on short notice.
- Politico-military cultures strongly influence predispositions to accept or reject particular policy options.
- The most elemental national security policy specifies civilian or military control of armed forces.
- Excessively centralized civilian control tends to undermine military effectiveness; excessively decentralized civilian control complicates strategic planning.
- The winner of competition between foreign and domestic priorities receives most national resources.
- Foreign policies help shape military strategies; military power contributes to foreign policy clout.
- Despots tend to rely heavily on military power; nonaggressive nations tend to emphasize diplomatic and economic leverage in the absence of imminent threats.
- Excessive emphasis on domestic matters may jeopardize objectives abroad; excessive emphasis on foreign affairs may invite trouble at home.
- Bold foreign policies unaccompanied by adequate military power encourage serious gaps between ends and means.

NOTES

1. U.S. joint and uniservice doctrines cover almost every conceivable circumstance. Foundation documents include *Joint Pub. 3-0, Doctrine for Joint Operations* (Washington: Office of the Chairman, Joint Chiefs of Staff, 1993); Field Manual (FM) 3-0, *Operations* (Washington: Department of the Army, June 14, 2001); Air Force Manual (AFM) 1-1, *Basic Aerospace Doctrine of the United States Air Force,* 2 vols. (Washington: Department of the Air Force, 1992); *From the Sea: Preparing the Naval Service for the 21st Century,* a White Paper (Washington: Department of the Navy, September 1992) and *Forward . . . From the Sea* (1994), both address the U.S. Navy and Marine Corps.

2. John Toland, *The Rising Sun: The Decline and Fall of the Japanese Empire, 1936-1945* (New York: Random House, 1970); William Manchester, *American Caesar: Douglas MacArthur, 1880-1964* (Boston: Little, Brown, 1978), 488-501.

3. Sir Robert Thompson, *No Exit from Vietnam* (New York: David McCay Co., 1969), Chapters VIII, IX; *U.S. Foreign Policy for the 1970s: A New Strategy for Peace,* A Report to the Congress by Richard M. Nixon, President of the United States (Washington: U.S. Government Printing Office, February 18, 1970), 68-72.

4. *American Military Culture in the Twenty-First Century* (Washington: Center for Strategic & International Studies, February 2000); Ken Booth, *Strategy and Ethnocentrism* (New York: Holmes and Meier, 1979); Yitzhak Klein, "A Theory of Strategic Culture," *Comparative Strategy,* vol. 10, 1991, 3-23.

5. Major General J. F. C. Fuller, *A Military History of the Western World,* 3 vols. (New York: Funk & Wagnalls, 1954), especially the chronicles that precede each chapter; Sun Tzu, *The Art of War,* ed. and trans. Samuel B. Griffith (New York: Oxford University Press, 1963); Frank A. Kierman, Jr. and John K.

Fairbank, eds., *Chinese Ways of Warfare* (Cambridge, MA: Harvard University Press, 1974), 1-26.

6. For takeover tactics, refer to Edward N. Luttwak, *Coup d'État* (New York: Alfred A. Knopf, 1969).

7. Brian Loveman and Thomas M. Davies, Jr., eds., *The Politics of Antipolitics: The Military in Latin America*, rev. and updated ed. (Wilmington, DE: Scholarly Resources, 1997); Abraham F. Lowenthal and J. Samuel Fitch, eds., *Armies and Politics in Latin America*, rev. ed. (New York: Holmes and Meier, 1986).

8. William Reno, *Warlord Politics and African States* (Boulder, CO: Lynne Reiner Publishers, 1998); Samuel Decalo, *Psychoses of Power: African Personal Dictatorships* (Boulder, CO: Westview Press, 1989).

9. Contexts are contained in Robert B. Asprey, *War in the Shadows: The Guerrilla in History*, vol. II (Garden City, NY: Doubleday & Co., 1975), 903-31; James R. Price, "Algeria, 1954-1962," in *Challenge and Response in Internal Conflict*, vol. III, *The Experience in Africa and Latin America*, ed. D. M. Condit and Bert H. Cooper, Jr., et al. (Washington: Center for Research in Social Systems, American University, April 1968), 177-203.

10. Admiral of the Fleet of the Soviet Union Sergei G. Gorshkov, *The Sea Power of the State* (Annapolis, MD: Naval Institute Press, 1976), 124-26.

11. Robert Conquest, *The Great Terror: A Reassessment* (New York: Oxford University Press, 1990), 182-213, 427-31, 450-53.

12. Allen F. Chew, "Beating the Russians in the Snow: The Finns and the Russians, 1940," *Military Review*, June 1980, 38-47; *Fighting the Russians in Winter: Three Case Studies*, Leavenworth Papers No. 5 (Fort Leavenworth, KS: U.S. Army Command and General Staff College, Combat Studies Institute, December 1981), 17-30.

13. Michael J. Deane, *Political Control of the Soviet Armed Forces: A Conflict of Interests* (New York: Crane, Russak and Co., 1977); Eugene D. Bétit, *Political Control of the Soviet Armed Forces: The Committee of People's Control*, unclassified (Washington: Defense Intelligence Agency, 1978).

14. Nikita S. Khrushchev, *Khrushchev Remembers: The Last Testament*, ed. and trans. Strobe Talbott (Boston: Little, Brown, 1974), 13-15; Otto Preston Chaney, Jr., *Zhukov*, rev. ed. (Norman: University of Oklahoma Press, 1996), 397-465.

15. Thomas W. Wolfe, *The Military Dimension in the Making of Soviet Foreign and Defense Policy* (Washington: RAND Corporation, October 1977).

16. Russell Weigley, "The American Military and the Principle of Civilian Control from McClellan to Powell," *Journal of Military History*, vol. 57, issue 5 (October 1993), 27-58.

17. William A. DeGregorio, *The Complete Book of U.S. Presidents: From George Washington to Bill Clinton*, 5th ed. (New York: Wings Books, 1997).

18. Walter Goerlitz, *History of the German General Staff, 1657-1945*. trans. Brian Battershaw (Westport, CT: Greenwood Press, 1975; reprint of the 1953 ed., published in New York by Praeger); Trevor N. Dupuy, *A Genius for War: The German Army and General Staff, 1807-1945* (Englewood Cliffs, NJ: Prentice-Hall, 1977).

19. Sections 133(a) and 134(a), Title 10, United States Code; Public Law 95-140, "Defense Department—Deputy and Under Secretaries of Defense, Position Changes" (October 21, 1977).

20. Public Law 81-788, September 18, 1950.

21. Overviews are available in Samuel P. Huntington, *The Soldier and the State: The Theory and Politics of Civil-Military Relations* (Cambridge, MA: the Belknap Press of Harvard University, 1959); Allan R. Millett, *The American Political System and Civilian Control of the Military: A Historical Perspective*, Mershon Position Papers in the Policy Sciences, no. 4 (Columbus: The Mershon Center of Ohio State University, April 1979).

22. Section 402, Title 50, United States Code; John Prados, *Keepers of the Keys: A History of the National Security Council from Truman to Bush* (New York: Morrow, 1991).

23. Wallace Earl Walker, "Congressional Resurgence and the Destabilization of U.S. Foreign Policy," *Parameters*, September 1988, 54-67.

24. War Powers Resolution of 1973, P.L. 93-148, 87 Stat. 555; "War Powers of Congress and the President—Veto," *Congressional Record*, November 7, 1973, S20093-S20116; *The War Powers Resolution: Relevant Documents, Correspondence, Reports*, Subcommittee on Arms Control, International Security, and Science of the Committee on Foreign Affairs, 100th Cong., 2d sess. (Washington: U.S. Government Printing Office, May 1988).

25. *Intelligence Authorization Act for FY 1990-91*, Rpt. No. 101-174, 101st Cong., 1st sess. (Senate Select Committee on Intelligence, September 18, 1989), 6-9, 18-33; Richard F. Grimmett, *Covert Actions: Congressional Oversight*, Issue Brief 87208 (Washington: Congressional Research Service, March 23, 1989).

26. Title 22, United States Code, Section 2151n, "Human Rights and Development Assistance."

27. John M. Collins, *America's Small Wars: Lessons for the Future* (Washington: Brassey's [U.S.], 1991), 91–92, 95–96, 101–10, 213, 214–15, 216–20.

28. Louis Morton, "Germany First: The Basic Concept of Allied Strategy in World War II," in *Command Decisions,* ed. Kent Roberts Greenfield (Washington: Office of the Chief of Military History, U.S. Army, 1960), 11–47.

29. Seweryn Bialer and Michael Mandelbaum, *Global Rivals: The Forty-Year Contest for Supremacy Between America and the Soviet Union* (New York: Vintage Books, 1988); John Lewis Gaddis, *Strategies of Containment: A Critical Appraisal of Postwar American National Security Policy* (New York: Oxford University Press, 1982).

30. *National Security Strategy of the United States* (Washington: The White House, August 1991); Stanley R. Sloan, *The U.S. Role in a New World Order: Prospects for George Bush's Global Vision,* Rpt. 294 RCO (Washington: Congressional Research Service, March 28, 1991).

31. President Bill Clinton, Address to the 48th Session of the United Nations General Assembly, September 27, 1993.

32. *A National Security Strategy for a New Century* (Washington: The White House, October 1998). Quotation on iv.

33. *Public Papers of the Presidents of the United States: Nixon, 1969* (Washington: U.S. Government Printing Office, 1971), 434.

34. Ilya Zemtsov and John Farrar, *Gorbachev: The Man and the System* (New Brunswick, NJ: Transaction Publishers, 1989); Mikhail Gorbachev, *Perestroika: New Thinking for Our Country and the World,* updated ed. (New York: Harper & Row, 1988); Lieutenant General William E. Odom, *The Collapse of the Soviet Military* (New Haven, CT: Yale University Press, 1998).

35. R. Ernest and Trevor N. Dupuy, *The Harper Encyclopedia of Military History: From 3,500 B.C. to the Present,* 4th ed. (New York: HarperCollins, 1993), 1–147.

36. Fred McGraw Donner, *The Early Islamic Conquests* (Princeton, NJ: Princeton University Press, 1981); Erik Hildinger, *Warriors of the Steppe: A Military History of Central Asia, 500 B.C. to 1,700 A.D.* (New York: Sarpedon, 1997); Robert Marshall, *Storm from the East: From Ghenghis Khan to Kublai Khan* (Berkeley: University of California Press, 1993).

37. See, for example, Byron Farwell, *Queen Victoria's Little Wars* (New York: Harper & Row, 1972); Douglas Porch, *The French Foreign Legion: A Complete History of the Legendary Fighting Force* (New York: HarperCollins, 1991).

38. General Colin L. Powell with Joseph E. Persico, *My American Journey* (New York: Random House, 1995), 576–77.

39. *NATO Facts and Figures* (Brussels, Belgium: NATO Information Service, any issue in the late 1970s to the mid-1980s).

40. General Bruce Palmer, Jr., *The 25-Year War: America's Military Role in Vietnam,* Lexington: University of Kentucky Press, 1984; Robert S. McNamara with Brian VanDeMark, *In Retrospect: The Tragedy and Lessons of Vietnam* (New York: Time Books, 1995).

PART II

FUNDAMENTALS OF MILITARY STRATEGY

6. Strategic Starting Points

Glendower: I can call spirits from the vasty deep.
Hotspur: Why, so can I, or so can any man;
but will they come when you do call
for them?

William Shakespeare
Henry IV, Part I

Strategies designed to achieve politico-military objectives are endlessly variable. Each demands different armed forces, incurs different costs, and runs different risks. Any given strategy "may be the best possible in certain situations and the worst conceivable in others," according to Général d'Armée André Beaufre, who accumulated a wealth of practical experience during his lengthy tenure as a strategic theoretician, planner, and practitioner for France.[1]

Proficient national security policy-makers and military strategists, like Hotspur, are well aware that "spirits from the vasty deep" come at required times and places only if the call is compelling. They therefore develop a range of innovative options designed to solve particular problems under given conditions, then select the course of action they believe most likely would elicit desired responses from friends, enemies, and fence-straddlers. Those who skillfully employ strategic building blocks, schools of thought, and other fundamentals generally enjoy the most consistent success.

STRATEGIC BUILDING BLOCKS

Strategic planners, knowingly or not, use theories, principles, policies, doctrines, and concepts as intellectual building blocks (Table 10 summarizes respective attributes).[2] Integrating processes, which are part art and part science, lean heavily on assumptions whenever facts are unavailable.

Strategic Theories

Intellectual pioneers in every field of endeavor develop theories that must be validated by trial and error or calculations. Their hypotheses, which expand the knowledge base with no particular applications in mind,[3] sometimes have serendipitous spin-offs with awesome implications. Albert Einstein's Special Theory of Relativity, the outgrowth of basic scientific research, for example, unexpectedly paved the way for nuclear weapons.

Creative thinkers since the Stone Age have left a legacy of creative ideas that successors continue to enrich.[4] The earliest on record was Sun Tzu, whose writings circa 500 B.C. profoundly influenced unconventional warfare in the twentieth century (Mao Zedong was his most prominent disciple).[5] Niccolò Machiavelli made a lasting mark on strategic skullduggery when he penned *The Prince* in 1513 (Lenin latched onto his ideas 400 years later).[6] Carl von Clausewitz, Alfred Thayer Mahan, and Giulio Douhet respectively influence U.S. land, sea, and air strategies to this very day.[7] Rear Admiral J. C. Wylie's unfulfilled quest for a general theory of power control left a target for ambitious innovators to shoot at.[8]

Table 10

Strategic Building Blocks

	Strategic Theories	Strategic Principles	Security Policies	Military Doctrines	Strategic Concepts
Properties	Hypotheses	Truths	Guidelines	Convictions	Options
Purposes	Open New Options	Control Quality	Regulate Applications	Standardize Procedures	Solve Problems
Sources	Imagination	Historical Experience	National Preferences	Practical Experience	Syntheses
Styles	Speculative	Declarative	Directive	Instructive	Applicative
Producers	Intellectual Pioneers	Politico-Military Scholars	Top Politico-Military Officials	Top Military Officials	Strategic Planners

Strategic Principles

Strategic principles are self-evident truths that politico-military scholars have distilled from historical studies over several millennia, but not all lists are alike. Entries expressed in one or two words (surprise, security, simplicity) are subject to dissimilar interpretations and, unlike some laws of physics, economics, and natural sciences, are neither immutable nor invariably applicable. Experienced strategists nevertheless use principles as checklists to help control the quality of theories, policies, doctrines, concepts, and plans (whether Proposal A violates the Principle of Surprise and, if so, what difference does it make is a typical question). Chapter 7 addresses Principles of Deterrence, Chapter 8 discusses Principles of War, and Chapter 9 deals with previously unexplored Principles of Preparedness.

Security Policies

Top civilian and military leaders review national security policy options (a few of which appear on Table 9 page 48), pick those that best serve stated purposes, then promulgate guidelines that officially affect almost every military strategy. Some policies, such as those that regulate military personnel recruitment standards and relations with civilian contractors, pertain to relatively narrow functions, whereas many have overarching ramifications.

The Kremlin's policy of "peaceful coexistence," which Nikita Khrushchev articulated at the 20th Communist Party Congress in February 1956, once typified entries in the latter category. That form of politico-military conflict, redesignated "détente" about 1972, employed psychological warfare, subversion, and disinformation programs on a grand scale in efforts to undermine non-Communist regimes around the world.[9] Countervailing U.S. policies drew sharper boundaries between war and peace, respected the spirit as well as the letter of laws, fought "fairly" in accord with traditional "rules," and found "dirty tricks" repugnant. Respective platforms for strategic competition thus differed markedly in most respects.

Military Doctrines

Military doctrines standardize strategic, operational, tactical, and logistical procedures in peacetime as well as war under offensive, defensive, and benign conditions. Doctrinal tenets, which are products of practical experience, indicate that certain behaviors produce best results for land, sea, air, amphibious, and space forces in given environments. Military doctrines, unlike policies, are instructive rather than directive in nature. Conformance is not required if common sense dictates otherwise.[10]

Each armed service establishes a doctrinal framework within which many subordinate doctrines reside.[11] Some address military operations in distinctive regions (arctic, equatorial, wet, dry, rural, urban, level, mountainous, and so on).[12] Others concern distinctive functions, such as antisubmarine warfare, close air support, and counterinsurgency.

Strategic Concepts

Strategic concepts, unlike theories, seek to solve specific problems. Formulation responsibilities rest with politico-military planners who fold relevant theories, principles, policies, and doctrines into various theses calculated to achieve security objectives effectively and efficiently despite perceived opposition. Decision-makers, after weighing pluses and minuses, bless what appears to be the best option.

Antiballistic missile concepts, for example, might rely mainly on point defenses or contemplate area defenses that feature boost phase, mid-course, or terminal intercepts using weaponry based on land, at sea, in space, or in some combination. Relative risks, costs, and technological complexities strongly influence inclinations to accept or reject any course of action under consideration.[13]

STRATEGIC SCHOOLS OF THOUGHT

Continental, maritime, air, space, and special operations forces embrace military cultures and strategic schools of thought that cause them to view strategic problems from different perspectives. The following summaries deliberately oversimplify salient characteristics to emphasize dissimilarities.[14]

Continental School

Adherents of the Continental School, who are direct strategic descendants of Clausewitz, tend to compartmentalize the globe into theaters of operation, regional areas of responsibility, and local zones of action. They contend that the defeat (even destruction) of enemy armed forces, mainly by manpower-intensive armies, is the ultimate object of war.[15]

Navies and air forces exist primarily to transport troops to scenes of action and support them after arrival. Land power will bring conflicts to conclusion and thereafter occupy enemy territory if required.

Maritime School

Continental methods of operation are fairly foreign to the Maritime School, whose members have a global reach. Many devotees favor the teachings of Alfred Thayer Mahan, who preached that control of high seas and littorals determines decisions ashore.[16] The basic objective is to dominate critical sea lanes and choke points that channelize forces afloat. Surface ships, submarines, and amphibious forces then can master land masses by blockades or the selective projection of power inland.

Aeronautical School

The Aeronautical School was founded in 1921 by Giulio Douhet, whose disciples now are legion.[17] Their fundamental beliefs are, first, that air power unaided can be decisive; second, that given a free hand air power could make protracted combat obsolete; and third, that control of the air and the destruction of the enemy's war-making potential, primarily population centers and industrial bases, are the most important missions. Air support for ground forces rates a much lower priority.

Astronautical School

Members of the embryonic Astronautical School promote innovative strategies, tactics, and force postures that complement those of land, sea, and air.[18] Their central theme is still indistinct, but space strategists believe that armed forces positioned at lunar libration points L4 and L5, 60 degrees ahead and behind Earth's moon in its orbit, could dominate the entire Earth-Moon System. If so, they may adapt Halford J. Mackinder's Heartland Theory with words much like these:[19]

Who rules circumterrestrial space commands
Planet Earth;
Who rules the Moon commands circumterrestrial space;
Who rules L4 and L5 commands the Earth-Moon System.

Special Operations School

The Special Operations School is populated by small teams distinctively prepared to perform overt, covert, and clandestine missions that orthodox armed forces could not accomplish as well, if at all. Its members, who mix force with fraud and finesse, offer decision-makers scalpels rather than sledge hammers for sensitive deterrent, persuasive, coercive, and war-fighting purposes.[20]

Unifying School

Inquisitive thinkers seek a Unifying School of strategic thought that could weld Continental, Maritime, Aeronautical, Astronautical, and Special Operations Schools together more tightly than joint military doctrines have yet been able to do. Parallel searches for superior ways to integrate all forms of military and nonmilitary power proceed along similar lines.[21] Military strategists meanwhile must sift claims from separate schools throughout planning and programming processes.

ELEMENTAL ALTERNATIVES

National purposes, styles, values, and geographic circumstances often govern military strategies. Switzerland and Sweden, for example, made neutrality stick during World Wars I and II, because no nation coveted their territories. Embattled Belgium along Germany's line of march tried the same tack and was swallowed both times.[22] Insular Britain banks primarily on sea power while France, just across the English Channel, looks landward. Military strategists nevertheless normally pick and choose from a tantalizing menu of elemental alternatives.[23]

Sequential and Cumulative Strategies

Sequential strategies comprise successive steps, each contingent on those that precede, until they reach the final objective. Typical linkages include defensive operations, followed by counteroffensives when circumstances permit. Cumulative strategies, in contrast, constitute concurrently conducted actions, none individually decisive, that eventually create crushing results.[24] Strategic bombardments and naval campaigns against enemy merchant ships are illustrative. The Soviet Union used cumulative techniques in a different vein during the 1940s when, one by one, Stalin incarcerated nine countries behind the Iron Curtain. No single loss seemed shattering to Free World leaders, but the Kremlin absorbed most of Central Europe before NATO blocked further encroachments.

Sequential and cumulative strategies usually are mutually reinforcing, as U.S. Armed Forces demonstrated during World War II when they pursued two interrelated courses of action against Japan. Sequential campaigns island-hopped across the Pacific Ocean toward Tokyo, while cumulative campaigns aimed at Japan's economy simultaneously severed air and sea lines of supply and communication.[25]

Direct and Indirect Strategies

Military strategies, like music, can be played in two keys.[26] Most employ both in favored combinations but the major key, which accentuates direct uses of force, has dominated since Cain killed Abel. Compellence still outranks posturing and persuasion when security interests are intense and time is short.[27] A lighter touch that incurs lower costs and risks even so may sometimes achieve objectives at least as well. Indirect strategies that rely less on brawn and more on brain power literally or figuratively replace frontal assaults with flank attacks, perhaps accompanied by deception and covert operations.[28]

Military strategists should remain aware that imprudent reliance on direct *or* indirect approaches invites trouble. Adolf Hitler's greatest triumphs, for example, were bloodless ones between 1933 and 1939, when he glued diplomacy, psychological warfare, subversion, bravado, geopolitics, science, and military capabilities into an offensive strategy that recognized no distinct boundary between war and peace. Reckless overemphasis on armed force after France fell in 1940 eventually led to Nazi Germany's defeat by numerically superior U.S., Soviet, and British opponents who were able to mass far greater military power.

Active and Reactive Strategies

Freedom of action is a universally cherished security interest. Active strategies that open and exploit opportunities consequently are preferable to reactive strategies that respond to enemy overtures. Offensive armed forces, which attack at times and places of their choosing, enjoy great advantage according to Sun Tzu, because if the enemy "does not know where I intend to give battle he must prepare in a great many places. And . . . those I have to fight in any one place will be [relatively] few. For if he prepares to the front his rear will be weak, and if to the rear his front will be fragile. If he prepares to the right his left will be vulnerable," and vice versa. "And when he prepares everywhere he will be weak everywhere."[29] Those wise words pertain equally well to nonlethal offensives for deterrent and defensive purposes. U.S. Massive Retaliation and Flexible Response strategies, for example, ceded initiative to the Soviet Union throughout the Cold War, yet accomplished bedrock objectives without firing a shot, because accompanying threats backed by nuclear capabilities restricted rational courses of enemy military action.[30]

Active strategies sometimes enable militarily weak nations to impose their will on powerful opponents whose passivity encourages assertiveness, as Hitler demonstrated soon after he became Chancel-

lor of Germany's Third Reich in January 1933. First, he repudiated the Versailles Treaty, reinstated compulsory military service in violation of its provisions, and began to build a *Luftwaffe* (Air Force). Next, he reoccupied the demilitarized Rhineland with a token force in March 1936 (French leaders merely protested to the impotent League of Nations). Hitler annexed Austria precisely two years later and, in October 1938, acquired Czechoslovakia's Sudetenland when British and French appeasers signed the Munich Pact. *Ein Volk, ein Reich, ein Führer* (one people, one nation, one leader) became more than a Nazi slogan at that point.[31]

Maneuver and Attrition Strategies

Attrition strategies aim to wear rivals down, then wear them out, whereas physical and intellectual maneuvers curtail enemy abilities to employ available power advantageously. Almost all military operations of high, mid, or low intensity bank on both, but purposes, policies, doctrines, and circumstances cause balances to differ.

Some coalitions and individual nations habitually rely on massed manpower and materiel to quash antagonists no matter how long it takes.[32] U.S. Armed Forces and their allies successfully emphasized attrition techniques against the Axis Powers in Europe for six long years (1940–1945) before they finally emerged victorious. Less muscular belligerents and subnational groups such as insurgents and terrorists employ ceaseless pinpricks to erode enemy will.[33] Nonviolent attrition can wear down will to resist until opponents decide to accede. That technique helped passive resistance specialist Mahatma Gandhi rid India of British rule in 1947 and Martin Luther King, Jr. to advance civil rights in the United States, largely because public opinion in each instance precluded the liberal use of firepower by opposing armed forces and police.[34]

Général d'Armée André Beaufre likens offensive and defensive military maneuvering to options that fencers favor: feint, thrust, follow through, parry, riposte, disengage. All ultimately aim to gain, regain, or deprive enemies of freedom of action.[35] "Decapitation" strategies that short-circuit command and control systems, for example, aim to leave rival armed forces leaderless and confused, while so-called "horizontal escalations" that unexpectedly widen the scope rather than the intensity of conflict seek to overcommit adversaries and shift strategic centers of gravity.[36]

Arms Control vs. Arms Competition

President Woodrow Wilson included general disarmament as one of the Fourteen Points in his peace proposal of January 8, 1918. The League of Nations later incorporated that aim in its Covenant. Interests in arms control intensified manyfold after nuclear weapons emerged in 1945.[37] Adversaries need not profit equally if compromise solutions benefit all concerned, but pacts seldom last long if any signatory feels slighted.

Arms control strategies are most attractive when costs of competition and risks of war seem excessive. Several purposes are prominent: improve positions vis-à-vis opponents; preserve the status quo; make adversarial relationships more predictable (verification capabilities and confidence-building measures are very important); conserve resources; save money; and prevent dangerous technological developments. The world might have been safer in the last regard if arms controllers had prohibited multiple independently targetable reentry vehicles (MIRVs), which caused U.S. and Soviet strategic nuclear warhead inventories to expand exponentially starting in 1970. Both sides thereafter intensified costly but fruitless searches for effective ballistic missile defenses.[38]

Arms competition strategies often pay off handsomely when one side cannot or will not keep pace, which happened in Korea after an uneasy truce settled over that war torn peninsula in 1953. U.S. military assistance policies, which discouraged South Korean ground forces from expanding proportionately or developing strong offensive capabilities, encouraged a one-sided arms race that by the 1990s vested smaller North Korea with almost twice as many men on active duty, more than twice as many main battle tanks, five times as many self-propelled artillery pieces, five times as many surface-to-surface missiles, and immense quantitative superiority in many other weapon categories. Approximate qualitative parity prevailed, but resultant military imbalances gave shudders to the Government in Seoul, which is barely twenty-five miles south of the Demilitarized Zone.[39]

POLITICO-MILITARY ASSUMPTIONS

Fallacious assumptions, whether tacit or consciously stated, can sabotage military strategies just as surely as enemy actions.[40] Seasoned planners consequently scrutinize all identifiable assumptions carefully and prepare backup positions for those that seem shaky. The dozen listed below illustrate a wide range of sensitive issues:

- The absence of direct military threats does (not) greatly reduce the importance of armed forces as foreign policy instruments
- The United States should (not) be the world's "policeman"
- Competition for scarce natural resources will (not) culminate in armed combat
- Warning time before war erupts will (not) be ample and unambiguous
- War in region A will (not) spread to or involve forces from regions B and C
- Transnational terrorists will (not) obtain and employ nuclear weapons
- National survival is (not) the only interest that justifies heavy casualties
- Public support for Plan A will (not) strengthen despite present opposition

- Policy-makers can (not) emphasize nonmilitary missions indefinitely without undercutting combat capabilities
- National will is (not) steadfast and allies will (not) stand firm
- Foreign flag merchant ships will (not) be available for use whenever required
- Meaningful multilateral arms control accords are (not) obtainable under current conditions

STRATEGIC PATHS AND PITFALLS

Sun Tzu counseled, "What is of supreme importance in war is to attack the enemy's strategy."[41] The main aim is to pit off-beat capabilities against vulnerabilities, and thereby nullify enemy plans, programs, and operations. Consistently successful practitioners emphasize asymmetrical approaches, shun strategic mismatches, and spurn extremist solutions. They concurrently guard against reprisals, because consequences akin to Newton's Third Law of Motion apply: to every action there is an equal counteraction.

Asymmetrical Strategies

Asymmetrical strategies employ ingenious capabilities, perhaps in exotic combinations, that adversaries are poorly prepared to defeat.[42] No nation now is well-prepared to deter or defend against biological warfare assaults. Transnational terrorists generally render traditional armed forces irrelevant. Cybernetic warfare specialists conceivably could "disarm" military giants who rely excessively on computers.

Atypical strategies that succeed not only outfox rival armed forces, but invalidate enemy investments. U.S. nuclear deterrent capabilities, for example, began to depend much more on ballistic missiles and much less on aircraft in the early 1960s. Relatively few B-52 bombers nevertheless were able to exploit Soviet fixations on homeland defense for the next quarter century with three beneficial effects: 1) Soviet air defenders needed to cover approaches from every direction, whether the U.S. bomber fleet was large or small; 2) Soviet decision-makers, who routinely expended billions of rubles to expand and improve that shield, deprived offensive programs that could directly endanger U.S. security; and 3) Soviet air defenses never degraded U.S. nuclear retaliatory capabilities predicated on ICBMs and SLBMs.[43]

Strategic Mismatches

Well-conceived strategies closely connect threats, objectives, policies, tactics, forces, and other strategies. Unrealistic requirements and discontinuities within or between any of those categories cause risks to soar and increase prospects for failure, as the following vignettes reveal.

Strategy-Threat Mismatches

The simplistic U.S. strategy called Massive Retaliation, which raised the specter of nuclear devastation, conserved money, manpower, materiel, and may have deterred a head-on collision with the Soviet Union, but it left many crucial interests uncovered. U.S. Armed Forces in the 1950s and early 1960s braced for worst-case outbursts that never occurred, while insidious foes who featured subversion, chicanery, and low-intensity conflicts scored consistently without tripping nuclear triggers. Stalin and his successors consolidated control over Central Europe, Mao took charge in China, and Communist-kindled conflagrations menaced other East Asian countries from Korea to Malaya. The United States, in short, was well-prepared to deter nuclear attacks, but could not counter ambiguous aggression without using nuclear mallets to drive tacks.[44]

Objective-Policy Mismatches

Israel's widely acclaimed counterterror tactics may be among the world's best, but its repressive strategy amplifies Arab animosities and creates terrorists faster than air strikes and hit teams can kill them. Questionable policies include illegal construction of settlements in Israeli-occupied territories, autocratic control over Islamic holy sites in Jerusalem, and reprisals that surpass the *Old Testament* prescription of an eye for an eye, a tooth for a tooth. Suspected terrorists may be shot on sight, arrested without charge, detained without trial, and deported without proof. Innocent persons suffer when troops demolish or seal suspected homes and hideouts. Severe restrictions on domicile, movement, employment, and free speech, plus rights of assembly and association, make Arab inhabitants second-class citizens. Internal security consequently remains an elusive Israeli objective with no solution in sight after more than fifty years of savage conflict.[45]

Strategy-Force Mismatches

NATO's Armed Forces essentially served as a "tripwire" for nuclear weapons when Massive Retaliation prevailed. Requirements for credible defensive capabilities increased severalfold when the Atlantic Alliance embraced a Flexible Response strategy in 1967, but deployments scarcely changed. U.S. Army contingents assigned to Allied Forces Central Europe still consisted of two corps that totaled five divisions plus support. U.S. Air Force, Europe (USAFE) listed twenty-one tactical fighter squadrons before and after the shift. Allied contributions also remained constant. Either the pre-1967 aggregate was larger than needed for a trip wire or the post-1967 aggregate was insufficient for defense. A marked strategy-force mismatch was evident in at least one event.[46]

U.S. military strategy in the 1960s called for forces that could fight full-scale wars with the Soviet Union *and* the People's Republic of China at the same time, yet have enough left over to handle a lesser contingency (2½ wars in popular parlance). That aspiration, which shrank to 1½ wars in 1969, required abilities to meet a major attack by the USSR *or* China, assist allies against non-Chinese aggression in Asia, and contend with a small conflict elsewhere. Ambitions by 1980 demanded assets able to cope concurrently with one major and one minor contingency.[47] The Clinton Administration's *Bottom-Up Review* in 1993 required forces sufficient to fight and win two major regional conflicts (MRCs) "almost simultaneously"

while minimizing U.S. casualties.[48] Strategy-force connections in every instance were unrealistic.

Secretary of Defense Donald Rumsfeld, who subsequently served President George W. Bush, concluded that the two MRC strategy unreasonably overstretched available resources. His testimony before Senate and House Armed Services Committees on June 21, 2001 therefore recommended less robust forces that could "defeat the efforts of any adversary to achieve its objectives by force or coercion," concurrently repel "attacks in a number of [other] critical areas, and also be capable of conducting a limited number of smaller-scale contingencies." Whether a skeptical Congress will fund sufficient assets to accomplish those scaled down but nevertheless ambitious aims was uncertain when this book went to press.[49]

Strategy-Tactics Mismatches

Viet Minh insurgents after World War II pursued a revolutionary war strategy that cost-effectively defeated France in 1954.[50] Ho Chi Minh and his henchmen, who thereafter struggled to reunify North and South Vietnam, met U.S. Armed Forces and their allies head-on in 1965 with traditional military tactics that blighted the countryside, devastated urban centers, and caused casualties to skyrocket on both sides. Communists scored a sweeping psychological victory during their Tet Offensive of February 1968, but virtually destroyed Viet Cong guerrilla units and undergrounds in the process. Heavy attrition continued for seven more years, until South Vietnam capitulated in 1975. Greater patience (normally a revolutionary war hallmark) coupled with prudent tactics might have consolidated the two countries under Communist rule at far less cost over a longer period.[51]

Strategy-Strategy Mismatches

NATO's strategy for the defense of Western Europe required rapid reinforcements and resupplies from the United States if Soviet Armed Forces and their Warsaw Pact associates invaded. Specific requirements existed in 1984 to "move six Army divisions, 60 tactical fighter squadrons, and one Marine Amphibious Brigade (MAB)—all with initial support—to their combat positions within 10 days."[52] Merchant ships had to transport virtually all heavy cargo, but neither U.S. nor allied naval strategies emphasized early control over essential sea lines of communication. Best estimates of arrival were measured in months, by which time the war might well have been over. Debates raged, but continental and maritime strategies remained mismatched until the Cold War ended.[53]

Extremist Strategies

Excessive reliance on *any* strategic theory, principle, school of thought, policy, concept, or elemental alternative invites avoidable problems. Pat solutions, whether simple or complex, warrant close inspection. There is little evidence, for example, that deter-rent and combat capabilities always are incompatible, that maneuver always should take precedence over attrition, or that budgets always should dictate strategies, as some commentators contend (the selection of the best alternative during Robert S. McNamara's days as Secretary of Defense invariably revolved around *the most appropriate economic criterion,*" according to one critic[54]).

"Either/or" strategies that arbitrarily exclude Option A at the expense of B or vice versa usually lack flexibility. Great Britain, France, and Germany paid terrible penalties when their military strategists overemphasized offensive operations during World War I, despite technological innovations that made frontal assaults against machine guns and massed artillery suicidal. French strategists deified defense two decades later and suffered early defeat. Mismatched strategies that disregard fundamentals or apply them poorly invite avoidable problems and risk failure.

KEY POINTS

- Strategic theoreticians pave the way for superior concepts and plans
- Principles distilled from historical study can foster strategic quality control
- Policy guidelines fundamentally influence military strategies
- Military doctrines distilled from practical experience standardize ways to perform various functions and operate in distinctive environments
- Concepts that integrate relevant theories, principles, policies, doctrines, and forces comprise the centerpiece of every strategic plan
- Continental, maritime, air, space, and special operations schools of thought may be most or least appropriate in any given situation
- Sequential strategies, which take consecutive steps, and cumulative strategies, which constitute concurrently conducted actions, usually are reinforcing
- Direct strategies normally emphasize force; indirect strategies stress finesse
- Active strategies that open and exploit opportunities are preferable to reactive strategies that respond to enemy overtures
- The balance between attrition and maneuver strategies depends on objectives, policies, doctrines, and circumstances
- Arms control strategies can sensibly confine costs and risks
- Asymmetrical strategies pit off-beat capabilities against enemy vulnerabilities
- Mismatched strategies that disregard fundamentals or apply them ineptly invite avoidable problems and risk failure

NOTES

1. Général d'Armée André Beaufre, *An Introduction to Strategy* (New York: Praeger, 1965), 11-15, 44-46, 135-38. Quotation is on 13.

2. Major General L. B. Holley, Jr., "Concepts, Doctrines, Principles: Are You Sure You Understand the Terms?," *Air University Review,* July-August 1984, 90-93; Yehoshafat Harkabi, *Theory and Doctrine in Classical and Modern Strategy,* Working Paper No. 13 (Washington: Woodrow Wilson Center, October 1981).

3. Lyman B. Kirkpatrick, Jr., "Eccles Strategy on Strategy," *Naval War College Review,* Summer 1977, 12-14.

4. Assorted anthologies include Thomas R. Philipps, ed., *Roots of Strategy: A Collection of Military Classics* (Westport, CT: Greenwood Press, 1982); Edward Meade Earle, ed., *Makers of Modern Strategy: Military Thought from Machiavelli to Hitler* (Princeton, NJ: Princeton University Press, 1943); Peter Paret, ed., *Makers of Modern Strategy: From Machiavelli to the Nuclear Age* (Princeton, NJ: Princeton University Press, 1986); George Edward Thibault, ed., *The Art and Practice of Military Strategy* (Washington: National Defense University, 1984).

5. Sun Tzu, *The Art of War,* trans. Samuel B. Griffith (New York: Oxford University Press, 1963), especially 66-71, 96-101.

6. Niccolò Machiavelli, *The Prince* (Chicago: University of Chicago Press, 1985).

7. Carl von Clausewitz, *On War,* ed. and trans. Michael Howard and Peter Paret (Princeton, NJ: Princeton University Press, 1976); Alfred Thayer Mahan, *The Influence of Sea Power Upon History, 1660-1783* (New York: Hill and Wang, 1969); Giulio Douhet, *The Command of the Air,* trans. Dino Ferrari (Washington: Office of Air Force History, U.S. Government Printing Office, 1983).

8. Rear Admiral J. C. Wylie, *Military Strategy: A General Theory of Power Control* (New Brunswick, NJ: Rutgers University Press, 1967).

9. Leo Gruliow, ed., *Current Soviet Policies—II: The Documentary Record of the 20th Party Congress and Its Aftermath* (New York: Praeger, 1957), 36-37; Richard H. Shultz and Roy Godson, *Dezinformatsia* (New York: Pergamon-Brassey's, 1984); Ladislav Bittman, *The KGB and Soviet Disinformation: An Insider's View* (New York: Pergamon-Brassey's, 1985).

10. For various views of doctrine, see Donald M. Snow and Dennis M. Drew, *Introduction to Strategy,* (Maxwell AFB, AL: Air Command and Staff College, 1982), 89-105.

11. Note 1, Chapter 5 identifies foundation doctrines of U.S. Armed Services.

12. Geographically oriented military doctrines are typified by Field Manual 30-70, *Basic Cold Weather Manual,* April 1968; Field Manual 90-3/Fleet Marine Force Manual 7-27, *Desert Operations,* August 19, 1977; Field Manual 90-5, *Jungle Operations,* August 16, 1982; Field Manual 90-6, *Mountain Operations,* June 30, 1980; Field Manual 90-10, *Military Operations in Urbanized Terrain,* August 15, 1979; and Field Manual 90-13, *River Crossing Operations,* September 30, 1992, all published by the Department of the Army. See also *U.S. Navy Cold Weather Handbook for Surface Ships* (Washington: Chief of Naval Operations, Surface Ship Survivability Office, May 1988); Air Force Doctrine Document 45, *Aerospace Weather Operations* (Washington: Department of the Air Force, August 31, 1994).

13. Conceptual disputes about ballistic missile defense are not new. See Charles Benson, "Deterrence Through Defense," *National Review,* March 9, 1971, 254-59; *Ballistic Missile Defense Technologies* (Washington: Office of Technology Assessment, 1985), 139-70.

14. Distillations are available in Wylie, *Military Strategy,* 37-75.

15. Clausewitz, *On War,* 75, 77, 90.

16. Alfred Thayer Mahan, *Naval Strategy Compared and Contrasted With the Principles and Practices of Military Operations on Land: Lectures Delivered at the Naval War College ... between the Years 1887 and 1911* (Westport, CT: Greenwood Press, 1975).

17. Douhet, *The Command of the Air;* Alexander P. DeSeversky, *Victory Through Air Power* (Garden City, NY: Garden City Publishing Co., 1943).

18. John M. Collins, *Military Space Forces: The Next Fifty Years* (New York: Pergamon-Brassey's, 1989), 41-71.

19. G. Harry Stine, *Confrontation in Space* (Englewood Cliffs, NJ: Prentice-Hall, 1981), 57, 58, 60-61, 86-87. For the original Heartland Theory, see Halford J. Mackinder, "The Geographical Pivot of History," *Geographical Journal,* vol. XXIII (1904), 421-44 and modifications in his *Democratic Ideals and Reality* (London: Constable & Co., 1919).

20. General Peter J. Schoomaker, *Special Operations Forces: The Way Ahead* (MacDill AFB, FL: U.S. Special Operations Command, March 1998); *SOF Vision 2020* (MacDill AFB, FL: U.S. Special Operations Command, January 1997).

21. Dissimilar searches for a unifying school of strategic thought are found in Wylie, *Military Strategy,* 65-

111 and Edward N. Luttwak, *Strategy: The Logic of War and Peace* (Cambridge, MA: Belknap/Harvard, 1987).

22. Bertil Haggman and Judi McCleod review the risks and costs of neutrality in *Defense of Freedom: Political Options* (Toronto: Mackenzie Institute, 1988).

23. Ken Booth, "New Challenges and Old Mind-sets . . .," in *The Uncertain Course: New Weapons, Strategies, and Mind-sets,* ed. Carl G. Jacobsen (New York: Oxford University Press for the Stockholm International Peace Research Institute, 1987), 39–65; Julian Lider, "Towards a Modern Concept of Strategy," *Cooperation and Conflict,* vol. XVI, no. 4 (1981): 217–35; Edward B. Atkeson, "The Dimensions of Military Strategy," *Parameters,* vol. 7, no. 1 (1977): 41–52.

24. Wylie, *Military Strategy,* 23–29.

25. *The War Reports of General of the Army George C. Marshall, General of the Army H. H. Arnold, and Fleet Admiral Ernest J. King* (New York: J. B. Lippincott, 1947), 209–46, 331–39, 384–400, 437–52, 514–57, 585–617, 660–92.

26. Beaufre, *An Introduction to Strategy,* 26–30, 42–44, 107–30, 134–35.

27. Thomas C. Schelling describes compellence in *Arms and Influence* (New Haven, CT: Yale University Press, 1966), 69–91.

28. Basil H. Liddell Hart unveiled his "strategy of the indirect approach" in *The Decisive Wars of History: A Study of Strategy* (Boston: Little, Brown, 1929) and elaborated in *Strategy,* 2d ed. (New York: Praeger, 1967). See also Robert J. Art, "To What Ends Military Power?" *International Security,* Spring 1980, 3–35; Charles W. Walter, "Interposition: The Strategy and Its Uses," *Naval War College Review,* June 1970, 72–84.

29. Sun Tzu, *The Art of War,* 98.

30. Secretary of State John Foster Dulles introduced Massive Retaliation in a speech before the Council on Foreign Relations in New York City on January 12, 1954 and clarified his remarks in "Policy for Security and Peace," *Foreign Affairs,* vol. XXXII (April 1954), 353–64. General Maxwell D. Taylor articulated the original rationales for Flexible Response in *The Uncertain Trumpet* (New York: Harper and Brothers, 1959). For NATO's adaptation, see Secretary of Defense Casper W. Weinberger, *Improving NATO's Conventional Capabilities: A Report to the United States Congress* (Washington: Department of Defense, June 1984), 1–19; J. Michael Legge, *Theater Nuclear Weapons and the NATO Strategy of Flexible Response* (Santa Monica, CA: RAND Corporation, 1983).

31. Robert T. Elson, *Prelude to War* (New York: Time-Life Books, 1976), 184–211.

32. Russell F. Weigley argues that attrition always has been *The American Way of War: A History of United States Military Strategy and Policy* (New York: Macmillan, 1973).

33. Mao Tse-Tung, *Basic Tactics* (New York: Praeger, 1966).

34. Penderel Moon, *Gandhi and Modern India* (New York: W. W. Norton, 1969); Martin Luther King, Jr., *Why We Can't Wait* (New York: Harper & Row, 1963), especially Chapter 5, "Letter From Birmingham Jail."

35. Beaufre, *An Introduction to Strategy,* 36–41.

36. Secretary of Defense Caspar Weinberger described horizontal escalation in *Annual Report to the Congress, Fiscal Year 1983* (Washington: Department of Defense, February 8, 1982), I-14, I-15, I-16. See also Joshua M. Epstein, "Horizontal Escalation: Sour Notes of a Recurrent Theme," *International Security,* Winter 1983/84, 19–31.

37. Trevor N. Dupuy and Gay M. Hammerman, eds., *A Documentary History of Arms Control and Disarmament* (New York: R. R. Bowker Co., 1973). For pros and cons, see Donald G. Brennen, *Arms Control, Disarmament, and National Security* (New York: G. Braziller, 1961).

38. Ted Greenwood, *Making the MIRV: A Study of Defense Decision Making* (Cambridge, MA: Ballinger, 1975).

39. Larry A. Niksch, "South Korea," *Fighting Armies,* ed. Richard Gabriel (Westport, CT: Greenwood Press, 1983), 133–34; Taek-Hyung Rhee, *U.S.-ROK Combined Operations: A Korean Perspective* (Washington: National Defense University Press, 1986), 26–28; *The Military Balance, 1998–1999* (London: Brassey's, for the International Institute of Strategic Studies, 1998), 185–88.

40. Henry E. Eccles, *Military Concepts and Philosophy* (New Brunswick, NJ: Rutgers University Press, 1965), 279–89.

41. Sun Tzu, *The Art of War,* 77–78.

42. Colonels Qiao Liang and Wang Xiangsoi, *Unrestricted Warfare* (Beijing: People's Liberation Army Literature and Arts Publishing House, February 1999).

43. See all nine annual editions of *Soviet Military Power* (Washington: Department of Defense, U.S. Government Printing Office, September 1981 through September 1990).

44. Henry A. Kissinger, *Nuclear Weapons and Foreign Policy* (New York: Harper and Brothers, 1957), 1–20, 316–61.

45. Ian Lustick, ed., *Palestinians Under Israeli Rule* (New York: Garland Publishing Co., 1994); Rashid

Khalid, *Palestinian Identity* (New York: Columbia University Press, 1997); Jacob M. Landau, *The Arab Minority in Israel, 1967-1991: Political Aspects* (New York: Oxford University Press, 1993).

46. *The Military Balance, 1966-67* and subsequent editions.

47. President Richard M. Nixon, *U.S. Foreign Policy for the 1970s: A New Strategy for Peace* (Washington: U.S. Government Printing Office, February 18, 1970), 128-29; Secretary of Defense Harold Brown, *Department of Defense Annual Report, Fiscal Year 1981* (January 20, 1980), 98, 99, 118.

48. Secretary of Defense Les Aspin, memorandum to selected addresses, *The Bottom-Up Review: Forces for a New Era* (September 1, 1993), amplified by *Report on the Bottom-Up Review* (Washington: Office of the Secretary of Defense, October 1993), 1-13.

49. Secretary of Defense Donald H. Rumsfeld and Chairman of the Joint Chiefs of Staff General Hugh Shelton, *Defense Strategy Review,* testimony before the Senate Armed Services Committee, June 21, 2001; Rowan Scarborough, "2-War Plan Outdated, Rumsfeld Tells Panel," *Washington Times* (June 22, 2001), A4.

50. Bernard B. Fall, "Indochina (1946-1954)," in *Challenge and Response in International Conflict,* vol. I, The Experience in Asia, ed. D. M. Condit, Bert H. Cooper, Jr., et al. (Washington: Center for Research in Social Systems, American University, February 1968), 237-69.

51. Literature on the Vietnam War is voluminous. A synopsis is available in Timothy Lomparis, "Giap's Dream, Westmoreland's Nightmare," *Parameters,* June 1988, 18-32.

52. Secretary of Defense Caspar W. Weinberger, *Annual Report to Congress, Fiscal Year 1985* (February 1, 1984), 175.

53. *The Maritime Strategy,* a special supplement to *U.S. Naval Institute Proceedings,* January 1986. See also David S. Sorenson, "Getting Back to Europe: Strategic Lift Needed Now More Than Ever," *Parameters,* June 1990, 64-74.

54. James M. Roherty, *Decisions of Robert S. McNamara* (Coral Gables, FL: University of Miami Press, 1970), 71-72.

7. Fundamentals of Deterrence

*Croesus said to Cambyses: That peace was better
than war, because in peace the sons did bury their
fathers, but in wars the fathers did bury their sons.*

Francis Bacon, 1625
Apophthegms, New and Old

Nobody since Croesus (circa 525 B.C.) has more clearly or succinctly stated the case for deterrence, which supports interests in peace.[1] Deterrent strategists endeavor primarily to convince adversaries that aggression of any kind is the least attractive of all alternatives. Deterrence secondarily aims to discourage unwelcome escalation and the continuation of ongoing conflicts that deterers or their allies prefer to terminate. A tertiary purpose, seldom enunciated but nonetheless important, is to dissuade friends and the unaffiliated from pursuing courses of action that could adversely affect the deterer's valued interests.

Pioneers in this esoteric field relied heavily on game theories, which are too abstruse for most national security policy-makers and military strategists. This study, in partial compensation, summarizes prevalent causes of conflict, then reviews principles and concepts that practitioners might find useful.

THE DYNAMICS OF DETERRENCE

Deterrence has utility across the national security spectrum from normal peacetime competition to unrestrained war with weapons of mass destruction.[2] Deterrent dynamics, unlike those of passive avoidance, feature threats, promises, or acts, not necessarily military in nature, that pledge punishment if deterees perform forbidden deeds and perhaps offer rewards if they abstain. Psychological assaults on enemy intentions leave enemy capabilities unscathed. Strategists seek answers to three key questions: Who deters whom from making what impermissible moves by what means with what motivations at what times in what situations? What countermoves will deterees most likely make? What counter-countermeasures seem advisable?[3]

Deterrent failures are obvious.[4] Communism, for example, made great gains during the 1950s when U.S. Armed Forces enjoyed a nuclear monopoly, because abilities to deter cataclysmic combat were powerless to prevent piecemeal encroachments. Israel predicated deterrence on repeated demonstrations of military superiority after it won independence in 1948, but undaunted Arab antagonists nevertheless fought two more major wars (1967, 1973) in futile attempts to retrieve lost territory and establish an Islamic state.

Precise reasons for deterrent successes often are difficult or impossible to prove, since self-deterrence rather than threats or promises frequently is the decisive factor. Deterees may never have intended to take proscribed actions, may have concluded that financial costs would be excessive, or may have refrained simply because predicted gains appeared too small. No deterer knows for sure why suicidal terrorists, who fear no retaliation, have never unleashed nuclear weapons that many suspect they possess.[5]

CAUSES OF CONFLICT

There is no one best way to prevent political, economic, psychological, technological, cybernetic, or military conflicts, because nationalism, imperialism, jurisdictional disputes, ideological, religious, and environmental disagreements, avarice, poverty, injustice, and revenge are just a few among many motivations.[6] Five causes that have little in common are representative: unprovoked aggression; provoked aggression; preemptive and preventive wars; regrettable blunders; and catalytic conflicts.

Unprovoked Aggression

Unprovoked aggression has been a common cause of armed conflict since pastoral and agricultural societies first clashed several thousand years ago. Quests for hegemony, territorial aggrandizement, cultural dominance, economic self-sufficiency, and greed, perhaps in some combination, prompted most such wars.[7] Opportunities generally look most inviting when victims are militarily weak, are otherwise unprepared to resist effectively, and perhaps seem predisposed to appease. Transnational terrorist attacks against targets in neutral countries fit into the last category.

Provoked Aggression

Shooting wars in response to perceived provocations erupt when one or more adversaries believe that armed combat is a tolerable (even desirable) way to resolve disputes. Weapons of mass destruction have dampened enthusiasm in some quarters, but aggravations still instigate international aggression and likely always will. Some amalgamation of political, economic, and social grievances, real or imagined, most often provokes insurgencies, coups d'état, and other intranational conflicts.[8]

Preemptive and Preventive Wars

Preemptive and preventive wars, occasionally called "anticipatory retaliation," explode when politico-military decision-makers on one side believe a showdown surely will occur sooner or later, and therefore find little to lose and perhaps something to gain by striking first. Lengthy preparations precede preventive wars, whereas threatened parties preempt on short notice to attenuate attacks they feel are imminent.

Reciprocal and intensifying fears are conceivable: Side A, who suspects B's motives, prepares to attack. B, in response, does likewise, even though its leaders originally entertained no such intention. A's fears thus become reinforced. The spiral stops only if A and B both cool off or one opens fire.[9]

Regrettable Blunders

Miscalculations, misperceptions, accidents, and other regrettable blunders sometimes cause senseless conflicts. Reasons range from erroneous intelligence estimates and net assessments through unsound assumptions to false warnings, bravado, and irrational behavior.[10] Ambiguous, ambivalent, and intentionally misleading signals also may trigger wars. Hitler, for example, did not believe that Britain and France would declare war when his troops invaded Poland in September 1939, because both countries acquiesced when he brazenly reoccupied the Rhineland (1936), annexed Austria, then swallowed Sudetenland (both 1938).[11]

Catalytic Conflicts

Catalytic conflicts are altercations that one nation or subnational group deliberately foments between two or more others to suit its own purposes. A hostile China, hoping to emerge as the world's only superpower, hypothetically might have catalyzed an ongoing U.S.-Soviet Cold War crisis by striking the United States with nuclear-tipped submarine-launched ballistic missiles, the true source of which would have been virtually unverifiable. Potentates in Teheran, hoping to eliminate archrivals in Baghdad, similarly might unleash a devastating anthrax or smallpox epidemic in Washington, D.C. during acrimonious disputes between the United States and Saddam Hussein about Iraq's multifaceted biological weapon programs.

Catalysis need not culminate in a shooting war. Israeli agents masquerading as anti-Western extremists, for example, sabotaged Anglo-American installations throughout Egypt in the summer of 1954 as one attempt to delay the impending British departure from Suez, obviate U.S. rapprochement with Egyptian President Gamal Nasser's new government, and thereby strengthen Israel's position at his expense.[12]

PRINCIPLES OF DETERRENCE

Theoreticians and planners who aim to deter conflicts succeed most consistently when they use sound principles to guide their research and review results.[13] There are no hard and fast rules like Bernoullian numbers and Boyle's Law of Gases, but military strategists can't go far wrong if they heed Principles of Deterrence described below.

Purpose	Preparedness
Credibility	Nonprovocation
Uncertainty	Prudence
Pain	Publicity
Pleasure	Paradox

Principle of Purpose

Conflict prevention is the basic objective, but deterrent strategists must specify politico-military purposes more precisely before they can focus effectively on any given center of gravity, because each demands different treatment. Schemes crafted to forestall naked aggression do little to discourage insidious operations and piecemeal encroachments. Needs to extend a deterrent umbrella over partners create special problems. So do time limitations—how soon deterrence must take effect and how long it must last often determine the optimum course of action.

Principle of Credibility

Credible deterrence, which raises costs of aggression unacceptably high, generally is achievable only if promised rewards or punishments seem logical. Put simply, you'd ignore me if, in the course of some minor tiff, I said, "Cross that line and I'll scuff your shoe shine." You'd scoff if I threatened to shoot, unless I'm a known psychotic. But if I said, "Take one more step and I'll bloody your nose," you'd have to ask yourself seriously, "Is what I want important enough to risk a broken beak?"

Deterrent strategies also are shaky if bold recipients rightly or wrongly suspect a bluff. British attempts to deter Argentina's occupation of the Falkland Islands failed in 1982, precisely because decision-makers in Buenos Aires never believed that Prime Minister Margaret Thatcher would wage war over those frigid wastelands, despite repeated assurances to the contrary.[14]

Principle of Uncertainty

Deterrence predicated on uncertainties is the fallback position if credibility for any reason seems unattainable.[15] The U.S. nuclear strategy of Mutual Assured Destruction, which promised to pulverize the Soviet Union provided Soviet Armed Forces struck first, must have made decision-makers in Moscow wonder whether counterparts in Washington D.C. *really would* risk national suicide regardless of provocation, but they couldn't afford to take a chance. The nuclear-armed French *Force de Frappe*, which was much smaller than its U.S. counterparts, performed a similar function.[16]

Principle of Pain

Painful penalties commonly underpin deterrent demands. Bloodthirsty threats, such as those associated with nuclear "balances of terror,"[17] occupy one pole with political, economic, and psychological pressures at the other. Promises to punish aggressors severely and concurrently keep them from achieving key objectives are complementary options calculated to make reckless enemy leaders think at least twice before they initiate impermissible acts.[18]

Principle of Pleasure

Blandishments sometimes make antagonists abandon undesirable tacks. Yasser Arafat momentarily renounced terrorism in December 1988 and recognized Israel's right to exist in return for "substantive dialogues" between senior U.S. officials and the Palestine Liberation Organization (PLO).[19] Insurgents often respond positively to reforms that alleviate or eliminate ideological, cultural, religious, economic, or social grievances. Rewards may also deter allies, other associates, and neutrals more readily than punitive threats. Prospects of additional U.S. aid, for example, encouraged Egyptian President Anwar as-Sadat to sign a peace treaty with Israel in 1979.[20]

Principle of Preparedness

Perpetual preparedness is one price of peace anywhere that virulent threats exist, because nothing tempts opportunists as conclusively as opponents with their guards down. Robust defenses and retaliatory capabilities as a rule reduce risks, but policy-makers and resource allocators who lack much institutional memory repeatedly learn hard lessons too late. The poorly armed, poorly equipped, badly outnumbered "Battered Bastards of Bataan" (1942) and benighted Task Force Smith in Korea (1950) bought time with their blood because deterrence failed, as unready U.S. Armed Forces did at the onset of several previous wars.[21] That failing is by no means confined to the United States, as military tombstones bear mute testimony in many other countries.

Principle of Nonprovocation

Military postures that rivals consider dangerously provocative can cause deterrence to collapse just as surely as unpreparedness. Strategists who hope to avoid that impression therefore shun "use 'em or lose 'em" forces that must strike first or risk ruin. They additionally favor deployments that deemphasize weapons of mass destruction and emphasize some or all of the following deterrent options: defense rather than offense; ready reserves rather than huge active contingents; and remote rather than forward basing. The proper mix is a matter of judgment, depending on circumstances.[22]

Principle of Prudence

Secretary of Defense Robert McNamara based U.S. nuclear strategy on the supposition that "it is the clear and present ability to destroy the attacker as a viable twentieth century nation and an unwavering will to use these forces in retaliation to a nuclear attack upon ourselves or our allies that provides the deterrent, and not the ability partially to limit damage to ourselves."[23] He may have been right, but no standoff between evenly matched disputants is eternally certain, because one side sooner or later almost always dominates. The Principle of Prudence consequently recommends military shields and civil defenses that could reduce casualties, limit damage, and make enemies pay dearly if, all efforts to the contrary, war supersedes peace.

Principle of Publicity

Neither fear of punishment nor promise of reward is possible if deterers keep relevant capabilities and intentions a secret. Policy-makers and strategists therefore must determine what information they should transmit to whom, how to do it, and when.[24] The U.S. Department of Defense in the 1980s, for example, advertised Stealth aircraft abilities to penetrate enemy airspace undetected and return unscathed, but guarded technological details that could expedite enemy abilities to duplicate such feats.

Communicators may convey messages directly or indirectly, verbally or nonverbally, officially or unofficially, formally or informally, explicitly or implicitly, publicly or privately, clearly or ambiguously, just once or repeatedly. Pronouncements by senior officials generally carry greater weight than off-the-cuff comments by subordinates. Public forums are more apt to reinforce deterrence than private remarks. Dramatic weapon demonstrations as a rule are more convincing than dialogues.

Principle of Paradox

Shooting wars occasionally can best assure peace, if armed conflict now discourages overconfidence among foes, encourages friends, and thereby forestalls future combat.[25] President Harry S Truman had that paradoxical principle implicitly in mind when he chose to side with the Republic of Korea after Communist troops swarmed south in 1950.[26] A second paradox confirms that vigorous defense of piddling interests produces disproportionately large deterrent benefits whenever so doing convinces predators that assaults against high-value objectives would be foolhardy.

DETERRENT THEORIES AND CONCEPTS

Strategists tailor theories, concepts, and plans to suppress specific causes of conflict. Threats, promises, and actions may play independent or complementary roles. Latitude for intellectual innovation is almost limitless, because few techniques are multipurpose, some are contentious, and schemes that aim to deter catalytic conflicts, terrorism, and cybernetic warfare are embryonic at best.[27] Most of Table 11 is self-explanatory, but confidence-building measures, peacekeeping, demonstrations, deception, tripwires, reciprocity in kind, and irrational acts bear embellishment.

Confidence-Building

Confidence-building measures, a form of arms control, promote deterrence provided A and B in good faith both agree to limit the likelihood of conflicts caused by apprehension, miscalculation, or misunderstanding. Information exchanges, "hot lines" between top decision-makers, and other communications improve abilities to anticipate problems and take corrective actions in time to short-circuit crises. Typical disclosures include advance notice of mis-

sile tests and large-scale maneuvers in sensitive areas. Free and easy on-site observation and inspection help verify various accords that constrain the quantity and quality of rival armed forces. Forbidden zones and restrictions on research may also limit potentially threatening activities.[28]

Peacekeeping

Peacekeeping, a United Nations (UN) specialty,[29] interposes nonviolent armed forces between belligerents by mutual consent to maintain a truce or otherwise deter hostilities. Mandates often prescribe the contingent's duties, size, composition, arms, dispositions, legal status, and impose various preconditions that usually include a time limit. Prowess at diplomacy, negotiations, mediation, and arbitration is more important than military power, because enforcement plays little or no part.[30]

Peacekeepers have kept the lid on conflicts around the world for many years, but abilities to do so are not limitless. Deterrence, for example, failed catastrophically when Sierra Leonean rebels breached a fragile cease-fire in May 2000, ran amok, amputated limbs from innocent bystanders, and held nearly 500 UN peacekeepers hostage.[31]

Demonstrations

Demonstrations, separate and distinct from garden variety shows of force, send psychological signals designed to deter opponents from initiating, continuing, or escalating conflicts of any kind. Displays most often feature specific capabilities that deterers could put into play if deterees refuse to desist. Invitations for high-ranking enemy officials to observe military maneuvers that unveil impressive capabilities transmit deterrent threats indirectly. NATO's contingency plans once called for a low-yield nuclear "shot across the bow" if the Warsaw Pact invaded West Germany, according to General Alexander M. Haig, Jr. when he was Supreme Allied Commander, Europe.[32]

Table 11

Deterrent Techniques Connected to Causes of Conflict

Deterrent Techniques	Unprovoked Aggression	Provoked Aggression	Preemptive, Preventive Wars	Regrettable Blunders	Catalytic Conflicts
Threats					
Retaliation	X	X			
Reciprocity in Kind	X	X			
Continued Conflict[1]	X	X			
Escalation	X	X			
Promises					
Rewards	X	X			
Reforms[2]		X			
Actions					
Diplomacy	X	X	X	X	X
Confidence-building			X	X	
Crisis Management	X	X	X	X	
Peacekeeping	X	X		X	
Posturing[3]	X	X			
Demonstrations[4]	X	X			
Deception	X	X	X		
Tripwires	X	X			
Irrational Acts[5]	X	X			

[1]Intrawar deterrence.
[2]Insurgencies, resistance movements, coups d'état.
[3]Shows of force, reinforcements.
[4]Symbolic and exemplary displays.
[5]"Brinkmanship" and games of "chicken."

Deception and Disinformation

Sun Tzu asserts that "All warfare is based on deception."[33] Deterrent strategies calculated to conceal truth and publicize lies are no exception. Scams that increase ambiguity strengthen deterrence through uncertainty. Those that build faith in erroneous beliefs foster false credibility. The basic purpose in either case is to misrepresent capabilities, intentions, or both in ways that make deterees pause.[34]

Nazi defenders deployed in the Pas de Calais moved much too late to meet Allied landings in Normandy on June 6, 1944, because Hitler feared that dummy armored divisions armed with full-scale inflatable "toys" would soon make the main crossing from England to France.[35] Soviet strategists in August 1957 (two months before *Sputnik*, their first space satellite, flew) began to boast about a "super-long-distance intercontinental multi-stage ballistic missile" that U.S. Armed Forces could not yet duplicate. The dangerous "missile gap" that became a serious issue during the 1960 presidential election never developed, but deceitful claims continued to strengthen Soviet deterrent powers for several years despite pronounced U.S. superiority in deliverable nuclear weapons.[36]

Tripwires

The term "trip wire" connotes a largely symbolic armed force that customarily is positioned in an allied country as visible indication of support. The nation to which that token, but highly valued, contingent belongs presumably would respond vigorously if enemies attacked it. One truncated U.S. Army division deployed between Seoul and the Korean Demilitarized Zone, for example, adds credibility to deterrence despite modest combat capabilities, because its presence astride a high-speed invasion route signals U.S. intent to honor treaty commitments if Communist troops once again head south.[37] The Kremlin and Fidel Castro used one so-called Soviet "combat brigade" in Cuba to invigorate deterrence through uncertainty from the early

1960s through the 1970s. President Carter in 1979 publicly found that small force "not acceptable," but took no action to remove it.[38]

Reciprocity in Kind

Fear of reciprocity in kind was one basis for mutual deterrence after the United States and Soviet Union became charter members of an "Atomic Club" in 1949. No country well equipped to retaliate in kind has been seriously subjected to CW assaults since 1918, mainly because masks and protective clothing impair military performance. Collective protection for armed forces and civilians is inconvenient as well as expensive, and decontamination requirements— including those for rivers of wash water—can become astronomical.[39] President Franklin D. Roosevelt and British Prime Minister Winston Churchill fortified deterrence during World War II with an ominous promise of immediate reprisals in kind if Nazi Germany and Japan employed lethal chemicals against the Allies.[40]

Intolerable consequences similarly discourage biological warfare (BW), provided both sides boast known or suspected capabilities (British experiments with anthrax in 1944 left Scotland's Gruinard Island uninhabitable for 100 years).[41] Possibilities of self-deterrence also are omnipresent, because the unpredictable effects of BW agents could backfire mercilessly against employers.

Irrational Acts

The "rationality of irrationality" comes into play when conniving strategists consciously strive to strengthen deterrence through uncertainty by promising retribution that only lunatics would implement.[42] Unequivocal commitments, automatic responses, and other illogical concepts that seemingly leave deterers little or no choice are typical. A recent record speckled with eccentric acts makes irrational strategies most plausible. Bravado may buttress uncertainties, if not underdone or overdone, but those who bluster too often or not at all benefit least.[43] Nations willing to run the greatest risks emerge victorious without resort to war, but deterrence is bound to fail if *both* sides play hazardous games of "chicken" and press "brinkmanship" until they collide.[44]

KEY POINTS

- Deterrent strategies strive to discourage aggressors from initiating, escalating, or continuing conflicts and to forestall other unwanted actions by friends and neutrals as well as enemies
- Threats, promises, rewards, and punishments are typical deterrent instruments
- Reforms, crisis management, shows of force, demonstrations, confidence-building measures, deception, tripwires, reciprocity in kind, and irrational acts are typical deterrent techniques
- Strategic theoreticians and practitioners succeed most consistently when they use Principles of Deterrence to steer research and shape plans
- Unprovoked and provoked aggression, preventive and preemptive wars, accidental, and catalytic conflicts require dissimilar deterrent strategies
- Credible deterrence predicated on clearly evident conflict dominance capabilities is most persuasive
- Deterrence predicated on uncertainty is the fallback position if credibility is unattainable
- Nothing tempts aggressors as conclusively as poorly prepared opponents
- Neither threats of punishment nor promises of reward deter unless employers publicize relevant capabilities and intentions
- Deterrent failures are obvious, but it is difficult (often impossible) to prove which ploys succeeded in the past

NOTES

1. Most literature addresses nuclear deterrent theories and concepts developed in the 1950s and 1960s, but basic tenets have wide applicability. Glenn H. Snyder cites several seminal articles in *Deterrence and Defense: Toward a Theory of National Security* (Princeton, NJ: Princeton University Press, 1961), 9n, 10-30, 225-38; Alexander L. George and Richard Smoke, *Deterrence in American Foreign Policy: Theory and Practice* (New York: Columbia University Press, 1974), 9-104; Bernard Brodie, *Strategy in the Missile Age* (Princeton, NJ: Princeton University Press, 1959), 264-304; Robert Jervis, "Deterrence Theory Revisited," *World Politics*, January 1979, 289-324.

2. Naval Studies Board, Commission on Physical Sciences, Mathematics, and Applications, National Research Council, *Post-Cold War Conflict Deterrence* (Washington: National Academy Press, 1997); Robert G. Joseph and John F. Reichart, *Deterrence and Defense in a Nuclear, Biological, and Chemical Environment* (Washington: National Defense University Press, 1999).

3. *The Nature of General War*, HI-1537-BN (Croton-on-Hudson, NY: Hudson Institute, November 5, 1971), 5 (Chart 2).

4. John J. Mearsheimer reviews five deterrent failures in *Conventional Deterrence* (Ithaca, NY: Cornell University Press, 1983); John Orme surveys eight in "Deterrence Failures: A Second Look," *International Security*, Spring 1987, 96-124.

5. NBC deterrent problems at the end of the twentieth century parallel those that Neil C. Livingstone and Joseph D. Douglas assessed in *CBW: The Poor Man's Atom Bomb* (Cambridge, MA: Institute for Foreign Policy Analysis, February 1984) and Brian M. Jenkins addressed in "Will Terrorists Go Nuclear?," *Orbis* (1985): 507-15.

6. Geoffrey Blaney, *The Causes of War* (New York: Free Press, 1973); R. J. Rummel, *Understanding Conflict and War*, vol. 4 (Beverly Hills, CA: Sage Publications, 1979), 241-315; John C. Stoessenger, *Why Nations Go to War*, 2d ed. (New York: St. Martin's Press, 1978); Michael T. Klare, *Resource Wars: The New Landscape of Global Conflict* (New York, Metropolitan Books, 2000).

7. R. Ernest and Trevor N. Dupuy, *The Harper Encyclopedia of Military History: From 3,500 B.C. to the Present*, 4th ed. (New York: HarperCollins, 1993); Major General J. F. C. Fuller, *A Military History of the Western World*, 3 vols. (New York: Funk & Wagnalls, 1954).

8. Michael Howard, "The Causes of War," *Wilson Quarterly*, Summer 1984, 90-103; G. D. Kaye, D. A. Grant, and E. J. Edmond, *Major Armed Conflict: A Compendium of Interstate and Intrastate Conflict, 1720 to 1985*, ORAE Rpt. No. R95 (Ottawa, Canada: Department of National Defense, November 1985).

9. Snyder, *Deterrence and Defense*, 104-6.

10. Ibid., 110-11; David Abshire and Brian Dickson, "War by Miscalculation: The Forgotten Dimension," *Washington Quarterly*, Autumn 1983, 114-24.

11. William L. Langer, ed., *An Encyclopedia of World History: Ancient, Medieval, and Modern* (Boston: Houghton Mifflin Co., 1968), 1011, 1016-19, 1021, 1127-30.

12. Clyde R. Mark, *The "Lavon Affair"* (Washington: Congressional Research Service, December 21, 1972).

13. General Andrew J. Goodpaster, "Deterrence: An Overview" in *Post-Cold War Conflict Deterrence*, 21-24; John M. Collins, "Principles of Deterrence," *Air University Review*, November-December 1979, 17-26, rebuttals, July-August 1980, 77-84, and reconsiderations, January-February 1981, 91-92.

14. Douglas Kinney, *National Interest, National Honor: The Diplomacy of the Falkland Islands Crisis* (New York: Praeger, 1989).

15. Herman Kahn christened uncertainty "the residual fear of war" in *Thinking About the Unthinkable* (New York: Horizon Press, 1962), 129. Henry A. Kissinger elaborated in *The Necessity for Choice* (New York: Doubleday and Co., 1962), 53-58. Thomas C. Schelling devoted a full chapter to "the threat that leaves something to chance" in *The Strategy of Conflict* (Cambridge, MA: Harvard University Press, 1960), 187-203.

16. Michael Harrison, *The Reluctant Ally: France and Atlantic Security* (Baltimore: Johns Hopkins University Press, 1981).

17. Albert Wohlstetter, "The Delicate Balance of Terror," *Foreign Affairs*, January 1959, 211-34.

18. Glenn H. Snyder, *Deterrence by Denial and Punishment*, Research Monograph No. 1 (Princeton, NJ: Center of International Studies, Princeton University, January 2, 1959).

19. Edward Cady, David B. Ottaway, and John M. Goshko, "U.S., in Shift, Agrees to 'Substantive Dialogue' with PLO," *Washington Post*, December 15, 1988, A1, A42, A44.

20. Ellen B. Laipson, *Egypt: U.S. Foreign Assistance Facts*, Issue Brief IB85060 (Washington: Congressional Research Service, May 5, 1988).

21. Charles E. Heller and William A. Stofft, eds., *America's First Battles, 1776-1965* (Lawrence, KS: University Press of Kansas, 1986).

22. F. Mike Miles, *Soviet Military Doctrine: Meeting the Criteria for a Defensive Orientation?*, Rpt. No. 89-561F (Washington: Congressional Research Service,

October 3, 1989); Michael D. Wallace, "Armaments and Escalation: Two Competing Hypotheses," *International Studies Quarterly*, March 1982, 37-56.

23. Secretary of Defense Robert S. McNamara, *Statement Before the Senate Armed Services Committee on the FY 1969-73 Defense Program and the 1969 Defense Budget*, February 1, 1968, 47.

24. Glenn H. Snyder, *Deterrence and Defense*, 239-58; Yehoshafat Harkabi, *Nuclear War and Nuclear Peace* (Jerusalem, Israel: Program for Scientific Translation, 1966) 124-31.

25. Thomas C. Schelling, *Arms and Influence* (New Haven, CT: Yale University Press, 1966), 78-81; Snyder, *Deterrence and Defense*, 33-40.

26. President Harry S Truman, *Years of Trial and Hope* (New York: Doubleday and Co., 1956), 339-40.

27. Theresa C. Smith, *Trojan Peace: Some Deterrence Propositions Tested*, Vol. 19, Book 2, Monograph Series in World Affairs (Denver: University of Denver, Graduate School of International Studies, 1982), 5-52, 63-84; R. Wagner Harrison, "Deterrence and Bargaining," *Journal of Conflict Resolution*, June 1982, 329-58.

28. John Borawski, ed., *Confidence-Building Measures for Crisis Stability* (Boulder, CO: Westview Press, 1986); William Lynn, "Confidence-Building Measures," in *Preventing Nuclear War: A Realistic Approach*, ed. Barry Blechman (Bloomington: Indiana University Press, 1985), 24-52.

29. See especially former United Nations Secretary-General Boutros Boutros-Ghali, *An Agenda for Peace: Preventive Diplomacy, Peacemaking and Peacekeeping*, A Report . . . Pursuant to the Statement Adopted by the Summit Meeting of the Security Council on 31 January 1992, 6-10, 29-36.

30. *Peacekeeper's Handbook* (New York: Pergamon Press for International Peace Academy, 1984), 21-41, 54-59.

31. Carl Ek, *Sierra Leone: Background and Issues for Congress*, Rpt. No. RL30367 (Washington: Congressional Research Service, November 8, 1999) and *Sierra Leone: Failed Peace?*, Rpt. No. RS20578, May 11, 2000.

32. *Strategic Weapons Proposals*, Hearings Before the Senate Committee on Foreign Relations, Pt. I, 97th Congress, 1st Sess. (Washington: U.S. Government Printing Office, 1981), 73-74.

33. Sun Tzu, *The Art of War*, trans. Samuel B. Griffith (New York: Oxford University Press, 1963), 66.

34. Donald C. Daniel and Katherine L. Herbig, eds., *Strategic Military Deception* (New York: Pergamon Press, 1981), 3-30; Michael J. Handel, "Intelligence and Deception," *Journal of Strategic Studies*, March 1982, 122-54.

35. Roger Hesketh, *Fortitude: The D-Day Deception Campaign* (Woodstock, NY: Overlook Press, 2001); Roy Hoopes, "World War II's Master of Deception," *Retired Officer*, January 1986, 36-41.

36. Charles H. Donnelly, *United States Defense Policies in 1959*, House Committee on Armed Services, 86th Cong., 2d sess. (Washington: U.S. Government Printing Office, May 27, 1960), 10-11, 14-16; *United States Defense Policies in 1960* (May 26, 1961), 10-11, 20-21; *United States Defense Policies in 1961* (June 7, 1962), 13-14.

37. Larry A. Niksch, *South Korea: Should the U.S. Withdraw?*, a paper prepared for a conference on United States Policy Toward the East Asian/Western Pacific Region (New York: Institute of Asian Studies, St. John's University, November 17-18, 1989).

38. Raymond L. Garthoff, *Reflections on the Cuban Missile Crisis* (Washington: Brookings Institution, 1989), 120; "Text of the President's Speech on U.S. Response to Soviet Military Force in Cuba," *New York Times*, October 2, 1979, A18.

39. *The Problem of Chemical and Biological Warfare*, vol. II, "CB Weapons Today" (New York: Humanities Press, Stockholm International Peace Research Institute [SIPRI], 1973).

40. John Ellis van Courtland Moon, "Chemical Weapons and Deterrence: "The World War II Experience," *International Security*, Spring 1984, 3-35.

41. *Department of Defense Biological Defense Program*, Report to the House Committee on Appropriations, May 1986; John Hubner, "The Hidden Arms Race," *San Jose Mercury News*, Sunday Supplement, April 15, 1984, 13.

42. Herman Kahn describes the rationality of irrationality in *On Thermonuclear War*, 2d ed. (New York: Free Press, 1960), 291-95.

43. John McDonald, *Strategy in Poker, Business, and War* (New York: W. W. Norton, 1950), 28-34, 70-74; Barton Whaley, *Strategem: Deception and Surprise in War* (Cambridge, MA: MIT Center for International Studies, 1969).

44. Kahn, *On Thermonuclear War*, 291-95; Bertrand Russell, *Common Sense and Nuclear Warfare* (New York: Simon and Schuster, 1959), 30-31.

8. War-Fighting Fundamentals

*A study of the laws of war is necessary. . . . To learn these is
no easy matter and to apply them is even harder; some officers
are excellent at paper exercises and theoretical discussions in
the war colleges, but when it comes to battle there are those
who win and those who lose.*

Mao Zedong
On the Study of War
1936

Union General William Tecumseh Sherman knew that "war is hell" long before his blue-clad divisions blighted a fifty-mile-wide swath between Atlanta and Savannah, Georgia, on their march to the sea in November–December 1864.[1] Woeful strategies make war even worse. The rigid Western Front that ran from Flanders to the Alps during World War I defied frontal assaults for more than four years. Millions died and millions more were maimed, because combat began for no sensible reason and terminated long after the best possible outcome was a Pyrrhic victory.[2]

Contemporary strategists can do better, as Mao was well aware, if they select wisely from war-fighting principles, theories, policies, and concepts that cover every conceivable contingency from start to finish during low-, mid-, and high-intensity conflicts on land, at sea, in Earth's atmosphere, and in space. Open options variously emphasize eager or reluctant resort to armed conflict; offense or defense; maneuver or attrition; power projection or forward deployments; destruction or dislocation; instantaneous or incremental escalation; and few or many self-imposed limitations, including those that concern collateral damage and casualties, weapons of mass destruction, and covert or clandestine operations.

PRINCIPLES OF WAR

Strategic trailblazers tacitly paid homage to Principles of War many centuries before Carl von Clausewitz compiled the first formal list in an 1812 memorandum for Prussia's Crown Prince Friedrich Wilhelm.[3] Current collections vary in length and composition (most U.S. catalogues contain nine[4]). The dozen described below, drawn from foreign and domestic compilations, are slanted to serve senior politico-military policy-makers and strategists, rather than practitioners of operational art and tacticians.

Purpose	Surprise
Initiative	Security
Flexibility	Simplicity
Concentration	Unity
Economy	Morale
Maneuver	Time

Principle of Purpose

Decisive, attainable political objectives and complementary military aims selected to satisfy valid national security interests form the foundation for military missions and strategic concepts. All should be consistent, clearly articulated, prioritized, and preferably directed against the enemy's strategic center of gravity. Plans and operations at every level should contribute to attainment; none should be contradictory.

Experienced national security decision-makers regularly review all purposes to ensure that they remain sound, because those expressed at the onset of war are subject to repeated alteration when emotions run high and unforeseen events unfold. U.S. objectives, for example, flip-flopped four times during the first full year of armed conflict in Korea. The initial aim was to survive a North Korean invasion (June–August 1950); then to reunite North and South Korea (September–November 1950); next to survive a Chinese invasion (December 1950–March 1951); and finally to restore the status quo ante-bellum (April 1951–July 1953).[5]

Principle of Initiative

Offensive operations, which enable wielders to act rather than react at times and places of their choosing, are the best way to gain and retain initiative while depriving adversaries of equal advantage. Successes result in freedom of action, which inspires friends, demoralizes foes, opens opportunities to exploit enemy vulnerabilities, and thereby controls the course of events.

Skillful strategists defend only until offensive options appear or reappear. Fabius Maximus Verrucosus Quintas the *Cunctator* (Delayer) harassed Hannibal for several years during the Second Punic War and avoided decisive encounters long enough for Roman legions to gain strength. Victory, however, arrived only after Scipio Africanus finally inaugurated an offensive strategy that defeated Carthage on its home ground in 202 B.C.[6] Russian resistance to Napoleon Bonaparte between June and October 1812 and Soviet delaying actions from June 1941 until November 1942 simply bought time until defenders could mount conclusive counterattacks.[7]

Principle of Flexibility

An inane efficiency expert who attended Franz Schubert's *Unfinished Symphony* observed that four oboe players often were idle, twelve violins played identical notes, and horns repeated passages that strings had previously played. He concluded that the composer "could have finished that opus long before he died, if he had eliminated superfluous instruments." Every music lover, however, knows that diversification and redundancies made Schubert's opus a masterpiece.

Armed forces, like orchestras, cherish flexibility. Planning for certitude in fact may be the most grievous of all military mistakes, because no one can consistently forecast the time, place, scope, tenor, intensity, and course of events. Purposes, policies, and procedures may change unexpectedly on one or both sides. Preferred concepts and capabilities may prove fallible. Players with only one plan thus run serious risks, for they have no fallback position if rivals nullify their only scheme.[8]

A spectrum of long-, mid-, and short-range strategies affords the best insurance against injurious surprise. U.S. contingency plans in the 1970s and early 1980s, for example, viewed the People's Republic of China from three perspectives: 1) China is friendly; 2) China is hostile; and 3) China remains neutral.[9] Relationships early in the twenty-first century might be described as 4) China steers an independent course that selectively welcomes and resists U.S. overtures.

Principle of Concentration

Abilities to concentrate overwhelming strength against vital enemy weakness expedite the attainment of decisive results, whether the strategic center of gravity be hostile armed forces, national will, industrial capacity, a capital city, the hearts and minds of common people, undergrounds that support guerrilla operations, or a charismatic leader. The side that possesses initiative has a huge advantage, because it can focus power on known objectives while rivals dissipate energies preparing for uncertain contingencies.

Quantitatively (even qualitatively) inferior forces may prevail, provided they concentrate while distracted opponents divide. Sun Tzu described that phenomenon with these words: "If I am able to use many to strike few at the selected point, those I deal with will be in dire straits." Insurgent and resistance movements have repeatedly put that principle into practice with considerable success ever since.[10]

Principle of Economy

Even superpowers have finite resources, so concentration at decisive times and places commonly requires economies of force elsewhere. Politico-military strategists establish priorities that allot minimum essential efforts and resources to secondary endeavors. The Principle of Economy, for example, prompted the U.S. and British decision to defeat Nazi Germany before turning full attention toward Japan during World War II.[11]

Prudent strategists take pains to avoid concurrent combat with two or more powerful adversaries, because they may not be able to economize anywhere without incurring outrageous risks. Hitler, who deliberately opened Eastern and Southern Fronts before he won in the West, belatedly learned that hard lesson to his nation's sorrow. Lean German forces in North Africa, Italy, and along the Atlantic Wall fought tenaciously, but were too few and finally lost.[12]

Principle of Maneuver

Maneuverability, which amalgamates mobility with agility, makes it possible to shift fluidly from one strategic mode to another and readily redeploy armed forces. Employers can concentrate, disperse, or disengage various forms of national power smoothly and rapidly to expand successes, abridge failures, exploit opportunities, and block vulnerabilities. Strategically significant flank attacks, horizontal or vertical envelopments (the latter from air or space), turning movements, and infiltrations that avoid enemy strengths are preferable to figurative or literal frontal assaults.

Astute strategists strive to maintain physical and intellectual momentum, so faltering opponents can-

not recuperate, then follow lines of least resistance en route to ultimate objectives.[13] Failure to pursue can have costly, long-term consequences. Whether General Eisenhower's broad front strategy in autumn 1944 unnecessarily prolonged war in Western Europe by giving disorganized German forces time to regroup remains a controversial topic many decades later.[14]

Principle of Surprise

Surprise does not vouchsafe success, but it vastly improves prospects. Secrecy, speed, deception, disinformation, originality, and audacity can produce results that far exceed efforts expended and thereby alter balances of power to great advantage. Shocked foes need not be caught wholly off guard, but only grasp the full significance of their predicament too late to respond effectively. Distraction (a psychological phenomenon) and disruption (a physical function) deprive rivals of initiative. Freedom of conception and freedom of action accordingly become twin casualties.[15]

Military surprise, such as the sneak attack on Pearl Harbor,[16] immediately comes to mind, but non-military forms sometimes have immense military implications. Political surprise of the first order occurred in 1989, when unexpected termination of the Cold War upended long-standing U.S. and NATO strategies.[17] Japan experienced shocking economic surprise after its political leaders signed a tripartite pact with Nazi Germany and Fascist Italy in September 1940, because President Franklin D. Roosevelt immediately embargoed much-needed scrap metal and petroleum shipments, then froze all Japanese assets in the United States.[18] Technological surprise "made potential enemies cringe in fright," according to Nikita Khrushchev, when *Sputnik I*, a basketball-sized Soviet space satellite, unexpectedly began to orbit Earth.[19]

Principle of Security

Nations and subnational groups, like prize fighters, must protect themselves at all times. Security, the flip side of surprise, preserves power and reduces probabilities that foreign and domestic enemies might jeopardize strategic plans, programs, or operations. Physical security shields populations, infrastructures, resources, and armed forces, increases freedom of action, and concurrently reduces vulnerabilities as well as risks. Positive intelligence programs concerning enemy capabilities and intentions guard against surprise. So do counterintelligence successes that dilute rival espionage efforts and expose subversion.

The Principle of Security by no means encourages timidity. On the contrary, bold offensives that move too fast for enemies to react effectively were popular before horse cavalry began to run rings around foot soldiers in ancient times. General George S. Patton, Jr. rewrote record books in 1944 when his armored columns, with "air cavalry" and French resistance forces protecting open flanks, sped from Brittany past Paris to Germany's western gateway in just fifty-five days, an operational feat of huge strategic significance.[20]

Principle of Simplicity

The military acronym KISS (keep it simple, stupid), which originated in the misty past, remains apropos, because the most complex theories and concepts can be couched in understandable terms. A simple book entitled $E = MC^2$, for example, long ago enlightened the author's grammar school son about Albert Einstein's Special Theory of Relativity. Strategic concepts expressed lucidly and concisely reduce opportunities for misinterpretations and decrease prospects for confusion in the fog of war.

General William C. Westmoreland, who received ambiguous guidance as long as he was Commander in Chief, U.S. Military Assistance Command, Vietnam (COMUSMACV), must have envied the crystal-clear directive that U.S. and British Combined Chiefs of Staff furnished General Eisenhower in February 1944: "You will enter the continent of Europe and, in conjunction with other United Nations, under-

take operations aimed at the heart of Germany and the destruction of her Armed Forces."[21] That marching order remained firm until armed conflict ceased.

Principle of Unity

The British Joint Chiefs of Staff in 1947 formally approved a Principle of War called "Co-operation," based on team spirit and good will.[22] Most military doctrines, however, promote Unity of Command, because central sources of authority are better able to assign responsibilities, promulgate policies, establish procedures, issue guidance, approve plans, set standards, supervise implementation, and settle disruptive disputes.

Disparate sources of policy and fragmented command arrangements invite dilemmas. No master plan, for example, ever integrated U.S. and South Vietnamese efforts. Commander in Chief, Pacific, headquartered in Hawaii, was responsible for the air war. COMUSMACV conducted ground operations. The U.S. Ambassador in Saigon handled diplomatic matters. Nearly forty South Vietnamese organizations engaged in rural reforms in 1966. The resultant patchwork made it impossible for U.S. Armed Forces and their allies to prosecute the Vietnam War most effectively.[23]

Principle of Morale

Clausewitz estimated that armed conflict is mainly "composed in equal parts of physical and moral causes and effects. One might say that the physical seem little more than the wooden hilt, while the moral factors are the precious metal, the real weapon, the finely honed blade." Napoleon Bonaparte, in his 115 Maxims, likewise noted that "The moral is to the material as three to one."[24]

War, whether hot or cold, tests the will of civilians as well as armed forces. Sturdy morale is imperative in times of great trouble, because all is lost if the urge to compete withers. Compelling purposes, leadership, discipline, and unflagging belief in a cause nurture such laudable traits as loyalty, élan, esprit de corps, confidence in capabilities, and tenacity. Pain and privation may do likewise, witness Britain's gritty stand in 1940 during the Blitz by Hermann Göring's *Luftwaffe* and subsequent German stoicism after Allied air forces began carpet bombing cities throughout the Third Reich.[25]

Principle of Time

The acronym METT (Mission, Enemy, Terrain, and Time) reminds national security decision-makers that relentless and irreplaceable time, which usually favors one side, constrains nearly every military course of action. Savvy strategists consequently try to determine whom time will benefit most, then shape concepts and plans accordingly.[26]

Time in some regards seemed unimportant to Lieutenant General Ulysses S. Grant who, while still in the Wilderness on his way to Spotsylvania and Cold Harbor, announced his intention "to fight it out on this line, if it takes all summer."[27] Tenacity similarly marked U.S. military performance during World Wars I and II, then in Korea, but public opposition to protracted war in Vietnam for questionable causes still makes the U.S. Government reluctant to engage in lengthy armed conflicts unless obviously vital interests are involved. That impatient attitude toward time, which preemptively closes options, puts U.S. strategists at a decided disadvantage when pitted against persistent antagonists.[28]

Composite Utility

Not all Principles of War are invariably relevant (Concentration and Economy compete for attention). Values vary with situations (offensive strategies may benefit most from Surprise, defensive strategies from Security). Some respected authorities seriously doubt that such precepts have practical utility.[29]

Principles of War, like Principles of Deterrence (pp. 73–75), nevertheless comprise convenient checklists with which to appraise strategic policies, concepts, plans, and operations. National security policy-makers and military strategists should evaluate risks and estimate costs before they knowingly violate any of the foregoing principles, because records show that winners by and large took heed, while losers—discounting those who clearly were out of their league—by and large did not.

PREMIER WAR FIGHTING POLICIES

Premier war-fighting policies prescribe basic conditions under which nations apply military power to achieve objectives. Relative priorities of force and finesse, preferences for offensive operations compared with defense, and peacetime deployment patterns are universally important.

Force vs. Finesse

Heavy-handed Chiefs of State, especially those in a hurry, tend to favor direct approaches and free use of armed force. Military strategies, plans, and operations take precedence over all other foreign and domestic policy instruments. Adherents, however, would do well to heed H. L. Mencken's admonition that "There is always an easy solution to every human problem—neat, plausible, and wrong," because over-reliance on brute strength leaves little room for games of intellectual judo that might mate ends and means equally well or better at less cost.

Strategists who prefer a lighter touch selectively apply political, economic, technological, psychological, cybernetic, and military power in consonance with Sun Tzu's belief that "to subdue the enemy without fighting is the acme of skill."[30] Special operations professionals who "think small" occasionally surmount obstacles that those who "think big" never could scale. *SS Hauptsturmführer* (Captain) Otto Skorzeny proved that point twice in little more than a twelvemonth, first when he rescued heavily-guarded Benito Mussolini, Italy's deposed *Il Duce*, from atop Gran Sasso Mountain deep in the Apennine Mountains (September 1943), then when his actions toppled Nicholas de Nagybánya Horthy, the side-switching Hungarian Regent (October 1944).

Both operations were strategically important, because Mussolini remained the titular head of a German-dominated Fascist Government in northern Italy, and Hungary, which previously prepared to defect from the Axis, remained Hitler's pawn until World War II ended in Europe.[31]

A reasonable balance between force and finesse, however desirable it may be, is difficult to maintain in the United States, where erratic mood swings coupled with frequent philosophical changes among senior officials in the Executive Branch and in Congress make consistent strategies elusive. Military power received scant consideration between World Wars I and II, figured prominently from the late 1940s through the late 1960s, sagged in the 1970s after public opposition to the Vietnam War brought that trend to a screeching halt, then revived during the 1980s. Willingness to use armed forces for humanitarian and peacekeeping missions soared after the shooting war with Iraq in January–February 1991, while inclinations to engage in armed combat declined.[32]

Offense vs. Defense

Policy decisions determine whether any country or coalition basically adopts an offensive or defensive posture. The choice has far-reaching ramifications for, as Sun Tzu observed, "Invincibility lies in the defense; the possibility of victory in the attack."[33] Overemphasis in either event is inadvisable, because offensive and defensive capabilities are complementary, like swords and shields.

Overemphasis on Offense

A good offense is the best defense in some circumstances, but a deadly liability under less favorable conditions. Devotees of the World War I doctrine dubbed *offense à outrance* (attack relentlessly and outrageously) stubbornly pitched endless waves of cannon fodder into awesome defensive firepower and field fortifications for more than four years. Many million dead and wounded littered battlefields between August 1, 1914 and November 11, 1918, when an armistice finally stopped the slaughter.[34]

Overemphasis on Defense

Fortified points and lines, typified by the Iron Curtain that separated Central from Western Europe throughout the Cold War, have strategic utility.[35] So do buffer zones and bastions, such as those that the Soviet Navy once maintained for its ballistic missile submarines in the Barents Sea and the Sea of Okhotsk.[36] Most military strategies and supporting force postures contribute to defense, but overemphasis (or total dependence, as some zealots propose[37]) reduces flexibility. NATO's member nations, for example, promised Warsaw Pact opponents that "none of our weapons will ever be used except in response to attack."[38] That declaratory policy allowed Communist troops to quash rebellions in East Germany (1953), Hungary (1956) and Czechoslovakia (1968) without worrying that NATO might intervene.[39]

Offensive Defense

Schizophrenic policies that are offensively defensive give intelligence analysts fits, because true intents are difficult to divine. The Brezhnev Doctrine, for example, rejected self-determination and reserved rights to conduct offensive operations in defense of Socialism wherever it faltered.[40] That policy justified Soviet aggression in Afghanistan (1979–1989) and fostered Cold War fears that, under duress, occupants of the Kremlin might order preemptive, damage-limiting, nuclear strikes to help defend Mother Russia. Soviet spokesmen denied such plans, but their long record of duplicity made disclaimers suspect.[41] Senior officials in Moscow expressed similar reservations about NATO's deterrent and defensive strategy, which emphasized deep counteroffensive strikes.[42]

Defensive Offense

Defensively offensive strategies that could confer decisive advantage are future possibilities. Put simply, offensive and defensive operations have alternately reigned supreme since the Stone Age. Defense occupied the top spot throughout World War I, but offense rebounded during World War II, nailed down first place with the advent of nuclear weapons in 1945, and has occupied that perch ever since. The first country to couple sound (not necessarily impervious) ballistic missile defenses with modest offensive capabilities will enjoy peerless capabilities until other nation-states duplicate that feat or offensive breakthroughs once again reverse the cycle. Whether resultant leverage would serve interests in peace or aggression depends on national security policies of the possessor.[43]

Peacetime Deployment Patterns

Policy-makers in nations that have extensive security interests well beyond their own borders must decide whether to deploy sizable armed forces abroad or maintain most at home ready to project the proper mix of military power on short notice whenever and wherever needed. Decisions to adopt either option strongly influence the size, shape, and characteristics of implementing armed services.

Forward Presence

Forward deployments put war-fighting forces in position to help friends and defuse budding crises before they balloon. Continuous presence ashore at the invitation of allies assures access to useful infrastructure, but is costly and may breed burden-sharing disputes (the House Committee on Armed Services activated a Defense Burden Sharing Panel in the 1980s for that reason). Offshore deployments, which are less visible, generate perpetual debates by vociferous proponents of land- and sea-based air power about the value of "being there" (physical presence) versus "being nearby" (virtual presence).[44]

U.S. Armed Forces in the 1980s were ensconced at nearly 1,700 large and small installations on foreign soil, mainly in Europe and along the edge of

East Asia. That collection included cantonments, airfields, seaports, supply depots, maintenance shops, troop training areas, gunnery ranges, communication centers, electronic listening posts, early warning sites, quarters, and dependent support facilities. Well over half of all such holdings (two-thirds of those in Europe) have closed, curtailed activities, or assumed standby status since the Soviet Union collapsed. Commensurate reductions in U.S. deterrent and quick-reaction combat capabilities followed.[45]

Power Projection

Military strategies that project expeditionary forces from positions in central reserve to cope with distant "come-as-you-are" contingencies create unique requirements. Airborne and amphibious assault capabilities sufficient to seize lodgments in hostile territory, then secure footholds until reinforcements arrive, often (not always) are essential. Needs frequently exist for enough transportation to move all follow-on combat and support personnel, weapons, equipment, and accompanying supplies from home stations to areas of operation on tight schedules, unload rapidly under primitive conditions if necessary, then sustain operations as long as directed. Prepositioned stocks sometimes lighten initial loads, but those located ashore are sitting duck targets, floating depots are hard to maintain in tip-top condition, and usefulness in either case is nil unless secure transfer sites are conveniently located.

Diminished forward presence, plus policy obligations to cope with two major regional contingencies that overlap, put unrealistic demands on U.S. long-haul airlift and sealift in the early 1990s. An exhaustive study that took into account Operations Desert Shield, Desert Storm, and several exacting scenarios emphasized needs to reach "hot spots" anywhere around the world before aggressors could "overrun key objectives" and build combat power before they "caused unacceptable attrition to U.S. forces, politically fractured the coalition [if any], or ravaged occupied territory." Whether U.S. mobility assets will satisfy those policy aims in the foreseeable future is problematic.[46]

WAR-FIGHTING THEORIES AND CONCEPTS

Most writings about war-fighting theories and concepts pertain to operational and tactical options (Table 12), but military strategists who think big can adapt a good deal. Brief expositions below address maneuver warfare, attrition, escalation, and de-escalation, then note the impact of policy restraints.

Table 12
Typical War-Fighting Options

Offense	Defense
Penetrations	Positional Defense
Standoff Attacks	Mobile Defense
Envelopments	Forward Defense
Infiltration	Defense in Depth
Surgical Operations	Buffers and Barriers
Interdiction	Bastions
Sieges	Scorched Earth

Strategic Maneuvers

Practically all tactical maneuvers have strategic utility when writ large.[47] The principal difference is perspective. Allied armies and air forces, for example, maneuvered at will after they burst from the Normandy beachhead in July 1944, but from strategic standpoints the advance was a frontal assault on Germany for ten consecutive months until May 8, 1945. Any Soviet attempt to seize Western Europe would have essentially been a straightforward thrust between the Baltic Sea and the Alps toward the Atlantic coast, no matter now many operational and tactical maneuvers campaign planners devised to expedite progress. Allied Command Europe (ACE) prepared to conduct locally significant delaying actions, but NATO's politically motivated forward defense policies forbade operations that would purposely trade German territory for time while ACE

tried to gain strength, regroup, and mount counter-offensives.[48]

Strategic Attrition

Sieges and blockades, which epitomize attrition, are among the most static forms of warfare. Their purpose is to sap well-defended enemies by deprivation over long periods, rather than root them out quickly at greater risk. Tactical sieges traditionally concentrate on points and small areas (castles once were typical targets). The Soviet blockade of Berlin, relieved by a massive U.S. airlift in 1948–49, exemplifies operational usage.[49]

Strategic sieges commonly occur on grander scales. Blockades ashore and afloat have been favorite instruments since ancient times. The United States Navy, in accord with President Lincoln's Anaconda Policy, began to quarantine the Confederacy on April 19, 1861. Constriction cut off almost all Confederate seaborne commerce before the Civil War ended, despite daring blockade runners like fictional Rhett Butler of *Gone With the Wind* fame.[50] Armed forces might similarly strangle opponents in space, perhaps adapting techniques the U.S. Pacific Fleet applied against Japan during World War II.[51] Mao Zedong and associate Lin Biao hoped to encircle enemy cities with rural revolutionary bases, then overcome industrial powers from strategic springboards in Asia, Africa, and Latin America.[52] Terrorists aim to put target governments and their citizens in states of strategic siege. Successes in that regard are starkly demonstrated in Washington, D.C., where police and protective barriers increasingly safeguard treasured monuments and national institutions at the expense of public access.

Escalation

Escalation entails competitions in risk taking and resolve. Escalation may begin before armed conflict commences (twenty of the forty-four rungs on Herman Kahn's original escalation ladder were in the "peacetime" crisis category).[53] Offensive and defensive belligerents thereafter may intensify combat, broaden the scope, or both. Available power, which need not be military, imposes the only physical constraint, although concern that rivals might over-react customarily limits incentives. Fainthearted war-fighters who face stalwarts usually lose in any case.

Vertical Escalation

Vertical escalation, which is most common, increases violence and perhaps speeds up tempos. Characteristic techniques reinforce committed forces, mobilize more combat power, employ or threaten to employ weapons of mass destruction, strike targets previously declared "off limits" (such as urban centers and privileged sanctuaries), and reduce intervals between major offensive operations.

Horizontal Escalation

Horizontal escalation, which supplements or supplants the vertical variety, spreads conflicts geographically.[54] Employers who possess sufficient reserves and mobility forces instigate actions in one or more regions that are well removed from the main battleground. Some initiatives are diversions, while others are decisive. The Athenian expedition to Sicily during the Peloponnesian War (415–413 B.C.), for example, remained a "side show," whereas Scipio's excursion across the Mediterranean Sea moved "center stage" from Rome to Carthage during the Second Punic War (204–202 B.C.).[55]

Protagonists who rely on allies or proxies can escalate horizontally at little cost, which Stalin tried to do in 1942 when he prematurely urged U.S. and British associates to open a second front in France.[56] Adversaries short on military means but skilled at psychological warfare also can spread conflicts far and wide, as Ho Chi Minh's henchmen did at the Paris peace table during the Vietnam War, with devastating effects in the United Nations and the United States.[57] Cybernetic warriors can play hob with com-puter dependent armed forces and societies anywhere in the world.[58]

Gradual Escalation

Gradual escalation is often confused with flexible response, but in fact is exceedingly rigid.[59] U.S. policy-makers and strategists verified that truism to perfection in Vietnam by increasing pressures in such small increments that recipients were able to adapt in much the same way that cancer patients learn to live with pain that would be intolerable if inflicted instantaneously.

De-escalation

Unilateral de-escalation transpires when excessive risks and costs lead Side A or Side B to believe that less aggressive operations would better serve its security interests, whereas reciprocal retrenchments normally necessitate inducements, concessions, and conciliation. Meaningful gestures may be implicit or explicit, large or small, practical or symbolic, expressed in words or deeds. The gradual U.S. withdrawal from Vietnam (1969–1972) was a classic case of de-escalation to curb domestic dissent and reduce casualties.

Overtures that do not decrease military capabilities include cooling-off periods, prisoner of war exchanges, and the replacement of officials that enemies despise. Military commanders in any event should remain alert while opponents de-escalate, because supposedly friendly signals sometimes mask hostile intentions. Hitler, for example, tried hard to mollify British Prime Minister Winston Churchill while Hermann Göring's *Luftwaffe* prepared to bomb London and other English cities.[60]

Policy Restraints

Brutes do battle without compunction. Ancient Assyrians, who amassed a mighty empire by storming, sacking, and demolishing cities throughout the Fertile Crescent, behaved so badly for several hundred years that a coalition of Medes and Chaldeans eventually obliterated Nineveh in 612 B.C., then eradicated the rest of the nation.[61] Ghenghis Khan, who ran roughshod across Eurasia in the 13th century A.D., believed "The greatest pleasure is to vanquish your enemies and chase them before you, to rob them of their wealth and see those dear to them be bathed in tears, to ride their horses and clasp to your bosom their wives and daughters."[62] The Japanese "Rape of Nanking" and Pol Pot's butchery in Cambodia represent large-scale atrocities in modern times.[63]

Cruel practices have by no means disappeared, but multilateral conventions, arms control accords, and other international laws currently restrict the conduct of "civilized" states during armed combat.[64] U.S. national security policy-makers additionally impose severe unilateral restraints on military strategists, of which the following four are illustrative.

War Power Restraints

Disapproval of the Vietnam War prompted Congress to pass the *War Powers Resolution* of 1973, which circumscribes the President's authority to introduce U.S. Armed Forces into hostilities or potentially hostile situations without a declaration of war or specific statutory authority and specifies withdrawal after sixty days unless Congress extends the deadline. Presidents Reagan, Bush, and Clinton respectively disregarded that edict during conflicts in Grenada (1983), Panama (1989–1990), the Persian Gulf (1990–1991), and Kosovo (1999), partly because the Supreme Court has never ruled on constitutionality, but U.S. politico-military strategists nevertheless must take war powers provisions into account.[65]

Covert Operations Restraints

Congressional condemnation of the "secret war in Laos" and other covert actions led to the Hughes–Ryan Amendment of 1974, which forbade the CIA to expend foreign assistance funds for any purpose "other than activities intended solely for obtaining necessary intelligence, unless and until the President finds that each such operation is important to the security of the United States and reports, in a

timely fashion . . . to the appropriate subcommittees of the Congress. . . ." The Oversight Act of 1980 retained and refined those requirements.[66]

Assassination Restraints

Several U.S.-sponsored or tacitly approved plots that culminated in successful, attempted, or suspected assassinations during the 1960s and early 1970s prompted congressional complaints.[67] President Gerald R. Ford in 1976 responded with Executive Order 11905, which declared that "No employee of the United States Government shall engage in, or conspire to engage in, political assassination"—a term that has never been officially defined. President Reagan's Executive Order 12333, which remains in effect, additionally forbids "anybody acting on behalf of the United States Government" and decrees that "no agency of the Intelligence Community shall participate in or request any person to undertake activities forbidden by this Order."[68] Those proscriptions never were intended to protect terrorists, but narrow interpretations thus far have made "up close and personal" hits impolitic, although U.S. policy-makers publicly approve "drive-by" cruise missile attacks on suspected locations, such as the August 1998 assault on Osama bin Laden's hideout in Afghanistan.[69]

Unrealistic Restraints

A U.S.-led coalition in January–February 1991 took just six weeks to defeat Iraq at the cost of 147 U.S. combat fatalities. Photographic records of that pristine triumph, repeatedly televised internationally in living color, left the unrealistic impression that U.S. Armed Forces could invariably employ precision-guided munitions with pinpoint accuracy in densely populated places, even if enemy leaders deliberately intermingle military targets with noncombatants.[70] Hypersensitive opinion-makers in the United States have considered collateral damage and casualties socially unacceptable ever since, and U.S. leaders remain extremely reluctant to launch operations that place American lives at risk.[71]

CONFLICT TERMINATION

Conflict termination, the ultimate form of de-escalation, occurs when one side capitulates or withdraws, belligerents arrange mutually agreeable terms, or outsiders impose a settlement.[72] Termination is relatively easy to achieve when victory, however defined, is decisive, but can be difficult when both sides fight for limited ends with limited means. Cessation becomes incredibly complex when combatants with asymmetrical vulnerabilities assign vastly different values to respective objectives, as commonly is the case when nations clash with subnational groups.[73]

Inhibitions

Every war indeed must end, but inducements must exceed inhibitions before authorities take serious steps to terminate.[74] Insistence on idealistic or ideologically motivated objectives (defeat evil; convert disbelievers) makes it much easier to start a war than to stop it. Struggles in such cases often continue long after rational cost-benefit relations cease to exist. Both sides may take turns escalating, which happened when U.S. and Chinese Communist forces fought from mid-1951 to mid-1953 trying to improve positions marginally.[75] Fear of defeat may have similar effects, if winners demonstrate scant compassion and losers spread atrocity tales to stiffen resistance. "Enjoy the war; the peace will be terrible" was *Reichsminister* Joseph Goebbel's slogan, while Hitler's "scorched earth" proclamation of March 19, 1945 directed the faithful to destroy all infrastructure in the Third Reich so no enemy could enjoy the fruits of victory.[76]

Horizontal escalation by definition creates two or more generically linked but widely separated conflicts that rival powers may have to extinguish individually. That condition, which pertained at the end of World War I, eventually required the Allies to conclude six treaties: Versailles (with Germany), St. Germain (with Austria), Trianon (with Hungary), Neuilly (with Bulgaria), Sèvres and later Lausanne (with Turkey).[77]

Inducements

Unacceptable casualties and damage, budgetary costs, shrinking resources, exhaustion, and prospects of stalemate or defeat are strong incentives to terminate unwanted wars. Nations normally try to conclude one conflict before they become embroiled in others. Additional inducements include diminishing domestic support and international disapproval. Public dissent rather than battlefield failures, for example, prompted the Nixon Administration to withdraw from Vietnam. Secretary of Defense Caspar Weinberger later listed as one of his six preconditions for future U.S. intervention "some reasonable assurance that we will have the support of the American people and their representatives in Congress."[78] French Minister of Interior François Mitterand, a few days after fighting started in Algeria, announced that, "the only negotiation is war," but President Charles de Gaulle granted every rebel demand seven years later, with overwhelming approval of the French people.[79] Serious attempts to terminate wars, in short, most commonly arise when one or both sides reevaluate objectives, conclude that the cause is no longer worth continued costs, and decide to settle for less than they would like, because peace seems preferable to further hostilities whether they win or lose.

Termination Techniques

Blurred distinctions between war and peace have caused conflict termination treaties to fall from favor since World War II. No legal document has ever ended any transnational terrorist, insurgent, or resistance movement; losers usually just fade away.[80] The most common techniques used to terminate orthodox conflicts currently are surrender, imposed settlements, compassion, and reconciliation.

Surrenders

Side A may maintain unbearable pressures or escalate until Side B capitulates. That course was popular in the distant past, when unconditional surrender terminated most conflicts and defeated people were dispatched or enslaved. The U.S. Civil War and World War II culminated in unconditional surrender, but victors in each case were benevolent. Conditional surrenders involve considerable give-and-take if losers retain enough strength to drive hard bargains.[81]

Imposed Settlements

Outsiders occasionally impose termination terms or otherwise encourage cessation of hostilities. President Eisenhower short-stopped the British-French-Israeli invasion of Egypt well before that coalition achieved its strategic objective, which was to regain control of the Suez Canal after President Gamal Abdel Nasser nationalized it on July 26, 1956.[82] The United Nations since its inception in 1946 has repeatedly applied political, economic, and military pressures to terminate wars, with varying degrees of success. Assorted regional associations, such as the Organization of American States and the Economic Community of West African States have done likewise.[83]

Compassion

Compassionate combatants may stop mauling opponents who clearly are beaten and ready to quit, but have not yet raised a white flag. U.S. Armed Forces, for example, spared terrified Iraqi troops who frantically scrambled to escape annihilation along the so-called "Highway of Death" between Kuwait City and Basra during Operation Desert Storm. President George Bush, speaking from the Oval Office on February 27, 1991, announced that, "Iraq's Army is defeated. Our military objectives are met. I am pleased to announce that at midnight tonight, Eastern Standard Time, exactly one hundred hours since ground operations commenced and six weeks since the start of Operation Desert Storm, all U.S. and coalition forces will suspend offensive combat operations."[84]

Reconciliations

Terminations predicated on compromise are trickiest. The timing and other conditions of cease-fires, boundary disputes, the disposition of territories, force withdrawals, prisoner exchanges, and reparations are cogent considerations.[85] Conciliation depends to great degrees on communications that minimize misunderstandings.[86] Domestic politics almost always play important roles, and often determine what concessions key officials, various elites, and the populace will accept.[87]

Table 13
Conflict Termination Related to Postwar Prospects

Conflict Termination		Postwar Prospects		
Outcomes	Terms	Control Opponents	Profit From Opponents	Lasting Peace Prospects
Victory	No Surrender	N/A	Variable[1]	Variable[2]
	Unconditional Surrender	Fine	Variable[1]	Variable[3]
	Conditional Surrender	Good	Variable[1]	Variable[4]
Compromise	Favor Self	Good	Good	Poor
	Impartial	Fair	Fair	Good
	Favor Rival	Poor	Poor	Poor
Stalemate	None	Poor	Poor	Poor[5]
Defeat	Benevolent	Poor	Good	Good
	Malevolent	Nil	Poor	Poor

[1]Good if loser's infrastructure remains reasonably intact. Otherwise fair to poor, depending on damage and casualties.
[2]Exterminating losers ensures lasting peace between belligerents, but resultant regional power balances may be unstable.
[3]Depends on the victor's postwar deportment.
[4]Depends on conditions imposed and the victor's postwar deportment.
[5]Exhaustion and other factors may cause peace to persist for some indefinite period after a stalemate.

Outcomes

The likelihood of lasting peace depends largely on the way winners treat losers (Table 13). Unsettled issues and harsh terms tend to impair postwar prospects. History is rife with wars fought to regain lost territories, as demonstrated in Alsace-Lorraine, which traded hands from France to Germany and back again in 1871, 1919, 1940, and 1945. Austria, Prussia, and Russia (later Nazi Germany and the Soviet Union) repeatedly partitioned Poland. True peace imposed by force is a rare exception to the general rule, because compellence leaves a residue of resentment. Tranquility is assured if victors eviscerate the vanquished, but they frequently destroy valuable spoils of war in the process. Bystanders moreover may kindle a new conflict to reshape regional balances of power.

Enlightened statesmen and politico-military strategists therefore try to frame terms that build "golden bridges" instead of "brick walls." Conflicts terminate most favorably when triumphant powers emphasize reconciliation and losers in the long run profit almost as much as winners. Reconstruction in the aftermath of the U.S. Civil War is exemplary, carpetbaggers notwithstanding.[88] The Marshall Plan, which worked miracles in Western Europe,[89] and U.S. benevolence toward Japan after World War II were even shinier. Those compassionate performances have led more than one comedian to say, "It's better to lose a war with the United States than to win!"

KEY POINTS

- Principles of War for strategic purposes demand different slants than those that pertain to operational art or tactics, but
- Almost all tactical war-fighting options have strategic utility when writ large
- Politico-military policies and international laws prescribe basic conditions under which nations apply military power to achieve war-fighting objectives
- Over-reliance on force leaves little room for games of intellectual judo that might mate ends and means equally well at less cost
- Strategies that overemphasize offense, defense, maneuver, or attrition usually are inadvisable, because immoderation as a rule increases risks
- Strategies that emphasize forward deployments at or near "hot spots" improve crisis response capabilities
- Strategies that project military power abroad from bases in the home country increase requirements for long-haul airlift, sealift, and forceable entry forces
- Vertical escalation intensifies conflicts physically or psychologically; horizontal escalation broadens the scope
- Unilateral de-escalation occurs when risks and costs become excessive; inducements, concessions, and conciliations encourage reciprocal de-escalation
- Wars end when one side capitulates or withdraws, belligerents come to mutually agreeable terms, or outsiders impose a settlement
- The likelihood of lasting peace depends on the way winners treat losers

NOTES

1. Burke Davis, *Sherman's March* (New York: Random House, 1980).

2. John Keegan, *The First World War* (New York: Alfred A. Knopf, 1999).

3. John I. Alger, *The Quest for Victory: The History of the Principles of War* (Westport, CT: Greenwood Press, 1982). For offbeat views, see Russell W. Glenn, "No More Principles of War," *Parameters*, Spring 1998, 48-66.

4. Former Chairman of the Joint Chiefs of Staff General Nathan F. Twining (1957-60) discusses Principles of War in *Neither Liberty nor Safety: A Hard Look at U.S. Military Policy and Strategy* (New York: Holt, Rinehart and Winston, 1966), 198-225. JCS Chairmen General Colin L. Powell (1989-93) and General John M. Shalikashvili (1993-96) discuss Principles of War in Joint Pub. 1, *Joint Warfare of the U.S. Armed Forces* (Washington: National Defense University Press), November 11, 1991, 21-35 and January 10, 1995, III-1 to III-9.

5. James F. Schnabel, *United States Army in the Korean War: Policy and Direction, the First Year* (Washington: U.S. Government Printing Office, 1972); *The Record on Korean Unification, 1943-1960: Narrative Summary with Principal Documents* (Washington: U.S. Government Printing Office, 1960), 15-22, 86-126.

6. Brian Cavan, *The Punic Wars* (New York: St. Martin's Press, 1980), 115-61; Basil H. Liddell Hart, *Scipio Africanus: Greater Than Napoleon* (New York: Biblo and Tannen, 1971), 123-203.

7. David G. Chandler, *The Campaigns of Napoleon* (New York: Macmillan, 1966), 739-861; Alexander Werth, *Russia At War, 1941-1945* (New York: E. P. Dutton & Co., 1964), 131-581.

8. Rear Admiral J. C. Wylie, *Military Strategy: A General Theory of Power Control* (New Brunswick, NJ: Rutgers University Press, 1967), 83-85.

9. For background, see President Richard M. Nixon, *U.S. Foreign Policy for the 1970s* (Washington: U.S. Government Printing Office, February 18, 1970), 140-42; (February 25, 1971), 105-9; (February 9, 1972), 26-37; (May 3, 1973), 16-25; Barton Gellman, "Reappraisal Led to New China Policy," *Washington Post*, June 22, 1998, A1.

10. Sun Tzu, *The Art of War*, trans. Samuel B. Griffith (New York: Oxford University Press, 1963), 98; Robert B. Asprey, *War in the Shadows: The Guerrilla in History* (Garden City, NY: Doubleday & Co., 1975).

11. Louis Morton, "Germany First: The Basic Concept of Allied Strategy in World War II," in *Command Decisions*, ed. Kent Roberts Greenfield (New York: Harcourt, Brace and Co., 1959), 11-47.

12. Percy Ernest Schram, *Hitler: The Man and the Military Leader* (Chicago: Quadrangle Books, 1971), 202.

13. Basil H. Liddell Hart, *Strategy*, 2d rev. ed. (New York: Praeger, 1967), 340-42, 348-50.

14. Roland G. Ruppenthal, "Logistics and the Broad Front Strategy," in *Command Decisions*, 419-27; David Irving, *The War Between the Generals* (New York: Congdon & Lattrès, 1981), 267-88.

15. Richard K. Betts, *Surprise Attack: Lessons for Defense Planning* (Washington: Brookings Institution, 1982); Klaus Knorr and Patrick Morgan, *Strategic Military Surprise: Incentives and Opportunities* (New York: National Strategy Information Center, 1982); Liddell Hart, *Strategy*, 340-42.

16. Gordon W. Prange, *At Dawn We Slept: The Untold Story of Pearl Harbor* (New York: McGraw-Hill, 1981).

17. *National Security Strategy of the United States* (Washington: The White House, August 1991), 1-6; *National Military Strategy of the United States* (Washington: Chairman of the Joint Chiefs of Staff, January 1992), 1-5.

18. Jerome B. Cohen, *Japan's Economy in War and Reconstruction* (Minneapolis: University of Minnesota Press, 1949), Chapter 3.

19. Nikita S. Khrushchev, *Khrushchev Remembers: The Last Testament*, ed. and trans. Strobe Talbott (Boston: Little, Brown, 1974), 47.

20. General George S. Patton, Jr., *War As I Knew It* (Cambridge, MA: Houghton Mifflin Co., 1947), 99-137; Staff Sergeant Mark Murphy, "Patton's Air Cavalry," *World War II in the Air: Europe*, ed. Major James F. Sonderman (New York: Bramhall House, 1963), 270-75.

21. Forrest C. Pogue, *The Supreme Command. The United States Army in World War II: The European Theater of Operations* (Washington: U.S. Government Printing Office, 1954), 53.

22. Twining, *Neither Liberty nor Safety*, 221, 225.

23. General Bruce Palmer, *The 25-Year War: America's Military Role in Vietnam* (Lexington: University Press of Kentucky, 1984), 193-96; Colonel Harry Summers, *On Strategy: The Vietnam War in Context* (Carlisle Barracks, PA: Strategic Studies Institute, U.S. Army War College, 1981), 87-96.

24. Carl von Clausewitz, *On War*, ed. and trans. Michael Howard and Peter Paret (Princeton, NJ: Princeton University Press, 1976), 184-85. Napoleon's 115 maxims appear in Thomas R. Philipps, ed., *Roots of Strategy: A Collection of Military Classics* (Westport, CT: Greenwood Press, 1982), 407-39.

25. Philip Ziegler, *London at War, 1939-1945* (New York: Alfred Knopf, 1995); David Irving, *The De-

struction of Dresden (New York: Holt, Rinehart and Winston, 1963).

26. Ajay Singh, "Time: The New Dimension in War," Joint Force Quarterly, Summer 1998, 124-29; Reginald Bretnor, Decisive Warfare: A Study in Military Theory (Harrisburg, PA: Stackpole Press, 1969), 72-98.

27. Lieutenant General Ulysses S. Grant, in a dispatch from Spotsylvania Courthouse to Army Chief of Staff Henry W. Halleck, May 11, 1864.

28. Frederick M. Downey and Steven Metz, "The American Political Culture and Strategic Planning," Parameters, September 1988, 35-36.

29. Liddell Hart, Strategy, 347.

30. Sun Tzu, The Art of War, 77, 79.

31. Glenn B. Infield, Skorzeny: Hitler's Commando (New York: St. Martin's Press, 1981), 29-45, 65-77; Charles Foley, Commando Extraordinary (New York: G. P. Putnam's Sons, 1955), 35-58, 83-100.

32. John A. Gentry, "Military Force in An Age of National Cowardice," Washington Quarterly, Autumn 1998, 179-91; Frederick M. Downey and Steven Metz, "The American Political Culture and Strategic Planning," Parameters, September 1988, 38-39.

33. Sun Tzu, The Art of War, 85.

34. Jack L. Snyder, The Ideology of the Offensive: Military Decision Making and the Disasters of 1914 (Ithaca, NY: Cornell University Press, 1984); Michael Howard, "Men Against Fire: The Doctrine of the Offensive in 1914," in Makers of Modern Strategy: From Machiavelli to the Nuclear Age, ed. Peter Paret (Princeton, NJ: Princeton University Press, 1986), 510-26.

35. Martin H. Bryce, Forts and Fortresses (New York: Facts on File, 1990); Ian Hogg, The History of Fortification (New York: St. Martin's Press, 1981).

36. Saul Bernard Cohen, Geography and Politics in a World Divided (New York: Random House, 1963), 193-203; Jan S. Breemer, "The Soviet Navy's SSBN Bastions," RUSI Journal, Winter 1989, 33-39.

37. Anders Boserup and Robert Neild, eds., The Foundations of Defensive Defense (New York: St. Martin's Press, 1990); Johan Galtung, "Transarmament from Offensive to Defensive Defense," Journal of Peace Research, vol. 21, no. 2, (1984), 127-39.

38. NATO and the Warsaw Pact: Force Comparisons (Brussels, Belgium: NATO Information Service, 1984), 1.

39. Stefan Brandt, The East German Rising (New York: Praeger, 1957); Richard Lettis and William E. Morris, The Hungarian Revolt, October 23-November 4, 1956 (New York: Scribner, 1961); Harry Schwartz, Prague's 200 Days: The Struggle for Democracy in Czechoslovakia (New York: Praeger, 1969).

40. S. Kovalev, "Sovereignty and the International Obligation of Socialist Countries," Pravda, September 26, 1968, 4. An English translation appeared in The Current Digest of the Soviet Press, October 16, 1968, 10-12.

41. For various views, see D. T. Yazov, "On Soviet Military Doctrine," Journal of the Royal United Services Institute (RUSI), Winter 1989, 4; Henry Trofimenko, "The 'Theology' of Strategy," Orbis, Fall 1977, 510; Fritz W. Ermarth, "Contrasts in American and Soviet Strategic Thought," International Security, Fall 1978, 152, 153; Benjamin S. Lambeth, How to Think About Soviet Military Doctrine (Santa Monica, CA: RAND Corporation, February 1978), 10-12.

42. New Technology for NATO: Implementing Follow-on Forces Attack (Washington: Office of Technology Assessment, U.S. Government Printing Office, June 1987), 49-52, 103-8.

43. Jack Swift, "Strategic Superiority Through SDI," Defense & Foreign Affairs, December 1985, 17, 36.

44. Bradford Dismukes, "The U.S. Military Presence Abroad," Strategic Review, Spring 1995, 49-58; Glenn W. Goodman, Jr., "Virtual Overseas Presence: Air Force Redefines the Strategic Security Landscape" and Commander Christopher M. Wode, "Beyond Bombers Vs. Carriers," both in Armed Forces Journal, April 1995, 12, 29-30; Michael W. Smith and Henry L. Eskew, Cost and Capability Differences in Land-Based and Sea-Based Tactical Aviation (Washington: Center for Naval Analyses, February 1995).

45. Pete Williams announced the first wave of U.S. base closings abroad in Pentagon Briefing (Washington: News Transcripts, Inc., July 30, 1991). See also Peter Grier, "The Flags Come Home," Air Force, October 1991, 32-35; Additional U.S. Overseas Bases to End Operations, News Release (Washington: Office of the Assistant Secretary of Defense [Public Affairs], August 18, 1994). Updated informally by author.

46. Conduct of the Persian Gulf War, Final Report to Congress (Washington: Department of Defense, April 1992), Appendix E and 24-29 of Annex F; Mobility Requirements Study (Washington: Department of Defense, January 23, 1992), vol. I, Conclusions and Recommendations, Unclassified Executive Summary.

47. Richard D. Hooker, Jr., ed., Maneuver Warfare: An Anthology (Novato, CA: Presidio Press, 1993); William S. Lind, Maneuver Warfare Handbook (Boulder, CO: Westview Press, 1985).

48. Secretary of Defense Caspar Weinberger reviews reasons for NATO's rigid defense policies in Improving NATO's Conventional Capabilities: A Report to the

United States Congress (Washington: D.C. Department of Defense, June 1984), 10–11.

49. Ann and John Tusa, *The Berlin Airlift* (New York: Atheneum Press, 1988).

50. E. W. Carter III, "Blockade," *U.S. Naval Institute Proceedings* (November 1990), 42–47.

51. Brent L. Gravatt, "Elements of Conventional War: Land, Sea, Air, and Space," *Naval War College Review* (May–June 1985, 13–14.

52. Lin Piao, "Long Live the Victory of People's War!" in *Mao Tse-Tung and Lin Piao: Post Revolutionary Writings*, ed. Kuang Fan (Garden City, NY: Anchor Books, 1972), 357–412.

53. Herman Kahn, *On Escalation: Metaphors and Scenarios* (New York: Praeger, 1965), 3–9, 37–51, 219.

54. Roger Beaumont, *Horizontal Escalation: Patterns and Paradoxes*, Stratech Studies Series (College Station: Center for Strategic Technology, Texas A&M, April 1993).

55. Major General J. F. C. Fuller, *A Military History of the Western World*, vol. I (New York: Funk & Wagnalls, 1954), 53–80, 115–45.

56. Leo J. Meyer, "The Decision to Invade North Africa (Torch)," in Greenfield, *Command Decisions*, 176–86.

57. Stanley Karnow, *Vietnam: A History* (New York: Viking Press, 1983), 623–70.

58. James Adams, *The Next World War: Computers Are the Weapons and the Front Line is Everywhere* (New York: Simon & Schuster, 1998); Edward Waltz, *Information Warfare: Principles and Operations* (Boston: Artech House, 1998).

59. General Curtis E. LeMay, *America Is in Danger* (New York: Funk & Wagnalls, 1968), 25.

60. Kahn, *On Escalation*, 230–43.

61. Stewart C. Easton, *The Heritage of the Past: From the Earliest Times to the Close of the Middle Ages* (New York: Rinehart & Co., 1958), 95–99.

62. James Charlton, ed., *The Military Quotation Book* (New York: St. Martin's Press, 1990), 92.

63. Iris Chang, *The Rape of Nanking: The Forgotten Holocaust of World War II* (New York: Basic Books, 1997); Ben Kiernan, *The Pol Pot Regime: Race, Power, and Genocide in Cambodia Under the Khmer Rouge, 1975–1979* (New Haven, CT: Yale University Press, 1998).

64. *Treaties in Force: A List of Treaties and Other International Agreements of the United States in Force on January 1, 1990* (Washington: U.S. Government Printing Office, 1990), 369–75; *Arms Control and Disarmament Agreements* (Washington: U.S. Arms Control and Disarmament Agency, 1982), 9–18, 120–31.

65. *The War Powers Resolution: Relevant Documents, Correspondence, Reports,* Subcommittee on Arms Control, International Security, and Science of the House Committee on Foreign Affairs, 100th Congress, 2d sess. (Washington: U.S. Government Printing Office, May 1988).

66. *Intelligence Authorization Act for FY 1990-91,* Rpt. No. 101-174, Senate Select Committee on Intelligence, 101st Cong., 2d sess. (Washington: U.S. Government Printing Office, September 18, 1989), 6–9, 18–33.

67. *Alleged Assassination Plots Involving Foreign Leaders*, an Interim Report of the Senate Select Committee to Study Governmental Operations With Respect to Intelligence Activities, 94th Cong., 1st sess. (Washington: U.S. Government Printing Office, November 20, 1975).

68. Executive Order 11905, February 8, 1976 (41 FR 7703), twice amended, signed by President Gerald R. Ford; Executive Order 12036, January 24, 1978 (43 FR 3674), signed by President Jimmy Carter; Executive Order 12333, December 4, 1981 (46 FR 59941), signed by President Ronald Reagan.

69. Raymond Close, "Hard Target: We Can't Defeat Terrorism With Bombs and Bombast," *Washington Post*, August 30, 1998, C1, C5.

70. General Colin L. Powell with Joseph E. Persico, *My American Journey* (New York: Random House, 1995), 506–28.

71. Peter D. Feaver and Christopher Gelpi, "How Many Deaths Are Acceptable? A Surprising Answer," *Washington Post*, November 7, 1999, B3.

72. Fred Charles Iklé, *Every War Must End* (New York: Columbia University Press, 1971); Stephen J. Cimbala and Keith A. Dunn, eds., *Conflict Termination and Military Strategy: Coercion, Persuasion, and War* (Boulder, CO: Westview Press, 1987); Paul R. Pillar, *Negotiating Peace: War Termination As a Bargaining Process* (Princeton, NJ: Princeton University Press, 1983); *How Wars End*, a special edition of *The Annals of the American Academy of Political and Social Science*, November 1970, 1–172.

73. Gordon A. Craig and Alexander L. George, *Force and Statecraft: Diplomatic Problems of Our Time* (New York: Oxford University Press, 1983), 220–22.

74. Ibid., 222–23; Iklé, *Every War Must End*, 9, 12.

75. General Matthew B. Ridgway, *The Korean War* (New York: Doubleday & Co., 1967), 185–225.

76. William L. Shirer, *The Rise and Fall of the Third Reich* (Greenwich, CT: Crest Books, 1962), 1432–33.

77. William L. Langer, ed., *An Encyclopedia of World History: Ancient, Medieval, and Modern* (Boston: Houghton Mifflin Co., 1968), 977–79, 1085–86.

78. "Excerpts from Address of Weinberger," *New York Times*, November 29, 1984, 5.

79. David and Marina Ottaway, *Algeria: The Politics of a Socialist Revolution* (Berkeley: University of California Press, 1970). Mitterrand's quotation is from Iklé, *Every War Must End*, 12.

80. Quincy Wright, "How Hostilities Have Ended: Peace Treaties and Alternatives," and Paul Seabury, "Provisionality and Finality," both in *How Wars End*, 51–61, 96–104.

81. Iklé, *Every War Must End*, 38–58; Paul Kecskemeti, *Strategic Surrender: The Politics of Victory and Defeat* (Stanford: Stanford University Press, 1958).

82. Kenneth Love, *Suez: The Twice Fought War* (New York: McGraw Hill, 1969), 333–700.

83. Sydney D. Bailey, ed., *How Wars End: The United Nations and the Termination of Armed Conflict, 1946–1964*, 2 vols. (New York: Oxford University Press, 1982); David M. Morriss, "From War to Peace: A Study of Cease-fire Agreements and the Evolving Role of the United Nations," *Virginia Journal of International Law*, vol. 36 (Summer 1996), 801–931.

84. Powell, *My American Journey*, 519–23.

85. Pillar, *Negotiating Peace*; Craig and George, *Force and Statecraft*, 227–29.

86. George H. Quester, "Wars Prolonged by Misunderstood Signals," in *How Wars End* (Annals), 30–38; Liddell Hart, *Strategy*, 371.

87. Iklé, *Every War Must End*, 59–105; Robert Rothstein, "Domestic Politics and Peacemaking," Robert Randle, "The Domestic Origins of Peace," and Morton H. Halperin, "War Termination As a Problem in Civil-Military Relations," all in *How Wars End* (Annals), 62–95.

88. Eric Foner, *Reconstruction: America's Unfinished Revolution, 1863–1877* (New York: Harper & Row, 1988); J. G. Randall, *The Civil War and Reconstruction* (Boston: D. C. Heath and Co., 1937).

89. "The Marshall Plan and Its Legacy: The 50th Anniversary," *Foreign Affairs*, Commemorative Section, vol. 76, no. 3 (May–June 1997), 157–221; Harry B. Price, *The Marshall Plan and Its Meaning* (Ithaca, NY: Cornell University Press, 1955).

9. Fundamentals of Military Preparedness

When your weapons are dulled . . . neighboring
rulers will take advantage of your distress.
And even though you have wise counsellors,
none will be able to lay good plans.

Sun Tzu
The Art of War

Superb military strategies are advantageous only if armed forces are properly organized, equipped, and trained to implement them successfully wherever, whenever, and however required for as long as necessary in peacetime and in war. Quantitative and qualitative considerations include military roles, functions, and missions, active and reserve force postures, manpower, materiel, education, training, infrastructure, technologies, modernization programs, industrial capacities, and other facets of military power. Efforts to satisfy present demands when resources are scarce may sacrifice future proficiency.

Military preparedneses moreover is situation specific. Weak U.S. Armed Forces, for example, were adequate before World War II erupted in Europe, since no enemy directly endangered the United States and capacities for rapid expansion were prodigious. Incomparably stronger U.S. forces subsequently outclassed Vietnamese opponents in most measurable respects, but initial preparedness for orthodox rather than unorthodox combat was a minus instead of a plus.

READINESS VS. SUSTAINABILITY

Readiness connotes immediate abilities to conduct military operations. Sustainability determines how long operations can last before casualties and the lack of consumables (munitions, fuel, food, repair parts) render units ineffective. Readiness and sus-

tainability are mutually indispensable components of military preparedness, because rapidly deployable forces that lack staying power risk early defeat, whereas durable forces that arrive too late are useless.[1] Armed forces unfortunately cannot become equally prepared for every eventuality. Nuclear, biological, chemical, traditional, and unconventional warfare are distinctive. Military operations other than war, such as peacekeeping, humanitarian assistance, disaster relief, drug interdiction, and noncombatant evacuation, demand different skills. So do uniservice, joint, and coalition endeavors.

PRINCIPLES OF PREPAREDNESS

Excessive attention to military preparedness yields armed forces that are unnecessarily expensive. A satisfactory balance between competing national needs therefore is advisable. Nine Principles of Military Preparedness, analogous to Principles of Deterrence and War described in Chapters 7 and 8, could help planners, programmers, and budgeteers fashion versatile forces at reasonable costs.

Principle of Purview

Postulation: Armed forces perform best when prepared to fulfill characteristic roles and functions.

Characteristic roles fundamentally shape military readiness and sustainability requirements. Armies prepare to operate primarily on land, air forces above land, navies on, under, over, or from the sea, amphibious forces along littorals, and space forces within Earth's circumterrestrial envelope or beyond. Characteristic combat and support functions influence preparedness requirements within each military service. Reasonable overlaps enhance flexibility, but revised roles and functions become essential whenever interservice competition generates undesirable redundancies.[2] The most recent U.S. reviews, for example, did not resolve Army and Air Force disputes about primary responsibility for theater missile defense,[3] battlefield interdiction,[4] and close air support.[5]

Principle of Regional Peculiarity
Postulation: Armed forces perform best when prepared for employment in particular geographic regions.

Every Area of Responsibility (AOR) is geographically unique in terms of physical and cultural geography. Armed forces expressly prepared for employment in any given environment normally function less well elsewhere until they complete time-consuming, often costly, transitions. They not only must become familiar with new friends, enemies, terrain, climate, demographic patterns, cultures, and social situations, but also tailor weapons, equipment, clothing, and supplies to suit new conditions. Frigid climes, for example, require parkas, insulated boots, lined sleeping bags, skis, snowmobiles, low-viscosity lubricants, and hot meals with high caloric contents, none of which are suitable in the tropics. Exotic diseases that decimate poorly prepared troops in equatorial rain forests are absent in deserts. Lowlanders who enter high altitude AORs on short notice suffer from oxygen deprivation (hypoxia) until they adapt.[6]

Principle of Quantitative Sufficiency
Postulation: Armed forces perform best when force levels and assigned missions are compatible.

General George Washington on September 15, 1780, told Congress that, "Our object ought to be . . . a good army rather than a large one." Practical limits nevertheless exist, because small armed forces are less able to control extensive territory, cannot absorb heavy casualties as easily, and possess less flexibility when unforeseen contingencies arise. Rapid operating tempos and lengthy forward deployments require larger establishments than routine operations at or near home stations.

Manpower Levels
Authorized personnel ceilings limit the number of divisions, air wings, naval ships, and other military units that a nation could field at or near full strength. Assigned personnel equal authorizations in the absence of conscription only if recruiting programs attract enough entry-level volunteers and retention programs keep commissioned, warrant, and enlisted pay grades at prescribed levels. Units that are required to commence operations at full strength must be authorized overstrengths in peacetime, because some personnel invariably are ill, on leave, AWOL, in transit, incarcerated, or in school. Legal waivers may eliminate others, such as single parents, HIV-positive individuals, conscientious objectors, and females who are pregnant or suffer postpartum depression.

Weapons, Equipment, and Supplies
Fully manned units perform optimally only if they possess all authorized weapons, equipment, and repair parts. Mundane items like dump trucks, fork lifts, field kitchens, hospital beds, power generators, and encryption devices count. Quantitatively ready forces additionally must possess enough supplies to sustain operations until replenishments become available. Needs differ for each type unit, each class of supplies, each mission, and each AOR. Ground forces, for example, consume more fuel and less ammunition during fluid offensive warfare than they do in defensive positions.[7]

Principle of Qualitative Superiority

Postulation: Armed forces perform best when personnel, weapons, equipment, and supplies are superior to those of the most capable opponents.

Preparedness requires professionally competent personnel and technologically competitive materiel. Outnumbered forces must maintain a significant qualitative edge in both respects or risk failure.

Competent Personnel

Reduced readiness is the penalty for failure to attract and retain well-disciplined personnel who can assimilate essential military instruction. Selection processes that impose high standards at the onset are imperative, because inculcation is time-consuming and expensive. Basic flight training for one U.S. pilot, for example, consumed about a year and cost more than $1 million in the late 1990s. It takes a decade to develop well-seasoned noncommissioned officers. Flag-rank commanders and high-level logisticians take twice that long. Efforts to retain the most promising, productive, and experienced individuals consequently deserve a high priority.

Competitive Technologies

Simple, yet qualitatively superior, weapons and equipment facilitate training, contribute to sustainability under combat conditions, and enable armed forces to achieve objectives more expeditiously with fewer casualties than otherwise would be possible. Prerequisites include research and development communities whose occupants create reliable, state-of-the-art implements that average military personnel can master with reasonable effort and industrial plants can mass-produce at reasonable costs.

Principle of AC-RC Complementarity

Postulation: Armed forces perform best when the active-reserve mix maximizes the strengths and minimizes the weaknesses of each component.

Active and reserve components (AC, RC) are complementary. A few small countries such as Israel and Switzerland rely mainly on reserves,[8] but overemphasis on either asset usually wastes money and impairs preparedness. Readiness moreover suffers when RC receive missions for which AC are better qualified, and vice versa.[9]

The optimum mix varies service by service. Reserve airlifters, who routinely hone requisite skills at civilian occupations, can answer calls on short notice, whereas reserve ground combat forces generally cannot. Active armies consequently are preferable when missions demand assured availability and rapid responsiveness to cope with contingencies that erupt abruptly and terminate quickly. Army reserves, in contrast, serve best when used during prolonged operations to expand or reconstitute AC capabilities with individual and unit replacements, communications, intelligence, and logistical support.

Principle of Compatibility

Postulation: Armed forces perform best when they prepare to participate in joint and combined operations.

Land, sea, air, amphibious, and space forces must work smoothly with each other and with allies. Uniservice, joint, and combined policies, strategies, doctrines, and tactics thus are imperative. More than 100 documents prescribe joint personnel, intelligence, plans, operations, logistics, and command/control doctrines for U.S. Armed Forces. Sixty-some publications serve similar purposes for NATO.[10]

Interchangeable or interoperable weapon systems, equipment, and supplies are just as important as compatible processes. Research, development, procurement costs, and logistical burdens soar unless high-volume items like rifle ammunition, air-to-surface missiles, and assorted repair parts suit more than one military service. Dangerous problems arise when uninational forces cannot communicate easily with each other, much less with coalition partners.[11]

Principle of Installations
Postulation: Armed forces perform best when diversified installations simplify training and support.

Ready, sustainable armed forces require home bases where they can adequately prepare to accomplish assigned missions. U.S. Armed Forces in 2001 occupied more than 3,000 major and minor properties in all fifty states and territories.[12] Several contained huge tracts for training (Nellis Air Force Base northeast of Las Vegas is only slightly smaller than Connecticut). Armed forces everywhere demand supply and maintenance depots. Other installations perform such assorted functions as administrative support, professional military education, communications, hospitalization, research, and development. Nations with regional or global responsibilities require similar assets abroad. Strategically situated U.S. outposts that girdled the globe during the Cold War peaked at 1,700. Sharp retrenchments during the early 1990s cut costs considerably, but drastically reduced operational flexibility.[13]

Principle of Foresight
Postulation: Armed forces are best prepared when decision-makers take future as well as current requirements into account.

Foresighted national security decision-makers, whose mission is to prepare forces for uncertain futures, seek insights from cycles, patterns, trends, intelligence estimates, threat assessments, and war games. Associated assumptions concern potential opponents and probabilities of war; conflict types, intensities, and durations; warning and reaction times; the responsiveness of reserves; the availability of allies; consumption rates for expendables; and industrial capacities. Results determine likely force modernization requirements, together with the best tradeoffs between research, development, acquisition, operations, and maintenance accounts. The

challenge is to preserve strategic, operational, tactical, and technological superiority, prevent block obsolescence, and revise war reserve stocks without endangering day-to-day preparedness.[14]

Principle of Resource Sufficiency
Postulation: Armed forces perform best when resource allocations enable them to implement prevalent military strategies effectively.

Military preparedness is an expensive proposition, especially in the absence of conscription. Readiness and sustainability lapse when unreasonably low force levels and insufficient funds create great gaps between ends and means. Indeed, any nation that sets its sights too high and pursues policies that defy successful implementation with available power may at best lose influence because of public embarrassment and at worst lose wars.[15] Wary resource allocators nevertheless recognize that unnecessarily large military budgets can undercut rather than strengthen national security. Occupants of the Kremlin, who failed to grasp that cogent fact, literally bankrupted the Soviet Union by the late 1980s and thereby caused the collapse of its Armed Forces along with the nation.[16]

PRESENT PREPAREDNESS
Widespread readiness and sustainability shortcomings indicate that few nations consciously honor the foregoing Principles of Preparedness or any others. Strategic, operational, personnel, materiel, logistical, and budgetary problems described below are illustrative.

Illogical Objectives
History records many instances in which qualitatively superior armed forces defeated much larger foes, but politico-military strategists who establish objectives for which force levels are unrealistically low create preparedness problems and implicitly accept unnecessarily shaky calculated risks. Hitler ultimately lost World War II because his superlative military machine was too small to achieve simultane-

ous victories on eastern, western, and southern fronts, given adversaries whose combined resources were vastly greater. British strategist Basil H. Liddell Hart summed up Hitler's predicament with these words: "Once America's strength developed, and Russia survived to develop hers, the . . . only uncertainties were—how long it would take, and how complete [the debacle] would be."[17]

Secretary of Defense Robert McNamara in the early 1960s proclaimed a 2½-war strategy that could best be described as ludicrous, given postulated requirements for relatively small U.S. non-nuclear forces, in conjunction with allies, to defeat the Soviet Union, China, and simultaneously douse a "brushfire." President Nixon, in efforts to "harmonize doctrine and capability," scaled back to a 1½-war strategy that called for assets able to handle Soviet *or* Chinese aggression and concurrently cope with one lesser contingency.[18] "One-plus" capabilities even so proved unattainable, according to Defense Secretary Harold Brown who, a decade later, conceded that, "We have never acquired the agility or mobility." Resource allocators instead settled "for a lower level of combat-readiness" and "economized (some would say scrimped) on the nuts and bolts needed to sustain a non-nuclear conflict . . . for more than a relatively short period of time. And our allies have been even more cavalier."[19]

Unrealistic U.S. ambitions continue. Defense Secretary Les Aspin's *Bottom-Up Review* of 1993 required abilities to fight and win two major regional conflicts nearly simultaneously with a high probability of success, while minimizing American casualties.[20] Even he, however, admitted that his efforts merely rationalized what President Clinton's defense budget would buy.[21] The 1997 Quadrennial Defense Review declared that "the United States now and for the foreseeable future [must] be able to deter and defeat large-scale, cross-border aggression in two distant theaters in overlapping time frames."[22]

Whether U.S. Armed Forces, much reduced during the 1990s, could comply if concurrent contin-

gencies arose, say, in Korea and the Persian Gulf depends heavily on dubious assumptions. Probabilities appear best only if warning times before War One were measured in weeks; if essential ports and airfields remained in friendly hands; if prepositioned stocks were adequate and conveniently located; if War Two started after War One deployments were complete; if War One was brief; if U.S. casualties and equipment losses were light; and if U.S. allies made meaningful contributions in both cases, while enemies received little or no assistance. Wrenching questions concerning which war should take priority otherwise would arise, and slighted friends would be righteously outraged.

Operations Other Than War

Rapid-response deployments enhance readiness in some respects during military operations other than war (MOOTW), but long-term pluses and minuses depend mainly on primary roles and missions. Some military formations selectively improve preparedness, while others lose their cutting edge.[23]

MOOTW Pluses

Armed forces gain practical experience during military operations other than war when they perform logistical and communications tasks for which they are organized, equipped, and trained. Operation Restore Hope (December 1992–May 1993) gave U.S. Air Mobility Command real-world, real-time opportunities to demonstrate global reach and upgrade austere airports in distant Somalia.[24] U.S. Army engineers who helped restore Nicaragua after Hurricane Mitch hit in November 1998 rebuilt washed-out roads, replaced a flooded hospital with a clinic, provided stricken communities with medical care, and advised the Ministry of Health regarding epidemics.[25] Special Operations Forces (SOF) possess assorted capabilities that dovetail with "peacetime" needs better than bullets and bayonets. Psychological operations (PSYOP) programs that mold public opinion and civic actions that elevate the lot of common people facilitate the attainment of national objectives. That happened in Haiti, where fewer than 1,200 SOF personnel became benefactors and de facto governors in more than 730 communities from 1994 into 1995.[26] Some combat forces enjoy comparable advantages. Explosive ordnance disposal units and land mine clearance teams, for example, accrue experience that they could not replicate during routine training.[27]

MOOTW Minuses

Military operations other than war nevertheless degrade preparedness in crucial respects. Cargo aircraft that repeatedly fly food, clothing, and medical supplies from Point A to Point B, land, unload, and return find little opportunity to practice low-level navigation, aerial delivery techniques, and assault landings or participate in joint airborne training with paratroopers. They also pay a price in terms of wear and tear, deferred depot maintenance, and availability to handle unexpected crises elsewhere. Airborne early warning and control (AWACS) aircraft that look for and try to track illicit narcotics flights across the Caribbean Sea have little time to practice battle management, their primary mission. Army combat troops take longer than other forces to recover after lengthy MOOTW operations (several months on the average), particularly when divisions unavoidably suspend battalion- and brigade-level training because large numbers deploy while the rest remain at home stations.[28]

Peacetime Operating Tempo

Six axioms illuminate relationships between peacetime operating tempo (OPTEMPO) and readiness:

- OPTEMPO increases when military missions expand, if force levels remain constant or decrease
- OPTEMPO increases when force levels decline, if military missions remain steady or subside at slower rates

- Rapid OPTEMPO increases strains on military manpower and materiel
- Rapid OPTEMPO increases the expenditure of repair parts and supplies
- Rapid OPTEMPO increases budgetary requirements
- Rapid OPTEMPO impedes training and otherwise impairs preparedness if prolonged (excessively slow OPTEMPO may do likewise)

More than ninety "named" operations consumed greater efforts by ever fewer U.S. Armed Forces during the 1990s, not counting innumerable small deployments. Well over half involved substantial operations for combat, peacekeeping, and humanitarian purposes. A dozen were active when the new millennium began: Joint Falcon and Eagle Eye in Kosovo; Deliberate Forge, Joint Forge, and Determined Forge in Bosnia; Northern Watch, Southern Watch, Desert Spring, and Arabian Gulf Maritime Intercept Operations related to Iraq; Multinational Force and Observers in the Sinai; Laser Strike and other counterdrug operations in the Western Hemisphere.[29] That hectic pace, accompanied by large-scale reliance on reserve components and repeated family separations, impinged on many aspects of military preparedness, including abilities to recruit, retain, and train qualified personnel.

Personnel Issues

Preparedness falters unless training programs invest draftees and volunteers with essential skills, professional military education programs develop leaders at every level, and enlightened personnel policies retain highly qualified officers, NCOs, and specialists who represent valuable investments. Intangibles also count, according to British Major General J. F. C. Fuller, because "Neither a nation nor an army is a mechanical contrivance, but a living thing, built of flesh and blood and not of iron and steel. . . . The more mechanical become the weapons with which we fight, the less mechanical must be the spirit which controls them."[30] Key considerations include attitude, morale, esprit de corps, a strong sense of belonging, and team play. Females and homosexuals in uniform both raise disciplinary and extremely emotional issues in such regards, with results that directly affect male bonding and unit cohesiveness.

Servicewomen

Hippolyte, queen of the Amazons and daughter of Ares, the Greek god of war, led a mythological race of warrior women that Homer cited in the *Iliad*. Legendary Jeanne d'Arc, the seventeen-year-old Maid of Orléans, gave France short-lived but nevertheless stunning victories over English adversaries in 1429 during the Hundred Years' War. Women in the Soviet Union and several other countries saw combat during World War II, when the male manpower pool was insufficient and national survival was at stake. Israel briefly considered, then discarded, similar usage.[31]

The United States at the onset of the twenty-first century was the only major military power that recruited women en masse as a matter of policy rather than expediency. The average percentage at that time approximated 15 percent (17–18 percent in the Air Force, 5–6 percent in the Marine Corps).[32] Related policies and practices pitted women's-rights advocates against defenders of tradition. Countless complaints about harassment and male abuses of power occasionally culminated in acrimonious trials.[33] Rising expectations concurrently caused U.S. servicewomen to complain about a "glass ceiling" that allegedly impeded rapid promotions, banned land combat billets, and reserved choice assignments for men. Males, in turn, resented political agendas, social engineering, and "gender-norming" that, as they saw it, undermined military preparedness and capabilities. Orders from female officers and NCOs made macho men chafe. Most objected to inconsistent physical standards that gave women high marks, despite obvious fitness and strength deficiencies. Pregnant and otherwise undeployable females ground masculine gears, because men did double duty to fill blank files.[34] Resultant military preparedness issues are disputatious.

Homosexuals

Many homosexuals have been fearsome warriors, including Alexander the Great, who amassed a mighty empire and won eternal fame. Others faced shame or, like British brevet Major General Hector "Fighting Mac" Macdonald, were literally hounded to death when their proclivities became public knowledge.[35] Animosities continue, because few countries have bridged the cultural gap that presently prevails.

A head-on collision between U.S. pro-con factions occurred in January 1993 when President Clinton, despite long-standing traditions and advice from the Joint Chiefs of Staff, officially announced his intent to tolerate homosexuality in U.S. Armed Forces.[36] No one knows how many homosexuals still serve quietly "in the closet," but vocal outsiders have caused constant turmoil ever since. Outraged colleagues who harass known or suspected "culprits" continue to make banner headlines, despite repeated reevaluations, "sensitivity" training, and jurisdictional disputes that reached the Supreme Court.[37] Whether deep-seated social issues involved are susceptible to coercive and legal solutions remains to be seen. Military preparedness meanwhile experiences adverse effects of uncertain but reportedly sizable proportions.[38]

Materiel Issues

Improperly maintained materiel neither works as well nor lasts as long as it should. Preventive maintenance is especially important when weapons and equipment are subject to hard usage under harsh conditions. Wind-blown grit, for example, fouls engines and abrades all moving parts in desert climes. Helicopters are particularly delicate, but all aircraft, motor vehicles, crew-served weapons, small arms, and electronics tend to malfunction in the absence of constant, intensive care. Ships, aircraft, and other major items that miss scheduled overhauls gradually become unreliable.

Incremental upgrades may substantially extend the life spans of proven systems, vest them with greater reliability, and restore their technological edge. Aging weapon systems and equipment nevertheless require replacement when maintenance becomes disproportionately frequent and costly, mean times between failures shorten significantly, accident rates increase, and block obsolescence looms.

The precipitous qualitative decline of hardware that Russia inherited from the USSR, caused by budgetary neglect for political, economic, and social reasons, serves as an object lesson for national security decision-makers who fail to preserve, upgrade, or replace materiel. Deployments remain quantitatively impressive, but non-nuclear capabilities that buttressed Soviet claims to superpower status ashore, aloft, and afloat disappeared in less than a decade.[39] Revitalization likely will take longer.

FUTURE PREPAREDNESS

Military superiority is perishable in a world wracked by fundamental changes that exacerbate existing security problems and create new concerns at breathtaking rates. Murphy's Law furthermore predicts that, "If anything can go wrong it will." Future military preparedness consequently depends primarily on farsighted policy-makers and strategists with penchants for conceptual and postural flexibility. Their multifaceted mission is to evaluate observable trends; estimate what capabilities might be most useful fifteen to twenty years hence, given anticipated threats; harness evolutionary and revolutionary technologies in innovative ways; alter military education, training, and the industrial base accordingly; then tailor existing institutions to orchestrate uniservice, joint, and coalition operations under envisaged conditions.[40]

The dust bins of history are loaded with losers whose 20/20 hindsight encouraged them to refight past wars against antagonists who forged ahead. The defeat of club-wielding cavemen by Neolithic enemies armed with spears perhaps was first. The quick victory of fast-moving German forces over French defenders, who in May 1940 occupied fixed positions reminiscent of World War I, was among the most famous, but by no means the last. National security policy-makers and military strategists should bear those debacles in mind and act accordingly, lest they add to the list.

KEY POINTS

- Superb military strategies are advantageous only if armed forces are properly organized, equipped, and trained to implement them successfully
- Readiness and sustainability are inseparable needs, because forces that lack staying power risk early defeat, while those that arrive too late are useless
- Principles of Preparedness could help planners, programmers, and budgeteers fashion versatile forces at reasonable costs
- Strategists who establish objectives for which force levels are unrealistically low create preparedness problems and implicitly accept shaky calculated risks
- Military operations other than war selectively improve the preparedness of most support forces and degrade most combat capabilities
- Rapid operating tempo impedes training and otherwise impairs preparedness if prolonged (excessively slow OPTEMPO may do likewise)

- Personnel preparedness considerations include attitude, morale, esprit de corps, team play, and other intangibles as well as education and training
- Preventive maintenance, regular overhauls, incremental upgrades, and timely replacement of military materiel benefit readiness and sustainability
- Future military preparedness depends primarily on farsighted policy-makers and strategists who estimate what capabilities might be most useful fifteen to twenty years hence, then foster flexible plans and programs

NOTES

1. Unpreparedness can be costly. See, for example, Charles E. Heller and William A. Stofft, eds., *America's First Battles: 1776-1965* (Lawrence: University of Kansas Press, 1986).

2. *Title 10, United States Code,* Section 153 (b) obligates the Chairman of the Joint Chiefs of Staff to review roles and functions at least once every three years. See Admiral William J. Crowe, Jr., *Roles and Functions of the Armed Forces,* a Report to the Secretary of Defense (Washington: Office of the Chairman, Joint Chiefs of Staff, September 28, 1989); General Colin L. Powell, *Roles, Missions, and Functions of the Armed Forces of the United States,* February 1993 and his memorandum to the Secretary of Defense, *Comments on the Commission on Roles and Missions of the Armed Forces Report "Directions for Defense,"* July 24, 1995.

3. *Theater Missile Defense* (Washington: Department of the Army, Roles and Missions Directorate, 1995); Air Force Chief of Staff General Merrill A. McPeak, *Presentation to the Commission on Roles and Missions of the Armed Forces* (Washington: U.S. Government Printing Office, January 1995), 157-83.

4. *Deep Battle* (Washington: Department of the Army, Roles and Missions Directorate, November 15, 1994); McPeak, *Presentation to the Commission on Roles and Missions of the Armed Forces,* 31-101.

5. *Close Air Support/Fire Support* (Washington: Department of the Army, Roles and Missions Directorate, January 10, 1995); McPeak, *Presentation to the Commission on Roles and Missions of the Armed Forces,* 103-22.

6. John M. Collins, *Military Geography: For Professionals and the Public* (Washington: National Defense University Press, 1998; republished by Brassey's, 1998), Chapter 6, "Regional Peculiarities," 93-136.

7. Operations Desert Shield and Desert Storm typify ground force sustainability requirements. See *Conduct of the Persian Gulf War: Final Report to Congress* (Washington: Office of the Secretary of Defense, April 1992), Appendices F and G; *Certain Victory* (Washington: Office of the Chief of Staff, U.S. Army, 1993), Chapter 2.

8. Nathaniel Lorch, *Shield of Zion: The Israeli Defense Forces* (Charlottesville, VA: Howell Press, 1991).

9. Debates about the mix of active and reserve components are not new. See Robert L. Goldich, *U.S. Army Combat-to-Support Ratios: A Framework for Analysis,* Rpt. 89-386F (Washington: Congressional Research Service, June 26, 1989). See also Goldich and David F. Burrelli, *Combat-to-Support Ratios in the U.S. Armed Forces: A Review and Summary of Selected Studies,* memorandum for the Senate Armed Services Committee (Washington: Congressional Research Service, May 15, 1985).

10. Joint Pub. 1-01.1, *Compendium of Publications* (Washington: Office of the Chairman, Joint Chiefs of Staff, April 23, 1999); a spokesman for the Director of Operational Plans & Interoperability (J-7) furnished updates and Allied Joint Publication statistics in January 2001.

11. "Interoperability," *Joint Doctrine Encyclopedia* (Washington: Office of the Chairman, Joint Chiefs of Staff, July 16, 1997), 352-54; *NATO Logistics Handbook,* 3d ed. (Brussels, Belgium: Senior NATO Logisticians' Conference Secretariat, October 1997), Chapter 17, "Standardization and Interoperability."

12. For a partial list, see *Guide to Military Installations Worldwide: More Than 300 Major Bases, Posts and Stations,* a supplement to the *Army Times, Navy Times,* and *Air Force Times,* November 2000.

13. *More U.S. Overseas Bases to End Operations* (Washington: Office of Assistant Secretary of Defense [Public Affairs], October 22, 1993).

14. Representative outlooks include *Project 2025* (Washington: Institute for National Strategic Studies, National Defense University, May 1992) and Paul Bracken, "The Military After Next," *Washington Quarterly,* Autumn 1993, 154-74.

15. Hans J. Morgenthau, *Politics Among Nations: The Struggle for Power and Peace,* 4th ed. (New York: Alfred A. Knopf, 1967), 139-40.

16. Lieutenant General William P. Odom, *The Collapse of the Soviet Military* (New Haven, CT: Yale University Press, 1998).

17. Basil H. Liddell Hart, *History of the Second World War* (New York: G. P. Putnam's Sons, 1971), 711-13.

18. *U.S. Foreign Policy for the 1970s: A New Strategy for Peace,* a Report to the Congress by President Richard Nixon (Washington: U.S. Government Printing Office, February 18, 1970), 128-29.

19. Harold Brown, *Department of Defense Annual Report, Fiscal Year 1981* (Washington: Office of the Secretary of Defense, January 1980), 98-99, 118. Quotation on 99.

20 Memorandum from the Secretary of Defense [to selected addressees,] Subject: *The Bottom-Up Review,* accompanied by *The Bottom-Up Review: Forces for a New Era,* September 1, 1993. Amplified by *Report on the Bottom-Up Review,* October 1993, 1-13.

21. Minutes from a press conference convened by Leon Panetta, Les Aspin, and Laura d'Andrea Tyson to discuss the Penny-Kasich bill, November 19, 1993; John T. Correll, "The Bottom-Down Review," *Air Force,* December 1993, 2; Kim R. Holme and Baker Spring, "Aspin's Defense Review: Top-Down, Not Bottom-Up," *Armed Forces Journal,* August 1993, 39-40.

22. *Report of the Quadrennial Defense Review* (Washington: Office of the Secretary of Defense, May 1997), 12.

23. Commander Ramé Hemstreet, *Small Worlds Missions: The Impact of Military Operations Other Than War on Combat Readiness* (Washington: National War College, May 10, 1999).

24. Ibid., 13-14.

25. Major Jeffrey R. Eckstein, "A Short and Successful Operation," *Army,* September 1999, 67-70.

26. *USSOCOM Pub. 1, Special Operations in Peacetime* (MacDill AFB, FL: U.S. Special Operations Command, January 1996), 2-24 to 2-27.

27. Hemstreet, *Small Worlds Missions,* 30; Gregory L. Bier, Stanley W. Grzyb, and M. Merrill Stevens, *Understanding and Expanding the United States Military Role in Humanitarian Demining Operations,* Landpower Essay Series No. 98-3 (Washington: Association of the United States Army, June 1998).

28. *Military Operations: Impact of Operations Other Than War on the Services Varies,* GAO/NSIAD-99-69, a report submitted to the Senate Armed Services Committee, Subcommittee for Military Readiness and Management Support (Washington: General Accounting Office, May 24, 1999).

29. *U.S. Participation in Military Operations, 1990-Present* (Washington: Office of the Chairman, Joint Chiefs of Staff, September 1999).

30. Major General J. F. C. Fuller, *Generalship: Its Diseases and Their Cure* (Harrisburg, PA: Military Service Publishing Co., 1936), 13.

31. Martin van Creveld, "Why Israel Doesn't Send Women Into Combat," *Parameters,* vol. 23, no. 1 (Spring 1993), 5-9.

32. *Selected Manpower Statistics for FY 1999* (Washington: Directorate for Information Operations and Reports, Washington Headquarters Services, Office of the Secretary of Defense).

33. Melissa S. Herbert, *Camouflage Isn't Only for Combat: Gender, Sexuality, and Women in the Military* (New York: New York University Press, 1998); Sidney J. Freedberg, Jr., "Taking Aim at GI Jane," *National Journal,* March 14, 1998, 590-91; Thomas E. Ricks, "General's Case Raises Worries on Harassment," *Washington Post,* April 5, 2000, A1, A9.

34. Stephanie Gutman, *The Kinder, Gentler Military: Can America's Gender-Neutral Fighting Force Still Win Wars?* (New York: Scribners, 2000); Geoffrey Norman, "Babes in Arms," *Men's Health,* vol. 11, no. 5 (June 1996), 50-52; "Women in Combat? Insights Worth Repeating," *Marine Corps Gazette,* vol. 81, no. 11 (November 1997), 73-74.

35. Byron Farwell, *Eminent Victorian Soldiers: Seekers of Glory* (New York: W. W. Norton, 1985), 294-98.

36. General Colin L. Powell with Joseph E. Persico, *My American Journey* (New York: Random House, 1995), 546-47, 563-64, 570-74.

37. *High Court Again Sidesteps "Don't Ask, Don't Tell" Controversy,* First Amendment Center Home Page, May 12, 1997; *Appeals Court Upholds Military "Don't Ask, Don't Tell" Policy,* Cable Network News (CNN), September 24, 1998.

38. For balanced views, see David F. Burrelli and Charles Dale, *Homosexuals and U.S. Military Personnel Policy: Current Issues,* Rpt. RL30113 (Washington: Congressional Research Service, March 17, 1999).

39. Lieutenant General William P. Odom, *The Collapse of the Soviet Military;* Stewart D. Goldman, *Russian Conventional Armed Forces: On the Verge of Collapse?* Rpt. 97-820-F (Washington: Congressional Research Service, September 4, 1997).

40. Admiral William A. Owens, *Lifting the Fog of War* (New York: Farrar, Straus, and Giroux, 2000).

10. Fundamentals of Arms Control

Can't anybody here play this game?

Casey Stengel
First Manager of the New York Mets
Outraged remark, 1962

Nations traditionally amass military power to protect strategic interests and support foreign policies. Intemperate competitions, which often ensue, foster quantitative and qualitative arms races that not only deplete resources, talents, and energies, but guarantee ever-greater violence if armed conflicts erupt. Proficient arms controllers advance assorted alternatives designed to discourage military one-upmanship without undermining required capabilities.[1]

Commentators with polarized opinions make strong cases for and against arms control. All such contentions, however, miss the mark, because historical records reveal that results since World War II have been less helpful than optimists hoped and less harmful than pessimists feared. One fact even so seems irrefutable: poorly qualified players unintentionally abet opponents more often than not, whereas arms controllers who know how to play complex games of give and take can usefully complement military power ashore, aloft, afloat, and in space.

ARMS CONTROL AIMS

Arms controllers, unlike arms accumulators, aim to verifiably limit numbers, types, technological characteristics, locations, and uses of major military formations, armaments, and stockpiled munitions. Advocates concurrently strive to trim military budgets, but recognize that steps to replace or redeploy provocative forces and implement other risk-reduction measures may increase rather than curb costs. Successes strengthen stability and foster the following strategic objectives:[2]

- Prevent lopsided military balances
- Enhance defensive capabilities
- Reduce offensive capabilities
- Alleviate international tensions
- Improve threat predictions
- Forestall accidental conflicts
- Reduce risks of surprise attack
- Minimize devastation if deterrence fails
- Contain costly escalation
- Preserve selected environments

QUANTITATIVE RESTRICTIONS

Quantitative restrictions reduce, retard, or preclude the deployment of selected armed forces, weapon systems, and munitions. Cuts, caps, and bans establish ceilings that may be as high or as low as advocates prefer and adversaries will accept. Counterproliferation strategies aim to confine or preclude horizontal spreads.*

Force Level Limitations

War fighters, who feel most comfortable with military superiority, are suspicious of strategies that limit force levels, but carefully calculated, effectively

---

*Chapter 11 covers nuclear, biological, chemical warfare, and radiological (NBCR) counterproliferation strategies.

monitored covenants sometimes serve national interests. Soviet leaders, for example, prized massive military deployments, but nevertheless ratified several arms control pacts that included numerical restraints.

Idealistic Disarmament

General and complete disarmament was the goal in 1928 when sixty-three nations ratified the Kellogg–Briand Pact. That idealistic edict, which obliged signatories to renounce war as an instrument of national policy, failed in practice because it contained no provisions for enforcing compliance. The League of Nations in 1932, following a decade of preliminary discussions, convened a World Disarmament Conference in Geneva, Switzerland. Its keystone proposal, contained in the so-called Hoover Plan, visualized the progressive elimination of offensive weapons, but major participants watered it down to a toothless statement of principles.[3] Pragmatic arms controllers, with those failures firmly in mind, currently conclude that Utopian injunctions of any kind could be undesirable as well as unattainable in a dangerous world where predators abound.[4]

Unilateral Reductions

Unilateral slashes that do nothing to redress unfavorable balances normally are inadvisable, but may be cost-effective and safe under favorable conditions. NATO's deterrent powers, for example, remained rock solid when President Carter removed 1,000 obsolescent nuclear weapons from Western Europe in 1979. President Reagan recalled 1,400 more in 1983, even though Moscow refused to reciprocate.[5]

Deep Force Reductions

Deep reductions normally demand discretion, because temptations to retain unauthorized forces as cushions can be strong and surreptitious violations might confer decisive military advantage on cheaters after all participants reach low levels. Relative power balances moreover may rapidly become lopsided if one party rearms unexpectedly and opponents are poorly prepared to compensate. Mutual force-reduction proposals designed to decrease nonnuclear deployments on both sides of the Iron Curtain, for example, long foundered because Soviet contingents repositioned in European Russia could regenerate combat power more rapidly than U.S. counterparts could return from bases in the United States and elsewhere overseas.[6] At least two preconditions consequently should precede deep reductions: reasonable abilities to verify compliance and alternative means to maintain security if treacherous rivals renege.

Force Caps

Force caps can prevent expensive, risky, and perhaps unrewarding arms races when militarily significant reductions appear impractical or impossible. Pacts that prohibit expansion are preferable to those that codify planned deployments and thereby permit signatories to increase holdings until they reach stipulated ceilings, which happened twice in rapid succession when U.S. and Soviet arms controllers concluded Strategic Arms Limitation Talks I and II. First, the 1972 SALT I Interim Agreement allowed Soviet ICBM silo construction to proceed on schedule. The SALT II Treaty of 1979 then entitled both sides to expand multiple independently targetable reentry vehicle (MIRV) inventories considerably.[7]

Negotiators should guard against pernicious side effects to the best of their abilities, because force caps can stimulate destabilizing attempts to fill power vacuums. The Washington Naval Treaty of 1922 and a follow-on conference in London, for example, established a 5 to 3.5 ratio between U.S. and Japanese battleships. Aircraft carriers, which rapidly replaced dreadnoughts thereafter, could conduct surprise attacks at vastly greater ranges, but initially were less survivable. The side that struck first thus gained great advantage.[8]

Force Freezes

Arms control moratoriums, which freeze forces or other militarily valuable assets at present levels, usually are acceptable only if adversaries possess approximately equal capabilities. Some participants otherwise must accept protracted (perhaps permanent) inferiority accompanied by chronic risks.

Arms controllers can elect various alternatives. The aforementioned Washington Treaty officially "froze" U.S., British, and Japanese fortifications, naval bases, maintenance facilities, and coastal defenses throughout the Pacific Basin.[9] Nuclear freeze proposals were popular during the Cold War. Moratoriums that follow force reductions in any case are preferable to freezes that preserve high levels.

Absolute Bans

Absolute bans, which prohibit selected weapon systems, are more stringent than force caps or freezes, because even one sighting constitutes a violation. The Seventh Book of Manu, published in Sanskrit circa 700 B.C., forbade weapons with barbed, poisoned, or flaming points many centuries before the Saint Petersburg Declaration of 1863 legally outlawed weapons that cause "unnecessary suffering." Article XXIII of Hague Regulation IV (1907) concentrated on venomous weapons, plus unspecified arms, projectiles, or materials that included saw-toothed bayonets and hollow-point bullets,[10] but arms controllers as yet have been able to proscribe few weapons of strategic importance. The Anti-Ballistic Missile Treaty of 1972, which allows token defenses, is subject to dispute at this writing.[11]

U.S. economist and financier Bernard Baruch tried and failed to outlaw nuclear weapons in 1946 when he presented the United Nations with a fourteen-point plan that, if adopted, would have "entrusted all phases of the development and use of atomic energy" to an International Atomic Development Authority. Proposed penalties stigmatized as international crimes the possession of weapon-grade nuclear materials and the manufacture or possession of nuclear armaments of any kind. "Devilish" nuclear programs, he concluded, take mankind back "not merely to the Dark Ages but from cosmos to chaos. If we find a suitable way to control atomic

weapons, it is reasonable to hope that we may also preclude the use of other weapons adaptable to mass destruction. When a man learns to say 'A' he can, if he chooses, learn the rest of the alphabet too."[12] Soviet dictator Joseph Stalin, who had other ideas, dashed those altruistic hopes when he refused to say "A." The Soviet Union vetoed the Baruch Plan, detonated its first nuclear device in 1949, and thereby precipitated the most perilous arms race in history.

Nuclear-Free Zones

Neither NATO nor the Warsaw Pact accepted Polish Prime Minister Adam Rapacki's 1957 proposal to designate a nuclear-free zone in Europe, because both espoused strategies that depended heavily on nuclear firepower. A Latin American nuclear-free zone, in force since 1967, held fast only after Argentina and Brazil cancelled robust programs. No non-African nation is party to an African nuclear-free zone treaty (France and the People's Republic of China, but not the USA, USSR, or UK, signed protocols). Only one nuclear-free zone has ever been established in a region where nuclear arms previously were acceptable: New Zealand did so unilaterally in February 1985, when its newly installed Labour Party posted coastal waters "Off Limits" to nuclear-armed warships. Nuclear-free zones in empty Antarctica, space, and on ocean floors have fared well thus far, but future international competition eventually may invalidate them. Biological, chemical, and radiological warfare-free zones remain nonexistent.[13]

Counting Rules

Figures don't lie, but liars figure and rascals warp military statistics to their advantage if unwary rivals allow. Arms controllers consequently should define categories precisely and establish clear counting rules before force level bargaining begins. Failure to do so invites avoidable misunderstandings, prolongs processes, and leaves legal loopholes that may cause serious acrimony concerning actions that violate the spirit, if not the letter, of concluded pacts.

Common Complexities

Number crunching can be incredibly complex. Paramilitary forces, such as Soviet Internal Security Troops (MVD) and Border Guards (KGB), share many characteristics with standard military formations. Reserve components are more important than regulars in Israel, Switzerland, and Sweden. Full strength divisions train as teams, whereas skeletons that consist primarily of commanders and staffs cannot function until inductees or reservists fill blank files. Whether forces with such disparate capabilities should count the same is questionable.

Multipurpose aircraft, missiles, and artillery that can deliver nuclear, chemical, and traditional munitions may occupy more than one category. Modern and obsolescent weapon systems vary in value. So do modifications that outperform standard models, much like stock racing cars run faster than commercial automobiles with the same external features. Dissimilar organizational structures further complicate equations. The U.S. Department of Defense, for example, relies extensively on civilians to supplement military personnel, whereas Soviet Armed Forces routinely used troops to operate railroads and harvest crops.

Nuclear Counting Problems

Nuclear arms controllers trapped in that maze struggle to concoct mutually acceptable databases. SALT II negotiations stalled repeatedly, because Soviet spokesmen insisted that the term "strategic" should embrace all nuclear-capable aircraft and missiles able to strike the other's homeland, whereas U.S. participants contended that forward-based systems ashore and afloat were "tactical." Both sides eventually recognized intercontinental ballistic missiles (ICBMs), submarine-launched ballistic missiles (SLBMs), and heavy bombers as strategic nuclear-delivery vehicles, but arguments continued until disputants decided what fit in each category. Land-based ballistic missiles able to reach 5,500 kilometers (about 3,000 nautical miles) counted as ICBMs.

U.S. B-1s and B-52s, along with Soviet Bears and Bisons, constituted heavy bombers, including many in "moth balls" or cannibalized for repair parts. So did smaller warplanes armed with air-launched missiles that could strike targets 600 km (325 nm) away. Variants configured for in-flight refueling, reconnaissance, antisubmarine warfare, and other "nonstrategic" purposes were exempt only if Functionally Related Observable Differences (FRODs), such as no bomb bay doors or missile pods, indicated that bombardment was impossible.[14]

Traditional Force Counting Problems

Counting questions also plague officials who seek to control traditional weapons. What criteria, pray tell, should bound a database for main battle tanks? Weight? Caliber of the primary weapon? Type of armor? The Treaty on Conventional Forces in Europe (CFE) counted tracked or wheeled armored vehicles that "weigh at least 16.5 metric tonnes unladen weight [18.2 short tons] and which are armed with a 360-degree traverse gun of at least 75 millimeters calibre." Armor with the same size gun but lesser weight occupied a separate category called "heavy armament combat vehicle." The CFE Treaty lumped tube artillery with all mortars and multiple rocket launchers of 100 mm or larger. Counting rules concerning many other weapons were equally convoluted.[15]

BW and CW Counting Problems

The 1972 Biological Weapons Convention counts microbial and other biological agents plus toxins only if quantities and types "have no justification for prophylactic, protective or other peaceful purposes." Those loose definitions leave great latitude for interpretation.[16]

The 1993 Chemical Weapons Convention explicitly prohibits toxic agents and precursors that can cause death, temporary incapacitation, or permanent harm to humans or animals. It also bans offensive (but not defensive) uses of riot control agents, which produce short-lived sensory irritations or disabling physical effects. Most illegal agents, however, have industrial, agricultural, research, pharmaceutical, protective, or domestic law enforcement applications, which the treaty condones. Different controls over production, stockpiling, and transfers pertain to each class. No international agreement controls incendiaries, such as napalm and white phosphorus.[17]

QUALITATIVE LIMITATIONS

Qualitative constraints in many respects are more elusive than quantitative controls. National security policy-makers and military strategists perpetually debate whether to restrict technological progress and, if so, what measures would achieve desired objectives most effectively.

Whether to Control Technology

Military hard-liners disapprove any curbs, firm in their conviction that national security depends on technological supremacy at every level. Their prescriptions, however, would guarantee cost-ineffective, open-ended competition. Counselors at the opposite pole prefer to restrain all technologies that conceivably could fuel arms races, though that course of action not only would penalize stabilizing and destabilizing weapon systems alike, but would block economic development and dual-purpose enterprises. Commercial airliners and stealth bombers, for example, use similar computers and microprocessors. Identical launch vehicles and space satellites serve military and civilian purposes. Compromise solutions consequently seem sensible most often.[18]

When to Control Technology

It is theoretically feasible to confine emerging technologies at six stages: research, development, test, evaluation, production, and deployment. Prospects in practice, however, are bleak before development begins and after evaluation is complete.

Effective restrictions are elusive during research, because it is difficult to detect secretive pioneering programs, identify security implications from sketchy data, and predict enemy prospects of success in given time frames. Promising programs are hard to suppress after production starts, because the most serious technological problems have already been solved, applications have been proven, financial investments have become large, and potential beneficiaries urge early deployment. Prime times for arms control consequently occur during experimental stages, when confidence in weapon system reliability is low. Optimum opportunities occur when technological problems are extensive, expenses are extravagant, and feasibility is uncertain regardless of cost. The United States and Soviet Union concluded the ABM Treaty of 1972 under those conditions.[19]

What Technology to Control

Arms controllers have long sought to clamp lids on antisatellite systems, particle beams, high-energy lasers, fast-trajectory ballistic missiles tipped with MIRVs, and other innovative weapon systems which, if perfected, might radically alter military balances of power. Munitions that reduce distinctions between nuclear and traditional warfare, such as extremely low yield fission warheads, enhanced radiation weapons, and fuel-air explosives, have been or still are candidates for restriction.

Technological characteristics that cause intense anxiety typically include range, accuracy, lethality, and reliability, but size and weight sometimes are central considerations. The 1922 Washington Naval Treaty, for example, forbade signatories to deploy capital ships larger than 35,000 tons and limited gun calibers to 16 inches or less. U.S. arms controllers got gas pains in the mid-1970s, when the Soviets deployed huge SS-18 ICBMs armed with eight to ten high-yield warheads apiece a full decade before MX Peacekeeper missiles vested Strategic Air Command with comparable capabilities.[20]

Revolutionary developments attract most attention, but arms controllers might also curb evolutionary modernization programs that transform performance dramatically over time. The first U.S. F-4 Phantom fighter/attack aircraft in 1962 looked essentially the same as the last model that came off assembly lines eleven years later, but much-improved engines, avionics, armaments, ordnance, and maneuverability gave the final version vastly improved capabilities.[21] M-1A1 Abrams main battle tanks, which resembled the M-1s they superseded, possessed much greater firepower and survivability, because designers replaced the original 105mm gun with a 120mm model, added depleted uranium armor and ammunition, thermal imaging sights, and a controlled environment for their crews.[22]

How to Control Technologies

Arms control agreements that interrupt or preclude experimentation during proof of principle or prototype stages make it difficult (perhaps impossible) for technologists to perfect experimental weapon systems or selected components. Pacts that forbid testing after weapons deploy inhibit modernization. Several test bans since the 1950s have sought to confine nuclear capabilities. Some have been successful, while others have flopped, as the following vignettes confirm.

Tacit Test Moratorium

The United States, which abided by the uninspected nuclear test moratorium of 1958, was caught flat-footed when the Soviet Union unilaterally abrogated that "gentlemen's agreement" with a spectacular series of atmospheric explosions in 1961. JCS Chairman General Nathan F. Twining complained that U.S. Armed Forces "lost Pacific bases for nuclear testing, lost the trained nuclear teams, lost the motivation in nuclear laboratories, and lost the capacity for producing meaningful and up-to-date plans."[23] His remarks in retrospect seem overstated, but that unhappy experience revealed at least three useful

lessons: unverifiable arms control agreements are precarious; tacit understandings are less reliable than treaties; and failure to anticipate and prepare for realistic contingencies constitutes inexcusable negligence.

Partial and Threshold Test Bans

U.S. arms controllers applied those lessons when, with Soviet counterparts, they concluded the Partial Test Ban Treaty of August 1963, which prohibits nuclear detonations in the atmosphere, in space, and under water. The Threshold Test Ban Treaty of July 1974 forbade subterranean nuclear explosions that exceed 150 kilotons. Those durable pacts solved many environmental problems, but signatories who cannot legally conduct practical experiments must validate nuclear weapon systems using computer simulations. They also must speculate about crippling side effects, such as communication blackouts caused by nuclear blasts in space, because few have been properly probed.[24]

Comprehensive Test Ban Treaty

Efforts to conclude a Comprehensive Test Ban Treaty (CTBT) that covers nuclear explosives for constructive* as well as destructive purposes have foundered since the 1950s, largely because military liabilities seem to outweigh benefits. Smaller, safer, more dependable nuclear weapon stockpiles allegedly would be impossible to create and maintain if all testing ceased. Only 26 of 44 countries with ongoing nuclear programs of any kind had ratified the CTBT when the United States Senate rejected it on October 13, 1999.[25]

---

*Innovators actively explored peaceable uses of nuclear explosives from the late 1950s into the 1970s. The U.S. Atomic Energy Commission in the late 1950s proposed Project Plowshare which, if approved, would have used nuclear munitions to expedite the excavation of an alternative to the Panama Canal, perhaps through Nicaragua. Other proposals included the rapid construction of harbors in Alaska and operations to loosen Canadian petroleum embedded in oil tar sands.

NEGOTIATING TECHNIQUES

Politics, ideologies, cultures, institutions, and leadership styles strongly influence negotiating techniques.[26] Objectives, team play, and tactics vary considerably. Open societies operate differently than autocracies. Personalities or procedures sometimes dominate. Delegations address issues sequentially or simultaneously in confrontational or cooperative ways. Proclivities to compromise may be strong or weak. Public opinion is crucially important in some countries, but almost inconsequential in others.[27]

Agreed Guidelines

Experienced arms controllers agree that negotiations should feature unambiguous objectives, carefully crafted agendas, bold gambits, unflagging attention to detail, and great patience. Negotiators sometimes wrangle for weeks, even months, over the phraseology of subordinate clauses. Optimal results additionally demand bright debaters with long institutional memories.

Unambiguous Objectives

Clearly conceived, consistent arms control aims are obligatory. Strategists and tacticians otherwise cannot devise sensible negotiating positions. Senior officials who disagree, as U.S. Executive and Legislative Branches often do, should resolve bureaucratic and political disputes behind closed doors before negotiations begin, because undisguised bureaucratic power struggles help antagonists achieve *their* goals.[28]

Agendas and Gambits

Arms control negotiators never should permit opponents to shape agendas unilaterally, because the side that does so determines what topics to discuss, when to discuss them, and thereby gains great initiative. Assertive opening moves that put adversaries on the defensive are more desirable than timid gambits, which leave little room for bargaining. Rigid negotiators stand pat regardless, while opponents prepared to give and take craft acceptable fallback positions before they tip their hand. Seasoned participants avoid self-imposed deadlines that might make them miscalculate and give rivals leverage with which to extract last-minute concessions (frantic U.S. efforts to conclude treaties before summit meetings were commonplace during the Cold War).[29]

Fine Print

Pitfalls frequently accompany "agreements in principle." Wary negotiators consequently give little ground without some positive response, particularly when antagonists might construe conciliatory gestures as lack of resolve. Those determined to avoid dangerous sins of omission or commission insist that treaty texts precisely define the meaning of every significant word, phrase, and punctuation mark. Professional interpreters and translators who are familiar with political jargon and military terminology are particularly helpful.[30]

Institutional Memories

Negotiators who study rival track records and historical contexts within which arms control debates take place are best able to emerge victorious. Andrei Gromkyo, who said "nyet" to seven U.S. presidents while he served as Soviet Foreign Minister for twenty-eight consecutive years (1957–1985), had an institutional memory second to none. The Soviet Union retained one delegation from 1972 to 1979, the period it took to conclude a SALT II Treaty, whereas U.S. leaders switched chief negotiators six times and repeatedly replaced senior support staff.[31] Assaults on slipshod U.S. performance began to erupt for those reasons before President Carter signed that pact.[32]

Perennial Disputes

Arms controllers argue endlessly concerning the importance of military superiority, bargaining chips, and linkage. A few short paragraphs adequately illustrate the most prevalent disagreements.

Importance of Military Superiority

President Ronald Reagan's arms controllers were convinced that they had to strengthen U.S. offensive nuclear forces before Soviet spokesmen would seriously consider mutual reductions. Lieutenant General Edward L. Rowny, shortly before his confirmation as chief of the U.S. Strategic Arms Reduction Talks (START) delegation in 1981, summarized that view in one sentence: "Either [the Soviets] come down of their own volition . . . or we have to go up in order to convince them they have to come down."[33] The notion that successful negotiations depend on military superiority or parity, however, is not invariably correct, as the Soviet SALT I team demonstrated conclusively in 1972, when it drove hard bargains even though the U.S. nuclear triad possessed far greater capabilities.[34]

Importance of Bargaining Chips

"Bargaining chips" are present, projected, or proposed weapons that are worth less to possessors than to opponents who, for real or imagined reasons, make momentous arms control concessions to cap, reduce, preclude, or eliminate them.[35] Soviet leaders in the early 1980s, for example, agreed to deep cuts during START, partly because they feared that U.S. decision-makers otherwise would abrogate the Anti-Ballistic Missile (ABM) Treaty and deploy highly publicized "Star Wars" missile defense systems that had barely begun gestation.[36] Bargaining chips unfortunately may become "necessities" if attempted tradeoffs fail. That happened in 1983, when NATO offered to forego the deployment of nuclear-capable Pershing II and ground-launched cruise missiles, then installed them because Moscow refused to eliminate SS-4, SS-5, and SS-20 counterparts.[37]

Importance of Linkage

Two schools of strategic thought debate whether to link arms control with other foreign policy and military issues. The first focuses each agenda on a single security problem. Leonid I. Brezhnev, in his capacity as First Secretary of the Soviet Communist Party, in May 1972 signed the SALT I Interim Agreement while U.S. bombers pummeled his North Vietnamese allies, because the nuclear balance took precedence. Arms controllers who belong to the second school refuse to negotiate with antagonists who engage in such nefarious practices as aggression and human rights abuse. President Lyndon B. Johnson postponed the opening session of SALT I in 1968 after Soviet Armed Forces crushed Czech resistance. The U.S. Senate postponed ratification of the SALT II Treaty at President Carter's request after Soviet troops invaded Afghanistan in December 1979.[38] Neither school is consistently satisfactory.

COMPLIANCE PROBLEMS

Strategists, tacticians, and technologists ceaselessly search for reliable ways to confirm compliance with arms control accords. They also dispute the best way to deal with violators.[39]

Confidence-Building Measures

Confidence-building measures (CBMs) include "hotlines" (point-to-point communications between national leaders), risk-reduction centers (clearinghouses for information exchange), and prior notification of missile test launches, military maneuvers, and other potentially provocative activities. Most CBMs still in effect were originally devised to reduce East-West tensions during the Cold War, but the precepts are applicable to other situations.[40]

Verification Procedures

Perfect verification may be impossible, even with the most intrusive forms of inspection.[41] Confidence in abilities to detect serious violations before hazardous situations develop consequently is the main aim. Dual benefits thereby derive: expectation of discovery discourages flagrant infractions; early warnings allow time for reflective responses.[42]

Satellite sensors, other national technical means, on-site inspections, espionage agents, and information exchanges all help intelligence communities collect clues. Skilled analysts nevertheless must evaluate incomplete, often ambiguous evidence and fill blank spots with inferences when hard facts are unavailable. Sensors in space can count ICBM silos, bombers on air bases, surface ships in port, and armored vehicles in motor pools, but cannot determine whether any given installation produces chemical warfare agents or pharmaceuticals. Assessments are additionally complex, because investigators must evaluate nonevents as well as events to prove or disprove cheating. Adverse political repercussions follow "false positives" that unjustly accuse innocent parties of serious violations, while "false negatives" that overlook genuine skullduggery may lead to gross inequities.[43]

Response to Violations

Verification is useless unless aggrieved governments take appropriate counteractions. Every nation in Europe knew for many years that Nazi Germany was illegally massing military power in violation of the Versailles Treaty, but all remained passive until Hitler invaded Poland on September 1, 1939.[44] Lesser deviations that offenders refuse to correct on request generally deserve rebukes, because they could be attempts to test enemy verification capabilities or resolve. Indeed, they might be the only indication of covert violations on grand scales that could dangerously disturb existing military balances unless challenged as soon as discovered.[45] Muteness nevertheless may be the best response to perceived violations if complaints could compromise sensitive sources of information or the political benefits obtainable from inaction seem to exceed incurred risks. Active countermeasures, in ascending order of severity, include "bribery," political or economic sanctions, treaty abrogations, and military retaliation.[46]

KEY POINTS

- Arms controllers limit numbers, types, technical characteristics, locations, and uses of military formations, armaments, and stockpiled munitions
- Unambiguous objectives, carefully crafted agendas, and meticulous attention to detail facilitate successful negotiations
- Caps, cuts, and bans establish quantitative ceilings that may be as high as advocates prefer and adversaries accept
- Deep force reductions demand discretion, because cheaters could gain great advantage
- Arms control pacts that freeze forces at current levels are preferable to those that permit signatories to increase holdings until they reach higher ceilings
- Treaties that prohibit weapons of mass destruction are exceptionally difficult to conclude if perceived enemies already are so armed
- Arms controllers who fail to establish precise, mutually agreeable counting rules invite legal loopholes and potentially dangerous misunderstandings
- Qualitative restraints often are elusive, because intangible considerations are extremely complex
- Prime times to control weapon system technologies occur before practicality has been proven and financial investments become large
- Reliable abilities to verify and enforce compliance with arms control accords are imperative

NOTES

1. Fundamental considerations are contained in James E. Dougherty, *How to Think About Arms Control and Disarmament* (New York: Crane, Russak, & Co., 1973); Thomas C. Schelling and Morton H. Halperin, *Strategy and Arms Control* (New York: Twentieth Century Fund, 1961).

2. Donald Brennen, "Setting and Goals of Arms Control," in *Arms Control, Disarmament, and National Security*, ed. Donald G. Brennan (New York: George Braziller, 1961), 19-22, 30-31; *Arms Control and National Security: An Introduction* (Washington: Arms Control Association, 1989), 10-15.

3. Baron Philip Noel-Baker, *The First World Disarmament Conference, 1932-1933 and Why It Failed* (New York: Pergamon Press, 1979).

4. Ken Booth, "Disarmament and Arms Control," in John Baylis et al., *Contemporary Strategy*, vol. I, *Theories and Concepts*, 2d ed. (New York: Holmes & Meier, 1987), 140-57.

5. Melissa Healy, "NATO Tallies Its Obsolete Nukes," *Defense Week*, January 14, 1985, 13, 16.

6. Mark M. Lowenthal, *The CFE Treaty: Verification and Compliance Issues*, Issue Brief 91009 (Washington: Congressional Research Service, 1991).

7. *Arms Control and Disarmament Agreements: Texts and Histories of Negotiations*, 6th ed. (Washington: United States Arms Control and Disarmament Agency, 1990), 150, 261.

8. Charles H. Fairbanks, Jr., and Abram N. Shulsky, "From Arms Control to Arms Reductions, The Historical Experience," *Washington Quarterly*, Summer 1987, 59-73.

9. U.S. Congress, *Building up of the United States Navy to the Strength Permitted by the Washington and London Naval Treaties*, Hearings . . . on S. 51, January 7, 8, 9, 1932, Senate Committee on Naval Affairs (Washington: U.S. Government Printing Office, 1932).

10. *The Law of War and Dubious Weapons* (Stockholm, Sweden: Stockholm International Peace Research Institute (SIPRI), 1976), 1-75; Leon Friedman, ed., *The Law of War: A Documentary History*, vol. I (New York: Random House, 1972), 192-93, 249-50, 318; Alva Myrdal, *The Game of Disarmament* (New York: Pantheon Books, 1976), 226-54.

11. *Arms Control and Disarmament Agreements: Texts and Histories of Negotiations*, 155, 181; Stephen Hildreth and Amy Woolf, *National Missile Defense*, Issue Brief 10034 (Washington: Congressional Research Service, January 16, 2001), updated periodically.

12. "The United States Proposals for the International Control of Atomic Energy, Presented to the United Nations Atomic Energy Commission by the United States Representative, Mr. Bernard M. Baruch, June 14, 1946", in *The International Control of Atomic Energy: Growth of a Policy,* Department of State Publication 2702 (Washington: U.S. Government Printing Office, 1946).

13. *Arms Control and Disarmament Agreements: Texts and Histories of Negotiations,* 20-30, 52-88, 107-17; "Big Flap Down Under," *Time,* February 18, 1985, 48-49; "Storm Signals Fly for U.S. in South Pacific," *U.S. News & World Report,* March 4, 1985, 31-33.

14. *SALT II Agreement: Vienna, June 18, 1979,* Selected Documents No. 12B (Washington: Department of State, Bureau of Public Affairs, July 1979), 10-12, 19, 56, 60-63.

15. *The Treaty on Conventional Armed Forces in Europe.* English translation (Washington: Department of State, November 19, 1990), 3-4.

16. *Arms Control and Disarmament Agreements: Texts and Histories of Negotiations,* 129.

17. Lisa Tabassi, ed., *OPCW [Organization for the Prohibition of Chemical Weapons]: The Legal Texts* (The Hague: TMC Asser Press, 1999), 3.

18. Christopher Lamb, *How to Think About Arms Control, Disarmament, and Defense* (Englewood Cliffs, NJ: Prentice Hall, 1988), 241-43.

19. Ibid., 239-40; Albert Carnesale and Richard N. Haass, "Lessons Learned from Superpower Arms Control," *Washington Quarterly,* Summer 1987, 31-33.

20. Voluminous volumes during the Cold War annually contained U.S. candidates for control, beginning in Fiscal Year 1978. For the most comprehensive, see U.S. Congress, *Fiscal Year 1983 Arms Control Impact Statements,* Joint Committee Print of the Senate Committee on Foreign Relations and the House Committee on Foreign Affairs, 97th Cong., 2d sess. (Washington: U.S. Government Printing Office, 1982).

21. Marcelle Size Knaack, *Encyclopedia of U.S. Air Force Aircraft and Missile Systems,* vol. 1, *Post World War II Fighters, 1945-1973* (Washington: Office of Air Force History, 1978), 264-85.

22. Christopher Foss, ed., *Jane's Armour and Artillery, 1990-1991* (Alexandria, VA: Jane's, 1990), 139-44.

23. General Nathan F. Twining, *Neither Liberty nor Safety: A Hard Look at U.S. Military Policy and Strategy* (New York: Holt, Rinehart and Winston, 1966), 136-39.

24. *Arms Control and Disarmament Agreements: Texts and Histories of Negotiations,* 37, 184.

25. *Comprehensive Test Ban Treaty,* Treaty Doc. 105-28, 105th Cong., 1st sess., September 23, 1997; Jonathan E. Medalia, *Nuclear Weapons: Comprehensive Test Ban Treaty,* Issue Brief 92099 (Washington:

Congressional Research Service, December 1999) and *Comprehensive Test Ban Treaty: Pro and Con,* Rpt. No. RS20351, October 19, 1999.

26. Lamb, *How to Think About Arms Control, Disarmament, and Defense,* 166-71.

27. For some contrasting styles, see Igor Lucas, "Managing U.S.-Soviet Arms Control Initiatives: Do We Speak the Same Language?," *Comparative Strategy,* vol. 6, no. 2 (1987), 164-84; William W. Tombaugh, "Some Thoughts on Negotiating with the North Vietnamese," *National Security Affairs Forum,* National War College (Spring/Summer 1975), 49-58; Sondra Snowdon, "How to Negotiate With the Japanese," *U.S. News & World Report* (September 28, 1987), BC-10.

28. M. Scott Davis, "Negotiating with Ourselves," *Foreign Service Journal,* November 1985, 29-33; Raymond L. Garthoff, "Negotiating with the Russians: Some Lessons from SALT," *International Security,* Spring 1977, 22-23.

29. Fred Charles Iklé, *How Nations Negotiate* (New York: Harper and Row, 1964), 238-53.

30. Ibid.; Lucas, "Managing U.S.-Soviet Arms Control Initiatives: Do We Speak the Same Language?," 169-76, 179-80.

31. Strobe T. Talbott, *Endgame: The Inside Story of SALT II* (New York: Harper & Row, 1979), passim. For Soviet SALT II negotiating techniques, see Joseph G. Whelan, U.S. Congress, *Soviet Diplomacy and Negotiating Behavior: Emerging New Context for U.S. Diplomacy,* House Foreign Affairs Committee Print, vol. I (Washington: U.S. Government Printing Office, 1979), 443-548.

32. Roger P. Labrie, ed., *SALT Hand Book: Key Documents and Issues, 1972-1979* (Washington: American Enterprise Institute for Public Policy Research, 1979), 667-704.

33. U.S. Congress, *Nomination of Edward L. Rowny,* Hearings before the Senate Committee on Foreign Relations, 97th Cong., 1st sess. (Washington: U.S. Government Printing Office, 1981), 23, 33.

34. John Newhouse, *Cold Dawn: The Story of SALT [I]* (New York: Holt, Rinehart and Winston, 1983).

35. Thomas C. Schelling, "A Framework for Evaluation of Arms Control Proposals," *Daedalus,* Summer 1975, 194-98.

36. President Ronald Reagan, "It Was 'Star Wars' Muscle That Wrestled Arms Race to a Halt," *Los Angeles Times,* July 31, 1991, B5; START, Treaty Doc. 102-20, 102d Cong., 1st sess., November 25, 1991.

37. Stanley R. Sloan, *NATO Nuclear Forces: Modernization and Arms Control* (Washington: Congressional Research Service, October 24, 1983).

38. Paul Johnson, "Arms Control and Managing Linkage," *Survival,* September/October 1986, 431-44.

39. For various overviews, see Allan R. Krass, *Verification: How Much Is Enough?* (Philadelphia: Taylor and Francis for Stockholm International Peace Research Institute [SIPRI], 1985); Seymour Melman, ed., *Inspection for Disarmament,* (New York: Columbia University Press, 1958).

40. John Borawski, ed., *Avoiding War in the Nuclear Age: Confidence-Building Measures for Crisis Stability* (Boulder, CO: Westview Press, 1986); Stanley R. Sloan and Mikaela Sawtelle, *Confidence-Building Measures and Force Constraints for Stabilizing East-West Military Relations in Europe* (Washington: Congressional Research Service, August 30, 1988).

41. Lewis A. Dunn and Amy A. Gordon, *On-Site Inspection for Arms Control Verification: Pitfalls and Promise* (Washington: Science Applications International Corporation, May 1989).

42. Jerome Wiesner, "Introduction to Arms Control," in *Arms Control and Verification: The Technologies That Made It Possible,* ed. Kosta Tsipis et al. (New York: Pergamon-Brassey's, 1986), xiii.

43. Admiral Noel Gayler, "Verification, Compliance, and the Intelligence Process" and William E. Colby, "The Intelligence Process," both in *Arms Control Verification: The Technologies That Made It Possible,* 3-13.

44. Trevor N. Dupuy, *A Genius for War: The German Army and the General Staff, 1807-1945* (Englewood Cliffs, NJ: Prentice-Hall, 1977), 192-52.

45. *Verification: The Critical Element of Arms Control* (Washington: U.S. Arms Control and Disarmament Agency, March 1976), 4-5, 28, 30.

46. Ibid., 7-8, 28-30; Lamb, *How to Think About Arms Control, Disarmament, and Defense,* 140, 143-46.

PART III

SPECIALIZED MILITARY STRATEGIES

11. Counterproliferation Strategies

It's not the size of the dog in the fight,
It's the size of the fight in the dog.

Apt Aphorism
Anonymous

Small nations and subnational groups, like scrappy little dogs with sharp teeth, could inflict grievous wounds with even one primitive nuclear explosive or a few radiological, biological, or chemical weapons. Large nations so endowed might do likewise. Current aspirants include insecure or outlaw states, terrorists, religious extremists, and rancorous ethnic groups whose aquisition prospects are improving despite global nonproliferation norms, diplomacy, export constraints, security assurances, and arms control accords.

So-called "weapons of mass destruction" (WMD)* are proliferating at different rates and pose different threats in different regions (Table 14).[1] Wise strategists consequently treat causes and symptoms case-by-case, because solutions that make sense in some situations are inane in others. Counterproliferators need to know what motivates each offender to acquire weapons of mass destruction before they can formulate meaningful plans. A reasonable feel for research, development, and deployment trends reveals how fast unfettered programs progress and simplifies prognoses.

CAUSES OF PROLIFERATION

Interests in security, power, prestige, and economy, often in some combination, spark WMD prolifera-

tion. Actual or possible possession commands respect, augments influence in regional (even global) affairs, increases bargaining leverage at conference tables, reduces military reliance on allies, and fosters national pride.

The urge to replicate becomes almost irresistible if adversaries possess capabilities that decisively alter military balances. The United States and the Soviet Union formed the original Nuclear Club in 1949, four years after Americans detonated the first atom bomb. Membership doubled as Great Britain and France acquired small nuclear arsenals to avoid impressions at home and abroad that they depended entirely on the United States for protection. China began to accumulate nuclear weapons in the 1960s, after Sino-Soviet relations soured.[2]

Insecurity remains the most common motivation among nations that feel threatened by unfriendly neighbors. Insufficient manpower, real or imagined provocations, and political isolation contribute. Pakistan, for example, never could match India's non-nuclear military machine, which contains twice as many active forces and could mobilize immensely more reserves. Some Arab states deployed chemical warfare (CW) weapon systems to offset Israel's unannounced but suspected nuclear capabilities. Burma and Ethiopia apparently procured CW munitions to cope with separatists and other insurgents.[3] Several other nations have allegedly used chemical agents in Afghanistan, Iran, Iraq, Cambodia, Kurdistan, Laos, and Yemen since the 1970s.[4]

---

*Nuclear weapons cause mass destruction. Radiological, biological, and chemical warfare weapons may cause mass casualties, but leave terrain and infrastructure intact.

Table 14

NBC Weapon Possession and Programs
(January 2001)

	Nuclear Weapons	Biological Weapons	Chemical Weapons	Longest Range Missile
NATO				
France	Confirmed	Ended	Ended	SLBM
United Kingdom	Confirmed	Ended	Ended	SLBM
United States	Confirmed	Ended	Confirmed	ICBM
Former USSR				
Kazakstan	Ended	Suspected	Suspected	SRBM
Russia	Confirmed	Confirmed	Confirmed	ICBM
East and South Asia				
China	Confirmed	Suspected	Confirmed	ICBM
India	Confirmed	None	Confirmed	MRBM
Pakistan	Confirmed	Suspected	Suspected	MRBM
North Korea	Suspected	Suspected	Confirmed	IRBM
South Korea	Ended	None	Confirmed	SRBM
Taiwan	Ended	Suspected	Suspected	SRBM
Thailand	None	None	Suspected	None
Vietnam	None	None	Suspected	SRBM
Middle East				
Egypt	None	Confirmed	Suspected	SRBM
Iran	Seeking	Suspected	Confirmed	MRBM
Iraq	Seeking	Confirmed	Confirmed	SRBM
Israel	Confirmed	Suspected	Confirmed	MRBM
Syria	None	Seeking	Confirmed	5RBM
Africa				
Ethiopia	Seeking	Seeking	Suspected	None
Libya	Ended	Ended?	Confirmed	MRBM
South Africa	Ended	None	Suspected	Ended
Latin America				
Argentina	Ended	None	None	None
Brazil	Ended	None	None	None

Key: Intercontinental ballistic missiles (ICBM)—3,400 miles (5,500 kilometers)
Intermediate-range ballistic missiles (IRBM)—1,850–3,400 miles (3,000–5,500 kilometers)
Medium-range ballistic missiles (MRBM)—625–1,850 miles (1,000–3,000 kilometers)
Short-range ballistic missiles (SRBM)—less than 625 miles (1,000 kilometers)
Submarine-Launched Ballistic Missiles—about 2,500 miles (4,000 kilometers)
Source: Robert Shuey, *Nuclear, Biological, and Chemical Weapons and Missiles: The Current Situation and Trends,* Rpt. Nr. RL30699 (Washington: Congressional Research Service, January 5, 2001).

Predators whose ambition is to project offensive military power beyond their borders covet nuclear, biological, chemical, and radiological (NBCR) weapons with which to cow opponents who cannot reciprocate in kind and to act as force multipliers if important objectives prove unobtainable without resort to armed combat. Iraqi President Saddam Hussein presses such programs with those motives in mind.[5] Terrorists thus far have refrained from using suitcase-sized nukes to achieve sociopolitical purposes, but counterproliferators cannot count on straight-line projections of that trend.

Nuclear Weapon Proliferation

A 19-kiloton (KT) demonstration shot atop a 100-foot tower at a desert test site near Alamogordo, New Mexico, ushered in the Nuclear Age shortly after daybreak on July 16, 1945. That astounding detonation, equal to 19,000 tons of TNT, made Dr. J. Robert Oppenheimer, the Chief Scientist of Project Manhattan, mutter a line from the Sanskrit epic *Bhagavad Gita:* "I am become Death, the shatterer of worlds." *Fat Man* and *Little Boy,* the first and only atomic bombs ever exploded in combat, obliterated huge areas within Hiroshima and Nagasaki three weeks later (August 6th and 9th, 1945) with yields that approximated fifteen and twenty-three KT respectively.[6] Japan capitulated quickly.

The First Surge (1949–1997)

Al Jolson, who starred in *The Jazz Singer* (the world's first "talking" picture), bragged, "You ain't seen nothin' yet!" His boast would have pertained even better to the arms race that accelerated sharply after Soviet scientists ended the U.S. nuclear monopoly in 1949. Fission weapon inventories multiplied rapidly and, by the early 1950s, both superpowers began to deploy thermonuclear (fusion) munitions with wallops measured in millions rather than thousands of tons apiece.[7]

Nuclear proliferation nevertheless proceeded at a much slower pace than President Kennedy predicted in March 1963, when he anticipated that fifteen to twenty-five nations would join the Nuclear Club within the next decade.[8] Confirmed members in fact remained five (USA, USSR, Britain, France, China) for more than thirty years. Belarus, Kazahstan, and Ukraine inherited ICBMs and atomic bombs when the Soviet Union collapsed in 1990, but Moscow retained operational control until all three recipients dismantled those arsenals. Argentina, Brazil, South Africa, South Korea, and presumably Taiwan discontinued promising nuclear weapon programs.

The Second Surge (1998–)

The second proliferative surge started in 1998 when India announced that it had converted prototype devices into workable nuclear weapons. Pakistan soon duplicated that feat. Israel remains undeclared,

but intelligence sources confirm a sizable stockpile. North Korea probably hoards a handful. Iraq, Iran, and Libya lag well behind, but clearly intend to follow suit. The Nuclear Club would surge from eight to twelve members if they succeed.[9]

The Prognosis

Probabilities that nuclear combat will occur for the first time since August 1945 loom larger than fearful observers would like to believe, because some latecomers and candidates are sworn enemies (India vs. Pakistan, Israel vs. Arab states). Some involve autocratic leaders with aggressive records. All possess suitable delivery vehicles. The U.S.-Soviet Cold War standoff thus seems stable in retrospect and the "Doomsday Clock" that U.S. atomic scientists reset repeatedly during those trying times has by no means stopped ticking.

Radiological Weapon Proliferation

Simple, inexpensive radiological munitions lack the blast and heat properties of traditional nuclear armaments, but shaped-charge explosives release a cloud of powdered plutonium oxide or depleted uranium that could render large urban areas radioactively uninhabitable for many years. Relatively easy production and deployment processes make such arms increasingly attractive to developing nations and subnational groups (including transnational terrorists) that lack the facilities and expertise to produce fission or fusion weapons.[10]

Biological Weapon Proliferation

The "popularity" of biological warfare (BW) weapons magnified immeasurably during the twentieth century.[11] Ten nations surely or probably possess significant capabilities early in the twenty-first century, including Russia, China, India, Pakistan, and pugnacious North Korea. None, however, causes greater anxieties than Iraq, where President Saddam Hussein systematically foils efforts to determine the status of suspected BW programs.[12]

Chemical Warfare Proliferation

History's first poison gas attack flopped on January 31, 1915 in East Prussia's Masurian Lake District, because chemical warfare (CW) agents became nearly inert in sub-zero temperatures, but a cloud of chlorine inflicted 15,000 British casualties near Ypres, Belgium less than three months later.[13] All major powers employed CW weapons before World War I was over, with such horrifying effects that the Geneva Protocol of 1925 banned further use and discouraged acquisition. Few confirmed cases occurred thereafter until Fascist Italy bedeviled barefoot Ethiopians with mustard gas in 1936. Saddam Hussein's use of chemicals during the 1980–1988 war with Iran, threats to do so during Operation Desert Storm in 1991, plus the subsequent dousing of Kurdish and Shiite dissidents make Iraq the most menacing nation.

Delivery Vehicle Proliferation

Various delivery vehicles can attack targets with nuclear, radiological, biological, or chemical weapons from locations on land, at sea, or in the air, whichever is most appropriate. WMD proliferators who possess ballistic missiles create the greatest anxieties (Table 14), because credible defenses appear infeasible for the foreseeable future, but cruise missiles and tactical combat aircraft also cause grave concerns.

INTELLIGENCE INDICATORS

Successful counterproliferation starts with intelligence estimates that accurately indicate which NBC threats are incipient, which are ripening rapidly, and which are mature. Hard data are difficult to acquire, because WMD proliferators try to mask their programs at every stage of research, development, production, storage, distribution, and deployment.

Communal R&D Clues

Few first-generation proliferators proceed independently. Imported nuclear physicists, industrial

chemists, and pharmacists sometimes supplement homegrown talent, but experts need not cross international borders to help, because computers and facsimile machines freely transfer essential information around the globe. BW and CW development processes both employ dual-use materials that can serve harmless and harmful purposes equally well. Neither needs conspicuous facilities. Field testing can easily be camouflaged as a civilian activity such as crop dusting and is difficult to detect at night. Unmarked biological and chemical munitions are indistinguishable from high-explosive bombs and artillery shells. Stringent structural defenses and round-the-clock security measures invariably seek to prevent unauthorized use, foil thieves, frustrate intrusion, and repel armed raiders. Secretiveness tends to rouse suspicions, but neither confirms nor denies NBCR activities.[14]

Unique R&D Clues

Nuclear/radiological, biological, and chemical weapon R&D programs not only differ remarkably from each other, but from all other military research and development. Intelligence communities nevertheless are hard-pressed to confirm proliferation and estimate the rapidity of progress.

Nuclear/Radiological R&D Indicators

All nuclear reactors produce plutonium,[15] an activity that requires conspicuous facilities, a large labor force, extensive radiation shielding, and radiates great heat. Other tip-offs include nitric acid and telltale radioactive isotopes of xenon, krypton, iodine, and argon. Uranium enrichment likewise is hard to conceal. Gas diffusion and centrifuges, which demand huge facilities and corrosion-resistant materials, expel heat into the atmosphere or nearby streams. Calutron plants and smaller gas diffusion installations both require specialized materials and parts that few neophyte proliferators possess.[16]

Less infrastructure is necessary if proliferators buy or steal test results, fissile feedstocks, even finished munitions. Opportunities are open, because it is difficult to safeguard thousands of nuclear weapons that are scheduled for, are undergoing, or have completed dismantlement in Russia. Smugglers might circumvent controls in anticipation of rich rewards.[17]

Biological Warfare R&D Indicators

Biological warfare agents are living microorganisms, viruses, rickettsias, bacteria, protozoa, fungi, and derivative infectious materials that cause fatal or incapacitating diseases in people, livestock, or vegetation. Most toxins are poisonous byproducts of metabolic processes, although some are synthetic.[18]

Nearly all equipment and supplies needed to mass-produce BW agents are commercially available through legitimate channels. Processes are exceptionally difficult to detect, partly because each agent is virtually indistinguishable from natural pathogens, partly because BW and commercial vaccine plants employ similar equipment and materials. Laboratory-sized facilities can generate products so quickly that intelligence collectors look fruitlessly for refrigerated storage vaults, which once were required but no longer are needed to preserve BW agents before they fill bombs, missile warheads, spray tanks, and artillery shells—a process that is easily concealed.[19]

Chemical Warfare R&D Indicators

Mustard gas and phosgene are easy to produce without specialized materials or elaborate facilities, because essential technologies have evolved very little since World War I. Precursor chemicals needed to manufacture nerve agents in contrast are commercially scarce, few civilians processes are readily transferable, and proliferators must master cyanation or alkylation reactions, depending on the type agent under development. Those who plan to produce agents solely for immediate use nevertheless can shorten R&D times considerably if they sacrifice long shelf life, safety, and sound waste disposal practices.[20]

CW agent production involves no "signature" equipment and essential facilities easily masquerade as commercial chemical complexes. Caches measured in tons are far more conspicuous than minuscule amounts of BW, but there is no visual way to identify unmarked packages in bulk storage or to differentiate chemical from traditional munitions (cylinders that contain Soman, for example, look like those filled with compressed air).[21] On-site verification teams search unsuccessfully for stockpiled CW agents if proliferators manufacture ingredients in separate facilities for use in binary munitions, which contain two nonlethal chemicals that unite and become toxic only when en route to targets.[22]

NBC Deployment Indicators

Signs that proliferators intend to deploy nuclear, biological, or chemical weapons include unique command and control arrangements; organizational innovations; the procurement of specialized transports and other equipment; pertinent strategies, tactics, and doctrines; unique military education and training, such as targeting techniques and troop safety; and logistical support, especially esoteric construction, supply, and maintenance. Detection of such indicators, however, may follow rather than precede first employment. None, for example, warned Japan before U.S. B-29 bombers ravaged Hiroshima and Nagasaki.

COUNTERPROLIFERATION

Conceptual disputes, plus the absence of attractive options, paint a bleak future for military operations designed to prevent the spread of mass destruction weapons. The field therefore remains wide open for innovative strategists, who will be enshrined forever if they solve proliferation problems.

Disputes About Desirability

Two schools of thought recommend drastically different strategies to prevent or confine proliferation. The first, fathered by French General Pierre Gallois and fostered by Raymond Aron, suggests that the uncontrolled spread of WMD might strengthen deterrence by reducing gains for aggression.[23] The second school, which boasts many more subscribers, concludes that the spread of NBC weapons would increase the incidence of "brinkmanship" and wars by miscalculation, encourage escalation, and otherwise destabilize international relations.[24] Compromisers contend that nations should feel free to proliferate essentially defensive weapon systems that decrease vulnerabilities without endangering rivals, but skeptics remind them that the purpose of some arms is ambiguous and open to unhappy interpretations. Soviet leaders, for example, viewed U.S. Strategic Defense Initiatives as thinly veiled attempts to acquire nuclear first-strike capabilities and their Russian successors implicitly concur.[25]

Nonmilitary Options

Nonmilitary disincentives embrace "carrots and sticks" in various combinations. Some kibitzers claim that current possessors could discourage proliferation if they drastically reduced (preferably abandoned) WMD inventories and thereby served as role models.[26] Rebutters, who believe that idealistic technique would allow cheaters to become military superpowers, cite the Nuclear Nonproliferation Treaty as a more pragmatic approach. Negative tactics include political ostracism, economic sanctions, withdrawal of foreign aid, test bans, "open skies" policies that permit aerial reconnaissance, on-site inspections, and other confidence-building measures. Neither nonmilitary enticements nor punishments, however, have worked well thus far.[27]

Military Options

The dearth of solid intelligence concerning surreptitious proliferation programs severely restricts military countermeasures, few of which hold much promise. Uncertainties regarding probabilities of success and cheerless consequences of failure accompany all seven options outlined below, which probably are the best of a discouraging lot.

Option 1: Intelligence Collection

Photographic and radar-imaging sensors high overhead depict activities on Earth's surface in exquisite detail, along with complementary "eavesdropping" equipment able to record all kinds of electronic transmissions. Seismic and acoustic "listening posts" report precise times and approximate locations of nuclear tests, except perhaps those of sub-kiloton yields. Space satellites in proper position can detect the characteristic double flash of light from any nuclear explosion above land or water.

"Spies in the sky" discovered a secret chemical warfare plant in Libya during the 1980s, then pinpointed probable nuclear weapon projects in North Korea,[28] but limitations nevertheless are considerable. Dual-use technologies make it difficult (often impossible) to identify illicit enterprises. Not even U.S. Armed Forces own enough satellites and aircraft to maintain constant vigilance over every probable proliferator, and the best they have are not always good enough. Space satellites equipped with state-of-the-art radar-imaging sensors, for example, failed to find subsurface power lines that linked the nuclear site at Tarmiya, Iraq with a distant substation.[29]

Clandestine on-site inspectors occasionally might corroborate clues that standoff "detectives" discover and fill in blank spots. Decision-makers nevertheless display little enthusiasm for this approach, because attempts to infiltrate laboratories, production plants, or storage facilities in search of specimens would be extremely hazardous, prospects for success would be poor, and political penalties for failure could be grim.

Option 2: Security Guarantees

Some strategists suggest that security guarantees, such as U.S. promises to extend a "nuclear umbrella" over allies,[30] could keep friends from deploying weapons of mass destruction. Assurances, however, did not keep Britain and France from acquiring nuclear capabilities in the 1950s, when the United States possessed overwhelming nuclear superiority, nor have they notably inhibited proliferation since then.

Option 3: Blockades

Nations concerned about NBCR proliferation could install blockades and conduct aerial interdiction operations to tighten economic sanctions or to deprive culprits of raw materials, technological expertise, and finished products they need to create and manufacture delivery vehicles as well as munitions. Prudent leaders even so ponder such measures carefully before they proceed, because blockades on land or at sea are costly. Cordons installed for counterproliferation purposes could last weeks, months, even years, and international laws consider blockades to be acts of war. Protracted sieges moreover might evoke defiance by adversaries and antagonize legitimate merchants.

Option 4: Eliminate Key Personnel

Key scientists, technologists, and program managers who participate in the development, production, and deployment of first-generation NBCR weapons epitomize "strategic centers of gravity," because progress would slow significantly or stop in their absence. Most, however, are civilians who ply their trade in "peacetime," and therefore constitute illegitimate targets according to international law, although they could influence future military capabilities as much as or more than uniformed soldiers, sailors, and airmen do during wars.

Option 5: Air Strikes

Aerial bombardment might be an acceptable option once or twice, but domestic support (much less international approval) for repeated strikes might be hard to muster. Minuses moreover often outweigh pluses, as the following illustrations confirm.

The Israeli Air Force bombed an Iraqi nuclear reactor under construction on bare ground south of Baghdad in June 1981. Success upset Saddam Hussein's timetable so seriously that international concerns did not resurface for several years,[31] but nuclear proliferation sites buried in bedrock would be much harder to destroy. Direct hits on active North Korean nuclear reactors might contaminate Seoul with radioactive fallout within a few hours, then cover southern Japan the next day. No such effects occurred during the Israeli air raid on Iraq, because the demolished reactor was inactive, while aerial bombardments during Operation Desert Storm avoided fissile stockpiles and left reactor cores intact.[32]

Biological and chemical warfare facilities pose different problems. "Shell games" make constantly moving installations extremely hard to find. Wind directions and velocities would determine the extent of collateral damage and civilian casualties during aircraft and missile strikes on BW and CW plants anywhere. Responsible parties could anticipate politically and morally counterproductive repercussions if many innocents were killed, infected, or contaminated.[33]

Option 6: Sabotage

Demolition experts skilled at sabotage might cost-effectively wreck NBCR weapon facilities, supplies, and products, given reliable intelligence about clandestine infiltration and exfiltration routes, physical layouts, vulnerable points, and installation security. An eleven-man demolition team in possession of filched floor plans, for example, hit Hitler's heavy water plant near Vermork, Norway during World War II. That audacious act denied Nazi Germany its main source of deuterium oxide, the only moderator then available for uranium-fueled reactors. One crafty agent soon thereafter set charges that sank a ferry loaded with all heavy water previously produced.[34]

The good news is that modern saboteurs, with far superior technology at their disposal and benefits derived from far more intensive training, should be able to challenge those spectacular performances during any stage of NBCR weapon development, production, or storage. The bad news is that auspicious conditions would be uncommon and participants could expect no mercy if captured.

Option 7: Invasion

A powerful invasion force could cancel embryonic or infant WMD proliferation projects in any country, but Option 7 seems inadvisable unless foreign and domestic opinion is favorable, solid support from a strong coalition is forthcoming, springboards in neighboring states are available, and heavy civilian as well as military casualties on both sides are acceptable. Political and economic costs are additional considerations. That combination of preconditions seems improbable, except in extenuating circumstances.

CURRENT OUTLOOK

Intelligence communities determined that Saddam Hussein had initiated nuclear weapon projects in the early 1980s, but senior recipients of repeated warnings dallied for nearly a decade, by which time Iraqi programs worth $7–10 billion employed more than 20,000 people (7,000 scientists and engineers), included two major uranium enrichment plants,

received direct foreign technical assistance, and benefited from massive foreign procurement. Iraqi biological and chemical warfare R&D programs received outside assistance without interruption during that same period.[35]

Ten countries have terminated nuclear, biological, or chemical warfare programs (Table 14, page 124), but political persuasion and economic sanctions thus far have failed to forestall threatening WMD proliferation in Iraq and other hot spots around the world. Unscrupulous possessors could use such weapons for coercive purposes and, if combat occurred, inflict unprecedented casualties on hapless civilians as well as rival armed forces. Outraged victims then would ask, "Why didn't counterproliferators take positive actions to prevent catastrophes?"

Formidable problems unfortunately plague all seven military courses of action profiled above. All are risk-laden. Some seem infeasible. That depressing outlook behooves national security policymakers and planners to improve NBCR deterrent techniques and to burnish war-fighting abilities for immediate application if preventive measures fail. Chapter 12 covers nuclear strategies, while Chapter 13 addresses biological and chemical warfare.

KEY POINTS

- Insecure nations, outlaw states, terrorists, religious extremists, and rancorous ethnic groups seek to possess nuclear, biological, chemical, and radiological weapons
- Sworn enemies, some of whom are unstable and exhibit aggressive tendencies, increase the likelihood of NBCR combat
- A few noted strategists believe that proliferation strengthens deterrence by increasing risks and reducing gains from aggression
- Most strategists believe that the spread of NBC weapons is extremely destabilizing and increases the likelihood of wars by miscalculation
- Successful counterproliferation demands intelligence estimates that accurately indicate which NBCR threats are incipient, which are ripening rapidly, and which are mature
- Sound intelligence is hard to acquire, because proliferators mask programs at every stage of research, development, production, storage, and deployment
- Political persuasion and economic sanctions thus far have failed to forestall the most threatening trends

- Serious questions concerning probabilities of success and consequences of failure make most military countermeasures unattractive
- That bleak outlook amplifies needs for new ways to deter NBCR proliferation and for war-fighting strategies if deterrence fails

NOTES

1. *Proliferation: Threat and Response* (Washington: Office of the Secretary of Defense, April 1996); George J. Tenet, *Statement by Director of Central Intelligence before the Senate Committee on Armed Services Hearing on Current and Projected National Security Threats,* February 2, 1999, passim.

2. William Epstein, "Why States Go—and Don't Go—Nuclear," *Annals of the American Academy of Political and Social Science,* March 1977, 17-28.

3. Anthony H. Cordesman, *Weapons of Mass Destruction in the Middle East* (London: Brassey's UK, 1991); Elisa D. Harris, "Chemical Weapons Proliferation in the Developing World," *Defense Yearbook, 1989* (Washington: Brassey's, 1989), 69, 75-76.

4. Edward M. Spiers, *Chemical Warfare* (Urbana: University of Illinois Press, 1989), 89-119.

5. Cordesman, *Weapons of Mass Destruction in the Middle East,* 60-81, 95-102.

6. Richard Rhodes, *The Making of the Atom Bomb* (New York: Simon and Schuster, 1968); Chuck Hansen, *U.S. Nuclear Weapons: The Secret History* (New York: Orion Books, 1988), 11, 14, 21.

7. Richard Rhodes, *Dark Sun: The Making of the Hydrogen Bomb* (New York: Touchstone Books, 1996). For U.S. and Soviet tests through 1962, see DA Pamphlet 39-3, *The Effects of Nuclear Weapons,* rev. ed. (Washington: U.S. Government Printing Office, February 1964), 672-81b.

8. *Public Papers of the Presidents of the United States: John F. Kennedy, 1963* (Washington: U.S. Government Printing Office, 1964), 280.

9. For a survey that amalgamates several official sources, see Robert D. Shuey, *Nuclear, Biological, and Chemical Weapons and Missiles: The Current Situation and Trends,* Rpt. No. RC 30699 (Washington: Congressional Research Service, January 5, 2001).

10. Victor L. Issraelyan, "Radiological Weapons: Possible New Types of Weapons of Mass Destruction," in Victor L. Issraelyan and Charles C. Flowerree, *Radiological Weapons Control: A Soviet and U.S. Perspective,* Occasional Page 29 (Muscatine, IA: Stanley Foundation, February 1982), 17-30.

11. Stephen Rose, "The Coming Explosion of Silent Weapons," *Naval War College Review,* Summer 1989, 6-29.

12. Michael Dobbs, "Soviet-Era Work on Bioweapons Still Worrisome," *Washington Post,* September 12, 2000, A1, A26; Barton Gellman, "A Futile Game of Hide and Seek," *Washington Post,* October 11, 1998, A1, A42-A43 and "Arms Inspectors 'Shake the Tree,' " October 12, 1998, A1, A16-A17.

13. Brigadier General S. L. A. Marshall, *The American Heritage History of World War I* (New York: Simon and Schuster, 1964), 88, 107-8.

14. Office of Technology Assessment, *Technologies Underlying Weapons of Mass Destruction* (Washington: U.S. Government Printing Office, December 1993), 37-38, 50-52, 100-2, 164-65.

15. For characteristics of nuclear reactors, see *Nuclear Proliferation and Safeguards,* vol. II, Part One (Washington: Office of Technology Assessment, June 1977), Appendix (Technical Description of Fuel Cycle Facilities and Evaluation of Diversion Potential), 72-101.

16. David Albright, "A Proliferation Primer," *Bulletin of the Atomic Scientists,* June 1993, 16-22.

17. David Hoffman, "Cure for Russia's Nuclear 'Headache' Proves to Be Painful Crisis: Spotty Data Hobble Bid to Secure Bomb Material," *Washington Post,* December 26, 1998, A1 and "Idled Arms Experts in Russia Post Threat: Many Take Talents to Developing States," December 28, 1998, A1.

18. *The Problem of Chemical and Biological Warfare,* vol. II, *CB Weapons Today* (New York: Stockholm International Peace Research Institute [SIPRI], 1993), 37-41, 42-43, 61-72.

19. Office of Technology Assessment, *Proliferation of Weapons of Mass Destruction: Assessing the Risks* (Washington: U.S. Government Printing Office, August 1993), 9-11, 38; *Technologies Underlying Weapons of Mass Destruction,* 50-51, 99-106; Stephen Rose, "The Coming Explosion of Silent Weapons," 7, 9.

20. Steven R. Bowman, *Chemical Weapons Convention: Issues for Congress,* Issue Brief 94029 (Washington: Congressional Research Service, January 12, 1999), 8-10.

21. *Technologies Underlying Weapons of Mass Destruction,* 16-27; *Proliferation of Weapons of Mass Destruction,* 10-11, 36.

22. *Technologies Underlying Weapons of Mass Destruction,* 38-51, 103, 105; Bowman, *Chemical Weapons Convention: Issues for Congress,* 8-10; *The Problem of Chemical and Biological Warfare,* vol. II, 3-6, 308.

23. General Pierre Gallois, *The Balance of Terror: Strategy for the Nuclear Age,* foreword by Raymond Aron (Boston: Houghton Mifflin, 1961); Kenneth N. Waltz, *The Spread of Nuclear Weapons: More May Be Better,* Adelphi Papers 171 (London: International Institute for Strategic Studies, Autumn 1981); Bruce Bueno de Mesquita, "An Assessment of the Merits of Selective Nuclear Proliferation," *Journal of Conflict Resolution,* June 1982, 283-306.

24. Richard N. Rosecrance, ed., *The Dispersion of Nuclear Weapons: Strategy and Politics* (New York: Columbia University Press, 1963), 21-26, 293-314.

25. *Soviet Propaganda Campaign Against the U.S. Strategic Defense Initiative* (Washington: U.S. Arms Control and Disarmament Agency, August 1986); David Hoffman and Charles Babington, "ABM Issue Unresolved As Summit Ends," *Washington Post,* June 5, 2000, A1, A10; Peter Baker, "No Deal Soon on Missile Defense Plan, Russia Says," *Washington Post,* September 6, 2001, A1.

26. George H. Quester, "Nuclear Proliferation: Linkages and Solutions," *International Organization,* Augumn 1979, 548-53.

27. Zachery S. Davis, *Nonproliferation Regimes: A Comparative Analysis of Policies* (Washington: Congressional Research Service, April 1, 1991); George H. Quester, "Reducing the Incentives to Proliferate," *Annals of the American Academy of Political and Social Science,* March 1977, 72-81. For the original "Open Skies" proposal, see *Public Papers of the Presidents of the United States: Dwight D. Eisenhower, 1955* (Washington: U.S. Government Printing Office, 1959), 715.

28. William C. Rempel and Robin Wright, "Libya Plant Found by Vigilance, Luck," *Los Angeles Times,* January 22, 1989, 1, 22; "Concern Rises About DPRK Nuclear Program," *Foreign Broadcast Information Service,* FBIS-EAS-91-043-A, March 5, 1991, 8.

29. David Kay, who headed several International Atomic Energy Agency (IAEA) inspections in Iraq: a presentation at the National Institute of Standards and Technology, Gaithersburg, MD, May 15, 1992; *Technologies Underlying Weapons of Mass Destruction,* 169.

30. Caspar W. Weinberger addressed the long-standing U.S. nuclear umbrella for NATO in *Improving NATO's Conventional Capabilities: A Report to the United States Congress* (Washington: Department of Defense, June 1984), 10. The Nixon Doctrine specified a nuclear shield for other U.S. friends in *U.S. Foreign Policy for the 1970s: Building for Peace* (Washington: U.S. Government Printing Office, February 25, 1971), 13-14.

31. Glenn Frankel, "Iraq Said Developing Nuclear Weapons," *Washington Post,* March 31, 1989, A1; James P. Wootten and Warren H. Donnelly, *Israeli Raid into Iraq,* Issue Brief 81103 (Washington: Congressional Research Service, July 2, 1981).

32. Mark Hibbs and Margaret Ryan, "Experts Say U.S. Weapons Can't Destroy DPRK Nuclear Facilities," *Nucleonics Week,* April 7, 1994, 15.

33. Leon Sloss, "Deterring the Acquisition, Exploitation, and Use of Weapons of Mass Destruction," in *The Niche Threat: Deterring the Use of Chemical and Biological Weapons,* ed. Stuart E. Johnson (Washington: National Defense University, 1997), 95-121.

34. Dan Kurtzman, *Blood and Water: Sabotaging Hitler's Bomb* (New York: Henry Holt, 1997). For demolition techniques, see FM 5-25, *Explosives and Demolitions* (Washington: Department of the Army, March 1996) and *Commando Operations* (Alexandria, VA: Time-Life Books, 1991), 98-109, "The Art of Blowing Things Up."

35. *Technologies Underlying Weapons of Mass Destruction,* 168-69.

12. Nuclear Warfare Strategies

Don'tcha worry, honey chile,
Don'tcha cry no more.
It's jest a li'l ole atom bomb
In a li'l ole limited war.
It's jest a bitsy warhead, chile
On a li'l ole tactical shell,
And all it's gonna do is blow us all
To a li'l ole limited hell.

Anonymous
Tactical Nukes

Knockout artist Joe Louis, who was famous for his shuffle rather than fancy footwork, repeatedly put opponents on the canvas because they could neither run far nor hide from his figurative atom bombs. Bantamweight nations endowed with nuclear weapons possess incomparably greater destructive capabilities.* Military strategists consequently need to know about the nature of nuclear warfare, which is fundamentally different than traditional combat. They then can turn their attention to a complex array of deterrent, war-fighting, and conflict termination options.

THE NATURE OF NUCLEAR WARFARE

Premeditated instigation of a nuclear war with any opponent prepared to retaliate in kind would involve serious soul-searching, because a single large-scale nuclear exchange could endanger far distant nonbelligerents as well as combatants, while even a few "primitive" weapons could cripple small coun-

---

*Chapter 14 links nuclear warfare with traditional combat. Chapter 15 connects nuclear warfare with domestic and transnational terrorism.

tries. "Winners," unable to withstand incomparable casualties and damage, might fare little better than "losers."[1]

Nuclear Explosive Characteristics

Nuclear and traditional high explosives both produce blast waves in air and shock waves if detonated below ground or underwater. Differences, however, are greater than similarities, because fission weapons are thousands and fusion weapons millions of times more powerful. Both emit searing heat and blinding light called thermal radiation. Both discharge transient rays in the form of initial nuclear radiation and, if activated on or near Earth's surface, deposit radioactive particles far from the burst point (measurable fallout that lasts weeks, months, or years may drift downwind thousands of miles). The distance that any given weapon transmits injurious effects depends on its yield calculated in kilotons (KT) or megatons (MT) and additional variables that Table 15 displays.[2]

Nuclear Casualties

Nuclear casualty estimates are iffy, because each battleground is unique and assumptions in lieu of

Table 15

Factors That Affect Nuclear Weapon
Effectiveness

- Timing of attacks (day or night, weekday or weekend)
- Magnitude of attacks (full-scale or limited)
- Targets (counterforce or countervalue)
- Type bursts (air, space, surface, subterranean, or underwater)
- Weapon accuracies (yards or miles; meters or kilometers)
- Weapon yields (kilotons or megatons)
- Warning times (minutes, hours, or days)
- Active defenses (types and effectiveness)
- Local topography (rugged or open terrain)
- Weather (calm or windy, cloudy or clear)
- Winds aloft (prevailing directions, seasonal variations)
- Soil (dry or wet; loose or compact)
- Vegetation (forested, grassy, or bare)
- Military deployments (concentrated or dispersed)
- Relevant military training (extensive or scanty)
- Demographic distribution (concentrated or scattered)
- Civil defense shelters (blast or fallout; natural or man-made)
- Civil defense training (extensive or scanty)

facts complicate most equations. Two conclusions even so are certain: a rain of traditional explosives would be required to kill and wound the same number of humans that one nuclear burst could incapacitate instantaneously; casualties caused by nuclear radiation would continue to mount long after combat ceased.

Immediate Medical Implications

Most nuclear warfare scenarios promise mass casualties that would immediately overwhelm medical facilities. The few centers that specialize in severe burn cases would be swamped with requirements that surpass capacities by many orders of magnitude, even in the best-equipped countries. Rapid triage would be required to maximize care where it might pay off most, a particularly trying task with regard to nuclear radiation, because similar symptoms accompany lethal and lesser doses.[3]

Rosy predictions in the mid-1970s anticipated 800,000 fatalities and innumerable injured in desperate need of emergency treatment if Soviet Armed Forces hit all 1,041 U.S. ICBM silos with 1 megaton

apiece. Appraisals predicated on a wider range of assumptions quadrupled those counts, which climbed across graphs almost vertically.[4] Modern weapon systems with lower yields, greater accuracies, and single-shot hard target kill probabilities would cause fewer civilian casualties if aimed at missile silos, but consequences would still be cataclysmic. The most optimistic estimates foresaw infinitely greater grief in the aftermath of Soviet assured destruction assaults on a series of U.S. urban centers such as New York, Chicago, and Los Angeles.[5]

Deferred Medical Implications

Experience in Japan indicates that some deferred medical miseries would arise within a day or two after the onset of any nuclear war, others after several years. Radiation, the principal culprit, attacks the central nervous system, lymphoid tissue, gastrointestinal tracts, and reproductive organs. Humans exposed to 1,000 REM or more all die within a few weeks at most. Perhaps three fourths expire if hit with half that amount. Those who survive customarily need to convalesce for more than a year.* Early symptoms usually include nausea, vomiting, and fatigue, followed by fever, diarrhea, emaciation, delirium, and convulsions. Wounds heal slowly and secondary infections increase among survivors, because severe radiation takes its toll on white blood cells and makes immune systems malfunction. Leukemia and abnormal numbers of cataracts, along with increased bone marrow, lung, kidney, thyroid, and breast cancers, crop up decades later.[6]

Nuclear Devastation

Allied aircraft loaded with iron bombs and incendiaries lambasted Hamburg, Germany six times be-

---

*Roentgens measure radiation doses; RADs measure absorbed radiation doses; REMs (roentgen equivalent mammal or man) measure the biological effects of radiation on human beings.

tween July 24 and August 3, 1943, with results that residents called *die Katastrophe*.[7] Japan felt incomparably greater shocks two years later, because one atomic bomb apiece immediately reduced Hiroshima and Nagasaki to piles of rubble.

Blast Damage

Blast waves that emanate from nuclear air and surface bursts cause the most direct damage. Effects therefrom not only radiate much farther than those that accompany traditional explosions but are incomparably more potent. Overpressures shove air outward from the fireball in every direction; reflected energies generally increase compression several times when shock waves hit solid objects; underpressures then reverse air flow during a suction phase. The resultant effects bend over, around, and envelop everything in their path.[8]

Targets most vulnerable to blast include institutional, industrial, commercial, administrative, and residential structures, motor vehicles, locomotives, rolling stock, aircraft, and ships. The radii of severe, moderate, and light damage vary with weapon yields, distances from ground zero, intervening obstacles (natural or man-made), the sturdiness of objects engulfed, and defensive measures (if any). Peak overpressures greater than 25 pounds per square inch (psi) generate winds far more violent than the worst tornadoes, but compression and suction together create devastating effects at much lower levels. Three psi, for example, severely damage unshielded aircraft, while 5 psi wrecks brick houses beyond repair. Nuclear blasts that rupture furnaces and natural gas lines, short-circuit electrical circuits, break water pipes, and block streets with rubble make fearsome fires hard to extinguish. Populations deprived of food, water, shelter, and electrical power suffer severely.[9]

Ruinous Radiation

Initial radiation from nuclear explosions in space can paralyze electrical equipment. Some phenom-

ena disrupt transmissions, while others render equipment inoperable. Intense ionization of Earth's atmosphere not only weakens high frequency (HF) radio and search radar signals, but makes them skip erratically, as demonstrated in August 1958 when U.S. megaton-sized TEAK and ORANGE test shots, detonated above Johnson Island in the central Pacific, degraded transmissions for several hours throughout a region several thousand miles in diameter. Electromagnetic pulse (EMP) surges toward ground at terrific speeds, then attacks electronic systems on land, at sea, and in the air. Ruinous, widespread damage likely would result, because few lightning arresters, power shunting switches, and other protective devices could respond fast enough to save solid state circuits, which may be a million times more vulnerable than vacuum tubes. Damage would be impossible to predict or control. Computers deprived of memories, for example, could obliterate national and local records of all kinds; paralyze communication links, power transmission facilities, and public utilities; misdirect missiles in flight; make avionics malfunction; and detonate time-fused munitions prematurely.[10]

NUCLEAR ARMS CONTROL

Havoc at Hiroshima and Nagasaki, coupled with seemingly insurmountable defensive problems, elevated arms control to a lofty level. "Ban the bomb" wasn't peacenik propaganda in the mid-1940s; it was official U.S. policy. The Truman–Attlee–King Declaration of November 15, 1945 recommended "the elimination from national armaments of atomic weapons and all other major weapons of mass destruction." It further advocated "effective safeguards by way of inspection and other means to protect complying states against the hazards of violation and evasions." A Soviet resolution dated December 27, 1945 expressed similar sentiments.[11]

Bernard Baruch, on behalf of the United States Government, on June 14, 1946, more specifically proposed that an International Atomic Development Authority under auspices of the United Nations be entrusted with the ownership, management, research, and development of all nuclear activities and possess powers to control, inspect, and license associated projects that might be "potentially dangerous to world security." A vigorous arms race ensued after the Soviet Union vetoed the Baruch Plan and detonated a nuclear device on August 29, 1949.[12]

Nuclear arms controllers have strained ever since to retard or prevent further nuclear proliferation, inhibit the spread of related raw materials and technologies, restrict or prohibit testing, restrain, freeze, or reduce weapon deployments, establish nuclear-free zones, and cut costs. Some successes have been sustained and spectacular. Antarctica became nuclear-free in 1959, followed by space and Latin America in 1967. More than eighty-five nations signed the 1968 Nonproliferation Treaty. Strategic Arms Reduction Talks (START) agreements later slashed U.S. and Soviet long-range inventories substantially. Both countries in May 1988 ratified an INF Treaty that eliminated their intermediate-range nuclear forces.[13]

Politico-military stumbling blocks nevertheless inhibit solutions to potentially grave problems, and likely will continue to do so for the foreseeable future. Deeper START reductions, for example, remained beyond reach when President Clinton and Russian President Vladimir Putin first discussed possibilities in June 2000.[14] Nuclear deterrent and warfighting strategies accordingly remain fashionable.

NUCLEAR DETERRENT STRATEGIES

Bernard Brodie in *The Absolute Weapon,* his groundbreaking book about nuclear strategy, concluded that deterrence had become the main military mission. Armed forces, as he saw it in 1946, could "have almost no other useful purpose."[15] Bernard Baruch, speaking before the United Nations General Assembly that same year, solemnly announced that, "We are come to make a choice between the quick and

the dead. . . . We must elect World Peace or World Destruction."

Even aggressive nations depend on deterrence to avoid nuclear war until they are ready, but optional ways of achieving that objective remain controversial after five decades of debate. Quirky concepts and various views about offensive and defensive force requirements compete for top billing.

Searches for Stability

Deterrent theoreticians, policy-makers, and planners strive to achieve strategic stability.[16] That elusive state, the nuclear deterrent equivalent of Nirvana, is attainable under two diametrically different conditions: 1) nations that could nuke opponents without risking destruction decline to do so; 2) no nation could nuke another without risking destruction. The United States occupied Category 1 from 1945 through the late 1950s, when no competitor could threaten its survival. Category 2 relationships with the USSR pertained thereafter, because U.S. and Soviet Armed Forces both deployed nuclear retaliatory forces that could inflict intolerable retribution after suffering a savage first strike. J. Robert Oppenheimer likened them to scorpions in a bottle—both would die if one stung the other.

Deterrent Effects of Defense

Policies and programs designed to defend homelands against nuclear attacks are exceedingly controversial. One faction firmly believes that antiaircraft, antimissile, civil defense, dispersion, site hardening, and other protective measures strengthen deterrence, whereas dissenters disagree (Figure 3 presents a tree of pro-con arguments).

Negative Views of Defense

U.S. civilian theoreticians shaped three distinctive schools of negative thought in the 1950s. One viewed the deterrent value of homeland defense through a philosophical prism, another took a technological tack, while the third cited arms control

Figure 3
Deterrent Effects of Homeland Defense

A Tree of Arguments

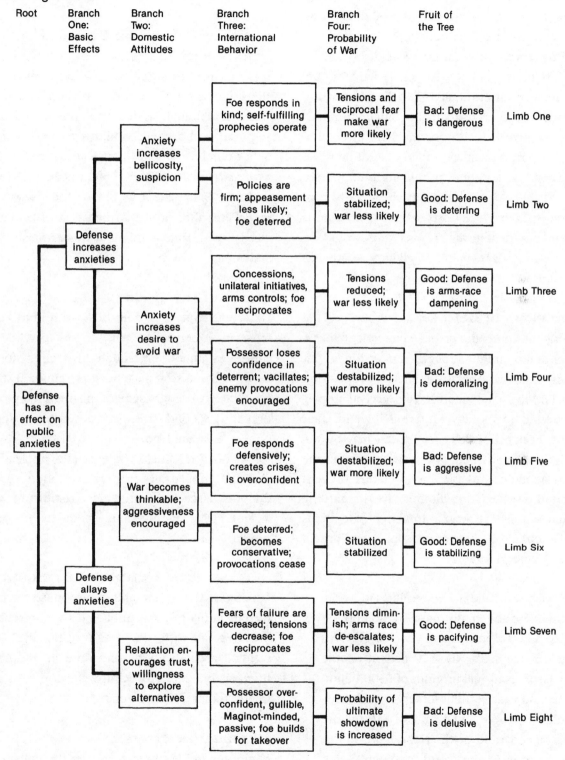

Adapted from a diagram in *Arms Control and Civil Defense*, edited by D.G. Brennan, The Hudson Institute, 1963.

and costs.[17] Patrons of School "A" contended that a "balance of terror" based on mutual vulnerability would best preserve deterrence by making meaningful victory impossible. Prospects of prodigious casualties were central to the concepts. Any move to mitigate the threat of reciprocal suicide would be counterproductive. School "B," less certain that defense is intrinsically undesirable, believed that impervious protection is unattainable, since saturation attacks could overload any system. School "C" contended that a porous shield indeed might increase casualties and devastation by inviting intemperate assaults. Stability, if attainable at all, would be at some stratospheric level. Costs incurred for dubious improvements in deterrent power thus would be unconscionable. Many politico-military strategists still subscribe to one of those schools.

Positive Views of Defense

Proponents of homeland defense concede that mutual vulnerability might strengthen deterrence, but only if opponents cooperate, a dubious proposition at best. Leaving vital interests in survival unprotected would be morally impermissible, in their judgment. Leak-proof defenses indeed may be unachievable at any cost, but porous protection at the very least would complicate enemy tactics, prevent unmitigated disasters, and diminish fears regarding accidental or nuisance attacks. Imperfect safeguards might also enhance postwar prospects, as Herman Kahn explained in 1960:

> "Both very sensitive and very callous individuals should be able to distinguish (and choose, perhaps) between a country which survives a nuclear war with, say, 150 million people and a Gross National product of $300 billion a year, and a nation that emerges with only 50 million people and a GNP of $10 billion. The former would be the richest and fourth largest nation in the world, and one which would be able to restore a reasonable facsim-

ile of the prewar society; the latter would be a pitiful remnant that would contain few traces of the prewar way of life."[18]

Effects of Defense on Extended Deterrence

U.S. promises to extend a "nuclear umbrella" over allies during the Cold War lacked credibility in the absence of homeland defense. Britain consequently acquired seaborne capabilities to help hedge its bets. French President Charles de Gaulle formulated a *force de frappe* in the 1950s, because he felt sure that no U.S. President would sacrifice New York to save Paris after Soviet Armed Forces brought nuclear-tipped ballistic missiles to bear on the United States.[19]

Effects of Defense on Stability

Deterrent strategists who believe in homeland defense must determine what to shield without disrupting stability. Prelaunch protection for land-based weapon systems tends to strengthen stability, because so doing suggests planned employment only for a second strike. The absence of safeguards conversely could be provocative, since first-strike forces need no shield. Defenses for nuclear forces plus the population, primary institutions, and production base could indicate attempts to survive a first strike with strong elements of national power intact.

Assorted Deterrent Concepts

Maximum, minimum, and compromise nuclear deterrent concepts, accompanied by different force postures and costs, compete for primacy. Each has claimed ascendancy at one time or another, but none seems likely to occupy the top spot permanently under all conditions.

Minimum Deterrence

Minimum and Finite Deterrence, the cheapest and least complex of all options, are predicated on the proposition that nuclear combat would be an unmitigated disaster for all belligerents. Proponents therefore see no need for numerous war-fighting weapon systems and decry homeland defense on grounds that mutually vulnerable populations encourage stability. They believe that the most durable nuclear deterrent is a "balance of terror" that holds cities on both sides at risk.[20]

Critics claim that Minimum Deterrence lacks credibility even as a declaratory policy, because it is based on threats that would be suicidal if implemented by any nation that spurns counterforce capabilities and disregards homeland defense. Dr. Donald G. Brennan, a prominent disbeliever who held sway at Herman Kahn's Hudson Institute, coined the acronym "MAD" for Mutual Assured Destruction, which he believed to be "almost literally mad."[21]

Maximum Deterrence

Maximum Deterrence at the opposite end of the strategic spectrum banks on abilities to win a nuclear war if required. Its prophets, who value flexibility and freedom of action, prescribe quantitatively and qualitatively superior retaliatory forces with first-strike capabilities, foolproof early warning systems, survivable command centers, and the best possible protection for cities. Resultant war-fighting postures are robust, but expensive and complex. Detractors claim that associated first-strike characteristics could prompt antsy opponents to preempt, would precipitate an endless arms race with those who hope to maintain a prudent balance, and cause costs to spiral upward unnecessarily, because considerably fewer resources and less money would ensure more than enough deterrence.[22]

Compromise Concepts

A procession of compromises amplify Minimum Deterrence, compress Maximum Deterrence, borrow peculiarities from one or both, and inject original ingredients. Concepts that Herman Kahn enunciated in 1960 may still be worth review. Finite Deter-

rence, Mostly Finite Deterrence, and Partial Damage Limitation afford increasingly greater reliability and flexibility than Minimum Deterrence. Counterforce as Insurance introduces "modest" war-fighting capabilities better able to discourage nuclear blackmail than any of those options, allegedly without incurring prohibitive costs or appearing as provocative as Maximum Deterrence.[23]

Deterrent Force Requirements

The size and composition of nuclear retaliatory forces required for deterrent purposes depends on the nature and magnitude of threats that they face. Some nations need extensive and variegated deployments, while others can sensibly settle for simple arrangements.

Force-Sizing Standards

The nuclear force-sizing scale ranges from inferiority to superiority, with parity midway between. Comparable statistical strengths are less important than corresponding capabilities. Marked preponderance may be essential in some regards, but inferiority is acceptable, provided it does not weaken deterrent powers militarily or psychologically.

Sufficiency, which tolerates asymmetries that leave stability undisturbed, probably is the most rational standard for, as President Nixon explained to Congress in 1971, "There is an absolute point below which our security forces must never be allowed to go. That is the level of sufficiency. Above or at that level, our defense forces protect national security adequately. Below that level is one vast undifferentiated area of no security at all."[24] He might have added that excessive nuclear deployments raise costs unnecessarily and perhaps deprive competing requirements of essential resources.

Retaliatory Force Composition

Retaliatory forces that implement deterrent strategies must be able to accomplish assigned missions after nuclear-armed enemies attack. Two functionally different weapon systems that decrease collective vulnerabilities, increase flexibility, complicate rival planning, and minimize prospects of technological surprise are preferable to any monad. Triads, quadrads, and pentads may buttress deterrence somewhat better, but the practical value of investments declines with each layer. Mirror-image deployments seldom are necessary. High-tech, affluent sea powers, for example, may rely mainly on highly survivable missile-launching submarines, while land powers emphasize delivery systems ashore.[25]

Possible Lessons Learned

All U.S. and Soviet nuclear deterrent concepts and force postures after the early 1960s left yawning gaps between ends and means. None reduced force levels or restrained costs significantly until the Cold War was almost over, but mutual deterrence persisted for thirty years. Three possible lessons emerge from that experience:

- National leaders who fully appreciate the horrific nature of nuclear warfare are fairly easy to deter, regardless of techniques employed.
- Risk-takers who disregard the nature of nuclear warfare may be difficult or impossible to deter, regardless of techniques employed.
- Deterrent techniques that incorporate nuclear war-fighting capabilities would serve national security interests best if preventive measures fizzle.

NUCLEAR WAR-FIGHTING STRATEGIES

Seasoned national security decision-makers are acutely aware that carefully crafted deterrent strategies may fail and prepare to cope if that happens. Nuclear war-fighting policies that specify opening gambits, target selections, and homeland defense strongly influence force requirements, costs, and outcomes.[26]

Opening Gambits

Huge benefits would accrue from a first strike at the onset of any nuclear conflict or from first use of nuclear weapons in traditional combat. Second-strike counterpunches accordingly must rapidly overcome initial disadvantages.

First-Strike Policies

Nuclear war–fighters who believe that a good offense makes the best defense rephrase an ancient axiom to read, "Do unto others before they do unto you." Major General Orville Anderson's public pronouncements in favor of preventive war cost him his job as Commandant of the Air War College in September 1950. U.S. Chief of Naval Operations Admiral Robert Carney and Air Force Vice Chief of Staff General Muir Fairchild, who wanted to squelch the Soviet Union while the United States still possessed overwhelming nuclear superiority, nevertheless beat that same drum with impunity four years later.[27] General Curtis E. LeMay and other early Commanders in Chief of U.S. Strategic Air Command (SAC) preferred first-strike policies that would shock, disorganize, and demoralize opponents, and thereby pave the way for quick victory.[28] They never received permission, because preventive and preemptive operations are laden with political liabilities and look unattractive after enemy forces acquire sizable nuclear capabilities.

Second-Strike Policies

The ability of truncated second-strike forces to perform assigned missions in chaotic postattack environments after absorbing the effects of nuclear blast, heat, and radiation would depend largely on enemy targeting priorities, the number of survivors, their states of training, and contingency plans. Launch-on-warning policies could safely maximize retaliatory capabilities only if infallible intelligence sources confirmed the source, magnitude, and probable impact areas of enemy nuclear attacks in progress, notified national command authorities in time for them to transmit permission, and enough minutes remained for recipients to react effectively.[29]

Targeting Policies

Targeting policies shape the nature of nuclear war. They also dictate the numbers, types, and attributes of weapon systems needed to execute stated strategies. Counterforce strategies embrace active, passive, offensive, and defensive measures calculated to degrade rival military capabilities. Countervalue strategies aim to obliterate civilian enterprises and undermine national will.

Counterforce Targeting

Counterforce targeting, which concentrates on enemy nuclear delivery systems, associated defenses, nerve centers, and weapon stockpiles, seeks to disarm opponents as quickly as possible. First-strike force requirements are simple and fairly inexpensive as long as opponents possess few nuclear-capable forces, all at known locations, all static, and none well-shielded. Complexities and costs rise when enemy inventories increase, superhard shelters dot landscapes, and mobile weapon systems supplement or replace those in fixed positions. General Curtis E. LeMay explained resultant problems this way in 1968: The U.S. "strategy of counterforce was basically defensive, [but] there was a catch to it. To get most of the enemy forces on the ground we would have to attack first," and "our force would have to be much larger than it is now."[30]

U.S. counterforce capabilities, for example, relied entirely on manned bombers from 1945 until 1959, when the first single-shot Atlas ICBMs and Polaris submarines became operational. Antisubmarine warfare hunter-killer teams soon began to sprout. Land- and sea-launched ballistic missiles laden with MIRVs blossomed to handle a plethora of aiming points in the Soviet Union. U.S. ICBMs eventually acquired single-shot kill probabilities against Soviet missile silos (some of which could withstand overpressures that approximated 10,000

psi), and the U.S. triad became a de facto pentad when nuclear-armed air- and sea-launched cruise missiles entered active service.

Countervalue Targeting

Countervalue targeting concentrates on urban centers, industries, resources, and institutions that constitute the fabric of enemy society. The principal intent is to deprive opponents of cherished possessions and staying power, break their spirit, and continue punishment until they quit. Force requirements are less demanding and costs are lower than those connected with counterforce, because primary targets are static and relatively "soft."

Countervalue operations nevertheless sound a sour note, since they disregard age-old advice from Sun Tzu, who contended that, "The worst policy is to attack cities."[31] Ethical considerations aside, there is good reason to agree, because assaults on metropoli would destroy assets that both sides need to recuperate and deprive "winners" of spoils that could embellish their postwar power base.

Amalgamations

Counterforce and countervalue operations are complementary. Counterforce-plus-avoidance strategies spare important military targets located inside cities, whereas counterforce-plus-bonus strategies deliberately maximize collateral casualties and damage.[32] Policy-makers at the pinnacle must determine the proper mix.

Defensive Options

Surveillance screens that cover every avenue of enemy approach, responsive command, control, and communication systems, interceptor aircraft, and surface-to-air missiles (SAMs) guard against enemy cruise missiles as well as manned bomber attacks. The best shields, however, are porous, and reliable ballistic missile defenses remain technologically infeasible at this writing. Passive defenses thus are imperative.

Protection for Retaliatory Forces

The number of nuclear delivery vehicles deployed before combat begins is less important than those left in mission-capable condition after being attacked. Second-strike policies multiply prelaunch survivability problems severalfold, as evidenced by the plight of static U.S. ICBMs after Soviet counter-silo capabilities began to pose insufferable threats.

Nuclear strategists in the Pentagon and at SAC Headquarters scrutinized thirty proposed basing modes that included open and covered trenches, launch sites submerged along the continental shelf or dug deeply into bedrock, a "drag strip," and a "race track." The latter concept called for 200 road-mobile ICBMs, each to circle constantly or wander randomly among twenty-three hardened launch sites along a fifteen to twenty mile oval at one of 200 self-contained installations. No foe could conduct a successful nuclear first strike without simultaneously smashing most of the 4,600 shelters, since bogus transports and safe havens made it impossible for satellite sensors to tell which targets were counterfeit. The "racetrack" and all other outlandish proposals were stillborn, because they invited saturation attacks on the United States, were impractical, excessively expensive, and would have taken years to complete.[33]

Population Protection

No country endangered by nuclear weapons can safely disregard civil defense. Nations that concentrate a high percentage of their citizens in capital cities such as Seoul, Pyongyang, Baghdad, Damascus, Riyadh, and Teheran are among the most needy, because a few well placed explosions would wipe out much of the populace along with industrial capacities, telecommunication nodes, and cherished institutions.

Well-stocked shelters in residential areas and workplaces would provide some protection against blast, heat, and radiation, provided warning times were adequate, but the best passive defense against

nuclear weapons is to be somewhere else when they detonate. City evacuation consequently received serious consideration in the United States and the Soviet Union during the Cold War,[34] but it soon became clear that inhabitants caught in the open would suffer more casualties than if they stayed home. One U.S. skeptic predicted "the biggest rush hour in history, and probably the last." First-strike strategies theoretically would allow aggressors to evacuate selected urban centers before nuclear combat began, but few citizens could survive long, even in mild weather, if nuclear reprisals smashed the cities they left and eradicated sources of sustenance.[35]

NUCLEAR WAR TERMINATION STRATEGIES

Nuclear wars could subside spontaneously, but starting may be much easier than stopping. The British Ministry of Defence, in a 1954 White Paper, envisaged "a period of broken-backed warfare . . . during which both sides would seek to recover their strength, carrying on the struggle in the meantime as best they might."[36] U.S. Admiral Robert B. Carney concurred. "With the passing of that initial phase," he opined, "tough people would carry on across the radioactive ashes and water, with what weapons are left."[37]

Belligerents in any case would do well to pose and postulate answers to key questions that concern cease-fire, truce, or armistice arrangements, "sideshows" that involve allies, postwar disarmament, and political settlements.[38] The prime prerequisite would be to maintain contact with enemy representatives who have the authority, abilities, and inclination to conclude nuclear hostilities. Target lists that aim to "decapitate" opponents by eradicating national nerve centers appear nonsensical when seen in that light. Nuclear war termination requirements on the contrary would better be met by actions that spare capital cities, alternative seats of government, and interconnecting telecommunications.[39]

KEY POINTS

- Even a few nuclear weapons could cause incomparable casualties and damage in large countries and cripple small ones
- The basic aim of nuclear deterrent strategies is to ensure a standoff called "stability," so no rational national leader could be tempted to strike first
- National leaders who fully appreciate the nature of nuclear war are much easier to deter than risk-takers who are ignorant of or ignore related perils
- The deterrent value of homeland defense is subject to serious dispute, whereas homeland defense is an undeniable war-fighting asset
- Force-sizing policies that call for "sufficiency" and stress essential military capabilities instead of statistical strengths are preferable to all other standards
- First-strike strategies give war-fighters great advantage; second-strike strategies designed to deter are relatively risky and expensive
- Numerous, well-protected enemy nuclear delivery systems make counterforce strategies a complex and costly proposition
- Countervalue strategies invite retaliation in kind and could culminate in the destruction of assets that "winners" as well as "losers" need to recuperate.
- "Decapitation" strategies that kill enemy leaders or sever communications with them might make it difficult or impossible to terminate disastrous nuclear combat

NOTES

1. Herman Kahn describes a series of hurdles in *On Thermonuclear War* (Princeton, NJ: Princeton University Press, 1960), Chapter 2.

2. DA Pamphlet 39-3, *The Effects of Nuclear Weapons*, rev. ed. (Washington: U.S. Government Printing Office, February 1964), 1–27, 473–75.

3. *Long-Term Worldwide Effects of Multiple Nuclear Weapons Detonations* (Washington: National Academy of Sciences, 1975); *The Fallen Sky: Medical Consequences of Thermonuclear War*, ed. for Physicians for Social Responsibility by Saul Aronow et al. (New York: Hill and Wang, 1963).

4. *United States and Soviet City Defense: Considerations for Congress*, prepared by the Congressional Research Service, Senate Document 94-268, 94th Cong., 2d sess. (Washington: U.S. Government Printing Office, September 30, 1976), 19–26. For a hypothetical account of casualties from a U.S. attack on the Kozelsk ICBM field 180 miles southwest of Moscow, see John Barry and Evan Thomas, "Dropping the Bomb," *Newsweek*, June 25, 2001, 28–30.

5. *The Effects of Nuclear War* (Montclair, NJ: Allenheld, Osmun & Co., for the Office of Technology Assessment, U.S. Congress, 1980), 15–46.

6. DA Pamphlet 39-3, *The Effects of Nuclear Weapons*, 577–626.

7. Martin Middlebrook, *The Battle of Hamburg* (New York: Charles Scribner's Sons, 1983).

8. DA Pamphlet 39-3, *The Effects of Nuclear Weapons*, 102–20.

9. Ibid., blast, 149–70, 196–274, 316–50; thermal radiation, 63–115.

10. Ibid., radioactivity, 502–31.

11. Frederick S. Dunn and William T. R. Fox present passionate pleas for arms control in *The Absolute Weapon: Atomic Power and World Order*, ed. Bernard Brodie (New York: Harcourt, Brace and Co., 1946), 13–17, 169–203. Quotation on 13.

12. "The United States Proposals for the International Control of Atomic Energy, Presented to the United Nations Atomic Energy Commission by the United States Representative, Mr. Bernard M. Baruch, June 14, 1946", in *The International Control of Atomic Energy: Growth of a Policy*, Department of State Publication 2702 (Washington: U.S. Government Printing Office, 1946).

13. Three-page summaries of many agreements, negotiations, and proposals are available in Amy Woolf, *Arms Control and Nonproliferation Activities: A*

Catalog of Recent Events, Rpt. RL30033 (Washington: Congressional Research Service, January 4, 1999).

14. David Hoffman, "Arms Control Reverts to a Waiting Game," *Washington Post,* June 6, 2000, A1, A23.

15. Brodie, *The Absolute Weapon,* 76.

16. Bernard Brodie, *Strategy in the Missile Age* (Princeton, NJ: Princeton University Press, 1959), 303-4; Yehoshafat Harkabi, *Nuclear War and Nuclear Peace* (Jerusalem: Israel Program for Scientific Translation, 1966), 48-50.

17. Stefan T. Possony and J. E. Pournelle, *The Strategy of Technology* (Cambridge, MA: Dunellen, 1970), 115-16.

18. Kahn, *On Thermonuclear War,* 13-20. Quotation on 19.

19. Charles de Gaulle, Discours et Messages, Tome II (Paris: Institut Charles de Gaulle), 524-25.

20. Kahn, *On Thermonuclear War,* 7-16.

21. Donald R. Brennen, quoted in Extension of Remarks by Representative John G. Schmitz, *Congressional Record,* September 13, 1971, E9439.

22. Brodie, *Strategy in the Missile Age,* 274-80.

23. Kahn, *On Thermonuclear War,* viii-x, 4-27.

24. President Richard M. Nixon, *U.S. Foreign Policy for the 1970s: Building for Peace* (Washington: U.S. Government Printing Office, February 25, 1971), 167.

25. John M. Collins, *Strategic Nuclear Delivery Systems: How Many? What Combinations?,* Rpt. No. 74-177F (Washington: Congressional Research Service, October 7, 1974) and *U.S. Strategic Nuclear Force Options: A Framework for Analysis,* Issue Brief 77046, November 2, 1983.

26. For seminal studies on nuclear warfare, see *The Absolute Weapon: Atomic Power and World Order.* Bernard Brodie and Eilene Galloway explored influences on land and naval strategies in *The Atom Bomb and the Armed Services,* Public Affairs Bulletin No. 55 (Washington: Legislative Reference Service, May 1947).

27. General Curtis E. LeMay, *America Is in Danger* (New York: Funk and Wagnalls, 1968), 59, 64-65, 84, 117.

28. Bernard Brodie discusses preventive and preemptive wars in *Strategy in the Missile Age,* 227-48.

29. "Sec. Brown: 'Launch on Warning or Launch Under Attack'?," *Defense/Space Daily,* November 11, 1977,

68. For elaboration, see Richard L. Garwin, "Launch Under Attack to Redress Minuteman Vulnerability?," *International Security,* Winter 1979-1980, 116-39; Robert G. Bell, *Launch on Warning: Pros and Cons* (Washington: Congressional Research Service, July 7, 1976).

30. LeMay, *America Is in Danger,* 83, 116.

31. Sun Tzu, *The Art of War,* trans. Samuel B. Griffith (New York: Oxford University Press, 1963), 78.

32. LeMay, *America Is in Danger,* 66-68.

33. *ICBM Basing Options: A Summary of Major Studies to Determine a Survivable Basing Concept for ICBMs* (Washington: Office of the Deputy Under Secretary of Defense for Research and Engineering [Strategic and Space Systems], December 1980); *The MX Weapon System: Issues and Challenges* (Washington: General Accounting Office, February 12, 1981), 38-39.

34. N. M. Titov et al., *Civil Defense,* ed. and trans. G. A. Cristy, Document ORNL-7R-2845 (Oak Ridge, TN: Oak Ridge National Laboratory, July 1975), v, vii, 25-28; Leon Gouré, *Soviet Civil Defense in the 1970s* (Coral Gables, FL: Center for Advanced International Studies, University of Miami, September 1975), 50-56.

35. "Warnke Against Civil Defense Program," *Defense/Space Daily,* November 30, 1978, 136; Ward Sinclair and Warren Brown, "Evacuation Could Bring Huge Traffic Jam," *Washington Post,* April 2, 1979, A1.

36. *Statement on Defence,* Command Paper #9075, Presented by the Minister of Defence to Parliament (London: Her Majesty's Stationery Office, February 1954), 5. For comments, see Brodie, *Strategy in the Missile Age,* 160-65.

37. Admiral Robert B. Carney, speech delivered in Cincinnati, OH on February 21, 1955, quoted in Brodie, *Strategy in the Missile Age,* 160n.

38. Thomas C. Schelling, *Arms and Influence* (New Haven, CT: Yale University Press, 1966), 204-20 and *The Strategy of Conflict* (Cambridge, MA: Harvard University Press, 1960), 53-80.

39. Harold Brown, *Department of Defense Annual Report, Fiscal Year 1982* (Washington: Office of the Secretary of Defense, January 19, 1981), 41-42.

13. Biological and Chemical Warfare Strategies

*The [Black Death], which was probably bubonic plague,
came out of the East in 1347 . . . and carried off a quarter
of the population of Europe. Its influences on society
were catastrophic.*

Major General J. F. C. Fuller
A Military History of the Western World
Chronicle 16, Volume I

Aggressors gifted with biological warfare (BW) agents even more virulent than the medieval Black Death lack powers to destroy hardware or real estate, but could exterminate or incapacitate human beings along with livestock and kill or contaminate crops on calamitous scales. Chemical warfare (CW) agents are somewhat more manageable, but all types could cause mass casualties. It therefore seems surprising that so few creative thinkers currently tackle biological and chemical warfare problems with anything like the intellectual intensities that Cold War theoreticians applied to nuclear strategies starting in 1945. Urgent needs still exist for military theories, concepts, policies, doctrines, tactics, plans, and programs designed to deter and deal with such malevolence.*[1]

BIOLOGICAL AND CHEMICAL WEAPONS

Traditional armed forces have fought most wars since the Stone Age. Future conflicts could be exclusively nuclear. Unique BW and CW capabilities could greatly amplify psychological shock and enhance operational flexibility during any form of armed conflict. Precise target locations would not be necessary, because agents blanket the landscape, then seep into nooks and crannies like water seeking the lowest level. Bonuses not obtainable from nuclear or conventional explosives include no urban rubble, no tree blow-down, and no other obstacles that could impede friendly ground forces.

BW Weapon Systems

Military strategists generally find biological warfare an unattractive form of combat, because most effects are delayed and unpredictable. Some BW agents cause lengthy, debilitating diseases from which stricken humans usually recover, while others, such as anthrax, botulism, ebola, hemorrhagic fever, plague, and smallpox, frequently are fatal. A third class blights sources of sustenance (Table 16).[2]

Most BW agents are best dispensed as aerosols, but the integration of aerial delivery vehicles with compatible munitions poses complex engineering problems. Microbial pathogens and toxins, for example, last only a few hours when exposed to heat and low humidity inside bombs, missile warheads, spray tanks, and artillery shells. Unstable agents cannot tolerate sharp strains associated with projec-

---

*Chapter 17 links biological and chemical warfare with domestic and transnational terrorism.

Table 16
Biological Warfare Agents

	Humans	Livestock	Crops
Viruses	Smallpox (30) Hemorrhagic Fever (80–90) Ebola (50–100) Encephalitis (5–60) Hepatitis (1) Influenza (1)	Hoof & Mouth (5–85) Poultry Plague (90–100) Avian Influenza (?) Rinderpest (15–95) Swine Fever (95–100) Mad Cow Disease (100?)	
Rickettsias	Tularemia (10–60) Typhus (10–40) Q-Fever (0–4) Spotted Fever (20–60)	Heart Water (50–60)	
Bacteria	Anthrax (20–100) Plague (30–100) Cholera (10–80) Glanders (50–100) Typhoid (4–20) Salmonella (?)	Anthrax (40–80) Brucellosis (5) Glanders (50–100)	Corn Blight Rice Blight
Protozoa	Amoebic Dysentery Malaria Sleeping Sickness	Coccidiosis (?)	
Fungi	Valley Fever (0–50)	Aspergillosis (50–90) Lumpy Jaw (50–90)	Cereal Mildew Cereal Rust Corn Rust Potato Blight Rice Blast
Toxins	Botulism (95–100) Ricin (?) Staph Infections (?) Mycotoxicosis (?)		

Figures in parentheses estimate the percent of fatalities in untreated cases. Wide fluctuations reflect different strains and degrees of resistance. Well-nourished populations are less susceptible to some diseases than impoverished people. Proper treatment would reduce rates dramatically, but no nation is well-prepared to cope with epidemics.

tile flights. The principal challenge therefore is to maintain potency throughout storage, delivery, and dissemination.[3]

Genetic engineers seek to tailor biological agents that act rapidly and are reasonably controllable. One aim is to increase the virulence and immunity of selected viruses, furnish them with prolific vectors, program them to multiply as required, then die after completing a specified number of cell divisions. Future BW threats could be mind-boggling if experimental psychotoxins that induce fear, fatigue, depression, or severe mental disorders supplement current incapacitants.[4]

CW Weapon Systems

CW weapons include incendiaries such as napalm, smokes, assorted riot control agents, and herbicides, of which the Vietnam-era Agent Orange is most notorious.[5] This text deals exclusively with lethal and incapacitating agents, none of which are designed to damage materiel, although corrosive chemicals may do so unless cleaned off quickly.

Nonpersistent aerosols and vapors include blood agents, asphyxiants, and nerve gasses, the most volatile of which linger no more than a few minutes even on calm days, whereas persistent vessicants and thickened nerve agents laid down as liquids

Table 17

Chemical Warfare Agents

	Symbol	State	Odor	Persistency
Nonpersistent				
Blood Agent				
Hydrogen Cyanide	AC	Vapor	Peach	Few Minutes
Asphyxiant				
Phosgene	CG	Vapor	Newly Mown Hay	Few Minutes
Nerve Agents[1]				
Tabun	GA	All Aerosol	Odorless	Minutes
Sarin	GB	or	Odorless	Hours
Soman	GD	Vapor	Odorless	Hours
Persistent[2]				
Nerve Agents[3]				
Soman (Thickened)[4]	GD(T)	Oily Liquid	Odorless	Days/Weeks
Agent VX	VX	Oily Liquid	Odorless	Days/Weeks
Vesicants				
Mustard	HD	Oily Liquid	Garlic	Days/Weeks
Lewisite	L	Oily Liquid	Geranium	Days/Weeks
Mustard-Lewisite	HL	Oily Liquid	Garlic	Days/Weeks

[1]Nonpersistent nerve agents are so lethal that protective clothing is essential, because small droplets may mingle with aerosols or vapor.
[2]All persistent agents are least tenacious in warm, windy, rainy weather.
[3]All persistent CW agents are toxic on unprotected skin, but lethal doses are much larger than those required to kill by inhalation.
[4]Thickened Soman remains lethal for long periods under arctic-like conditions, but less so than in temperate climates.

remain hazardous to human health for several days, even weeks (Table 17). CW delivery vehicles commonly include aircraft, missiles, artillery, mortars, rocket launchers, and hand-laid chemical land mines.[6]

Casualties occur when victims inhale, ingest, or absorb CW agents. Mustard mixed with Lewisite sears eyes first, then nasal passages, throat, lungs, and exposed skin. Fast-acting hydrogen cyanide (often used for gas chamber executions) makes it impossible for human bodies to consume oxygen carried by red blood cells, whereas delayed-reaction phosgene attacks respiratory tracts. Tabun, Sarin and Soman, which last somewhat longer in free states, induce neuroparalysis in the absence of an immediate antidote. Amounts required to incapacitate or kill usually vary with concentration densities, dosage times, individual sensitivities, temperatures, and physical activities of those afflicted. Rapid respi-

ration brought about by strenuous exertion, for example, increases vapor intake and reduces abilities to hold breath while masking. Perspiration promotes blisters. Prolonged exposure to relatively low toxic levels can disable personnel just as surely as fleeting encounters with larger doses.

BIOLOGICAL AND CHEMICAL ARMS CONTROL

The number of potential enemies armed with BW and CW weapons made many statesmen nervous enough to emphasize arms control immediately after World War I, when the 1925 Geneva Protocol prohibited usage. The Biological Weapons Convention of 1972, which will wither away if current trends persist,[7] obligated signatories to "destroy, or divert to peaceful purposes . . . all [BW] agents, toxins, weapons, equipment, and means of delivery." The 1993 Chemical Weapons Convention, which imposed similar restrictions on CW activities, mandated on-site inspections and penalties for countries that fail to comply.[8] One glance at Table 14 (page 124) nevertheless confirms that, counterproliferation constraints notwithstanding, BW- and CW-capable nations still abound, of which some are extremely hostile toward perceived adversaries near and far. Current numbers will increase if unfulfilled programs in progress reach fruition.

BIOLOGICAL WARFARE STRATEGIES

Pressing needs exist for creative BW strategies, because deterrent and war-fighting concepts are deficient. Requirements would remain urgent if proliferation ceased, because unprincipled possessors already retain appalling capabilities that they could employ at times and places of their choosing.

BW Deterrent Techniques

Deterers with little compunction or whose survival is at stake might credibly announce intentions to "go nuclear" if opponents initiate biological warfare, but threats of that sort would be less believable under most other conditions. If, as unconfirmed reports indicated, U.S. officials so warned Iraq during the Persian Gulf War of 1990–1991, Saddam Hussein probably was unimpressed, because senior U.S. officials seem much more reluctant to wreak havoc than their World War II predecessors (General Curtis E. LeMay reaped ridicule in the mid-1960s when he advocated bombing Vietnam "back to the Stone Age"[9]). The first nuclear detonation in combat since 1945 moreover would set an imprudent precedent, and could provoke the first nuclear exchange in history if opponents could reciprocate in kind.

Non-nuclear forces that fail to deter traditional conflicts seem no more likely to discourage biological warfare. Aggressors indeed might decide that BW campaigns would increase their leverage without raising risks significantly. Operation Desert Storm, for example, might have culminated quite differ-

ently if Saddam Hussein had seized Kuwait, then promised to strike Saudi Arabian cities with BW-capable Scuds unless the U.S.-led coalition dissolved and allowed him to retain ill-gotten gains. That threat would have been credible, given defective defenses against Iraqi missiles.[10]

Threats to destroy enemy BW installations and stockpiles or retaliate in kind offer faint hope of success, partly because it is very difficult to find lucrative targets. Elusive Iraqi Scuds and many BW facilities, for example, escaped unscathed throughout Desert Storm, despite their positions on flat terrain that is almost devoid of vegetation or other natural cover.[11] Future tricksters situated on rough topography covered with forests would find it easier to fool any adversary. Military strategists moreover could anticipate politically as well as morally unfortunate repercussions if successful attacks indiscriminately covered friends and noncombatants with poisonous clouds. Fear that biological warfare may backfire hence may offer the best incentives for potential deployers to refrain.

Biological Combat

No nation has ever fought a war in which biological weapons played a prominent part, but urgent needs for BW war-fighting techniques clearly exist if the following assumptions are even close to correct:

- The proliferation of BW weapons will continue, despite preventive measures
- Deterrent techniques will remain deficient
- Rash leaders, coupled with resultant possibilities for miscalculation, make biological warfare increasingly likely
- Observable sickness would be the earliest indication that BW agents have infected humans, livestock, and crops until better warning devices become available
- Casualties could overwhelm available medical services

- Damaged crops would take months or years to replenish

BW Offensive Options

Biological weapons are not well adapted for offensive use on battlefields, because wholesale delivery poses huge problems, incubation periods are measured in days or weeks, and required results would be hard to synchronize with nuclear, traditional, or chemical operations. Attacks even so could be timed to take effect on or about any given date. Natural epidemics normally start slowly and usually can be confined (AIDS and influenza are two prominent exceptions), whereas biological warfare agents would afflict all or most of a population almost simultaneously. Flight to avoid contagious neighbors and infected cadavers could quickly broadcast diseases far beyond their original borders.[12]

BW Defensive Options

Neither active nor passive BW defenses hold much promise at this moment.[13] Shocking casualties could occur if even a few enemy aircraft or missiles leaked through a sophisticated but pervious screen, which clearly can happen. A teenage German daredevil, for example, penetrated Soviet air defenses undetected on May 28, 1987, buzzed Lenin's tomb, then landed just off Red Square; an adventurous pilot crash-landed a light plane on the White House lawn in September 1994.[14]

Mass vaccinations to protect civilian populations as well as military personnel against particular BW threats appear impractical and, if accomplished, probably would prompt enemies to elect equally effective substitutes. Subtle genetic alterations might make agents of choice resistant to customary innoculations.[15]

Biological warfare accordingly seems most attractive to megalomaniacs who care little for human life even in their own country. Most military strategists meanwhile find other forms of armed combat more attractive until scientists and technologists open much better BW options.

CHEMICAL WARFARE STRATEGIES

Chemical warfare strategies, which have undergone many modifications since 1915, are more mature than BW counterparts. Some characteristics are similar, but those that differ demand unique treatments.

CW Deterrence

Most students of the subject doubt that chemical warfare deterrent strategies should rely heavily on threats to retaliate with nuclear or traditional weapons, for reasons already described. Abilities to respond in kind, however, look promising, because no country with extensive offensive capabilities has suffered CW attacks since 1918.[16]

The explanation is simple: chemical warfare bestows few assured benefits on initiators, who face reciprocal risks, reduced capabilities, and expense. Masks impair breathing, obstruct vision, and muffle communications. It takes several minutes for well-trained individuals to don cumbersome suits that are subject to rips and act as impromptu saunas in warm weather. Fatigue sets in fast. Time to complete routine tasks, like loading trucks and digging foxholes, may double or triple. Troops wearing gloves fumble with rifle sights, toggles, switches, and dials that demand tactile dexterity. Personnel need "sanitized" shelters to work, eat, sleep, relieve bladder and bowels, or merely blow noses. Extensive CW operations could overload supply and maintenance systems. Tons of decontaminants (bleach slurries, absorbent powders, detergents) and something like 200,000 gallons of wash water per armored division would be required after each attack that dispensed persistent agents. Expectation of retaliation in kind consequently dampens temptations to initiate chemical combat against opponents who are organized, equipped, and trained to give as good as they get or better.[17]

Chemical Combat

Chemical warfare agents have never been decisive, even when disseminated wholesale during World War I. National security policy-makers and military strategists currently possess vastly improved CW capabilities, but nonetheless would be well advised to weigh offensive advantages against defensive disadvantages carefully before they decide to initiate chemical combat against rivals who are likewise armed.

Offensive CW Options

The offensive utility of chemical warfare weapons is considerable, given a wide variety of potential delivery vehicles. U.S. intelligence analysts in the 1980s, for example, concluded that each Soviet BM-21 battery of eighteen forty-tube 122mm rocket launchers (now owned by Russia) could bombard enemy positions with 720 rounds of nonpersistent Sarin or hydrogen cyanide in a single 20-second salvo, reload, and replicate that strike 10 minutes later. Short-range cruise missiles containing thickened Soman could contaminate targets 180 miles distant without endangering aircraft or crews.[18]

Volatile agents that disperse quickly are well-suited for surprise attacks against troop concentrations, strong points, and command centers, because defenders must don full protective regalia until they identify the threat, while assault forces who know what agent is involved need no gear save gas masks. Lethal agents laid down as liquids can restrict avenues available to poorly prepared opponents, protect the flanks of friendly ground forces, and saturate enemy logistical installations along with ports, airfields, and surface ships at sea.

Defensive CW Requirements

Most modern armed forces are reasonably well-prepared to defend against unstealthy aircraft. Sound missile defenses, however, await scientific breakthroughs and abilities to intercept artillery projectiles in flight appear improbable, given the most optimistic long-range forecasts. Passive defenses accordingly bear heavy burdens.

Detection Defenders need near real-time detection devices to warn forces downwind of chemical attacks, differentiate agents, measure intensities, predict persistencies, and tell commanders when to signal "all clear." Instigators, who must safeguard against capricious wind shifts and avoid self-inflicted casualties while traversing contaminated terrain, have identical demands. Instruments range from simple litmus-type papers to ultrasensitive alarms that detect chemicals in the air, but few items deployed at the turn of the twenty-first century discriminate among CW threats or measure concentrations very accurately.[19]

Individual Protection Individual protection against chemical warfare agents starts with custom-fitted masks designed to filter out known vapors and aerosols. The best have voice transmitters, devices that enable wearers to sip beverages, and tubes that facilitate mouth-to-mouth resuscitation. Complete encapsulation against vesicants and nerve agents includes hood, suit, socks, shoes, and gloves made of impervious materials. Antidotes administered expeditiously reduce deaths from nerve agents that are inhaled or absorbed.

Forces that fight in full ensemble regrettably lose 30–60 percent effectiveness almost immediately and deteriorate rapidly thereafter, even under ideal conditions. Constant wear of protective clothing to cover all contingencies is impractical. Standing procedures that specify reduced states of readiness spell trouble if troops are caught by surprise. The price paid in stress and diminished combat capabilities consequently is high.[20]

Collective Protection Sterilized shelters are essential, because individuals who remove masks or loosen clothing even momentarily during chemical combat otherwise could become casualties. Collective accommodations ashore and afloat feature toxic-free command posts, communication centers, medical facilities, maintenance shops, assorted other installations, and "citadels" aboard surface ships. CW filters, pumps, and other defensive devices protect some vans, tanks, and infantry fighting vehicles.

Shortcomings nevertheless are extensive. Ventilating systems are especially vulnerable. Inflatable shelters, seemingly ideal for fluid warfare, are subject to punctures; permanent structures are expensive and infeasible for mobile forces; tanks and self-propelled gun carriages cannot replenish ammunition without risking chemical contamination; casualties endanger doctors, nurses, and other patients unless medics scrub them before admittance. R&D specialists labor to reduce the list of such liabilities, but successes thus far have come slowly.[21]

Medical Care

First aid is the first order of business after any chemical attack. Requirements vary with degrees of surprise, states of training, human failures, and faulty equipment, such as leaky masks, garments, and collective shelters. Most afflicted personnel must make their own diagnoses and treat themselves if medics are too few to handle mass casualties. Nerve agent antidotes, which have debilitating side effects, could reduce combat power during crises if injected needlessly.

Decontamination

Armed forces can "fight dirty" for brief periods, but soon must remove persistent chemical agents from doused troops, arms, equipment, supplies, and important properties or accept increased attrition accompanied by decreased combat effectiveness. Soap and water suffices for personnel, provided they gingerly remove polluted clothing. Slick surfaces

pose few decontamination problems, but irregular shapes like aircraft cockpits take much longer to scrub. Soviet Armed Forces during the Cold War fielded a mobile "car wash" with truck-mounted jet engines on a turntable to facilitate hot air drying. Difficult cases demand bleach slurries, absorbent powders, and detergents that damage metal, rubber, and electronics unless cleaners take precautions.[22] Flexibility was lacking during Operation Desert Storm, because U.S. water-based decontamination systems intended for use in Europe were unsuitable in the arid Middle East.[23]

Cleanup

Cleanup crews can "sanitize" flatlands, including airfields, by broadcasting neutralizers, turning ground with bulldozers, and burning vegetation, although forces downwind must guard against fumes in the latter event. Labor, implements, materials, and tactical situations limit how much can be reasonably purged from rough topography if such action becomes necessary.

NEEDS FOR CREATIVE CONCEPTS

No nation presently is well-prepared to deter or deal effectively with biological warfare threats that may be more ominous than those associated with nuclear weapons. Chemical warfare problems are more localized and better understood, but shortcomings could tip regional balances of power in favor of ruthless wielders. Proper employment in any case requires creative strategies coupled with high-priority programs developed expressly to eliminate prominent gaps and improve existing offensive and defensive BW/CW capabilities.

KEY POINTS

- BW and CW warfare weapons that can incapacitate or kill humans and animals also can contaminate or kill crops on calamitous scales, but do not destroy hardware or real estate
- Some BW agents cause widespread debilitating diseases, others frequently are fatal, while a third class blights sources of sustenance
- Military strategists generally find biological warfare unattractive, because many agents are unstable and most effects are delayed, uncontrollable, and unpredictable
- Lethal and incapacitating CW agents are better understood, somewhat more manageable, and their effects are comparatively localized
- BW- and CW-capable nations still abound, despite international arms control conventions
- Biological warfare threats may be more ominous than nuclear weapons, but deterrent, offensive, and defensive strategies have barely begun to incubate
- CW capabilities are well suited for offensive missions that other armed forces cannot accomplish equally well
- Armed forces prepared to retaliate in kind are best able to deter chemical warfare, because they confront aggressors with reciprocal risks, reduced abilities, and expense
- Individual and collective protective measures make CW operations an inconvenient form of warfare for attackers and defenders if each deploys chemical weapons
- Persistent CW agents make postattack cleanup a hazardous, time-consuming, costly process

NOTES

1. Stuart E. Johnson, ed., *The Niche Threat: Deterring the Use of Chemical and Biological Weapons* (Washington: National Defense University Press, 1997).
2. For tutorials, see *The Biological-Chemical Weapon Warfare Threat* (Washington: Central Intelligence Agency, 1998), 1–22; Javed Ali, Leslie Rodriques, and Michael Moodie, *U.S. Chemical-Biological Defense Guidebook* (Alexandria, VA: Jane's Information Group, 1998), 92–126; Abram S. Benenson, ed., *Control of Communicable Disease Manual*, 16th ed. (Washington: American Public Health Association, 1995). *The Problem of Chemical and Biological Warfare*, vol. II, *CB Weapons Today* (New York: Stockholm International Peace Research Institute (SIPRI), 1973), 37–41, 42–43, 61–72.
3. Ibid.
4. Charles Pillar and Keith Yamamoto, *Gene Wars* (New York: William Morrow, 1988); Macha Levinson, "Custom-Made Biological Weapons," *International Defense Review*, November 1986, 1615.
5. Institute of Medicine, National Academy of Science, *Veterans and Agent Orange: Health Effects of Herbicides Used in Vietnam* (Washington: National Academy Press, 1994).
6. Ali, Rodriques, and Moodie, *U.S. Chemical-Biological Defense Guidebook*, 36–74; *The Problem of Chemical and Biological Warfare*, vol. II, 33–35, 42–43, 47–48.
7. Ambassador Donald A. Mahley, *Statement by the United States to the Ad Hoc Group of Biological Weapons Convention States Parties* (Washington, D.C.: Office of International Information Programs, U.S. Department of State, July 25, 2001), Web site http://usinfo.state.gov, with transcript, *Mahley News Conference on Biological Weapons Protocol*.
8. *The Arms Control Reporter* (Cambridge, MA: Institute for Defense and Disarmament Studies, updated monthly); *Chem-Bio Weapons & Defense Monitor* (Washington: Exchange Monitor Publications, published biweekly).
9. General Curtis E. LeMay with MacKinlay Kantor, *Mission With LeMay: My Story* (Garden City, NY: Doubleday, 1965), 565.
10. John J. Arquilla, *Constraints on Regional Deterrence After the Cold War*, RR-466-A/AF (Santa Monica, CA: RAND Corporation, August 1993), 8–9, 16, 17, 19.

11. Thomas A. Keany and Eliot A. Cohen, *Gulf War Air Power Survey: Summary Report* (Washington, D.C.: U.S. Government Printing Office, 1993), 78-90, 137, 138; Jonathan B. Tucker, "Lessons of Iraq's Biological Programme," *Arms Control,* December 1993, 229-71.

12. William C. King, IV, *Biological Warfare: Are U.S. Armed Forces Ready?,* Land Warfare Papers No. 34 (Washington: Association of the U.S. Army, October 1999), 1-14; Office of Technology Assessment, *Proliferation of Mass Destruction Weapons: Assessing the Risks* (Washington: U.S. Government Printing Office, August 1993), 53-54.

13. King, *Biological Warfare,* 15-24.

14. "Mathias Rust," *Collier's Yearbook,* 1987; "Pilot Crashes Small Plane on White House Lawn," *Facts on File Yearbook* (1994), 657-58.

15. *Biological Warfare,* vol. 4 (Washington: Defense Nuclear Agency, Summer 1994), iii, 72-78; Robert Harris, "Towards a Theory of Biological Deterrence," *World Outlook,* Summer 1990, 95-102.

16. John Ellis van Courtland Moon, "Chemical Weapons and Deterrence: The World War II Experience," *International Security,* Spring 1984, 3-35, 36-54.

17. FM *21-40, Chemical, Biological, and Nuclear Defense* (Washington: Department of the Army, October 15, 1977), Chapter 5 and Appendix B.

18. Charles J. Dick, "The Soviet Chemical and Biological Warfare Threat," *Royal United Services Institute (RUSI),* March 1981, 48; A. F. Graveley, "Defense or Deterrence? The Case for Chemical Weapons," *RUSI,* December 1981, 14; Gary Eifried, "Russian CW: Our Achilles' Heel in Europe", *Army,* December 1979, 25.

19. Ali, Rodriques, and Moodie, *U.S. Chemical-Biological Defense Guidebook,* 165.

20. Ibid., 197-206.

21. FM 21-40, *Chemical, Biological, and Nuclear Defense,* 5-33 through 5-36; Eylert Haup, "DSK: NBC Protection in the German Navy," *National Defense,* May-June 1984, 88, 91-92, 94, 96.

22. Ali, Rodriques, and Moodie, *U.S. Chemical-Biological Defense Guidebook,* 181-86; Dick, "The Soviet Chemical and Biological Warfare Threat," 51; K. G. Benz, "NBC Defense: An Overview," *International Defense Review,* Part II, *Detection and Decontamination,* February 1984, 164.

23. *Conduct of the Persian Gulf War: Final Report to Congress* (Washington: Department of Defense, April 1992), Q9.

14. Traditional Forces and Strategies

*Tradition: A historical line of conventions, principles,
and attitudes characteristic of a school [or] social group;
a long-established custom or practice.*

Webster's New World College Dictionary
4th Edition

Traditional warfare, which has been in vogue for eons, spurns nuclear, biological, chemical, and radiological (NBCR) weapons, yet otherwise spans the conflict spectrum from minor engagements to combat on the scale of World War II. Military lexicons commonly call such strife "conventional," but that term is a misnomer, because innovative strategies, tactics, plans, and operations produce best results. So-called "general purpose forces" that perform traditional roles, functions, and missions ashore, afloat, aloft, and in space also are mislabeled, because respective responsibilities are specialized. Deterrent and war-fighting concepts and plans consequently must integrate their efforts creatively.

COMPLEMENTARY FORCE CONTRIBUTIONS

Armed forces that engage in traditional warfare are far more diversified and costly in compilation than NBCR counterparts. Roles, functions, and missions are much more diversified. All military services contribute offensive, defensive, and deterrent capabilities, but none can bear every burden alone.[1]

Land Power Peculiarities

Armies are the largest, most versatile military component in most countries, primarily because humanity, treasured institutions, industries, and the most easily accessible resources are located terrestrially. Ground forces are best able to seize, secure, and

occupy (even govern) hostile territories for prolonged periods. They routinely perform assorted logistical functions for expeditionary air forces and naval elements ashore. Major elements of the United States Marine Corps, for example, leaned heavily on the U.S. Army for support when committed far from salt water during World War I (1917–1918), in Korea (1950–1953), and in Vietnam (1965–1971).[2] Armies additionally perform internal security missions in many countries. Debilitating deficiencies even so are evident, because armies rely extensively on sister services for aerial reconnaissance, surveillance, and firepower as well as long-haul airlift and sealift.

Sea Power Peculiarities

The foremost naval functions have eternally been to exercise command over selected seas, to ensure that critical sea lines of communication (SLOCs) remain open for friends but not for foes, and to project naval power against hostile shores.[3] No truly new responsibility has emerged in the last 2,500 years, but modern missiles and aircraft launched from platforms afloat can strike targets several hundred miles inside hostile territory. Sea control facilitates international commerce, an essential element of national power and prosperity. Permanent or intermittent offshore presence near hot spots puts naval forces in position to respond expeditiously if crises occur. Only navies and merchant marines can deploy, redeploy, and sustain massive armed forces in foreign countries overseas.[4] Sea power, like land power, nevertheless exhibits glaring limitations. Top-of-the-line naval combatants are the most costly of all military hardware and, except for those with nuclear propulsion, expend fossil fuels at prodigious rates. Transit times for the speediest ships are measured in weeks over long distances. Naval forces moreover perform most administrative and logistical functions at vulnerable installations ashore.

Air Power Peculiarities

Aerial reconnaissance, surveillance, strategic bombardment, interdiction, close air support for land forces, and resupply became air force roles and functions before World War I ended on November 11, 1918.[5] Offensive counter-air operations retain top priority, because failure to establish and maintain air superiority can have calamitous consequences. Hitler's *Luftwaffe,* for example, paved the way for panzer spearheads on June 22, 1941, when it destroyed approximately 1,800 Soviet aircraft between dawn and dusk. Defenders, deprived of air cover, suffered demoralizing defeats on every front during the first week of war.[6] Air forces unfortunately are no more able to escape shortcomings than land and sea services. Most land-based aircraft still rely on elaborate installations that may not be conveniently located or politically accessible, require extensive logistical support during lengthy operations, and perform better when targets are situated on bare, level terrain rather than in mountains or woodlands.

Space Power Peculiarities

Modern armed forces have become increasingly dependent on multifaceted space operations since the Soviet scientific satellite called *Sputnik* electrified the world in 1957. Intelligence functions feature reconnaissance, surveillance, missile warning, target acquisition, tracking, nuclear detonation detection, poststrike assessments, signal interception, mapping, meteorological information, and verification of compliance with arms control accords. Navi-

gational satellites help armed forces locate themselves precisely anywhere on Earth. Military communicators routinely route long-range signals through relay stations in circumterrestrial space.[7] Unrestricted access, however, is scarcely assured. Cybernetic assaults already are feasible. Additional vulnerabilities will arise as soon as enemies deploy lethal antisatellite (ASAT) weapons and will persist until technologists perfect countermeasures.

Synergistic Capabilities

Armed combat normally involves two or more military services, perhaps from two or more nations, that can be most effective only if teamwork prevails. Joint/combined policies, doctrines, plans, and operations that integrate and synchronize the input from all contributors create synergistic capabilities that are much greater than the sum of separate parts, because common actions focus on common objectives. Combined strengths accordingly offset individual weaknesses, provided implementing commanders practice what harmonizers preach.[8]

COMPARATIVE FORCE POSTURES

Military balance sheets, which measure the combat power available to competing countries or coalitions, are tricky to compile, because data almost always are incomplete and reliability varies considerably. Results sometimes are suspect, because appraisers for various reasons may slant findings to create preferred impressions. Pentagon publications entitled *Soviet Military Power*[9] and the Kremlin's rebuttals dubbed *Whence the Threat to Peace,*[10] for example, emphasized enemy assets and slighted enemy liabilities. All net assessments and threat assessments even so start with quantitative and qualitative comparisons.

Quantitative Balances

British Admiral Horatio Nelson, a naval wizard during the Napoleonic Wars, noted that "numbers annihilate." His conclusion is not completely correct, but few war-fighters question the value of quantitative superiority, which enables possessors to absorb heavy casualties without becoming ineffective and affords flexibility available from no other source. The war-fighting balance in West-Central Europe was badly skewed throughout the Cold War, because the Warsaw Pact deployed many more divisions, tanks, and tactical aircraft than NATO did.[11] Readily available reinforcements from Poland and European Russia far outnumbered NATO counterparts. General Bernard W. Rogers, when he was Supreme Allied Commander, Europe, doubted that NATO could hold the line very long against a concerted Soviet offensive without employing nuclear weapons, which "would invite at least as much devastation" on defenders as on invaders.[12]

Qualitative Balances

Badly outnumbered but qualitatively superior armed forces sometimes prevail. British Prime Minister Winston Churchill, in a speech before the House of Commons on August 20, 1940, paid tribute to the Royal Air Force (RAF) with these stirring words: "Never in the field of human conflict was so much owed by so many to so few." Valiant RAF fighter pilots won the Battle of Britain, because short-range German escorts based in France were unable to protect Göring's vulnerable bombers against British interceptors that ground controllers vectored from English airdromes using tips that the world's first early warning radar network provided. That triumph caused Hitler to cancel Operation Sea Lion (the planned German invasion of Britain) and preserved the British Isles as a springboard for the Allied invasion of Normandy in June 1944.[13]

Strategists who routinely rely on qualitative supremacy to offset numerical inferiority even so can expect some rude surprises, because good large forces generally defeat good small ones. Overwhelming weight more than any other factor crushed the best that Germany and Japan had to offer during the Second World War, when both nations illogically bit off more than they could chew: Hitler tangled simultaneously with the Soviet Union, United States, Britain, France, and lesser European allies.[14] General Hideki Tojo, in his capacities as Premier, Minister of War, and Army Chief of Staff, took on China, the United States, Britain, the Netherlands, Australia, New Zealand, and assorted associates along Asia's southern rim.[15]

Beneficial Balances

Costly efforts to match opposing armed forces statistically or technologically are militarily meaningless when the practical value of superiority in any given category is neutral, immaterial, or negative.[16] NATO, for example, felt no need for more men under arms when the twenty-first century opened, even though Russian personnel strengths still exceeded a million, because dilapidated weapons and low morale made it difficult for Russia to subdue tiny Chechnya, much less menace Western Europe.[17] The best military balances, which concentrate on required capabilities rather than mirror images, enable nations to implement chosen strategies, accomplish missions, and satisfy objectives without wasting resources.

TRADITIONAL DETERRENCE

Strategic theories and concepts that traditional armed forces employ to prevent unwanted wars remain skimpy compared with literature that deals with nuclear deterrence.[18] Policy-makers, planners, and practitioners nevertheless agree that obvious abilities to make aggression unattractive and willingness to act decisively if provoked are cornerstones. Advantageous deployments, periodic demonstrations, and partnerships that augment military power contribute, but intangibles make it difficult to determine how much of what is required under specific conditions.

Incalculable Force Requirements

First-rate armed forces contribute to deterrence, but degrees to which they do so are arguable. Congress, for example, appropriated about $1 trillion to improve, operate, and maintain the U.S. military establishment during President Reagan's first Administration, but members of the House Armed Services Committee remained perplexed after they held hearings to determine how much deterrence those dollars bought. One witness doubted that anybody in the U.S. intelligence community knew. "A whole lot was bought, paid for, and deployed before 1981," he explained. "A lot of that trillion bucks is still in the pipeline. It may influence deterrence in the future, but it has not yet." Only one group can authoritatively tell whether taxpayers got their money's worth, he continued: "The Politburo in Moscow, and for some reason or other they aren't talking."[19]

National security policy-makers and military strategists, who nonetheless must try to calculate how much of what is needed for traditional deterrence, consequently tend to make conservative decisions. President Richard M. Nixon couched requirements as follows in a commencement address at the U.S. Air Force Academy on June 4, 1969: "I do not consider my recommendations infallible. But if I have made a mistake, I pray that it is on the side of too much and not too little. If we do too much, it will cost us our money. If we do too little, if may cost us our lives."[20]

Force Deployment Options

Permanent, large-scale presence near present and potential trouble spots is expensive in terms of manpower, materiel, and money, while distant "fire brigades" reduce responsiveness. The best deterrent strategies consequently couple forward deployments with reinforcements that can answer 911 calls rapidly. Optimum combinations take the imminence, intensity, and nature of perceived threats into account.

Permanent Presence

Large garrisons permanently deployed at strategic locations are best able to demonstrate resolve, prevent power vacuums, preserve regional balances, contain incipient threats, and defend vigorously if deterrence fails. Tiny "tripwires" nevertheless can serve useful purposes under favorable conditions. Soviet Armed Forces could have swamped the U.S. Berlin Brigade any time the Kremlin gave a green light, but so doing would have risked a nuclear war with NATO. The deterrent value of that minute contingent consequently was immense compared with its combat capabilities.[21]

Case-by-case assessments are essential, because it is difficult to determine beforehand what advantages permanent presence will provide. U.S. on-site forces helped maintain equilibrium in Europe throughout the Cold War and continue to do so in Korea, whereas Saddam Hussein began to mount operations against Iraqi Kurds and Shiite minorities before any U.S. forces returned home after Operation Desert Storm.[22] Host nation restrictions still dilute the deterrent and war-fighting abilities of U.S. Armed Forces in Saudi Arabia—Defense Minister Prince Sultan bin Abdul-Aziz on December 31, 1998, publicly declared that if the United States should ask permission to launch air strikes against Iraq from Saudi bases, "We will not agree."[23]

Power Projection

Deterrent strategies crafted to defuse budding contingencies before they balloon demand fast-reflex forces that are ready to fight on arrival. Proven abilities to assemble the proper mix of military power on short notice and project it wherever required can give aggressors pause, as demonstrated in August 1990 when U.S. Armed Forces swooped into Saudi Arabia from distant departure bases, first to establish a tripwire between Kuwait and Persian Gulf oil fields farther south, then to build a bulwark.[24]

Significant liabilities even so limit leverage. Power projection may aggravate rather than dampen incipient crises if opponents detect preparations, interpret them correctly, and take counter-actions quickly. Political restraints sometimes diminish the deterrent value of forces based in foreign countries, because they can launch out-of-area expeditions only if host nations concur. U.S. logisticians, for example, had to resupply Israel from the United States rather than from Western Europe during the Yom Kippur War of 1973, because most NATO members found continued access to Arab petroleum more important than Israel's security. Portugal allowed landings in the Azores, but no other ally let U.S. cargo ships and transport aircraft use its facilities.[25]

Periodic Demonstrations

Large-scale military maneuvers, exercises, rapid deployments, reserve call-ups, and other demonstrations that periodically offer visible proof of impressive capabilities make all but the most wooden-headed opponents wonder whether the price of aggression would be excessive. Deterrent failures paradoxically may do likewise. The Democratic People's Republic of Korea, for example, has long been able to strike south in great strength with little or no warning, but Kim Il Sung learned a hard lesson in 1950–1953 when, after spectacular early successes, North Korea would have ceased to exist without massive military intervention by Chinese "volunteers."[26] He and Kim Jong Il, his successor, have avoided a decisive shootout with South Korea ever since, although two splendid opportunities arose when traditional U.S. forces were heavily committed elsewhere: first during massive U.S. involvement in Vietnam (1965–1972), then during Operations Desert Shield and Desert Storm (1990–1991).

Collective Security

Alliance systems, including multinational coalitions under UN and other international banners, can significantly lighten deterrent force requirements and financial burdens of each member state. They also strengthen political will and furnish useful infrastructure, provided mutual interests are at stake, all are of one mind concerning politico-military courses of action, and geographic situations are favorable.

Clear Intentions

Potent traditional capabilities provide a powerful deterrent only if accompanied by indisputable intentions to employ them if provoked. Vacillation not only undercuts credibility but weakens deterrence through uncertainty. Serbian President Slobodan Milosevic consequently felt free to savage Albanian rebels who sought to separate Kosovo from Greater Serbia in 1998–1999, because frequent threats by the United States and NATO to take military countermeasures proved empty until March 24, 1999.[27]

TRADITIONAL WAR-FIGHTING

Traditional war-fighting requirements differ in many respects from those of deterrence. Policy-makers must decide what volitional limitations to approve, while military strategists decide how to proceed if nuclear warfare overlaps.

Volitional Limitations

General Nathan F. Twining, while Chairman of the Joint Chiefs of Staff (1957–1960), longed for the good "old days [when] war was war and peace was peace." No one asked, "Is this a 'limited war,' or a 'general war,' or a 'total war'?" before the inconclusive collision in Korea. "Americans did what was necessary to win." U.S. joint doctrine still declares that, "If deterrence fails, then our single objective is **winning the nation's wars.** When we fight, we fight to win."[28]

There nevertheless are valid reasons for restrictions when "winning" seems too costly in terms of irreplaceable lives and precious resources. Astute strategists in such circumstances scale back political objectives, military aims, participating forces, weaponry, targets, and areas of operation, singly or in some combination.[29] Bargaining, which may be implied or explicit, manipulates promises, threats, counterthreats, proposals, counterproposals, offers, assurances, and concessions. One criterion, however, remains constant: negotiated settlements invariably involve terms that both sides are willing to accept.[30]

Limited Ends

Limited wars demand mutual willingness to settle for less than any belligerent would like without undercutting crucial security interests. Compromises replace unconditional surrender as the ultimate objective. President Truman, for example, abandoned efforts to reunify Korea after China intervened, but steadfastly sought to contain Communism and preserve the South Korean Government. Choosing goals calls for special caution when foes possess weapons of mass destruction, because rash decisions risk disasters.[31]

Limited Means

Strategists who strive to circumscribe the scope and severity of war limit means as well as ends. Defensive, support, and advisory troops are less provocative than offensive combat power. Confrontations between proxies are apt to be less incendiary than clashes between principals. Air and naval forces disengage more easily than those on the ground. Multinational alliances make it difficult for dominant nations to take actions that partners disapprove.

Twenty Free World countries contributed to the United Nations Command during the Korean War.[32] Their presence blurred the edges of a struggle between the United States and China, which steadfastly clung to the fiction that its contingents south of the Yalu River were "volunteers." Soviet training teams, service troops, surface-to-air missile crews, and interceptor aircraft pilots later flooded the Nile Delta to protect Moscow's massive investments in military aid to Egypt, but Leonid Brezhnev let Arab clients lose their Six-Day War with Israel in 1967 rather than furnish offensive reinforcements.[33] Cuba at the height of the Cold War was a de facto Soviet surrogate in several African countries that overlook maritime lines of communication—25,000 Cuban combat troops, plus 6,000-7,000 advisers and tech-

nicians, pursued Communist aims in Angola alone, according to U.S. intelligence estimates.[34]

Nuclear, biological, and chemical weapons by definition are taboo during traditional wars, although practical applications are apparent. General Twining believed that if the United States Air Force had "dropped one A-bomb on a tactical target during the Korea War . . . there might have been no Chinese invasion. . . ."[35] Low-yield nuclear detonations might have sealed off mountain passes along the Ho Chi Minh Trail and obliterated Communist base areas in isolated locales many miles from the nearest urban centers in Vietnam, Laos, and Cambodia. The nuclear genie nevertheless has remained in the jug since 1945, partly because abstinence is less ambiguous than limitations on allowable yields and employment practices, and partly because nuclear combat might become commonplace if any belligerent broke the long-standing moratorium.[36]

Limited Methods

Duels designed to limit armed combat have been scarce since about 980 B.C., when Israeli King Saul bet that little David could defeat the Philistine giant Goliath, who promised, "If he be able . . . to kill me" in one-on-one, winner-take-all combat, "then we will be your servants: but if I prevail . . . then ye shall be our servants, and serve us." David's victory prevented a pitched battle between opposing armies, for "when the Philistines saw their champion dead, they fled."[37]

Modern Chiefs of State, who deal with much greater complexities, tend to disregard military advice that they fear might conflict with political requirements in sensitive situations. Wrangling with Secretary of Defense Robert S. McNamara over ways to block Soviet sea lines of communication in the Caribbean Sea nearly cost U.S. Admiral George Anderson his job as Chief of Naval Operations during the Cuban missile crisis (he failed to receive a second two-year term).[38] Policies that President Lyndon Johnson imposed on U.S. military operations in

Southeast Asia (1965–1972) violated virtually every Principle of War to avoid provoking China or the Soviet Union and to promote peace talks with Hanoi.[39] Military strategists at such times earn their pay only if they devise strategic options that work acceptably well despite severe restrictions.

Limited Arenas

Limited wars generally are confined geographically. The United States Navy, which supported Chinese Nationalist defenders on beleaguered Quemoy Island in the early 1950s, freely transferred cargo from transport ships to Taiwanese landing craft that came under fire only after they crossed an imaginary line three miles offshore. U.S. Seventh Fleet in turn never attacked installations on the Chinese Communist mainland.[40] Those arrangements were satisfactory, but sanctuaries are more easily recognized if demarked by national boundaries, lines of latitude and longitude marked on everyone's maps, or clearly defined terrain features such as roads, railroads, large streams, and seashores. The Yalu River, which separates China from Korea, was a logical place for UN forces to stop in November 1950, because crossing that "Rubicon" would have initiated a new conflict.[41]

City limits sometimes serve well. Rome escaped unscathed in June 1944, because Allied and Axis leaders declared Italy's ancient capital an open city.[42] Paris enjoyed equal status before German occupation troops took possession in May 1940, but escaped destruction in August 1944 only because General Dietrich von Choltitz courageously refused to follow directives from his Führer, who wanted to incinerate that beautiful city.[43]

Risk Control

Limited war strategists, like tightwire walkers, pursue a ticklish trade. Excessive audacity by either side risks showdowns that neither wants. Excessive timidity invites adversaries to extort concessions that individually seem inconsequential, but can be devastating in compilation. The trick is to keep limitations and risks within reason until rival governments reach mutually agreeable settlements that need not be equitable.

NUCLEAR WARFARE NEXUS

Nuclear nations, whose members are expanding, might be tempted to use weapons of mass destruction rather than engage in protracted traditional combat or accept defeat.[44] Military strategists, in concert with practitioners of operational art, accordingly should review related problems and devise fresh solutions in light of technological developments.

Perceived Problems

Theater nuclear weapons in the early 1950s made threatened countries reconsider military doctrines, tactics, and standing operating procedures. Skeptics questioned whether traditional land and amphibious forces in particular could survive on nuclear battlefields, much less accomplish essential missions.

Proposed Solutions

The United States Army, whose only nuclear-capable adversary then was the Soviet Union, planned to disperse self-contained combat battalions three to five miles apart on a nonlinear battlefield to a depth of 100 miles or more, each prepared to move forward, laterally, or backwards like chess pieces. The intent was to assemble requisite forces rapidly at critical times and places, deliver decisive blows, then separate. "Mass for combat, scatter to survive" became the formula for victory.[45]

Lieutenant General Roy S. Geiger, an amphibious warfare expert who witnessed nuclear tests at Bikini Lagoon in June–July 1946, advised the Commandant of the Marine Corps that "a small number of atomic bombs could destroy an expeditionary force as now organized, embarked, and landed." A naval board the following December concluded that "the answer lies in a wide dispersion of our attack force, a rapid concentration of our landing force by means other than small boats or amphibians and thereafter maintaining close contact with the enemy."[46] Heliborne assault troops, coupled with carrier-based and vertical takeoff/landing (VTOL) aircraft for fire support, became prescribed centerpieces. Colonel Robert E. Cushman, Jr., a future Commandant, opined that resultant capabilities would "cut down the danger from that of disaster to that of calculated risks."[47]

Practical Impediments

Serious obstacles arose when U.S. Armed Services tried to put those principles into practice. Abilities to control quick concentrations, strikes, and dispersals on envisaged scales were nonexistent. Neither the Army's target acquisition systems nor its direct fire weapons could cover three- to five-mile intervals between isolated combat battalions. Artillery was quantitatively and qualitatively unable to compensate. Theater nuclear weapons would have endangered defenders almost as much as foes, if used to take up the slack. Enemy forces consequently might have been able to operate with considerable impunity in the voids, perhaps even surround and eliminate each "island." Logistical vulnerabilities loomed, because supply lines that depended on aerial distribution were unreliable. So were the aircraft upon which amphibious doctrine depended in the 1950s.[48]

Present Prospects

Revolutionary changes have alleviated or eliminated most of the shortcomings just described. Technological improvements in the mill promise further improvements. Military strategists as a result might realistically reconsider discarded options to determine whether present and impending ways to shoot, move, communicate, and sustain might make modern armed forces more viable if nuclear and traditional warfare overlap.

TRADITIONAL WARFARE FULCRUM

Traditional deterrent and war-fighting strategies demand far greater versatility than those that feature nuclear, biological, or chemical weapons. Traditional forces, like symphony orchestras, perform best when they possess alternative means to attain required ends. Land, sea, air, amphibious, and space forces bereft of multiple options can neither cope with known problems nor contend with unanticipated contingencies most effectively. Flexibility, in short, is the fulcrum.

KEY POINTS

- No military service is best suited for all purposes under all conditions
- Traditional deterrent and war-fighting strategies offer far greater flexibility than those that feature nuclear, biological, or chemical weapons
- Traditional military capabilities in large measure reflect how well land, sea, amphibious, and air forces mesh
- Well-balanced traditional forces enjoy much greater freedom of action than those that excessively rely on land, sea, or air power
- Highly capable, clearly visible forces that are permanently positioned to block aggression are better able to bolster deterrence than those that appear intermittently
- Deterrence additionally benefits from strong expeditionary forces that are initially self-sufficient and ready to fight on arrival
- Potent capabilities contribute most to deterrence only if accompanied by obvious will to employ that power if provoked
- Qualitative superiority can offset quantitative inferiority up to some undefinable point, but good large forces generally defeat good small ones
- Limited wars demand willingness to settle for less than any combatant would like
- The trick is to keep limitations and risks within reason until rival governments reach agreeable settlements that need not be equitable
- Unique strategic and tactical problems would arise if traditional and nuclear warfare overlap

NOTES

1. Martin Blumenson, "Of Land Powers and Sea Powers" and Sir Julian Corbett, "Inherent Differences in the Conditions of War on Land and on Sea," both in *The Art and Practice of Military Strategy,* ed. George Edward Thibault (Washington: National Defense University Press, 1984), 36–41, 169–72.

2. Allen R. Millett, *Semper Fidelis: The History of the United States Marine Corps,* rev. ed. (New York: Macmillan, 1991), 287–318, 475–517, 559–606.

3. Excerpts from "Alfred Thayer Mahan," ed. Allen Westcott, 103–5, 114–17; Sir Julian Corbett, "Some Principles of Maritime Strategy," 161–74; and Admiral of the Fleet of the Soviet Union Sergei G. Gorshkov, "The Sea Power of the State," 224–32, 239–44, 248–54, all in Thibault, *The Art and Practice of Military Strategy.*

4. Clark G. Reynolds, *Command of the Sea: The History and Strategy of Maritime Empires* (New York: Morrow, 1974); Michael H. H. Evans, *Amphibious Operations: The Projection of Sea Power Ashore* (Washington: Brassey's, 1990).

5. David R. Mets, *The Air Campaign: John Warden and the Classical Airpower Theorists* (Maxwell AFB, AL: Air University Press, 1998); Andrew G. B. Vallence, *The Air Weapon: Doctrines of Airpower Strategy and Operational Art* (New York: St. Martin's Press, 1996); John Gooch, ed., *Airpower: Theory and Practice* (Portland, OR: F. Case, 1995).

6. Alexander Boyd, *The Soviet Air Force Since 1918* (New York: Stein and Day, 1997), 110–114; Alan Clark, *Barbarossa: The Russian-German Conflict, 1941–1945* (New York: William Morrow and Co., 1965), 44–76.

7. Paul B. States, *Space and National Security* (Washington: Brookings Institution, 1987), 45–72; Thomas C. Brandt, "The Military Uses of Space," in *America Plans for Space* (Washington: National Defense University Press, 1986), 81–91.

8. Joint Pub. 1, *Joint Warfare of the Armed Forces of the United States* and Joint Pub. 0-2, *Unified Action Armed Forces* lay the foundation for U.S. joint doctrine (Washington: Office of the Chairman, Joint Chiefs of Staff). Joint Pubs. 1-0, 2-0, 3-0, 4-0, 5-0, and 6-0 respectively address Personell and Administration, Intelligence, Operations, Logistics, Plans, and C⁴ Systems.

9. *Soviet Military Power* (Washington: U.S. Government Printing Office, nine editions between 1981 and 1990 (none in 1982); *Military Forces in Transition* (Washington: Department of Defense, 1991).

10. *Whence the Threat to Peace?* (Moscow: Military Publishing House, USSR Ministry of Defense), 1st ed., January 1982; 2d ed., July 1982; 3d ed., August 1984.

11. Statistics are contained in John M. Collins, *U.S.-Soviet Military Balance, 1980-1985* (Washington: Pergamon-Brassey's, 1985), 260-63.

12. Quotation is from "General Bernard W. Rogers," *Armed Forces Journal,* September 1983, 80. See also General Bernard W. Rogers, "Raising the Nuclear Threshold," *Defense,* June 1984, 2, 4-6; *NATO: Can the Alliance Be Saved?,* Report of Senator Sam Nunn to the Senate Committee on Armed Services, 97th Cong., 2d sess. (Washington: U.S. Government Printing Office, 1982), 2-3.

13. Richard Hough, *The Battle of Britain: The Greatest Air Battle of World War II* (New York: W. W. Norton, 1990); Peter Fleming, *Operation Sea Lion* (New York: Simon and Schuster, 1957).

14. Trevor N. Depuy, *A Genius for War: The German Army and General Staff, 1807-1945* (Englewood Cliffs, NJ: Prentice-Hall, 1977), 253-99; Barrie Pitt, *The Battle of the Atlantic* (New York: Time-Life Books, 1977).

15. John Toland, *The Rising Sun: The Decline and Fall of the Japanese Empire, 1936-1945* (New York: Random House, 1970), 34-284.

16. *United States/Soviet Military Balance: A Frame of Reference for Congress,* Senate Committee on Armed Services, 94th Cong., 2d sess. (Washington: U.S. Government Printing Office, January 1976), 21-26.

17. Lieutenant General William P. Odom, *The Collapse of the Soviet Military* (New Haven, CT: Yale University Press, 1998); Stuart D. Goldman, *Russian Conventional Armed Forces: On the Verge of Collapse?* Rpt. 97-820-F (Washington: Congressional Research Service, September 4, 1997).

18. Recent writings include Naval Studies Board, Commission on Physical Sciences, Mathematics, and Applications, National Research Council, *Post-Cold War Conflict Deterrence* (Washington: National Academy Press, 1997); Gary L. Guertner, Robert Haffa, Jr., and George Questor, *Conventional Forces and the Future of Deterrence* (Carlisle Barracks, PA: Strategic Studies Institute, U.S. Army War College, May 20, 1992).

19. *What Have We Got for $1 Trillion?,* Hearings Before the Defense Policy Panel of the House Committee on Armed Services, 99th Cong., 1st sess. (Washington: U.S. Government Printing Office, 1987), 49-51. Quotation on 50.

20. "Address at the Air Force Academy Commencement Exercises in Colorado Springs, Colorado," *Public Papers of the Presidents of the United States: Nixon, 1969* (Washington: U.S. Government Printing Office, 1971), 436.

21. The U.S. Berlin Brigade's predicament is pungently described in Thomas C. Schelling, *Arms and Influence* (New Haven: CT: Yale University Press, 1966), 47.

22. Alfred B. Prados, *The Kurds of Iraq: Status, Protection and Prospects,* Rpt. 94-423F (Washington: Congressional Research Service, May 12, 1994); Kenneth Katzman, *Iraq: Marsh Arabs and U.S. Policy,* Rpt. 94-320F (Washington: Congressional Research Service, April 13, 1994).

23. "Saudi Not to Allow Use of Territory for Iraq Attacks," *Reuters News Wire,* (December 31, 1998, 00:55 AET).

24. Lieutenant General William G. ("Gus") Pagonis, *Moving Mountains: Lessons in Leadership and Logistics from the Persian Gulf War* (Boston: Harvard Business School Press, 1992), 6-7, 95-140; *Gulf War Air Power Survey,* vol. V, *A Statistical Compendium and Chronology* (Washington: U.S. Government Printing Office, 1993), Chapter 3 summarizes personnel strengths, strike aircraft arrivals, airlift, and sealift.

25. Insight Team of the London *Sunday Times, The Yom Kippur War* (Garden City, NY: Doubleday & Co., 1974), 423-27.

26. T. R. Fehrenbach, *The Kind of War* (New York: Macmillan Co., 1963); Roy E. Appleman, *United States Army in the Korean War: South to the Naktong, North to the Yalu* (Washington: U.S. Government Printing Office, 1960).

27. Steven R. Bowman, *Bosnia and Kosovo: U.S. Military Operations,* Issue Brief 93056 (Washington: Congressional Research Service, April 1999).

28. General Nathan F. Twining, *Neither Liberty nor Safety: A Hard Look at U.S. Military Policy and Strategy* (New York: Holt, Rinehart and Winston, 1966), 102-14, 118. Quotations on 104-5.

29. Early writings include: Robert Endicott Osgood, *Limited War: The Challenge to American Strategy* (Chicago: University of Chicago Press, 1957); Henry A. Kissinger, *Nuclear Weapons and Foreign Policy,* 132-202, 224-33. More recently, see Christopher M. Gacek, *The Logic of Force: The Dilemma of Limited War in American Foreign Policy* (New York: Columbia University Press, 1994); Major General

Robert H. Scales, Jr., *Firepower in Limited War,* rev. ed. (Novato, CA: Presidio Press, 1994).

30. Bernard Brodie, *Strategy in the Missile Age* (Princeton, NJ: Princeton University Press, 1959), 308, 312–14, 334; Thomas C. Schelling, "Bargaining, Communication and Limited War," *Journal of Conflict Resolution,* vol. 1, no. 1 (March 1957) and *Arms and Influence,* 131–45, 19–203, 215–20.

31. Robert McClintock, *The Meaning of Limited War* (Boston: Houghton Mifflin Co., 1967), 205.

32. For land, sea, and air forces under the UN banner in Korea see Colonel Harry G. Summers, Jr., *Korean War Almanac* (New York: Facts on File, 1990), 288–91.

33. Colonel Trevor N. Dupuy, *Elusive Victory: The Arab-Israeli Wars, 1947–1974* (New York: Harper & Row, 1978), 237–38.

34. *Soviet Military Power,* 3d ed., April 1984, 123–24.

35. Twining, *Neither Liberty nor Safety,* 117.

36. Schelling, *Arms and Influence,* 131–35.

37. Old Testament, 1 Samuel 17. For analyses, see Major General Yigal Yadin, *The Art of Warfare in Biblical Lands,* vol. 2 (Jerusalem: International Publishing Co., 1963), 265–67.

38. David Detzer, *The Brink: Cuban Missile Crisis, 1962* (New York: Thomas Y. Crowell, 1979).

39. Rationales are available in Neil Sheehan et al., *The Pentagon Papers* (New York: Quadrangle Books, 1971).

40. Henry A. Kissinger, *Necessity for Choice: Prospects of American Foreign Policy* (New York: Anchor Books, Doubleday & Co., 1962), 63.

41. Schelling, *Arms and Influence,* 132–33, 134, 135.

42. Martin Blumenson, *Mark Clark* (New York: Condon & Weed, 1984), 213–16.

43. Alistair Horne, *To Lose a Battle: France, 1940* (Boston: Little, Brown, 1969), 94, 381–94, 561–64, 573; Larry Collins and Dominique Lapierre, *Is Paris Burning?* (New York: Pocket Books, 1965), 25–29, 79–80, 195–97, 275–80, 301–3, 316–20.

44. Kissinger, *Necessity for Choice,* 78–101.

45. General Willard C. Wyman, "Highlights of Army Doctrine," *Armor,* March–April 1958, 16; Lieutenant Colonel A. J. Bacevich, *The Pentomic Era: The U.S. Army between Korea and Vietnam* (Washington: National Defense University Press, 1986), 67–68, 104–5, 115–17; Lieutenant Colonel Jerry M. Sollinger, *Improving U.S. Theater Nuclear Doctrine* (Washington: National Defense University Press, 1983), 15.

46. Lieutenant Colonel Kenneth J. Clifford, *Progress and Purpose: A Developmental History of the United States Marine Corps, 1900–1970* (Washington: History and Museums Division, Hq. U.S. Marine Corps, 1973), 71–72.

47. Colonel J. D. Hittle, "Amphibious Warfare," *Marine Corps Gazette,* June 1954, 19; Colonel Robert E. Cushman, Jr., "Amphibious Warfare Tomorrow," *Marine Corps Gazette,* April 1955, 30–34.

48. Bacevich, *The Pentomic Era,* 68, 70, 117–18.

15. Insurgency Strategies

If a man does not keep pace with his companions,
perhaps it is because he hears a different drummer.
Let him keep step to the music which he hears,
however measured or far away.

Henry David Thoreau
Walden, XVIII, 1854

Insurgents defy established authorities and invaders for political, ideological, economic, social, religious, ethnic, or cultural reasons.[1] All march to different drummers than those whose mission is to deny them success, but not all forms of insurgency are of equal interest to military strategists. Conspiratorial coups d'état usually succeed or fail too quickly for national security policy-makers and planners to shape outcomes.[2] Abilities to stop spontaneous uprisings seem equally slim, as demonstrated during the Russian Revolution of 1917, a political time bomb that exploded in Petrograd, then gained irreversible momentum almost immediately.[3]

This chapter concentrates on three types of insurgency that are similar in every respect save opponents: revolutionary wars; counterrevolutions; and resistance movements, which aim to oust occupying powers. Concluding discussions address insurgent support for traditional military operations.[4]

THE NATURE OF INSURGENCIES

Insurgencies arguably are the most agile, sophisticated form of conflict. Opportunistic practitioners with infinite persistence and unstructured approaches to problem-solving thrive on chaos that they deliberately engender. Skilled craftsmen gain leverage from second-, third-, even fourth- and fifth-

level effects that unfold unpredictably. Trends toward ever greater complexity are evident.

Classical Insurgencies

Insurgent concepts, policies, plans, programs, and employment practices are so unlike those associated with traditional warfare that untutored onlookers fail to identify any rules at all, but patterns are perceptible (Table 18). Traditional conflicts, which emphasize military power, normally ignite abruptly to capitalize on surprise, whereas the transition from peace to war during most insurgencies is almost imperceptible, because instigators at the onset possess little clout, and thus must inch their way onto center stage. Belligerents and nonbelligerents traditionally remain separate and distinct, while combatants and noncombatants intermingle during insurgencies that admit no front lines or rear areas. Some insurgencies feature passive resistance,[5] but mass military insurrections, which are more common, recognize few restraints. Newsworthy acts of sabotage, ambushes, shootouts at barricades, assassinations, abductions, and hostage seizures attract most attention, even though political, economic, social, and psychological instruments are more important than armed force. Insurgents in any event benefit more from protracted confrontations than incum-

Table 18
Characteristics of Classical Insurgency

- Three stages are evident: preparation, progressive expansion, and culmination
- Preparations commonly are covert or clandestine
- Organizations typically include full-time cadres and part-time auxiliaries
- Cellular structures foster tight security
- Initial overtures usually are low-key and insidious
- Both sides seek support from or acceptance by the same population
- Primary battlefields thus lie within human minds
- There are no noncombatants or neutrals in the traditional sense
- Belligerents mingle with bystanders
- All must choose sides or accept dangerous consequences
- Military and paramilitary battlefields lack sharply defined boundaries
- Operations commonly are protracted
- Politico-military strategies employ finesse as well as force
- Psychological offensives are more important than military power
- Subversive activities take precedence over head-on collisions
- Psychological operations precede, accompany, and follow armed combat
- Inexpensive paramilitary forces possess sharp teeth and short logistical tails
- Political victory, however defined, invariably is the main aim
- Ends invariably justify means
- Complexities continue to increase

bent governments, because they have a lot less to lose and everything to gain.[6]

New Wave Insurgencies

Characteristics described above have become less clean-cut since religious fanatics, aggrieved ethnic groups, criminal gangs, clans (such as those that vie for ascendancy in Somalia), and other nongovernmental groups began to compete with nation-states in the post–Cold War world. "Good guys" and "bad guys" are more difficult to distinguish. Many of them conduct offbeat operations to achieve unorthodox objectives. Drug cartels in Colombia, for example, would rather control illicit narcotics traffic than replace the Government in Bogotá, which suffers from king-sized bureaucratic headaches. Conditions will

become increasingly complex and incidents likely will increase, if pronounced trends early in the twenty-first century are any indication.[7]

Cross-Purpose Insurgencies

Revolutions, counterrevolutions, and resistance movements that proceed concurrently at cross-purposes may introduce additional complications. French irregulars with Allied assistance, for example, uniformly opposed Nazi occupation forces and the puppet government in Vichy from mid-1940 until August 1944. Some continued to fight for nine more months, but whether Gaullists or Communist competitors would rule France in the aftermath generated bitter disputes until General Charles de Gaulle finally consolidated control after World War II ended in Europe.[8] Communist and non-Communist factions fought each other for eventual control of Yugoslovia[9] and the Philippines[10] during the same general time frame.

REVOLUTIONARY WARFARE

Revolutionary wars, which may be predominantly urban or rural, occasionally crop up in sophisticated countries, but spawn most often in impoverished, underprivileged societies. The classical aim is to convince a majority of the population that insurgent programs are preferable to those of the ruling regime, which allegedly disregards their needs and is powerless to protect misguided adherents. Supporting objectives and implementing actions variously seek to isolate governments from constituents and foreign countries, ruin their credits, overextend their resources, perhaps replace social structures, and ultimately seize power.[11]

Grievances

Revolutions rarely plague countries where the populace is too tired, hungry, downtrodden, and fearful to rebel.[12] Instead, they flourish most often where the will to revolt replaces passive acceptance of flagrant injustice. Emotional causes such as freedom, human rights, and equal opportunity need not be realistic or attainable, provided people are willing to die for them. Idealistic Chinese students who demanded democratic reforms knew that success was unlikely, but defiantly disregarded authorities who told them to cease and disperse. The People's Liberation Army on June 3–4, 1989, killed hundreds in Beijing's Tiananmen Square and wounded or arrested thousands more.[13] Dedicated revolutionaries moreover disdain time. Ho Chi Minh and his successors in Hanoi, for example, fought from 1945 to 1975 until they finally reunified Vietnam on Communist terms, despite staggering casualties and incalculable damage.[14]

Tribal rivalries remain the root of many uprisings in Africa, where only five out of thirty-two states (Cameroon, Ivory Coast, Senegal, Tanzania, and Tunisia) avoided at least one violent change of government between 1963, when President Sylvanus Olympio of Togo was assassinated, and 1997, when President Mobutu Sese Seko fled Zaire one leap ahead of Laurent Desiré Kabila's bloodthirsty guerrillas.[15] Unpopular regimes in any case invite insurgencies if they can't control exploitable frictions between rich and poor, old and young, peasants and proletariat, adversarial ethnic groups, and antagonistic religions.[16]

The Declaration of Independence by colonial North Americans espoused the right of self-determination as its cause. "We hold these rules to be self-evident," its signatories asserted, "that all men are created equal, that they are endowed by their Creator with certain unalienable rights, that among these are life, liberty and the pursuit of happiness. . . . That whenever any form of government becomes destructive of these ends, it is the right of the people to alter or to abolish it." All fifty-five signers thereby did "pledge to each other our lives, our fortunes, and our sacred honor."[17] That historic document has inspired oppressed peoples the world over since 1776, starting with the French Revolution, which began on July 14, 1789, when mobs stormed the Bastille.[18]

Guidance

Dreams without direction are useless. Blind passion may bind headless multitudes together temporarily, but charismatic leaders must fan the fires of revolution and focus frustrations to generate maximum power. Influential idealists and other fellow travellers, whom Lenin called "useful idiots," often assist. Hard-core adherents need not be numerous, according to T. E. Lawrence, whose guerrillas ran rings around Turkish troops in the Arabian Desert during World War I—rebellions, he opined, "can be made by 2 percent active in a striking force, and 98 percent passively sympathetic."[19]

Some prophets and exponents of revolutionary war put thoughts on paper, others are warriors, while a gifted few wield sword and pen equally well. Karl Marx and Friedrich Engels theorized that corrupt governments must be razed and replaced.[20] Vladimir Lenin and Leon Trotsky put those postulations into practice.[21] Mao Zedong, who shaped and implemented strategies suitable for China's peasantry, composed classic treatises on protracted war and guerrilla warfare while he confronted Chiang Kai-shek's Nationalist Government.[22] Ho Chi Minh and General Vo Nguyen Giap adapted Mao's politico-military doctrines to suit circumstances when they accosted the duly elected Government of South Vietnam.[23] Fidel Castro and Che Guevara slanted similar concepts for use in rural Latin America before they ousted Cuban dictator Fulgencio Batista.[24] Brazilian firebrand Carlos Marighella blazed the way for urban guerrillas everywhere about that same time.[25]

Organizations

Revolutionary organizations are like icebergs. Paramilitary guerrillas and a few direct action auxiliaries are merely the visible tips of vastly larger covert and clandestine undergrounds that plan, control, and sustain insurrections. Together, they comprise a team that rarely works well without close collaboration by all participants.

Undergrounds and Auxiliaries

Most undergrounds consist of a hard-core cadre that recruits, indoctrinates, and trains personnel for its own purposes and for guerrilla groups. Additional duties involve intelligence production, counterintelligence, munitions manufacture, transportation, communications, and fund-raising. Many part-time auxiliaries who lead otherwise normal lives perform special tasks (such as surreptitious message deliveries and newspaper printing) and special assignments (such as sabotage and assassination). Sympathetic lawyers defend accused revolutionaries in courts of law. Psychological warfare (PSYWAR) experts in the perception management business circulate petitions and feed stories to members of the news media. They also spread rumors designed to brighten rebel images and discredit the government. Threats, intimidation, coercion, and emotional stress all help create converts when logic and inducements fail. Revolutionary propaganda holds a heavy advantage, because rebels are judged by promises, not what they produce, while incumbents must run on their records.[26]

Cellular structures enhance security (Figure 4). Rudimentary undergrounds commonly open with a multipurpose nucleus that seldom exceeds ten individuals, and may be somewhat smaller. The least successful self-destruct or stagnate at that stage, while others mature as multifaceted syndicates with numerous offshoots. Groups grow by adding cells instead of expanding those extant to minimize compromise. Intermediaries called "cutouts" separate "chiefs" from "indians" and cells from each other, so prisoners who crack under interrogation can furnish captors with few lucrative leads. Some organizations perform support tasks step-by-step in series to keep cells small. Cell 1 might buy material to make munitions, while Cell 2 manufactures components, Cell 3 assembles weapons, and Cell 4 disseminates finished products.[27]

Tight control from top to bottom decreases duplication of effort but forfeits flexibility, because high-level leaders with limited appreciation for local peculiarities are poorly positioned to determine what tools and techniques might be most useful at any given time or place. Excessive centralization also reduces the ability of cell chiefs to attack targets of opportunity and make other time-sensitive decisions. Vulnerabilities burgeon, because frequent meetings and increased communication requirements make cabals unnecessarily conspicuous (whether access to the Internet will exacerbate or cure that problem remains uncertain). Succession can pose prickly problems if "kingpins" become casualties. Most groups accordingly favor "steering committees" that prescribe policies, concepts, procedures, and priorities, but let subordinate cells act on their own initiative.

Guerrilla Groupments

The term "guerrilla," which means "little war," entered military lexicons in the early 1800s, when Spanish and Portuguese *guerrilleros* helped Wellington drive Napoleon Bonaparte's forces from the Iberian Peninsula back into France.[28] Paramilitary bands specialize in sabotage, hit-and-run raids, and ambushes, but seldom try to hold terrain against determined opposition. Guerrillas, like undergrounds from which they draw strength, emphasize political education and issue awareness. They habitually assign high priorities to agitation and propaganda, because victory is obtainable only if they enlist mass support for insurgent causes.[29]

Guerrillas generally establish bases and conduct operations within geographical areas of responsibility where they live. Units that deploy farther afield need intelligence from regional commanders who are intimately familiar with local terrain, customs, and enemy activities.[30] Organizational structures usually parallel those of regular armed forces, tailored to suit available manpower pools and prevalent situations. Fidel Castro, for example, employed squads, platoons, and companies,[31] whereas Mao mustered undersized formations that, for propa-

Figure 4
Cellular Underground Organizations

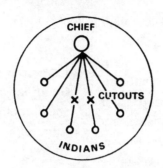

SIMPLE SETUP
Nothing But a
Multipurpose Nucleus

COMPLEX SETUP
Mature and Multifaceted

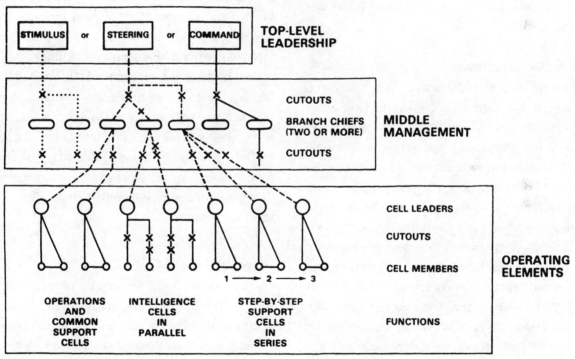

LEGEND

——— Central control
– – – – Centralized policy, decentralized operations
········· Decentralized control

Cell operations always are solid lines

NOTES:
1. Branch chiefs are required only if there are many cells.
2. Threats to group security dictate the number of cutouts.
3. The number of cells varies; members average 3 - 10, rarely more.
4. Operations and support cells function as teams.
5. Intelligence cells function as individuals.
6. Leaders at any level may enlist solitary specialists.
7. Members from several cells may make up a temporary task force.
8. Operations and support cells may be single or multipurpose.
9. Step-by-step support requires sequential collaboration.
10. Part-time auxiliaries and informal support functions do not show.

ganda purposes, he called battalions, regiments, and divisions.[32] Captured weapons, equipment, and supplies reduce needs for elaborate logistical depots.

Revolutionary Phases

Mao Zedong pursued a three-phase revolutionary strategy during China's protracted war against Japan: Strategic Defensive; Preparation for Counteroffensive; Strategic Counteroffensive. Different phases proceeded concurrently in different parts of the country. When rebels ran into stiff resistance, they changed tactics or retrenched, then rejuvenated.[33] Undergrounds and guerrillas around the world subsequently adapted Mao's concepts to suit revolutionary requirements in vastly different environments. Preparation, Expansion, and Culmination best describe the three phases associated with most modifications.

Phase I: Preparation

Underground activities dominate during Phase I, which lays the foundation for expansion. Insurgents first recruit cadres, investigate social class structures, identify complaints, and accumulate intelligence files needed to formulate propaganda themes and plans. To gain support, they infiltrate and subvert grassroots organizations such as schools, clubs (including Boy Scouts and Campfire Girls or equivalents), unions, cooperatives, business associations, police, armed forces, intelligence communities, and governmental offices at every level. Activists establish new cliques where few or none exist and attack those that resist. No institution that grants contact is too ostentatious or too obscure. Success ensures access to, and influence over, ranks and files.

Rebel leaders, when ready, labor to establish a system of "dual power," wherein a subversive shadow government vies with duly constituted authority for control. Coercion goes hand-in-glove with persuasion. Well-organized insurgents begin to sponsor widespread boycotts, black markets, insidious rumor campaigns, demonstrations, strikes, riots,

and other disorders that are cheap to produce and costly to counter. Unchecked operations eventually become so disruptive and responses so repressive that afflicted populations tend to endorse revolutionary programs rather than endure continued chaos.

Phase II: Expansion

Guerrilla warfare gains momentum during Phase II. Small, mobile groups rely on raids to secure arms, ammunition, medical supplies, and radios while civilian sympathizers furnish food, clothing, shelters, and a steady stream of current intelligence concerning governmental capabilities, intentions, plans, and ongoing operations.

Mao, a master of simulation and dissimulation, heeded Sun Tzu, his mentor many times removed.[34] "Avoid the solid," he advised, and "attack the hollow." Guerrillas, he continued, should "withdraw when [a stronger enemy] advances; harass him when he stops; strike him when he is weary; pursue him when he withdraws."[35] Discreet insurgents who disperse to survive and concentrate to fight at times and places of their choosing thus may be outnumbered ten to one, yet incessantly pit ten against one during minor engagements that create demoralizing results in compilation.

Phase III: Culmination

Classical insurgents during Phase III seek conclusive victory. Traditional armed forces augment guerrillas in efforts to defeat government troops decisively and thereby culminate conflict on their own immutable terms. Stubborn negotiators, who steadfastly pursue parallel paths that lead toward victory, tend to compromise only when so doing undercuts opponents, fosters favorable public opinion, otherwise supports revolutionary programs, or deflects impending defeat.[36] New wave insurgencies in contrast rarely require decisive shootouts. Iranian revolutionaries, for example, toppled Shah Mohammed Reza Pahlavi in January 1979 without engaging his vaunted armed forces.[37]

Outside Support

Insurgencies sometimes succeed without any outside assistance, but material and moral support in the form of military education, training, advice, PSYOP, logistical gifts, funds, and/or armed forces gives rebels a great boost. Patrons, however, must determine whether pluses outweigh minuses before they decide to contribute. Consider, for example, the Iraqi Liberation Act, which President Clinton signed on October 31, 1998. It vested him with discretionary authority over $97 million in military aid for use by factions that hope to unhorse Iraqi President Saddam Hussein. The Fiscal Year 1999 Defense Appropriations Bill reportedly included funds with which to shape related public opinion in Iraq and neighboring countries; organize, equip, and train a liberation army; then progressively expand territories under opposition control.[38] Skeptical General Anthony C. Zinni, then Commander in Chief of U.S. Central Command, told the Senate that arming any of the ninety-one opposition groups could be destabilizing. The Turkish Government, which perennially confronts Kurdish separatists along its borders, agreed.[39] Dissenters conversely contend that relatively small U.S. investments could reap large benefits, because Iraqi countermeasures would be costly in terms of money, manpower, materiel, time, and effort, whether would-be "liberators" won or lost.

Offbeat Approaches

National security policy-makers and military strategists should remain aware that not all revolutionaries mimic Mao's three classical phases. Aung San Suu Kyi, the 1991 Nobel Peace Prize recipient, advocates and practices nonviolent defiance of the brutal military junta that governs Myanmar (Burma). Phase I is an overt operation; Phases II and III play no part in her plans.[40] Castro's guerrilla bands, which never

numbered much more than 2,000 lightly armed men, compelled the Cuban Government to capitulate in December 1958 after a few Phase II engagements.[41] The U.S. Civil War opened on April 12, 1861 when Confederate forces fired on the tiny Federal garrison at Fort Sumter, South Carolina. Undergrounds and guerrillas played strategically insignificant roles throughout that four-year Phase III conflict, which terminated on April 9, 1865 when General Robert E. Lee surrendered to General Ulysses S. Grant at Appomattox Court House, Virginia.[42]

COUNTERREVOLUTIONS

Some insurrections produce results that satisfy concerned populations. Others prompt counterrevolutions designed to restore the original government and social order or replace them with substitutes that most citizens consider palatable. Strategies, tactics, forces, and techniques are indistinguishable in most respects from those that revolutionaries employ.

Soviet Experiences

Occupants of the Kremlin, long before and during the Cold War, rejected rights of national self-determination. Associated policies, eventually enshrined in the Brezhnev Doctrine, opposed counterrevolutions anywhere in the Socialist sphere and promised swift retribution for infractions.[43] That adjudication justified repressive actions on four occasions: three inside the "Soviet Empire," plus one on its periphery.

Successes in Central Europe

The first clash occurred in East Berlin, where anti-Communist rioters on June 17, 1953 hurled brickbats and Molotov cocktails at Soviet tanks before troops crushed their brief rebellion.[44] Hungarian insurgents surfaced in October 1956, when Premier Imre Nagy repudiated the Warsaw Pact and proclaimed an independent, neutral nation. Soviet Armed Forces routed mostly leaderless mobs after internal security agents abducted, then executed, Nagy and Pal Maleter, his Minister of Defense.[45] Warsaw Pact troops from the Soviet Union, Poland, Hungary, and Bulgaria converged on Czechoslovakia in August 1968, deposed Prime Minister Alexander Dubcek, and reestablished a cooperative Communist government.[46] NATO protested vigorously in each instance, but never threatened to intervene militarily, because risks of nuclear war seemed unacceptable.

Failure in Afghanistan

Catastrophic failure followed those three successes when Leonid Brezhnev invoked his own doctrine on Christmas Eve 1979 after Mujahideen insurgents in neighboring Afghanistan put Moscow's puppet regime at risk. The ensuing conflict lasted longer than the Great Patriotic War against Nazi Germany, but "victory" remained elusive despite awesome Soviet military power and merciless tactics. The Soviet rear guard withdrew on February 15, 1989 after Mikhail Gorbachev concluded that ends and means were badly mismatched.[47]

Sandinista Experiences

Anastasio Somoza's family rode roughshod over Nicaragua and lined their pockets with ill-gotten gains for forty years until 1978, when the Inter-American Commission on Human Rights and the United Nations General Assembly censured atrocities they attributed to Anastasio Junior's National Guard. That despot, bereft of politicomilitary support, fled on July 17, 1979, one step ahead of left-leaning Sandinista insurgents who launched their final offensive from sanctuaries in Costa Rica.[48]

Foreign policy problems cropped up almost immediately between the anti-Communist Reagan Administration and Marxists in Managua, who received arms, equipment, supplies, and advice from Cuba and the Soviet bloc. Whether U.S. military aid might have enabled counterrevolutionary Contra guerrillas

to defeat the Sandinistas in battle became moot after 1984 when Congress, which had been ambivalent from the beginning, forbade "assistance of any kind, either directly or indirectly, to any person or group engaging in an insurgency or other act of rebellion against the Government of Nicaragua."[49]

The infamous Iran-Contra affair ensued when frustrated officials in the U.S. National Security Council sought to outflank that congressional injunction. First, they sold TOW antitank missiles to Iran at inflated prices, then illegally funneled surplus funds to their Contra clients. Cover-up efforts failed and heads rolled when facts surfaced,[50] but severe sanctions coupled with Sandinista economic ineptitude and war costs caused Nicaragua's GNP to dive and inflation to soar. Mediation efforts by a colloquium of Central American nations culminated with internationally supervised elections on February 26, 1990, which counterrevolutionaries won decisively.[51]

RESISTANCE MOVEMENTS

Anticolonial sentiments inspired many resistance movements in the twentieth century. Military occupation motivated most of the remainder (Table 19). All possessed popular support. All copied revolutionary strategies, tactics, and techniques, but no operations progressed beyond Phase II, save those during Mao's struggle to eject Japanese invaders (1935–1945) and Ho Chi Minh's efforts to free Indochina from France (1946–1954).[52]

Resistance movements commonly become thumb-in-the-eye, knee-in-the-groin, winner-take-all contests that would sicken the Marquis of Queensbury. Compassionless Mau Maus butchered neutral and intolerant countrymen along with British landholders and livestock in Kenya (1952–1960).[53] One group of Croatian sadists, who sided with Hitler's henchmen in Yugoslavia during World War II, chopped off noses, ears, breasts, and limbs, poured salt into wounds, and buried or burned vic-

Table 19
Typical Resistance Movements in the Twentieth Century

Resist Colonial Rule		Resist Military Occupations	
Europe		**Europe**	
Ireland vs. Britain	(1916–21)	Poland vs. Nazi Germany	(1939–44)
Cyprus vs. Britain	(1954–58)	France vs. Nazi Germany	(1940–44)
		Norway vs. Nazi Germany	(1940–45)
		Belgium vs. Nazi Germany	(1940–44)
		Denmark vs. Nazi Germany	(1940–45)
		Netherlands vs. Nazi Germany	(1940–45)
		USSR vs. Nazi Germany	(1941–44)
		Yugoslavia vs. Nazi Germany	(1941–44)
		Greece vs. Italy, Nazi Germany	(1942–44)
Asia		**Asia**	
Philippines vs. United States	(1899–1902)	China vs. Japan	(1934–45)
India vs. Britain	(1942–47)	Burma vs. Japan	(1942–45)
Indochina vs. France	(1945–54)	Philippines vs. Japan	(1942–45)
Indonesia vs. Netherlands	(1946–49)	Tibet vs. China	(1951–60)
Malaya vs. Britain	(1948–60)		
Middle East		**Middle East**	
Israelis vs. Britain	(1945–48)	Arabs vs. Ottoman Turks	(1916–18)
Africa		**Africa**	
Southwest Africa vs. Germany	(1904–07)	Boers vs. Britain	(1899–1902)
Morocco vs. Spain	(1921–26)	Ethiopia vs. Fascist Italy	(1937–41)
Kenya vs. Britain	(1952–60)		
Northern Rhodesia vs. Britain	(1953–64)		
Algeria vs. France	(1954–62)		
Congo vs. Belgium	(1957–60)		
Portuguese Guinea vs. Portugal	(1959–74)		
Angola vs. Portugal	(1961–75)		
Mozambique vs. Portugal	(1964–75)		

tims alive. Ante Pavelic, their leader, once brandished a wicker basket filled with gouged out eyeballs. "You Germans use bullets," his spokesman boasted, "but we use hammers, clubs, ropes, fire, and quicklime. It's less expensive."[54]

Proclivities to compromise are low during such high stakes endeavors, as they are during revolutionary wars and counterrevolutions, because resistance leaders who waver lose the confidence of people whose support they seek to enlist. Outlooks consequently appear pessimistic for statesmen and well-meaning mediators whose mission is to craft peace accords that all belligerents seem likely to honor.

TRADITIONAL WARFARE NEXUS

Insurgents in the midst of traditional wars often act as "force multipliers" that delay, deceive, disorganize, and otherwise disrupt enemy military operations. Undergrounds and guerrillas not only furnish regular armed forces with invaluable intelligence, but make life miserable for adversaries along vulnerable lines of communication and in lightly defended rear areas.[55]

Subversive Activities

Foreign correspondents with Spanish Nationalist General Emilio Mola Vidal in November 1936 asked which of his four converging columns would be in the vanguard when he captured Madrid. My "Fifth Column," he replied, which was composed of subversives, espionage agents, saboteurs, and rabble-rousers already inside the city. Similar accomplices infested Bilbao, Cartegena, Gijón, Santander, and Valencia. Missions in each instance were to infiltrate policy-making machinery and news media, foment disaffection, undermine morale, and otherwise assist or obviate traditional military operations against key cities. Successes contributed significantly to Generalissimo Francisco Franco's victory.[56] Fifth Columns subsequently arranged flower-strewn welcomes for Hitler's Storm Troopers in the Rhineland (1936), Austria (1938), and the Sudetenland (1938).[57] Comparable subversion assisted Soviet takeovers in several countries between the Baltic and Black Seas shortly after World War II subsided.[58]

Coordinated Combat

Guerrillas and regular armed forces have been complementary on many occasions. Linkages are tight in some instances, intentionally loose in others. Light touches sometimes accomplish more than heavy hands. National security policy-makers and military strategists must decide which tack to take.

Tight Surface-to-Surface Ties

Partisans who jeopardized German lifelines in European Russia during World War II habitually increased operational tempo immediately before and during Soviet ground combat offensives. Saboteurs on the night of June 19–20, 1944, demolished more than 10,000 targets that ran through and around the Pripet Marshes. Main efforts severed all rail lines that served the Third Panzer Army, which Marshal Georgy Zhukov attacked the next day. German Army Group Center, engaged in a titanic struggle with the First, Second, and Third White Russian Fronts, collapsed a week later, partly because there was no way to deliver supplies fast enough in sufficient quantities to sustain high-pressure combat. Rear-area security requirements before and after that momentous event deprived German frontline divisions of much needed arms, equipment, supplies, and at least 100,000 men.[59]

Tight Surface-to-Air Ties

OSS Detachment 101, which consisted of a small U.S. nucleus and 10,000 Kachin tribesmen, killed more than 5,000 Japanese soldiers and severed enemy supply lines in northern Burma during World War II. Linkage with Allied ground forces was nearly nonexistent, but Detachment 101 fed the Tenth U.S. Air Force with precise information concerning the size, location, dispositions, and movement of enemy troops that aerial observers could not find in dense jungles. Unique search and rescue capabilities retrieved scores of air transport crews that Japanese gunners shot down as they flew from India to China and back again across the Himalayan "Hump."[60]

Intentionally Loose Ties

Lawrence of Arabia operated independently from 1916 through 1918 along a line that ran from Medina near the Red Sea to Damascus, partly by choice, but primarily because his guerrilla war against the Ottoman Turks "was so odd and far away that coy Authority left us to ourselves. We had no base machinery, no formal staff, no clerks, no government, no telegraphs, no public opinion, no troops of British nationality." Contact between Lawrence's legions and General Sir Edmund Allenby's expeditionary forces was nil. When peace came, Lawrence's will-o'-the-wisp Arab guerrillas had killed, wounded, or worn out about 35,000 Turks; captured an equal number; imposed immense static security burdens along the Hejaz Railroad; and occupied 100,000 square miles of Turkish territory at minimal cost to themselves. That "side-show of a side-show," which deliberately avoided armed combat whenever possible, almost won the Middle East war without major battles.[61]

KEY POINTS

- Insurgencies demand fundamentally different treatment than traditional warfare
- Insurgencies originate most often in societies where flagrant injustices, real or imagined, inflame the populace and inspire rebellion
- Strong rebel leaders normally must focus the energies of emotional masses who are willing to die for political, ideological, economic, social, religious, ethnic, or cultural causes
- Underground cells plan, control, and sustain insurrections from havens inside urban or rural communities
- Guerrillas generally conduct paramilitary raids, ambushes, and sabotage within areas of operation that they know well
- Psychological offensives normally are more important than armed combat
- Insurgent strategies often proceed from Phase I (Preparation) through Phase II (Expansion) to Phase III (Culmination) but, except for Phase I, rebels alter that sequence to suit circumstances
- Foreign patrons who furnish material and moral support give rebels a great boost, but must decide beforehand and periodically review whether benefits outweigh liabilities
- Insurgents tend to compromise only when so doing undercuts opponents, fosters favorable public opinion, otherwise promotes their programs, or deflects defeat
- Insurgents who delay, deceive, disorganize, and disrupt enemy operations sometimes augment traditional military capabilities at crucial times and places

NOTES

1. For a concise review of valuable references, see Robert T. Bunker, "Unconventional Warfare Philosophers," *Small Wars and Insurgencies,* vol. 10, no. 3 (Winter 1999), 136-49.

2. Edward N. Luttwak, *Coup d'État* (New York: Alfred A. Knopf, 1969).

3. Richard Pipes, *The Russian Revolution* (New York: Alfred A. Knopf, 1990).

4. Robert S. Asprey, *War in the Shadows: The Guerrilla in History,* vol. I and II, (Garden City, NY: Doubleday & Co., 1975); Doris M. Condit, Bert H. Cooper, Jr., et al., eds., *Challenge and Response in International Conflicts* (Washington: Center for Research in Social Systems, American University), vol. 1, *The Experience in Asia* (February 1968); vol. II, *The Experience in Europe and the Middle East* (March 1967); vol. III, *The Experience in Africa and Latin America* (April 1968); *Supplement,* Dominican Republic, Haiti, Laos (September 1968).

5. For passive resistance precepts, see Penderel Moon, *Gandhi and Modern India* (New York: Norton, 1969); Martin Luther King, Jr., *Why We Can't Wait* (New York: Harper & Row, 1963), especially Chapter 5, "Letter From Birmingham Jail."

6. Sir Robert Thompson, *Revolutionary War in World Strategy, 1945-1969* (New York: Taplinger Publishing Co., 1970), 16-18, 19-20, 21-22; Robert Taber, *The War of the Flea* (New York: Lyle Stuart, 1965), 45-46, 57.

7. Comments on a draft of this chapter by U.S. Special Operations Command, September 1999.

8. Charles B. McDonald, "France (1940-1944)," in Condit, Cooper, et al., *Challenge and Response in International Conflicts,* vol. 2, 112-50; Blake Erlich, *Resistance: France 1940-1945* (Boston: Little, Brown, 1965).

9. Earl Ziemke, "Yugoslavia (1941-1944)," in Condit, Cooper, et al., *Challenge and Response in International Conflicts,* vol. II, 320-51; Ronald H. Bailey, *Partisans and Guerrillas* (New York: Time-Life Books, 1978), 74-151.

10. Edward Geary Lansdale, *In the Midst of Wars* (New York: Harper and Row, 1972), 6-9; Robert Ross Smith, "The Philippines (1946-1954)," in Condit, Cooper, et al., *Challenge and Response in International Conflicts,* 474-507.

11. John Shy and Thomas W. Collier, "Revolutionary War," in *Makers of Modern Strategy: From Machiavelli to the Nuclear Age,* ed. Peter Paret (Princeton,

NJ: Princeton University Press, 1986), 815-62; Thompson, *Revolutionary War in World Strategy, 1945-1969,* 4, 5-6, 25.

12. Ted Robert Gurr, *Why Men Rebel* (Princeton, NJ: Princeton University Press, 1970); Eric Hofer, *The True Believer: Thoughts on the Nature of Mass Movements* (New York: HarperCollins, reissue 1989); Franz Fanon, *The Wretched of the Earth* (New York: Grove Press, 1963); Clarence Crane Brinton, *The Anatomy of Revolution* (New York: Random House, 1966).

13. For a recount of actions at Tiananmen Square, see Nicholas D. Kristof, "China Update: How the Hardliners Won," *New York Times Magazine,* November 12, 1989.

14. Bernard B. Fall, "Indochina (1946-1954)" and "South Viet-Nam (1956-1963)," in Condit, Cooper, et al., *Challenge and Response in Internal Conflict,* vol. I, 237-69, 321-75; Asprey, *War in the Shadows,* vol. II, 977-1391.

15. John Reader, *Africa: A Biography of the Continent* (New York: Alfred A. Knopf, 1998).

16. Thompson, *Revolutionary War in World Strategy, 1945-1969,* 6, 8-9; Taber, *The War of the Flea,* 11, 13-14.

17. Vincent Wilson, Jr., ed., "The Declaration of Independence," in *The Book of Great American Documents,* 3d ed. (Brookville, MD: American History Research Associates, 1993), 11-19.

18. William Doyle, *The Oxford History of the French Revolution* (New York: Oxford University Press, reprint 1990).

19. T. E. Lawrence, "The Evolution of a Revolt," *Army Quarterly and Defense Journal,* October 1920; reprinted in Stanley and Rodelle Weintraub, eds., *Evolution of a Revolt: Early Postwar Writings of T. E. Lawrence* (University Park, PA: Pennsylvania State University, 1968), 100-19. Quotation on 119.

20. Karl Marx, *Capital, The Communist Manifesto and Other Writings,* ed. Max Eastman, with an unpublished essay on Marxism by Lenin (New York: Modern Library, 1932), 315-55; Robert C. Tucker, ed., *The Marx-Engels Reader* (New York: Norton, 1978).

21. Stefan T. Possony, ed., *Lenin Reader* (Chicago: H. Regnery, 1966), especially 310-498; Vladimir Il'ich Lenin, *What Is to Be Done?,* trans. S. V. and Patricia Utechin, ed. S. V. Utechin (Oxford: Clarendon Press, 1963); Dimitrii A. Volkogonov, *Trotsky: The Eternal Revolutionary,* trans. and ed. Harold Shukman (New York: Free Press, 1996).

22. Mao Zedong, *Chairman Mao Tse-tung on People's War* (Beijing: Foreign Languages Press, 1967). Also,

Mao, *On Protracted War,* 2d ed. (Beijing: Foreign Languages Press, 1960) and *On Guerrilla Warfare,* trans. and with an introduction by Samuel B. Griffith (New York: Praeger, 1961).

23. Ho Chi Minh, *On Revolution: Selected Writings, 1920-1966,* ed. Bernard Fall (Boulder, CO: Westview Press, 1984); General Vo Nguyen Giap, *People's War, People's Army* (New York: Praeger, 1962).

24. Roland E. Bonachea and Nelson P. Valdéz, eds., *Revolutionary Struggle, 1947-1958: Selected Works of Fidel Castro,* vol. 1 (Cambridge, MA: MIT Press, 1972), especially 155-59, 341-449; Che Guevara, *On Guerrilla Warfare* (New York: Praeger, 1961).

25. Carlos Marighella, *Minimanual of the Urban Guerrilla* (Vancouver, Canada: Pulp Press, 1974).

26. *The Organizer's Manual* (Boston: O. M. Collective, undated); Andrew R. Molnar et al., *Undergrounds in Insurgency, Revolutionary, and Resistance Warfare* (Washington: Special Operations Research Office, American University, November 1963); DA Pamphlet No. 550-104, *Human Factors Considerations of Undergrounds in Insurgencies* (Washington: Headquarters, Department of the Army, September 1966).

27. Alexander Foote, *Handbook for Spies,* 2d ed. (London: Museum Press, 1953), 53-74; Molnar, et al., *Undergrounds in Insurgency, Revolutionary, and Resistance Warfare,* 52-54; *Human Factors Considerations of Undergrounds in Insurgencies,* 19-28.

28. Asprey, *War in the Shadows,* vol. I, 125-34; Leroy Thompson, *Ragged War: The Story of Unconventional and Counter-revolutionary Warfare* (London: Arms and Armour Press, 1974), 7-14.

29. *General Grivas on Guerrilla Warfare,* trans. A. S. Pallis (New York: Praeger, 1965).

30. Franklin M. Osanka, ed., *Modern Guerrilla Warfare* (New York: Free Press of Glencoe, 1967).

31. Guevara, *On Guerrilla Warfare,* 38.

32. Mao, *On Guerrilla Warfare,* 71-87.

33. Mao, *On Protracted War,* 43-65.

34. Sun Tzu, *The Art of War,* trans. Samuel B. Griffith (New York: Oxford University Press, 1963), 66-71.

35. Mao, *On Guerrilla Warfare,* 46.

36. Sir Robert Thompson, *No Exit from Vietnam* (New York: David McKay, 1969), 77-87.

37. John T. Stempel, *Inside the Iranian Revolution* (Bloomington: Indiana University Press, 1981).

38. H.R. 4655, *The Iraq Liberation Act of 1998* (PL 105-338), passed by the House of Representatives on October 5, 1998, by the Senate on October 20, 1998, and signed by President Clinton on October 30,

1998; Kenneth B. Katzman, *Iraq's Opposition Movements,* Rpt. 98-179F (Washington: Congressional Research Service, updated March 2, 1999); John Lancaster, "U.S. Gives Go-Ahead to Iraqi Opposition," *Washington Post,* January 14, 2001, A1, A22.

39. Vernon Loeb, "General Wary of Plan to Arm Groups in Iraq" and Thomas W. Lippman, "U.S. Builds Support for Ouster of Saddam," *Washington Post,* January 29, 1999, A19, A22; Scott Peterson, "Iraqi Dissident Groups Called Part of the Problem," *Washington Times,* December 2, 1998, A15.

40. Aung San Suu Kyi, *Freedom from Fear and Other Writings,* ed. Michael Aris (New York: Penguin Books, 1995). For perspectives, see Bertil Lintner, *Burma in Revolt: Opium and Insurgency Since 1948* (Boulder, CO: Westview Press, 1994).

41. John Heins, "Cuba (1953-1959)," in Condit, Cooper, et al., *Challenge and Response in International Conflicts,* vol. III, 435-61.

42. Shelby Foote, *Civil War: A Narrative,* 3 vols. (New York: Random House, 1974).

43. S. Kovalev, "Sovereignty and the International Obligation of Socialist Countries," *Pravda,* September 26, 1968, 4. Reprinted in *The Current Digest of the Soviet Press,* October 16, 1968, 10-12.

44. Stefan Brant, *The East German Rising, 17th June 1953,* trans. Charles Wheeler (New York: Praeger, 1957); Wolfgang H. Kraus, "East Germany (June 1953)," in Condit, Cooper, ed. al., *Challenge and Response in International Conflicts,* vol. II, 458-96.

45. David Pryce-Jones, *The Hungarian Revolution* (New York: Horizon Press, 1969); Leonard Bushkoff, "Hungary (October-November 1956)," in Condit, Cooper, et al., *Challenge and Response in International Conflicts,* vol. II, 530-78.

46. Harry Schwartz, *Prague's 200 Days: The Struggle for Democracy in Czechoslovakia* (New York: Praeger, 1969).

47. Joseph J. Collins, *The Soviet Invasion of Afghanistan: A Case Study in the Use of Force in Soviet Foreign Policy* (Lexington, MA: Lexington Books, 1986); David C. Isby, *War in a Distant Country, Afghanistan: Invasion and Resistance* (New York: Sterling Publishing Co., 1989).

48. Robert A. Pastor, *Condemned to Repetition: The United States and Nicaragua* (Princeton, NJ: Princeton University Press, 1987), 49-187; Shirley Chris-

tian, *Nicaragua: Revolution in the Family* (New York: Random House, 1985), 34-118.

49. James P. Seevers, "Key Congressional Actions," Annex B to John M. Collins, *America's Small Wars: Lessons for the Future* (Washington: Brassey's [U.S.], 1991), 256-58.

50. Peter Kornbluh and Malcolm Byrne, eds., *The Iran-Contra Scandal: The Declassified History (The National Security Archive Document)* (New York: New Press, May 1993).

51. Pastor, *Condemned to Repetition,* 191-320, 348-79; Robert F. Turner, *Nicaragua v. United States: A Look at the Facts* (New York: Pergamon-Brassey's, 1987).

52. Michael Lindsay, "China (1927-1937)" and "China (1937-1945)"; Bernard B. Fall, "Indochina (1946-1954)," all in Condit, Cooper, et al., *Challenge and Response in International Conflicts,* vol. I, 30-68, 138-77, 238-69.

53. Robert Ruark, *Something of Value,* reprint (New York: Buccaneer Books, 1991); Doris M. Condit, "Kenya (1952-1960)," in Condit, Cooper, et al., *Challenge and Response in International Conflicts,* vol. III, 270-311.

54. Bailey, *Partisans and Guerrillas,* 87, 104-13.

55. Russell Miller, *The Resistance* (New York: Time-Life Books, 1979).

56. Hugh Thomas, *The Spanish Civil War* (New York: Harper & Brothers, 1961), 317, 446-47, 470, 480, 591-92, 602.

57. Robert T. Elson, *Prelude to War* (New York: Time-Life Books, 1976), 185-211.

58. Saul Bernard Cohen, *Geography and Politics in a World Divided* (New York: Random House, 1963), 193-203.

59. DA Pamphlet 20-240, *Rear Area Security in Russia: The Soviet Second Front Behind the German Lines* (Washington: Department of the Army, July 1951), 1, 2, 13-35.

60. Lieutenant General William R. Peers and Dean Brelis, *Behind the Burma Road: The Story of America's Most Successful Guerrilla Force* (Boston: Little, Brown, 1963).

61. Weintraub, *Evolution of a Revolt,* 100-19. See also T. E. Lawrence, *Seven Pillars of Wisdom: A Triumph* (Garden City, NY: Garden City Publishing, 1938).

16. Counterinsurgency Strategies

I know of two types of warfare: mobile warfare and positional warfare. I never heard of revolutionary war.

General Charles de Gaulle
Quoted by Bernard B. Fall
Street Without Joy

French Armed Forces had been actively engaged against Viet Minh undergrounds and guerrillas for several years when General de Gaulle chastised a subordinate with that snide remark in 1950. Widely shared scorn for revolutionary warfare doctrine was still in vogue[1] when President René Coty, Premier Joseph Laniel, Foreign Minister Georges Bidault, General Henri Navarre (Commander in Chief, Indochina), Major General René Cogny (who commanded French troops in Tonkin), and Colonel Christian de Castries (on-site commander) presided over the debacle at Dien Bien Phu in May 1954, which terminated French suzerainty in Southeast Asia.[2] Algerian freedom fighters won their war for independence from France (November 1954–March 1962), partly because callous counterinsurgent forces antagonized common people, whose good will was essential.[3]

Latter-day Chiefs of State and their advisers who fail to appreciate the unique nature of revolutionary warfare, counterrevolutions, and resistance movements are apt to make equally expensive mistakes, because political, economic, social, psychological, and military operations are mutually dependent. Irresolute or irresponsible policy-makers can prevent or squander military victories, whereas myopic generals who ignore the primacy of nonmilitary programs make meaningful triumphs impossible.

THE NATURE OF COUNTERINSURGENCY

Indigenous governments mount counterinsurgency operations to forestall or defeat insurrections, whether rebel motives be anticolonial (nationalists vs. Britain in Malaya, 1948-1960[4]); secessionist (Eritrean separatists vs. Ethiopia, 1961-1993[5]); reformist (Iranian radicals vs. Mohammed Reza Shah Pahlavi, 1978-1979[6]); reactionary (Taliban fundamentalists vs. Islamic moderates in Afghanistan, 1994-1998[7]); ideological (Viet Cong Communists vs. embryonic democracy in South Vietnam, 1955-1975[8]); or some combination thereof. Invaders employ analogous techniques against resistance movements (undergrounds vs. Nazi Germans throughout occupied Europe, 1940-1945[9]).

Common Characteristics

There is no one best way to cope with all forms of insurrection,[10] but the foremost requirement should be to eradicate root causes and thereby reduce incentives for uprisings to flower. Contributory programs, based on first-rate intelligence, feature some combination of coercion and persuasion designed to justify national and local governments as the only legitimate sources of authority, eradicate underground infrastructures, squelch subversion, separate insurgents from sources of sustenance, and protect loyal segments of the populace against depredations by rebels.

Counterinsurgencies Compared with Traditional Conflicts

Counterinsurgencies share few characteristics with traditional warfare, and therefore demand different techniques (Table 20). Body counts on battlefields are less important than battles for human hearts and minds. Brutal tactics that quash the symptoms of insurrection but leave noxious causes intact may suppress rebellions for long periods, but strategists who hope to heal national wounds employ armed force primarily as a shield behind which benevolent programs give disaffected people genuine prospects for liberty, justice, security, and prosperity. Outsiders who hope to govern occupied territories peacefully pursue comparably benevolent policies.

Counterinsurgencies Compared with Insurgencies

Insurgents advocate radical change, whereas counterinsurgents aim to preserve or restore internal stability. Both seek voluntary support from or, at worst, passive acceptance by, the populace, because neither can achieve or retain control indefinitely if most citizens oppose their programs (Table 21). Beyond that, however, respective characteristics are asymmetrical at the onset.

Will-o'-the-wisp rebels nearly monopolize initiative during early stages of any insurrection. Small groups break cover and attack targets where and when they choose, seldom defend territory after

they become robust, and abide by few rules. Countermeasures, in contrast, are initially reactive, relatively large-scale, costly endeavors. "Ins" possess luxurious resources but, unlike "Outs," must protect people and property, plus the political, economic, and military trappings of national power that include industrial facilities, farmlands, communication nodes, command posts, logistical installations, lines of communication, and information repositories. Legal, moral, and ethical constraints limit permissible courses of action in democratic countries.[11]

ANTI-UNDERGROUND STRATEGIES

Insurrections, like cancer, can be countered best if detected and treated early. Enlightened rulers address grass-roots causes before malignancies appear. Governments that tarry invite subversion and, if corrective strategies fail, guerrilla warfare may flourish.

Tailored Intelligence

Incipient threats demand integrated political, military, economic, social, and psychological countermeasures that capitalize on incumbent credits and exploit insurgent liabilities, but radicals on the fringe of respectability are hard to recognize and preliminary evidence is subject to assorted interpretations. Strategic dilemmas commonly develop, because drastic crackdowns could damage the regime's reputation, while prolonged leniency could encourage full-fledged rebellions.

Counterinsurgency operations consequently demand descriptive and predictive intelligence concerning undergrounds, auxiliaries, and proclivities

Table 20

Counterinsurgencies Compared with Traditional Conflicts

	Traditional Conflicts	Counterinsurgencies
Initial Threats	Obvious	Ambiguous
Basic Objectives	Military Victory	Internal Stability
Decisive Strategies	Direct	Indirect
Decisive Power	Military	Sociopolitical
Technological Superiority	Telling	Trivial
Decisive Action	Defeat Enemy Forces	Ensure Popular Support
Conflict Duration	Variable	Protracted

Table 21

Counterinsurgencies Compared with Classical Insurgencies

	Insurgencies	Counterinsurgencies
Interests	Radical Change	Status Quo
Basic Objectives	Replace Authority	Preserve Authority
Infrastructrures	Relatively Meagre	Extensive
Tangible Resources	Few	Many
Armed Forces		
Regular Forces	None in Phase I or II	Yes
Security Forces	None	Yes
Police	None	Yes
Guerrillas	Phases II and III	No
Allied Forces	Sometimes	Sometimes
Operations	Mainly Covert	Mainly Overt
Legal, Moral Restraints	Few	Many*
Terrorism	Usually Acceptable	Usually Taboo*
Financial Costs	Low	High
Popular Support	Crucial	Crucial

*In democratic countries

of the populace to assist or resist insurgents. Military and civilian intelligence communities accumulate insights concerning insurgent hierarchies, strategies, tactics, successes, and failures, together with reasons therefor. They also amass basic data about races, creeds, customs, cultures, and other demographic matters that might motivate rebels to defect. Police, who are familiar with residents and routines, as a rule are better suited than armed forces to compile dossiers on known and suspected dissidents, their domiciles, families, friends, movements, methods of operation, and current activities. Intelligence agents most easily insinuate themselves into insurgent cells when undergrounds launch large-scale recruitment programs, because opportunities to do so diminish thereafter.[12]

Velvet Glove Operations

Executive, legislative, and judicial operations that emphasize finesse instead of force promote public safety and public welfare. Complementary programs in each category feature law enforcement, reforms, and civic actions.

Law Enforcement

Nascent insurgencies often tempt the most benevolent government officials to bend or break legal rules, because due processes and constitutional safeguards seem excessively restrictive. The British High Commissioner during anticolonial uprisings in Malaya, for example, promulgated emergency regulations that vested police with authority to detain suspects for two years without trial, to search without warrants, and banish suspected subversives. Other nations under siege by insurgents have restricted rights of free speech and assembly, banned publications, outlawed renegade organizations, and issued scrips or altered currencies to frustrate rebel financiers.[13]

Agreeable lines between subversion and legitimate public opposition to governmental policies nevertheless are hard to draw. Law-abiding citizens everywhere resent widespread arrests, preventive detention, mandatory death penalties for rebels who bear arms, harsh prison terms for lesser offenses, and the suspension of habeas corpus. Banned organizations tend to reappear under deceptive banners. Public trials that turn into sounding boards for insurgent causes often discredit the State and disillusion constituents.[14]

Realistic Reforms

Force frequently fails to curb insurrections unless coupled with reforms. Sandinista outcasts prevailed in Nicaragua, even though President Somoza's *Guardia Nacional* and security forces maintained military superiority from start to finish. Ruthless French troops clearly outclassed insurgents in Algeria, but finally lost that war. Counterinsurgency strategies that aim to manage rather than resist positive change offer greater flexibility. Typical reforms reapportion political influence, enhance economic opportunities, dampen social discontent, control corruption, and terminate uncivilized practices. Successes rally loyal factions, convert fence straddlers, preempt rebel causes, and reduce the insurgents' reservoir of recruits.[18]

Reforms indeed shortstopped rampant civil disobedience in the United States during the late 1960s and early 1970s, when radicals collectively called the "New Left" preached revolutionary replacement of the "Establishment." Students for a Democratic Society (SDS), who opposed racial discrimination, poverty, conscription, and U.S. involvement in the Vietnam War, promoted "participatory democracy." Its wild-eyed Weatherman Faction and militant Black Power proponents openly advocated violence. "Off the pigs" (kill police) was one popular slogan. Draft dodgers chanted, "Hell no, we won't go," and publicly destroyed registration cards. "Burn, baby, burn" was the rallying cry of rioters who torched Watts (a suburb of Los Angeles), downtown Washington, D.C., and other cities in 1968. Dissenters provoked pitched battles with police during the 1968 Democratic national convention in Chicago,[16] but U.S. national security decision-makers never advocated cluster bombs or napalm to suppress any of those uprisings. The reviled "Establishment" instead put teeth into civil rights legislation, substituted an All-Volunteer Force for conscription, cut U.S. casualties in an unpopular war, and incrementally exited Vietnam. Widespread disturbances soon ceased, because the New Left lacked compelling causes and public support disappeared.

Accommodations unfortunately are impossible between governments that are willing to tackle the

elemental causes of insurgencies and rebel leaders who refuse to abandon their objectives for any reason. Religious fanatics bent on establishing a theocratic state in Algeria during the late 1990s and illicit narcotics cartels that strive to convert Colombia and Peru into criminal communities are illustrative.[17] Reforms moreover usually fail whenever insurgents can control outcomes. Land redistribution programs, for example, flop if recipients risk torture, death, or both as the penalty for acceptance.

Civic Actions

The fundamental aim of civic actions for counterinsurgency purposes is to improve living conditions of poverty-stricken people. Public works and agricultural projects take top priority. Civil and military engineers construct houses and schools; build, upgrade, and repair roads that lead to and from markets; install electricity; and dig water wells in backward regions. Sanitation specialists expand and modernize waste-disposal facilities to reduce the incidence of insects and rodents that transmit infectious diseases. Doctors, nurses, and paramedics provide medical and dental care where such services previously were inadequate or nonexistent (proper instruction drastically reduces mortality among infants and their mothers in underdeveloped nations).[18]

Ramon Magsaysay, first as Secretary of National Defense, then as President of the Philippines in the 1950s, played civic actions like Artur Rubinstein played grand pianos, as a few of his actions indicate:

- Greedy landlords fleeced impecunious peasants in land courts until Magsaysay directed military judge advocates to furnish free legal assistance
- Usurers put tenant farmers permanently in debt until he liberalized rural credit
- Magsaysay promulgated new laws that authorized sharecroppers 70 percent of the yields they produced

- He resettled landless peasants in Pampanga Province, an erstwhile stronghold of Hukbalahap (Huk) Communists

Civic actions, in short, helped turn impending defeat into victory. Tycoons and ultraconservatives disapproved, but their disparagement did not dim Magsaysay's popularity with common people throughout the Philippines. Huk insurgents, who lacked public approval, laid low from 1955 until President Ferdinand Marcos's second term in 1972, when political corruption, economic crises, crumbling social structures, and human rights abuses helped them stage a brief comeback.[19]

Benevolence nevertheless has limitations. Civic actions in regions under insurgent control seldom pay large dividends, because rebels not only reap related benefits but try to take credit. Program managers moreover must make sure that left hands know what right hands are doing. Economists in South Vietnam, for example, established price controls on pork to guard against the ravages of inflation, but set ceilings so low that producers refused to market their products.[20]

Iron Fist Operations

Iron fists complement velvet gloves nicely against undergrounds and auxiliaries, provided practitioners avoid excessive force and obey laws of the land. Governments that punish groups instead of individuals, treat captives cruelly, or otherwise abuse civil rights may subdue insurgencies for long periods, but simultaneously tarnish images they hope to brighten at home and abroad. Strategies that Nazi Germany, Argentina, and the U.S.-led coalition in Vietnam once employed to repress or eradicate insurgent infrastructures are edifying in such regards.

Nazi German Reprisals

Nazi German Gestapo agents and SS troops remorselessly used reprisals to rein in resistance throughout occupied Europe during World War II. Cold-blooded killers executed citizens wholesale in retaliation for sabotage and other subversive acts.[21] The most infamous incident occurred in June 1942, when hit squads killed or incarcerated 10,000 innocents (largely intelligentsia), liquidated the population of Lidice, and leveled that village after Czech assassins slew Reinhard Heydrich, the "Butcher of Prague," who was *Reichsprotektor* of Bohemia and Moravia, Deputy Chief of the Gestapo, and commanded the *Sicherheitsdienst* (Security Forces called SD).[22]

Such tactics drastically reduced underground effectiveness, but Nazis responsible for criminal misconduct paid a high price after Germany surrendered. An International Military Tribunal in 1947 sentenced a dozen policy-makers to death by hanging and handed harsh prison sentences to seven more (Heinrich Himmler committed suicide to avoid indictment; Hermann Göring killed himself hours before his scheduled execution). Subsequent trials severely punished many subordinates.[23]

Argentine Atrocities

Argentina's military junta dissolved parliament, imposed martial law, ruled by decree, and viciously suppressed political opponents among their own people during a "dirty war" that lasted from 1977 to 1983. Ultraconservatives, convinced that savage measures were required to excise a "Communist conspiracy," spirited several thousand alleged leftists (including Catholic clergy) into secret prisons from which few emerged alive. Torture and other atrocities were commonplace. Perpetrators murdered "subversive" mothers immediately after they gave birth, then passed newborn babies to ideologically reliable parents. Two decades later, affiliates of an organization called "Mothers of the Plaza de Mayo" still sought countless "*desaparecidos,*" who had disappeared without a trace.[24]

Argentine countersubversion tactics that featured blunt force did little to endear the junta to its constituents. Atrocities, coupled with a chaotic economy (inflation exceeded 900 percent), caused that group to collapse soon after it instigated and lost a disastrous war with Britain over the barren Falkland/Malvinas Islands.[25] The Argentine Commission on Human Rights accused ring leaders of criminal acts and Raúl Alfonsín, who won the 1983 presidential election, convened courts that sentenced them to long prison terms for multiple murders, abductions, and assorted barbarisms. Pardons for many in 1990 excluded former Army Chief of Staff Major General Carlos Suárez-Mason, dubbed "*El Señor de Vida y Muerte*" (the Lord of Life and Death), because Alfonsín believed that premature release would set "a very bad precedent" favoring "those who would try to install authoritarian regimes in Argentina."[26]

U.S. Phoenix Program

President Ngo Dinh Diem's secret police (Cong An) virtually eradicated the Communist Party in newly created South Vietnam following the 1954 cease-fire, but that truncated shadow government regained strength after his assassination in 1963. Underground organizations by mid-decade probably counted 80,000–150,000 full- and part-time members who variously engaged in political agitation, propagandized, collected intelligence, established covert communication networks, developed logistical complexes, extorted taxes, executed uncooperative local leaders, and unleashed terrorist attacks designed to discredit the Government of South Vietnam (GVN).[27] President Nguyen Van Thieu in July 1968 therefore officially welcomed the U.S. Phoenix program, which was to advise, support, and assist *Phuong Hoang,* its GVN counterpart. Specific individuals, such as Communist Party officials and key cadre, constituted top priority targets. The Phoenix charter explicitly prohibited "assassinations or other violations of the rules of land warfare," but regular army units, paramilitary formations, and police were "entitled to use such reasonable military force as [was] necessary to obtain the goals of rallying, cap-turing, or eliminating the Viet Cong Infrastructure [VCI]."[28]

Phoenix accomplished its mission. Statistical data are subject to dispute, but by 1972 several thousand members of the VCI who once controlled hamlets, villages, and interconnecting routes throughout South Vietnam had defected, fled, been captured, or were killed. The People's Revolutionary Party probably lost fifteen members for every new recruit. Occasional atrocities, such as those that characterized operations in Nazi-occupied Europe and junta-ruled Argentina, unquestionably occurred, but none reflected official policies. One CIA participant explained lapses this way: "It gets pretty damn intense. Sometimes we made mistakes, we went in the wrong direction, we screwed up, but there was no evil intent." Congressional hearings in 1971 seemed to confirm his contention, despite lurid testimony to the contrary.[29]

COUNTERGUERRILLA STRATEGIES

Counterinsurgency strategists must engage enemy undergrounds, auxiliaries, and guerrillas concurrently if insurgents gain enough strength to mount locally or nationally significant paramilitary operations. Flexible concepts are advisable, because each requirement is unique.

Optional Approaches

Offensive military operations aim to close with and defeat guerrilla formations. Defensive operations seek to safeguard civilian communities within selected territories. Strategies that borrow bits from both approaches may favor the first, the second, or neither, but all opt to seal off external support so that foreign sympathizers cannot substantially reinforce guerrilla capabilities with arms, equipment, supplies, and funds.

Search and Destroy

Search and destroy strategies directed against insurgent armed forces strive to gain, retain, or regain initiative, deny opponents freedom of action, compel them to react rather than act, and separate guerrillas from sources of sustenance. Success, however, is by no means assured, because irregulars who play hide and seek are difficult to find, fix, and fight to the finish.

General William C. Westmoreland mounted massive search and destroy missions against Viet Cong guerrillas and North Vietnamese infiltrators in South Vietnam, beginning with Operation Starlight in August 1965, when U.S. Marines decimated the 2d Viet Cong Regiment near Chu Lai. Soon thereafter, he directed the U.S. Army's 1st Cavalry Division "to seek and destroy the enemy force in Pleiku Province." Close combat that pitted one U.S. brigade against three North Vietnamese regiments in the Ia Drang Valley ensued in mid-November.[30] Sweeps on grander scales continued but, despite meticulous plans, the percentage that ran guerrillas to ground was small compared with efforts expended. Such expeditions often wearied airmobile troops to no avail, while enemy foot soldiers familiar with escape routes eluded cordons, led counterinsurgents on wild goose chases, then reoccupied abandoned positions as soon as pursuers departed.

Clear and Hold

Clear and hold strategies, which orient on friendly population and production centers instead of enemy armed forces, aim to "sanitize" the most important sectors first, then expand like oil slicks until they control all key areas. Counterinsurgents do battle where *they* choose, under conditions most favorable to themselves. Successes isolate guerrillas from indigenous supporters and create secure environments within which governments can promote political, economic, and social programs designed to strengthen ties with neutrals and disaffected citizens.

Successive commanders in chief of Britain's East Africa Command relied mainly on clear and hold operations during Mau Mau uprisings in Kenya

(1952–1960), because search and destroy sweeps were hopeless against guerrillas in jungle hideouts that bordered contested areas (it cost the equivalent of $28,000 to kill one insurgent in 1955, of whom something like 5,000 remained at large). Actions to restore stability in Nairobi, the capital city, and throughout white-held highlands came first, followed by steps to reconstitute governmental control over Kikuyu tribal reserves, which were analogous to nineteenth-century American Indian reservations. Military mop-ups ceased in November 1956, after which indigenous police assumed full responsibility for internal security.[31]

Hold and Harass

Strategies that overemphasize search and destroy operations leave key areas uncovered while counterinsurgents chase elusive foes. Strategies that rely excessively on clear and hold operations allow guerrillas to gain strength undisturbed, then strike where and when least expected. Hold and harass concepts, which borrow from both, call for implementing forces to seize, secure, and expand key areas, yet badger opponents often enough to keep them off balance.

Separate Guerrillas from Outside Support

Guerrillas who receive extensive outside assistance may prosper, whereas otherwise they would perish. Counterinsurgent strategists accordingly endeavor to isolate them from the outside world to the greatest extent possible, but few find it easy to do so. Strong border guards are essential along lengthy frontiers, unless topographic features limit access to a few points inland and along coasts. Politically touchy problems arise whenever powerful nations nourish insurgencies or guerrillas establish sanctuaries inside neighboring countries.

Remote and insular locations are easiest to isolate. Chinese Communists, hidden from most foreign news media and buttressed behind the Himalayan wall, decimated rebels in Tibet (1956–1960) while frustrated Free World leaders wrung their hands.[32] Insurgents who unsuccessfully sought to unseat Indonesian President Sukarno and oust the Communist Party from that archipelago in 1958–1961 received little foreign aid.[33] It is infinitely more difficult to seal off outside support when battlegrounds abut sympathetic neighbors. Massive U.S. and allied efforts, for example, failed to stop North Vietnam from furnishing Viet Cong insurgents with wholesale supplies and reinforcements.[34]

Primacy of Land Power

Counterguerrilla operations rely mainly on land power. Naval spheres of influence during such conflicts seldom extend far from coastal and inland waterways. Fixed-wing aircraft and helicopters routinely insert, redeploy, and extract ground forces, supply isolated outposts, conduct psychological operations, and augment the firepower of units in close contact, but scarce, fleeting targets dilute other doctrinal applications. Counterinsurgents generally achieve air superiority by default, because rebels rarely possess many aircraft. The absence of guerrilla "heartlands" and industrial installations greatly reduces benefits obtainable from strategic bombing. Interdiction missions also pay smaller than average dividends, because vulnerable observers find it difficult to distinguish "good guys" from guerrillas, even if they fly low and slow (under 1,500 feet at no more than 125 knots).[35]

Requisite Force Ratios

Counterguerrilla force requirements are difficult to calculate, because the resilience of rebel bands and their abilities to replenish combat losses may vary radically within any given country or area of responsibility. Body counts (which commonly include noncombatants) and numbers of captured weapons seldom make credible progress indicators for similar reasons.

Some theorists claim that counterinsurgents can

prevail only if force ratios favor them by at least 10-to-1, because they must defend crucial urban centers, industrial infrastructures, essential lines of communication, and vulnerable bases. Experience, however, proves that great quantitative superiority is not universally required. Seasoned military strategists consequently view such contentions warily until net assessors compare qualitative strengths and weaknesses on both sides. Relevant factors include topography, climate, vegetative cover, the number and location of core areas, firepower, mobility, communications, training, morale, and leadership.

Ratios in Yugoslavia (1941–1944)

Force ratios in Yugoslavia from summer 1941 until autumn 1944 never favored Axis invaders by much more than 2-to-1 (perhaps 450,000 vs. fewer than 200,000 guerrillas). Italian divisions disposed along the Dalmatian coast from Slovenia to Albania were spiritless, while German divisions were understrength and poorly equipped. Most of their officers and NCOs were middle-aged, few had seen combat since 1918, and counterinsurgency training was nil. Nevertheless, they crushed all opposition in 1943, partly because Communist partisans under Josip Broz Tito and monarchist Chetniks under Colonel Draza Mihailovic wasted energy fighting each other. Impoverished guerrilla bands that thereafter lived hand-to-mouth gained strength only after Italy capitulated on September 9, 1943, withdrew its nineteen divisions, and allowed insurgents to seize huge stocks of arms and supplies. A few additional *Wehrmacht* divisions even so plugged the gap until October 1944, when Soviet Armed Forces overran Belgrade and threatened to sever German escape routes.[36]

Ratios in Indochina (1946–1954)

Force ratio requirements are by no means one-sided. Tenacious guerrillas may win by not losing, but they generally need great quantitative superiority to achieve military victory against otherwise well-matched opponents. French Union Forces, for example, were only slightly more numerous than Viet Minh guerrillas in Indochina from 1946 through May 1954 (basically 1-on-1), according to Bernard Fall, a keen student of that conflict. "The real surprise," he observed, "was not that the French were defeated, but that it took eight years for [that] to happen."[37] Wrong. That war might have lasted many more years if French "crapshooters" hadn't bet a bundle on one cosmic roll of the dice and thrown snake eyes at Dien Bien Phu.

PACIFICATION PROGRAMS

Pacification programs implement policies and practices that are responsive to, and involve participation by, a majority of the people in any nation that insurgents infest. Successes, which ensure the legitimacy of national and grass-roots governments, simultaneously discredit insurgents and brand them as criminals unworthy of support.

Principles in Practice

Coercive practices may deter or crush rebellions, but democratic governments generally favor strategies that mingle force with finesse. Armed services, paramilitary formations, and police conduct tactically offensive albeit strategically defensive operations against undergrounds and guerrillas. Strategically offensive pacification programs aim to eliminate root causes of insurgency and thereby restore governmental authority at national, regional, and local levels.

Members of the United States Marine Corps, who implicitly understood those demands, covered themselves with glory battling guerrillas in the Caribbean between 1915 and 1934. Long-term stability, however, would have been elusive without complementary pacification programs that received little publicity. Gyrenes in Haiti, for example, established a gendarmerie and augmented meager infrastructure with much-needed roads, sanitation facilities, hospitals, and telecommunication links. They also revised an antiquated legal code and boosted the school population from 16,000 to 100,000 between 1917 and 1920, while halving costs. Similar civic actions helped suppress insurgencies in the Dominican Republic.[38] Wisecracking U.S. Army soldiers in Vietnam, who fifty years later quipped, "Grab 'em by the balls, their hearts and minds will follow," had to relearn the hard way that lasting gains demand politico-military collaboration.[39]

Politico-Military Team Play

Governmental organizations that participate in pacification include foreign equivalents of most U.S. Cabinet-level departments. Economic ministries fight inflation and encourage private enterprise. Agricultural ministries promote crop improvement and animal husbandry programs. Ministries of education endeavor to reduce illiteracy, broaden intellectual perspectives, and otherwise develop well-informed electorates. Military forces and civilians share most other public welfare responsibilities, of which the following are representative:

- Military and civilian intelligence communities track enemy policies, plans, programs, force postures, operations, and key individuals
- Military and civilian counterintelligence communities seek to foil subversives, saboteurs, and espionage agents
- Military and civilian PSYOP specialists seek to influence the behavior of friendly, enemy, and neutral audiences at home and abroad
- Military and civilian personnel receive, control, tend, and resettle refugees, while others try to rehabilitate defectors
- Military and civilian construction teams build, rebuild, repair, and maintain urban and rural infrastructure
- Military and civilian medics practice preventive and curative medicine, particularly in re-

gions that otherwise would lack proper health support

Consolidation and Coordination

Armed force and pacification programs are parts of one package that can be fully effective only if overseers point all participants in the same direction at the same time to avoid wasteful duplication and avoidable gaps. No amount of money can compensate for serious institutional imperfections, as U.S. strategists discovered in Vietnam, where poorly coordinated activities floundered for several years with everyone and no one in overall charge short of President Lyndon B. Johnson.[40]

PRESCRIPTIONS FOR SUCCESS

Insurgencies are primarily political, social, and psychological operations in which military power plays tactically offensive but strategically defensive roles.

Attainable goals, actions that permanently deprive insurgents of voluntary public support, and reforms designed to prevent the resurrection of rebel causes are prescriptions for success. The side that wins the people eventually wins the war.

Classical insurgents generally "negotiate" only to publicize victories, avoid debacles, or open promising psychological fronts. Counterinsurgent strategists seated at conference tables consequently serve their country best when they scrutinize insurgent agendas carefully and remain aware that seemingly innocuous concessions could uncover vital interests. Patience is imperative, because overly ambitious projects and false expectations of early victory undermine confidence and the will to persist, whereas beleaguered governments prepared for protracted war are better able to tolerate temporary reversals and may triumph more rapidly than leaders anticipate.[41]

KEY POINTS

- There is no one best way to defeat all forms of insurrection, but experienced counterinsurgent strategists consistently attack causes as well as symptoms
- Governments that abuse civil rights may suppress insurgencies for long periods, but they simultaneously strengthen rather than weaken rebel causes
- Combat operations and pacification are inseparable parts of one package
- Actions to eradicate insurgent undergrounds demand timely, detailed intelligence concerning key individuals and their current activities
- Counterguerrilla strategies that combine search and destroy with clear and hold operations generally are superior to those that overemphasize either polarized approach
- Counterinsurgents strive to separate guerrillas from their power base in the populace and from foreign sources of support
- Civic actions and reforms often encourage loyal factions to rally, convert fence straddlers, and cause insurgents to defect, but rarely thrive in areas that rebels control
- Factors that influence military force levels needed to defeat insurgencies include geographic environments, weapons, equipment, training, morale, and leadership
- Savvy counterinsurgents negotiate warily, because rebels who agree to parley normally have ulterior motives and seldom compromise
- Patience is imperative, because counterinsurgency is a protracted process; disappointments await participants who expect early gratification

NOTES

1. Bernard B. Fall, *Street Without Joy: Insurgency in Indochina, 1946-1963*, 3d rev. ed. (Harrisburg, PA: Stackpole, 1963), 352-53.

2. Bernard B. Fall, *Hell in a Very Small Place* (Philadelphia, PA: Lippincott, 1966).

3. Alistair Horne, *A Savage Peace: Algeria 1954-1962* (New York: Viking, 1978).

4. Donald MacKay, *The Malayan Emergency, 1948-60: The Domino That Stood* (Washington: Brassey's, 1997).

5. Dan Connell, *Against All Odds: A Chronicle of the Eritrean Revolution* (New York: Red Sea Press, 1997); Roy Patman, *Even the Stones Are Burning* (New York: Red Sea Press, 1998).

6. James A. Bill, *The Shah, the Ayatollah, and the United States* (New York: Foreign Policy Association, 1988).

7. For insights concerning the Taliban, see Kenneth B. Katzman, *Afghanistan: Current Issues and U.S. Policy Concerns,* Rpt. 98-106F (Washington: Congressional Research Service, April 13, 1999).

8. Douglas Pike, *Viet Cong: The Organization and Techniques of the National Liberation Front of South Vietnam* (Cambridge, MA: MIT Press, 1966) and *War, Peace, and the Viet Cong* (MIT Press, 1969).

9. Russell Miller, *The Resistance* (New York: Time-Life Books, 1979).

10. Mark Moyer, *Phoenix and the Birds of Prey: The CIA's Secret Campaign to Destroy the Viet Cong* (Annapolis, MD: Naval Institute Press, 1997), Chapter 27, "Theories of Revolutionary Warfare"; Roger Trinquier, *Modern Warfare: A French View of Counterinsurgency* (New York: Praeger, 1964); Noel Barber, *The War of the Running Dogs: The Malayan Emergency, 1948-1960* (New York: Weybright and Talley, 1972).

11. David Galula, *Counterinsurgency Warfare: Theory and Practice* (New York: Praeger, 1964), 5-16; Robert Taber, *The War of the Flea: A Study of Guerrilla Warfare Theory and Practice* (New York: Lyle Stuart, 1965), 18-21.

12. Andrew R. Molnar discusses intelligence requirements in DA Pamphlet 550-104; *Human Factors Considerations of Undergrounds in Insurgencies* (Washington: Special Operations Research Office, American University; U.S. Government Printing Office, September 1966), 233-51.

13. Ibid., 261; *The Emergency Regulation Ordinance, 1948, With Amendments Made Up to 31 March 1953* (Kuala Lumpur: Federation of Malaya; Government Press, 1953), 3-11.

14. Galula, *Counterinsurgency Warfare: Theory and Practice,* 65-66.

15. Roger Darling, "Analyzing Counterinsurgency," *Military Review,* June 1974, 54-55, 58-59.

16. Massimo Teodori, ed., *The New Left: A Documentary* (New York: Bobbs-Merrill, 1969); *The Politics of Protest,* A Report Submitted by Jerome H. Skolnick, Director, Task Force on Demonstrations, Protests, and Group Violence, to the National Commission on the Causes and Prevention of Violence (Washington: U.S. Government Printing Office, 1969); Price M. Cobbs and William H. Grier, *Black Rage* (New York: Basic Books, 1968); Milroad I. Popov, "The American Extreme Left: A Decade of Conflict," *Conflict Studies,* no. 29 (December 1972), 1-19.

17. Joshua Sinai, "A Conflict Resolution-Based Counterinsurgency Strategy for Resolving Protracted Rebellions," *SO/LIC News,* National Defense Industrial Association, vol. 8, no. 2 (December 1998), 4.

18. Molnar, *Human Factors Considerations of Undergrounds in Insurgencies,* 269-76; Michael J. Wagner, *Hershey Bar Diplomacy: The Employment of Military Forces in Humanitarian Operations,* 3d ed. (Maxwell AFB, AL: Air University, 1994).

19. Robert Ross Smith, "The Philippines (1946-1954)," in Doris M. Condit and Bert H. Cooper, Jr., et al., eds., *Challenge and Response in International Conflicts,* vol. I, The Experience in Asia (Washington: Center for Research in Social Systems, American University, February 1968), 476-78, 494-95, 496, 501-2; Edward Geary Lansdale, *In the Midst of Wars* (New York: Harper and Row, 1972), 47-49, 75-76; David Joel Steinberg, *The Philippines: A Singular and Plural Place* (Boulder, CO: Westview Press, 1982), 99-130.

20. Galula, *Counterinsurgency Warfare,* 74-79.

21. For graphic evidence, see Miller, *The Resistance,* 114-25; Ronald H. Bailey, *Partisans and Guerrillas* (New York: Time-Life Books, 1978), 104-13.

22. Callum MacDonald, *The Killing of Reinhard Heydrich: The SS "Butcher of Prague"* (New York: Da Capo Press, 1998).

23. Robert H. Jackson, *The Case Against the Nazi War Criminals* (New York: A. A. Knopf, 1946) and *The Nürnberg Case* (New York: A. A. Knopf, 1947).

24. Donald C. Hodges, *Argentina's "Dirty War": An Intellectual Biography* (Austin: University of Texas Press, 1991); Amaranta Wright, "Children of a Dirty War: Argentina Struggles With the Legacy of a Horrible Crime," *U.S. News & World Report,* December 7, 1998, 34-36.

25. Douglas Kinney, *National Interest, National Honor: The Diplomacy of the Falklands Crisis* (New York: Praeger, 1989).

26. Cynthia Gorney, "Argentine Atrocities Described," *Washington Post,* March 29, 1988, A14; "Argentina," *Collier's Yearbook,* 1987, 1988, 1989.

27. Moyer, *Phoenix and the Birds of Prey,* 3-55; Dale Andrade, *Ashes to Ashes: The Phoenix Program and the Vietnam War* (Lexington, MA: Lexington Books, 1990), 1-13.

28. Moyer, *Phoenix and the Birds of Prey,* 59-146; William Colby with James McCargar, *Lost Victory: A Firsthand Account of America's Sixteen Year Involvement in Vietnam* (New York: Contemporary Books, 1989), 244-51, 280-81.

29. Colby with McCargar, *Lost Victory,* 330-34; Moyer, *Phoenix and the Birds of Prey,* 235-78, quotation on 365; *U.S. Assistance Programs in Vietnam,* 22d Report, together with Separate and Additional Views, U.S. Congress, House Committee on Government Operations (Washington: U.S. Government Printing Office, 1972).

30. Admiral U. S. G. Sharp and General William C. Westmoreland, *Report on the War in Vietnam: As of 30 June 1968,* Section II, *Report on Operations in South Vietnam, January 1964-June 1968* (Washington: U.S. Government Printing Office, 1968), 109-10; Lieutenant General Harold G. Moore and Joseph L. Galloway, *We Were Soldiers Once . . . and Young: Ia Drang—The Battle That Changed the War in Vietnam* (New York: Random House, 1992).

31. Doris M. Condit, "Kenya (1952-1960)," in Condit, Cooper, et al., *Challenge and Response in International Conflict,* vol. III, The Experience in Africa and Latin America, 270-311; Fred Majdalany, *State of Emergency: The Full Story of Mau Mau* (Boston: Houghton Mifflin, 1963).

32. William C. Johnstone, "Tibet (1951-1960)," in Condit, Cooper, et al., *Challenge and Response in International Conflict,* vol. I, 536-57; John Kenneth Knaus, *Orphans of the Cold War: America and the Tibetan Struggle for Survival* (New York: Public Affairs, 1999).

33. Genevieve Collins Linebarger, "Indonesia (1958-1961)," in Condit, Cooper, et al., *Challenge and Response in International Conflict,* vol. I, 402-38.

34. John Prados, *The Blood Road: The Ho Chi Minh Trail and the Vietnam War* (New York: John Wiley & Sons, 1999).

35. Dennis M. Drew, "U.S. Airpower Theory and the Insurgent Challenge: A Short Journey to Confusion," *Journal of Military History,* October 1998, 809-32.

36. Earl Ziemke, "Yugoslavia (1941-1944)," in Condit, Cooper, et al., *Challenge and Response in International Conflicts,* vol. II, The Experience in Europe and the Middle East, 320-51; DA Pamphlet 20-243, *German Antiguerrilla Operations in the Balkans (1941-1944)* (Washington: Department of the Army, August 1954), 17, 20-27, 36-38, 44-45, 50-52, 64-69.

37. Bernard B. Fall, "Indochina (1946-1954)," in Condit, Cooper, et al., *Challenge and Response in International Conflicts,* vol. I, 238-69, quotation on 265.

38. Rayford W. Logan, "Haiti (1918-1920)" and Siegfried Garbuny, "Dominican Republic (1916-1924)," both in Condit, Cooper, et al., *Challenge and Response in International Conflict,* Supplement (September 1968), 2-57; Dana G. Munro, *Intervention and Dollar Diplomacy in the Caribbean, 1900-1921* (Princeton, NJ: Princeton University Press, 1964), 269-387.

39. Sir Robert Thompson, *No Exit from Vietnam* (New York: David McKay, 1969), 145-61.

40. Richard A. Hunt, *Pacification: The American Struggle for Vietnam's Hearts and Minds* (Boulder, CO: Westview Press, 1995); Thomas W. Scoville, *Reorganizing for Pacification Support* (Washington: Center of Military History, U.S. Army, 1982); Robert Shaplen, *Time Out of Hand: Revolution and Reaction in Southeast Asia,* rev. ed. (HarperColophon Books, 1970), 451-53.

41. Thompson, *No Exit from Vietnam,* 77-87, 176-78; Galula, *Counterinsurgency Warfare,* 77-78.

17. Sociopolitical Terrorism

Al ain't sellin' excuses. . .
Al's sellin' whiskey.

Attributed to Frank Nitti
Al Capone's "Enforcer"

Scarface Al Capone, like fictional Godfather Vito Corleone, made customers an offer they couldn't refuse when he promised broken bones, bombs in miscreant cabarets, and sudden death to repeat offenders who refused to buy his bootleg booze. Fearful retailers far beyond Al's headquarters in Cicero, Illinois became true believers as soon as his goon squads began to gun down defiant entrepreneurs and destroy their property.

Sociopolitical terrorists, who murder, maim, and demolish indiscriminately rather than selectively, make Capone seem kindly by comparison. Their purpose is to inspire such widespread fear and confusion within afflicted countries that national leaders must make a no-win decision: capitulate or lose popular support. Increasingly sophisticated weapons, a profusion of lucrative targets, and innovative tactics greatly enhance the capabilities of each successive generation.[1]

THE NATURE OF SOCIOPOLITICAL TERRORISM

Louis de Saint-Just, a Jacobin who lopped off many heads during the French Revolution before a guillotine decapitated him in turn, firmly believed that "Violence in itself is neither rational nor lawful, but there's no better way of making people respect reason and law."[2] Not all violence, however, involves terrorism, and not all terrorists employ public, impersonal, repetitive violence to accelerate sociopolitical change. John W. Hinckley, Jr. was not a terrorist when he tried to assassinate President Ronald Reagan in March 1981, because his rampage purposely put only one senior U.S. official in peril (wild shots wounded three others).[3] Osama bin Laden clearly qualified after he declared a Jihad (Holy War) against the United States in February 1998.[4] Malicious assaults on a few isolated schools, churches, or synagogues constitute common crime, whereas methodical attempts to outlaw abortion, recast educational systems, or combat religious beliefs using identical tactics constitute sociopolitical terrorism.[5]

Domestic terrorism originates within and is directed against one country or bloc. Hitler's Gestapo discouraged dissent in Germany and in occupied territories. "Papa Doc" Duvalier's Ton Ton Macoutes kept the lid on dissidents inside Haiti. The KGB and its predecessors performed similar functions inside the Soviet Union and its satellite states.[6] Transnational terrorists, in contrast, strike without warning anywhere in the world, then return to distant sanctuaries. Air transportation makes freewheeling attacks particularly attractive. All terrorists commonly exploit mass news media (especially television) to ensure that the widest possible audience receives the full psychological impact of their sociopolitical messages almost instantaneously.

ATYPICAL TERRORISTS

Typical terrorists don't exist, because hereditary characteristics, personalities, occupations, lifestyles, motivations, and methods vary remarkably. Pragmatists mingle with madmen, idealists with mercenaries, true believers with opportunists.[7] Brazilian firebrand Carlos Marighella, in *Minimanual of the Urban Guerrilla,* his textbook on terrorism, prized offensive spirit, initiative, stamina, and capacities to dissemble. He also lauded individuals who are amoral, adventurous, action-oriented, brave, cool, clever, creative, idealistic, imaginative, patient, and patriotic in some sense.[8]

Terrorists generally believe that cherished ends justify any feasible means. Attacks on innocent men, women, and children make sense when seen in that light, because intimidated populations tend toward capitulation if security forces cannot protect them. Terrorists who sound tocsins before they assault seldom weep if officials disbelieve or disobey their warnings. Zionist Menachem Begin, who led Irgun guerrillas against British rule in Palestine, for example, told British officials on July 22, 1946 that his organization was about to blow up the King David Hotel in Jerusalem, then disclaimed responsibility for 136 dead and wounded because they disregarded his heads up (Begin later served as Israeli Prime Minister, 1977–1983).[9]

"Personnel officers" who recruit terrorists as a rule avoid mentally unstable, impulsive individuals whose motives are personal rather than sociopolitical and whose actions are uncontrollable. Many idealists, however, welcome martyrdom for spiritual or religious reasons.[10] Kozo Okamoto, a fanatical member of the Japanese Red Army (JRA) group that killed twenty-eight and injured sixty-seven more at Lod Airport near Tel Aviv in May 1973, displayed a death wish before and after he made this romantic statement during his trial: "When I was a child, I was told that when people died they became stars. . . . We three Red Army soldiers wanted to become Orion when we died. . . . As the revolution goes on, how the stars will multiply!"[11]

TYPICAL TERRORIST ORGANIZATIONS

Terrorist organizations, like insurgent undergrounds that Chapter 15 describes, favor cellular structures that range from simple to complex, depending on personnel strengths and operational requirements. It generally is hard to join, because paranoid members recruit selectively, are exceedingly suspicious of outsiders, and use stringent tests to weed out weaklings along with phonies; some groups, for example, order aspirants to commit a random murder. Disengagement is even more difficult for those who decide to quit, since death is the usual sentence for defectors.[12]

TERRORIST TOOLS

Nuclear, biological, chemical, and radiological weapons would give sociopolitical terrorists great powers[13] but, at the turn of the twenty-first century, most groups still favor rugged, reliable implements that cell members can employ adroitly with minimum training. Exotic tools analogous to those that fictional James Bond featured in his capacity as Agent 007 are rare exceptions.

Preferred Weapons

Stocks in trade include small arms and automatic weapons with silencers. "Snooperscopes" simplify night sniping. Explosives range from relatively primitive to sophisticated devices equipped with miniature, remote, delayed detonators. Some cells possess small, self-contained, highly destructive, easily concealed antiaircraft missiles. Mobility means include long- and short-haul public transportation systems as well as privately owned automobiles, aircraft, and motorboats.[14]

Technologists provide constant improvements. Assault rifles and automatic pistols currently accommodate armor-piercing ammunition that can penetrate protective vests and lightly armored limousines. "Gas guns" project incapacitating or lethal aerosols. Terrorists can camouflage plastic explosives such as Semtex into seemingly benign objects, such as suitcases and children's toys. Water-based slurry and emulsion explosives defy vapor pressure detectors. Search and disposal problems multiply when terrorists use four or five switches in different combinations to trigger any given device. Booby traps, for example, may respond to tilt, tremble, pressure, or release. Barometric, acoustic, and light-sensitive charges may detonate on command.[15]

"How To" books make it easy for terrorists to improve commercial armaments and concoct munitions, as a quick scan of any Delta Press catalogue indicates. *The Anarchist Cookbook,* in its twenty-ninth printing since 1971, contains well-illustrated chapters that cover various weapons, explosives, and electronics for anyone who wants to build silencers for submachine guns or make cacodyl, a virulent amalgam of arsenic and methyl for use in Molotov cocktails. Other titillating titles promise greater breadth and depth: *Improvised Munitions Handbooks* (three volumes); *Assorted Nasties;* and *OSS/CIA Assassination Device: Plans for a .22 Caliber Cigarette Lighter.*[16] Computer users need not visit a library, because the Internet is a wide-open textbook.

Nuclear Weapons

Unscrupulous state sponsors who share terrorist aims are potential sources of easily concealed, portable nuclear weapons, but increasingly attractive alternatives exist. Unclassified documents outline basic technologies. Porous controls, black markets, and impecunious possessors of essential expertise in several countries open additional opportunities for terrorists to buy, steal, or otherwise acquire fissile materials, finished components, and know-how with which to fashion crude nuclear weapons. Even low-grade radiological materials, such as cobalt-60, strontium-90, and cesium-137 in lieu of plutonium or highly enriched uranium, could wreak local havoc if wrapped around traditional munitions and incendiary devices.[17] Terrorists who lack nuclear capabilities of any kind might create widespread radioactive fallout if, Kamikaze-style, they crashed a light plane loaded with explosives into a nuclear power plant or otherwise sabotaged poorly protected commercial reactors. Serbia in the early 1990s, for example, reportedly threatened to create

the equivalent of "several Chernobyls" in Europe if sufficiently provoked.[18]

Sociopolitical terrorists, whose specialties are "propaganda by deed" and "theater in the round" on grandiose scales, "want a lot of people watching, not a lot of people dead," according to one respected school of thought. Their leaders surely must understand that even a well-handled nuclear hoax could pay huge propaganda dividends if it spread panic among senior officials as well as ostensibly imperiled populations, but self-restraint thus far has prevailed for reasons that remain obscure.[19] There nevertheless is scant cause for complacency, because racial, ethnic, religious, tribal, and ideological fanatics who commit mass murders without compunction fuel trends toward increased violence.[20] President Bill Clinton in his annual address to the United Nations General Assembly on September 21, 1999, indeed deplored "hot-blooded hatreds and stone-cold hearts" which, "—when married to advanced weaponry and terrorism—threaten to destroy the greatest potential for human development in history, even as they make a wasteland of the soul."[21]

Biological Weapons

The list of biological warfare (BW) agents is long (see Table 16, page 146), but degrees of lethality, transmission problems, logistical difficulties, antidotes, and treatments limit the number of mass-casualty producers that terrorists might employ successfully. Relatively few people, for example, would be afflicted if terrorists laced food with lethal salmonella at a well-attended Shriners' convention. It would take several tons of highly toxic ricin to infest fifty square miles, whereas a few pounds of contagious aerosols with a wider downwind spread could kill or incapacitate far more people under identical conditions. BW authorities currently believe that anthrax and smallpox constitute the most dangerous threats, followed by tularemia, pneumonic plague, and hemorrhagic fever. Crude atomic bombs wielded by terrorists could wreak local havoc but, as one BW pundit put it, smallpox (which killed perhaps 300 million unimmunized humans in the twentieth century) could quickly engulf the globe. Rapid intercontinental transportation systems and the absence of adequate vaccine since scientists controlled that scourge make smallpox most menacing.[22]

"Agro-terrorists" could assault crops and livestock. Veterinarians are most fearful of mad cow disease; foot and mouth disease, which afflicts cattle, hogs, and sheep; infectious swine fever, for which no vaccine exists; and a deadly variant of avian influenza, which caused the U.S. Department of Agriculture to kill $63 million worth of chickens during a six-month-long outbreak in the 1980s. BW laboratories have developed other agents designed to decimate fruits, grains, and vegetables. Some produce toxins that endanger humans who ingest them. The United States is painfully vulnerable, because selective livestock breeding drastically reduces diversity, high concentrations on fewer farms facilitate the spread of contagious diseases, and many seed stocks originate in foreign countries under loosely controlled conditions.[23]

Intelligence analysts doubt that any nation as yet has furnished terrorists with biological agents, but renegade groups beholden to no government conceivably could pilfer them from poorly guarded stockpiles or produce their own instruments, perhaps with assistance from unscrupulous pharmacologists or scientists who underpinned BW programs in the former Soviet Union.[24] Members of the Aum Shinrikyo cult nevertheless discovered that mass dissemination is difficult, when they released botulin toxin and anthrax in densely populated central Tokyo during the early 1990s, yet failed to create any casualties.[25] Ultraviolet rays devitalize most agents, which can't survive exposure to sunlight; explosive devices sterilize them; aerosols that cling to dust particles in damp air are too large to inhale, while those in excessively dry air shrivel and die. Filtration and chlorine reduce dangers to municipal water supplies. Cooking kills most pathogens, but raw and improperly stored foods invite finagling.[26] Practical problems accordingly restrain BW terrorism somewhat, but trends toward increased violence coupled with improved technologies make prospects seem bleak.[27]

Chemical Weapons

Chemical warfare (CW) agents are easier to produce than nuclear weapons and easier than BW munitions to deliver, despite meteorological sensitivities.[28] The world received a wake-up call on March 20, 1995, when Aum Shinrikyo thugs in Tokyo released homemade sarin (a lethal nerve agent) inside five subway trains at fifteen widely separated stations. Vapors killed twelve, hospitalized nearly 1,000, traumatized thousands more, and sent psychological shock waves throughout Japan.[29] Similar incidents on stupefying scales are pragmatic possibilities.

TERRORIST TARGETS AND TACTICS

Terrorism epitomizes a strategically indirect approach that enables individuals and small groups to exert great influence at minimal cost. Perpetrators assault neutral nations as well as known enemies whenever so doing serves useful purposes. Factions that favor a Palestinian homeland, for example, have often attacked European countries sympathetic to Israel.

Tempting Targets

Calamities would occur in large cities if commercial and computer traffic ceased for long periods, skyscraper ventilation systems failed, perishable products spoiled, and chaotic conditions encouraged looters. Information storage and transfer sites, communication centers, transportation nodes, petrochemical plants, electrical power and water distribution systems present tempting targets. Symbolically significant structures, such as the U.S. Capitol, the White House, the Supreme Court building, the Pentagon, the Washington Monument, and the Library of Congress (all in Washington, D.C.), are particularly appealing, because demolition would make thunderous sociopolitical statements. The same is true for embassies, military compounds, and ships in harbors. Prominent public figures who oppose terrorist programs also run high risks. Chiefs of State, their advisers, senior military commanders, influential members of the news media, educators, other opinion shapers, police, and judges are potential bull's-eyes.

Tried and True Tactics

Terrorists strive to attract and retain attention with high-profile acts that shock public sensibilities. Tried and true tactics emphasize assassinations, abductions, hostage-takings, hijackings, and demolitions, separately or in some combination. Technological progress is opening a sixth option: cybernetic terrorism (see Chapter 19, page 210).

Assassination

Assassination, defined herein as premeditated murder for sociopolitical purposes, is a direct, discriminating, economical way to achieve potentially decisive results. Secret Service agents in the White House on New Year's Eve 1980 collared a female tourist with a pistol in her purse and a demented intruder harmlessly accosted Queen Elizabeth in her Buckingham Palace boudoir in July 1982,[30] but it generally takes proficient planners and gimlet-eyed killers with exceptional expertise to penetrate professional security systems, accomplish strategically important missions, and escape unscathed.

"Termination" techniques vary considerably. Georgi Markov, a Bulgarian defector who opposed the dictatorial regime in Sofia, died in London on September 11, 1978 when an assassin lanced him with a ricin-coated umbrella tip.[31] Frederick Forsyth's novel *The Day of the Jackal* described in great detail how a skilled sniper might have assassinated French President Charles de Gaulle after he prom-

ised freedom for Algeria.[32] Viet Cong (VC) terrorists elevated assassination to a much broader plain when they murdered more than 6,000 province chiefs, judges, policemen, and lesser functionaries between 1959 and 1964. VC "death squads" additionally slaughtered educators who taught pupils to love their country and resist Communism. Executioners often disemboweled and decapitated family members along with perceived offenders to ensure that no witnesses missed their message.[33]

Abduction

It is much harder to abduct closely guarded moguls than to hit marks with telescopic rifles or with poisoned pellets at point-blank range. Abductions, however, can enrich terrorist coffers, publicize causes, and spur authorities to free imprisoned compatriots.

Italy's Red Brigades, whose constituents had lost faith in existing institutions, kidnapped Christian Democrats and pillars of Italian society. They snatched former Prime Minister Aldo Moro in 1978, convened a "people's tribunal," condemned him to death as an enemy of the proletariat, riveted world attention for fifty-four days, then dumped his bullet-ridden body in an abandoned automobile when the Government refused to release thirteen incarcerated terrorists. Brigadier General James L. Dozier, the highest ranking U.S. officer at NATO's headquarters in Verona, Italy, narrowly escaped harm after Red Brigade goons grabbed him in December 1981. Abductors, who blamed Dozier for "American massacres in Vietnam," held him subject to "proletarian justice" for forty-two days, before a massive manhunt found the General in a secret "people's prison" and Italian counterterrorist teams retrieved him safely.[34]

The Symbionese Liberation Army (SLA), which never numbered more than ten members, put an altruistic spin on abduction when they spirited newspaper heiress Patricia Hearst from her Berkeley, California, apartment on February 4, 1974. Their ransom note demanded that her wealthy father furnish $70 worth of food to "all people with welfare cards, Social Security pension cards, food stamp cards, disabled veteran cards, medical cards, parole or probation papers, and jail or bail release slips." Expenditures would have totaled at least $250 million (may be twice that much) in California alone. The SLA initially accepted his counteroffer of $2 million, then promised to turn Patty loose within seventy-two hours if he donated $4 million more. He agreed, but the gang soon got a grand propaganda bonus, because "brainwashed" Patty joined its ranks, voluntarily renounced her birthright, took the revolutionary name Tania, participated in a bank robbery that netted the SLA $10,600, sprayed a store front with machine-gun bullets, and eluded capture until September 1975.[35]

Hostage-Taking

Sociopolitical terrorists who accumulate hostages en masse hope to use them as human "bargaining chips" with which to extort desired concessions. Techniques are similar to those associated with abductions, except hostage-takers rarely move victims from known locations, whereas kidnappers usually transport them surreptitiously to safe houses.

Radical "students" beholden to the Ayatollah Khomeini seized the U.S. Embassy in Tehran on November 4, 1979. They forthwith released thirteen hostages who were female or black, but retained fifty-three others for 444 days pending receipt of an official U.S. apology for previously supporting Mohammed Reza Shah Pahlavi, deportation of the ailing Shah to face trial in Iran, and return to Iran of billions that he allegedly had stashed abroad. The U.S. Government never met those demands, but the protracted stalemate publicly weakened President Jimmy Carter and his Administration. Khomeini contrastingly strengthened his position politically and psychologically by holding all fifty-three hostages until Ronald Reagan replaced Carter as President on January 20, 1981.[36]

The Libyan-based Democratic Revolutionary Movement for the Liberation of Arabistan (currently called Khuzestan) fared less well when affiliated terrorists stormed the Iranian Embassy in London on April 30, 1980. Six heavily armed thugs, who quickly overwhelmed four British and twenty-five Iranian occupants, demanded regional autonomy for Khuzistan Province (which abuts Iraq at the head of the Persian Gulf), plus freedom for ninety-one prisoners by noon the next day. Two such deadlines and several days passed while police and media representatives sought to resolve the crisis peacefully, until frustrated terrorists on May 5 finally killed a hostage and heaved his body out the front door. Three elite Special Air Service (SAS) teams soon thereafter swept through the building and, during an eleven-minute battle, killed five gunmen, captured the sixth, and rescued all hostages, only a few of whom were wounded.[37]

Hijacking

Skyjackings peaked at about eighty per year between 1969 and 1972, with mixed results before, during, and after that period. Shia fundamentalists fared well in June 1985, when they skyjacked TWA Flight 847, a Boeing 727 en route from Athens to Beirut, then offered to exchange 108 hostages for 700 prisoners that Israel captured in southern Lebanon three years earlier. That deal fell flat and the terrorists eventually turned all hostages loose (save one murdered in midair), but they went scot-free and got a propaganda bonanza from the resultant media circus.[38] The Popular Front for the Liberation of Palestine (PFLP), a splinter group of the Palestinian Liberation Organization (PLO), fared poorly after it commandeered three airliners over international airspace on September 6, 1970. Two landed at Dawson Field northeast of Amman, Jordan, the third in Cairo. PFLP pirates diverted the fourth transport to Jordan three days later, terrorized passengers and crew, then blew all four aircraft to smithereens while commentators and television cameras beamed their rampage around the world. Those forays backfired badly, because "Black September" ensued. King Hussein's Arab Legion battled Palestinian radicals in Jordan, Syrian tanks intervened, and Israel made compensatory countermoves along its de facto frontiers. U.S. and Soviet intervention on behalf of respective clients seemed conceivable. The dust settled short of a full-scale war on September 29, after which surviving PFLP terrorists released the last six hostages in exchange for seven guerrillas in Western Europe and twelve Arabs in Israel.[39]

Hijackers prey on cruise ships and railway trains as well as aircraft. The Italian liner *Achille Lauro* netted Palestinian terrorists more than 400 hostages in October 1988.[40] Radicals who sought independence for Molucca (formerly a Dutch colony but legally part of Indonesia since 1949) confiscated a train for twelve days in 1976. A second spectacular started on May 23, 1977, when one group of terrorists stopped an express in northeast Holland and herded forty-nine hostages into first-class compartments. Conspirators simultaneously snared 110 teachers and pupils in a nearby elementary school, but sent 106 of them home when a virus sickened the children. Ringleaders insisted that the Netherlands support Moluccan separatism, liberate twenty-one prisoners, and promise safe passage for all, including themselves. The resultant standoff, which lasted three weeks, terminated when counterterrorists killed six hostage-holders and broke both sieges.[41]

Demolitions

Terrorists always have displayed a penchant for demolitions. The most fatalities ever recorded occurred on June 23, 1985, when Sikh extremists blew 329 humans to bits in an Air India jet over the Atlantic Ocean. A suitcase bomb that Libyan baggage handlers loaded aboard Pan Am Flight 103 obliterated 259 passengers over Lockerbie, Scotland, in December 1988 and debris killed eleven more innocents on the ground.[42] Buildings also are vulnerable. Suicidal bombers slaughtered 220 U.S. Marines,

eighteen sailors, two Army soldiers, and sixty French paratroopers in their Beirut barracks on October 23, 1983.[43] Timothy McVeigh, a right-wing militiaman, killed 168 and injured 850 in the most deadly onslaught inside the United States when he gutted Oklahoma City's Alfred P. Murrah Federal Building on April 19, 1995.[44] A fanatical attack on the U.S. Air Force compound at Khobar Towers near Dhahran, Saudi Arabia, left nineteen dead and 500 wounded on June 25, 1996.[45] Twin assaults on U.S. embassies in Nairobi, Kenya, and Dar es Salaam, Tanzania, initially left eighty-one dead and more than 1,700 wounded on August 7, 1998.[46] Lesser calamities have been legion, slaughters continue, and terrorists armed with weapons of mass destruction could make past tolls seem minuscule.

Explosions that cause few fatalities can saddle cities with gigantic costs and grievous confusion, as terrorists demonstrated on February 26, 1993, when they hit the 110-story twin-tower World Trade Center in New York City during business hours. Blast effects killed six persons and injured more than 1,000 when an enormous device detonated in the subterranean parking garage, but that was barely the beginning. A crater several stories deep and 200 feet wide threatened to topple the entire structure. Electrical short circuits and inoperable elevators trapped 50,000 employees and thousands more visitors for hours in pitch black, smoke-filled stairwells. A humongous traffic jam tangled lower Manhattan when police cars, fire engines, and ambulances tried to converge on the scene. Perhaps 350 businesses, banks, brokerage houses, law firms and other tenants were displaced for at least a month. Revenues lost during that period totalled more than $1 billion, according to off-the-cuff calculations. Lloyds' of London and a consortium consequently faced huge liability, property, and business interruption claims. New York City police investigated 364 bomb threats during the first five days after the blast (five or six per day was normal) and anxieties rippled all the way to the U.S. Pacific coast.[47]

Nightmare Scenarios

The World Trade Center debacle could have been much worse. No terrorist group took credit or stipulated what the U.S. Government must do to avoid recurrences. Imagine what might have happened if the explosive charge had contained radioactive material or instigators had orchestrated similar events in rapid succession across the country. They might, for example, have demolished the pyramid-shaped Transamerica Building in San Francisco on Day Two, followed by Chicago's Sears Tower on Day Three, then promised continued destruction on a grand scale if the President of the United States refused to comply with demands A, B, C, and D before their nonnegotiable deadline elapsed. No showdown on such a scale has ever arisen anywhere in the world, but such scenarios give counterterrorists nightmares.

SPONSORSHIP AND SUPPORT

State sponsorship and support for de facto proxies can telescope the time it takes terrorists to become proficient and affords flexibility for professionals. Benefactors who provide operational bases as well as expertise and funds are particularly valuable.[48]

Cost-effective largesse generally includes training facilities, instruction, difficult-to-detect arms, intelligence, and safe havens to which transnational terrorists return when their missions are complete. Most patrons also furnish false documents that mask the true identities of surrogates (plastic surgeons in Czechoslovakia reportedly altered facial features to make hit men unrecognizable during the Cold War).[49] The former Soviet Union, some of its Warsaw Pact surrogates, Afghanistan, Algeria, Cuba, Iran, Iraq, Lebanon, Libya, North Korea, and Syria typify countries that once organized, equipped, and directed transnational terrorist activities, or do so now.[50]

Sociopolitical terrorists who lack state sponsors or other affluent sympathizers generally finance their operations with ill-gotten gains from criminal activities such as bank robberies, embezzlements, kidnappings, expropriations, counterfeiting, illicit drug deals, and fraudulent "tax" collections akin to Mafia "protection" rackets. Profits range from picayune to prodigious. One Argentinean group in April 1974 established a ransom record that may never be beaten: $14,200,000 in return for Victor E. Samuelson, an Exxon Oil Company executive it held captive for 144 days.[51]

KEY POINTS

- Sociopolitical terrorism, which epitomizes a strategically indirect approach, enables individuals and small groups to exert great influence at minimal cost
- Terrorists aim to cause anguish so intense and widespread that authorities cannot cope, and consequently comply with their demands
- Massacres make sense to domestic and transnational terrorists, who believe that the ends they cherish justify any feasible means
- Typical terrorists don't exist, because pragmatists mingle with madmen, idealists with mercenaries, true believers with opportunists
- Tightly knit terrorist organizations, which are exceedingly suspicious of outsiders, screen recruits carefully and kill defectors
- Most groups still favor simple, rugged, reliable weapons that members can employ well with minimal training
- Ruthless terrorists could employ nuclear and radiological munitions or dispense biological and chemical weapons more liberally
- Tempting targets include prominent public figures, economically important nerve centers, military compounds, ships in harbors, and symbolically significant structures
- Tried and true tactics emphasize assassinations, abductions, hostage-takings, hijackings, and demolitions
- State sponsorship, funds, safe havens, and other forms of support can telescope the time it takes terrorists to become proficient and facilitate transnational operations

NOTES

1. For overviews, see Anthony H. Cordesman, *Asymmetric Warfare Versus Counterterrorism: Rethinking CBRN and CIP Defense and Response* (Washington: Center for Strategic and International Studies, September 2000); Walter Laquer, *The New Terrorism: Fanaticism and the Arms of Mass Destruction* (New York: Oxford University Press, 1999); Bruce Hoffman, *Inside Terrorism* (London: Victor Gollancz, 1998); Martin Shubik, "Terrorism, Technology, and the Socioeconomics of Death," *Comparative Strategy*, October–December 1997, 399–414.

2. Louis de Saint-Just, *Oeuvres Choisies* (Paris: Avant-propos de Dionys Mascolo, 1968), 327.

3. William A. DeGregorio, *The Complete Book of U.S. Presidents: From George Washington to Bill Clinton,* 5th ed. (New York: Wings Books, 1997), 651–52.

4. Bernard Lewis, "License to Kill: Usama bin Ladin's Declaration of Jihad," *Foreign Affairs,* November/December 1998, 14–19.

5. John M. Collins, "Definitional Aspects," in *Political Terrorism and Energy: The Threat and Response,* ed. Yonah Alexander and Charles K. Ebinger (New York: Praeger, 1982), 1–14.

6. *Hitler's Enforcers: The Gestapo and SS Security Service in the Nazi Revolution* (New York: Oxford University Press, 1996); Bernard Diederich and Al Burt, *Papa Doc: Haiti and Its Dictator* (London: Bodley Head, 1970); Robert Conquest, *The Great Terror: A Reassessment* (New York: Oxford University Press, 1991).

7. Gavin Cameron, *Nuclear Terrorism: A Threat Assessment for the 21st Century* (New York: St. Martin's Press, 1999), 17–56; Laqueur, *The New Terrorism,* 90–104; Konrad Kellen, *Terrorists: What Are They Like? How Some Terrorists Describe Their World and Actions,* RAND Note N-1300-SL, prepared for Sandia Laboratories (Santa Monica, CA: RAND Corporation, November 1979), 2–6, 34, 39.

8. Carlos Marighella, *Minimanual of the Urban Guerrilla* (Vancouver, Canada: Pulp Press, 1974), 2–5.

9. Menachem Begin, *The Revolt: Story of the Irgun* (New York: Henry Schuman, 1951, 212-30.

10. Laqueur, *The New Terrorism*, 81-90, 127-55.

11. Patricia Steinhoff, "Kozo Okamoto," *Asian Survey*, vol. 16, no. 9 (September 1976), 830-45.

12. Kellen, *Terrorists: What Are They Like?*, 35-44, 51-52, 56-63, 65-66; Richard E. Rubenstein, *Alchemists of Revolution: Terrorism in the Modern World* (New York: Basic Books, 1987), 3-16.

13. *Assessing the Threat,* First Annual Report to the President and the Congress of the Advisory Panel to Assess Domestic Response Capabilities for Terrorism Involving Weapons of Mass Destruction (Santa Monica, CA: RAND Corporation, December 15, 1999); Jonathan B. Tucker, ed., *Toxic Terror: Assessing Terrorist Use of Chemical and Biological Weapons* (Cambridge, MA: MIT Press, 2000).

14. Richard Clutterbuck, *Terrorism in An Unstable World* (New York: Routledge, 1994), 26-54; Jimmie C. Oxley, "Non-Traditional Explosives: Potential Detection Problems," in *Technology and Terrorism,* ed. Paul Wilkinson (London: Frank Cass, 1993), 30-47.

15. Wayne Biddle, "It Must Be Simple and Reliable," *Discover,* Special Report on the Technology of Terrorism (June 1986), 22-31.

16. William Powell, *The Anarchist Cookbook* (New York: L. Stuart Press, 1971); *Catalogue,* vol. 37 (Eldorado, AK: Delta Press, Ltd., 1998), especially 3-14, 29-31, 42-43, updates available on the Internet, http://www.infogo.com/delta.

17. John B. Roberts, II, "Will Terrorists Go Nuclear?," *American Spectator,* July/August 2000, 36-39; Stanley S. Jacobs, "The Nuclear Threat As a Terrorist Option," *Terrorism and Political Violence,* vol. 10, no. 4 (Winter 1998), 150-156; Cameron, *Nuclear Terrorism,* 131-34, 143.

18. Vince Cannistraro and Robert Kupperman, "U.S. Must Measure Possibility of Terrorism," *Christian Science Monitor,* March 2, 1993, 19.

19. Jacobs, "The Nuclear Threat As a Terrorist Option," 156-60; Brian Jenkins, "Will Terrorists Go Nuclear?" *Orbis,* Fall 1985, 507-15, quotation on 511.

20. Bruce Hoffman and David Claridge, "The RAND-St. Andrews Chronology of International Terrorism and Noteworthy Domestic Incidents, 1996," *Terrorism and Political Violence,* vol. 10, no. 2 (Summer 1998), 135-180; Cameron, *Nuclear Terrorism,* 77-130.

21. Bill Sammon, "Clinton Decries 'Scarred' Century," *Washington Times,* September 22, 1999, A1.

22. W. Seth Carus, *Bioterrorism and Biocrimes: The Illicit Use of Biological Agents in 20th Century* (Washington: Center for Counterproliferation Research, National Defense University, 1999), 21-25; Mark G. Kortepeter and Gerald W. Parker, "Potential Biological Weapons Threats," *Emerging Infectious Diseases,* Special Issue, vol. 5, no. 4 (July–August, 1999), 523-27, plus additional articles devoted to anthrax and smallpox; Richard Preston, "The Demon in the Freezer," *New Yorker,* July 12, 1999, 44-61.

23. Judith Miller, "Administration Plans to Use Plum Island to Combat Terrorism," *New York Times,* September 22, 1999, 1; *Bioterrorism May Be Threat to U.S. Agriculture* (Columbus: Ohio State University, http://www.osu.edu, posted August 10, 1999).

24. Carus, *Bioterrorism and Biocrimes,* 17-19, 32, 35-38; Ken Alibek with Stephen Handelman, *Biohazard: The Chilling Story of the Largest Covert Biological Weapons Program in the World, Told from the Inside by the Man Who Ran It* (New York: Random House, 1999), 270-76. Judith Miller, "U.S. Told to Spend More to Neutralize Soviet Germ Scientists," *New York Times,* December 10, 1999, 14.

25. "Aum Shinrikyo: Once and Future Threat?," *Emerging Infectious Diseases,* Special Issue, 513-16.

26. Carus, *Bioterrorism and Biocrimes,* 21-23, 38; Ned Dolan, *BW Research* (MAJUSMCRET@aol.com, July 28, 1999).

27. Bruce Hoffman, "Terrorist Targeting: Tactics, Trends, and Potentialities," in Wilkinson, *Technology and Terrorism,* 14-19.

28. Javed Ali, Leslie Rodriques, and Michael Moodie, *U.S. Chemical-Biological Defense Guidebook* (Alexandria, VA: Jane's Information Group, 1998), 138-50.

29. "Aum Shinrikyo: Once and Future Threat?" 513-16.

30. "Intruder Talks to Queen in Her Bedroom At Palace," *New York Times,* July 12, 1982, A5; *Facts on File Yearbook* (New York: Facts on File, Inc., 1982), 513-14.

31. *Facts on File Yearbook* (1978), 748-49; Laqueur, *The New Terrorism,* 163.

32. Frederick Forsyth, *The Day of the Jackal,* reissue ed. (New York: Bantam Books, 1982); also a 1973 movie, same title, starring Edward Fox.

33. Major General Edward Lansdale, "Vietnam: Do We Understand Revolution?," *Foreign Affairs,* XLIII, no. 1 (October 1964), 81; Bernard B. Fall, *The Two Vietnams: A Political and Military Analysis* (New York: Praeger, 1963), 360; Denis Warner, *The Last Confucian* (New York: Macmillan, 1963), 137.

34. Walter N. Lang, *The World's Elite Forces: The Men, Weapons, and Operations in the War Against Terrorism* (London: Salamander Books, 1987), 112, 137-39; Richard Drake, *The Aldo Moro Murder Case* (Cambridge, MA: Harvard University Press, 1995).

35. Albert Perry, *Terrorism from Robespierre to Arafat* (New York: Vanguard Press, 1976), 342-64; Patricia Campbell Hearst and Alvin Moscow, *Patty Hearst: Her Own Story* (New York: Avon, mass market paperback ed., 1988).

36. Gary Sick, *All Fall Down: America's Tragic Encounter with Iran* (New York: Random House, 1986); Warren Christopher et al., *American Hostages in Iran: The Conduct of a Crisis* (New Haven, CT: Yale University Press, 1986).

37. Lang, *The World's Elite Forces,* 132-33.

38. Clutterbuck, *Terrorism in An Unstable World,* 178.

39. Major General James Lunt, *Hussein of Jordan* (New York: William Morrow, 1989), 131-43. For context, see Henry A. Kissinger, *The White House Years* (Boston: Little, Brown, 1979), 609-31.

40. Antonio Cassese, *Terrorism, Politics, and Law: The Achille Lauro Affair,* trans. S. J. K. Greensleeves (Princeton, NJ: Princeton University Press, 1989); Lang, *The World's Elite Forces,* 146-47.

41. Lang, *The World's Elite Forces,* 122-24.

42. Rodney Wallis, *Lockerbie: The Inside Story* (New York: Praeger, 1999); Clutterbuck, *Terrorism in An Unstable World,* 167-68.

43. *Report of the DoD Commission on Beirut International Airport Terrorist Act,* October 23, 1983, commonly called The Long Report (Washington: Department of Defense, December 20, 1983).

44. *Alfred P. Murrah Federal Building Bombing, April 19, 1995, Final Report* (Stillwater, OK: International Fire Service Training Association, November 1996).

45. William J. Perry, *Force Protection: Report to the President and Congress on the Protection of U.S. Forces Deployed Abroad* (Washington: Department of Defense, September 15, 1996).

46. Alan Cooperman, "Terror Strikes Again," *U.S. News & World Report,* August 17, 1998, 10-17.

47. *World Trade Center Bombing: Terror Hits Home,* Hearings before the Subcommittee on Crime and Criminal Justice of the Committee on the Judiciary, House of Representatives, 103d Cong., 1st sess. (Washington: U.S. Government Printing Office, March 9, 1993); related accounts in the *New York Times* between February 27 and March 3, 1993.

48. Laqueur, *The New Terrorism,* 156-83.

49. Ernest Evans, *Calling a Truce to Terror* (Westport, CT: Greenwood Press, 1979, 43-46; Leroy Thompson, *Ragged War: The Story of Unconventional and Counter-revolutionary Warfare* (London: Arms and Armour Press, 1994), 315-16.

50. For state sponsorship during the Cold War, see Claire Sterling, *The Terror Network: The Secret War of International Terrorism* (New York: Holt, Rinehart, and Winston Reader's Digest, 1981); Uri Ra'anan et al., eds., *The Hydra of Carnage: International Linkages of Terrorism* (Lexington, MA): Lexington Books, 1986).

51. Perry, *Terrorism from Robespierre to Arafat,* 266-67.

18. Counterterrorism Strategies

*"I don't think they play at all fairly," Alice began,
in a rather complaining tone . . . "and they don't
seem to have any rules in particular: at least, if
there are, nobody attends to them—and you
have no idea how confusing it is. . . ."*

Lewis Carroll
Alice in Wonderland

Counterterrorism is confusing, precisely because there aren't many rules in particular. Opponents, like the ethereal Cheshire Cat, appear and disappear at will. "Off with its head," the Queen cried, but no one knew quite where to chop. The executioner claimed that "you can't cut off a head unless there's a body to cut it off from," the King believed that "anything with a head could be beheaded," and the grinning cat faded from view while disputes continued. Debates about the best ways to combat sociopolitical terrorism also remain unresolved. This primer explores conflicting rationales to help sharpen issues and facilitate cost-effective tradeoffs between avoidable vulnerabilities and perfect protection, which probably is unattainable.

THE NATURE OF COUNTERTERRORISM

Policies, plans, programs, and operations designed to deter and combat terrorism occupy three complementary tiers.* Tier One provides passive protection

---

*U.S. practitioners reserve the term "counterterrorism" for offensive measures and call defensive measures "antiterrorism." The term "combating terrorism" embraces both, but those definitions are not widely accepted elsewhere. This treatise refers to offensive and defensive counterterrorism for simplicity's sake.

for people, selected assets, and lines of communication. Tier Two actively responds to terrorist attacks. Tier Three puts terrorists and their sponsors on the defensive.[1] Auspicious campaigns at all three levels feature centralized planning, decentralized execution, timely intelligence, meticulous training, and interagency (preferably international) teamwork. Advanced technologies facilitate otherwise infeasible missions, but flexible policies and proficient personnel with a flair for improvisation are more important.

PARTICIPANTS AND CONTROL

Counterterrorists must identify and evaluate threats, manage crises, assess postattack situations, cope with consequences, and counterattack or strike first. Military and civilian participants typically include intelligence agents and analysts, police, firefighters, rescue squads, teams that disarm explosives, specialists who dispose of hazardous materials (HAZMAT), and power projection forces.

Dictatorial Regimes

Armed services, paramilitary formations, and secret police commonly perform counterterrorism functions for dictatorial regimes. Soviet leaders relied heavily on the Committee for State Security (KGB), which kept close tabs on every facet of life in all fifteen Soviet Socialist Republics and thereby discouraged domestic dissent. KGB personnel also protected senior Communist Party officials, secured key installations (such as nuclear storage sites), patrolled lengthy Soviet frontiers to intercept intruders, nurtured a network of informants inside the Ministry of Defense to prevent military coups, and monitored the Ministry of Internal Affairs (MVD), which furnished a pervasive national police force.[2]

Democratic Governments

Counterterrorism is foremost a law enforcement function in most democratic countries. Paramilitary gendarmeries or their functional equivalents assist in nearly every nation save the United States, which traditionally disapproves military power as a domestic security instrument, except under exigent circumstances. Federal laws and Department of Defense regulations forbid U.S. Armed Forces (other than the Coast Guard) to participate directly in search, seizure, and arrest operations or otherwise act as a *posse comitatus* for law enforcement purposes, except as authorized expressly by the Constitution or Congress. The Department of Justice rules that such restrictions apply only within the United States but, at this writing, Secretaries of Defense have approved only one exception: the 1990 apprehension of Panamanian strong man General Manuel Noriega during Operation Just Cause.[3]

Orchestration

A mind-numbing array of U.S. players practice counterterrrorism at home and abroad. The Federal Bureau of Investigation (FBI) and Federal Emergency Management Agency (FEMA) lead the national list of forty some elements that deal with domestic terrorism. The Department of State and Central Intelligence Agency (CIA) exercise responsibilities overseas. State and local government participants, who numbered about 2,000,000 in 1999, populated 17,000 law enforcement agencies, 32,000 fire departments, 8,000 emergency medical services, and various other affiliates.[4] All countries require well-orchestrated command/control systems that integrate civil and military capabilities from top to bottom. Wasteful redundancies otherwise occur and conflicting requirements labeled "foreign," "domestic," "law enforcement," and "homeland defense" slip through jurisdictional cracks.[5]

Experience indicates that counterterrorists normally perform best when executives at the top of the pyramid synchronize strategic policy guidance, plans, research-development-procurement programs, and budgets. Centralized training ensures uniform standards while saving time, money, and instructors. Too tight a rein, however, inhibits initiative, fosters inflexibility, and risks regrettable decisions, because directors far from ongoing actions cannot be universally well informed or keep abreast of fast-moving situations, no matter how closely they communicate with commanders on the scene. Senior officials thus are well advised to delegate operational control and tactical decisions to trusted subordinates.

OVERARCHING ISSUES

Three overarching issues strongly influence deterrent, defensive, and offensive strategies: fixed versus flexible policies; violence versus nonviolence; and preemption versus response. Prescribed approaches determine whether counterterrorism strategies are predominantly active or reactive, favor force or finesse, and make it easy or hard for terrorists to predict implementing operations.

Fixed Versus Flexible Policies

Inflexible counterterrorist policies are undesirable, because crises that superficially seem similar in most respects often are fundamentally different. Excessive flexibility not only complicates decision making when emergencies leave little time for deliberation, but opens opportunities for unscrupulous acts.

Insufficient Flexibility

Declaratory policies that prohibit concessions under any conditions might strengthen deterrence by promising terrorists that their objectives are unachievable, but rigidity rules out responses that might be wiser in some situations. Refusal to ransom the Director of Central Intelligence or Chairman of the Joint Chiefs of Staff, for example, could jeopardize national security secrets on a catastrophic scale. It also would take senior decision-makers with steel nerves to ignore reports that terrorists had seeded any skyscraper with a nuclear weapon.

Excessive Flexibility

Excessive flexibility can be just as detrimental as too little. The Omnibus Diplomatic Security and Antiterrorism Act of 1986, for example, denied any items on the U.S. Munitions List to countries that, according to the Secretary of State, sponsored terrorism.[6] Freewheeling Marine Corps Lieutenant Colonel Oliver North, in direct violation, nevertheless negotiated illicit arms sales to Iran with blessings from President Reagan's National Security Adviser Robert C. McFarlane and his successor Vice Admiral John M. Poindexter, partly because they hoped that so doing might encourage Iran's Ayatollah Khomeini to help free hostages whom Shiite Muslim henchmen held in Lebanon. That ploy boomeranged badly: captors not only kept all pawns for several more years,[7] but resultant scandals shook the Reagan Administration to its foundations when news hounds, congressional hearings, and the final report of independent prosecutor Lawrence E. Walsh revealed that anti-Communist Contra guerrillas in Nicaragua received profits derived from those illegal transactions.[8]

Violence Versus Nonviolence

Firepower is suitable and feasible in many situations, but invites adverse political repercussions if targeting intelligence is inadequate. Political pressures and economic sanctions are pointless against groups that lack patron states. Ill-conceived sanctions against nation-states may cause more problems than they solve at home and abroad. Experienced leaders therefore weigh each case on its merits, determine what combination of "carrots" and "sticks" appears most appropriate, then craft strategies and tactics accordingly.

Preemption Versus Retaliation

Counterterrorists may preempt, if intelligence reports indicate that terrorist attacks are imminent, or initiate preventive strikes, if policy-makers conclude that terrorists eventually will attack. Both options invoke the right of self-defense. Both offer great military advantage. Retaliation, in contrast, forefeits initiative, but poses fewer public relations problems. Hot pursuit while culprits are clearly identifiable best assures approval at home and abroad, but does nothing to prevent the havoc that terrorist already have wreaked.

DETERRENT DILEMMAS

Counterterrorists, unlike nuclear strategists, can test theories and refine concepts by trial and error, but the dynamics of deterrence still defy full understanding. No one at this writing can convincingly explain why sociopolitical terrorists use awesome capabilities so sparingly or are so circumspect about escalatory opinions that conceivably could include nuclear, biological, chemical, or radiological (NBCR) weapons.

Political, economic, and social reforms designed to alleviate or eliminate root causes of conflict rarely sway sociopolitical terrorists, who generally demand concessions too great for afflicted governments to accept. Radicals motivated by religious fundamentalism and deep-seated ethnic animosities defy intimidation. Nothing seems to faze suicidal fanatics who welcome death. Combative counterterrorists promise swift retribution, but strong rhetoric unintentionally increases the prestige of terrorist groups and may provoke rather than discourage attacks.[9] Flexible strategies that selectively apply offensive and defensive countermeasures consequently seem to bolster deterrence best.

DEFENSIVE COUNTERTERRORISM

Defensive countermeasures strive to discourage terrorist acts and to mitigate damage and casualties if deterrence fails. Faultless intelligence and broad spectrum strategies are required, because conventional, NBCR, and cybernetic threats pose markedly different problems.

Passive Defense

Passive measures comprise the bedrock upon which defensive counterterror strategies rest. Plans, programs, and operations invariably seek to shield very important persons (VIPs), strengthen public safety, safeguard nationally valuable infrastructure, and enhance cybernetic security.

VIP Protection

Terrorists who specialize in surgical strikes threaten to assassinate or abduct military and civilian VIPs. The best-protected luminaries live and work within walled compounds on large, well-illuminated, heavily guarded grounds where state-of-the-art anti-intrusion devices include visible light and infrared surveillance cameras that ceaselessly project sharp images on closed-circuit television sets. Redundant communications serve heavily armed, highly trained rapid reaction forces.[10]

Security-conscious VIPs select random departure times, routes, destinations, and points of debarkation whenever they leave sanctuaries by automobile, helicopter, boat, or on foot and disseminate "classified" schedules only to those subordinates who absolutely need to know. Wheelmen who excel at combat driving commonly chauffeur heavily armored yet agile limousines replete with bulletproof glass, an inner carapace (turtle shell) of laminated composite materials, explosion-proof fuel tanks, au-

tomatic fire extinguishers, and other protective devices.[11] Scouts secure intersections and defiles along hazardous routes before caravans with armed escorts fore and aft speed by.

Public Safety

Comparable protection for common people is impractical. Barricades and stringent security checks shield some public buildings, but shopping malls, supermarkets, theaters, tourist Meccas, sport stadiums, cathedrals, schools, and other centers that attract large crowds comprise attractive targets. No nation is well prepared to cope with mass casualties in the aftermath of terrorist attacks that employ NBCR weapons. Biological warfare agents for which neither antidotes nor cures are available might be worst, because victims could communicate contagious diseases countrywide, even worldwide, before symptoms appear.[12]

Public education programs that inform rank-and-file military personnel as well as civilians about terrorist tactics and enlighten them about "street smart" countermeasures consequently are important. Experience indicates that low-key but routine involvement by news media, schools, colleges, and "think tanks" could pay big dividends. Careless campers, for example, set countless wild fires that cost the United States Government about $1 billion per year in the 1950s, before "Smokey Bear" campaigns dramatically reduced accidental incinerations, preserved valuable timber, and coincidentally saved $17 billion during the next three decades.

Infrastructure Protection

High-value infrastructures that invite terrorist attacks require adequate physical security, because they form the foundation of modern societies. Key components include governmental, industrial, commercial, and military assets, plus interconnecting transportation and telecommunication links. Close collaboration between public and private sectors is essential.[13] Shrines, monuments, and other cultural icons also are potential targets.[14]

Military Installations Command posts, barracks, ports, airfields, and logistical depots typify installations that armed forces must defend against terrorist attacks without compromising military missions. Experienced counterterrorists accordingly take several precautions that have universal applicability:[15]

- Regularly reevaluate intelligence estimates concerning the types, imminence, and intensities of terrorist threats
- Use findings to educate assigned military personnel (plus dependents, if any) and train counterterror teams
- Locate garrisons and outlying facilities in secluded areas to the greatest extent possible, consistent with essential missions
- Harden structures, install shatterproof glass, and secure perimeters to strengthen local security
- Surround cores with concentric exclusion zones to reduce dangers from standoff attacks
- Restrict access routes, and protect points of entry with guard posts in depth and heavy-duty barriers
- Maintain security force manning levels commensurate with perceived threats; avoid stultifying periods of guard duty, which decrease alertness
- Establish flexible standing operations procedures (SOPs) and rules of engagement (ROE)
- Assign sectors of responsibility, then repeatedly rehearse optional responses to each type of threat, assess performances, and refine procedures
- Conduct frequent, unannounced inspections

to ascertain the readiness of counterterror teams and defensive facilities
- Work closely with local law enforcement agencies and, if in a foreign country, with host nation counterterror specialists

Civilian Installations Civilian infrastructure is harder to protect, because fewer courses of action are open. Embassies and consulates must remain where they are well able to represent respective governments. Installations that provide electrical power, light, water, and petroleum products to industrial, commercial, agricultural, financial, and residential consumers not only occupy fixed positions, but rarely can restrict access routes, designate surrounding areas "Off Limits," or establish defenses in-depth. Neither owners nor users can adequately protect isolated facilities, such as water reservoirs, radio relay stations, and bridges along arterial routes.

Inexpensive countermeasures include corporate vulnerability surveys, reductions in force at risky sites, and crisis reaction cells, whose members recommend policies, develop defensive plans, and supervise implementation.[16] Stringent airport security measures have drastically reduced hijackings and shootouts at terminals since the 1970s.[17]

No country, however, can safeguard all assets equally well at home and abroad. Most U.S. embassies, consulates, and cultural centers remain vulnerable to vehicle-borne explosives, because a vast majority (including prestigious posts in London, Paris, and Rome) are 100 feet or less from busy thoroughfares. The United States Government could close shop in the most dangerous foreign countries, accredit envoys regionally, and ensconce them centrally at safer locations,[18] but abilities to promote U.S. foreign policies would suffer. Defenders also could fortify Capitol Hill, the Pentagon, the State Department, official residences, national landmarks, and other potential targets. The nation, however, would pay a heavy price, because budgets would balloon, America's image as a free society would sag under siege, and terrorists would thereby achieve strategically significant bloodless victories. Painful compromises thus seem inevitable.

Cybernetic Security

Concerns for cybernetic security are intensifying at logarithmic rates, given boundless dependence on telecommunications, computers, and the World Wide Web. Multiple points of entry, coupled with inexpensive but nevertheless sophisticated intrusion techniques, invite sociopolitical terrorists to acquire, destroy, transform, or manipulate critical information and codes with devastating effects that could ripple through or across national infrastructures. Laptop computers and telephone connections to any Internet Service Provider enable assailants to conduct electronic reconnaissance surveys, locate security loopholes, breach "firewalls," then insert viruses that obliterate passwords, delete files, and invade emergency service sites. Physical attacks and cybertage (electronic sabotage) conducted concurrently against key military and civilian targets conceivably could undercut all forms of national power.[19]

Defenses against cybernetic attacks are woefully deficient at the turn of the twenty-first century. Victims seldom could discern intrusions during early stages, much less respond in time to escape serious injury. Contributing factors include incomplete appreciation of cybernetic threats, legal impediments, and reluctance to share politically, economically, and militarily sensitive information. Acceptable protection awaits centralized operation centers that are organizationally and technologically prepared to collect information about the nature and extent of cybernetic attacks, determine implications, and implement appropriate countermeasures before damage becomes extensive.[20]*

---

*For additional discussion, see section entitled Cybernetic Warfare in Chapter 19.

Active Defense

Active defenses feature hostage rescue operations and actions to disarm explosives that terrorists emplace. Both missions are among the trickiest that counterterrorists or any other forces ever perform.

Rescue Hostages

Hard-liners consider hostages expendable, and thereby render them valueless for bargaining purposes, but most national leaders are more compassionate. Nonviolent options include diplomatic overtures, prolonged debates, and political, economic, or social payoffs. Force, which completes the package, almost always takes precedence if holders harm hostages.

Assorted variables determine suitable tactics and tools. Hostages, for example, might be one, few, or many; healthy, sick, or sedated; cooperate with rescuers or resist, if the so-called Stockholm Syndrome compels them to sympathize with captors.[21] Loose rules of engagement seldom work well if safety is essential. It makes a difference whether terrorists vacillate or show resolve, hold hostages in known or unknown, single or multiple, static or mobile sites that are large or small, heavily or lightly defended, near or far, aloft, afloat, or ashore in domestic, foreign, friendly, or hostile territory where final approaches are open or covered.

Flexible strategies are invaluable, because patience is preferable on some occasions, while speed, surprise, and physical prowess take precedence under different conditions.[22] The July 1976 Israeli success in Uganda and fruitless U.S. efforts to extricate prisoners from Tehran in April 1980 both involved long-distance raids into hostile lands, but Baader-Meinhof and Palestinian hijackers conveniently concentrated hostages at Entebbe International Airport, whereas Iranian revolutionaries scattered captives throughout the U.S. Embassy compound in the midst of a metropolis.[23] Hanafi radicals with relatively modest demands released 134 pawns in Washington on March 11, 1977, at the behest of ambassadors from Egypt, Iran, and Pakistan, whereas British Special Air Service (SAS) teams had to storm the Iranian Embassy in London on May 5, 1980 after negotiations with hard-core Marxist-Leninist counterrevolutionaries broke down.[24]

Neutralize Explosives

Ordnance disposal teams aim to seize, disarm, destroy, or otherwise neutralize explosive devices that terrorists hide within buildings. Searchers who rummage through rooms may give terrorists time to detonate munitions before they arrive, even if intelligence reports pinpoint locations. Demolition experts fortunate enough to find concealed explosives before they blow cannot always neutralize foreign models that may be armed and fused differently than domestic counterparts.[25] On-site defenders, booby traps, and anti-tampering devices compound their dangers. Chances of success hence are slim.

OFFENSIVE COUNTERTERRORISM

Offensive counterterrorism normally amalgamates political and economic power with some sort of armed force. Impeccable intelligence is the key in any case, because poorly informed counterterrorists can neither find elusive foes nor accurately identify patrons who provide sanctuaries and support.

Nonviolent Options

Political, commercial, and financial pressures, censorship, and ostracism may put terrorists on the defensive or reduce their offensive options without resort to violence. All generally require great patience over lengthy periods of time, because expectations of early success are seldom assured.

Political Pressures

Political pressures applied to avenge terrorist atrocities and prevent repetition span a spectrum of possibilities. Rungs on that escalation ladder include steps to suspend normal relations with states that subsidize transnational terrorism, revoke favored nation trade status, close bothersome enemy embassies to prevent misuse of diplomatic immunity, deny passports and visas to or deport individual suspects, interrupt ongoing education and training programs, or abrogate treaties. Political countermeasures of greatest severity might sever relations, even withdraw recognition, which would deprive offenders of rights normally available under the offended nation's laws. Psychological warfare (PSYWAR) specialists conduct concurrent campaigns that expose culprits to public censure, incite international communities to curb connections with offending nations, encourage dissident groups to overthrow renegade governments, and otherwise seed uncertainties in terrorist camps.

Censorship and Ostracism

Trees that fall in forests may frighten campers nearby, but don't make enough noise to scare anybody beyond earshot. The most atrocious terrorist acts similarly would lack strategic significance if television, radio, and newspaper reporters refused to transmit substantive and symbolic messages far and wide. Counterterrorists would like to deny opponents that privilege, but prospects are nearly nil for two reasons: censorship is anathema in societies that value freedom of the press; and banner headlines and captivating broadcasts help members of the news media climb promotion ladders.[26]

Chiefs of State and their spokesmen give priceless publicity to sociopolitical terrorists with whom they meet, but benefits sometimes outweigh liabilities, because ostracism eliminates opportunities for productive dialogue. President Clinton in October 1994 therefore lifted the official ban on U.S. Government contacts with Sinn Fein, the provisional political wing of the Irish Republican Army (IRA), which periodically employed terrorist tactics in efforts to separate Northern Ireland from the United Kingdom. Clinton then dined with Sinn Fein President Gerry Adams at the White House in efforts to broker a peace agreement. Adams and British Prime Minister Tony Blair discussed IRA demands at 10 Downing Street in December 1997 (the first such meeting since David Lloyd George negotiated with IRA guerrilla chieftain Michael Collins in 1921), after which Adams helped draft a historic power-sharing pact that the Irish Republic and Northern Ireland approved on May 22, 1998.[27]

Economic Sanctions

Economic sanctions under favorable conditions can exert painful pressures on nations that nurture terrorists. Restrictions on trade (especially boycotts and embargoes), foreign assistance, technology transfers, export credits, tourism, capital transactions, and access to commercial facilities (including ports and airfields) are among the most common penalties. Severe limitations nevertheless are evident. Economic blockades are theoretically possible, but frequently flounder because key countries won't forego profits or fear retaliation. Mind-boggling legal tangles commonly allow individuals and nongovernmental organizations to escape prosecution if they traffic with terrorist states. Do U.S. businessmen, for example, break laws when they deal with Arab states that underwrite violence-prone "freedom fighters" whose sociopolitical aim is an independent Palestine? Reliable answers to such questions are nonexistent.

Violent Options

The most direct, decisive, expeditious ways to eradicate terrorism involve violence. Actions to eliminate ringleaders, eviscerate terrorist groups, exact retribution, and punish patron states are among the most popular options. Only Courses One and Two require skilled counterterrorists, but all demand timely, accurate intelligence.

Kingpin Killings

"The only good Indian is a dead Indian" was General Philip H. Sheridan's oft-quoted comment when Comanche Chief Toch-a-way said, "Me good Indian."

Some (maybe most) counterterrorists similarly contend that "the only good terrorist is a dead one." Lethal force, as they see it, is quick, cost-effective, and eternally deters each dead terrorist. They cite the Principle of Military Necessity, which invokes "the right to compel submission of the enemy with the least possible expenditure of time, lives, and money."[28] Their message to terrorist kingpins is unmistakable: "Desist, or we will hunt you down wherever you try to hide and kill you without compunction."

Lethal force clearly is allowable when counterterrorists catch small fry red-handed. Chiefs of State, however, are reluctant to hire headhunters as matters of national policy, because so doing might expose them to counterattacks in kind, martyred terrorists might serve their cause better dead than alive, and replacements might be more dangerous than top dogs they supplant. Terrorism in such cases would intensify instead of subside.[29]

Blast Terrorist Bases

"Drive-by shootings" that blast terrorist bases may be politically embarrassing, if intelligence reports falsely identify targets. Saudi Arabian expatriate Osama bin Laden, for example, allegedly bankrolled transnational terrorist groups whose members demolished U.S. embassies in Nairobi, Kenya, and Dar es Salaam, Tanganyika, on August 7, 1998. President Clinton on August 20th authorized simultaneous cruise missile strikes against his hideout in Afghanistan and the Al Shifa Pharmaceutical Plant on the outskirts of Khartoum, Sudan. The latter, according to U.S. intelligence analysts, produced Empta, a precursor for VX nerve agents, with technological assistance from Iraq.[30]

The attack that demolished Al Shifa facilities was a tactical success but a public affairs disappointment. Osama bin Laden's involvement proved unproveable. Sudanese officials, who swore that the plant manufactured nothing but medications, enjoyed a propaganda bonanza when they invited foreign news media representatives to inspect the rubble. The well-respected international Organization for the Prohibition of Chemical Weapons contradicted State Department testimony that Empta is a "substance not used in [any] commercial applications," and anonymous diplomats in Khartoum testified that Iraqis in cahoots with the Sudanese Government indeed were developing chemical agents, but at another location nearby.[31]

Eviscerate Terrorist Groups

Intelligence needed to eviscerate terrorist groups is scarce, because paranoid cells are practically impenetrable by outsiders. Leaders take pains to conceal their identities, move frequently, disregard geographic frontiers, and plan each action meticulously. Skillful sleuths rely on interagency and international cooperation, since no single source monopolizes leads concerning terrorist command structures, memberships, movements, and methods of operation.

Most target dossiers are flawed and findings have short shelf lifes, but counterterrorists nevertheless have eradicated a number of notorious groups since the 1970s. The tiny Symbionese Liberation Army, which kidnapped and converted newspaper heiress Patricia Hearst to its cause, lasted barely six months (November 6, 1973–May 17, 1974) before "General" Donald DeFreeze and five companions roasted to death following a shootout with FBI agents and Los Angeles police. All three survivors, including Patty (aka Tania) Hearst, eluded capture until the following year.[32] The Baader-Meinhof gang ran amok in West Germany for more than a decade beginning about 1969, then disintegrated because diligent counterterrorists had killed the most militant or put them behind bars.[33] Red Brigades in Italy brutally assaulted "reactionary" politicians, police, journalists, and industrialists during approximately that same period. The high-profile murder of former Prime Minister Aldo Moro in 1978 and the abduction of U.S. Army Brigadier General James Dozier in 1981

were among their most infamous exploits before political and legal reforms knocked props from beneath their programs. Many members were killed, incarcerated, or recanted until nothing remained except a few impotent splinters.[34]

Attack Patron States

Sovereign states that shelter and sustain transnational terrorists deserve reprisals, but reasonable proof of complicity often is hard to acquire and prudent counterterrorists avoid provoking powerful adversaries that could bite back. U.S. Armed Forces, for example, never tried to quash camps where the Soviet Union and its East European satellite states trained terrorists,[35] because so doing might have precipitated World War III. Retaliation against less potent opponents may produce negative or ambiguous as well as positive results, depending on circumstances.

Rancorous relations between the United States and Libya began about 1970, when Mu'ammar al-Qadhafi evicted the U.S. Air Force from Wheelus Air Base, assisted revolutionary groups around the globe, encouraged transnational terrorism, tried to topple pro-Western neighbors, and established close ties with the Soviet Union.[36] Proven and alleged provocations peaked with the terrorist bombing of a night club in Berlin. More than 100 U.S. aircraft retaliated against five target areas near Tripoli and Benghazi on April 15, 1986, despite objections by France and Spain, which refused overflight rights. Those raids, which lasted eleven minutes, have made Libyan terrorism more circumspect ever since, but lessons learned remain ambiguous, because U.S. officials still don't know for sure why Qadhafi chose not to respond with untraceable attacks.[37]

DEMOCRATIC CONSTRAINTS

Legal, moral, and cultural considerations strongly constrain counterterrorist activities in democratic countries. Key issues include civil liberties, allowable courses of punitive action, and the disposition of detained terrorists. Costs calculated in terms of operational flexibility sometimes are severe.

Civil Liberties

Amendment I to the U.S. Constitution promises freedoms of speech, the press, peaceful assembly, and the right "to petition the Government for a redress of grievances." Amendment IV guards against "unreasonable searches and seizures." A *Posse Comitatus* Act forbids the U.S. Army to enforce laws within the United States[38] but, at the behest of the President and the Attorney General, that Service began to collect domestic intelligence when civil rights and anti-Vietnam War demonstrations surged in the late 1960s, because workloads exceeded FBI capacities. Army surveillance files in scores of data banks eventually covered 100,000 individuals and virtually every dissenting organization from far right to far left, of which the following are representative: the Ku Klux Klan; the John Birch Society; the American Civil Liberties Union (ACLU); the National Association for the Advancement of Colored People (NAACP); the Southern Christian Leadership Conference; the Anti-Defamation League of B'nai Brith; the National Committee for a Sane Nuclear Policy; Clergy and Laymen Concerned About the War; and the National Organization for Women (NOW). Those practices ceased in 1971, after investigative reporters engendered public outrage and Congress clamped on a lid.[39]

Calls for Draconian countermeasures that threaten individual and organizational freedoms resurfaced in the late 1990s when the specter of terrorists armed with nuclear, biological, chemical, or radiological weapons caused increasing concerns. The ACLU and other civil libertarians contend that roving wiretaps, secret court orders that authorize intelligence agents to trace telephone calls or obtain business records, and expanded internal security roles for U.S. Armed Forces represent unwarranted assaults on the Constitution.[40] Secretary of Defense William S. Cohen, in testimony before the Senate Armed Services Committee on September 16, 1999, justified selective infringements with these words: "We need greater intelligence . . . here at home. That is going to put [the U.S. Government] on a collision course with rights of privacy. And it's something that democracies have got to come to grips with. . . . How much are we willing to give up in the way of intrusion into our lives?"[41] The first terrorist attack that causes casualties and damage on unprecedented scales likely will clear minds rapidly in that regard.

Legal Dispositions

Public trials followed by the imprisonment or execution of sociopolitical terrorists respect due processes, but conceptual disputes and sluggish bureaucracies impose stumbling blocks in free societies. International conventions ostensibly regulate criminal jurisdictions of contracting States, yet foreign nations rarely extradite fugitive felons on request (a judicial procedure) or deport them (an executive procedure), unless doing so seems to satisfy their best interests.[42] Members of the Palestine Liberation Front (PLO), for example, strained U.S. diplomatic relations with Egypt and Italy after PLO gunmen hijacked the *Achille Lauro* cruise ship in October 1985, murdered a crippled American passenger, and dumped him overboard. The terrorists surrendered to authorities in Cairo, who figuratively washed their hands of the matter, then put the culprits aboard an Egyptian airliner bound for Algeria. Four U.S. Navy F-14 Tomcat fighters intercepted that flight in international airspace and force it to land in Sigonella, Sicily, whereupon the Italian Government released the key felon without trial and favored the rest with lenient sentences.[43] Jurisdictional disagreements and legal loopholes likely will continue to complicate proper disposition of apprehended terrorists until foreign and domestic lawmakers enact legislation that leaves less opportunity for interpretation.

KEY POINTS

- Counterterrorism benefits from centralized preparation and decentralized operations
- Counterterrorism is foremost a law enforcement function in most democratic nations
- Legal, moral, and cultural constraints strongly influence counterterrorism in democratic countries
- Timely, accurate intelligence is invariably indispensable
- Rigid counterterrorism policies that prohibit concessions under any conditions may rule out sensible actions in crucial situations
- Counterterrorists, unlike nuclear strategists, have not yet devised widely accepted deterrent concepts
- Personnel security programs provide poorer protection for the public than for VIPs, because financial costs and inconvenience are excessive
- Civilian infrastructure is much harder to protect than military installations
- Terrorist attacks, including cybertage (electronic sabotage), could undercut all forms of national power
- Cybernetic and infrastructure protection demand close collaboration between public and private sectors
- Hot pursuits are more easily justified than delayed counterattacks or preemptive strikes, because terrorists are clearly identifiable
- Counterterrorists who grapple daily with complex problems understand that sound, simple solutions are rare

NOTES

1. For overviews, see Anthony H. Cordesman, *Asymmetric Warfare Versus Counterterrorism: Rethinking CBRN and CIP Defense and Response* (Washington: Center for Strategic and International Studies, September 2000); Karl A. Segar, *The Anti-Terrorism Handbook* (Novato, CA: Presidio Press, 1990); Neil C. Livingstone, *The Cult of Counterterrorism: The "Weird World" of Spooks, Counterterrorists, Adventurers, and the Not Quite Professionals* (Lexington, MA: Lexington Books, 1990).

2. John Barron, *KGB: The Secret Work of Soviet Agents* (New York: Reader's Digest Press, 1974), 80-85, 451-53; Amy W. Knight, "The KGB's Special Departments in the Soviet Armed Forces," *ORBIS*, Summer 1984, 257-80; Harriet Fast and William F. Scott, *The Armed Forces of the USSR* (Boulder, CO: Westview Press, 1979), 218-22.

3. Title 18, United States Code, Section 1385, "Use of the Army and Air Force as Posse Comitatus"; Title 10, United States Code, Sections 375 and 379; *Legal Memorandum: The Extraterritorial Applica-* *tion of the Posse Comitatus Act and Chapter 18 of Title 10, U.S. Code* (Washington, Office of the Chief Counsel, Maritime and International Law Division, U.S. Coast Guard, December 22, 1989; Secretary of Defense Dick Cheney, memorandum entitled *Modification of DoD Directive 5525.5,* "DoD Cooperation with Civilian Law Enforcement Officials," December 20, 1989; Charles Doyle, *Use of the Military to Enforce Civilian Law: Posse Comitatus Act and Other Considerations,* Rpt. No. 95-964S (Washington: Congressional Research Service, September 12, 1995).

4. *Combating Terrorism: Use of National Guard Response Teams Is Unclear,* letter report to congressional requesters, GAO/NSIAD-99-110 (Washington: General Accounting Office, June 21, 1999); Ron Laurenzo, "GAO: Time to Reassess Guard Anti-Terror Teams," *Defense Week,* July 6, 1999, 1.

5. Ashton Carter, John Deutch, and Philip Zelikow, "Catastrophic Terrorism: Tackling the New Danger," *Foreign Affairs,* vol. 77, no. 6 (November-December 1998), 82-83.

6. *Export Administration Act*, 100 Stat. 853 at 874 (P.L. 99-399), January 1986; *Omnibus Diplomatic Security and Antiterrorism Act of 1986*, HR 4151, August 27, 1986.

7. Clyde R. Mark, *Lebanon: U.S. Hostages, An Overview and Chronology, February 10, 1984-December 27, 1991*, Rpt. No. 92-398F (Washington: Congressional Research Service, April 7, 1992). For reminiscences, see Terry Anderson, *Den of Lions: Memoirs of Seven Years* (New York: Crown Books, 1993); Brian Keenan, *An Evil Cradling: The Five-Year Ordeal of a Hostage,* 1st American edition (New York: Viking, 1993).

8. Peter Kornbluh and Malcolm Byrne, eds., *The Iran-Contra Scandal: The Declassified History,* The National Security Archive Document (New York: New Press, May 1993).

9. Brian M. Jenkins, *Fighting Terrorism: An Enduring Task* (Santa Monica, CA: RAND Corporation, February 1981), 4-5; Neil C. Livingstone, "Terrorism: What Should We Do?," in *This World,* Fall 1985, 62; Conor Cruise O'Brien, "Thinking About Terrorism," *Atlantic,* June 1986, 9-10; John M. Oseth, "Combatting Terrorism: The Dilemmas of a Decent Nation," *Parameters,* Spring 1985, 68.

10. Neil Livingstone, *The Complete Security Guide for Executives* (Lexington, MA: Lexington Books, 1989); Brian M. Jenkins, *Terrorism and Personal Protection* (Boston: Butterworth Publishers, 1985); Richard Clutterbuck, *Terrorism in an Unstable World* (New York: Routledge, 1994), 83-86.

11. Roger Davies, "Protective Technology for VIP Limousines," *Intersec: The Journal of International Security,* June 1991, 51-52.

12. John Donnolly, "CIA Sees Threat in Global Diseases," *Boston Globe,* June 20, 2000, 1; Jessica Stern, "Is That an Epidemic—or a Terrorist Attack? A Lethal Weapon We Must Learn to Recognize," *New York Times,* October 16, 1999, 19; Secretary of Defense William S. Cohen, "Preparing for a Grave New World" [no pun intended], *Washington Post,* July 26, 1999, A19.

13. *Critical Foundations: Protecting America's Infrastructures,* (Washington: Commission on Critical Infrastructure Protection, October 13, 1997), 3-6.

14. Arthur Santana, "Monuments Are Found Vulnerable to Attack," *Washington Post,* July 2, 2000, A1, A8.

15. *Force Protection: Global Interests, Global Responsibilities,* Report to the President and Congress (Washington: Secretary of Defense, September 15, 1996), especially Secretary Perry's cover letter; basic report, 6-10, 14; and Annex A, 24-68; Bonne Chance, "Bases Weigh Terror Risk, Security Costs: Bill for Upgrades May Be Billions," *Atlanta Journal and Constitution,* July 4, 2001, 8.

16. *Critical Foundations,* 93-99; Brooks McClure, "Corporate Vulnerability—and How to Assess It," in *Political Terrorism and Energy,* ed. Yonah Alexander and Charles K. Ebinger (New York: Praeger, 1982), 209-27.

17. John D. Baldeschwieler, "Explosive Detection for Commercial Aircraft Security" and Paul Wilkinson, "Designing an Effective International Aviation Security System," in *Technology and Terrorism,* ed. Paul Wilkinson (London: Frank Cass, 1993), 81-122; Clutterbuck, *Terrorism in an Unstable World,* 194-206.

18. Thomas W. Lippman, "Report on Terrorism Suggests Closing Some U.S. Embassies," *Washington Post,* January 9, 1999, A14; Vernon Loeb, "U.S. Spent $3 Billion to Protect Embassies," *Washington Post,* July 23, 2001, A20; Eli Lake, "$5 Billion Eyed for Embassy Security," *Washington Times,* July 30, 2001, A13.

19. *Critical Foundations,* 15-20, A2-A7; Anthony Forster, "Hi-Tech Terrorists Turn to Cyber Warfare," *Jane's Intelligence Review,* September 1999, 46-49.

20. *Critical Foundations,* 27-33, 89-91, A2-A10.

21. Leo Ettinger, "The Effects of Captivity," and Thomas Strantz, "The Stockholm Syndrome," in *Victims of Terrorism,* ed. Frank M. Ochberg and David A. Soskis (Boulder, CO: Westview Press, 1982), 73-93, 149-63.

22. Walter N. Lang, *The World's Elite Forces* (New York: Salamander Books, 1987), 18-85, 114-47; Leroy Thompson, *The Rescuers: The World's Top Ten Anti-Terrorist Units* (Boulder, CO: Paladin Press, 1986), 19-54.

23. William Stevenson, *90 Minutes at Entebbe* (New York: Bantam Books, 1976); Charles Beckwith and Donald Knox, *Delta Force* (New York: Harcourt Brace and Jovanovich, 1983), 187-300.

24. *Facts on File Yearbook, 1977,* 192, 396, 711; Doug Campbell, "SAS Dares and Wins: A Raid That Worked," *Soldier of Fortune,* September 1980, 26-29.

25. Optional ways to arm and fuse nuclear munitions are contained in Chuck Hanson, *U.S. Nuclear Weapons: The Secret History* (New York: Orion Books 1988), 225-27. See also Tony Capaccio, "Commando Role in Countering Nukes Will Grow," *Defense Week,* December 20, 1993, 5.

26. Rod Paschall, *LIC 2010: Special Operations & Unconventional Warfare in the Next Century* (Washington: Brassey's [U.S.], 1990), 107-8.

27. Karen Donfried, *Northern Ireland: The Peace Process and the IRA Cease-Fire of August 31, 1994,* Rpt. 96-763F (Washington: Congressional Research

Service, September 10, 1996) and *Northern Ireland: The Talks Process as Prelude to the April 1998 Peace Agreement,* Rpt. 98-542 (Washington: Congressional Research Service, May 25, 1998).

28. Morris Greenspan, *The Modern Law of Land Warfare* (Berkeley: University of California Press, 1959), 313-14. See, for example, Robert F. Turner, "In Self-Defense, U.S. Has Right to Kill Terrorist bin Laden," *USA Today,* October 26, 1999, 17A.

29. Stuart Taylor, Jr., "Is the Assassination Ban Dead?" *National Journal,* November 21, 1998, 2758-59; Harry Levins, "Military Experts Debate Moral Ramifications of Killing Leaders," *St. Louis Post-Dispatch,* August 3, 2001, 10.

30. Clyde Mark and Ted Dagne, *Terrorist Attacks on U.S. Embassies in Africa: Aftermath and U.S. Retaliation,* Issue Brief 98042 (Washington: Congressional Research Service, September 16, 1998).

31. *Facts on File,* vol. 58, no. 3013 (September 3, 1998), 608-9 and no. 3018 (October 8, 1998), 710.

32. Albert Parry, *Terrorism from Robespierre to Arafat* (New York: Vanguard Press, 1976), 361-62.

33. Julian Becker, *Hitler's Children: The Story of the Baader-Meinhof Terrorist Gang* (Philadelphia: Lippincott, 1977).

34. Raimondo Catanzaro, ed., *The Red Brigades and Left-Wing Terrorism in Italy* (New York: St. Martin's Press, 1991); Richard O. Collin and Gordon L. Freedman, *Winter of Fire: The Abduction of General Dozier and the Downfall of the Red Brigades* (New York: Dutton, 1990).

35. Director of Central Intelligence William J. Casey, *Remarks Before the Symposium on Terrorism and Industry: Threats and Responses* (Washington: Stanford Research Institute and the Center for Strategic and International Studies, October 14, 1985), 3-5, 17 and "The International Linkages: What Do We Know?" in *Hydra of Carnage: International Linkages of Terrorism,* ed. Uri ra'anan et al. (Lexington, MA: Lexington Books, 1986), 8-9, 11.

36. P. Edward Haley, *Quddafi and the United States Since 1969* (New York: Praeger, 1984); Daniel P. Bolger, *Americans at War: An Era of Violent Peace, 1975-1986* (Novato, CA: Presidio Press, 1988), 169-89, 383-441.

37. David Turndoff, "The U.S. Raid on Libya: A Forceful Response to Terrorism," *Brooklyn Journal of International Law,* vol. 14, no. 1 (1988), 187-221; Frederick Zilian, Jr., "The U.S. Raid on Libya—and NATO," *ORBIS,* Fall 1986, 499-524; Anthony Cordesman, "After the Raid: The Emerging Lessons from the Attack on Libya," *Armed Forces Journal,* August 1986, 355-60.

38. See Note 3.

39. *S. Rept. 94-755: Supplementary Detailed Staff Reports on Intelligence Activities and the Rights of Americans,* Final Report, Book III, Senate Select Committee to Study Governmental Operations with Respect to Intelligence Activities, 94th Cong., 2d sess., April 23, 1976, 785-834.

40. *National Commission on Terrorism,* Final Report, June 5, 2000.

41. Bill Gertz, "Inside the Ring," *Washington Times,* September 17, 1999, A7.

42. David Freestone, "International Cooperation Against Terrorism and the Development of International Law Principles of Jurisdiction," in *Terrorism and International Law,* ed. Rosalyn Higgins and Maurice Flory (New York: Routledge, 1997), 43-67.

43. *Facts on File Yearbook* (New York: Facts on File Publications, 1986), 29, 518-19.

19. Nonlethal Warfare Strategies

*Military affairs, in the broad sense, can seldom
be taken up in isolation. . . . And that is why a
general theory of strategy must, I believe, be
a theory of power in all its forms, not just a
theory of military power.*

Rear Admiral J. C. Wylie
Military Strategy

Political, economic, technological, psychological, and cybernetic means of waging nonlethal warfare commonly supplement armed force in pursuit of national security objectives and replace military power when conditions are favorable.* Future quests for victory indeed may take place mainly on nonviolent battlefields, if prognostications by Chinese Colonels Qiao Liang and Wang Xiansui are even close to correct. High-intensity conflict, as they see it, "is now escaping from the bounds of bloody massacres and exhibiting a trend toward low casualties, or even none at all . . . and there is almost no domain which does not have warfare's offensive pattern."[1]

Parallel views are widespread in the Western World. Whether those contentions are premature or pundits overstate their case remains to be seen, but present-day politico-military policy-makers and strategists are consciously melding lethal and non-

lethal capabilities more effectively than their predecessors. Only Grade A students of such subjects, however, pick the best possible blends by choice instead of by chance.

THE NATURE OF NONLETHAL WARFARE

Machiavelli theorized about nonlethal warfare half a millennium ago.[2] Hitler put theories into practice with spectacular success in the 1930s, before armed force replaced finesse as his forte.[3] Stalin, who specialized in insidious actions, subsequently annexed or dominated most of Central Europe without resort to large-scale shootouts.[4] Creative thinkers since then have explored innovative techniques that, coupled with heretofore nonexistent cybernetic warfare, add exotic complexities. The trick is knowing which option(s) will reap the greatest advantages under what conditions.

Nonlethal warfare objectives typically aim to enfeeble foes at home and abroad under Cold and Hot War conditions:[5]

- Shake public confidence in rival governments
- Separate rivals from their friends and allies
- Disrupt rival command, control, and communication systems

---

*Chapter 19 excludes tactically rather than strategically significant nonlethal weapons, such as stun guns, water cannons, nonpenetrating projectiles (rubber bullets), irritants, calmatives, tranquilizers, adhesives ("stickums"), antitraction agents ("slickums"), combustion modifiers, metal embrittlements, specialty foams, thermal barriers, odiferous substances, high-powered microwaves, low-energy lasers, particle beams, strobe lights, holographs, infrasound, ultrasound, and other acoustic devices.

- Separate rivals from foreign raw materials and finished products
- Undermine rival financial structures
- Cripple rival corporations at home and abroad
- Alter perceptions, attitudes, and behavior of friends, foes, and neutrals
- Deprive rivals of accurate information and feed them misinformation
- Deny rivals benefits from technological breakthroughs

Prospects normally are most favorable when employers maximize shock effects at the onset. Success is less likely if early achievement of objectives is essential, important allies disapprove, or adversaries believe that costs of compliance would outweigh benefits. Nonlethal warfare is least effective against risk-taking autocrats, who not only enhance their reputations by resisting but hope to win by not losing.[6]

POLITICAL WARFARE

Political warfare practitioners manipulate international relations offensively and defensively to strengthen their stance and sap opponents. They typically may cancel state visits, restrict cultural interchanges, boycott international athletic events, abrogate treaties, recall ambassadors, close embassies to prevent misuse of diplomatic immunity, deny entry to or deport offensive officials, sever diplomatic relations and, if additional clout is required, withdraw recognition, which deprives transgressors of legal rights. Adroit moves with potent military implications enable political warriors to block enemy diplomatic initiatives, foster flexibility, facilitate surprise attacks, and defang defeated foes.

Block Enemy Initiatives

Political warriors covet abilities to block vexatious enemy initiatives. The United Nations charter, which empowers the Security Council to order po-

litical, economic, and/or military countermeasures against any aggressor, offers opportunities to do so at the highest levels, because Chapter V authorizes the five permanent members (originally USA, USSR, UK, France, and Nationalist China) to veto any resolution they disapprove, even if all others vote favorably.[7]

The Soviet Union exercised veto privileges forty-three times before January 10, 1950, when its spokesman, Jakob Malik, stalked out and stayed away after the Security Council refused to oust Nationalist China. That rash move made it impossible for Stalin to reject UN resolutions that in rapid succession condemned North Korea's invasion of South Korea in June 1950, and authorized a United Nations Command to intervene. Malik returned on July 27, but to no avail, because the General Assembly rather than the Security Council in October 1950 authorized UN operations north of the 38th Parallel after General MacArthur's amphibious landings at Inchon outflanked Communist forces farther south. No permanent member of the Security Council since then has relinquished its veto powers even momentarily.[8]

Foster Strategic Flexibility

Implicit and explicit agreements may favor one party or distribute benefits among two or more, but all bear close scrutiny, because short-term advantages sometimes become long-term liabilities. The Soviet-German nonaggression pact of August 23, 1939, for example, gave each signatory great latitude to carry out nefarious plans without interference by the other. Hitler's armed forces poured into Western Poland one week after Foreign Ministers V. M. Molotov and Joachim von Ribbentrop affixed their signatures. Stalin's troops occupied the remainder of that country, then annexed parts of Finland, the Baltic States, Galicia, western Belorussia, and northern Bukovina.[9] Both sides achieved short-range objectives at minimal costs, but Stalin's euphoria turned sour when Nazi invaders violated the nonaggression agreement and drove spearheads deep into the Soviet Union on June 22, 1941. Two years elapsed before Soviet troops launched strategically significant counteroffensives after they turned the tide at Stalingrad.[10]

Deceive Adversaries

"All warfare is based on deception," according to Sun Tzu.[11] Maybe not, but clever strategists made good use of deceit long before he made that observation and their descendants do so today. The mythological Trojan horse that infiltrated Troy facilitated a world-famous infiltration circa 1184 B.C.[12] General George S. Patton, Jr.'s fictitious First U.S. Army Group, which deployed in East Anglia 3,128 years later, led German defenders to conclude that Allied cross-channel attacks would concentrate on the Pas de Calais, which was more accessible than Western Normandy.[13]

Political deceit can be just as devastating, as Japanese diplomats demonstrated immediately before the raid that wrecked Pearl Harbor and put a huge proportion of the United States Navy out of commission on December 7, 1941. The first supersecret segments of a fourteen-part message from Foreign Minister Shiganori Togo to unwitting Ambassador Kishisaburo Nomura in Washington left Tokyo on December 6, when Vice Admiral Chuichi Nagumo's carrier task force was already close to Hawaii. U.S. signals intelligence specialists by the next morning had intercepted, deciphered, translated, and disseminated all fourteen transmissions, the last of which declared that "it is impossible to reach an agreement through further negotiations." Alarm bells, however, really began to ring only after separate correspondence from Togo told Nomura to deliver the complete packet, preferably to Secretary of State Cordell Hull, "at 1:00 PM on the 7th, your time" (8:00 AM at Pearl Harbor, where the first attack wave hit a few minutes earlier). All of that transpired on Sunday, which was not a duty day for the U.S. diplomatic corps or Armed Forces. Pearl Harbor was already in ruins when Ambassador Nomura and

Special Envoy Suburo Kurusu finally arrived in Hull's office. Strategic as well as tactical surprise was close to complete.[14]

Defang Defeated Enemies

Decrees that aim to defang defeated enemy forces by political means are a fairly recent phenomenon. Victors who impose severe terms on the vanquished sow seeds of future conflict if they relax vigilance and lose control, whereas benevolent winners who rehabilitate as well as disarm losers are more likely to nurture true peace. Relationships that followed World Wars I and II are instructive in such regards.

Destructive Constraints

The Treaty of Versailles, which emasculated Germany's military establishment after World War I, stripped away huge territorial holdings in Europe plus all colonial possessions, required staggering reparations, and robbed that nation of its self-respect.[15] General Hans von Seeckt, who served as de facto chief of an illegal German General Staff from 1920 until 1926, observed the 100,000-man Army personnel ceiling but, in violation of treaty provisions, almost immediately created cadres for rapid expansion, organized 20,000 paramilitary auxiliaries, covertly established a high-quality military education system, and conducted "paper maneuvers" to exercise commanders and staffs. Iron men drilled with wooden weapons and trucks that simulated tanks during his tenure. The League for Air Sports trained glider pilots who later crewed *Luftwaffe* aircraft. The German Navy illicitly laid keels for three "pocket battleships" that exceeded the 10,000-ton treaty limit and secretly constructed submarines in Finland, the Netherlands, and Spain.[16]

Covert violations became overt on March 16, 1935, when Hitler repudiated arms restrictions that the Treaty of Versailles imposed, then revived the Great General Staff, the *Kriegsakademie* (War College), and universal military service, despite perfunctory complaints from Britain, France, and a toothless Allied Control Commission. More than 1,000,000 German warriors wore military uniforms before Hitler invaded Poland on September 1, 1939, with almost as many in reserve. Appeasers finally stood fast, but it was too late to avoid catastrophic combat in Europe.[17]

Constructive Constraints

Allied powers occupied West Germany from 1945 until 1955, when the former enemies officially became friends. Restrictions on the *Bundeswehr,* over which NATO thereafter exercised operational command, established 495,000 as the manpower ceiling and strictly limited offensive weaponry, especially armored vehicles. Nuclear, biological, and chemical capabilities were verboten.[18] U.S. troops occupied Japan from 1945 until 1952. Article IX of that nation's post–World War II constitution declared that "the Japanese people forever renounce war as a sovereign right of the nation. . . . Land, sea, and air forces, as well as other war potential, will never be maintained. The right of belligerency of the State will not be recognized." Pacifism remains fashionable more than fifty years later.[19]

ECONOMIC WARFARE

Economic warriors primarily wield commercial and financial weapons against adversarial countries, coalitions, nongovernmental organizations, corporations, and individuals. They also coerce friends as well as neutrals whenever incentives and cajolery fail to produce required results. Economic warfare rucksacks contain assorted sanctions, preclusive purchases, export/import controls, and blacklists.[20]

Economic Sanctions

No adversary is self-sufficient in every respect. All need access to markets, resources, and capital. Nations that are most vulnerable to economic sanctions depend extensively on external sources of raw materials, finished products, or both, suffer from rampant inflation, and would become insolvent absent heavy foreign investments. Those that engage in aggression, spurn democracy, align themselves with enemies, violate human rights, sponsor terrorism, deal in illicit drugs, and proliferate weapons of mass destruction are open to countermeasures that deny goods, services, and funds if they refuse to rectify or forswear obnoxious behavior.[21]

Commercial Sanctions

Market manipulations, embargoes, boycotts, prohibitive tariffs, foreign aid annulments, and asset seizures enable economic warriors to attack targets from unexpected angles. Implementing actions typically limit, suspend, cancel, or deny licenses and procurement contracts, abrogate or reduce trade agreements, curtail or terminate attractive quotas, and withhold or withdraw most favored nation trade status. Confiscations not only prevent antagonists from exchanging stock shares for merchandise but enable sanctioning governments to oust managers who deal with enemies.[22]

Positive and negative techniques are available. Soviet strategists, for example, employed foreign aid offensively throughout the Cold War. More than thirty recipients eventually relied almost exclusively on the USSR for modern military hardware. Long-term loans in lieu of grants generated perpetual dependence by recipients and paved the way for base rights, access to military facilities, and political penetration.[23] America's Mutual Defense Assistance Act of 1951 (the Battle Act) conversely cut off U.S. assistance to countries that furnished the Soviet Union and its Warsaw Pact partners with arms, munitions, military equipment, and other "strategically significant" items, unless commercial sanctions clearly would impair U.S. national security.[24]

Financial Sanctions

Financial sanctions focus on investment restrictions, credit cancellations, fiscal cutoffs, freezes, seizures, liquidations, suspensions of payment, unannounced devaluations, and malicious manipulations of foreign exchange rates. Economic warriors who influence international financial institutions such as the World Bank cast negative votes when offenders request grants, loans, or credit. Other means designed to disrupt the financial stability of targeted states include incitements to capital flight, monetary speculation, refusal to underwrite investments, counterfeiting, finagling with foreign exchange reserves, and hampering abilities to acquire hard currencies, especially U.S. dollars.[25]

Preclusive Purchases

Wealthy governments and coalitions occasionally buy crucially important products at prices that enemies are unwilling or unable to pay. That option was worth every penny the Allied Powers spent on Iberian wolframite (tungsten) ore during World War II, when aggressive sanctions might have driven Spain's pro-Nazi Generalissimo Francisco Franco into the Axis camp. Spain and Portugal both expanded production in response to increased demands, but preemptive purchases by 1943 drastically reduced Nazi Germany's ability to produce electrical contacts, tenacious steel alloys for armor plate, armor-piercing ammunition, and high-speed cutting tools, because Hitler had no alternative other than overworked wolframite mines in Austria.[26]

Economic Controls

Allegedly neutral nations that traffic with aggressors are subject to commercial and financial sanctions, whereas governments that unwittingly give aid and comfort are not. Export/import controls and blacklists stand guard in such cases.[27]

Export/Import Controls

The United States and Britain imposed "paper blockades" to discourage traffic between neutral seaports and the Axis Powers during World War II. Respective consuls at key locations furnished ship captains with navigation certificates (navicerts) that approved cargoes, routes, passengers, and crews. They also issued warrants that authorized owners and masters with clean bills of health to purchase provisions, fuel, and insurance from sources that the United States and Britain largely controlled. Merchantmen that departed without a navicert or warrant in their possession were subject to interception at sea, followed by search in an Allied port, a costly, time-consuming procedure, even if captors discovered no contraband.

Export controls are less effective when neutral nations abut offenders with whom they normally trade or enemies control sea routes thereto. Leverage then depends on degrees to which neutrals rely on friendlies for sustenance, abilities of adversaries to pay, and relative power positions of belligerents and bystanders at any given time. Shipments to Nazi Germany from and through Sweden, for example, flowed freely until the tide turned in favor of Allied Armed Forces and Third Reich coffers became bare.

Blacklists

Greedy companies, corporations, and carriers that put profits before national security risk the commercial equivalent of suicide if powerful countries or coalitions blacklist them because they patronize enemies. The United States not only maintained a domestic list during World War II, but one for Latin America as well. Britain did likewise for the United Kingdom, Commonwealth members under Allied control, and uncommitted countries in Europe.[28]

Pragmatic Expectations

Pragmatic national security policy-makers and military strategists understand that economic warfare alone seldom solves foreign policy problems. Allies and neutrals normally must cooperate, unless instigators nearly monopolize banned products. Guilty parties moreover must be vulnerable to sanctions. The UN Security Council, for example, froze Afghan funds and other financial resources in November 1999 to make the Taliban Government expel transnational terrorist Osama bin Laden, but rulers of that already impoverished nation, who worry little about the welfare of common people, steadfastly refuse to comply.[29] Lenient policy-makers limit "strategic materials" to items of obvious military value, such as arms, munitions, computers, petroleum products, and scarce minerals, whereas hardliners contend that almost all consignments are strategic. North Korean Chief of State Kim Jong Il, for example, never needed to shift much time, money, and effort from military preparedness to agriculture in the late 1990s, because compassionate outsiders alleviated severe food shortages in his destitute country.[30]

Pernicious side effects sometimes injure friends and onlookers worse than they hurt intended targets.[31] The Clinton Administration, in response to complaints that U.S. wheat farmers would lose sales worth $250,000,000, shelved sanctions designed to punish India and Pakistan after both nations detonated nuclear devices in May 1998.[32] The United Nations in December 1996 initiated petroleum-for-food exchanges with Iraq, because commercial and financial restrictions reportedly were depriving blameless Iraqi civilians of adequate nourishment and medical supplies. That humanitarian move unfortunately *strengthened* Saddam Hussein, who convinced hungry people that foreigners rather than his regime were responsible for their plight, and it weakened sanctions designed to squelch his nefarious weapon programs.[33]

Economic warfare pluses nevertheless often outweigh minuses, even when desired results remain elusive. North Korean military power, for example, might be immeasurably greater if unfettered by international sanctions for the last half century. Saddam Hussein still ruled Iraq with an iron hand when this book went to press, but multinational export/import restrictions in 1990 surely undercut that country's combat capabilities before Operation Desert Storm erupted. Subsequent trade embargoes have made it infinitely more difficult for his regime to perfect nuclear weapons or amass militarily sig-

nificant biological and chemical warfare stockpiles. Well-conceived economic pressures, in brief, can contribute considerably to deterrence and help confine carnage if armed conflicts occur.[34]

TECHNOLOGICAL WARFARE

Technological warfare, which connects science with strategies, operational art, and tactics, endeavors to make rival armed forces uncompetitive, preferably obsolete. Technological surprise occurs when innovations burst on the scene without warning or deploy more rapidly than intelligence analysts estimate. Victorious challengers unveil technological superiority so pervasive and pronounced that adversaries can neither cope nor catch up.[35]

Abilities to predict whether friendly (much less enemy) experiments will succeed, and if so when, are fallible at best. A shortsighted study entitled *Technological Trends and National Policy* in 1937 overlooked nuclear weapons, which eight years later terminated World War II. Doctor Vannevar Bush, who directed the Office of Scientific Research and Development during World War II, missed the mark widely in December 1945 when he told the Senate Committee on Atomic Energy that intercontinental ballistic missiles were "impossible." Skeptics in 1961 doubted that astronauts would soon land on the moon and return safely, but the Apollo 11 crew did so before the decade ended.[36] Today's intellectual giants, armed with infinitely sharper R&D tools, make mind-boggling breakthroughs conceivable in breathtaking time. Being ahead thus is crucially important in technological fields that could decisively alter military balances.

Pathways to Superiority

Two diametrically different, yet complementary, research, development, test, and evaluation (RDT&E) paths point toward superiority. One is marked "Incremental Progress," the other "Quantum Leaps." Overemphasis on either is inadvisable.[37]

Incremental Progress

Incremental progress slowly but steadily modernizes deployed arms and equipment to maintain preeminence or eliminate troublesome quality gaps. Aviators understand that even a slight superiority in target-acquisition capabilities and air-to-air missile ranges enables interceptor aircraft to detect and destroy intruders that are faster and more maneuverable.[38] Increases in nuclear warhead yields amplify lethality considerably, even when accuracies remain constant. The single-shot kill probability of each 335-kiloton Mark 12-A warhead atop U.S. Minuteman III ICBMs approximated 48% against moderately hard Soviet silos (4,000 psi), compared with 35% for 170-kiloton Mark 12 predecessors.[39] Nazi Germany lost the Battle of Britain between July and October 1940, largely because *Luftwaffe* bombers lacked adequate escorts. Messerschmitt ME-109s carried barely enough fuel to fly from France to England and back, while twin-engined ME-110s were sluggish compared with Royal Air Force (RAF) Supermarine Spitfires and Hawker Hurricanes. Both sides took a shellacking before daylight bombardment ceased, but Britain survived.[40] The same *Luftwaffe* proved superior the following summer, when it swept Stalin's primitive Air Force from the skies.

Quantum Leaps

Quantum leaps, which emphasize technological pioneering, aim to render enemy military capabilities irrelevant. Technological warriors who take that path engage in speculative projects that are truly revolutionary. RDT&E and procurement costs range from modest to immense, as the following vignettes indicate.

One traditional warfare study in 1992 noted that precision-guided munitions already could destroy virtually any visible target, and consequently concluded that "while it may not be time to slay ... sacred cows," such as armored vehicles, manned aircraft, and major surface combatants, "it probably is time to prevent them from breeding." Aircraft carriers, for example, "stood out as clearly as billiard balls on green felt" when viewed from space, according to Apollo 11 astronaut Michael Collins.[41] Recommended replacements include sophisticated, but relatively inexpensive, autonomous land crawlers, airmobile drones, assorted submersibles, and small orbiting satellites, plus millions of tiny sensors, emitters, and micro-projectiles.[42]

Offense and defense have taken turns on top since the Stone Age. Only the timing of the next flip-flop is unpredictable. "Star Wars" programs similar to those that President Reagan initiated in March 1983[43] could total several trillion dollars when all components are perfected and deployed, but results would be cost-effective, because nuclear-capable possessors could present nuclear aggressors two options: desist or commit suicide. They would in fact be able to impose their will without fighting, an achievement that Sun Tzu called "the acme of skill" twenty-five centuries ago.[44]

Prudent Compromises

Modest technological improvements commonly become obsolescent soon after and sometimes before deployment, whereas quantum leaps delay useful upgrades indefinitely. Competitors who wait too long for elevators marked "Decisive Military Advantage" may lag dangerously behind those who climb technological stairs one at a time. Wise competitors consequently recognize that temporary solutions to present problems and ambitious programs that promise future superiority are inseparable parts of the same package.

Technological Shortcuts

Phase I (basic research) of the RDT&E process probes for scientific truths. Phase II (applied technologies) translates findings into practical programs. Phase II falls flat if Phase I fizzles. Costs of creativity lamentably are high in terms of talent, resources, foresight, and funds. Bureaucratic, institutional, doctrinal, and industrial impediments have lengthened lead times considerably since the 1950s.[45] Even the most competent technological warriors therefore seek outside assistance that might help them avoid blind alleys, bypass bottlenecks, perfect countermeasures, and expedite deployments. Nations and subnational groups that lack high-tech R&D capabilities must rely mainly on purchases, espionage, thievery, or the largesse of patrons.

Purchase Technology

Legitimate purchases invigorate research and development, but governmental "salesmen" must reconcile commercial interests with reasonable controls that safeguard national security.[46] Computers, software, encryption devices, and other dual- or multipurpose items that foreign armed forces might find useful are most controversial, but technological transfers that involve written instructions and oral advice may be equally inadvisable. Loral Space and Communications Ltd. and Hughes Electronics Corporation, for example, became subjects of a criminal investigation shortly after their representatives told Chinese clients why a Long March (*Chang Zheng*) missile booster exploded on its launch pad in February 1996, because critics claimed that such information might enable China to improve the performance of closely related East Wind (*Dong Feng*) ICBMs.[47]

Commandeer Technology

Wernher von Braun and his team of rocket scientists sired Nazi Germany's V-2 weapon system, which became the antecedent of every land-based ballistic missile and space launch vehicle. That incomparable cadre surrendered to U.S. troops at the end of World War II and, after scrupulous screening, 127 "wizards" arrived in the United States, together with 100 V-2 missiles, priceless records that totaled fourteen tons, and visionary aims of incalculable value. The Soviet Union scavenged a larger lot, but only a few

were skilled technologists. Von Braun personally presided over or inspired extraordinary achievements from 1946 until he retired in 1972 as Deputy Associate Administrator for Planning at the National Aeronautics and Space Administration (NASA).[48]

Purloin Technology

Most nations that covet technological superiority pay espionage agents to expedite progress. America's nuclear weapon monopoly lasted only four years, partly because U.S. and British spies passed secrets to Soviet R&D specialists, who detonated a fission device on August 1949, much sooner than the U.S. intelligence community predicted. A Soviet thermonuclear explosion followed precisely two years later, just 9 months and 12 days after the United States tested its first hydrogen bomb. Julius and Ethel Rosenberg in 1953 received death sentences for treason. Donald Maclean, Kim Philby, and Guy Burgess, who fed the Kremlin vital information about U.S. nuclear programs and employment policies from perches in the British Foreign Office and military intelligence service (MI6), defected to the Soviet Union before they could be caught.[49] Clandestine quests to acquire U.S. nuclear know-how have proliferated ever since. China, for example, reportedly tried to extract neutron and miniaturization technologies from Lawrence Livermore, Los Alamos, and Sandia Laboratories during the late 1990s.[50]

Friends as well as enemies tend to purloin technological secrets when so doing seems to suit their best interests. Jonathan Jay Pollard, a U.S. citizen who worked for naval intelligence, received a life sentence in 1986, soon after the FBI nailed him for passing masses of classified information to the Israeli Bureau of Scientific Relations (his wife served five years for espionage). Less well publicized Israeli connivings have involved militarily useful semiconductor chips, electronic timing devices called krytrons, optical image processors, and "green salt," a uranium compound.[51]

Dangers of Overdependence

Overdependence on any given technology may be foolhardy if companion capabilities cannot compensate sufficiently for its shortcomings. Armed forces that forget how to read maps and use sextants could regret those deficiencies if enemies destroy Global Positioning System satellites. Solid-state circuitry packed into the smallest feasible space is a million times more vulnerable to electromagnetic pulse than antiquated vacuum tubes, because miniature components cannot tolerate high currents. Eavesdropping devices are useless against opponents who communicate mainly by word of mouth or in writing rather than by radios or telephones. Penchants for computers that lack less sophisticated backup systems invite disasters.

PSYCHOLOGICAL WARFARE

Strategic psychological warfare (PSYWAR) primarily concerns the planned use of propaganda and rumors to influence the opinions, emotions, attitudes, and behavior of hostile governments and nongovernmental groups on grand scales. Opening salvos commonly land during "peacetime" and, if armed combat erupts, psychological warriors continue to support politico-military objectives as long as necessary after hostilities cease. Mass communications enable skilled practitioners to attack targets far beyond military areas of operation.[52]

Words and Pictures as Weapons

Propagandists use words and pictures as nonlethal weapons to exploit successes, minimize failures, and make the most of mixed results. Some target specific audiences via television, radio, movies, theater, the World Wide Web, newspapers, magazines, and books, while others orate from podiums, pulpits, and soap boxes wherever crowds congregate. Rumor-mongers seed thoughts throughout the body politic, as opposed to particular groups. White, gray, and black propaganda all may deal in fraudulent data, but differ in most respects.

White Propaganda

White propaganda disseminates information for which purveyors are fully accountable. The U.S. Information Agency (USIA) throughout the Cold War was obligated by law "to promote a better understanding of the United States in other countries" and routinely publicized "policies promulgated by Congress, the President, the Secretary of State, and other officials associated with foreign affairs."[53] Occupants of the Kremlin openly trumpeted propaganda from 1917 until the Soviet Union collapsed in 1991. Two newspapers (*Pravda* and *Izvestia*), two periodicals (*New Times* and *International Affairs*), *Tass* news service, Novosti Press, and Radio Moscow parroted Communist Party lines. The World Peace Council (about 140 branches), the World Federation of Trade Unions (which boasted maybe 200 million members), the International Organization of Journalists, other fronts, and prominent fellow travelers routinely assisted.[54]

Gray Propaganda

Gray propaganda, whose source is concealed, is well-suited to feed enemies misleading information, float trial balloons, and disseminate messages that recipients believe come from close friends rather than outsiders. U.S. psywarriors during Operation Urgent Fury (October–November 1983) for the latter reason led residents of Grenada to believe that Spice Island Radio beamed messages from the Organization of Eastern Caribbean States instead of U.S. Armed Forces.

Black Propaganda

Black propaganda falsifies sources. Discovery can be politically embarrassing, even compromise crucial policies and plans, but spectacular successes are possible. Covert U.S. actions to evict Guatemalan President Arbenz Guzmán in June 1954 culminated quickly and cost-effectively in a nearly bloodless victory, largely because the bogus Voice of Liberation made 150 ragtag rebels and a few antiquated aircraft seem far larger and more capable than they actually were. The Guatemalan high command capitulated in the face of seemingly certain defeat, although its Armed Forces could have repulsed the invaders easily if ordered to counterattack.[55]

Rumor Campaigns

Rumors, unlike propaganda delivered directly to handpicked audiences, spread as unpredictably as oil slicks. Details may disappear during that process, but embellishments tend to sharpen original messages after repeated retellings.[56] German and British PSYWAR practitioners both used rumors advantageously before and during World War II. One story, originally planted in a Parisian bistro, alleged that an English tourist driving through Bavaria had collided with a wood and canvas "tank" mounted on a Volkswagen chassis. That canard, which soon appeared in a reputable motor magazine, then in a classified War Office intelligence summary, supported pacifist contentions that Britain need not rearm in 1938. Psywarriors in neutral capitals after the debacle at Dunkirk (May–June 1940) convinced gullible agents that Britain planned to defeat invasion forces with walls of fire in coastal waters. That falsehood caused the German Navy to sheath experimental barges with asbestos and visions of flaming surf must have given designated assault troops a bad case of the shakes.[57]

PSYWAR Targets

Relationships between PSYWAR stimuli and responses are erratic, because urban and rural, literate and illiterate, military and civilian, male and female, old and young audiences react differently. So do leaders and followers, haves and have-nots, skeptics and true believers. Influences that affect target selections within any given area of interest include political peculiarities, "pecking orders," economic conditions, religious preferences, ethical values, and folkways.

Detailed intelligence analyses direct psychological warfare professionals toward targets that simultaneously seem to be *vulnerable* (exploitable weaknesses are evident), *susceptible* (ways to exploit those weaknesses are evident), and *consequential* (successful exploitation promises rich rewards). Groups that appear vulnerable to rumors and propaganda unfortunately may not be susceptible, while those that seem susceptible often lack enough clout to make psychological offenses worthwhile. Prospects generally are best among urban intelligentsia, especially governmental decision-makers and opinion-shapers who constitute strategic centers of gravity.[58]

PSYWAR Themes

PSYWAR themes, tailored to support strategic objectives, seek to divide, convert, or consolidate public opinion and promote specific responses. Aggressors commonly advocate self-serving arms control agreements to create false hopes for peace and international stability. Themes that encourage divisiveness typically try to capitalize on ethnic antagonisms, religious animosities, racial rancor, social caste systems, and economic inequalities. Themes that deal with domestic disloyalty and the dubious allegiance of allies urge enemies to switch sides or surrender. Hitler, for example, might have purged top levels of the Nazi hierarchy and weakened war efforts after Rudolf Hess parachuted into Scotland with peace proposals on May 10, 1941, if British broadcasts had announced that other senior Nazi officials were about to defect.[59] NATO's propagandists likewise might have done more to drive wedges between Soviet Armed Forces and their Warsaw Pact partners, whose ranks were loaded with reluctant conscripts.[60]

PSYWAR Techniques

PSYWAR propaganda and rumors are intrinsically neither true or false, good or bad. Information, disinformation, and distraction programs enlighten, deceive, or confuse, depending on objectives. Shrewd psychological warriors think big, keep messages simple, and are consistent as well as persistent. Adolf Hitler, who appealed to gut feelings of the German people, understood those prescriptions perfectly when he penned *Mein Kampf:* "All effective propaganda has to limit itself to only a few points and to use them like slogans until even the very last man is able to imagine what is intended. . . ."[61]

Information

Fanatical Japanese troops, hungry for news during World War II, snapped up Allied leaflets that reliably reported their increasingly desperate situation and blamed incompetent commanders for human-wave assaults that sacrificed them senselessly. Nearly 20,000 surrendered, a pittance compared with wholesale German and Italian capitulations, but that figure otherwise might have been closer to zero.[62] Truth also can be a potent weapon in peacetime. Indeed, it was the most prominent U.S. instrument during the Cold War, when USIA beamed sixty-two themes on seven subjects to recipients on every inhabited continent.[63]

PSYWAR specialists who deal in unclassified facts nevertheless should assess the predilections of target audiences carefully before they proceed, because truth seldom sways true believers.[64] Chinese governments that cling to Communist ideologies, for example, still disregard democratic themes that have prompted change for more than fifty years. Concerted psychological campaigns thus far have failed to overcome ethnic, cultural, and religious animosities that make peace seem unlikely in Bosnia-Herzegovina and Kosovo after UN peacekeepers withdraw.

Disinformation

Lewis Carroll, in his satire *Through the Looking Glass,* explained the essence of disinformation exquisitely: "When *I* use a word," Humpty-Dumpty said in a rather scornful tone, "it means just what

I choose it to mean—neither more nor less." "The question is," said Alice, "whether you can make words mean so many different things." "The question is," huffed Humpty-Dumpty, "which is to be *Master*—that's all."

The Soviet Committee for State Security (KGB) to that end disseminated disinformation, even when "peaceful coexistence" was in full flower. No programs have ever exceeded its scope, which employed smear tactics, false alarms, oversimplified slogans, statements out of context, misleading comparisons, skewed cause/effects relationships, and other logic traps on a global scale (Table 22).[65] KGB propagandists routinely planted bogus stories that gained legitimacy after reputable foreign news agencies repeated them endlessly. U.S. and allied defenders frequently unmasked frauds, but refutations seldom received as much publicity as phony reports

Table 22
Typical PSYWAR Techniques

- **Quicksand** Big lies, "popularized" by Dr. Joseph Goebbels, Hitler's Minister of Propaganda, make antagonists struggle to refute damaging allegations
- **Halo and Horns** Perpetrators paint themselves as saints, opponents as sinners. "We are progressive, they are reactionary" is one popular theme
- **Baited Hook** Phony claims fool gullible observers. The Soviet Constitution, for example, falsely promised freedom of speech, press, and worship
- **False Label** Misrepresentation distorts the meaning of words. Totalitarian governments, for example, call themselves "People's Democratic Republics"
- **Albatross** Pejorative adjectives around the necks of innocent nouns can discredit persons, ideas, and actions. "Dirty dollars" and "puppet politicians" are illustrative
- **Bandwagon** Charlatans claim that "all the good guys are doing it," so everybody who wants to be a "good guy" should join the group
- **Time Machine** Inverting the sequence of past events can mislead audiences concerning causes and effects
- **ABC** Slogans like "ban the bomb" and "power to the people" promote oversimplified solutions to complex problems
- **Court Room** Smear tactics tar judges, juries, and judicial systems, while insisting on changes in venue.

SOURCE: Robert S. Byfield, *The Fifth Weapon* (New York, The Bookmailer, 1954)

and the tightly controlled Soviet news media were virtually invulnerable to counterattacks in kind.[66]

Distraction

PSYWAR experts excel at intellectual judo and games of one-upmanship designed to muddle minds, confuse issues, and keep opponents off balance. Patience is a virtue; impatience is a sin. Nonlethal weapons include obstruction, procrastination, legal monkey wrenches, and *Roberts' Rules of Order.* Sharp, unanticipated policy switches alternately raise enemy hopes, then dash them.

Sportsmanlike peacemakers are wide open to such assaults. Communist negotiators in Korea began to play physical and semantic tricks on U.S. counterparts during the first session in July 1951, when Vice Admiral C. Turner Joy, the UN's chief delegate, sank out of sight in a seat that had short legs, while North Korean General Nam Il glowered down from a chair a foot or so higher. Participants ultimately signed an armistice agreement after 575 wearisome meetings and countless battlefield casualties, but the war of words at Panmunjom continues unabated five decades later.[67]

The first Vietnam War ended in 1954 on terms that bisected the country when France capitulated.[68] "Talks about talks" to settle the second Vietnam War began in Paris on May 10, 1968, where the shape of the table (like the height of chair legs at Panmunjom) assumed huge psychological proportions.[69] Palavering continued until October 1972, when Henry A. Kissinger, the chief U.S. delegate, jubilantly announced that "peace is at hand. . . . What remains to be done can be settled in one more negotiating session. . . ."[70] The coveted covenant nevertheless was elusive. Frustration replaced euphoria well before peace talks collapsed on December 14. Communist propagandists screamed "aggression" when U.S. aircraft launched massive attacks against Hanoi and Haiphong four days later; adverse world opinion blossomed; antiwar sentiments revived in the United States; and Congress cut funds. The fragile

cease-fire that followed on January 27, 1973 rid the region of U.S. military combat power, but left Communist power in place, with predictably adverse results.[71] Psychological warfare was decisive.

Democratic Restrictions

Political, cultural, and practical factors restrain psychological warfare options in every country,[72] but most notably in democracies. "Propaganda," for example, has pejorative connotations in the United States, where "disinformation" is a dirty word. Investigators ferret out and publicize black programs. Freedom of speech gives enemies information with which to concoct themes that concern political scandals, economic woes, crime, and drug abuse. PSYWAR even so complements U.S. military capabilities nicely on occasion.

CYBERNETIC WARFARE

Cybernetic knights armed with computers instead of lethal weapons selectively or indiscriminately attack information terminals, networks, and repositories to acquire useful facts and disable, disrupt, or spoof opponents. Destructive and instructive computer viruses, Trojan horses, trapdoors, and worms constitute cyberwar ammunition. Offensive, defensive, and deterrent policies, strategies, doctrines, tactics, and techniques still are in formative stages, but the "infosphere" has already become an environmental medium commensurate with land, sea, air, and space.[73]

Cyberwar Schools of Thought

Information dominance vastly improves the speed and confidence with which military commanders at every level can complete what U.S. Air Force Colonel John R. Boyd called "OODA Loops" that sequentially observe enemy activities (O), orient on situations (O), decide what to do (D), and act accordingly (A).[74] Many senior officers consequently value cyber warfare as a "force multiplier" that enables wielders to launch asymmetrical, unattributable attacks in "peacetime" as well as war. The first (and thus far the only) acknowledged test during combat occurred in 1999, when U.S. Armed Forces successfully assaulted Yugoslav air defense command and control systems.[75]

Insurgents, terrorists, common criminals, renegade corporations, egomaniacal "hackers," and other nongovernmental zealots who have little or no traditional military power to multiply set cyberwar sights mainly on national infrastructures, rather than rival armed forces. Some nation-state strategists also champion that school of thought, firm in their convictions that societal disruptions on a grand scale would undermine enemy military capabilities indirectly and simultaneously weaken civilian will to resist.[76]

Neither of those polarized approaches is sufficiently flexible to satisfy all purposes under assorted conditions. Chiefs of State and their politico-military advisers for that reason likely will elect blends that take particular circumstances into account.

Cyberwar Targets

Military command, control, communications, computer, and intelligence (C^4I) networks contain profuse target arrays, the disablement or disruption of which would immeasurably amplify the fog of war and correspondingly impede timely, accurate decision-making in enemy camps. Successful offensives could shut down intelligence sensors, block access to data storage facilities, and sever electronic connections between commanders and subordinates. Cybernetic warriors could incapacitate communication relays in space faster and at far less cost than currently envisioned antisatellite (ASAT) systems or pass signals through those way stations to make computerized weapons malfunction on Earth.

Governmental installations, commercial telecommunications, financial institutions, public utilities, and emergency services are a few among many attractive civilian infrastructure targets. Chaos would reign if widespread cyberwarfare attacks mis-

routed railway trains, rescheduled airline flights, erased credit records, altered stock exchange statistics, turned off computerized water taps, and blacked out urban centers.[77]

Attractive Offensive Options

Computer viruses take advantage of standardized software, message formats, and data links to infiltrate networks, then replicate like contagious diseases. "Trojan horses," which piggyback on enemy files, lie dormant and difficult to detect until human handlers tell them to extract information, delete files, or alter stored data. "Bacteria," sometimes called "rabbits," reproduce exponentially until they occupy all processor capacity, memory, and disc storage space. Individuals who carelessly share programs, even work stations, hasten the spread. "Worms" that travel from computer to computer and across network connections cause no mischief, but they carry codes that do. Defenders must safeguard assets against all kinds of incursion, because the most insidious viruses mount dissimilar assaults simultaneously.[78]

Denial of Service (DOS) attacks, unlike viruses, flood the Internet with illegitimate message traffic. Sharply focused versions cause specific terminals to "crash," because they can't handle the influx of packets that are improperly matched, arrive out of sequence, or simply overload receivers. "Smurf" offensives, in contrast, flood entire networks, regardless of size or bandwidths, until they innundate innocent bystanders along with intended targets. Distributed Denial of Service (DDOS) assaults emanate clandestinely from many sites on several different networks. Perpetrators first infiltrate a slew of unwitting hosts, assume their identities, turn their computers into unwitting accomplices called Zombies, then install malicious programs that they activate at will. Defenders consequently find it difficult to identify and disable offensive machines, much less intercept innumerable packets that crisscross countless paths.[79]

Cyberwar Benefits and Liabilities

Offensive cyber warriors obtain huge benefits, because they determine the battlefields where info wars will be fought and strike without warning. Their operations leave targets physically intact and directly cause no collateral damage or casualties. Acquisition costs, logistical support, and basing requirements are minuscule compared with traditional weapon systems.

Potentially serious liabilities nevertheless are evident. Employment doctrines and rules of engagement are rudimentary at this stage.[80] So are defensive countermeasures.[81] Thousands conceivably could die if hackers interrupted food, water, fuel, and power distribution systems for long periods or bollixed emergency medical services. Police and firefighters would perform poorly if fooled. The validity of damage assessments proved speculative in September 1999, when Russian cyber warriors penetrated Pentagon firewalls. Whether they gained access to classified information is anybody's guess, despite interagency investigations.[82] Neither great powers nor non-state actors express much interest in cybernetic arms control at this moment.[83] Legal differentiations between combatants and noncombatants remain muddy.[84]

Poorly prepared defenders already must reckon with anonymous cyber warriors, who are almost immune to military reprisals and allow no privileged sanctuaries. Confrontations between nations could escalate unpredictably.[85] Russia in September 1995, for example, flatly stated that it "retains the right to use nuclear weapons first against the means and forces of information warfare, and then against the aggressor state itself." Continued cyber attacks in such event might make crisis management and early termination of hostilities impossible.[86]

Highly computerized countries (especially the United States) possess the greatest cyberwar capabilities, but paradoxically are most vulnerable. Their national security policy-makers and military strategists consequently should think problems through thoroughly before they open Pandora's Box any wider.[87]

KEY POINTS

- Political warfare consistently reinforces military power, and vice versa
- Cagey diplomatic deals often foster military flexibility and facilitate surprise attacks
- Statesmen who impose harsh terms on the vanquished but appease violators invite renewed warfare
- Sanctions are most effective when friends and neutrals cooperate
- Sanctions that injure innocents more than guilty parties are hard to maintain
- Being ahead technologically is crucially important in fields where breakthroughs could decisively alter military balances
- Incremental improvements that ensure current technological superiority and innovations that promise future supremacy are essential parts of one package
- Psychological warriors use words as weapons
- The most lucrative PSYWAR targets are vulnerable, susceptible, and consequential
- The most influential psychological warriors selectively employ truthful information *and* disinformation
- Cybernetic warfare is more cost-effective and harder to counter than most forms of lethal conflict
- Highly computerized countries that possess the greatest cyberwar capabilities also are most vulnerable

NOTES

1. Colonels Qiao Liang and Wang Xiangsui, *Unrestricted Warfare: Assumptions on War and Tactics in the Age of Globalization,* trans. Foreign Broadcast Information Service (Beijing: PLA Literature Arts Publishing House, February 1999), Chapter 7, "Ten Thousand Methods Combined As One: Combinations That Transcend Boundaries," 195-222.

2. Niccolò Machiavelli, *The Prince,* ed. Peter Bondanella, trans. by Mark Musa (New York: Oxford University Press, 1998) and *Discourses,* ed. Bernard Crick, trans. Leslie J. Walker (New York: Viking Press, 1985).

3. William L. Shirer, *The Rise and Fall of the Third Reich: A History of Nazi Germany* (Greenwich, CT: Crest Books, 1962), Book Three, "The Road to War," 385-823.

4. Saul Bernard Cohen, *Geography and Politics in a World Divided* (New York: Random House, 1963), 193-203; Malcolm Macintosh, *Evolution of the Warsaw Pact,* Adelphi Papers, No. 58 (London: Institute for Strategic Studies, June 1969).

5. Robert S. Byfield, *The Fifth Weapon* (New York: The Bookmailer, 1954), 9-10, 19, 22.

6. Alexander L. George, *Forceful Persuasion: Coercive Diplomacy As an Alternative to War* (Washington: United States Institute of Peace Press, 1991), 3-14, 67-84; Stephen Biddle and Wade Hinkle, *Using Coercive Force More Effectively,* Background QDR Brief for OSD/SO/LIC (Washington: Institute for Defense Analyses, March 7, 1997).

7. *United Nations Charter,* Chapter V, Article 27, Paragraph 3.

8. Security Council Resolutions S/1501, June 25, 1950, S/1511, June 27, 1950, and S/1588, July 7, 1950; Rosalyn Higgins, *United Nations Peacekeeping, 1946-1967,* vol. 2, *Asia* (London: Oxford University Press, 1970), 159-64; General J. Lawton Collins, *War in Peacetime: The History and Lessons of Korea* (Boston: Houghton Mifflin Co., 1969), 9-24, 148-49.

9. Alexander Werth, *Russia At War, 1941-1945* (New York: E. P. Dutton & Co., 1964), 40-65; Cohen, *Geography and Politics in a World Divided,* 193-203.

10. Alan Clark, *Barbarossa: The Russian-German Conflict, 1941-1945* (New York: William Morrow and Co., 1965), 3-273.

11. Sun Tzu, *The Art of War,* trans. Samuel B. Griffith (New York: Oxford University Press, 1963), 66-69.

12. Homer, *The Iliad,* trans. Robert Fagles (New York: Penguin Books, 1998).

13. Roger Hesketh, *Fortitude: The D-Day Deception Campaign* (Woodstock, NY: Overlook, 2000); Carlo

d'Este, *Patton: A Genius for War* (New York: HarperCollins, 1995), 593-94.

14. Gordon W. Prange, *At Dawn We Slept: The Untold Story of Pearl Harbor* (New York: McGraw-Hill, 1981), 466, 483-87, 502; Howard W. French, "Pearl Harbor Truly a Sneak Attack, Papers Show," *New York Times,* December 9, 1999, A3.

15. Fred L. Israel, ed., *Major Peace Treaties of Modern History: 1648-1967,* vol. II (New York: Chelsea House Publishers, in association with McGraw-Hill Book Co., 1967), 1235-1534, especially 1288-1311, 1348-80.

16. Trevor N. Dupuy, *A Genius for War: The German Army and General Staff, 1807-1945* (Englewood Cliffs, NJ: Prentice-Hall, 1977), 181-222; Shirer, *The Rise and Fall of the Third Reich,* 167-262.

17. Dupuy, *A Genius for War,* 223-52; Shirer, *The Rise and Fall of the Third Reich,* 263-790.

18. *London and Paris Agreements,* Department of State Publication 5659 (Washington: Department of State, November 1954); Catherine M. Kelleher, "Fundamentals of German Security: The Creation of the Bundeswehr—Continuity and Change," in *The Bundeswehr and Western Security,* ed. Stephen F. Szabo (London: Macmillan, 1990).

19. William Manchester, *American Caesar: Douglas MacArthur, 1880-1964* (Boston: Little, Brown, 1978), 497-506.

20. Yuan-li Wu, *Economic Warfare* (New York: Prentice-Hall, 1952); David L. Gordon and Royden Dangerfield, *The Hidden Weapon: The Story of Economic Warfare* (New York: Harper & Brothers, 1947).

21. For lists of U.S. laws that authorize, require, and waive sanctions, see Dianne E. Rennack and Robert D. Shuey, *Economic Sanctions to Achieve U.S. Foreign Policy Goals: Discussion and Guide to Current Law,* Rpt. 97-949 (Washington: Congressional Research Service, September 21, 1999), 10-22.

22. Ibid., 5-6; *The Economics of National Security,* vol. XV, *Economic Warfare and Economic Intelligence* (Washington: Industrial College of the Armed Forces, 1958), 11-12, 17-19.

23. *The Soviet Union and the Third World: A Watershed in Great Power Policy?,* A Report to the House Committee on International Relations by Joseph G. Whelan and William B. Inglee, 95th Cong., 1st sess. (Washington: U.S. Government Printing Office, May 8, 1977), 68-74; Anthony H. Cordesman, "The Soviet Arms Trade: Patterns for the 1980s," *Armed Forces Journal,* Part One, June 1983, 96-97, 100, 102, 103-105 and Part Two, August 1983, 34-35, 38, 40-41, 44, 69.

24. *The Economics of National Security,* 17-19.

25. Wu, *Economic Warfare,* Chapters 4 and 5.

26. *The Economics of National Security,* 12-13.

27. Ibid., 4-5, 6-8, 9-10.

28. Ibid. 8-9.

29. *United Nations Security Council Resolution 1267,* October 15, 1999, effective November 15, 1999.

30. Wu, *Economic Warfare,* 10-13; Larry A. Niksch, *North Korean Food Shortages: U.S. and Allied Responses,* Rpt. 97-551 F (Washington: Congressional Research Service, May 30, 1997).

31. Rennack and Shuey, *Economic Sanctions to Achieve U.S. Foreign Policy Goals,* 1-9.

32. Barbara LePoer et al., *India-Pakistan Nuclear Tests and U.S. Response,* Rpt. 98-570 F (Washington: Congressional Research Service, November 24, 1998) and Jeanne Grimmett, *Nuclear Sanctions: Section 102(b) of the Arms Control Export Act and Its Application to India and Pakistan,* Rpt. 98-486 A (Washington: Congressional Research Service, September 21, 1999).

33. Lois McHugh, *Iraq: Humanitarian Needs, Impact of Sanctions, and the "Oil for Food" Program,* Rpt. 98-570 F (Washington: Congressional Research Service, August 13, 1998) and Kenneth Katzman, *Iraq: Oil-for-Food Program,* Rpt. RS2022S (Washington: Congressional Research Service, June 4, 1999).

34. For positive views, see David E. Weekman, "Sanctions: The Invisible Hand of Statecraft," *Strategic Review,* Winter 1998, 39-45.

35. Stefan T. Possony and J. E. Pournelle, *The Strategy of Technology* (Cambridge, MA: Dunellen, 1970), 1-20, 55.

36. *Joint Experimentation Campaign Plan 2000 (OPLAN 00)* (Norfolk, VA: U.S. Atlantic Command, September 20, 1999); George Heilmeier, "Guarding Against Technological Surprise," *Congressional Record,* June 22, 1976, S10139; Thomas K. Adams, "Radical Destabilizing Effects of New Technologies," *Parameters,* Autumn 1998, 99-111.

37. Fred E. Saalfeld and John F. Petrik, "Disruptive Technologies: A Concept for Moving Innovative Military Technologies Rapidly to Warfighters," *Armed Forces Journal International* (May 2001), 48-52; Joseph L. Bower and Clayton M. Christensen, "Disruptive Technologies: Catching the Wave," *Harvard Business Review* (vol. 73, no. 1, January–February 1995), 43-53; Clayton M. Christensen, *The Innovator's Dilemma: When New Technologies Cause Great Firms to Fail* (New York: Harper Business, an imprint of HarperCollins, 2000).

38. Possony and Pournelle, *The Strategy of Technology,* 30, 38, 39.

39. Electronic System Division, General Electric Co. produced the Missile Effectiveness Calculator that an analyst used to compute single-shot kill probabilities for Minuteman III, using criteria in John M. Collins, *U.S.-Soviet Military Balance, 1980-1985* (Washington: Pergamon-Brassey's, 1985), 175.

40. Basil H. Liddell Hart, *History of the Second World War* (New York: G. P. Putnam's Sons, 1971), 87-108.

41. Michael Collins, *Resources, Technology, and Future Space Battlefields,* a conference paper (Washington: Center for Strategic and International Studies symposium, October 27-29, 1987), 3, 14-16.

42. *Project 2025* (Washington: Institute for National Strategic Studies, National Defense University, May 1992), 54-61, 78-79, quotation on 85.

43. U.S. "Star Wars" programs opened with "President's Speech on Military Spending and a New Defense," *New York Times,* March 24, 1983, 20.

44. Jack Swift, "U.S.: Strategic Superiority Through SDI," Part I, *Defense & Foreign Affairs Daily,* vol. XIV, no. 223 (November 18, 1985), 17-18.

45. Klaus Knorr and Oskar Morgenstern, *Science and Defense: Some Critical Thoughts on Military Research and Development* (Princeton, NJ: Princeton University Press, 1965), 19-27.

46. *International Transfer of Technology: An Agenda of National Security Issues,* Committee Print, prepared by the Congressional Research Service for the House Subcommittee on International Security and Scientific Affairs of the Committee on International Relations, 95th Cong., 2d sess., February 13, 1978.

47. Shirley A. Kan, *China: Possible Missile Technology Transfers from U.S. Satellite Export Policy—Background and Chronology,* Rpt. 98-485 F (Washington: Congressional Research Service, November 3, 1999).

48. Frederick I. Ordway, III, and Michell Sharpe, *Rocket Team* (Cambridge, MA: MIT Press, 1982); Wernher von Braun and Frederick I. Ordway, III, *History of Rocketry & Space Travel* (New York: Thomas Y. Crowell, 1966), 106-119, 140.

49. David Holloway, *Stalin and the Bomb: The Soviet Union and Atomic Energy, 1939-1956* (New Haven, CT: Yale University Press, 1994); Ronald Radosh and Joyce Milton, *The Rosenberg File* (New Haven, CT: Yale University Press, 1997); Verne W. Newton, *The Cambridge Spies: The Untold Story of Maclean, Philby, and Burgess in America* (Lanham, MD: Madison Books, distributed by National Book Network, 1993).

50. Shirley A. Kan, *China: Suspected Acquisition of U.S. Nuclear Weapon Data,* Rpt. RL30134 (Washington: Congressional Research Service, February 7, 2000)

and *China's Technology Acquisitions: Cox Committee's Report—Findings, Issues and Recommendations,* Rpt. RL30220, June 8, 1999.

51. Wolf Blitzer, *Territory of Lies: The Exclusive Story of Jonathan J. Pollard, the American Who Spied on His Country for Israel and How He Was Betrayed* (New York: Harper and Row, 1989); Edward T. Pound and David Rogers, "An Israeli Contract with a U.S. Company Leads to Espionage," *Wall Street Journal,* January 17, 1992, 1; Charles Babcock, "Computer Expert Used Firm to Feed Israel Technology," *Washington Post,* October 31, 1986, A1, A24.

52. Lieutenant General William P. Yarborough and Stanley Sandler, "Psychological Operations," in *International Military and Defense Encyclopedia,* ed. Colonel Trevor N. Dupuy et al. (Washington: Brassey's [U.S.], 1993), 1445-70; Paul M. A. Linebarger, *Psychological Warfare,* 2d ed. (New York: Duell, Sloan and Pierce, 1954); Robert T. Holt and Robert W. van de Velde, *Strategic Psychological Operations* (Chicago: University of Chicago Press, 1960), 17-72.

53. *Public Law 80-402* [H.R. 3342], 62 Stat. 6; *Title 22, United States Code,* 1431-42, approved January 27, 1948, known as the United States Information and Education Exchange Act of 1948, as amended.

54. Richard H. Shultz, Jr. and Roy Godson, *Desinformatsia: Active Measures in Soviet Strategy* (New York: Pergamon-Brassey's, 1984), 20, 25-31; "The Soviet Press," *World Press Review,* June 1986, 8; Wallace Spaulding, "Communist Fronts in 1985," *Problems of Communism,* March/April 1986, 72-78.

55. Richard H. Immerman, *The CIA in Guatemala* (Austin: University of Texas Press, 1982), 161-177.

56. Gordon W. Allport and Leo Postman, *The Psychology of Rumor* (New York: H. Holt and Co., 1947); S. Schlachter and H. Burdick, "A Field Experiment on Rumor Transmission and Distortion," *Journal of Abnormal and Social Psychology* (May 1955), 363-69.

57. John Baker White, *The Big Lie* (New York: Crowell, 1955), 1-10, 28-29.

58. Holt and van de Velde, *Strategic Psychological Operations,* 49-69.

59. Hans Speier, "Psychological Warfare Reconsidered," in *Propaganda in War and Crisis,* ed. D. Lerner (New York: G. W. Stewart, 1951), 485.

60. Daniel N. Nelson, *Soviet Allies: The Warsaw Pact and the Issue of Reliability* (Boulder, CO: Westview Press, 1984); Teresa Rakowska-Harmstone, *Warsaw Pact: The Question of Cohesion* (Ottawa, Canada: Department of Defence (ORAE), vol. I, February 1984; vol. II, November 1984).

61. Adolf Hitler, *Mein Kampf,* trans. Ralph Mannheim (New York: Houghton Mifflin, 1950), Chapter VI, "War Propaganda;" Lieutenant General William P. Yarborough, "The Power of Persuasion: Some Historical Vignettes," *Special Warfare,* Spring 1998, 24-26.

62. Allison B. Gilmore, *You Can't Fight Tanks with Bayonets: Psychological Warfare Against the Japanese Army in the Southwest Pacific* (Lincoln: University of Nebraska Press, 1999).

63. *Field Support Requests: Summary and Themes 1-7* (Washington: U.S. Information Agency, May 1986).

64. Holt and van de Velde, *Strategic Psychological Operations,* 35-38.

65. Paul W. Blackstock, *The Strategy of Subversion* (Chicago: Quadrangle Books, 1964); Byfield, *The Fifth Weapon,* 7-51.

66. Ladislav Bittman, *The KGB and Soviet Disinformation: An Insider's View* (New York: Pergamon-Brassey's, 1985); *Soviet Covert Action (The Forgery Offensive),* Hearings before the House Subcommittee on Oversight of the Permanent Select Committee on Intelligence, 96th Cong., 2d sess. (Washington: U.S. Government Printing Office, 1980); Shultz and Godson, *Desinformatsia.*

67. Vice Admiral C. Turner Joy, *How Communists Negotiate* (New York: Macmillan, 1955); William H. Vatcher, Jr., *Panmunjom: The Story of the Korean Military Armistice Negotiations* (New York: Praeger, 1958). For terms of the treaty, see *Major Peace Treaties of Modern History: 1648-1967,* 2657-2688.

68. *Major Peace Treaties of Modern History: 1648-1967,* 2689-2708.

69. Sir Robert Thompson, *No Exit from Vietnam* (New York: David McKay, 1969), 76-87.

70. Henry A. Kissinger, White House Press Conference, October 26, 1972; "Talks At Impasse, Kissinger Says," *Washington Post,* December 17, 1972, A1, A6.

71. Larry A. Niksch, *Issues and Agreement in the Paris Negotiations on Vietnam, January 1972-January 1973* (Washington: Congressional Research Service, April 2, 1973).

72. Linebarger, *Psychological Warfare,* 48-61; Holt and van de Velde, *Strategic Psychological Operations,* 41-48.

73. For overviews, see John Arquilla and David Ronfeldt, eds., *Athena's Camp: Preparing for Conflict in the Information Age* (Santa Monica, CA: RAND Corporation, 1997), especially 1-22; James Adams, *The Next World War: Computers Are the Weapons and the Front Line is Everywhere* (New York: Simon & Schuster, 1998); Edward Waltz, *Information War-*

fare: Principles and Operations (Boston: Artech House, 1998).

74. Air Force Manual 2025, *Information Operations: A New War-Fighting Capability* (Washington: Headquarters United States Air Force, December 11, 1996), Chapter 2. The first written reference to OODA probably appears in Colonel John R. Boyd's unpublished paper "Patterns of Conflict," (December 1986), 5, within a collection called *A Discourse on Winning and Losing,* August 1987. Contact Marine Corps University's Research Center at Quantico, VA (http://www.mcu.mil/MCRCweb/archive5a .html).

75. David Fulghum, "Yugoslavia Successfully Attacked by Computers," *Aviation Week & Space Technology,* August 23, 1999, 31-32.

76. Robert J. Bunker, *Information Operations and the Conduct of Land Warfare* (Washington: Institute of Land Warfare, Association of the United States Army, October 31, 1998), 10-11.

77. John Arquilla, "The Great Cyberwar of 2002," *Wired,* February 1998, 122-27.

78. Steve Steinke, "Moron Attacks," *Network Magazine,* April 2000, 1; Ralph Roberts, *Computer Viruses* (Greensboro, NC: Computer! Books, 1988), 17-29; Eugene H. Spafford et al., *Computer Viruses: Dealing With Electronic Vandalism and Programmed Threats* (Arlington, VA: ADAPSO, 1989), 7-30.

79. Brian Martin, *Have Script, Will Destroy (Lessons in DOS),* Hacker News Network, February 11, 2000; Anick Jesdanun, " 'Denial of Service' Attack Proves Hard to Pin Down," *Washington Times,* January 10, 2000, A20.

80. JP 3-13, *Joint Doctrine for Information Operations* (Washington: Office of the Chairman, Joint Chiefs of Staff, October 9, 1998).

81. "U.S. Forces Need Rules of Engagement for Cyberwar, Admiral Says," *Aerospace Daily,* July 5, 2000, 1; "DoD Secretary Creates Own Joint Task Force on Information Warfare Defense," *Inside the Pentagon,* December 24, 1999, 3.

82. "We're in the Middle of a Cyber War," *Newsweek,* September 20, 1999, 52.

83. *An Assessment of International Legal Issues in Information Operations* (Washington: Department of Defense, Office of General Counsel, May 1999), 48-49.

84. Ibid., 6-25, 32-34, 41-47; Commander Byard Q. Clemmons and Major Gary D. Brown, "Cyberwarfare: Ways, Warriors and Weapons of Mass Destruction," *Military Review,* September-October 1999, 35-45.

85. David Alberts, *The Unintended Consequences of Information Age Technologies: Avoiding Pitfalls, Seizing the Initiative* (Washington: National Defense University Press, April 1996).

86. Stephen J. Cimbala, "Nuclear Crisis Management and Information Warfare," *Parameters,* Summer 1999, 123-27, quotation on 119.

87. James Adams, "Virtual Defense: The Weakness of a Superpower," *Foreign Affairs* (May/June 2001), 98-112.

20. Coalition Warfare Strategies

True it is that politics
makes strange bedfellows

My Summer in a Garden
Fifteenth week
Charles Dudley Warner, 1870

Birds of a feather normally flock together. Nations and subnational groups on the contrary often establish long- or short-term ties to preserve peace, win wars, or pursue other purposes despite incompatible philosophies, policies, and values.[1] Coalitions vary remarkably (Table 23) but, regardless of characteristics, each member of every coterie must make strategically momentous decisions that concern the compatibility of partners, the merits of formal versus informal mergers, command/control arrangements, and respective contributions. Foreign policies, domestic politics, ideological links, perceived threats, geographic circumstances, anticipated benefits, probable liabilities, personalities, and other diversified factors affect the formation, configuration, cohesion, utility, and longevity of every coalition. Periodic reviews to ensure that original judgments remain valid are imperative.[2]

Table 23
Diversified Coalition Characteristics

De Jure	Or	De Facto
Large	Or	Small
Simple	Or	Complex
Weak	Or	Strong
Local	Or	Regional
Loose	Or	Tight
Formal	Or	Informal
Overt	Or	Covert
Bilateral	Or	Multilateral
Voluntary	Or	Involuntary
Short-term	Or	Long-term
Patronage	Or	Partnership

COLLECTIVE SECURITY INCENTIVES

Governments must determine whether collective security serves their purposes better than nonalignment (no ties to any other nation), complete neutrality (never take sides on international issues), or selective neutrality (occasionally take sides). Those able to achieve objectives at acceptable costs without incurring obligations generally go it alone. So do pariahs who have no useful friends. Most others tend to coalesce.

Nonalignment and Neutralism

Countries pay no penalty for nonalignment or neutrality, provided they are able to cope single-handedly with serious threats. Weak nations willing to withdraw from world affairs may remain aloof only if no acquisitive neighbor covets their territory or powerful guardians discourage aggression against them.[3] U.S., British, French, and Soviet Armed Forces occupied Austria from 1945 until 1955, but that tiny state remained nonaligned for the rest of the Cold War, partly because neither NATO nor the Warsaw Pact believed its real estate was vital, partly because neither wanted Austria within the other's sphere of influence.[4]

The Case for Collective Security

Well-conceived collective security arrangements encourage the development of common strategic concepts, the publication of common plans, and the generation of common preparations for coordinated action against common enemies. Obvious benefits include larger armed forces with greater capabilities, intelligence exchanges, maneuver room, base rights, overflight permission, and access to local labor. Intangibles like goodwill and mutual understanding are equally (often more) important. Every quid, of course, has a quo. Historical records suggest that leaders who promise no more than they can deliver, but produce a little extra whenever possible, do a lot to cement close relationships. All should amiably accept implicit as well as explicit rules from the start, so that little is left to imagination when moments of truth arise.[5]

COLLECTIVE SECURITY CHOICES

Two supranational coalitions have sought to ensure or restore world peace. The League of Nations was a washout between 1920 and 1946. The United Nations has reaped mixed results ever since. Sovereign states consequently tailor bilateral and multilateral lash-ups as required to satisfy specific needs and exert greater control.

League of Nations

President Woodrow Wilson and other idealists who conceived the League of Nations concluded that the world community in concert could deter armed aggression by any single country. The unified front that they envisioned invariably failed to materialize in the clutch, because a working majority of member states never agreed on who the enemy was and what action, if any, the League should take. Required commitments were more binding than most sovereign states were willing to make. Japan invaded Manchuria with impunity (1931); a bloody war between Bolivia and Paraguay raged in the Chaco (1932–1935); Mussolini ravaged and annexed primitive Ethiopia (1935–1936); Hitler's troops illegally reoccupied the Rhineland (1936); then seized Austria and Czechoslovakia (1938). No victim of Axis

aggression anywhere called on the League of Nations for help after World War II erupted. Few mourned when that inept organization vanished officially on April 19, 1946.[6]

United Nations

Pragmatists who shaped the United Nations learned useful lessons from those experiences. Member states furnish unarmed observers, "police forces," and large military formations with offensive combat capabilities that have helped maintain or restore peace at selected trouble spots around the world since 1948. The UN peacekeeping record has been admirable in many respects, but institutional, bureaucratic, and budgetary limitations are severe. All five permanent members of the Security Council, which is the only organ that can order peacekeeping or peacemaking operations, must approve every resolution. Consensus is by no means assured, because how many actions of what kind to take in which sovereign states raise contentious issues. Funds are sufficient to cover only a small fraction of all cases that request UN assistance. Ad hoc planning predominates, pending activation of a permanent military staff to replace the Security Council's dysfunctional Military Staff Committee. Some nations, including the United States, are reluctant to put troops under UN command. Early solutions to such thorny problems seem unlikely.[7]

International Coalitions

Nation-states create bilateral and multilateral coalitions to ensure favorable balances of power and thereby attain local, regional, hemispheric, or global objectives more rapidly and at less cost than otherwise would be possible. Countries that hope to dominate or strongly influence decisions tend to coalesce with coequal or lesser powers. Less sturdy states normally align primarily for protection, but may possess potent leverage if coalition leaders value cohesion.[8]

Relatively weak states that bandwagon with bullies ordinarily lose freedom of action and risk domination by their "benefactors," but opportunists who hop on bandwagons sometimes share otherwise unobtainable bonanzas. Benito Mussolini did so on June 10, 1940, when he declared war on France, which Hitler's blitzkrieg was rolling up like a rug. Stalin belatedly attacked Japan on August 8, 1945, just one week before Emperor Hirohito told his people that World War II was over. Cost-benefit ratios in each case were favorable.[9]

COMPATIBILITY PROSPECTS

Experienced politico-military policy-makers and strategists are acutely aware that prospects for compatibility vary from good to poor. Probabilities are best when security interests, objectives, strategic concepts, ideological convictions, reliability, and ethics are harmonious. Coalitionists can anticipate trouble whenever their views and those of colleagues differ sharply in even one of those categories.

Politico-Military Purposes

Common purposes pertained during Operations Desert Shield and Desert Storm, when the United States, solidly backed by UN Security Council Resolutions, persuaded thirty other countries to thwart aggression after Iraq seized Kuwait in August 1990. National pride, prestige, and cultural problems caused squabbles, but basic objectives (defend Saudi Arabia; defeat Saddam Hussein; free Kuwait) never were in doubt.[10]

Cross-purposes occur when strategists prompt partners to perform functions unrelated to the coalition's rationale. Only one NATO ally (Portugal) granted U.S. transport aircraft overflight or landing rights to and from Israel during the Yom Kippur War in 1973; others feared that if they did so outraged Arabs might deny them much-needed petroleum.[11]

Strategic Perspectives

Common purposes prevailed during NATO's lengthy confrontation with the Warsaw Pact (1949-

1991), but U.S. leaders and their European allies locked horns repeatedly because they viewed vital interests from different perspectives. Formidable military formations east of the Iron Curtain directly endangered the survival and independence of Western Europe, but not North America. Those geographic circumstances made it difficult for NATO to formulate mutually agreeable strategies in the mid-1960s, when Soviet ICBMs and SLBMs able to strike the United States made European members question whether any U.S. President would risk a full-scale nuclear exchange to ensure their survival.[12]

Ideological Persuasions

Desperate nations with few potential partners may coalesce with countries that champion detestable ideologies. Winston Churchill demonstrated that phenomenon with his famous statement that, "If Hitler invaded Hell, I should at least make a favorable reference to the devil in the House of Commons."[13] Most Americans reviled the Soviet Union throughout the 1920s and 1930s for many valid reasons, but despotic Stalin became "Uncle Joe," a valued U.S. ally, in the midst of World War II.[14] The United States supported several unsavory Chiefs of State during Cold War with the Soviet Union simply because they were antiCommunist. Rafael Trujillo (Dominican Republic), Anastasio Somoza (Nicaragua), Fernando Marcos (the Philippines), and Mohamad Reza Shah Pahlavi, who occupied Iran's Peacock Throne, were prominent.[15]

Reliability

Coalitions that remain intact only by dint of coercion are notoriously unreliable. Cold War occupants of the Kremlin can so attest, because it took repeated applications of force to keep rebellious non-Soviet members of the Warsaw Pact in line. Stalin dispatched tanks to quell antiCommunist riots in East German (1953). His successors dealt harshly with Hungarian mutineers (1956), then crushed Czechoslovakia in 1968, when Moscow's "puppet" governments tried to defect.[16]

Few coalition members relish unreasonably high risks or cling to losing sides if acceptable alternatives are available. King Victor Emmanuel III's war-weary Italian Government, with such thoughts in mind, first ousted Mussolini, then surrendered in September 1943, after which Nazi Germany conducted delaying actions alone in the Apennines. Hungarian Regent Miklós Horthy de Nagybánya in October 1944 likewise tried to negotiate a separate peace, which would have allowed a Soviet tidal wave to pour into Central Europe, but alert Nazis incarcerated him before his plan took effect, then installed a more compliant government.[17]

Scruples

Machiavelli counseled that "a wise leader cannot and should not keep his word when keeping it is not to his advantage or when reasons that made him give it are no longer valid."[18] Unscrupulous leaders before and since have used accomplices as cat's-paws, buffers, and pawns. Disciples in the Kremlin gave evidence, when they sacrificed third-country assets throughout the Cold War to attain Soviet ends or frustrate Western adversaries. The best way to avoid lamentable experiences is to review the records of prospective partners before forming any relationship, but ostensibly reliable allies even so may renege. That happened in 1975, when U.S. politico-military policy-makers abandoned their Vietnamese, Laotian, and Cambodian comrades who had battled Communist aggression for many years.

FORMAL AND INFORMAL COALITIONS

All alliances are coalitions, but not all coalitions are alliances. The latter require treaties that, according to international law, are legally binding on every member. Signatories consequently need to craft terms with great care. Tacit partnerships, in contrast, imply mutual responsibilities, but linkages re-

main informal. Coalition architects choose formal or informal ties, depending on governing factors and requirements.

Alliance Treaties

The Law of Diminishing Returns imposes practical limits on the size of each alliance and the number that each nation can sensibly instigate or join, taking political, economic, military, and geographic considerations into account. Treaties to which any nation is party moreover should be consistent. The League of Nations Covenant, for example, claimed that no signatory to the General Treaty for the Renunciation of War could lawfully enter, or remain in, an offensive alliance. Articles 52 and 103 of the United Nations Charter contain similar stipulations.[19]

Authentic Needs

The optimum size of any alliance system inherently depends on national purposes and perceived threats. Countries that confine their interests to a single region normally need belong to no more than one coalition. Great powers with global ambitions or responsibilities may find several alliances useful, but nevertheless should concentrate on key requirements because "pactomania" almost always is counterproductive. Some observers during the Cold War accused U.S. statesmen of collecting allies like postage stamps, whether partners were strategically well-situated or not, strong or weak, developed or undeveloped.[20]

Bilateral Alliances

Bilateral alliances, which minimize disputes concerning policies, plans, operations, and force postures, are most manageable. Organizational structures and coordination are comparatively simple. Both parties even so must work to maintain smooth relations, much like spouses in successful marriages. All eggs in one basket moreover is risky business, because bilateral coalitions dissolve if one member defects, and collapse if one suffers defeat. States that belong to more than one pact must decide which associates to support, if enemies attack more than one friend or "friends" attack each other (rancorous relations between Greece and Turkey, for example, have repeatedly given NATO cause for concern).

Multilateral Alliances

Multilateral alliances offer more flexibility, but disputes usually multiply. Sovereign states often squabble over control. Weak partners may be more trouble than they are worth, unless they contribute badly needed assets, such as strategic location. Efficiency, even effectiveness, becomes increasingly elusive as membership swells.[21] NATO for those reasons weighed benefits and liabilities at length before it admitted Poland, Hungary, and the Czech Republic on March 12, 1999.[22] Their armed forces, which were organized, equipped, and trained to suit Warsaw Pact purposes, may take a decade or more to recast in NATO's mold, but two geopolitical pluses apparently outweighed all minuses: those three countries provide springboards in Central Europe from which to mount and sustain military operations in the Balkans and beyond; their territory would comprise a useful buffer zone between Eastern and Western Europe if relations with Russia ever turn sour.

Treaty Terms

Every alliance should serve a clear purpose within recognizable geographic confines. The North Atlantic Treaty, crafted in 1949 for deterrent purposes, identifies its main aim as the "capacity to resist armed attack" against the territory, armed forces, ships, or aircraft of any member in Europe, North America, Eurasia, Turkey, the North Atlantic Ocean, or the Mediterranean Sea. Stated terms disregard internecine conflicts, subversion, and peripheral civil wars. The Inter-American Treaty of Reciprocal Assistance (Rio Pact), which covers most of the Western Hemisphere, addresses indirect as well as direct aggression and, "in the case of conflict between two or more American States," pledges to maintain or reestablish peace and security.[23]

Treaty terms that specify basic obligations precisely leave least room for misinterpretation, but sacrifice flexibility and demand repeated revisions as situations evolve. Excessively loose stipulations allow signatories immoderate autonomy. Signatories of the North Atlantic Treaty, which takes an intermediate tack, agree that "an attack against one or more of them . . . shall be considered an attack against them all," but the text does not stipulate specific responses at particular times and places. Each member simply takes "such action as it deems necessary, including the use of armed force."[24] Individual contributions remain matters for consultation. Germany furnished most land power during the Cold War, the United States and Great Britain most forces afloat. Iceland contributed bases and facilities, but no military formations.

Informal Coalitions

Informal coalitions, like formal alliances, may be bilateral or multilateral, long- or short-term, rigidly structured or free form. Many tacit, even extemporaneous, partnerships have enjoyed great longevity. No security treaty commits the United States to safeguard Israel against external threats, but tight emotional and moral ties have outlasted four Arab-Israeli wars and endless disputes since 1948, when the Truman Administration recognized that nation within minutes after it proclaimed independence.

Mercenaries

Niccoló Machiavelli 500 years ago warned Chiefs of State about the dubious value of mercenaries, whom he considered disloyal, poorly disciplined, and subject to defection when nations need them most.[25] The absence of legal obligations nevertheless need not make "hired guns" unreliable. The legendary French Foreign Legion and Gurkhas in the British army are prominent exceptions,[26] along with Montagnards, Nungs, and Cambodians who fought shoulder-to-shoulder beside U.S. Army Special Forces in Southeast Asia.[27]

Surrogates

National or subnational surrogates sometimes do "dirty work" for patrons with whom they have little in common beyond beliefs that "the enemy of my enemy is my friend," because all concerned hope to achieve cherished objectives that otherwise might be unattainable. Symbiotic partnerships even so are lopsided, because sponsors remain aloof while de facto proxies suffer casualties and take much of the blame for failures. Patrons benefit most when they synchronize politico-military operations and least when surrogates pursue cross-purpose agendas.[28] Benefactors in Moscow indeed must have been miffed when Fidel Castro sided with Argentine insurgents despite contrary Soviet intents, then assisted Eritrean "freedom fighters" against the Ethiopian Government, which the Kremlin favored.[29]

There are no hard and fast formulas for counter-proxy warfare, because each case is unique. National security policy-makers and military strategists must decide whether to oppose subsidizers, surrogates, or both in operational areas or their homelands. The prime prerequisite is accurate intelligence concerning patron-proxy relationships and respective vulnerabilities.[30]

COMMAND AND CONTROL

Bilateral coalitions experience command and control problems, even if both parties are friends of long standing whose racial, linguistic, ethical, and cultural characteristics are nearly identical.[31] Commanders and staffs are acutely concerned at every level that employs land, sea, air, amphibious, or space forces from more than one country, because complexities multiply logarithmically when diversities increase.

High Commands

Coalitions sometimes, but not always, integrate high commands that formulate grand strategies, prepare broad plans, and allocate resources to subordinates, given guidance from respective governments, then issue instructions to military commanders in chief

(CINCs). Principal participants determine how much authority high commands may exercise over forces from their countries. Some prefer semiautonomous components, whereas others favor central control. Coalition members must resolve serious disagreements to the satisfaction of all concerned or anticipate potentially dangerous disagreements at inopportune moments.

Major Military Commands

Major military commands that control combat and support forces within assigned areas of responsibility (AORs) generally perform operational and tactical rather than strategic functions. The choice of commanders in chief, organizational structures, and provisions for proper liaison all are important.

Commanders in Chief and Staffs

Coalition commanders in chief establish policies, set standards, prepare operational plans, and direct their implementation in peacetime and in war. Candidates ideally should possess political as well as military acumen; enjoy the confidence of political supervisors; deal with them tactfully and diplomatically; and be capable arbiters. The best-qualified officers display command presence, sound judgment, and superior decision-making abilities in troublesome times. Deputy CINCs, preferably from different countries and different services, should complement commanders. Similar prescriptions apply to subordinate commanders and coalition staffs. All perform best when they cultivate close professional and personal relationships with allied colleagues. There is no place for ethnocentric arrogance.

Unity of Command

Coalitions organize assigned armed forces in conformance with situations. Unity of command is preferable but not essential, provided collaboration is close, continuous, and comprehensive, as disparate allies demonstrated during Operations Desert Storm and Desert Shield. General H. Norman Schwarzkopf, who headed U.S. Central Command (CENTCOM), took charge of U.S., British, and French contingents in and adjacent to objective areas. His Royal Highness Lieutenant General Khalid bin Sultan of Saudi Arabia led a Joint Arab Islamic Force.[32] Integration is unnecessary whenever one nation furnishes all forces within any given AOR, or allied sectors are noncontiguous. Japan, for example, continued to operate independently in East Asia and the Pacific Basin after it joined far-distant Germany and Italy as part of the Axis Powers during World War II. Organizations in any event should ensure the smoothest possible transition from peace to war in the shortest possible time.

Coordination Techniques

Savvy CINCs maintain tight liaison with foreign associates to facilitate vertical and horizontal coordination. General Schwartzkopf accordingly sent 109 small teams from CENTCOM's Army Special Operations Task Force to assist Saudi General Sultan, whose Joint Arab Islamic Force represented twenty-three nations with disparate languages, customs, religions, arms, equipment, doctrines, and capabilities. Each team conducted individual and unit training that emphasized tactics, fire coordination, air support, minefield breaching, maintenance, and medical evacuation. Each team additionally installed radio links and, after armed combat began, controlled U.S. air strikes, which simplified targeting and reduced the likelihood of casualties from "friendly" fire by coalition partners.[33]

RESPECTIVE CONTRIBUTIONS

Affluent and needy members of security coalitions ceaselessly debate respective roles, which are not subject to simple calculations. Military and economic assistance strengthens weak partners who are willing but unable to contribute as much as allies would like. Equitable burden-sharing ensures that no member, large or small, carries disproportionately large loads.

Foreign Aid

Foreign aid takes many forms: money, weapons, equipment, supplies, advice, education, training, construction, and services furnished free of charge or paid for in cash, on credit, even by barter, perhaps at favorable rates over lengthy periods of time. Leases and loans are allowable. Short-, mid-, and long-term programs tailored to suit each worthy recipient are essential, because some need tactical instruction more than hard currency, while others need infrastructure more than materiel. Multiyear apportionments, carefully prioritized, consistently applied, and coupled with effective control mechanisms, regularly reap best results.[34]

Objectives

Foreign aid administrators variously endeavor to preserve or improve regional balances of power, advance ideological principles (democracy, Communism), ensure access to foreign bases or facilities, guarantee continued dependency of client states or, in the case of sales, alleviate balance-of-payment problems. Status quo powers generally assist junior partners in ways that enhance deterrence, defense, self-reliance, and internal stability, while predators give coalition partners greater offensive capabilities.[35] Those roles, however, may reverse on short notice. Soviet and Cuban logistical support, for example, helped Sandinista insurgents oust Nicaraguan President Anastasio Somoza in 1979, then furnished the newly installed Sandinista Government with the wherewithal it needed to fend off U.S.-backed Contras.[36]

Objections

Skeptics object to most foreign aid, which they contend may encourage commitments not otherwise intended, detract from the donor's military readiness, permit autocrats to quash legitimate opposition inside their own countries, and widen gaps between rich and poor through waste, fraud, and abuse. Assistance, they assert, too often becomes thinly veiled bribery or de facto rent and seldom provides enough

243

political clout and regional stability to make it cost-effective. Critics additionally claim that rising expectations breed resentment, unless benefactors meet beneficiaries' expanding demands expeditiously.[37] Enlightened policies make the best rebuttals.

Burden-Sharing

President John F. Kennedy, in his Inaugural Address on January 20, 1961, "let every nation know, whether it wishes us well or ill, that we shall pay any price, bear any burden, meet any hardship, support any friend, oppose any foe to assure the survival and success of liberty." President Richard M. Nixon, in his State of the World message less than a decade later (January 1970), declared that "America cannot—and will not—conceive *all* the plans, design *all* the programs, execute *all* the decisions and undertake *all* the defense of the free nations of the world." Those polarized pronouncements confirm that even the richest country in history can question its input to any coalition.

Facile burden-sharing formulae indeed are nonexistent. Quantifiable considerations include ratios between each coalition member's abilities to contribute and actual contributions (gross domestic products vs. defense budgets, population profiles vs. military manpower, and so on).[38] Skilled statisticians may assign relative weights and rank countries accordingly, but raw comparisons are deceptive and attempts to redress perceived wrongs can become acrimonious. NATO's members in May 1978, for example, generally agreed to increase defense spending by 3% annually in real terms. Several of them failed to meet that objective but, even if all had complied, there was no assurance that respective capabilities would increase proportionally, because no document specified how additional funds were to be spent.[39]

Few countries can project military power far beyond their borders, however capable they may be close to home. Those who cannot reach distant theaters alone need help from coalition partners. Two first-rate South Korean divisions that fought

beside U.S. Armed Forces in Vietnam routinely required long-haul transportation, logistical support, and financial subsidies. Their contributions were commendable, but costs to the United States were considerable.[40]

Burden-sharing that is calculated entirely in concrete terms discounts intangibles. Critical terrain, maneuver room, infrastructure, local labor forces, and shared intelligence surely count. So should comparative exposure to peril. The Federal Republic of Germany long played host to an immense concentration of foreign armies and air forces that intermingled with densely packed populations and industrial sites. Its people repeatedly suffered severe property damage during peacetime maneuvers and would have sacrificed civilian lifeblood and national treasure during any war with the Warsaw Pact.[41] National security policy-makers and military strategists consequently should build comprehensive cases before they allege that certain partners fail to bear their fair share, because false accusations weaken coalitions.

REQUIREMENTS FOR REVIEW

Historical experience confirms requirements to review coalitions, lest they quietly outlive their usefulness. Multinational alliances established to fight World War II, as well as those assembled for combat in Korea, Vietnam, and the Persian Gulf, dissolved soon after shooting stopped and situations stabilized. Many Cold War partnerships, in contrast, persist unchanged.[42] Nearly all seem overripe for review to reconfirm or redefine the purpose and scope of those retained, scrap the rest, and determine whether new affiliations would be advisable.

NATO, the most complex coalition of all time, has been assessing requirements since July 1990, because present challenges are quite different from those it faced before the Soviet Union collapsed. The primary military mission, which is "to guarantee the security and territorial integrity of member states," remains unchanged. Article 5 of the North Atlantic Treaty still specifies that "an attack against one or more of them in Europe or North America

shall be considered an attack against them all."
NATO's new strategic concept, consecrated in the
November 1991 *Rome Declaration on Peace and
Security,* nevertheless acknowledges that "the
threat of a simultaneous, full-scale attack . . . no
longer provides the focus." On the contrary, remaining risks "are multi-faceted in nature and multidirec-
tional." Salient concerns include transnational terrorism and the proliferation of nontraditional
weapons coupled with political, economic, social,
ethnic, and religious rivalries.[43] Strategic questions
such as those listed below await firm answers:

- Should U.S. military contributions to NATO
  be proportionately greater, less, or remain
  essentially the same as they have been since
  1949?
- Should Canada and Iceland continue to participate?

- Should NATO place a lid on membership or
  embrace all that clamor for acceptance?
- Should NATO extend security guarantees to
  Latvia, Estonia, and Lithuania, which are far
  removed from power centers in Western
  Europe?
- Where, for what purposes, under what circumstances, and to what extent should
  NATO apply military power beyond the borders of member states?
- Should NATO intervene militarily if war
  should erupt between members (such as
  Greece and Turkey)?
- Under what circumstances should NATO
  intervene militarily when internal conflicts
  afflict its members? Corsican, Basque, and
  Kurdish separatists currently raise such
  issues in France, Spain, and Turkey
  respectively.[44]

KEY POINTS

- Governments must decide whether collective security serves their purposes better than nonalignment or neutrality
- Supranational coalitions that seek to preserve or restore world peace experience severe institutional, bureaucratic, and budgetary problems
- Bilateral and multilateral coalitions with less ambitious aims consequently are common
- Prospects for success are best when coalition members share security interests, objectives, strategic concepts, ideologies, and ethics
- Unity of purpose is hard to maintain when coalition leaders prompt partners to perform functions unrelated to the coalition's rationale
- Alliance treaties are legally binding, whereas tacit partnerships merely imply mutual responsibilities
- The Law of Diminishing Returns imposes practical limits on the size of every coalition and the number of alliances any nation can sensibly maintain
- Bilateral lash-ups minimize disputes about policies, plans, and operations, whereas multilateral accords usually offer more flexibility but complicate coordination
- Military unity of command is preferable but not essential, provided collaboration is close, continuous, and comprehensive
- Equitable contributions by coalition members are not subject to simple calculations

NOTES

1. Maurice Matloff described one set of strange bedfellows in *The United States Army in World War II: Strategic Planning for Coalition Warfare, 1943-1944,* (Washington: Center for Military History, United States Army, 1994), 1-8. For a coalition made up of competitors who disliked each other, see Diana Preston, *The Boxer Rebellion: The Dramatic Story of China's War on Foreigners That Shook the World in the Summer of 1900* (London: Waker & Co., 2000).

2. Ken Booth, "Alliances," in *Contemporary Strategy: Theories and Concepts,* ed. John Bayles et al., vol. 1, 2d ed. (New York: Holmes & Meier, 1987), 258-76; Ole R. Holsti, P. Terrence Hopmann, and John D. Sullivan, *Unity and Disintegration in International Alliances: Comparative Studies* (New York: John Wiley and Sons, 1973), 249-277.

3. Robert L. Rothstein, *Alliances and Small Powers* (New York: Columbia University Press, 1968), 30-45, 47-49, 248-54; George Liska, *Nations in Alliance: The Limits of Independence* (Baltimore: Johns Hopkins Press, 1968), 202-54; Bruce George and Laurel David Lister, "Considerations for a 'Weak' Nation in Choosing Partners for an Alliance," *Jane's Defence Weekly,* October 12, 1985, 789, 791.

4. William B. Bader, *Austria between East and West, 1945-1955* (Stanford, CA: Stanford University Press, 1966).

5. Admiral Arleigh A. Burke, "A Critical Evaluation of U.S. Strategy," lecture delivered at the National War College, December 20, 1970.

6. George J. Lankevich, series ed., *Partners for Peace: International Cooperation Towards Peace in the Twentieth Century;* Gary B. Ostrower, *The League of Nations: From 1919 to 1929* and George Gill, *The League of Nations: From 1929 to 1946* (Garden City, NY: Avery Publishing Group, 1996).

7. John Hillen, *Blue Helmets: The Strategy of UN Military Operations* (New York: Brassey's, 1998); Colum Lynch, "Overhaul of UN Peacekeeping Is Urged," *Washington Post,* August 24, 2000, A18; Betsy Pisik, "Panel Hits UN on Military Planning," *Washington Times,* August 24, 2000, A1, A9.

8. Roslyn L. Simowitz, *The Logical Consistency and Soundness of the Balance of Power Theory,* Monograph Series in World Affairs, vol. 19, book 3 (Denver: University of Denver, Graduate School of International Studies, 1982).

9. Stephen M. Walt, *The Origins of Alliances* (Ithaca, NY: Cornell University Press, 1987), 17-33, 147-80; Dennis Mack, *Mussolini* (New York: Alfred A. Knopf, 1982), 234-35, 246, 250; Adam B. Ulam, *Expansion and Coexistence* (New York: Praeger, 1972), 394-98.

10. Norman Friedman, *Desert Victory: The War For Kuwait* (Annapolis, MD: Naval Institute Press, 1991).

11. Lester A. Sobel, ed., *Israel and the Arabs: The October 1973 War* (New York: Facts on File, 1974), 104.

12. Statement by Secretary of Defense Robert S. McNamara before the Senate Armed Services Committee on The Fiscal Years 1969-73 Defense Program and the 1969 Defense Budget, February 1, 1968, 27-32. See also, Daniel S. Papp, *The Soviet Perception of the American Will* (Carlisle Barracks, PA: Strategic Studies Institute, U.S. Army War College, January 30, 1979).

13. Winston Churchill, *The Second World War,* vol. III, *The Grand Alliance* (Boston: Houghton Mifflin Co., 1950), 370.

14. Thomas A. Bailey, *America Faces Russia: Russian-American Relations from Earliest Times to Our Day* (Ithaca, NY: Cornell University Press, 1950), 239-334.

15. *Ibid.,* 335-46; John M. Collins, *America's Small Wars: Lessons for the Future* (Washington: Brassey's, 1991), 77-78, 147-48, 177-78, 197-98.

16. Stefan Brant, *The East German Rising, 17th June 1953,* trans. Charles Wheeler (New York: Praeger 1957); David Pryce-Jones, *The Hungarian Revolution* (New York: Horizon Press, 1969); Harry Schwartz, *Prague's 200 Days: The Struggle for Democracy in Czechoslovakia* (New York: Praeger, 1969).

17. Robert Wallace, *The Italian Campaign* (New York: Time-Life Books, 1978), 48-54; Ernest C. Helmreich, *Hungary* (New York: Praeger, 1957), 366-69.

18. Niccoló Machiavelli, *The Prince,* trans. and ed. Thomas C. Bergin (Arlington Heights, IL: Harlan Davidson, 1947), 51-52.

19. Clive Parry, John P. Grant et al., eds., *Encyclopaedic Dictionary of International Law* (New York: Oceana Publications, 1986), 17.

20. John Spanier, *Games Nations Play: Analyzing International Politics,* 3d ed. (New York: Holt, Rinehart and Winston, 1975), 83; Hans J. Morgenthau, "Alliances and National Security," *Perspectives in Defense Management,* Autumn 1973, 15-24.

21. William H. Riker, "The Size Principle," and Karl W. Deutsch and Morton W. Kaplan, "The Limits of International Coalitions," both in *Alliance in International Politics,* ed. Julian R. Friedman et al. (Boston: Allyn and Bacon, 1970), 261-67. For multilateral alliances that mainly involve small states, see Leslie H.

Brown, "Regional Collaboration in Resolving Third-World Conflicts," *Survival*, May/June 1986, 208-20.

22. *Study on NATO Enlargement* (Brussels, Belgium: NATO Headquarters, September 1995); Stanley R. Sloan and Steven Woehrel, *NATO Enlargement and Russia: From Cold War to Cold Peace*, Rpt. 95-594S (Washington: Congressional Research Service, May 15, 1995).

23. *Legislation on Foreign Relations Through 1988* [not yet superseded], Joint Committee Print, vol. V, *Treaties and Related Material*, Senate Committee on Foreign Relations and House Committee on Foreign Affairs (Washington: U.S. Government Printing Office, December 1989), "North Atlantic Treaty," 363-66; "Inter-American Treaty of Reciprocal Assistance," 293-298.

24. *Legislation on Foreign Relations Through 1988*, 364.

25. Machiavelli, *The Prince*, 33-38.

26. Douglas Porch, *The French Foreign Legion: A Complete History of the Legendary Fighting Force* (New York: Harper Personal Library, 1992); Byron Farwell, *The Gurkhas* (New York: W. W. Norton & Co., 1984).

27. Shelby L. Stanton, *Green Berets at War: U.S. Army Special Forces in Southeast Asia, 1956-1975* (New York: Dell, 1985).

28. Philip Towle, "The Strategy of War by Proxy," *RUSI Journal*, March 1981, 21-26; Victor H. Krulak, "The Strategic Limits of Proxy War," *Strategic Review*, Winter 1994, 52-57; Richard Shultz, Jr., "Soviet Use of Surrogates to Project Power in the Third World," *Parameters*, Autumn 1986, 32-42.

29. Mark N. Katz, "The Soviet Cuban Connection," *International Security*, Summer 1983, 88-112.

30. William J. Taylor, Jr., and James J. Townsend, "Soviet Proxy Warfare," in *Strategic Requirements for the Army to the Year 2000*, eds. Robert K. Kupperman and William J. Taylor, Jr. (Lexington, MA: Lexington Books, 1984), 214-25.

31. For U.S. and British debates about command authority, see Forrest C. Pogue, *The United States Army in World War II. The European Theater of Operations: The Supreme Command* (Washington: U.S. Government Printing Office, 1954), 36-45.

32. General H. Norman Schwarzkopf, *It Doesn't Take a Hero* (New York: Bantam Books, 1992), 373-374; HRH General Khalid bin Sultan, *Desert Warrior* (New York: HarperCollins, 1995), 189-216, with command relationship charts on 244-48.

33. Conversation in June 1998 with Colonel James W. Kraus, who commanded CENTCOM's Army Special Operations Task Force during Operations Desert Shield and Desert Storm; Captain Chadwick W. Storlie, "The Liaison Coordination Element: Force Multiplier for Coalition Operations," *Special Warfare*, Spring 1999, 40-46.

34. *Commitment to Freedom: Security Assistance as a U.S. Policy Instrument in the Third World*, a paper by the Regional Conflict Working Group submitted to the Commission on Integrated Long-Term Strategy (Washington: U.S. Government Printing Office, May 1988), 32-33, 48-53.

35. Elliot L. Richardson, "The Case for Security Assistance to Other Nations," News Release (Washington: Office of Assistant Secretary of Defense [Public Affairs], March 30, 1973); Larry Q. Nowels, *Foreign Aid: Answers to Ten Frequently Asked Questions* (Washington: Congressional Research Service, August 21, 1986).

36. Morris Rothenberg, "The Soviets and Central America," in *Central America: Anatomy of Conflict*, ed. Robert S. Leiken (New York: Pergamon Press, 1984), 131-36, 139-44.

37. Senator Frank Church, "A Farewell to Foreign Aid," *Washington Post*, November 7, 1971, B1, B4; Karen DeYoung, "Generosity Shrinks in an Age of Prosperity," *Washington Post*, November 25, 1999, A1, A31.

38. For quantifiable indicators, see Caspar W. Weinberger, *Report on Allied Contributions to the Common Defense*, a report to the U.S. Congress (Washington: Department of Defense, March 1985).

39. Stanley R. Sloan, *Defense Burden-sharing: U.S. Relations with NATO Allies and Japan* (Washington: Congressional Research Service, June 24, 1988), 12-14; Anthony H. Cordesman, "Defense Burden Sharing: A Brief Scorecard on Our Major Allies (and Ourselves)," *Armed Forces Journal*, October 1982, 64, 66, 68, 70, 72, 90.

40. *United States Security Agreements and Security Commitments Abroad*, Part 6, Republic of Korea, Hearings before the Subcommittee on United States Security Agreements and Commitments Abroad of the Senate Committee on Foreign Relations, 91st Cong., 2d sess. (Washington: U.S. Government Printing Office, February 1970, 1532-74.

41. *Burden-Sharing: The Benefits, Costs, and Risks of Collective Security*, Special Report (Washington: Association of the United States Army, October 22, 1982); Robert W. Komer, "How to Get Less from the Allies," *Washington Post*, October 22, 1982, 21.

42. For U.S. treaties in force, see *Legislation on Foreign Relations Through 1988*, 293-511.

43. Senator William V. Roth, Jr., *NATO in the 21st Century* (Brussels, Belgium: North Atlantic Assembly, September 1998), quotations on 63, 68; Stanley R. Sloan, *The United States and European Defense,* Chaillot Papers 39 (Paris: Institute for Strategic Studies, April 2000).

44. William Drozdiak, "U.S., European Allies Divided Over NATO's Authority to Act," *Washington Post,* November 8, 1998, A33.

PART IV

KEYS TO STRATEGIC SUPERIORITY

21. Strategic Trailblazers

Thinking is the hardest work there is,
which is the probable reason why so
few people engage in it.

Henry Ford
Interview
February 1929

The arrogant Philistine giant named Goliath, "whose height was six cubits and a span" (at least 8 feet 11 inches, maybe more), wore a brass helmet, a coat of mail, carried a sword, and brandished an iron-tipped spear. He disdained little David, armed with a sling and five smooth stones from a nearby brook, until Swish!—the first shot dropped him in a heap, then he literally lost his head. One shot, one kill.[1] The moral of that tale might be, "Who Thinks Wins."

Creative thinkers are scarce, no matter what their occupation. Strategic trailblazers are no exception. One common characteristic nevertheless is evident, despite diversified origins, upbringing, interests, aptitudes, races, creeds, education, professional experience, and temperaments: all are problem-solvers who, like Alexander the Great, cut Gordian knots that inferior techniques never could unravel.

ILLUSTRATIVE ROLE MODELS

Some politico-military strategists in uniform and mufti are strictly theoreticians, others are practitioners, while a handful of switch-hitters wield pens as well as swords. Ten thumbnail sketches below identify role models in each category who flourished during different periods in different environments, addressed distinctive segments of the conflict spectrum, and displayed unique styles. Additional candidates qualify, but brilliant strategic stars have never been numerous.

Strategic Theoreticians

Strategic pioneers create theories, concepts, and other intellectual tools for use by doers who prepare overarching plans and conduct implementing operations. The written legacy includes works by such luminaries as Antoine Henri Jomini, Basil H. Liddell Hart, Giulio Douhet, Alfred Thayer Mahan, and Bernard Brodie, the world's first nuclear strategist. Sun Tzu, Carl von Clausewitz, and Herman Kahn, who made admirable contributions that still influence offensive, defensive, and deterrent schemes, represent three different countries and time periods.

Sun Tzu

Sun Tzu, who put strategic thoughts on paper in China circa 500 B.C., is history's first theoretician in that sparsely populated field. His concise treatise, entitled *The Art of War*, is the soul of simplicity, transcending time and place. No one in the twenty-five centuries since has had a better feel for strategic interrelationships, considerations, and constraints. Steadfast admirers on every continent except Antarctica still revere Sun Tzu, quote him at length, and consider him a relevant tutor.[2]

Carl von Clausewitz

Clausewitz, who had little formal education, joined the Prussian Army at age twelve, quickly won a commission, and served seventeen years as a staff officer. His deathless reputation, however, derived not from campaigns against enemies but as Director of the *Kriegsakademie* (War College), where he wrote his magnum opus *On War,* which was published posthumously in 1832. That classic continues to influence more students of strategy than any book before or since, with the possible exception of Sun Tzu's thirteen essays.[3]

Herman Kahn

Extroverted Herman Kahn was a citizen-soldier whose three years of military service during World War II terminated at the grade of sergeant. His education emphasized mathematics and physics, which seem odd starting points for a military theorist, but he built a towering reputation in the 1960s with such seminal works as *On Thermonuclear War,* which delved deeply into that topic. *On Escalation: Metaphors and Scenarios,* still a standard textbook, covers the entire conflict spectrum.[4]

Strategic Practitioners

A second group of politico-military strategists perform practical feats on land, at sea, in the air, and surely will do so in space, but never publish theories or concepts for enthusiasts to study. Thucydides, Hannibal, Genghis Khan, and Admiral Isoroku Yamamoto, who masterminded Japanese naval victories early in World War II, are a few of the famous names that left indelible marks. The trio selected for exemplification spotlights Cyrus the Great, Napoleon Bonaparte, and General of the Army George C. Marshall, who respectively served ancient Persia, postrevolutionary France, and the United States during its early days as an international power.

Cyrus the Great

Cyrus the Great, whose reign ended almost 200 years before Alexander's conquests began, was the progenitor of all strategic practitioners. He mopped up the Medes in 559 B.C., subjugated Babylon as described in the Book of Daniel, then pieced together a prototype Persian Empire between the Aegean Sea and the Indus River. His holdings were larger and lasted longer than any before, partly because his enlightened policies placated defeated peoples and made elaborate coalitions possible.[5]

Napoleon Bonaparte

Napoleon Bonaparte, who was Emperor of France and Supreme Commander of the *Grande Armée* for fifteen years, is renowned primarily as a peerless practitioner of operational art, but he strategically melded diplomacy and military power in ways that confounded opponents until his gigantic reach exceeded his grasp in 1814. He employed universal conscription (*levées en masse*) to wage war on unprecedented scales, played opponents one against another to isolate each politically, and thereby facilitated the defeat of numerically superior foes.[6]

George C. Marshall

General of the Army George C. Marshall participated in Allied policy-making conferences at Casablanca, Cairo, Teheran, Yalta, and Potsdam. He was a principal military adviser to Presidents Franklin Roosevelt and Harry Truman during World War II and a key architect of Allied global strategies (Winston Churchill called him the "organizer of victory"). The Marshall Plan thereafter helped reconstruct war-ravaged Europe and concomitantly stemmed the spread of Communism west of Stalin's Iron Curtain.[7]

Creative Practitioners

Strategic theorists who practice what they preach are rare indeed. Frederick the Great, French Marshal Hermann Maurice de Saxe, V.I. Lenin, Vietnamese General Vo Nguyen Giap, and space visionary Wernher von Braun typify the few who qualify. The selected four represent continental, naval, aeronautical, and revolutionary warfare schools of thought during the twentieth century. Two of them (Billy Mitchell and Admiral Sergei Gorshkov) excelled despite concerted counteractions by powerful opponents in their own countries.

André Beaufre

Général d'Armée André Beaufre, who was the youngest officer on the French General Staff in 1935, later became Deputy Commander in Chief of French forces in Indochina, commanded troops in Algeria, led the French corps that assaulted Suez in 1956, and subsequently occupied senior posts within NATO. Liddell Hart called his *Introduction to Strategy* "the most comprehensive and carefully formulated treatise on strategy. . .that has appeared in this generation—and in many respects surpasses any previous treatise."[8]

Sergei Gorshkov

Admiral of the Fleet of the Soviet Union Sergei G. Gorshkov took command of the Soviet Navy in 1956, when it was a coastal defense force. He produced a first-class "blue water" navy during the next thirty years, despite strong opposition by superiors who preferred land power and the absence of naval traditions in a nation that lacked ice-free access to open oceans. Gorshkov's *The Sea Power of the State* expressed strategic concepts and implementing force postures that gave U.S. opponents a bad case of jitters well before he retired.[9]

Billy Mitchell

Highly decorated Brigadier General Billy Mitchell, a flamboyant and vociferous proponent of airpower, expounded his views in print, on speaker's platforms, and eyeball-to-eyeball with star-studded disbelievers. He conceived vertical envelopment (parachute assaults) in 1918 and proposed that General Pershing prepare a division for such purpose. Three years later he demonstrated the potency of bombers against battleships. A court-martial convicted him of insubordination in 1925, but World War II vindicated his strategic visions.[10]

Mao Zedong

Mao Zedong concentrated on political thought, social studies, and the military history of China's classical kingdoms before he became Chairman of the Chinese Communist Party and a hard-bitten field commander (Sun Tzu was his mentor several times removed). Mao fathered fundamental concepts of revolutionary and guerrilla warfare, then proved their worth in battle against Japanese invaders and Chiang Kai-shek's Kuomintang troops. Students of those subjects consider the *Selected Works of Mao Tse-Tung* to be required reading.[11]

COVETED CHARACTERISTICS

"Scouts," whose mission is to earmark potentially talented military strategists by design instead of by accident, look for coveted characteristics that academic transcripts, personal histories, résumés, fitness reports, and other personnel records rarely reveal. Graduate degrees and war college diplomas merely indicate that possessors have been exposed to relevant instruction. Personal interviews fill some gaps, but are not foolproof. Promising candidates need not exhibit all attributes described below, but they cannot lack many.[12]

Intelligence

Native intelligence is indispensable. No reliable statistics are available, but nearly every strategic wizard is a genius in the broadest sense of that word, which *Webster's New World Collegiate Dictionary* defines as "great mental capacity and inventive ability; especially great and original creative ability at some art or science." Each is just as innovative in his or her own way as Thomas A. Edison and Alexander Graham Bell, even though their outputs are intangible rather than material.

Intellectual Activism

Much of the world's wit lies permanently fallow or is wasted on underachievers, whereas freethinking strategists possess inquisitive minds. They understand that Uncle Remus was right when he warned, "It ain't the things you don't know what gets you in deep trouble. It's the things you knows for sure what ain't so!" Their search for fundamental truths therefore features enlightened skepticism that makes them challenge all premises, attack all shibboleths, and explore all identifiable alternatives. They sift opinions from pole to pole, aware that nobody is invariably right or wrong, then discard junk and retain intellectual jewels.

Analytical Acumen

Analytical acumen is a coveted characteristic, because facts require interpretation before full meanings emerge. Gifts of discernment and sound judgment are indispensable when national security policy-makers and military strategists seek reliable answers to subjective questions like, "How much is enough?" and "How great is the risk?" Successful military strategists, like chess players, minimize rash acts only if they anticipate several sequential enemy moves and shape optional responses accordingly.

Broad Knowledge Base

Most superlative politico-military strategists are generalists whose professional knowledge base is exceedingly broad. They acquire depth as required from the detailed wisdom of experts in relevant disciplines. Herman Kahn's fame, for example, might have been confined to some esoteric subject, such as theories of gaming, if math and physics had remained his fortes. Instead, he ranged far and wide in social sciences for more than twenty-five years and left indelible marks on several levels of strategic thought.

Tenacity

Tenacity is a prized trait, because strategic trailblazers often suffer multiple failures during their search for transcendental ideas. Self-confident searchers explore multiple avenues until they find the right route to success, whereas impatient pioneers are prone to quit prematurely.

Salesmanship

Innovative strategists who are not Chiefs of State or their trusted advisers must be supersalesmen if they expect to enlist the support of skeptical superiors. Priceless theories and concepts otherwise gather dust. Admiral Gorshkov, to wit, wheedled and cajoled until he got his way, whereas Billy Mitchell's abusive frontal assaults reaped outrage until senior officers cashiered him.

COMPOSITE REQUIREMENTS

No catalog of characteristics could ever be complete without reminding readers that strategy formulation is an intricate act. Masters possess all or most of the attributes described in this brief chapter, but consistent success additionally demands generous injections of a priori apperception, divine revelation, intuition, and God-given common sense.

KEY POINTS

- Brilliant military strategists have never been numerous
- Some politico-military strategists are theoreticians, others are practitioners, while a handful of switch-hitters wield pens as well as swords
- Strategic pioneers create theories, concepts, and other intellectual tools
- Strategic practitioners incorporate theories and concepts into offensive, defensive, and deterrent plans
- Switch-hitting strategists, a rare breed indeed, are theorists who practice what they preach
- Scouts in search of potentially sharp strategists should concentrate on candidates who are smart, inquisitive, imaginative, skeptical, open-minded, persistent, and articulate
- A review of strategic role models in each category nevertheless reveals that personal characteristics, education, and practical experiences vary considerably
- Aptitudes and problem-solving abilities constitute the most common threads
- Common sense is the quintessential requirement
- Who thinks, wins

NOTES

1. *The Holy Bible,* First Book of Samuel, "David and Goliath."

2. Sun Tzu, *The Art of War,* trans. Samuel B. Griffith (New York: Oxford University Press, 1963).

3. Carl von Clausewitz, *On War,* ed. and trans. Michael Howard and Peter Paret (Princeton, NJ: Princeton University Press, 1976); Michael I. Handel, *Sun Tzu & Clausewitz Compared* (Carlisle Barracks, PA: Strategic Studies Institute, U.S. Army War College, 1991).

4. Herman Kahn, *On Thermonuclear War* (Princeton, NJ: Princeton University Press, 1960) and *On Escalation: Metaphors and Scenarios* (New York: Praeger, 1965).

5. Harold Lamb, *Cyrus the Great* (Garden City, NY: Doubleday, 1960); *Royal Persia: A Commemoration of Cyrus the Great and His Successors on the Occasion of the 2500th Anniversary of the Founding of the Persian Empire* (London: British Museum, 1971).

6. Jay Luvaas, ed., *Napoleon on the Art of War* (New York: Free Press, 1999); Peter Paret, "Napoleon and the Revolution in War," in *Makers of Modern Strategy: From Machiavelli to the Nuclear Age,* ed. Peter Paret (Princeton University Press, 1986), 123–42.

7. Forrest C. Pogue, *George C. Marshall,* vol. 2, *Ordeal and Hope, 1939–1942;* vol. 3, *Organizer of Victory, 1943–1945* (New York: Viking, 1966, 1973); Leonard Mosley, *Marshall: Hero for Our Times* (New York: Hurst Books, 1982).

8. Général d'Armée André Beaufre, *An Introduction to Strategy* (New York: Praeger, 1965), Liddell Hart's quotation is on page 10.

9. Admiral of the Fleet of the Soviet Union Sergei G. Gorshkov, *The Sea Power of the State* (Annapolis, MD: Naval Institute Press, 1979).

10. Brigadier General William Mitchell, diary entitled *From Start to Finish of Our Greatest War,* ed. and published posthumously as *Memoirs of World War I* (New York: Random House, 1960), vertical envelopment views on 268; Burke Davis, *The Billy Mitchell Affair* (New York: Random House), 1967.

11. *Selected Works of Mao Tse-Tung* (London: Lawrence and Wishart, 1954–56); Robert Payne, *Portrait of a Revolutionary: Mao Tse-Tung* (New York: Albard-Schuman, 1961).

12. A slightly different version of coveted characteristics originally appeared in John M. Collins, *Grand Strategy: Principles and Practices* (Annapolis, MD: Naval Institute Press, 1973), 222–25.

22. Strategic Stepping-Stones

'Tis Education forms the common mind;
Just as the twig is bent the tree's inclined.

Alexander Pope
Moral Essays, Epistle I
1733

Stepping-stones to strategic superiority start with intuitive, insightful minds and other attributes that Chapter 21 describes, but full development of innate potential demands environments conducive to creativity, progressive politico-military education, incisive research techniques, and a wealth of practical experience. Front-runners seize and maintain intellectual initiative, which facilitates freedom of action in strategic arenas.

CREATIVE ENVIRONMENTS

Niccolò Machiavelli penned *The Prince* and *Discourses* on the family farm near San Casiano during a period of idleness after the Medici ousted him from his Florentine office in 1512.[1] Alfred Thayer Mahan wrote *The Influence of Sea Power Upon History* while he was cloistered at the U.S. Naval War College (1886–1893).[2] Mao's strategic concepts took shape during the 1930s in a cave near Bao'an at the end of the Long March, while his army regrouped, reinforced, resupplied, and retrained far from the worries of war.[3] Most towering strategic theorists before and since similarly enjoyed intellectual freedom and tranquil opportunities to think.[4]

Intellectual Freedom

Strategic theorizing is to strategic planning as basic scientific research is to applied technology. Creative thinkers, whose aim is originality, flourish best under conditions that encourage flights of fancy. Di-

rected approaches that specify what tacks to take are "the kiss of death." The world would still be waiting for Einstein's Special Theory of Relativity if initiation of that multipurpose project had hinged on instructions from wheelers and dealers who are preoccupied with "practical matters."

Enlightened overseers, even in closed societies such as a Communist China, eschew any need for strategic trailblazers to justify, defend, support, or parrot official policy.[5] On the contrary, they encourage unconventional experimentation, prize opinions that "rock the boat," and tolerate repeated false starts, because intellectual pioneers are apt to be timid if punishment is the reward for failure. Learned senior officials also understand that strict deadlines discourage creative thought—neither Beethoven nor any other virtuoso could have promised to compose a masterpiece for the House of Habsburg by 1530 hours on a Friday afternoon.

Unregimented Regimens

Clock-punchers limit their productivity to rigidly budgeted schedules, while drudges nailed to desks become brain-dead. Strategic geniuses, who shun either regimen, generally immerse themselves in projects more or less continuously, wherever they may be. They make contact with progressive ideas at odd intervals in bedrooms or baths, at breakfast, on buses, and in bars. Day in and day out, they rack up more fruitful hours than regimented counterparts, but at paces tailored to suit their temperaments.

Prolific Contacts

Most of the old masters conceived innovative ideas in isolation, but few distinguished theorists do so today, because scopes have expanded exponentially and problems have become immeasurably more complex. The importance of formal and informal team play thus has magnified manyfold since Sun Tzu and Clausewitz produced strategic showpieces.

Security classifications, which strategic planners treasure, stultify theoreticians. Trailblazers who synthesize and expand ideas acquired from passive attendance at, or active participation in, assorted open forums consequently flower most profusely. Rigorous peer reviews during incubation stages are advisable, provided they avoid enforced compromise and committee solutions, which thwart creativity just as surely as castigation. Critique sessions and reactions to "trial balloons" serve best when they air opposing opinions and expose weak arguments, but leave originators free to adopt or disregard advice as they see fit.

Continuity

Professional theoreticians and concept formulators should welcome periodic acquaintanceships with "the real world" to broaden perceptions, identify unsolved problems, and broaden knowledge bases. Extensive experience nevertheless suggests that innovative strategists who stray from "ivory towers" too long may lose their magical touch.

STRATEGIC EDUCATION

Some of history's most eminent military strategists had no formal education of any kind, while others garnered degrees unrelated to the profession of arms. Self-instruction and practical experience prepared such luminaries as Alexander, Hannibal, his nemesis Scipio Africanus, Julius Caesar, Genghis Khan, Suleiman the Magnificent, Jomini, Douhet,

and Giap.[6] Pertinent tutelage nevertheless could give the most gifted performers a flying start and progressively embellish their competence.

Conspicuous Deficiencies

Civilian academic communities the world over award undergraduate and graduate degrees in political science and related fields that focus on international relations. Several hundred colleges in the United States currently address such disciplines.[7] Many other nations offer similar courses of instruction. The pool of foreign policy aspirants accordingly is large.

U.S. senior service colleges, in contrast, survey so many subjects in one academic year that none have time to explore strategic theories and concepts in depth across the conflict spectrum, much less develop alternatives. Penetrating reviews in the late 1980s revealed shortcomings[8] that stubbornly persist.[9] Professional military education systems in most foreign countries encountered comparable afflictions during the latter half of the twentieth century, with one prominent exception: the Voroshilov Academy of the Soviet General Staff in Moscow employed active-duty marshals, generals, and admirals as faculty, the student body embraced junior generals, and instruction lasted two years.[10] That august institution produced many notable products, of which Marshal of the Soviet Union V.D. Sokolovskiy's *Soviet Military Strategy* was just one.[11]

Corrective Actions

A self-sustaining core of superlative politico-military strategists (not a Prussian General Staff–style corps with operational responsibilities[12]) requires well-rounded career patterns and progressive education programs that repeatedly expose handpicked students to topics of increasing complexity. The identification, selection by competitive examination, and initial development of young officers who show great promise should start at an early stage[13] and culminate at a national center for strategic studies.

The Charter

The charter for such a center, according to Admiral William J. Crowe, Jr., when he was Chairman of the Joint Chiefs of Staff, should concentrate on the roots of national security strategies, contemporary international systems, worldwide trends, and judgments that concern where, when, and how to employ armed forces most effectively.[14] Courses on the evolution of strategic thought, followed by comparative analyses of past, present, and proposed concepts, could comprise additional cornerstones.[15]

The Commandant

The commandant, who sets policies, precedents, and standards for the recommended center, also picks faculty members, shapes research programs, and supervises implementation. Irreducible credentials should include:

- A national (preferably international) reputation sufficient to attract and retain top talent
- Proven competence as a politico-military strategist
- Demonstrated interest in, and aptitudes for, education (neither attribute would be adequate without the other)
- Thorough familiarity with national security decision-making processes at home and abroad

The Faculty

Faculty members must possess similar qualifications to command the respect of student bodies that consist of generals, admirals, other senior officers drawn from all military services, and high-ranking civilians. The faculty's mission, given guidance from the commandant, should be to:

- Customize curricula for resident, correspondence, refresher, and cram courses
- Prepare instructional materials that synthesize the full range of opinion on each topic, so students can absorb maximum information in minimum time
- Conduct classroom instruction and lead student debates that dissect strategic principles and practices across the conflict spectrum

The first National War College staff and faculty (1946–1947), which featured a mix of towering theoreticians and practitioners, might well serve as a model. Major General Alfred Gruenther, the Deputy Commandant, had been General Eisenhower's Deputy Chief of Staff during World War II. He later became the first Director of the U.S. Joint Staff, then Supreme Allied Commander, Europe (SACEUR). George F. Kennan, his civilian counterpart, conceived the U.S. Cold War concept of containment at the National War College, then penned "The Sources of Soviet Power," which *Foreign Affairs* published anonymously in 1947.[16] Dr. Bernard Brodie wrote the original works regarding nuclear strategy.[17] Dr. Sherman Kent's treatise entitled *Strategic Intelligence* became a globally acclaimed textbook.[18] Major General Lyman L. Lemnitzer succeeded General Gruenther, then became Army Chief of Staff, Chairman of the Joint Chiefs of Staff, and SACEUR. Lieutenant General Andrew J. Goodpaster, who briefly was Commandant, later wore four stars as SACEUR, but the stature of replacements has been less imposing ever since.[19]

Tenures

The initial cadre and General Goodpaster left the National War College after one academic year. General Lemnitzer watched the classes of 1948 and 1949 graduate, then departed. Those terms were too short to make indelible marks. Five-year tenures might be a reasonable minimum for the recommended center's commandant as well as faculty. Longer terms predicated on laudatory performance would allow supervisors to retain the best and periodically weed out the rest.

STRATEGIC RESEARCH

Professional military education and related research are inseparable. No national center for strategic studies could become a fountainhead of strategic knowledge without access to a constant stream of innovative theories and concepts that resident intellectuals and outsiders produce. Problems range from comparatively simple to incredibly complex as investigators feel their way into the future using traditional and nontraditional techniques.

Present Problems

Official and freelance think tanks produce truckloads of thoughtful reports, but few dreamers, heretics, and gadflies in their employ have probed strategic frontiers since Herman Kahn held sway at the Hudson Institute in the 1960s. Sample topics that cry for concerted exploration include reliable ways to deter terrorism, halt the proliferation of nuclear, biological, chemical, and radiological (NBCR) weapons, and defend against cybernetic warfare. National security issues connected with global pollution and resource despoliation pose other thorny problems. Under what conditions, pray tell, should aggrieved nations use armed force to handle sovereign states that wantonly raze rain forests, use petroleum for economic warfare purposes, divert precious water resources that neighbors desperately need, pillage fisheries along continental shelves, carelessly dispose of hazardous waste, or otherwise injure neighbors, even international communities?[20]

Future Problems

Strategic researchers need to anticipate problems before crises arise, an intimidating task at best. Alternative visions of the future comprise the starting point,[21] but the reliability of assumptions that shape optimistic and pessimistic projections decreases with the distance that seers peer into the future. Experienced strategists consequently tend to confine their outlooks to fewer than twenty-five years and limit scenarios to no more than three; some prefer a single trunk with multiple offshoots.[22] Postulations predicated on generally agreed trends, such as the quintet below, generate the fewest arguments:

- Asymmetrical strategies likely will enable nongovernmental groups to compete ever more effectively with nation-states
- Technologies of military significance likely will continue to accelerate at hypersonic paces
- Natural resources likely will become increasingly scarce in a world that likely will become increasingly interdependent
- Racial, ethnic, religious, and territorial rivalries, coupled with population explosions and increasing economic gaps between "haves" and "have-nots," likely will lead to armed conflicts of regional, even global, gravity
- Traditional armed forces and terrorists likely will employ NBCR weapons within the foreseeable future

Nontraditional Techniques

French Général d'Armée André Beaufre, a creative thinker who also was a skilled practitioner, several decades ago claimed that strategists should discard hypotheses based on precedents and probabilities. "No artist," he noted, "has ever painted a picture by following a complete set of theoretical rules."[23] Beaufre may have been a bit hyperbolic, but futurists Alvin and Heidi Toffler reinforced his sentiments with these words: "We believe that the promise of the twenty-first century will evaporate if we continue using the intellectual weapons of yesterday. It will vanish even faster," they continued, "if we ever forget" Leon Trotsky's admonition that "You may not be interested in war, but war is interested in you."[24]

Nonlinear Outlooks

Real life is messy, but most military strategists remain fond of linear cause-and-effect relationships that introduce order into otherwise disorderly situations. Chaos theories, in contrast, deal with frictions that exert disproportionately large influences over almost every aspect of human life.[25] Hectic preparations, uncooperative weather, unexpected casualties, last-minute mission changes, and fear often make armed combat an iffy proposition, as Clausewitz explained in his classic *On War.*[26]

Complexity theorists study interactions among elements on the edge of chaos, between order and confusion, a dynamic, unstable environment that displays both characteristics. Proponents of that discipline contend that locally unpredictable occurrences are structured, coherent, and cohesive when viewed from broader perspectives. Their mission is to discern behavioral patterns despite the clutter, determine how local turmoil affects "big pictures," improve predictability, and thus enable adaptive organizations to manipulate disorder more effectively than presently is possible.[27]

Military strategists are just beginning to connect chaos and complexity theories with war, which is inherently chaotic, complex, dynamic, and nonlinear. Concerted applications of those intriguing intellectual tools might enable current and future researchers to attack crucial problems from radically different directions than their predecessors. Fresh insights conceivably could create conceptual "force multipliers" that consistently rather than hapazardly vest military formations with combat capabilities equal to more than the sum of their parts, so that $1+1=2.5$ or 3.[28]

Unconventional Outreach

The finest strategic research institutes permanently employ, and maintain intermittent contact with, only a tiny fraction of the world's innovative talent. Outreach programs designed to tap the broadest possible spectrum of opinion, then screen, synthesize, and refine responses, thus could expand pres-

ent knowledge bases quickly and cost-effectively. Specialized clearinghouses could feed research facilities at a national center for strategic studies. U.S. Special Operations Command (USSOCOM) indeed activated a prototype in January 1994.[29]

Data collection campaigns, unclassified from start to finish, solicit contributions from active, reserve, and retired military personnel, plus selected civilians (Figure 5 is illustrative). Conduits include telephonic connections, professional publications that routinely reach targeted audiences, "snail mail," e-mail, and the World Wide Web.

USSOCOM's initial advertisement posed the following questions: "How many times have you or your people had a better way of doing a job than current procedures dictate? When was the last time someone in your unit said, 'If I were a general for a day, I'd. . . ?' Well, here's your chance to change the world. The only limits to this process are your imagination and creativity."[30] Strategic researchers operate on a different plane, but similarly keep requests simple, because polished input is less important than seminal ideas. Oral communications, skeleton outlines, and legibly scribbled foolscap are preferable to lengthy papers, provided they capture the essence. Prodigies who cannot write or lack free time consequently could participate. Clearinghouse staffs should also accept anonymous offerings from individuals who are forbidden to express advocative or provocative views in public.

No-holds-barred brainstorming produces a few jewels buried beneath piles of junk. Each clearinghouse consequently must sift every batch in search of useful thoughts, giving open-minded consideration to "far out" flights of fancy before they accept or reject submissions. A wide variety of knowledgeable critics should embellish or rebut the best contributions, because audience participation ensures second- and third-generation refinements. Decisionmakers ultimately approve or reject strategic options that clearinghouse staffs package with pro-con appraisals for their convenience.

Figure 5
SAMPLE CLEARINGHOUSE ADVERTISEMENT

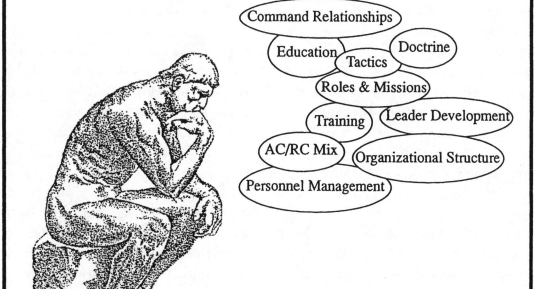

Who thinks, Wins!
US Special Operations Command Needs Your *Ideas*

- *What should we be doing that we aren't doing now?*
- *What are we doing that's no longer relevant?*
- *How can we do what we're doing better?*

Write or call:

The SOF Clearinghouse
Hq USSOCOM/J5-O
7701 Tampa Point Blvd
MacDill AFB, FL 33621-5323

(813) 828-4205
DSN 968-4205
FAX 968-3485

KEY POINTS

- Environments conducive to creativity feature intellectual freedom, tranquil opportunities to think, unregimented regimens, and prolific contacts
- Directed approaches, strict deadlines, security classifications, punishment for failure, and needs to support official policies inhibit strategic trailblazers
- Strategic education gives the most gifted strategists a flying start and progressively embellishes their competence
- Many civilian colleges confer degrees in political science, but no war college specializes in military strategy
- Every major military power could benefit greatly from a national center for strategic studies
- The evolution of strategic thought, strategic processes, comparative analyses of past, present, and proposed concepts, and politico-military trends would make solid cornerstones for such centers
- The stature of tenured commandants and faculty should command the respect of handpicked senior officials who study strategy under their supervision
- No national center for strategic studies could comprise a cutting edge without constant access to innovative theories and concepts
- The best strategic research centers mingle traditional and nontraditional techniques
- Strategic clearinghouses that tap the broadest possible spectrum of opinion could expand present knowledge bases quickly and cost-effectively.

NOTES

1. Niccolò Machiavelli, *The Prince,* ed. Peter Bondanella, trans. Mark Musa (New York: Oxford University Press, 1998) and *Discourses,* ed. Bernard Crick, trans. Leslie J. Walker (New York: Viking Press, 1985).

2. Alfred Thayer Mahan, *The Influence of Sea Power Upon History, 1660–1783* (New York: Hill and Wang, 1969).

3. Mao Tse-Tung, *On Guerrilla Warfare,* trans. Brigadier General Samuel B. Griffith (New York: Praeger, 1961).

4. A slightly different version of creative environments originally appeared in John M. Collins, *Grand Strategy: Principles and Practices* (Annapolis, MD: Naval Institute Press, 1973), 226–31.

5. See, for example, Colonels Qiao Liang and Wang Xiangsui, *Unrestricted Warfare,* ed. and trans. Foreign Broadcast Information Service (FBIS) (Beijing: PLA Literature and Arts Publishing House, February 1999).

6. Alan Axelrod and Charles Phillips, *The Macmillan Dictionary of Military Biography* (New York: Macmillan, 1998); Peter Paret, ed., *Makers of Modern Strategy: From Machiavelli to the Nuclear Age* (Princeton, NJ: Princeton University Press, 1986).

7. *Peterson's Guide to 4 Year Colleges* (Princeton, NJ: Peterson's, 1998), 1174–75.

8. *Professional Military Education,* Hearings before the Panel on Military Education of the House Armed Services Committee, HASC 100-125, 100th Cong., 1st and 2d sess. (Washington: U.S. Government Printing Office, 1991); *Report of the National Defense University Transition Planning Committee* (The Long Committee), submitted to the Chairman, Joint Chiefs of Staff, August 25, 1989.

9. Lieutenant General Richard Chilcoat, "The Revolution in Military Education," *Joint Force Quarterly,* Summer 1999, 59–63; Lieutenant General Leonard D. Holder and Williamson Murray, "Prospects for Military Education," *Joint Force Quarterly,* vol. 18 (Spring 1998), 81–90.

10. Harriet Fast Scott and William F. Scott, *The Armed Forces of the USSR* (Boulder, CO: Westview Press, 1979), 331–32, 354–56.

11. Marshal of the Soviet Union V. D. Sokolovskiy, *Soviet Military Strategy,* ed. Harriet Fast Scott (New York: Crane Russack, 1968).

12. Trevor N. Dupuy, *A Genius for War: The German Army and General Staff, 1807-1945* (Englewood Cliffs, NJ: Prentice-Hall, 1977).

13. Major Kelly C. Jordan and Major Thomas Goss, "Producing Strategists for the 21st Century," *Army,* June 1999, 45-49; General John R. Galvin, "What's the Matter with Being a Strategist?" *Parameters,* March 1989, 2-10.

14. Admiral Crowe's proposals appear in *Professional Military Education,* 1401-31.

15. John M. Collins, "How Military Strategists Should Study History," *Military Review,* vol. LXIII, no. 8 (August 1983), 31-44.

16. Mr. X [George F. Kennan], "The Sources of Soviet Power," *Foreign Affairs,* July 1947, 566-82.

17. Bernard Brodie, ed., *The Absolute Weapon: Atomic Power and World Order* (New York: Harcourt, Brace, 1946). Bernard Brodie and Eilene Galloway explored possible influences on land and naval strategies in *The Atom Bomb and the Armed Services,* Public Affairs Bulletin No. 55 (Washington: Legislative Reference Service, May 1947).

18. Sherman Kent, *Strategic Intelligence* (Princeton, NJ: Princeton University Press, 1965).

19. *Directory of National War College Graduates, 1999* (Washington: NWC Alumni Association, April 1999).

20. Connections between environmental aggravations and armed force are not new. See Robert Leider, *From Choice to Determinant: The Environmental Issue in International Relations* (Washington: Strategic Research Group, National War College, February 15, 1972). Susan A. Fletcher addresses contemporary problems in *International Environment: Current Major Global Treaties,* Rpt. No. 96-884ENR (Washington: Congressional Research Service, November 5, 1996).

21. *New World Coming: American Security in the 21st Century* (Washington: United States Commission on National Security/21st Century, September 15, 1999), 133-39.

22. Alvin and Heidi Toffler, *Future Shock* (New York: Bantam Books, 1970), *The Third Wave* (New York: Bantam Books, 1980), and *War and Anti-War: Survival at the Dawn of the 21st Century* (New York: Little, Brown, 1993); Steven Metz, *Armed Conflict in the 21st Century: The Information Revolution and Post-Modern Warfare* (Carlisle Baracks, PA: U.S. Army War College, Strategic Studies Institute, April 2000).

23. Général d'Armée André Beaufre, *An Introduction to Strategy,* trans. Major General R. H. Barry (New York: Praeger, 1965), 44-46.

24. Toffler, *War and Anti-War,* 252.

25. James Gleick, *Chaos: Making a New Science* (New York: Penguin, 1988).

26. Carl von Clausewitz, *On War,* ed. and trans. Michael Howard and Peter Paret (Princeton, NJ: Princeton University Press, 1976), 119-21.

27. M. Mitchell Waldrop, *Complexity: The Emerging Science at the Edge of Order and Chaos* (New York: Touchstone Books, 1993).

28. Colonel Glenn M. Harned, *The Complexity of War: The Application of Nonlinear Science to Military Science,* a research paper (Quantico, VA: Marine Corps War College, June 9, 1995); Lieutenant Colonel Robert P. Pellegrini, *The Links between Science and Philosophy and Military Theory: Understanding the Past; Implications for the Future* (Maxwell AFB, AL: School of Advanced Air Power Studies, June 1995).

29. Brigadier General William F. (Buck) Kernan, "USSOCOM Creates Clearinghouse for New Ideas," *Special Warfare,* April 1994, 21. *Night Flier* and *Full Mission Profile,* published respectively by USSOCOM's air and naval component commands, contained similar notices about the same time.

30. Ibid.

PART V

APPLIED STRATEGIES

23. Balkan Tar Babies

Brer Rabbit butted, but his head stuck in de tar.
Now Brer Rabbit's two fists, his two behind
foots, an his head wuz all stuck in de Tar-Baby.
He push an he pull, but de more he try to get
unstuck-up, de stucker-up he got. Soon Brer
Rabbit is so stuck up he can't scarcely move
his eyeballs.

Joel Chandler Harris
"De Tar-Baby"
Uncle Remus

Wily Brer Rabbit, a peerless con artist, escaped that predicament when his gullible captors fell for a phony story, but peacekeepers and peacemakers stucked-up in contested territories that once belonged to Yugoslavia haven't been that lucky. The cold-hearted foes they face are shrewd, calculating, tenacious, thumb-in-the-eye, knee-in-the-groin politico-military brawlers who never give up gracefully and rebound repeatedly after defeats.

This case study of ongoing operations that opened in the 1980s applies factors that previous chapters synopsized. It first reviews tragic events that originally motivated the United Nations to intervene, then methodically compares competitive security interests, objectives, force postures, policy options, and interactions of all parties involved. Concluding critiques summarize strategic successes and failures, contrast principles with practices, and speculate about probable outcomes after intervening armed forces withdraw. The ultimate aim is to demonstrate techniques that might have helped UN, U.S., and NATO strategists prepare better estimates of the situation and cost-benefit evaluations before, rather than after, they embraced Tar-Babies in Bosnia-Herzegovina and Kosovo.

POLITICO-MILITARY BACKDROP

Occupants of lands that constituted Yugoslavia during most of the twentieth century have seldom enjoyed centralized self-government. Romans, Ostrogoths, Bulgars, Venetians, Byzantines, Ottomans, Austrians, and Hungarians held sway at various times until World War I terminated. Each left indelible marks that continue to nurture intense political, ethnic, religious, linguistic, and social animosities within arbitrarily imposed boundaries that make little practical sense.[1]

Cultural Crazy Quilt

Orthodox Christian Serbs and Roman Catholic Croats are prominent among more than fifteen distinctive entities. They have repeatedly crossed swords with each other as well as with Albanian and Slavic Muslims who, with good reason, distrust them both. Serbians, who use a Cyrillic alphabet, speak a different language than Croatians, Slovenians, and Albanians, all of whom prefer Latin letters. Countless dialects further complicate communications. The greatest diversification prevails in Bosnia-Herzegovina, which remains a hotbed of rivalries rather than a melting pot, but antagonisms elsewhere are intense. Bitter feuds, much like those in the 1880s between hillbilly Hatfields and McCoys, keep fighting spirits bright when inhabitants aren't battling invaders.[2]

Tito's Fragile Federation

Josip Broz, better known as Tito, glued those diversified factions together in 1946 to form the Socialist Federal People's Republic of Yugoslavia, which incorporated Serbia, Croatia, Slovenia, Macedonia, Montenegro, and Bosnia-Herzegovina (Map 1). He ruled that fragile lash-up with an iron fist and quashed latent nationalism for thirty-four years, but a crumbling economy caused tensions to mount before he died in May 1980. Vicious power struggles ensued thereafter, partly because the Yugoslav Constitution of 1974 prescribed collective leadership rather than a clear-cut line of succession.[3]

Serbian President Slobodan Milosevic in 1989 forcibly reasserted control over autonomous Kosovo, a rebellious province whose Albanian majority has always balked at governance by Belgrade. Brief skirmishes occurred when Slovenia seceded from the Serb-dominated federation in 1991. Macedonia opted out without incident, but breakaway Croatia temporarily lost a big chunk of territory to Serb rebels within its boundaries before seven months of civil war ceased in January 1992. Serbian residents of Bosnia, with assistance from Belgrade, seized three fourths of that would-be country from Croats and Muslims the following May, then besieged Sarajevo, its capital city.[4]

Recognizable front lines and rear areas were nonexistent, because the civilian mix in most neighborhoods was bewildering. Five heterogeneous armed factions that totaled perhaps 170,000 intermingled: the Bosnia-Serb army; Bosnia-Serb irregulars; Croat defense forces; Bosnia-Croat irregulars; and Bosnian Muslims. Nearly twenty self-serving warlords, who controlled several hundred to several thousand combatants apiece, made matters even more confusing.[5] Mediation by the United Nations and the European Community (now the European Union) failed to stop mass murders, gang rapes, widespread destruction, concentration camps, evictions, and other forms of "ethnic cleansing" that caused a tidal wave of refugees to swamp several European nations. That chain of events motivated nine United Nations Security Council Resolutions that established, deployed, enlarged, and expanded the responsibilities of a blue-helmeted UN Protection Force (UNPROFOR) in 1992. Battalions occupied key positions from Croatia through Bosnia to Macedonia, while reconnaissance troops patrolled connecting routes.[6]

PEACEKEEPING IN BOSNIA

Bosnia's dire straits and uncertain future compelled the United Nations, European members of NATO, and the United States to make an elemental decision in 1992: do nothing or do something. The determination to do something in that nearly landlocked country (Map 2) created dilemmas concerning what to do, how to do it, who should do it, and what factors should define success. Security interests, objectives, policies, strategic courses of action, and risk-benefit ratios all came into play.

Comparative Interests

Security interests of the Bosnian Government and its Muslim majority were truly vital, because the survival of each was at stake (Table 24). That newly independent country would cease to exist if Serbian and Croatian enemies subdivided its territory or if one winner took all and evicted or eradicated objectionable ethnic groups. Lust for power motivated Serbs and Croats alike, both of whom valued peace and stability only on their own terms. The former yearned to establish a greater Serbia. Croats, who were somewhat less ambitious, hoped to hold what they had and clutch whatever they could in Bosnia-Herzegovina.

The United Nations, the United States, and NATO's European members feared that warfare would spread beyond Bosnia, perhaps beyond for-

Map 1

The Former Yugoslavia and Neighboring Countries

Karamales 2001

Map 2

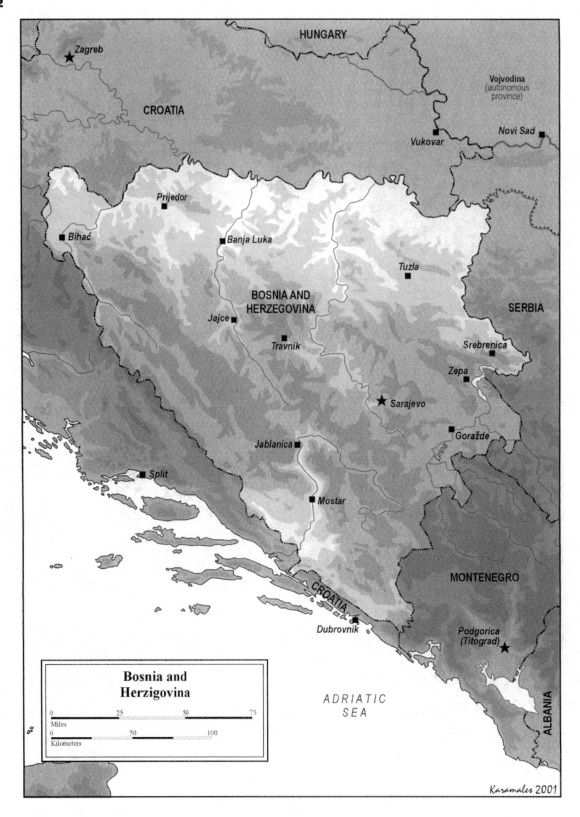

Table 24
Comparative Purposes in Bosnia

	Serbs	Croats	Muslims
Interests			
Survival			x
Power	x	x	
Objectives			
Control Most of Bosnia	x		
Control Bits of Bosnia		x	
"Cleanse" Bosnia	x	x	
Avoid Defeat			x
Preserve Noncombatants			x

	UN	NATO
Interests		
Peace	x	x
Stability	x	x
Compassion	x	x
Objectives		
Stop Ethnic Cleansing	x	x
Prevent Conflict Spread	x	x
Terminate Armed Combat	x	x
Preserve Peace	x	x
Repatriate Refugees	x	x
Alleviate Privation	x	x
Rebuild Bosnia	x	x
Catch War Criminals		x
Punish War Criminals	x	x

mer Yugoslavia if the flood of refugees overtaxed neighboring states. They therefore espoused interests in peace and regional stability. The televised plight of hungry, homeless victims who feared for their lives inspired strong humanitarian interests.

Comparative Objectives

Offensive, defensive, and counteractive aims that promoted the cherished interests just described ranged from egomaniacal to altruistic, with assorted shades between. Bosnian Muslims sought to avoid defeat until help arrived, because that was the only way to ensure survival. Serbian President Milosevic's equally unswerving objectives were aggressive:

seize most of Bosnia and convert it into an "ethnically clean" province under his jurisdiction. Croatia initially sought to incorporate adjoining parts of Bosnia but, after brutal battles with Islamic Bosnians, reluctantly settled for a federation of eight cantons, of which Muslims would govern half, contingent on recovery of territory from Serbian rivals who occupied about two thirds of the country by 1994.

UN, U.S., and NATO's European decision-makers generally agreed on several goals that, if achievable, would satisfy respective security and humanitarian interests. Efforts to stop ethnic cleansing, keep armed combat from spilling into adjacent countries, and terminate conflict quickly implicitly led the list. Less urgent aims sought to preserve peace once it was established, repatriate refugees, alleviate privation, help rebuild Bosnia's war-ravaged infrastructure, apprehend war criminals, and punish them appropriately.

Policy Options in Bosnia

Observers in late summer 1992 speculated that Serb leaders would talk any time, anywhere, at any level, because they basically had what they wanted, but evidence at hand also indicated that Milosevic intended to continue intense pressures if and when palavering commenced. The President of Bosnia-Herzegovina conversely found proposed cease-fires and partition plans unpalatable, because acceptance would split his country.[7] Croats, whose objectives were less hidebound, were willing to fight when conditions seemed favorable and back off when they did not.

Unimpeachable humanitarian motives underpinned urges to intercede, but potentially adverse repercussions counseled caution. Policy-makers in the United Nations, the United States, and Western European countries consequently reviewed risks, costs, and possible outcomes carefully before they decided to intervene in strength. Cheerless characteristics and poor prospects accompanied all but the first of eight options outlined below. The rest, which formed a rude escalation ladder with unevenly spaced rungs, required increasing amounts of military power.

Option 1: Police a Negotiated Settlement

A negotiated settlement acceptable to all belligerents would have satisfied every coveted security and humanitarian objective. Hopes, however, were dim, because one or more parties for various reasons rejected every proposal as time dragged on from 1992 into 1995, with few signs that expectations would improve.[8]

Option 2: Withdraw UNPROFOR

Compassionate bystanders deplored bloodshed (some called it genocide) in Bosnia. Canadian Major General Lewis MacKenzie, soon after he relinquished command of UN peacekeepers in Sarajevo, saw "no military solution . . . no way that intervention will do anything but escalate the fighting and more people will be killed." U.S. General John R. Galvin, who was NATO's Supreme Allied Commander when battles began, expressed similar sentiments: "If there's a political way to stop all this, then that's the way to do it without sinking into a morass of military operations that have no end."[9] Senior U.S. military officials concurred.[10] Noninvolvement would have abandoned every expressed objective, but proponents of withdrawal were prepared to accept that penalty.

Option 3: Reduce UNPROFOR Vulnerabilities

Redeployment of widely scattered United Nations peacekeepers to fewer, more defensible sites would have made UNPROFOR more secure, but its abilities to accomplish assigned missions would have plummeted. "Bad guys" would have enjoyed greater freedom of action and Bosnian noncombatants clearly would suffer.

Option 4: Shepherd Truck Convoys

UN Resolution 770 (August 13, 1992) recommended "all measures necessary" to guarantee safe delivery of food and medical supplies from Sarajevo International Airport to needy communities throughout Bosnia-Herzegovina.[11] Route security, however, posed grave risks, because spiraling escalation seemed likely if soldiers "riding shotgun" got hit. Serbs who surrounded the airport might massacre the tiny UN contingent (1,400 men 200 miles from the nearest reinforcements) or hold some hapless village hostage.[12] The United States, Britain, and France on August 24, 1992 consequently shelved plans to shepherd truck convoys.[13]

Option 5: Expand Peacekeeping

Peacekeeping, by definition, involves nonviolent efforts of a military force, interposed between belligerents by mutual consent, to maintain a truce or otherwise discourage armed conflict until true tranquility can be restored. Intermingled combatants and noncombatants, the absence of front lines, and general intransigence, however, had frustrated UN "peacekeepers" from the first day of insertion in 1992, because they found no peace to keep and, in fact, feared for their lives. Expanded missions accordingly seemed questionable until all belligerents respected a cease-fire.

Option 6: Level the Playing Field

UN Resolution 713 imposed an arms embargo against all former Yugoslavian states on September 25, 1992.[14] Results froze military imbalances of power, because Serbia had previously inherited most of the armor, artillery, and other heavy weapons that once belonged to Tito's army.[15] Influential members of Congress believed that the United States could prevent an early Serb victory, and thereby encourage a negotiated settlement, if it unilaterally shipped arms to the Muslim-led Bosnian Government.[16] Skeptics, however, feared that independent U.S. actions to "level the playing field" could have adverse repercussions. Rifts with U.S. allies might have resulted. Cooperation by Croatia, which owned all seaports along the Adriatic coast, was not assured. Serbian forces not only controlled all airfields and supply lines in Bosnia, but might have redoubled efforts to "win" before consignments arrived.

Option 7: Isolate Bosnian Battlegrounds

Actions to isolate Bosnian battlegrounds from outside assistance seemed attractive at first glance, but drawbacks were daunting. Economic sanctions proved insufficient. Blockades required collaboration by six neighbors of former Yugoslavia: Austria, Hungary, Romania, Bulgaria, Greece, and Albania. Success was by no means assured, even if all complied, because the landscape had been littered since World War II with concealed bunkers that, in conformance with Tito's national defense concepts, contained weapon and munition caches.

Option 8: Impose Peace

Military operations by a UN-U.S.-NATO coalition could have terminated large-scale combat and rid Bosnia-Herzegovina of the most antagonistic intruders. Estimated force requirements unfortunately ranged from a few divisions to one or more field armies (200,000 ground troops were mentioned most often), plus complementary airpower. The most sanguine assessments predicted widespread property damage along with extensive casualties among belligerents and noncombatants. Prolonged occupation after hostilities ceased seemed likely. Opponents of Option 8 accordingly outnumbered proponents by many to one.

Darkness Before Dawn

Conditions in Bosnia as of midsummer 1992 got worse before they got better.[17] UN Security Council Resolutions 824 and 836 in May and June 1993 prescribed "safe havens" at Bihac, Gorazde, Srebrenica, Sarajevo, Tuzla, and Zepa,[18] but outmanned outgunned UNPROFOR troops provided little protec-

tion for any of them.[19] Sarajevo and Tuzla experienced repeated shellings. NATO bombed Serb emplacements around Sarajevo in May 1995 to relieve pressures on the airport, whereupon Serb soldiers seized more than 300 UN peacekeepers and temporarily held them hostage. The worst European massacre since World War II left 7,000 dead at Srebrenica in July 1995.[20] Then, the very next month, Croats and Muslims in concert overran most of western Bosnia and handed Serb adversaries their first major defeat. That setback set the stage for serious peace negotiations, which had proved elusive during the previous three years.

Dayton Peace Agreement

Opportunities to police a negotiated settlement, the policy option that UN, U.S., and NATO European officials preferred, opened on November 25, 1995, when signatories of peace accords that conferees drafted in Dayton, Ohio agreed to "recreate as quickly as possible normal conditions of life" in war-torn Bosnia. Provisions of particular interest to military strategists were:[21]

- Bosnia-Herzegovina remained an independent state that retained Sarajevo as its capital and contained two semiautonomous "entities" (Map 3)
- The predominantly Muslim-Croat Federation of Bosnia-Herzegovina comprised approximately 51 percent of its territory
- The predominantly Bosnian-Serb Republic of Srpska comprised approximately 49 percent
- Boundaries in each instance generally coincided with cease-fire lines
- Peacekeepers were to patrol a narrow buffer zone between the two "entities" and secure a corridor within the Gorazde salient
- All armed forces "not of local origin" were to withdraw from Bosnia-Herzegovina within thirty days, except for peacekeepers
- All indigenous forces were to remain within

Map 3

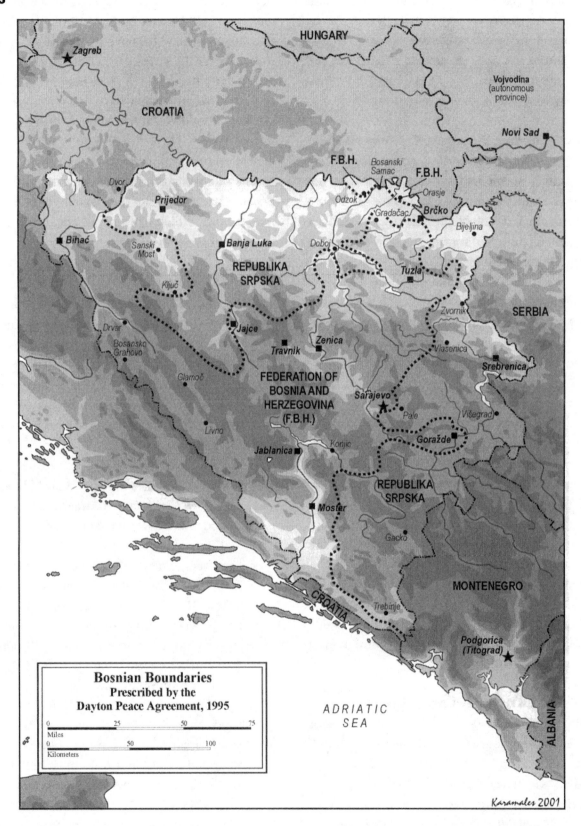

Bosnian Boundaries
Prescribed by the
Dayton Peace Agreement, 1995

designated locations and demobilize assets that prescribed facilities could not accommodate
- All armed civilian groups were to disband
- All refugees had the right to return home without risk of harassment, intimidation, or persecution for ethnic, religious, or political reasons

Implementation and Stabilization

An ancient proverb, often attributed to Homer, notes that "there is many a slip 'twixt the cup and the lip." Needs consequently existed for impartial armed forces that could guarantee immediate compliance with the Dayton Peace Agreement, then stabilize reconstituted Bosnia-Herzegovina until its nascent government became strong enough to maintain internal security without extensive outside assistance.

Implementation Force

UN Security Council Resolution 1031 on December 15, 1995 authorized a multinational, NATO-led Implementation Force (IFOR) to replace UNPROFOR and mandated it to maintain the cease-fire, control key landlines and airspace, monitor the movement of weapons and equipment into approved cantonments, inspect those sites periodically, and exercise other military responsibilities within Bosnia-Herzegovina for one year. Eighteen of nineteen NATO nations, plus eighteen other countries, contributed a total of 54,000 troops, which accomplished most missions handily (Iceland provided medical support). U.S., British, and French forces, which carried the biggest burdens, occupied politically- rather than militarily inspired areas of responsibility, with respective headquarters at Tuzla, Banja Luka, and Mostar (Map 4).[22]

Stabilization Force

UN Security Council Resolution 1088 approved a NATO-led Stabilization Force (SFOR) when IFOR's

mandate expired on December 20, 1996. The original intent was to withdraw in June 1996, but prudence extended that deadline indefinitely, subject to biannual review. Approximately 19,300 troops from thirty-four nations (4,300 U.S.) still performed routine security missions in 2001, with no end in sight.[23]

International Police Task Force

Neither IFOR nor SFOR was responsible for law and order. The Dayton Peace Agreement instead requested, but did not prescribe, an International Police Task Force (IPTF), which was much too small, slow to arrive, poorly qualified, insufficiently equipped, and underfunded. Its mission was simply to help restructure local police, many of whom had committed war crimes. IPTF as late as mid-2001 still totaled a paltry 1,830 from 45 countries, replete with disparate languages and questionable skills that made it difficult to deal with large-scale crime and human rights violations. "The top 10 percent [of the 60-man U.S. contingent] were fantastic," according to one observer, "but the bottom 10 percent made your eyes water." Incompetence and corruption were commonplace. Other contributions, most of them much smaller (1 man from Estonia, 2 from Tunisia, 3 apiece from the Czech Republic and Iceland), were comparable.[24]

PEACEMAKING IN KOSOVO

Peacekeepers had barely stabilized Bosnia before the kettle boiled over in Kosovo, a landlocked province in southernmost Serbia (Map 5). Orthodox Christian Serbs, who call that contested region the cradle of their civilization, have collided for centuries with largely Islamic Albanians, who trace their occupancy to pre-Roman Illyrium more than 2,000 years ago.[25]

Prewar Situation

Albanian residents boycotted the 1991 census, but reasonably reliable estimates indicate that they then

Map 4

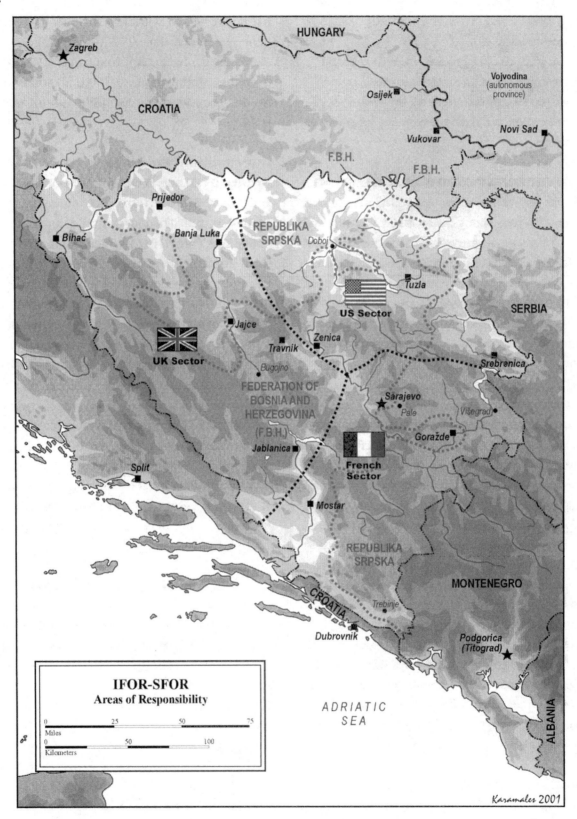

Map 5

Kosovo and Vicinity

Karamales 2001

constituted more than 80 percent of almost 2,000,000 Kosovars, whereas Serbs comprised fewer than one tenth. The province was nearly autonomous from 1974 until 1989, when Serb President Milosevic revoked that privilege and cracked down on dissenters. Defiant Albanians seceded in 1991, established their own parliament and, after the Dayton accords in late November 1995 dashed their hopes for independence, launched a classic insurgency with the newly formed Kosovo Liberation Army (KLA) as the cutting edge. The brutal Serbian backlash that began early in 1998 drove Kosovo's embryonic government into exile and swamped nearby nations with refugees.[26]

The United Nations, aghast at human suffering and fearful that armed conflict would engulf neighboring states, called for a cease-fire on March 31, 1998 and imposed an arms embargo that applied to Kosovo as well as the rest of Serbia. The UN, at the behest of six Contact Group countries (United States, Britain, France, Russia, Germany, and Italy), made additional demands on September 23d, still to no avail. NATO threatened air strikes the following month, but deferred when Milosevic agreed to comply with both UN Resolutions. He reneged, however, and in March 1999 disregarded a peace proposal that French, British, U.S., Russian, and European Union negotiators drafted at Rambouillet, France.[27] Cross-purposes at that point left the UN and NATO with two polarized options: put up or shut up. Security interests, objectives, and policies, plus courses of action open to Serb and Albanian protagonists, shaped Operation Allied Force.

Comparative Purposes

Serbs and the KLA both viewed power as a vital interest. Supporting objectives ensured vicious combat, because both sought control over Kosovo and both had regional aspirations beyond that beleaguered province. Serbia hoped that stubborn resistance would weaken NATO's will to persevere and thereby split the Atlantic Alliance, while the Kosovo

Table 25

Comparative Purposes in Kosovo
Before, During, and After Operation *Allied Force*

	UN	NATO	Russia	Serbs	KLA
Interests					
Power			x	x	x
Peace	x	x	x		
Stability	x	x	x		
Credibility	x	x	x	x	x
Respect	x	x	x	x	x
Compassion	x	x	x		
Objectives					
Control Kosovo	x	x		x	x
Cleanse Kosovo				x	x
Stop Ethnic Cleansing	x	x			
Prevent Conflict Spread	x	x	x		
Alleviate Privation	x	x			
Cause Regional Turmoil				x	x
Promote Tranquility	x	x	x		
Split NATO*				x	
Solidify NATO*			x		
Russian Participation					
Full Partnership			x		
Junior Partnership		x			
Defang Serbia	x	x			x
Win War		x		x	x
Exert Regional Influence	x	x	x	x	x
Repatriate Refugees**		x			
Maintain Law and Order**	x				
Rebuild Kosovo**	x				
Apprehend War Criminals		x			
Punish War Criminals	x				

* Primarily during Operation *Allied Force*
** Primarily after Operation *Allied Force*

Liberation Army sought increased assistance from NATO with which to win its war. Proclivities for compromise in each case remain exceedingly low (Table 25).[28]

Less-compelling interests in peace, regional stability, and compassion motivated the UN and NATO much the same as they did in Bosnia, but concerns about their own credibility overshadowed that list, because the world might become more dangerous if they failed to subdue economically- and militarily-backward Serbia. They decided to commit armed forces, since success would keep the conflict from spreading, terminate ethnic cleansing, allow humanitarian programs to flourish, facilitate the repatriation of refugees, and relieve Serbian pressures on neighboring states.[29] NATO's solidarity was essential. General Wesley K. Clark, in his capacity as Supreme Allied Commander Europe (SACEUR), declared that "the cohesion of the Alliance was more important than any single target we struck. . . ."[30]

Russia, which wanted a piece of the action, sought respect as a regional power[31] and opposed military action against Slavic Serbia, for which it felt compassion. Its spokesmen, like those who represented China, stuck thorns in NATO's side in 1998 and limited options open to the UN Security Council, of which both were members. Occupants of the Kremlin nevertheless shared important interests and objectives with the United Nations and NATO. They therefore became collaborators as soon as the crisis began to heat up.

NATO's Policy Options

NATO's politico-military policy-makers might have opted for survival of the fittest, in consonance with Charles Darwin's opus *On the Origin of Species by Means of Natural Selection,* but they never seriously considered letting nature take its course, because doing so would have deserted every security aim that Table 25 depicts. Realistic options reduced basic debates to complete reliance on airpower versus air-ground operations in assorted combinations.

Air Combat Operations

Exclusive employment of land- and sea-based combat airpower appeared attractive for several reasons. It was immediately available and spectacular successes against Iraq during Operation Desert Storm suggested to some senior officials that all objectives might be achievable a few days after bombardment began, with minimum casualties among NATO's armed forces and the least possible collateral damage. Ethnic cleansing, they contended, would stop as soon as havoc compelled President Milosevic to negotiate seriously. Reconciliations then could commence, and resettlements could proceed apace.[32]

Ground Combat Operations

Ground combat operations, including hit-and-run raids to harass Serb forces in Kosovo, looked a lot less inviting.[33] Numbers bandied about indicated that it might take 100,000–200,000 troops to clear Kosovo (approximately eight divisions), plus 100,000 for rear-area security and support during a lengthy war of attrition. More would have been needed to subdue the rest of Serbia.[34]

Casualty estimates ran high, assembly times would take months, the few staging bases that could accommodate contemplated forces were widely scattered, and most access routes were rudimentary. Romania and Bulgaria were remotely located, Greece and Hungary were reluctant, Montenegro and Macedonia forbade NATO troops to transit their sovereign territory, and hard-won stability would have been endangered if Bosnia became a springboard. Albania was obliging, but ports and airfields in that poverty-stricken country were primitive. The best road from Tirana inland was a logistician's nightmare that led through mountainous terrain where saboteurs could pick and choose from scores of bridges and tunnels that, if badly damaged, would be costly and time-consuming to restore. New construction would require cuts in bedrock, trestles, culverts, and retaining walls. Detours would demand lengthy delays.

Operation Allied Force

NATO's decision-makers, with those facts in mind, picked airpower to implement Operation Allied Force.[35] Bombing began on March 24, 1999, whereupon Serb adversaries accelerated ethnic cleansing in Kosovo.[36] NATO's policy-makers never resolved arguments about targeting priorities and incremental escalation before Milosevic and his cronies capitulated.

Targeting Priorities

SACEUR's first priority targets consisted of Serbian forces inside Kosovo, even though they were well-hidden, heavily defended against air attacks, and often benefited from ground fog and clouds that masked targets and made flying risky in mountainous terrain. His three-star air component commander, in contrast, never considered Serb ground forces to be a center of gravity. "Body bags coming home from Kosovo" wouldn't bother Milosevic a bit, he opined. Go straight for the gut, he recommended. Let leaders in Belgrade wake up in ruins after the first strike. Resultant operations first favored one, then the other. Aircrews received instructions to remain above 15,000 feet in any case, which reduced vulnerabilities to Serb air-defense weapons but degraded the accuracy of some precision-guided air-to-surface munitions during frequent periods of foul weather.[37]

Escalation Control

NATO's air campaign escalated cautiously, primarily for political reasons designed to sustain Alliance cohesion despite assorted sensitivities.[38] Phased attacks first concentrated on Serbia's Integrated Air Defense System and command/control apparatus, then on scattered Serb ground forces within Kosovo. Milosevic's military-industrial infrastructure, news media, and most other strategic targets were taboo until NATO's nineteen member nations authorized assaults at a summit meeting on April 23, 1999, a month after the bombing started (blasé Serbians conducted business as usual and jubilant crowds held rock concerts in downtown Belgrade not long before that meeting). NATO's North Atlantic Council expressed increasing concern for collateral damage and civilian casualties as its attrition strategy progressed.[39]

Serb Capitulation

Round-the-clock pummeling continued for seventy-eight days. It terminated on June 10, 1999 after Milosevic began to comply with terms that looked much like NATO's original demands: withdraw all Serbian military, paramilitary, and police forces from Kosovo; allow refugees to return home safely; per-

mit humanitarian organizations to minister unhindered; and let NATO-led peacekeepers ensure compliance. The main differences were that Russia helped draft provisions and an international protectorate with NATO at its core invited non-NATO nations to participate.[40]

Why wily Milosevic finally found acquiescence preferable to continued resistance is speculative. Mounting damage and evidence that NATO would persist, coupled with UN sanctions and the loss of Russian support, probably contributed. Russian Envoy Viktor Chernomyrdin and Finnish President Martti Ahtiaari may have convinced him that the offer they transmitted on June 3 was the best he would ever get. He may even have believed it wise to cut current losses, retain power at all costs, and try to recoup later.[41]

Postwar Situation

United Nations Security Council Resolution 1244, which on June 10 reaffirmed Serbia's sovereignty and territorial integrity, established postwar goals that aimed to cope with humanitarian crises, create a climate conducive to peace in Kosovo, and achieve a durable settlement. Progress in such regards remains uneven at this writing.[42]

Kosovo Force (KFOR)

The Kosovo Force (KFOR) under NATO's command originally numbered nearly 50,000 troops, of which ten percent or so deployed in Albania, Macedonia, and Greece. That peak strength, however, soon sagged to about 37,250. Those in Kosovo occupy U.S., British, French, German, and Italian Areas of Responsibility that include contingents from other nations. Russia requested, but did not receive, its own AOR. Some of its troops share the U.S. sector, along with forces from Poland, Greece, Ukraine, the United Arab Emirates, and Lithuania. Other Russian troops are deployed mainly in French and German domains (Map 6) with a few in U.K. and Italian sectors.[43]

KFOR successfully monitored, verified, and en-

Map 6

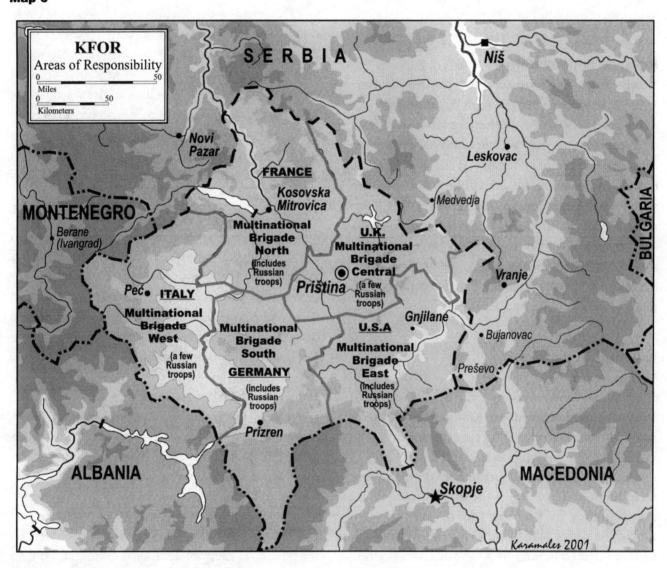

KFOR
Areas of Responsibility

SERBIA
Niš

0   50
Miles
0   50
Kilometers

Novi Pazar

FRANCE
Kosovska Mitrovica
Leskovac
Medvedja

MONTENEGRO
Berane (Ivangrad)

Multinational Brigade North
(includes Russian troops)

U.K.
Multinational Brigade Central
(a few Russian troops)

Vranje

Pristina

Peć
ITALY
Multinational Brigade West
(a few Russian troops)

Multinational Brigade South

GERMANY
(includes Russian troops)

U.S.A
Multinational Brigade East
(includes Russian troops)

Gnjilane
Bujanovac
Preševo

Prizren

ALBANIA

Skopje

MACEDONIA

BULGARIA

Karamales 2001

forced the withdrawal of Serbian forces from Kosovo, but demilitarization of the Kosovo Liberation Army hit snags. Many members still bear undeclared arms. Kosovar-Albanian guerrilla bands continued to conduct cross-border raids into Serbia proper as well as within Kosovo. Substantial numbers reportedly belong to criminal groups that terrorize traumatized citizens and fill power vacuums.[44]

Refugee Repatriation

Nearly 1,000,000 Albanians fled Kosovo by June 1999, according to the UN High Commissioner for Refugees (UNHCR). Several hundred thousand more wandered within that wretched province. Most returned to ravaged communities, where they became charity cases unable to survive the coming winter without food, clothing, and shelter that UNHCR furnished. Perhaps 240,000 Kosovar Serbs, who justifiably feared Albanian retribution, simultaneously took flight. Their absence likely will be prolonged, because conditions conducive to peaceful coexistence have not begun to develop.[45]

Law and Order

Military police, who specialize in crowd control, constabulary operations, and the apprehension of criminals, are shorthanded in Kosovo.[46] So are Multinational Specialized Units (gendarmeries). The United Nations, which possesses no civilian police, recruited fewer than half the number needed. Some were inept and most knew next to nothing about alien cultures in Kosovo. The so-called Kosovo Protection Corps, which consists mainly of present and former members of the KLA, caused more problems than it solved.[47] Combat troops that are organized, equipped, and trained to apply overwhelming force are poorly prepared and ill-disposed to maintain law and order in chaotic Kosovo, but do so by default in accord with UN Security Council Resolution 1244, until a United Nations Interim Mission in Kosovo (UNMIK) becomes fully operational.[48]

War Crimes Resolution

UN Security Council Resolution 808 on May 25, 1993 established the International Criminal Tribunal for the Former Yugoslavia (ICTY), the first such body to prosecute war criminals since post-World War II trials in Nürnberg and Tokyo. ICTY initially charged a good many low- to mid-level Bosnian Serbs, Croats, and Muslims with genocide, war crimes, and crimes against humanity.[49] Then, on May 27, 1999, ICTY indicted Serb President Slobodan Milosevic for similar atrocities in Kosovo. Imprisonment followed. The Yugoslav Cabinet on June 23, 2001 agreed to extradite him. Incarceration in Scheveningen detention center and trial at The Hague in the Netherlands followed.[50]

STRATEGIC CRITIQUES

After-action reports that praise or condemn peacekeeping in Bosnia and peacemaking in Kosovo cover strategic, operational, tactical, and logistical aspects.[51] This critique summarizes strategic successes and shortcomings, then offers a checklist that might help national security decision-makers determine whether military intervention in future foreign disputes is appropriate.

Strategic Successes

Successes enshrined in politico-military postmortems often reflect political, bureaucratic, institutional, or doctrinal biases. Wishful thinking sometimes kindles questionable conclusions. One might, for example, challenge assertions by the U.S. Department of Defense that the buildup of NATO ground combat power near Kosovo, visible preparations for the deployment of additional forces, and public discussions about their possible use "undoubtedly contributed to Milosevic's calculations that NATO would prevail at all costs."[52] Successes listed below stick to rock-solid facts that no reputable assessment has sought to refute:

- Stopped systematic ethnic cleansing in Bosnia

- Stopped ethnic cleansing by Serbs in Kosovo
- Stabilized Bosnia and reduced violence in Kosovo
- Rid Kosovo of Serbian military, paramilitary, and police forces
- Conducted one of the most precise military campaigns in history
- NATO remained resolute under pressure
- Suffered no Allied casualties during armed combat with Serbia
- Minimized civilian casualties and collateral damage in Serbia
- Terminated armed combat on UN and NATO terms
- Kept warfare from spreading to neighboring states
- Degraded Serb military capabilities to some debatable degree
- Repatriated many refugees, then ministered to them
- Repaired a good deal of damage in Bosnia and Kosovo
- Brought Serbian President Milosevic and a few other war criminals to trial

Strategic Shortcomings

Several strategically significant shortcomings violate one or more Principles of War, Principles of Preparedness, or both. Disregard for historical precedents, asymmetrical interests, misplaced priorities, shortsighted planning, failure to apply airpower against a decisive center of gravity, risky commitments, incoherent areas of responsibility, and the absence of a realistic exit strategy are prominent.

Historical Precedents

Top-level politico-military decision-makers evidently misconstrued or lightly regarded historical precedents that determined probabilities of success before the United Nations and NATO sought to placate

adversarial groups whose irreconcilable goals have fractured along ethnic, religious, and cultural fault lines. The best that peacekeepers in Bosnia and Kosovo can hope to do under those conditions is treat symptoms, while the causes of conflict remain ready to re-erupt the moment pacifiers depart.[53]

Asymmetrical Interests

The United Nations and NATO apparently paid scant attention to the Law of Asymmetrical Interests before they dispatched troops to the Balkans. None expressed urgent national security concerns. Instead, they pitted nonvital interests in regional peace, stability, and human rights against intense quests for politico-military power, which motivates Serb, Croatian, and Albanian aggressors. Incentives to persevere over the long haul consequently remain imbalanced.

Misplaced Priorities

The United Nations and NATO sought to halt humanitarian disasters. That basic objective was self-satisfying in Bosnia, where ethnic cleansing ceased after the Dayton Peace Agreement took effect in November 1995, but bloodlettings intensified in Kosovo after peacemakers intervened, because NATO's air campaign neither deterred atrocities nor defended intended victims. Political aims and military mission priorities thus were sorrowfully mismatched.

Inflexible Plans

Admiral J.C. Wylie's wise words that "planning for certitude is the greatest of all military mistakes"[54] escaped NATO's North Atlantic Council, whose members never approved Plans B and C for use if Plan A failed to achieve required results in reasonable time. Operation Allied Force initially "focused on brief, single-dimensional combat," according to the joint force commander on the scene. "Lack of the credible threat of ground invasion probably prolonged the air campaign," but NATO's only approved option remained "more of the same . . . with more assets."[55]

Airpower Restraints

NATO's nineteen nations comprised a committee that reduced every strategic decision to its lowest common denominator. Having decided to rely solely on airpower, they imposed restraints that made optimum employment impossible. Campaigns that pilots called "Rolling Blunder" instead of "Rolling Thunder" produced no sensible pattern, because decision-makers never agreed on a strategic center of gravity, the destruction or disruption of which would expedite the accomplishment of agreed objectives.

Serb defenders often may have known in advance the time that particular targets were about to be hit, because NATO's strike aircraft, which lacked compatible encryption devices, communicated over clear channels. Damage inflicted on Serbian Armed Forces reportedly was a lot less than original estimates indicated.[56] Gradual escalation allowed enemies ample time to adjust.[57] Concerns for civilian casualties and collateral damage left lucrative targets "off limits." NATO's reluctance to accept a single casualty among its military personnel further impeded mission accomplishment. Retired U.S. Marine Corps Lieutenant General Paul Van Riper summed up that syndrome as follows: "Those who take an oath to defend others were held out of harm's way while the very people they were to defend were in many ways viewed as 'expendables.' What does this say for the Western warrior ethic when future contingencies arise?"[58]

Concurrent U.S. Requirements

President Clinton's *National Security Strategy for a New Century* stipulated that U.S. Armed Forces "for the foreseeable future . . . must have the capability to deter and, if deterrence fails, defeat large-scale, cross-border aggression in two distant theaters in overlapping time frames." Said document expected them to do so despite "substantial levels of peacetime engagement as well as multiple smaller-scale contingency operations,"[59] such as Bosnia and Kosovo. The Secretary of Defense and Chairman of the Joint Chiefs of Staff in October 1999 nevertheless told Congress that they "could not have continued the intense campaign in Kosovo" if required to quell aggression by North Korea and Iraq.[60] Many critics contend that U.S. combat operations in North Korea *or* Iraq would have created the same effect. NATO's peacekeeping/peacemaking expedition in the Balkans almost certainly would have disintegrated if U.S. participation ceased at any stage.

Areas of Responsibility

Military areas of responsibility in Bosnia bear no resemblance to that country's political boundaries (Map 3, page 274). Split responsibilities avoid the appearance of favoritism to any indigenous faction, but complicate civil-military relationships, because occupation forces must deal with more than one domestic jurisdiction. The deployment of forces from some countries to more than one AOR in Kosovo violates unity of command. French forces patrol hotter spots than those of the United States, which currently is the world's sole military superpower (Map 5, page 277).

Exit Strategy

The United Nations had no realistic exit strategy when it earnestly embraced two Balkan Tar Babies in 1992. Neither did NATO when it intervened. The June 1996 deadline set for withdrawal from Bosnia was extended, then disappeared. No departure date has ever been prescribed for Kosovo. There was no plan to oust Milosevic or ensure self-sustaining regional peace after peacekeepers depart at some distant date. General Wesley Clark, the outgoing SACEUR, surmised that occupation forces would be required at least until a democratic government emerges in Belgrade. General Klaus Reinhart, KFOR's commander in March 2000, predicted five to ten years.[61] The patience of peacekeepers and the taxpayers who support them could wear thin somewhat sooner, given non-vital interests at stake.

Causes of Conflict Unresolved

Bosnia-Herzegovina and Kosovo continue to fester, because the causes of conflict remain unresolved. Vojislav Kostunica achieved a landslide victory during Serbian presidential elections on September 24, 2000 and deposed Slobodan Milosevic awaits trial for malfeasance in office at this writing, but Serbian radicals still lust for regional power. Albanian extremists harbor opposing aspirations in a climate that features appalling economic conditions and rampant crime.[62]

Macedonia came under fire in March 2001.[63] Other tinderboxes abound. "There is no military solution," according to Brigadier General Kenneth Quinlan, the U.S. Commander in Eastern Kosovo. "The military's job here is to provide time and space" for statesmen to establish true peace, which could take a very long time.[64] Winner-take-all armed combat and ethnic cleansing could spread uncontrollably, unless NATO maintains a politically and economically unattractive protectorate with strong U.S. participation. Secretary of State Colin L. Powell, who on April 11, 2001 saw "no end point," accordingly assured the European Community that "We came in together and we will come out together."[65]

The most important lesson learned from Balkan Tar-Babies thus may be found in Samuel Butler's *Hudibras,* penned in 1663: "Look before you ere you leap; for as you sow, ye are like to reap."

INTERVENTION CHECKLIST

Decisions to intervene militarily in altercations such as those that still plague Bosnia-Herzegovina and Kosovo call for subjective judgments. Former Secretary of Defense Caspar W. Weinberger prescribed "six major tests to be applied when we are weighing the use of U.S. combat forces abroad": the presence of "vital" U.S. or allied interests; clear intent to win;

precise objectives and ways to accomplish them; reasonable assurance of public support; military action as a last resort; and continual readjustments as required.[66] Those preconditions received mixed reviews, because authoritative rules may not always be advisable. The following checklist, which recognizes that each case is unique, features questions rather than answers.

National Interests

Military intervention in the absence of highly valued (not necessarily vital) interests is difficult to justify. The advisability of armed action is most evident when strong political or economic interests are at stake. Humanitarian and intangible interests such as national credibility may muster immediate support, but are much harder to sustain. Relevant questions in such regards could include:

- ✔ Which compelling national interests are involved?
- ✔ Are they compatible with those of potential allies?
- ✔ Which of them are worth fighting for?
- ✔ What price is the nation willing to pay in lifeblood and treasure?

Threats to National Interests

Decision-makers who hope to avoid wrong wars at wrong times with wrong enemies cannot rationally take military action until they consider alternatives, appraise probable risks, and prioritize each perceived threat. Those processes demand intelligence estimates that evaluate enemy intentions, capabilities, and limitations. Relevant questions in such regards could include:

- ✔ Which threats menace national interests most severely?
- ✔ Which of those threats seem susceptible to mainly military solutions?

✔ How would enemy cultures, capabilities, and geography affect operations?

✔ How would enemies likely react to military intervention?

Political Aims and Military Missions

Political aims and military missions prescribe what armed forces must do to satisfy national interests despite perceived threats. They are best developed in collaboration to ensure compatibility. Sound objectives not only seek a better situation than prevailed before intervention, but must be achievable in acceptable time at permissible costs. Relevant questions in such regards could include:

✔ Are political aims clearly expressed and militarily attainable?

✔ Are allied objectives harmonious?

✔ Would accomplishment of proposed missions solve the most serious problems?

✔ What political, military, and economic costs would accompany failure?

Strategic Policy Guidelines

Some strategic policies simplify the accomplishment of political aims and military missions, while others introduce complications. Neither lenient nor strict guidelines are constantly preferable. Early rather than last-resort use of armed force, for example, occasionally quells crises before they become intractable. Relevant questions in such regards could include:

✔ Are proposed policies compatible with political aims and military missions?

✔ Which policy restrictions could be safely relaxed?

✔ What costs are acceptable in terms of casualties and collateral damage?

✔ Should statesmen impose time limits on proposed military operations?

Contingency Plans

National security planners balance interests, objectives, and available power against risks and costs, taking policy guidance into account, as they search for feasible, suitable, and politically acceptable solutions to intervention problems. Contingency plans reduce prospects of injurious surprise if crises explode unexpectedly. Relevant questions in such regards could include:

✔ Where, when, how, and in what strength should intervention take place?

✔ What force mix is required, and which forces should phase in first?

✔ How could allied forces best divide the "workload?"

✔ Are Plans B and C on tap if Plan A fails to produce required results?

Resource Allocation

The best laid strategic plans are valid only if ends (desired outcomes) and means (forces and funds) match reasonably well with enough in reserve to cope if other threats loom large. Resource allocators must reduce requirements, add assets, or both if shortfalls create unwarranted risks. Relevant questions in such regards could include:

✔ Are allocated resources ample for the current contingency?

✔ Could remaining resources successfully handle other likely crises?

✔ How many reserve component forces of what kinds are required?

✔ How could allies best contribute? Would they?

Public Support

Public support in democratic countries ideally should precede rather than follow military intervention, but that is not always possible. Prior approval moreover may be transitory. Statesmen therefore must rally and sustain support that is not spontaneous. Compelling interests, sensible objectives, and reasonable prospects for timely success assist official salesmen. Relevant questions in such regards could include:

✔ Has the Chief of State lucidly explained the purpose of intervention?
✔ Are those purposes compelling enough to retain public approval?
✔ To what extent should unfavorable world opinion influence decisions?

✔ Are enemies more or less skillful at information warfare?

Recurrent Reappraisals

Military intervention, no matter how innocuously it begins, may escalate unexpectedly. Original rationales may be overtaken by unforeseen events. Experienced Chiefs of State and their advisers therefore scrutinize pertinent factors repeatedly after they barge in to ascertain whether soldiers, sailors, airmen, and marines lay their lives on the line for legitimate reasons.

KEY POINTS

- Hard and fast rules that prescribe when military intervention is advisable cannot be universally applicable, because every contingency is unique
- Historical precedents, such as centuries-old ethnic, religious, and cultural animosities in Bosnia and Kosovo, strongly influence probabilities that military intervention will succeed or fail
- Peacekeeping operations are improvident unless all belligerents, by mutual consent, agree to refrain from armed conflict
- Peacekeeping and peacemaking operations seldom reach satisfactory conclusions if the interests of aggressors are more intense than those of interventionists
- Peacekeeping and peacemaking operations normally are inconclusive unless termination terms alleviate causes as well as symptoms of conflict
- Peacemakers who concentrate power against strategic centers of gravity accomplish objectives most efficiently as well as effectively
- Exclusive reliance on any form of combat power usually is inappropriate, because land, sea, air amphibious, and space capabilities are synergistic
- Prudent interventionists prepare Plans B and C for implementation if preferred Plan A cannot produce required results in reasonable time
- Resource allocators commit cardinal sins if they leave little in reserve to cope with other important contingencies that may erupt
- Peacekeeping operations for which there is no realistic exit strategy are not perpetually supportable

NOTES

1. Rebecca West, *Black Lamb and Grey Falcon: A Journey Through Yugoslavia,* Twentieth Century Classics, reprint (New York: Penguin Books, 1995); For time lines, see Zeljan Suster, *Historical Dictionary of the Federal Republic of Yugoslavia,* European Historical Dictionaries, No. 29 (New York: Scarecrow Press, 1999).

2. DA Pamphlet 550-99: *Yugoslavia: A Country Study,* ed. Glenn E. Curtis (Washington: Federal Research Division, Library of Congress, 1992), 69–88.

3. Ibid., 42–58, 200–10.

4. Laura Silber and Allen Little, *Yugoslavia: Death of a Nation* (New York: TV/Penguin Books, 1996).

5. *The Situation in Bosnia and Appropriate U.S. and Western Responses,* Senate Armed Services Committee Hearing, August 11, 1992, Reuters transcript, 13–15, 19, 42–44, 52.

6. Marjorie Ann Browne, *Yugoslavia: UN Security Council Resolutions: Texts and Votes—1991-1992,* Rpt. No. 92-659F (Washington: Congressional Research Service, October 28, 1992), 61–76, 79–114, 119–28, 135–36, 143–50.

7. *The Situation in Bosnia and Appropriate U.S. and Western Responses,* 24, 40–41, 47, 48, 53–54.

8. For assorted peace proposals considered and discarded in 1993, see Steven Woehrel, *Bosnia-Hercegovina's Partition and U.S. Policy,* Rept. Nr. 93-904F (Washington: Congressional Research Service, September 24, 1993).

9. *The Situation in Bosnia and Appropriate U.S. and Western Responses,* 41, 50–51; "No Military Quick Fix," interview with General John R. Galvin, *USA Today,* August 10, 1992, 7.

10. Michael R. Gordon, "Limits of U.S. Role," *New York Times,* August 11, 1992, 6; Barton Gellman, "Defense Planners Making Case Against Intervention in Yugoslavia," *Washington Post,* June 13, 1992, A16.

11. UN Resolution 770, in Marjorie Ann Browne, *Yugoslavia: UN Security Council Resolutions: Texts and Votes—1991-1992,* 115–16.

12. *The Situation in Bosnia and Appropriate U.S. and Western Responses,* 16–17, 36, 41, 42, 45, 51–52; Daniel Benjamin, "Hatred Ten Times Over," *Time,* August 17, 1992, 25.

13. Trevor Rowe, "Allies Drop Plans for Military Role in Bosnia," *Washington Post,* August 25, 1992, A1.

14. UN Resolution 713, in Marjorie Ann Browne, *Yugoslavia: UN Security Council Resolutions: Texts and Votes—1991-1992,* 9–12.

15. James Gow, "The Remains of the Yugoslav People's Army," *Jane's Intelligence Review,* August 1992, 359–62; *The Military Balance, 1991-1992* (London: International Institute for Strategic Studies, 1991), 96–97.

16. See, for example, S.21 and related bill H.R. 1172, January 4, 1995. President Clinton vetoed them on August 11, 1995.

17. Steven Woehrel, *Bosnia-Hercegovina and Former Yugoslavia: Chronology of Events, June 1, 1994-July 16, 1995,* Rpt. No. 95-823F (Washington: Congressional Research Service, July 18, 1995) and *Chronology of Events, July 19, 1995-May 31, 1996,* 1–6.

18. *UN Security Council Resolution 824,* May 6, 1993, prescribed six safe havens. *Resolution 836,* June 4, 1993, extended UNPROFOR's mandate to include all six.

19. Major General Michael Rose describes the exasperating circumstances in *Fighting for Peace: Bosnia 1994* (London: Harvill Press, 1998).

20. David Rhode, *End Game: The Betrayal and Fall of Srebrenica, Europe's Worst Massacre since World War II* (Boulder, CO: Westview Press, 1998).

21. *Summary of the Dayton Peace Agreement,* Fact Sheet (Washington: Department of State, December 11, 1995); *Bosnia Peace Accord and NATO Implementation Force: Questions and Answers,* Rpt. No. 95-1186F (Washington: Congressional Research Service, March 8, 1996), 1–10. For full text of the Dayton peace agreement, see State Department web page at www.state.gov/www/regions/eur/bosnia/index.html.

22. Steven R. Bowman, *Bosnia: U.S. Military Operations,* Issue Brief 93056 (Washington: Congressional Research Service, March 2000), 1–4; *Bosnia Peace Accord and NATO Implementation Force: Questions and Answers,* 12–22.

23. *History of the NATO-Led Stabilization Force (SFOR) in Bosnia and Herzegovina,* SFOR (Joint Forge) Fact Sheet (Brussels, Belgium: NATO Headquarters, October 1, 1999); *SHAPEJOC Assessment Report,* January 7, 2001.

24. Julie Kim, *Bosnia: Civil Implementation of the Peace Agreement,* Rpt. No. 96-177F (Washington: Congressional Research Service, January 16, 1997), 25–32; Colum Lynch "Misconduct, Corruption by U.S. Police Mar Bosnia Mission," *Washington Post* (May 29, 2001), A1, A11.

25. Noel Malcolm, *Kosovo: A Short History,* 1st Harper Perennial ed. (New York: HarperCollins, by arrangement with New York University Press, 1999).

26. Steven Woehrel and Julie Kim, *Kosovo and U.S. Policy,* Issue Brief 98041 (Washington: Congressional Research Service, August 19, 1998).

27. Ibid.; Julie Kim, *Kosovo Review and Analysis of Policy Objectives, 1998–June 1999,* Rpt. RL30265 (Washington: Congressional Research Service, July 21, 1999), 3–5, 6, 7.

28. For apparent KLA objectives, see "Balkan Futures," *Weekly Global Intelligence Update* (Austin, TX: STRATFOR.COM, March 20, 2000), 1, 2.

29. *Kosovo/Operation Allied Force After-Action Report,* to Congress (Washington: Offices of the Secretary of Defense and the Chairman of the Joint Chiefs of Staff, January 31, 2000), 1–17.

30. Erin Q. Winograd, "Clark Says Air Campaign Wasn't Slowed by Coalition Requirements," *Inside the Army,* August 9, 1999, 2.

31. Stuart D. Goldman, "Russia's Goals during the Kosovo Conflict," in *Kosovo Lessons Learned,* Memorandum to Hon. William Roth (Washington: Congressional Research Service, September 3, 1999), 11–14.

32. Elaine M. Grossman, "U.S. Military Debates Link between Kosovo Air War, Stated Objectives," *Inside the Pentagon,* April 20, 2000, 1, 6–9.

33. Doyle McManus, "Clinton's Massive Ground Invasion That Never Was," *Los Angeles Times,* June 7, 2000, 1; Colonel Edward F. Bruner, *Kosovo: Possible Ground Force Options,* Rpt. Nr. RS20188 (Washington: Congressional Research Service, May 4, 1999).

34. Patrick Theros, "Ground War Fog," *Washington Times,* April 18, 1999, B3; Dana Priest, "A Decisive Battle That Never Was," *Washington Post,* September 19, 1999, A1, A30.

35. *Kosovo/Operation Allied Force After-Action Report,* 78–79.

36. *Erasing History: Ethnic Cleansing in Kosovo* (Washington: Department of State, 1999).

37. *Kosovo/Operation Allied Force After-Action Report,* 21–24; John A. Tirpak, "Short's View of the Air Campaign: What Counted Most for NATO's Success in the Balkans Was the Reduction of Strategic Targets, Not 'Tank Plinking' in Kosovo," *Air Force Magazine,* September 1999, 43–47; Dana Priest, "Tension Grew With Divide Over Strategy," *Washington Post,* September 21, 1999, A1, A16.

38. John F. Harris, "Berger's Caution Has Shaped Role of U.S. in War" and William Drozdiak, "NATO's Cautious Air Strategy Comes Under Fire," both in *Washington Post,* May 16, 1999, A1, A24, A26.

39. Colonel Edward F. Bruner, "Application of Force: Escalate or Overwhelm?" in *Kosovo Lessons Learned,* 4–6; Secretary of Defense William S. Cohen and General Henry H. Shelton, *Joint Statement on the Kosovo After Action Review,* (Washington: Office of Assistant Secretary of Defense (Public Affairs), October 14,

1999), 3–4; Tirpak, "Short's View of the Air Campaign," 45.

40. *Kosovo/Operation Allied Force After-Action Report,* 8–9; Kim, *Kosovo Review and Analysis of Policy Objectives, 1998–June 1999;* 5–6; appendices to *UN Security Council Resolution* 1244, June 10, 1999.

41. *Kosovo/Operation Allied Force After-Action Report,* 10–12; Woehrel, "Why did Milosevic Agree to Withdraw His Forces from Kosovo?" in *Kosovo Lessons Learned,* 7–9.

42. Kim, *Kosovo Review and Analysis of Policy Objectives, 1998–June 1999,* 6–9.

43. *Ibid.,* 8; Steve Bowman, *Kosovo: U.S. and Allied Military Operations,* Issue Brief 10027 (Washington: Congressional Research Service, March 30, 2000), 6, 7, 8; *COMKFOR Situation Report,* January 2001.

44. Bowman, *Kosovo: U.S. and Allied Military Operations,* 8; Steven Woehrel and Julie Kim, *Kosovo and U.S. Policy,* Issue Brief 98041 (Washington: Congressional Research Service, April 19, 2000), 4, 5.

45. Woehrel and Kim, *Kosovo and U.S. Policy,* 3–4, 8–9.

46. Colonel Don M. Snider, "Let the Debate Begin: The Case for a Constabulary Force," *Army,* June 1998, 14–16; David Wood, "Are MPs the Force of Choice? *Army Times,* March 27, 2000, 15.

47. Woehrel and Kim, *Kosovo and U.S. Policy,* 4.

48. Matthew Cox, "You Call This Soldiering?" *Army Times,* March 27, 2000, 14, 15.

49. Margaret Mikyung Lee, Raphael Perl, and Steven Woehrel, *Bosnia War Crimes: The International Criminal Tribunal for the Former Yugoslavia and U.S. Policy,* Rpt. 96-404F (Washington: Congressional Research Service, April 23, 1998).

50. R. Jeffrey Smith, "Yugoslavia Moves to Extradite Milosevic," *Washington Post,* June 24, 2001, A1, A19; R. Jeffrey Smith, "Serb Leaders Hand Over Milosevic for Trial by War Crimes Tribunal," *Washington Post,* June 29, 2001, A1, A26.

51. For a cross section, see General Wesley K. Clark, *Waging Modern War: Bosnia, Kosovo, and the Future of Combat* (New York: Public Affairs, 2001); *Kosovo/Operation Allied Force After-Action Report;* Admiral James O. Ellis, *A View from the Top,* briefing by Commander in Chief, U.S. Naval Forces, Europe, who commanded Joint Task Force Noble Anvil during Operation Allied Force; Ivo H. Daalder and Michael O'Hanlon, *Winning Ugly: NATO's War to Save Kosovo* (Washington: Brookings Institution, 2000); Walter N. Anderson, *Peace Without Honor: Enduring Truths, Lessons Learned, and Implications for a Durable Peace in Bosnia,* Land Warfare Papers No. 33 (Arlington, VA: Association of the United

States Army, September 30, 1999); Dr. Carl Mueller, *Operation Allied Force: Air Strategy Comments* (Maxwell AFB, AL: School of Advanced Air Power Studies, April 29, 1999).

52. *Kosovo/Operation Allied Force After-Action Report,* 11.

53. Dusko Doder, "Yugoslavia: New War, Old Hatreds," *Foreign Policy,* vol. 21 (Summer 1993), 3–23.

54. Rear Admiral J. C. Wylie, *Military Strategy: A General Theory of Power Control* (New Brunswick, NJ: Rutgers University Press, 1967), 85.

55. Ellis, *A View from the Top,* slides 7, 11.

56. John Barry and Evan Thomas, "The Kosovo Cover-up," *Newsweek,* May 15, 2000, 22–26.

57. Joseph Fitchett, "Clark Recalls 'Lessons' of Kosovo," *International Herald Tribune,* May 3, 2000, 1; Elaine M. Grossman, "Ralston Sees Potential for More Wars of Gradual Escalation," *Inside the Pentagon,* September 16, 1999, 1; William M. Arkin, "Smart Bombs, Dumb Targeting," *Bulletin of the Atomic Scientists,* May/June 2000, 46–53; John T. Correll, "The Use of Force: Gradual Escalation—Supposedly Dead After Vietnam—Is Staging a Comeback," *Air Force Magazine,* vol. 82, no. 12 (December 1999), 37–39.

58. Jeffrey Record, "Gutless Giant?" Commentary, *U.S. Naval Institute Proceedings,* March 2000, 2; Tom Bowman, "Cost of War: A New Accounting," *Baltimore Sun,* March 22, 2000, 2A. Lt. Gen. Van Riper is cited in Elaine M. Grossman, "For U.S. Commander in Kosovo, Luck Played Role in Wartime Success, *Inside the Pentagon,* September 9, 1999, 1, 12–13.

59. *A National Security Strategy for a New Century* (Washington: The White House, December 1999), 19.

60. *Kosovo/Operation Allied Force After-Action Report,* 120–21; Elaine Grossman, "Pentagon Crafts Balkan Disengagement Plan in Event of Major War," *Inside the Pentagon,* September 7, 2000, 1.

61. "General Says U.S. Troops in Balkans Indefinitely," *Washington Times,* February 18, 2000, A4; Yann Tessier, "Peacekeepers May Be in Kosovo 10 Years or More," *Washington Times,* March 18, 2000, A9.

62. Steven J. Woehrel, *Serbia and Montenegro: Current Situation and U.S. Policy,* Rpt. No. RL30371 (Washington: Congressional Research Service, November 13, 2000); Curt Tarnoff, *The Federal Republic of Yugoslavia: U.S. Economic Assistance,* Rpt. No. RS20737 (Washington: Congressional Research Service, January 8, 2001) and *Kosovo: Reconstruction and Development Assistance,* Rpt. No. RL30453, August 18, 2000.

63. Louise Branson, "It's Only a Lull in the Balkans Drama," *Washington Post,* April 15, 2001, B2; General Wesley K. Clark, "Don't Delay in Macedonia," *Washington Post,* March 20, 2001, A27; Peter Finn, "Macedonians Shell Rebel Positions," *Washington Post,* March 23, 2001, A19.

64. Sean D. Naylor, "Gunfighters and Guerrillas," *Army Times,* April 20, 2001, 14–18. The Quinlan quotation is on 16.

65. Alan Sipress, "Balkans Uprisings Condemned," *Washington Post,* April 12, 2001, A27; Elaine Monaghan, "Powell Affirms Role in Balkans," *Washington Times,* April 12, 2001, A13.

66. For Defense Secretary Weinberger's speech, plus nine other official views, see Steven Daggett and Nina Serafino, *The Use of Force: Key Contemporary Documents,* Rpt. No. 94-805F (Washington: Congressional Research Service, October 17, 1994).

24. Final Reflections

And one final warning to those of you
who are on the threshold of your careers
as strategic planners. After all your plans
have been perfected, all avenues explored,
all contingencies thought through, then
ask yourself one final question:
"What have I overlooked?"

Philip A. Crowl
"The Strategist's Short Catechism," in
The Art and Practice of Military Strategy

Damon Runyon shrewdly observed that races may not always be to the swift nor battles to the strong, but that's the way to bet. Optimum military power, however, is obtainable only if creative thinkers survey strategic forests instead of tactical trees, challenge entrenched assumptions, subordinate special interests, estimate what capabilities might be most useful given present and projected threats, then paint geostrategic pictures that statesmen and commanders in chief can use to guide military operations of all kinds in peacetime as well as war.

This entire tome, which features a structured approach, is predicated on convictions that seasoned as well as neophyte strategists who are familiar with fundamental theories, concepts, principles, schools of thought, historical experience, and assorted practices are apt to overlook less than colleagues who favor informal techniques. Conscious consideration of national security interests, threats, objectives, alternatives to military power, and other relevant factors indeed is the best way to make ends and means match consistently well regardless of missions. Bullets on the following page recapitulate ten crucially important points that appeared at the end of previous chapters.

TEN CRUCIAL POINTS RECAPITULATED

- The value of most national security interests varies significantly from time to time and place to place
- The most dangerous enemy capabilities imaginable constitute dangerous threats only if accompanied by hostile intentions
- Nothing weakens deterrence and encourages aggressors more surely than poorly prepared opponents
- Excessive reliance on force leaves little room for intellectual judo that might mate ends with means equally well or better at less cost
- Military victories achieved at the expense of important political objectives may weaken rather than strengthen national security
- Excessively centralized civilian control tends to undermine military effectiveness; excessively decentralized civilian control may undermine political aims
- Foreign policies help shape military strategies; military power imposes practical limits on foreign policies
- Nuclear strategies that aim to "decapitate" governments may eliminate the only enemy leaders authorized to terminate mutually disastrous combat
- Limited wars demand mutual willingness to settle for less than complete fulfillment of cherished objectives
- Prudent strategists prepare Plans B and C for implementation if preferred Plan A cannot produce required results in reasonable time

Appendix A
Strategic Terminology

abduction The kidnapping of individuals or groups for sociopolitical purposes.

active components Military organizations that serve national governments full time. *See also* reserve components

aggression The unprovoked initiation of political, military, paramilitary, economic, technological, psychological, or cybernetic warfare weapons to achieve objectives. *See also* first strike

aim *See* national security objectives

alliance Any coalition codified by a treaty that is legally binding on every member. *See also* coalition; collective security

antiterrorism Defensive counterterrorism. *See also* counterterrorism; terrorism

AOR *See* area of responsibility

applied research The innovative use of basic scientific knowledge to solve technological problems; the exploitation of strategic theories to create innovative concepts. *See also* basic research

area of operations Territory within which armed forces perform assigned missions. Such plots may lie within another organization's area of responsibility. *See also* area of responsibility

area of responsibility Territory within which a military commander exercises authority over, and is accountable for, all activities by armed forces under his or her control. *See also* area of operations

armed force The employment of military or paramilitary formations for offensive, defensive, or deterrent purposes. *See also* armed forces

armed forces Armies, navies, air forces, amphibious forces, and space forces that are organized, equipped, and trained to accomplish national security missions. Law enforcement and paramilitary forces occupy other categories. *See also* armed force; law enforcement; paramilitary

arms control Explicit or implicit international agreements that govern the numbers, types, characteristics, deployment, and employment of particular armed forces and armaments. *See also* arms limitations; disarmament

arms limitations Agreements to restrict quantitative holdings of, or qualitative characteristics of, specific armaments and weapon systems. *See also* arms control; disarmament

assassination Premeditated murder of selected, usually prominent, individuals for political, ideological, cultural, or religious reasons.

assumptions Suppositions concerning current situations and future events, presumed to be true in the absence of contrary evidence.

assured destruction Highly reliable abilities to inflict unacceptable damage on any individual adversary or combination of adversaries, even after absorbing a savage nuclear first strike.

asymmetrical warfare Conflict during which opposing sides employ different strategies, tactics, and weapons. Otherwise weak adversaries, for example, might gain great advantage from biological or cybernetic assaults against opponents who possess traditional military superiority.

attrition strategies Concepts that call for protracted operations designed to degrade rival capabilities and gradually erode enemy will.

auxiliaries Part-time participants in insurgencies and resistance movements who perform special functions and undertake special missions for undergrounds. *See also* underground

bargaining chips Present, projected, or proposed weapons that are worth less to possessors than to opponents. Adversaries sometimes make momentous arms control concessions to cap, reduce, terminate development of, prevent deployment, or eliminate such items.

basic intelligence Facts about political, economic, military, social, cultural, geographic, scientific, technological, biographic, and other characteristics of a country. *See also* intelligence; strategic intelligence

basic research All efforts to embellish knowledge about natural environments and scientific phenomena; the development of innovative strategic theories. *See also* applied research; strategic theories

battle A tactical collision between opposing armed forces. *See also* campaign; war

biological warfare The use of living organisms (such as bacteria and viruses), toxic agents derived from dead microorganisms, and plant-growth regulators to produce lethal or nonlethal casualties among humans, livestock, or plants; defenses against such attacks. *See also* chemical warfare

black propaganda Public information deliberately disseminated in ways that conceal the true sponsor and purportedly identify a false source. *See also* gray propaganda; propaganda; white propaganda

blockade Prolonged severance of land, sea, and/or air lines of communication to prevent the passage of commercial shipments and military traffic to and from a country, coalition, or geographic area. Such sieges constitute acts of war when initiated in peacetime

burden-sharing Contributions to coalitions by members whose inclinations and abilities may vary considerably. Typical considerations include money, manpower, materiel, and intelligence, together with such intangibles as maneuver room, infrastructure, labor pools, and respective risks.

BW *See* biological warfare

calculated risks The deliberate acceptance of gaps between ends and means, because dangerous enemy actions seem unlikely. *See also* risks

campaign A series of theater-level military actions that may or may not be strategically significant. *See also* battle; war

capabilities Abilities to take particular actions against particular opponents at particular times and places. *See also* intentions

capability plans Concept formulations that seek to solve strategic, operational, or tactical problems using existing armed forces and other existing assets. *See also* requirement plans

catalytic conflict War between two countries or coalitions that a third party maliciously instigates.

cell A small compartment, usually part of a larger organization (single-cell structures are rare), whose members engage in clandestine or covert activities. *See also* compartmentation

center of gravity *See* strategic center of gravity

chemical warfare The use of asphyxiating, poisonous, or corrosive gases, flames, aerosols, liquid sprays, and various smokes to produce lethal or nonlethal casualties among humans and livestock, kill crops, or damage materiel; defense against such attacks. *See also* biological warfare

circumterrestrial space   A region that abuts Earth's atmosphere at an altitude of about 60 miles (95 kilometers) and extends to about 50,000 miles (80,000+ kilometers). Most military space missions currently are confined therein. *See also* space

civic action   Political, economic, and social programs undertaken to strengthen the internal security of a nation-state or territory. Typical projects involve public works, construction, health, sanitation, communications, agriculture, education, and training. *See also* civil affairs.

civil affairs   Interactions of specially organized, equipped, and trained armed forces with governments, nongovernmental groups, and populations in friendly, neutral, or hostile areas before, during, after, or in lieu of other military operations. Civil affairs may perform governmental functions in occupied countries or when indigenous authorities are unable or unwilling to do so satisfactorily. *See also* civic action

civil defense   Shelters and other passive measures designed to minimize casualties and damage from enemy attacks on population centers and production bases; emergency steps to repair or replace vital utilities and facilities.

clandestine operations   Activities conducted so secretly that no one but sponsors, planners, and implementers know of their existence. *See also* overt operations; covert operations

coalition   A formal or informal, long- or short-term, rigidly structured or free form partnership of two or more nations. *See also* alliance; collective security

Cold War   Mainly nonviolent conflict between the United States, the Soviet Union, and their respective allies from 1946 until 1989–1990; any prolonged period of rancorous international relations that confines armed conflict to minor incidents and skirmishes.

collateral casualties and damage   Physical harm that nuclear, biological, chemical, radiological, and traditional weapons incidentally inflict on persons and property collocated with, or adjacent to, military targets. Such effects may be welcome or unwanted, depending on circumstances.

collective security   Bilateral and multilateral alignments that involve two or more partners who strive to accomplish respective deterrent, offensive, or defensive objectives at reduced risk and costs. *See also* alliance, coalition

combating terrorism   *See* counterterrorism; terrorism

combat power   *See* military power

combined (forces; operations)   Military activities that involve armed forces from two or more nations. *See also* joint (forces; operations); unified operations

command and control   An arrangement of facilities, equipment, personnel, and procedures used to acquire, process, and disseminate information that commanders and staffs need to plan and direct military operations.

commitments   *See* national security commitments

compartmentation   Internal security arrangements that make it possible for personnel to know about colleagues and activities elsewhere in their organization only if leaders furnish information on a need-to-know basis. *See also* cell

concepts   *See* strategic concepts

confidence-building   Arms control measures designed to reduce international tensions and help control crises. Representative initiatives include telecommunication "hot lines," risk-reduction centers, and prior notification of potentially provocative maneuvers.

conflict spectrum   A continuum of hostilities that ranges from nonviolent warfare to the most violent form of global (eventually intergalactic) combat.

constabulary   A military or paramilitary police force that occupying powers or other outsiders employ to maintain law and order, mainly throughout rural regions (villages, hamlets, and interspaces) in foreign countries. *See also* gendarmerie

contingency   An event that politico-military authorities anticipate might occur or that erupts unexpectedly. *See also* contingency plans and operations

contingency plans and operations   Preparation to deal with anticipated events and thereby reduce probabilities of injurious surprise; actions in case such events occur. *See also* contingency

conventional   *See* traditional (forces, operations, warfare, weapons)

core area   Any strategically significant territory the seizure, retention, destruction, or control of which would give adversaries a marked or decisive advantage.

cost-effectiveness   A condition that matches ends with means in ways that create maximum capabilities at sensible (preferably minimum) expense

costs   Prices paid, or to be paid, in terms of money, other resources, time, politico-military penalties, and other intangibles.

counterforce strategies   War-fighting concepts that concentrate on the destruction or neutralization of enemy armed forces and military infrastructure. *See also* countervalue strategies

counterinsurgency   Political, economic, social, military, and paramilitary measures that indigenous governments and associates or occupying powers use to forestall or defeat counterrevolutions, insurgencies, resistance movements, and

revolutions. *See also* counterrevolution; insurgency; pacification; resistance; revolutionary war

counterintelligence   Information gathered and activities conducted to safeguard classified information from foreign agents and to guard against subversion, sabotage, and assassinations. *See also* intelligence

counterproliferation   All measures designed to prevent the spread of particular weapons and delivery vehicles, especially those that contribute to nuclear, biological, chemical, and radiological warfare capabilities. *See also* proliferation

counterrevolution   Operations that losers and associates conduct against the winners of successful insurgencies. *See also* insurgency

counterterrorism   Deterrent, offensive, and defensive measures, both active and passive, designed to deter, diminish the effects of, or defeat terrorism. *See also* antiterrorism; terrorism

countervalue strategies   War-fighting concepts that call for the destruction or neutralization of enemy population centers, industries, resources, and high-value institutions. *See also* counterforce strategies.

coup d'état   Brief violence or bloodless action by a small, conspiratorial group to overthrow a government and seize political power.

covert operations   Activities that conceal the identity of sponsors and facilitate plausible denial of involvement if perpetrators are detected and accused. *See also* clandestine operations; overt operations

credibility   Clear evidence that adversaries not only can but will convert threats and promises into actions if required.

crisis   A national or international emergency with adverse security implications. *See also* crisis management

crisis management   Emergency actions that politico-military leaders take to control events that could jeopardize important national interests or prevent the attainment of crucial objectives.

cumulative strategies   Concepts that call for a collection of individual, random actions that seemingly are unrelated, but in sum create synergistic results. *See also* sequential strategies

CW   *See* chemical warfare

cybernetic warfare   Electronic operations that selectively or indiscriminately attack computer terminals, networks, and repositories, then acquire data and disable, disrupt, or spoof opponents; operations that deter and defend against such activities. *See also* information warfare

decapitation   Operations designed to kill key enemy leaders, destroy their command and control systems, or both.

deception   Measures designed to mislead enemies by manipulation, distortion, or falsification of evidence. Successes induce reactions prejudicial to enemy interests. *See also* disinformation

defensive concepts and operations   *See* strategic defense

deployment   *See* force deployment

détente   Words and actions that formally or informally reduce international tensions.

deterrence   Steps taken to discourage deterrees from initiating unwelcome actions and to inhibit escalation if they disregard. Promises of punishment and reward both may contribute.

development   *See* research and development

diplomacy   Skill in furthering foreign policy objectives during peacetime and in war, especially the settlement of disputes and the development of mutually satisfactory agreements through representations, negotiations, and other dialogue.

direct approach   Any security strategy that literally or figuratively features brute force, frontal assaults, and attrition. Military power most often predominates. *See also* indirect approach

disarmament   The disposal of all or specified armed forces and armaments as a result of unilateral initiatives or international agreements. *See also* arms control; arms reduction

disinformation   Propaganda deliberately calculated to deceive a particular audience. *See also* deception; propaganda

doctrine   *See* military doctrine

economic assistance   Money, supplies, equipment, advice, education, training, infrastructure construction, and other nonmilitary aid, provided free of charge or paid for by cash, credit, or barter. The main purpose is to strengthen allies and other friends. *See also* humanitarian assistance; military assistance; security assistance

economic power   The sum total of a nation's commercial, financial, industrial, and other capabilities that contribute to the production, distribution, and consumption of goods and services. The share that is, or could be, devoted to national security matters is most important to politico-military policy-makers and strategists. *See also* military power; national power; political power

economic sanctions   Commercial and financial punishments, undertaken unilaterally or multilaterally, to convince opponents that they should cease undesirable practices or otherwise bow to the wielder's will. *See also* economic warfare

economic warfare   The purposeful manipulation of trade, foreign aid programs, financial transactions, and other tools that influence the production, distribution, and consumption of goods and services with the intent to coerce or weaken adversaries. *See also* economic sanctions

employment   *See* force employment

ends   *See* national security objectives; military missions

escalation A deliberate or unpremeditated increase in the scope or intensity of any type conflict. *See also* horizontal escalation; vertical escalation

estimates *See* intelligence estimates; strategic estimates

expeditionary forces Any military force designed to operate in foreign countries.

fifth column Covert or clandestine groups that infiltrate a country or form therein, usually before armed combat begins, to conduct subversive, sabotage, and other special operations.

first strike The first offensive move of a war. *See also* aggression; first use; second strike

first use The initial employment of any capability in wartime. One side, for example, might be the first to employ nuclear weapons during traditional combat. *See also* first strike

flexibility Capabilities that afford a range of options and facilitate smooth transitions when situations change.

force deployment The procurement and disposition of military materiel and organizations; the movement to areas of operation and subsequent positioning of armed forces therein. *See also* force employment

force employment The strategic, operational, or tactical use of armed forces. *See also* force deployment

force freezes Arms control moratoriums that maintain armed forces or other militarily valuable assets at present levels. *See also* arms control

forces *See* armed forces

foreign aid Aid to an ally or other associate for political, economic, humanitarian, and/or security reasons that may be altruistic or self-serving. *See also* economic assistance; humanitarian assistance; military assistance; security assistance

foreign policy The fundamental philosophy, implicit and explicit propositions, and strategies that focus the international relations of every nation-state.

forward presence Strategies that deploy armed forces near potential hot spots to deter aggression, help defuse budding conflicts and, if that fails, to terminate combat quickly on favorable terms. *See also* power projection

freezes *See* force freezes

functions *See* military functions

gendarmerie A national paramilitary police force that indigenous governments employ to maintain law and order, mainly throughout rural regions (villages, hamlets, and interspaces). *See also* constabulary

general-purpose forces *See* traditional forces and warfare

general war Armed conflict of global proportions, during which the survival of one or more world powers is in jeopardy.

graduated response Incremental applications of national power that allow enemies time to adjust between each escalatory step. Sometimes called "piecemealing."

grand strategy The art and science of employing national power to achieve national security objectives under all circumstances. Favored instruments include force, threats of force, diplomacy, economic pressures, psychological operations, subterfuge, and other imaginative means. *See also* military strategy; national strategy

gray propaganda Public information disseminated in ways that do not specifically identify any source. *See also* black propaganda; propaganda; white propaganda

guerrillas and guerrilla warfare Predominantly indigenous insurgent or resistance groups that conduct paramilitary hit-and-run operations against regular armed forces, other irregulars, or noncombatants. *See also* insurgency; resistance

guidance   *See* planning guidance

homeland defense   *See* strategic defense

horizontal escalation   An increase in the scope, but not necessarily the intensity, of any conflict. *See also* escalation; vertical escalation

hostage   Any person or property illegally held captive or in peril until redeemed, rescued, or voluntarily released. *See also* hostage rescue

hostage rescue   Diplomacy, negotiations, sanctions, and armed action, singly or in some combination, to secure the safe release of persons or property held for redemption. *See also* hostage

humanitarian assistance   Disaster relief and other aid designed to alleviate privation and suffering, especially food, clothing, shelter, medical care, sanitation, utilities, and rudimentary surface transportation.

incidents   Brief, small-scale armed clashes at the lower end of the conflict spectrum. *See also* limited war; war

indirect approach   Any strategy that literally or figuratively features envelopments, flank attacks, and intellectually innovative maneuvers. Political, economic, psychological, and cybernetic pressures often take precedence over armed force. *See also* direct approach

information   Knowledge; unprocessed facts and reports, regardless of type or derivation, that analysts can convert into intelligence. *See also* intelligence

information systems   The methodical collection, processing, transmission, dissemination, and storage of knowledge by automated and manual means.

information warfare   Actions to degrade enemy information systems and preserve the effectiveness of friendly counterparts. *See also* cybernetic warfare; information systems

infrastructure   Organizations, fabrications, facilities, and installations that control and support civilian, military, paramilitary, law enforcement, or subversive activities.

instability   *See* strategic stability

insurgency   Protracted, organized efforts by indigenous groups to overthrow the established order (not necessarily a government), seize power by subversive and coercive means, and sometimes (not always) alter social systems. Political, ideological, economic, social, religious, ethnic, and cultural motivations are common. *See also* counterrevolution; resistance

insurrection   *See* counterrevolution; insurgency; resistance

intelligence   The official interpretation of information after professional analyses. *See also* basic intelligence; information; strategic intelligence

intentions   The determination of a country or coalition to employ capabilities in specific ways at particular times and places. *See also* capabilities

interdiction   Military operations to prevent or impede enemy use of selected areas or routes.

interests   *See* national interests; national security interests

joint (forces; operations)   Military activities that involve armed forces from two or more military services. *See also* combined (forces; operations); unified operations

law enforcement (forces; operations)   Police, gendarmeries, constabularies, border guards, coast guards, and other organizations designed to maintain order within particular countries or territories in accord with national, and sometimes international, legal mandates.

limited war   Armed encounters, exclusive of incidents, during which one or more major powers or their proxies voluntarily exercise various types and degrees of restraint to prevent unmanageable escalation. Objectives, forces, weapons, targets, and operational areas all are subject to restriction. *See also* incidents; war

lines of communication   Land, sea, air, and space routes essential to the conduct of national security affairs, especially the deployment, redeployment, and logistical support of armed forces.

linkage   An arms control policy that addresses force limitation and reduction issues in context with other politico-military problems, rather than in isolation.

LOC   *See* lines of communication

logistics   The design, development, acquisition, storage, movement, distribution, maintenance, and evacuation of military materiel; the medical care of military personnel; the construction, maintenance, operation, and disposition of facilities; and the acquisition or furnishing of services.

long-range plans   Any plan that covers a period more than ten years in the future. *See also* mid-range plans; short-range plans

means   *See* resources

mercenaries   Paid proxies. *See also* proxy warfare

mid-range plans   Any plan that covers a period three to ten years in the future. *See also* long-range plans; short-range plans

military aid   *See* military assistance

military assistance   Money, weapons, equipment, supplies, advice, education, training, construction, services, and other aid provided free of charge or paid for by cash, credit, or barter. The main purpose is to improve the military capabilities of allies and other friends. *See also* economic assistance; security assistance

military balance   The comparative combat power of competing countries or coalitions. *See also* military power; military posture; strategic balance

military doctrines   Tenets that standardize strategic, operational, tactical, and logistical procedures under offensive, defensive, and benign conditions. Military doctrines, unlike policies, are instructive rather than directive in nature. *See also* national security policies

military forces   Regular, active, and reserve land, sea, air, and space forces of a nation, the primary purposes of which are to deter, defeat, or otherwise deal with the full range of armed aggression wherever and whenever required. Secondarily, they perform law enforcement missions as directed. *See also* armed forces; law enforcement; paramilitary forces

military functions   Tasks that land, sea, air, and space forces routinely perform in conformance with their roles. Some tasks are uniservice, while two or more services share others. Aerial interdiction, antisubmarine warfare, intelligence collection, and psychological operations are typical. *See also* military missions; military roles

military missions   Instructions to particular armed forces that clearly indicate actions required at particular times and places in particular situations. *See also* military functions; military roles

military operations other than war   The employment of armed forces for nation-building, peacekeeping, humanitarian assistance, disaster relief, and other benign or benevolent purposes. Some definitions include counternarcotic operations and counterterrorism in this category.

military policies   *See* national security policies

military posture   The strength, disposition, and preparedness of armed forces to accomplish assigned missions despite particular opposition. *See also* military balance; military power

military power   A compilation of capabilities related to the military balance between particular countries or coalitions. Ingredients include numbers, types, and organizational structures of armed forces; technological attributes of weapons and equipment; discipline, morale, pride, confidence, élan, loyalty, and hardiness of personnel; education, training, and combat experience; readiness and sustainability; command and control arrangements; and leadership. Military power is useless unless accompanied by national will to use it appropriately. *See also* military balance; national power; national will

military preparedness   The readiness of armed forces to accomplish particular missions on short notice and sustain operations as long as necessary. *See also* readiness; sustainability

military requirements   Assets needed to accomplish national security objectives and military missions. *See also* military resources; requirement plans

military resources   Money, manpower, and raw materials needed to develop, operate, and maintain ready, sustainable armed forces that possess required capabilities. *See also* military requirements

military roles   Broad, enduring purposes that differentiate armies, navies, air forces, and space forces. Requirements to conduct prompt and sustained operations ashore, aloft, or afloat are typical. *See also* military functions; military missions

military strategy   The art and science of employing armed forces (not necessarily armed force) under all conditions to attain national security objectives during peacetime and in war. *See also* military tactics; operational art

military tactics   The detailed employment of military formations, including the arrangement and maneuvering of units in relation to each

other and the enemy. Battles and engagements predominate, if armed combat occurs. *See also* battle; engagement; military strategy; operational art

missions   *See* military missions

MOOTW   *See* military operations other than war

narco conflict   Hostilities associated with military and law enforcement operations designed to reduce (preferably eradicate) the production and distribution of illegal drugs.

national interests   Highly generalized expressions of a nation-state's compelling wants and needs. Survival, security, peace, prosperity, and power are representative. *See also* national security interests

national objectives   Fundamental purposes toward which nation-states direct policies and expend energies. *See also* national security objectives

national policies   Positive and negative proclamations, public and private, that guide governmental officials in pursuit of national objectives. *See also* national security policies

national power   The sum total of any country's present and projected capabilities derived from political, economic, military, social, scientific, technological, and informational resources in context with geographical circumstances. *See also* military power

national security   Measures taken by a country to safeguard interests and achieve objectives despite foreign and domestic threats of any kind. Strong institutions, economies, and social systems often are more important than military power.

national security commitments   Formal or informal promises to assist allies and other friends under general or specific conditions. Resultant obligations may be qualified or unqualified.

national security interests Interests that are primarily concerned with preserving a state from harm. *See also* national interests; vital interests

national security objectives Aims that are primarily concerned with shielding national interests from foreign and domestic threats. *See also* national objectives

national security policies Guidelines for attaining national security objectives. *See also* national policies

national security strategy *See* grand strategy

national strategy The art and science of employing national power under all circumstances to achieve national objectives. *See also* national power; national security strategy

national will The proclivity of a government and its people to support politico-military policies, strategies, and operations despite intense, sustained pressures.

nation-building Activities of a developing country, unilaterally or with outside assistance, to create or strengthen popular acceptance of political, economic, legal, social, and other institutions and thereby enhance internal security.

net assessments The dispassionate comparison of competing countries or coalitions to ascertain which seems best able to achieve its objectives despite opposition by the other. *See also* threat assessments

nongovernmental groups Civilian associations, foundations, multinational businesses, and other organizations whose members may approve or oppose strategic policies, plans, and operations.

nonlethal warfare The use of political, economic, social, technological, psychological, and cybernetic "weapons" to achieve national security objectives. Military forces may deploy to impress opponents, but armed combat is taboo.

nonproliferation *See* counterproliferation

nuclear-free zone A geographic area where nuclear weapons are prohibited by international agreement.

objectives *See* national objectives; national security objectives

offensive concepts and operations *See* aggression, counteroffensive; strategic offensive

operating tempo The pace of military operations, which intensifies when missions increase, available forces decrease, or both. Unreasonably rapid or slow OPTEMPOs impair preparedness, if prolonged.

operational art Military plans and operations that implement military strategies at theater level. Campaigns predominate if armed combat occurs. *See also* campaign; military strategy; military tactics

operations other than war *See* military operations other than war

OPTEMPO *See* operating tempo

overt operations Activities conducted openly, without any attempt to conceal the identity of the sponsor or participants. *See also* clandestine operations; covert operations

pacification Counterinsurgency operations that aim to establish or reestablish national and grassroots governments that are responsive to, and involve participation by, indigenous populations. *See also* counterinsurgency

paramilitary (forces; operations) Land, sea, and air forces, such as constabularies, gendarmeries, and border guards, that perform internal security functions and supplement regular armed forces as required; guerrillas and other irregulars that use quasi-military tactics and techniques. *See also* armed forces; guerrillas and guerrilla warfare; law enforcement; military forces

parity A condition that pertains when the capabilities of particular armed forces and weapon systems are approximately equal in effectiveness to those of enemy counterparts under comparable conditions. *See also* sufficiency; superiority

peace Domestic and international relationships characterized by the absence of hostile activities and intent. *See also* war

peace enforcement *See* peacemaking

peacekeeping Nonviolent efforts of armed forces, interposed between belligerents by mutual consent, to maintain a truce or otherwise discourage hostilities. *See also* peacemaking

peacemaking Military efforts to prevent armed conflict in a specified locale or to terminate ongoing hostilities by force. *See also* peacekeeping

perception management Overt, covert, or clandestine employment of deception, controlled disclosures, military demonstrations, psychological operations, and psychotropic agents to influence and exploit the emotions, thoughts, and motives of targeted governments, groups, and individuals in ways that help users achieve objectives. *See also* psychological warfare

planning guidance Policies, assumptions, directions, decisions, and instructions that help shape strategic, operational, and tactical concepts.

plans *See* capability plans; contingency plans; long-range plans; mid-range plans; requirement plans; short-range plans

policies *See* military doctrines; national policies; national security policies

politico-military The integration of foreign and domestic policies with military strategies.

political power A nation's abilities to promote foreign and domestic policies and achieve national objectives using diplomatic inducements and coercion as instruments. *See also* economic power; military power; national power

political sanctions Diplomatic punishments, undertaken unilaterally or multilaterally, to convince opponents that they should cease undesirable practices or otherwise bow to the wielder's will. *See also* political warfare

political warfare The malicious manipulation of international relations to discredit, coerce, deceive, defang, or otherwise degrade enemy influence and power.

posture *See* military posture

power *See* economic power; military power; national power; political power

power projection Strategies that dispatch expeditionary forces from positions in central reserve to cope with distant contingencies. *See also* forward presence

preemptive war Armed conflict initiated because decision-makers believe that enemy attacks are imminent. *See also* preventive war

preparedness *See* military preparedness

preventive war Armed conflict initiated because decision-makers believe that enemy attacks are inevitable and delays would magnify risks. *See also* preemptive war

principles of deterrence A checklist, distilled from historical experience, that skilled strategists consider when they formulate concepts designed to keep foes, friends, and neutrals from adopting unwelcome courses of action. *See also* principles of preparedness; principles of war

principles of preparedness A checklist, distilled from historical experience, that skilled planners, programmers, and budgeters consider during efforts to deploy ready and sustainable armed forces. *See also* principles of deterrence; principles of war; readiness; sustainability

principles of war A checklist, distilled from historical experience, that skilled strategists consider when they formulate concepts designed to achieve offensive and defensive objectives during conflicts of any kind. *See also* principles of deterrence; principles of preparedness

priorities *See* strategic priorities

programming A process that appraises options, then selects a mix of military organizations, weapons, and equipment with which to implement strategic plans, within limits prescribed by available funds and other resources. *See also* strategic plans

proliferation The spread of particular weapons and delivery vehicles, especially those that possess nuclear, biological, chemical, and radiological warfare capabilities. *See also* counterproliferation

propaganda Any form of communication that directly or indirectly influences the opinions, emotions, attitudes, or behavior of enemies, neutrals, and friends at home and abroad in ways that suit the sponsor. *See also* black propaganda; gray propaganda; propaganda of deeds; psychological operations; psychological warfare; white propaganda

propaganda of deeds Armed actions, especially terrorist attacks, that seek to influence the opinions, emotions, attitudes, and behavior of targeted audiences. *See also* propaganda

proxy warfare A form of limited war in which sponsors who seek to reduce costs and risks rely on de facto or de jure surrogates to accomplish selected missions.

psychological operations The planned use of propaganda to induce or reinforce the attitudes and behavior of enemy, friendly, and neutral audiences in ways that facilitate the accomplishment of security objectives during peacetime and in war. *See also* propaganda; psychological warfare

psychological warfare The planned use of psychological operations to induce or reinforce enemy attitudes and behavior in ways that facilitate the accomplishment of security objectives. *See*

also perception management; propaganda; psychological operations

PSYOP *See* psychological operations

PSYWAR *See* psychological warfare

purpose *See* national security interests; national security objectives

Pyrrhic victory Any triumph that incurs ruinous costs. *See also* victory

R&D *See* research and development

readiness The ability of armed forces to perform assigned missions on short notice wherever and whenever required. *See also* military preparedness; sustainability

rebellion An armed uprising against an incumbent government or other established authority. *See also* insurgency; resistance

reforms Political, economic, social, institutional, and other renovations designed to strengthen the security of nation-states beset by internal dissension.

requirement plans Concept formulations that seek to solve strategic and tactical problems using armed forces and other assets. Authors count unavailable resources, without which stated objectives would be unachievable. *See also* capability plans; military requirements

research and development Explorations, experimentations, validations, engineering, tests, and evaluations that create new military materiel. *See also* applied research; basic research

requirements *See* military requirements

research *See* applied research; basic research

resistance Organized efforts by undergrounds, auxiliaries, guerrillas, and sympathizers to importune and, if possible, oust occupying powers. *See also* auxiliaries; guerrillas and guerrilla warfare; insurgency; underground

resources *See* military resources

retaliation Military responses to offensive enemy actions. *See also* aggression; first strike; first use

revolutionary warfare *See* counterrevolution; insurgency

risks The danger of disadvantage (even defeat) that results from gaps between ends and means. *See also* calculated risks

roles *See* military roles

rules of engagement Authoritative directives that permit armed forces to instigate combat without further orders under specified conditions and limit permissible actions thereafter.

sanctions *See* economic sanctions; political sanctions

sanctuaries Geographically distinctive territories within which one or more belligerents allow opponents to rest, regroup, resupply, and retrain without fear of attack.

second-strike Retaliation after an aggressor initiates armed hostilities. *See also* aggression; first strike; first use

security *See* national security

security assistance Foreign aid provided primarily to improve the ability of allies and associates to resist internal or external aggression or contribute more effectively to a coalition. *See also* economic assistance; humanitarian assistance; military assistance

sequential strategies Concepts that call for a series of discrete steps, each carefully planned and appraised in terms of required results. Strategists usually must reshape consequent plans if any stage fails to materialize or is altered substantially. *See also* cumulative strategies

short-range plans Plans that cover periods no more than two years in the future. *See also* long-range plans; mid-range plans

shows of force military operations taken to influence opponents, allies, or neutrals in desired ways without resort to armed combat.

space The universe and all of its contents, except Earth and its atmosphere. *See also* circumterrestrial space

stability *See* strategic stability

strategic area *See* core area

strategic balance The comparative power of two competing countries or coalitions, taking political, economic, military, and other relevant factors into account. *See also* military balance

strategic center of gravity Any crucially important objective, the achievement of which promises a favorable conclusion to any given campaign or war. Typical examples include capital cities, key leaders, crucial industries, and enemy will.

strategic concepts Judgments concerning ways that armed forces might best perform respective functions and accomplish assigned missions, taking relevant theories, facts, assumptions, and policies into account. *See also* strategic theories

strategic defense Concepts and forces designed primarily to protect a nation's people and production base against armed attacks. *See also* strategic offense

strategic education Systematic instruction that imparts knowledge concerning the evolution of strategic thought; the framework of modern military strategy, with particular attention to politico-military relationships; prominent theories, concepts, and other fundamentals; rationales that underpin specialized strategies across the conflict spectrum; interfaces with nonmilitary forms of national power; and strategic research techniques.

strategic intelligence Evaluated, integrated, interpreted information required for the development of national security objectives, policies, strategies, plans, and programs. *See also* basic intelligence; intelligence

strategic mobility   Abilities to shift armed forces and supplies rapidly from home bases to and between distant theaters of operation.

strategic offense   Concepts and forces designed primarily to destroy an enemy's war-making capabilities or degrade them until opposition collapses. *See also* strategic defense

strategic principles   *See* principles of deterrence; principles of preparedness; principles of war

strategic research   Efforts to expand the strategic knowledge base and thereby expedite the development of creative theories and concepts. *See also* applied research; basic research

strategic stability   A state of equilibrium that encourages prudence by opponents who contemplate aggression, because none possess significant advantage.

strategic theories   Conjecture concerning innovative ways that armed forces might perform particular functions or accomplish difficult missions. *See also* strategic concepts

strategy   *See* grand strategy; military strategy; military tactics; national strategy; operational art; tactics

subversion   Insidious, mainly psychological, operations intended to undermine the morale, discipline, loyalty, and will of populations and otherwise degrade popular support for incumbent regimes.

sufficiency   A condition that pertains when military capabilities are neither unduly excessive nor inadequate to achieve objectives. *See also* parity; superiority

superiority   A condition that pertains when military capabilities are markedly greater than those

of opponents, overall or in particular categories. *See also* parity; sufficiency

surrogate warfare   *See* proxy warfare

susceptibility   The proclivity of particular targeted audiences to respond favorably to particular psychological operations. *See also* vulnerability

sustainability   The ability of armed forces to perform assigned missions effectively as long as necessary wherever and whenever required. *See also* military preparedness; readiness

tactics   *See* military tactics

targets   people that belligerents plan to kill, capture, or influence; property that they plan to seize or destroy; areas that they plan to control or deny; countries, areas, organizations, groups, and individuals against which intelligence and counterintelligence personnel direct activities.

technological warfare   Ceaseless efforts to produce qualitatively superior materiel that confers decisive military advantage over adversaries. *See also* technological surprise

technological surprise   The perfection of potentially decisive military materiel that deploys unexpectedly or more rapidly than enemy intelligence analysts anticipate. *See also* technological warfare

terrorism   Public, repetitive violence or threats of violence to achieve sociopolitical objectives by inspiring widespread fear among people not present at the scene. The ultimate aim is to disrupt national routines so severely that compliance with terrorist demands seems preferable to further disorder. *See also* counterterrorism; terrorist

terrorist   Anyone who practices terrorism, regardless of motive. *See also* terrorism

theater of operations   A major politico-military or geographic area (such as Western Europe or the Middle East) for which military commanders in chief prepare plans and conduct operations. *See also* area of responsibility

theories *See* strategic theories

threats The capabilities, intentions, and actions of perceived enemies that currently endanger national interests and objectives or seem likely to do so.

threat assessments The dispassionate comparison of foreign and domestic perils to determine which seem most imminent and intense. Decision-makers then establish priorities that concentrate on the greatest perceived hazards. *See also* net assessments

traditional forces and warfare Armed forces and methods of operation that exclude nuclear, biological, chemical, and radiological weapons.

tripwire A small, vulnerable, but symbolically significant deterrent force positioned in a friendly foreign country that adversaries threaten. Owners advertise intents to retaliate if their token contingent is attacked.

underground An illegal organization that surreptitiously plans and controls an insurgency or resistance movement; conducts covert or clandestine operations, such as subversion, sabotage, and terror; and provides guerrillas with administrative and logistical support. *See also* auxiliaries; guerrillas and guerrilla warfare

unified operations The terms "joint" and "combined" do not intrinsically connote unity of command. That condition pertains at national and international levels only when national or coalition leaders confer full responsibility and authority on one commander in chief. The Principle of Cooperation otherwise predominates. *See also* combined (forces; operations); joint (forces; operations)

verification Reconnaissance, surveillance, and on-site inspections that seek to confirm or deny compliance with arms control agreements.

vertical escalation An increase in the intensity of any conflict. *See also* escalation; horizontal escalation

victory The achievement of objectives during battles, campaigns, and wars. Ultimate triumph terminates hostilities. *See also* Pyrrhic victory

vital interests Interests that involve national survival, including the preservation of assets that make survival meaningful. *See also* national security interests

vulnerability Weaknesses of any kind that enemies could exploit by any means; the susceptibility of particular targeted audiences to psychological warfare. *See also* susceptibility

war Declared or undeclared combat of strategic significance that exposes one or more nations to defeat. *See also* battle; campaign; incidents; peace; warfare

warfare The use of lethal and nonlethal instruments, perhaps in combinations, to degrade, damage, or defeat adversaries. *See also* cybernetic warfare; economic warfare; information warfare; nonlethal warfare; political warfare; psychological warfare; technological warfare.

weapons of mass destruction Nuclear explosives; biological, chemical, and radiological munitions, which destroy nothing but cause widespread casualties among exposed humans, livestock, and crops.

white propaganda Public information disseminated in ways that identify the sponsor. *See also* black propaganda; gray propaganda; propaganda

will *See* national will

Appendix B
Abbreviations

AC	active component	**MT**	megaton
AOR	area of responsibility	**MVD**	Ministry of the Interior (USSR)
ASAT	antisatellite	**NATO**	North Atlantic Treaty Organization
BMD	ballistic missile defense	**NBC**	nuclear, biological, and chemical
BW	biological warfare	**NBCR**	nuclear, biological, chemical, and radiological
CIA	Central Intelligence Agency		
CINC	commander in chief	**NCO**	noncommissioned officer
CW	chemical warfare	**OODA**	observe, orient on, decide, act
DOS	Denial of Service	**PFLP**	Popular Front for the Liberation of Palestine
DDOS	Distributed Denial of Service		
EMP	electromagnetic pulse	**PLO**	Palestine Liberation Organization
FBI	Federal Bureau of Investigation	**PSYOP**	psychological operations
FEMA	Federal Emergency Management Agency	**PSYWAR**	psychological warfare
		RC	reserve component
GNP	gross national product	**R&D**	research and development
GVN	Government of Vietnam	**RDT&E**	research, development, test, and evaluation
ICBM	intercontinental ballistic missile		
IFOR	Implementation Force	**SACEUR**	Supreme Allied Commander, Europe
IPTF	International Police Task Force		
JCS	Joint Chiefs of Staff	**SALT**	Strategic Arms Limitation Talks
KGB	Committee for State Security (USSR)	**SFOR**	Stabilization Force
		SLA	Symbionese Liberation Army
KFOR	Kosovo Force	**SLBM**	submarine-launched ballistic missile
KLA	Kosovo Liberation Army	**SLOC**	sea line of communication
KT	kiloton	**SOF**	Special Operations Forces
MIRV	multiple independently targetable reentry vehicle	**SOP**	standing operating procedures
		START	Strategic Arms Reduction Talks
MOOTW	military operations other than war	**UK**	United Kingdom

UN	United Nations	**USSR**	Union of Soviet Socialist Republics
UNHCR	United Nations High Commissioner for Refugees	**VC**	Viet Cong
		VCI	Viet Cong Infrastructure
UNPROFOR	United Nations Protection Force	**WMD**	weapons of mass destruction
U.S.	United States		

Appendix C
A Bookshelf for Military Strategists

This bookshelf for military strategists emphasizes foundation documents. Many citations, therefore, date back decades or more. For additional detail, see endnotes that terminate each chapter, footnotes, and bibliographies that accompany the many references cited below, and the *Air University Library Index to Military Periodicals, 1963–2000,* distributed on CD-ROM by EBSCO Publishing, Peabody, MA 01960.

MASTERWORKS

Carl von Clausewitz, *On War,* ed. and trans. Michael Howard and Peter Paret (Princeton, NJ: Princeton University Press, 1976).

Giulio Douhet, *The Command of the Air,* trans. Dino Ferrari (Washington: Office of Air Force History, 1983).

Baron de Jomini, *The Art of War,* trans. G.H. Mendell and W. P. Craighill (Westport, CT: Greenwood Press, 1974).

Niccolò Machiavelli, *The Prince,* ed. Peter Bondanella, trans. Mark Musa (New York: Oxford University Press, 1998) and *Discourses,* ed. Bernard Crick, trans. Leslie J. Walker (New York: Viking Press, 1985).

Alfred Thayer Mahan, *The Influence of Sea Power Upon History, 1660–1783* (New York: Hill and Wang, 1969).

Mao Tse-Tung, *On Protracted War,* 2d ed. (Beijing: Foreign Languages Press, 1960) and *On Guerrilla Warfare,* trans. and with an introduction by Samuel B. Griffith (New York: Praeger, 1961).

Sun Tzu, *The Art of War,* trans. Samuel B. Griffith, (New York: Oxford University Press, 1963).

WORKS ABOUT MASTERS

Theodore Ayrault Dodge, *Caesar: A History of the Art of War Among the Romans Down to the End of the Roman Empire, With a Detailed Account of the Campaigns of Gaius Julius Caesar* (New York: De Capo Press, 1995).

Frederick the Great, on the Art of War, ed. by Jay Luvaas (New York: Free Press (Macmillan & Co.), 1966).

Basil H. Liddell Hart, *Scipio Africanus: Greater Than Napoleon* (Novato, CA: Presidio Press, 1992).

Paul Ratchnevsky, *Genghis Khan: His Life and Legacy,* trans. Thomas Nivison Haining (New York: Blackwell Publishing Co., 1993).

Robert B. Strasser, ed., *The Landmark Thucydides: A Comprehensive Guide to the Peloponnesian War* (New York: Free Press, 1996).

ANTHOLOGIES

Edward Mead Earle, ed., *Makers of Modern Strategy: Military Thought from Machiavelli to Hitler* (Princeton, NJ: Princeton University Press, 1943).

Arthur F. Lykke, ed., *Military Strategy: Theory and Application* (Carlisle Barracks, PA: U.S. Army War College, 1989).

Peter Paret, ed., *Makers of Modern Strategy: Military Thought from Machiavelli to the Nuclear Age* (Princeton, NJ: Princeton University Press, 1986).

George Edward Thibault, ed., *The Art and Practice of Military Strategy* (Washington: National Defense University Press, 1984).

OTHER OVERVIEWS

Colin Gray, *Modern Strategy* (New York: Oxford University Press, 2000).

Colonels Qiao Liang and Wang Xiangsui, *Unrestricted Warfare: Assumptions on War and Tactics in the Age of Globalization,* trans. Foreign Broadcast Information Service (Beijing: PLA Arts Publishing House, February 1999).

Edward N. Luttwak, *Strategy: The Logic of War and Peace* (Cambridge, MA: Belknap/Harvard, 1987).

Marshal of the Soviet Union V. D. Sokolovskiy, *Soviet Military Strategy,* ed. Harriet Fast Scott, 3d ed. (New York: Crane, Russak & Co., 1968).

FRAMEWORK OF MILITARY STRATEGY
Security Interests

Bernard Brodie, *Strategy and National Interests: Reflections for the Future* (Washington: National Strategy Information Center, 1971).

George C. McGhee, ed., *National Interests and Global Goals* (Lanham, MD: University Press of America, 1989).

Threats

Richard K. Betts, "Analysis, War, and Decision: Why Intelligence Failures Are Inevitable," *World Politics,* vol. 31, no. 1 (October 1978), 14-20.

John M. Collins, "Essentials of Net Assessment," in *U.S.-Soviet Military Balance: Concepts and Capabilities, 1960-1980* (Washington: McGraw-Hill Publishers, 1980), 3-14.

Global Trends 2015: Dialogue About the Future with Nongovernment Experts, NIC 2000-02 (Washington: paper prepared under the direction of the National Intelligence Council for publication by the National Intelligence Board, December 2000).

Sherman Kent, *Strategic Intelligence* (Princeton, NJ: Princeton University Press, 1965).

Security Objectives

Marc Cancian, "Centers of Gravity Are a Myth," *U.S. Naval Institute Proceedings,* September 1998, 30-34.

Lieutenant General Raymond B. Furlong, "On War, Political Objectives, and Military Strategy," *Parameters,* December 1993, 2-10.

Basil H. Liddell Hart, *Strategy,* 2d rev. ed. (New York: Praeger, 1967), Chapter XXI, "National Object and Military Aim."

Steven Metz and Frederick M. Downey, "Centers of Gravity and Strategy Planning," *Military Review,* April 1988, 27-33.

Politico-Military Policies

Ken Booth, *Strategy and Ethnocentrism* (New York: Holmes and Meier, 1979).

Joseph Collins, *American Military Culture in the Twenty-First Century* (Washington: Center for Strategic & International Studies, February 2000).

Samuel P. Huntington, *The Soldier and the State: The Theory and Politics of Civil-Military Relations* (Cambridge, MA: the Belknap Press of Harvard University, 1959).

Yitzhak Klein, "A Theory of Strategic Culture," *Comparative Strategy,* vol. 10, (1991), 3-23.

Allan R. Millett, *The American Political System and Civilian Control of the Military: A Historical Perspective,* Mershon Position Papers in the Policy Sciences, No. Four (Columbus: the Mershon Center of Ohio State University, April 1979).

FUNDAMENTALS OF MILITARY STRATEGY
Introductions

Général d'Armée André Beaufre, *An Introduction to Strategy* (New York: Praeger, 1965).

Donald M. Snow and Dennis M. Drew, *Introduc-*

tion to Strategy (Maxwell Air Force Base, AL: Air Command and Staff College, 1982).

Geomilitary Schools of Thought

John M. Collins, *Military Geography: For Professionals and the Public* (Washington: National Defense University Press, 1998; reprinted, Brassey's, 1998).

Sir Julian Corbett, *Some Principles of Maritime Strategy* (Annapolis, MD: Naval Institute Press, 1982).

Halford J. Mackinder, *Democratic Ideals and Reality* (New York: Henry Holt and Co., 1942).

David R. Mets, *John Warden and the Classical Air Power Theorists* (Maxwell Air Force Base, AL: Air University Press, 1996).

G. Harry Stine, *Confrontation in Space* (Englewood Cliffs, NJ: Prentice-Hall, 1981).

Theories and Concepts

Henry Eccles, *Military Concepts and Philosophy* (New Brunswick, NJ: Rutgers University Press, 1965).

Colonel Glenn Harned, USMC, *The Complexity of War: The Application of Nonlinear Science to Military Science* (Quantico, VA: Marine Corps University, June 5, 1995).

Rear Admiral J. C. Wylie, *Military Strategy: A General Theory of Power Control* (New Brunswick, NJ: Rutgers University Press, 1967).

Fundamentals of Deterrence

Geoffrey Blaney, *The Causes of War* (New York: Free Press, 1973).

Bernard Brodie, *Strategy in the Missile Age* (Princeton, NJ: Princeton University Press, 1959), 264-304.

Alexander L. George and Richard Smoke, *Deterrence in American Foreign Policy: Theory and Practice* (New York: Columbia University Press, 1974).

Michael Howard, "The Causes of War," *Wilson Quarterly* (Summer 1984), 90-103.

Richard G. Joseph and John F. Reichart, *Deterrence and Defense in a Nuclear, Biological and Chemical Environment* (Washington: National Defense University Press, 1999).

Glenn H. Snyder, *Deterrence and Defense: Toward a Theory of National Security* (Princeton, NJ: Princeton University Press, 1961).

John G. Stossenger, *Why Nations Go to War* (New York: St. Martin's Press, 1978).

War-Fighting Fundamentals

John I. Alger, *The Quest for Victory: The History of the Principles of War* (Westport, CT: Greenwood Press, 1982).

Roger Beaumont, *Horizontal Escalation: Patterns and Paradoxes,* Stratech Studies Series (College Station: Center for Strategic Technologies, Texas A&M, 1993).

Richard K. Betts, *Surprise Attack: Lessons for Defense Planning* (Washington: Brookings Institution, 1982).

Anders Boserup and Robert Neild, ed., *The Foundations of Defensive Defense* (New York: St. Martin's Press, 1990).

Donald C. Daniel and Katherine L. Herbig, ed. *Strategic Military Deception* (New York: Pergammon Press, 1981).

Russell W. Glenn, "No More Principles of War," *Parameters,* Spring 1998, 48-66.

Richard D. Hooker, Jr. ed., *Maneuver Warfare: An Anthology* (Novato, CA: Presidio Press, 1993).

Herman Kahn, *On Escalation: Metaphors and Scenarios* (New York: Praeger, 1965).

Klaus Knorr and Patrick Morgan, *Strategic Military Surprise: Incentives and Opportunities* (New York: National Strategy Information Center, 1982).

War Termination Fundamentals

Stephen J. Cimbala and Keith A. Dunn, ed., *Conflict Termination and Military Strategy: Coercion,*

Persuasion, and War (Boulder, CO: Westview Press, 1987).

"How Wars End," a special edition of *The Annals of the American Academy of Political and Social Science* (November 1970).

Fred Charles Iklé, *Every War Must End* (New York: Columbia University Press, 1971).

David M. Morris, "From War to Peace: A Study of Cease-fire Agreements and the Evolving Role of the United Nations," *Virginia Journal of International Law,* vol. 36 (Summer 1996).

Fundamentals of Military Preparedness

Martin van Creveld, *Supplying War: Logistics from Wallenstein to Patton* (Cambridge, UK: Cambridge University Press, 1979).

Charles E. Heller and William A. Stofft, ed., *America's First Battles: 1776–1965* (Lawrence: University of Kansas Press, 1986).

Ramé Hemstreet, *Small Worlds Missions: The Impact of Military Operations Other Than War on Combat Readiness* (Washington: National War College, May 10, 1999).

Lieutenant General William G. Pagonis, *Moving Mountains: Lessons in Leadership and Logistics from the Persian Gulf War* (Boston: MA: Harvard Business School Press, 1992).

Fundamentals of Arms Control

Donald G. Brennan, *Arms Control, Disarmament, and National Security* (New York: G. Braziller, 1961).

Trevor N. Dupuy and Gay M. Hammerman, ed., *A Documentary History of Arms Control and Disarmament* (New York: R. R. Bowker Co., 1973).

Fred Charles Iklé, *How Nations Negotiate* (New York: Harper and Row, 1964).

Christopher Lamb, *How to Think About Arms Control, Disarmament, and Defense* (Englewood Cliffs, NJ: Prentice Hall, 1988).

Thomas C. Schelling and Morton H. Halperin, *Strategy and Arms Control* (New York: Twentieth Century Fund, 1961).

Kosta Tsipis et al., ed., *Arms Control and Verification: The Technologies That Make It Possible* (New York: Pergamon-Brassey's, 1986).

SPECIALIZED MILITARY STRATEGIES
Counterproliferation

Stuart E. Johnson and William H. Lewis, ed., *Weapons of Mass Destruction: New Perspectives on Counterproliferation* (Washington: National Defense University Press, 1995).

Office of Technology Assessment, *Proliferation of Mass Destruction Weapons: Assessing the Risks* (Washington: U.S. Government Printing Office, August 1993) and *Technologies Underlying Weapons of Mass Destruction* (December 1993).

Kenneth N. Waltz, *The Spread of Nuclear Weapons: More May Be Better,* Adelphi Papers 171 (London: International Institute for Strategic Studies, Autumn 1981).

Nuclear Warfare

Bernard Brodie, ed., *The Absolute Weapon: Atomic Power and World Order* (New York: Harcourt, Brace, and Co., 1946).

DA Pamphlet 39-3: *The Effects of Nuclear Weapons,* rev. ed. (Washington: U.S. Government Printing Office, February 1964).

The Effects of Nuclear War (Montclair, NJ: Allenheld, Osmun, & Co., for the Office of Technology Assessment, 1980).

Leon Gouré, *War Survival in Soviet Strategy* (Coral Gables, FL: Center for Advanced International Studies, University of Miami, 1976).

Herman Kahn, *On Thermonuclear War* (Princeton, NJ: Princeton University Press, 1960).

Henry A. Kissinger, *Nuclear Weapons and Foreign Policy* (New York: Harper & Brothers, 1957).

Biological and Chemical Warfare

Javed Ali, Leslie Rodrigues, and Michael Moodie, *U.S. Chemical-Biological Defense Guidebook* (Alexandria, VA: Jane's Information Group, 1998).

The Biological Chemical Warfare Threat (Washington: Central Intelligence Agency, 1998).

Robert Harris, "Toward a Theory of Biological Deterrence," *World Outlook* (Summer 1990), 952–102.

The Problem of Chemical and Biological Warfare, 6 vol. (New York: Swedish Institute for Peace Research (SIPRI), 1973).

Traditional Warfare

Christopher M. Gacek, *The Logic of Force: The Dilemma of Limited War in American Foreign Policy* (New York: Columbia University Press, 1994).

Michael T. Klare, *Resource Wars: The New Landscape of Global Conflict* (NY: Metropolitan Books, 2000).

Robert Endicott Osgood, *Limited War: The Challenge to American Strategy* (Chicago: University of Chicago Press, 1957).

Clark G. Reynolds, *Command of the Sea: The History and Strategy of Maritime Empires* (New York: Morrow, 1974).

Major General Robert H. Scales, Jr., *Firepower in Limited War,* rev. ed. (Novato, CA: Presidio Press, 1994).

Andrew G. B. Vallence, *The Air Weapon: Doctrines of Air-power Strategy and Operational Art* (New York: St. Martin's Press, 1996).

Naval Strategies

Merrill L. Bartlett, ed., *Assault from the Sea: Essays on the History of Amphibious Warfare* (Annapolis, MD: Naval Institute Press, 1983).

Admiral of the Fleet of the Soviet Union Sergei G. Gorshkov, *The Sea Power of the State* (Annapolis, MD: Naval Institute Press, 1976).

Michael H. H. Evans, *Amphibious Operations: The Projection of Power Ashore* (Washington: Brassey's, 1990).

Mackubin Thomas Owens, "Toward a Maritime Grand Strategy: Paradigm for a New Security Environment," *Strategic Review,* Spring 1993, 7–19.

Clark G. Reynolds, *Command of the Sea: The History and Strategy of Maritime Empires* (New York: Morrow, 1974).

B. Mitchell Simpson, ed., *The Development of Naval Thought: Essays by Herbert Rosinski* (Newport, RI: Naval War College Press, 1977).

Insurgency

Robert S. Asprey, *War in the Shadows: The Guerrilla in History,* 2 vol. (Garden City, NY: Doubleday & Co., 1975).

Doris M. Condit and Bert H. Cooper, Jr., ed., *Challenge and Response in Internal Conflict* (Washington: Center for Research in Social Systems, American University, vol. I, February 1968; vol. II, March 1967; vol. III, April 1968; Supplement, September 1968).

Martin van Creveld, ed., *The Encyclopedia of Revolutions and Revolutionaries: From Anarchism to Zhou Enlai* (New York: Facts on File, 1996).

Franz Fanon, *The Wretched of the Earth* (New York: Grove Press, 1963).

Ted Robert Gurr, *Why Men Rebel* (Princeton, NJ: Princeton University Press, 1970).

Andrew R. Molnar et al., *Undergrounds in Insurgency, Revolution, and Resistance Warfare* (Washington: Special Operations Research Office, American University, 1963).

Robert Taber, *War of the Flea: A Study of Guerrilla Warfare Theory and Practice* (New York: Lyle Stuart, 1965).

Counterinsurgency

Center of Military History, U.S. Army, *Reorganizing for Pacification Support* (Washington: U.S. Government Printing Office, 1982).

Doris M. Condit and Bert H. Cooper, Jr. ed., *Challenge and Response in Internal Conflict.* See section on Insurgency for a full citation.

David Galula, *Counterinsurgency Warfare: Theory and Practice* (New York: Praeger, 1964).

Alistair Horne, *A Savage Peace: Algeria, 1954–1962* (New York: Viking Press, 1978).

Major General Edward Geary Lansdale, *In the Midst of Wars* (New York: Harper and Row, 1972.

Mark Moyer, *Phoenix and the Birds of Prey: The CIA's Secret Campaign to Destroy the Viet Cong* (Annapolis: Naval Institute Press, 1997).

Roger Trinquier, *Modern Warfare: A French View of Counterinsurgency* (New York: Praeger, 1964).

Terrorism

Gavin Cameron, *Nuclear Terrorism: A Threat for the 21st Century* (New York: St. Martin's Press, 1999).

Richard Clutterbuck, *Terrorism in an Unstable World* (New York: Routledge, 1994.

Bruce Hoffman, *Inside Terrorism* (London: Victor Gallancz, 1998).

Walter Laqueur, *The New Terrorism: Fanaticism and the Arms of Mass Destruction* (New York: Oxford University Press, 1999).

Albert Perry, *Terrorism from Robespierre to Arafat* (New York: Vanguard Press, 1976).

Jonathan B. Tucker, ed., *Toxic Terror: Assessing Terrorist Use of Chemical and Biological Weapons* (Cambridge, MA, MIT Press, 2000).

Paul Wilkinson, ed., *Technology and Terrorism,* London: Frank Cass, 1993).

Counterterrorism

Critical Foundations: Protecting America's Infrastructure (Washington: Commission on Critical Infrastructure Protection, October 13, 1997).

Force Protection: Global Interests, Global Responsibilities, Report to the President and Congress (Washington: Office of the Secretary of Defense, September 15, 1996).

Neil C. Livingstone, *The Complete Security Guide for Executives* (Lexington, MA: Lexington Books, 1989).

Neil C. Livingstone, *The Cult of Counterterrorism: The "Weird World" of Spooks, Counterterrorists, Adventurers, and the Not Quite Professionals* (Lexington, MA: Levingston Books, 1990).

Brian M. Jenkins, *Terrorism and Personal Protection* (Boston: Butterworth Publishers, 1985).

Karl A. Sagan, *The Anti-terrorism Handbook* (Novato CA: Presidio Press, 1990).

Nonlethal Warfare

David Alberts, *The Unintended Consequences of Information Age Technologies: Avoiding Pitfalls, Seizing the Initiative* (Washington: National Defense University Press, April 1996).

John Arquilla and David Ronfeldt, ed., *Athena's Camp: Preparing for Conflict in the Information Age* (Santa Monica, CA: RAND Corporation, 1997).

The Economics of National Security, vol. XV, *Economic Warfare and Economic Intelligence* (Washington: Industrial College of the Armed Forces, 1958).

Alexander L. George, *Forceful Persuasion: Coercive Diplomacy As an Alternative to War* (Washington: United States Institute of Peace Press, 1991).

Robert T. Holt and Robert W. van de Velde, *Strategic Psychological Operations* (Chicago: University of Chicago Press, 1960).

Klaus Knorr and Oskar Morgenstern, *Science and Defense: Some Critical Thoughts on Research and Development* (Princeton, NJ: Princeton University Press, 1965).

Paul M. A. Linebarger, *Psychological Warfare,* 2d ed. (New York: Duell, Sloan, and Pierce, 1954).

Stefan T. Possony and J. E. Pournelle, *The Strategy of Technology* (Cambridge, MA: Dunellen, 1970).

Edward Waltz, *Information Warfare: Principles and Operations* (Boston: Artech House, 1998).

Yuan-li Wu, *Economic Warfare* (New York: Prentice-Hall, 1952).

Coalition Warfare

Ken Booth, "Alliances," in *Contemporary Strategies: Theories and Concepts,* ed. John Bayles et al., vol. I, 2d ed. (New York: Holmes & Meier, 1987).

Julian R. Friedman et al., ed., *Alliance in International Politics* (Boston: Allyn and Bacon, 1970).

Ole R. Holsti, P. Terrence Hopmann, and John D. Sullivan, *Unity and Disintegration in Internal Alliances: Comparative Studies* (New York: John Wiley and Sons, 1973).

Stephen M. Walt, *The Origins of Alliances* (Ithaca, NY: Cornell University Press, 1987).

STRATEGIC RESEARCH

Paul Bracken, "The Army After Next," *Washington Quarterly*, Autumn 1993, 154–174.

John M. Collins, "How Military Strategists Should Study History," *Military Review*, vol. LXIII, no. 8 (August 1983).

Professional Military Education, Hearings before the Panel on Military Education of the House Armed Services Committee, HASC 100-125, 100th Cong., 1st and 2d sess. (Washington: U.S. Government Printing Office, 1991); *Report of the National Defense University Transition Planning Committee* (The Long Committee), submitted to the Chairman, Joint Chiefs of Staff, August 25, 1989.

Project 2025 (Washington: Institute for National Strategic Studies, National Defense University, May 1992).

Alvin and Heidi Toffler, *War and Anti-war: Survival At the Dawn of the 21st Century* (Boston: Little, Brown, 1993).

BALKAN TAR-BABIES

General Wesley K. Clark, *Waging Modern War: Bosnia, Kosovo, and the Future of Combat* (NY: Public Affairs, 2001).

Ivo H. Daalder, *Getting to Dayton: The Making of America's Bosnia Policy* (Washington: Brookings Institution, 2000).

Admiral James O. Ellis, *A View from the Top,* a briefing by Commander, Joint Task Force Noble Anvil during Operation Allied Force, undated (September 1999).

Kosovo/Operation Allied Force After-Action Report, report to Congress (Washington, Offices of the Secretary of Defense and the Chairman of the Joint Chiefs of Staff, January 31, 2000.

Karl Mueller, *Operation Allied Force Air Strategy Comments,* a briefing (Maxwell Air Force Base, AL: School of Advanced Air Power Studies, April 29, 1999).

Major General Michael Rose, *Fighting for Peace: Bosnia, 1994* (London: Harvill Press, 1998).

Rebecca West, *Black Lamb and Grey Falcon: A Journey Through Yugoslavia,* Twentieth Century Classics reprint (New York: Penguin Books, 1995).

STUDY AIDS

R. Ernest and Trevor N. Dupuy, *The Harper Encyclopedia of Military History: From 3,500 B.C., to the Present,* 4th ed. (New York: HarperCollins, 1993).

Charles W. Freeman, Jr., *The Diplomat's Dictionary* (Washington: National Defense University, 1994).

Major General J. F. C. Fuller, *A Military History of the Western World,* 3 vol. (New York: Funk & Wagnalls, 1954), especially the chronicles that precede each chapter.

Clive Parry, John P. Grant, et al., ed., *Encyclopaedic Dictionary of International Law* (New York: Oceana Publications, 1986).

Index

1½ or 2½ war strategy, 66, 103.
  See also major regional contingencies

abductions
  Brig. Gen. James Dozier, 197
  Patricia Hearst, 197, 198, 213
  Skorzeny excels at, 85-86
  terrorist tactics in, 197-99
  See also hostages
Acheson, Dean, on Korea, 27
Achille Lauro hijacking, 199, 214
active strategies, 63
aeronautical school of thought, 61
air defenses, porous, 235
air power in Kosovo, 279, 284
Albright, Madeleine, urges intervention in Bosnia, 53
Algeria
  De Gaulle grants independence to, 49, 91
  French counterinsurgency in, 181
alliance treaties, membership and terms, 240-41
amphibious operations during nuclear war, 161-62
Anderson, Adm. George, dispute with McNamara, 160
Anderson, Maj. Gen. Orville, preventive war advocate, 140
Andropov, Yuri, on peaceful coexistence, 16
AOR. *See* areas of responsibility
Arafat, Yasser, temporarily renounces terrorism, 74
areas of responsibility, 293
  Bosnia-Herzegovina, 274, 275
  Kosovo, 280-81, 284
Argentina, counterinsurgency in, 185-86

armed forces
  active-reserve relationships, 29-30, 101
  air power peculiarities, 39, 40, 156
  civil vs. military control, 49-51
  deterrent value of, 157-58
  force ratios for counterinsurgency, 188-89
  functions during counterinsurgencies, 188
  future preparedness of, 102, 106
  geographic influences, 100
  homosexuals in, 105
  interdependence of, 155-56, 162
  land power peculiarities, 39, 40, 155
  military balances, 156-57
  and operating tempos, 104
  power projection, 87-88, 158-59
  presence overseas, 87, 158
  qualitative considerations, 23-25, 30, 100-01, 113-14, 157
  quantitative considerations, 23, 28-30, 100, 112-13, 156-57
  resource allocations, 102
  responsiveness to change, 25
  sea power peculiarities, 39, 40, 155-56
  servicewomen, 105
  space power peculiarities, 39, 40, 156
  teamwork in, 25
  U.S. Cold War deployments, 87, 102
  U.S. contingency force requirements, 87-88, 103
  value of obsolescent forces, 29
  See also coalition warfare; military functions; military missions; military preparedness; military roles
arms control, 293
  agendas, 115
  bans, 111
  bargaining chips, 116
  biological and chemical warfare, 18, 147-48
  confidence-building measures, 116
  Conventional Forces in Europe (CFE) Treaty, 112
  counting complexities, 111-13
  disarmament, 64, 110
  force caps, 110
  freezes, 110-11
  Geneva Conventions, 18
  Hague Conventions, 18, 111
  linkage, 116
  mutual reductions in Europe, 110
  negotiating techniques, 115-16
  nuclear-free zones, 111
  objectives, 109, 115
  Strategic Arms Limitation Talks, 110, 112, 115, 116
  Strategic Arms Reduction Talks, 116, 136
  technological controls, 113-14
  test bans and moratoriums, 114
  unilateral reductions, 110
  verification, 116-17
  versus arms competition, 64
  See also counterproliferation; nuclear arms control
Aron, Raymond, on proliferation, 127
Aspin, Les, *Bottom-Up Review*, 103
assassination
  Aldo Moro, 197
  "kingpin" targets, 42, 78-79, 82

assassination, *continued*
Phoenix program, 186
President Reagan, 193
Reinhard Heydrich, 185
terrorist tactic, 197
U.S. prohibitions, 90
assumptions
defined, described, 7, 293
influence on net assessments, 30
influence on strategic research, 260
politico-military samples, 64-65
astronautical school of thought, 61
asymmetrical strategies, 65
attrition strategies, 63
Aum Shinrikyo, use of biological and chemical agents, 196
Aung An Suu Kyi, 173

Baader-Meinhof Gang, 213
ballistic missile defense, strategic significance of, 87, 128
bargaining chips, 116
Baruch, Bernard, and nuclear arms control, 111, 135-36
bastions, Soviet submarine, 86
Battle of Britain
preserves springboard for Normandy invasion, 157
technological factors, 225
Beaufre, Général d'Armée Andre
freedom of action as aim, 16, 63-64
strategic trailblazer, 59, 253, 260
Begin, Menachim, as Irgun terrorist, 194
biological warfare (BW)
agents, 127, 145-46, 148-49, 195-96
and arms control, 18, 147
attributes, 145
and Aum Shinrikyo, 196
catalytic conflicts, 72
consequences of, 148-49
credible and incredible threats, 148
defense against, 149, 151
defined, 294
delivery vehicles, 145
deterrence, 77, 148
genetic engineering, 146

proliferation, 124, 125
R&D installations as poor targets, 148
research and development, 127
terrorism, 195-96
Weapons Convention, 112
blockades
in Bosnia, 273
as counterproliferation option, 129
and Cuban missile crisis, 160
defined, 294
as type of attrition warfare, 88
Blair, Tony, dialogue with Irish Republican Army, 212
Bosnia-Herzegovina
blockades in, 273
Colin Powell on, 53
combatants, 268
Dayton Peace Agreement, 273-75
ethnic cleansing, 268
Implementation Force, 275, 276
interests of, 268-69
International Police Task Force, 275
negotiated settlement as early option, 272
peacekeeping prospects, 272
peacemaking force requirements, 273
policy options, 271-73
route security, 272
U.N. arms embargo, 272-73
U.N. safe havens, 273
U.S. objectives towards, 271
war begins in 1992, 268, 273
Bottom-Up Review, 103
Boyd, Col. John, OODA loops, 230
Bradley, Gen. Omar, interest in peace, 16
Braun, Wernher von, trailblazer in space, 226
Brennen, Donald G., coins acronym MAD, 139
Brezhnev, Leonid
counterrevolutionary doctrine, 86, 173-74
limits support for Arab clients, 160
brinkmanship, 77, 128

Brodie, Bernard
National War College faculty member, 259
strategic trailblazer, 136, 251
broken-back warfare, nuclear scenario, 142
Brown, Harold
1½ war deficiencies, 103
on Soviet buildups, 17
Broz, Josip (Tito), forms modern Yugoslavia, 268
budgets
influence strategies, 7
McNamara's cost-effectiveness criteria, 67
burden-sharing, 294
in coalitions, 87, 243, 244
Bush, President George Herbert Walker
disregards War Powers Resolution, 90
New World Order, 52
terminates *Desert Storm,* 92

capabilities, foreign, intelligence estimates of, 25-28
Carter, President James Earl, Jr. (Jimmy)
and hostages in Teheran, 198
human rights advocate, 18
theater nuclear reductions, 110
Castro, Fidel
guerrilla organizations, 170-72, 173
and Soviet patrons, 242
casualty avoidance, U.S. and NATO, 280, 284
catalytic conflicts, 72-73, 294
causes of conflict, 72-73
related to war termination, 92-93
unresolved in Kosovo, 283, 285
center of gravity. *See* strategic centers of gravity
CFE (Treaty on Conventional Forces in Europe), counting problems, 112
chaos theories, 261
chemical warfare
agents, 146-47, 150
arms control, 147-48

decontamination, medical care, and cleanup, 151
defensive measures, 150–51
delivery vehicles, 147, 150
detection, 150
deterrence, 149
individual and collective protection, 150–51
proliferation, 123, 124, 126
research and development, 127
retaliation in kind, 149
and terrorism, 196
unique attributes of, 145, 146–47
weapons convention, 112–13
China, military strengths and weaknesses, 24
Choltitz, Gen. Dietrich von, declares Paris open city, 161
Churchill, Prime Minister Winston
against chemical warfare, 77
coalition partners, 239
lauds RAF, 157
victory is Britain's aim, 14
city evacuation, civil defense option, 142
civic action, counterinsurgency technique, 184–85
civil defense, nuclear warfare option, 142
civil–military control
civilian control in autocracies, 49–50
civilian control in democracies, 50–51
military control, 49
Soviet system, 49–50
U.S. system, 50–51
Civil War, insurgency by separatist states, 173
Clark, Gen. Wesley K.
air power priorities in Kosovo, 279–80
NATO's cohesion is critical, 279
occupation forces for Kosovo, 284
Clausewitz, Carl von
and continental school of thought, 61
on national will, 25
on physical vs. moral factors, 84

on strategic centers of gravity, 41, 43
as strategic trailblazer, 9, 251–52
Clemenceau, Georges, on war, 8
Clinton, President William J. (Bill)
attacks terrorist installations, 212
deplores terrorism, 195
dialogue with Irish Republican Army, 211
disregards War Powers Resolution, 90
Iraqi Liberation Act, 173
national security strategy, 52
Strategic Arms Reduction Talks, 136
coalitions, 237
Axis alliance, 243
bilateral and multilateral treaties, 240–41
burden-sharing, 87, 244, 294
case for collective security, 237–38
commanders in chief and staffs in, 242
compatibility prospects within, 101–2, 239–40
coordination within, 243
deterrent value of, 159
foreign aid to, 243–44
high commands, 242
in Korean War, 160, 220
League of Nations, 63, 238
in limited wars, 160
major military commands, 242–43
and nonalignment/neutralism, 237
optimum size of, 240
periodic reviews of, 244–45
in Persian Gulf War, 242–43
purposes of, 239, 241
reliability of, 239–40
surrogates in, 240, 241–42
treaties, 240–41
unity of command, 242–43
See also North Atlantic Treaty Organization; United Nations
Cohen, William S., on intelligence for counterterrorism, 214
collateral casualties and damage, 295
concerns in Kosovo, 280, 284

collective security, case for, 237–38. See also coalitions
command and control
in coalitions, 242–43
in counterterrorism, 205–6
in insurgencies, 169–71
in terrorism, 194
See also civil-military control
commitments, compared with policies, 47
complexity theories, 261
Comprehensive Test Ban Treaty, 114
concepts. See strategic concepts
confidence-building measures, 75, 116
conflicts of interest, 18
conflict spectrum, 21–22, 295–96
conflict termination
in counterinsurgencies, 190
deescalation, 89
inducements, inhibitions, terms, 91–93
in limited wars, 160
in nuclear war, 142
Treaty of Versailles, 117, 221
World War II, 15, 222
See also deescalation
Congress
civil-military control, 50–51
forbids aid to Contras, 174
Iraqi Liberation Act, 173
restrains covert operations, 90
Tonkin Gulf Resolution, 35
War Powers Resolution, 90
Contact Group, membership, 278
contingency plans
intervention checklist, 286
major regional contingencies, 66, 87, 103, 284
NATO in Kosovo, 283–84
threat assessment, 30
U.S. plans for China, 82
continental school of thought, 61
Contras, 174, 207, 243
Conventional Forces in Europe, counting problems, 112
counterforce targeting, 141
counterinsurgencies, 181, 296
in Argentina, 185–86
civic actions, 184–85

counterinsurgencies, *continued*
 clear and hold strategies, 187
 compared with insurgencies,
  182, 183
 compared with traditional conflicts, 182
 force ratios, 188-89
 French in Algeria, Indochina, 181
 hold and harass strategies, 187
 intelligence, 182-83
 law enforcement, 183
 Malaya, 183
 Nazi German atrocities, 185
 New Left, 184
 outside support, 187-88
 pacification programs, 189-90
 prescriptions for success, 190
 primacy of land power in, 188
 with reforms, 183-85
 search and destroy strategies,
  186-87
 Soviet-Cuban support for Sandinistas, 243
 termination of, 190
 unity of effort, 189-90
counterproliferation strategies, 296
 air strikes, 129
 blockades, 129
 disputes about desirability,
  127-28
 intelligence indicators, 126-27
 intelligence collection, 128
 invasion of offending states, 130
 nonmilitary options, 128
 Nonproliferation Treaty, 128, 136
 prognosis for, 130
 sabotage, 129-30
 security guarantees, 128-29
 See also proliferation
counterrevolutions, 173, 296
 Soviet operations in Afghanistan,
  174
 Soviet operations in Europe, 86,
  173-74, 239-40
 See also counterinsurgencies
counterterrorism, 205, 296
 Achille Lauro hijacking, 199, 214
 attack patron states, 213
 attack terrorist bases, 212-13
 censorship and ostracism,
  211-12

 centralization vs. decentraliza-
  tion, 206
 civilian installation security,
  209-10
 civil liberties restraints, 214
 control mechanisms, 205-6
 cybernetic security, 210, 232
 deterrent dilemmas, 207-8
 disarming of explosives, 211
 "drive-by shooting," 212
 economic sanctions, 212
 fixed vs. flexible policies, 206-7
 hostage rescues, 210-11, 214
 intelligence in, 213, 214
 Iran-Contra affair, 207
 Israeli strategy and tactics, 65-66
 killing of terrorist leaders, 212
 legal considerations, 206, 214
 military installation security, 209
 political countermeasures, 211
 preemption vs. retaliation, 207
 and public safety, 208
 U.S. and Soviet participants,
  205-6
 violence vs. nonviolence, 207
 and VIP protection, 208
 See also terrorism
countervalue targeting, 141
covert operations, congressional restraints on, 90
credibility
 national security interest in,
  15-16
 Principle of Deterrence, 73
Croatia
 resistance movement in World
  War II, 174-75
 interests in Bosnia, 268, 271
Cuba
 missile crisis, 38
 Soviet surrogate, 160, 242
 Soviet tripwire in, 76-77
cumulative strategies, 62
Cushman, Col. Robert E., on amphibious operations during nuclear war, 162
cybernetic warfare, 230, 297
 benefits and liabilities, 232
 countermeasures, 232
 innovative capabilities, 26
 offensive options, 231
 participants, 231

 schools of thought, 230-31
 targets, 231
 terrorism and counterterrorism,
  210
Cyrus the Great, as strategic trailblazer, 252

Dayton Peace Agreement, 273-75
"decapitation" strategies, 64, 142
deception
 deterrent technique, 76
 missile gap, 76
 political warfare, 221
 in Normandy, 76
 and surprise, 83
Declaration of Independence, revolutionary document, 169
deescalation, 89. *See also* conflict
  termination
defense
 against chemical warfare agents,
  150-51
 civil defense, 142
 defensive offensives, 86-87
 and deterrence, 74
 of homeland, 15, 138
 against nuclear warfare, 74,
  136-38
 offensive defensives, 86
 purposes, 83-84
 Sun Tzu evaluates, 86
De Gaulle, Charles
 force de frappe, 138
 frees Algeria, 49, 91
 ignorant of revolutionary war,
  181
 versus communist insurgents during World War II, 168
demonstrations, deterrent technique, 75, 159
deterrence, 71, 297
 of biological warfare, 77, 148
 of chemical warfare, 149
 compared with avoidance, 71
 credibility in, 73
 by deception and disinformation,
  76
 and defense, 74
 by demonstrations, 75, 159
 extended deterrence, 138
 NATO's policies for, 53
 by nonprovocation, 74

by nuclear threats, 148
by permanent presence, 158
from power projection, 158-59
Principles of Deterrence, 73-75
and publicity, 74-75
purposes of, 71
rewards as incentives to, 74
success hard to prove, 71
techniques for (summarized), 76
theories of, 75-77
traditional requirements for, 157
tripwires, 76-77
by uncertainty, 73, 77
vacillation deflates, 159
by wars, 75
See also nuclear deterrence
Diem, Ngo Dinh, against Viet Cong, 186
direct strategies, 62-63
disinformation
    contributes to surprise, 83
    as deterrent technique, 76
    Soviet specialty, 229-30
doctrines. *See* military doctrines
domestic tranquility as universal interest, 15
Dominican Republic, U.S. counterinsurgency, 189
Douhet, Brig. Gen. Guilio, aeronautical school of thought, 61
Dozier, Brig. Gen. James L., abduction of, 197
Duvalier, "Papa Doc," domestic terrorism of, 193

economic warfare
    blacklists, 223
    export/import controls, 223
    limitations and successes, 223-24
    OPEC oil embargo, 17
    preclusive purchases, 223
    sanctions, 222-23
Eisenhower, Gen. Dwight D.
    broad front strategy, 83
    directive from Combined Chiefs of Staff, 37, 84
    resigns commission, 50
    in Suez crisis, 92
electromagnetic pulse, 135
Elizabeth II, and intruder in boudoir, 197
EMP, effects of, 135

ends and means, 3, 5, 8
    See also resource allocation
escalation
    controlled in Kosovo, 280
    ladder, 88-89
    vertical, horizontal, and gradual, 64, 89, 91
    See also deescalation
Estes, General Howell, III, on intelligence requirements, 22-23
ethnic cleansing
    in Bosnia, 268, 271
    in Kosovo, 279, 283
extended deterrence in homeland defense, 138

Fairchild, Maj. Gen. Muir, preventive war advocate, 140
Fall, Bernard, on French vs. Viet Minh force ratios, 189
female service members, disputes concerning, 105
fifth columns, in Spain, 176
Flexible Response
    compared with gradual escalation, 89
    NATO's shortcomings in, 66
flexibility, principle of, 82
force de frappe, 73, 138
Ford, President Gerald R., forbids assassination, 90
foreign aid
    objectives and objections, 243-44
    South Korean forces in Vietnam, 499
foreign policies
    compete with domestic policies, 51
    military power supports, 52-53
    Soviet priorities, 52
    U.S. priorities, 51-52
forward presence, value of, 87-88, 103, 158
freedom of action
    benefits, 16, 63-64, 82, 83
    security interest, 16
Fuller, Maj. Gen. J. F. C., on importance of morale, 104
functions. *See* military roles and functions

Gallois, Gen. Pierre, on proliferation, 127
Galvin, Gen. John R., about intervention in Bosnia, 272
Gandhi, Mahatma, on passive resistance, 63
Geiger, Lt. Gen. Roy S., on amphibious operations during nuclear war, 161-62
Geneva Conventions, on arms control, 18
geography
    in Cuban missile crisis, 38
    influence on preparedness, 100
    influence on strategies, 62
    as national security interest, 17-18
Germany
    contribution to NATO, 244
    in Treaty of Versailles, 117, 221
Gorbachev, Mikhail, reforms destabilize USSR, 52
Gorshkov, Fleet Adm. Sergei G.
    on Soviet naval needs, 17
    strategic trailblazer, 253, 254
gradual escalation, in Vietnam and Kosovo, 89, 280, 284
Grant, Gen. Ulysses S., tenacity of, 85
grand strategy, 4, 298
grand tactics. *See* operational art
Gromyko, Andrei, institutional memory of, 115
Guatemala, U.S. PSYOP feat in, 227-28
guerrillas
    assist traditional forces, 172
    in European Russia, 176
    organizations, 170, 172, 173
    outside support for, 187-88
Guzmán, Arbenz, PSYOP defeat of, 227-28

Hague Conventions, 18, 111
Haig, Gen. Alexander M., Jr., on nuclear "shot across the bow," 75
Haiti, U.S. counterinsurgency in, 189
Hearst, Patricia, abduction and terrorist activities of, 197, 198, 213

Heydrich, Reinhard, "Butcher of Prague," 185

hijackings as terrorist tactic, 198-99

Hitler, Adolf
  appeasement undermined deterrence of, 72
  deceived in Normandy, 76
  and domestic terrorism, 193
  Mein Kampf, 27
  nonaggression pact with USSR, 220-21
  and nonlethal warfare, 219
  overcommitted German Armed Forces, 83, 102-3, 157
  repudiated Treaty of Versailles, 117, 221
  skill in indirect strategy, 63

"hollow" armed forces, 25

homeland defense as universal interest, 15

homosexual service members, disputes concerning, 105

Hoover Plan for world disarmament, 110

horizontal escalation, 64, 89
  complicates conflict termination, 91
  second front in World War II, 89

hostages
  in Teheran, 198
  ransoms for, 197-98, 200
  rescues of, 197, 210-11
  terrorist tactics, 197-98
  UN peacekeepers in Bosnia, 273

Hukbalahaps (Huks), Philippine insurgents, 185

human rights, conventions regarding, 18

ideology, as national security interest, 17

IFOR. *See* Implementation Force

Implementation Force, 275, 276

indirect strategies, 62-63

Indochina
  French counterinsurgency in, 181
  French vs. Viet Minh force ratios, 188-89
  See also Vietnam War

information warfare, and deterrence, 74-75. *See also* cybernetic warfare

INF Treaty, 136

insurgencies, 299
  in Africa, 169
  in Burma, 173, 176
  causes, 168-69
  cellular organizations, 169-70, 171
  classical characteristics, 167-68
  command and control in, 169-72
  compared with traditional conflicts, 182
  Declaration of Independence as, 169
  during traditional conflicts, 176
  French Revolution, 169
  increasing complexities of, 168
  Mao Zedong's Phases I-III, 172-73
  motives, 181
  objectives, 168
  opposing each other, 168
  outside support, 173
  psychological warfare, 170
  Soviet/Cuban support for Sandinistas, 243
  subversion of, 175-76
  undergrounds, 170, 171
  See also counterinsurgencies; resistance

intelligence
  counterinsurgency, 182-83
  counterterrorism, 213, 214
  of enemy capabilities, 23-26
  enemy intentions, 26-27
  estimates, 6-7, 25-28
  proliferation indicators, 126-27
  proliferation site inspections, 128
  in psychological warfare, 228
  qualitative military considerations, 23-25, 30
  quantitative military considerations, 23, 28-30
  second opinions advisable, 28
  strategic guidance, 22-23, 260
  strategic vs. tactical, 27-28
  technological espionage, 226
  technological forecasting, 224

intentions
  difficult to divine, 26-27
  related to deterrence, 159

Intermediate-Range Nuclear Forces Treaty, 136

intervention checklist, 285-87. *See also* Weinberger

IRA. *See* Irish Republican Army

Iran
  in catalytic conflict, 72
  Iran-Contra affair, 174, 207
  hostages rescued in London, 198
  hostages held in Teheran, 198

Iraq
  in catalytic conflict, 72
  Desert Storm termination, 92
  Iraqi Liberation Act, 173
  See also Saddam Hussein

Irish Republican Army, U.S.-British dialogues with, 211-12

Israel
  counterterrorism strategy, 65-66
  reliance on reserves, 30
  in technological espionage, 226
  terrorism by and against, 194

Japanese Red Army, attacking LOD Airport, 194

Johnson, President Lyndon B.
  interest in credibility, 16
  public approval sours, 35
  Vietnam policies, 48, 160-61

Joy, Vice Adm. C. Turner, Panmunjom negotiator, 230

Kahn, Herman
  on defense against nuclear weapons, 138
  escalation ladder, 88-89
  on nuclear victory, 14
  as strategic trailblazer, 252

Kellogg-Briand Pact, 110

Kennedy, President John F.
  on burden-sharing, 244
  on nuclear proliferation, 125

Kent, Sherman
  on enemy intentions, 27
  National War College faculty member, 259

Kenya, Mau Mau insurgency, 187

KFOR. *See* Kosovo Force

Khmer Rouge, genocide in Cambodia, 18

Khobar Towers, terrorist attack at, 199

Khomeini, Ayatollah Ruhollah
    and hostages in Teheran, 198
    U.S. arms sales to, 207
Khrushchev, Nikita
    peaceful coexistence, 60
    sacks Marshal Zhukov, 50
Kim Il-Sung, deterred, 27, 159
Kim Song-Il, deterred, 159
King, Martin Luther, Jr., and passive
    resistance, 63
"kingpins," as strategic centers of
    gravity, 42
Kingston, Gen. Robert C., on intelli-
    gence requirements, 22
Kissinger, Henry A., Vietnam War
    negotiations, 230
Korea. See Korean War; North Ko-
    rea; South Korea
Korean War
    decision to resist invasion, 27, 75
    U.N. coalition in, 160, 220
Koster, Maj. Gen. Samuel, "doers"
    overshadow thinkers, 1
Kosovo
    air power option, 279–80
    air power restraints, 280, 284
    areas of responsibility in, 280–
        81, 284
    causes of conflict unresolved,
        285
    collateral casualties and damage,
        280, 284
    concurrent U.S. contingency re-
        quirements and, 284
    ethnic cleansing in, 279
    exit strategy from, 284–85
    geographic isolation of, 279
    gradual escalation in, 280–84
    ground combat force require-
        ments, 279
    law and order in, 282
    misplaced priorities in, 283
    prewar situation, 275, 278
    refugee repatriation, 282
    security interests, 278–79, 283
    strategic shortcomings, 283–85
    strategic successes, 282–83
    war criminals, 282
    war termination, 280
Kosovo Force, NATO command,
    280–82

Kosovo Liberation Army
    demilitarization of, 282
    formation of, 278
    police responsibilities of, 282

launch-on-warning nuclear retalia-
    tory policy, 140–41
Lawrence, T. E.
    active vs. passive insurgents, 169
    operations in Arabia, 176
League of Nations
    disarmament aim, 64, 110
    impotence of, 63
LeMay, Gen. Curtis E.
    bomb "back to Stone Age," 148
    preventive war, 140
Lenin, Vladimir
    on importance of national will,
        42
    on peaceful coexistence, 16
    quantity is a quality, 29
    on "useful idiots," 169
    writings reveal intentions, 27
Libya, terrorism and counterterror-
    ism, 213
Liddell Hart, Basil H.
    on centers of gravity for coali-
        tions, 43
    on military conservatism, 25
    predicted Allies would defeat
        Axis, 103
    on primacy of strategy over tac-
        tics, 5
    on victory, 38
limited war, 299–300
    allowable methods and means,
        160–61
    allowable objectives, 160
    geographical restrictions, 161
    nuclear nexus, 161–62
Lin Biao, encircle cities concept, 88
linkage, arms control technique,
    116
Lincoln, Abraham, on domestic tran-
    quility, 15

MacArthur, Gen. Douglas, and war
    without victory, 38–39
Machiavelli, Niccolò, 257
    on mercenaries, 241
    on morality, 18, 59, 240

McNamara, Robert S.
    2½ war strategy, 103
    assessing Soviet capabilities, 30
    cost-effectiveness criteria, 67
    disputes Adm. Anderson, 160
    spurns nuclear defense, 74
MacKenzie, Maj. Gen. Lewis, op-
    poses intervention in Bosnia,
    272
Mackinder, Halford J., heartland the-
    ory applied to space, 61–62
MAD. See Mutual Assured De-
    struction
Magsaysay, Ramon, counterinsur-
    gency techniques, 184–85
Mahan, Capt. Alfred Thayer, 257
    maritime school of thought, 61
major regional contingencies, U.S.
    requirements, 66, 87–88, 103,
    284
Malaya, British counterinsurgency
    in, 183
Malik, Jakob, leaves UN Security
    Council, 220
manpower. See military manpower
Mao Zedong, 257
    disciple of Sun Tzu, 59
    encircle cities concept, 88
    guerrilla organizations of, 170,
        172
    strategic trailblazer, 253
    three-phase insurgent strategy,
        172–73
    writings reveal intentions, 27
Marcos, Ferdinand, and Huks, 185
Marighella, Carlos, on beneficial ter-
    rorist attributes, 194
maritime school of thought, 61
Marshall, Gen. George C.
    Congress waives eligibility re-
        quirements for, 50–51
    strategic trailblazer, 252
Marshall Plan, promotes postwar
    peace, 93
Massive Retaliation
    strategic shortcomings, 65
    tripwire featured, 66
Mau Mau, Kenyan insurgents, 187
mercenaries, value of, 241
Meyer, Gen. Edward C. (Shy), on
    "hollow" Army, 25

military bases, related to preparedness, 205
military doctrines, 300
  basic attributes, 60-61
  compared with policies, 47
  compatibility required, 101
military education. *See* strategic education
military functions. *See* military roles and functions
military manpower, preparedness of, 100, 101
military materiel, preparedness of, 100, 101
military missions, 40-41, 300
  intervention checklist, 286
  mission creep, 41
  See also military roles and functions
military objectives
  influence on preparedness, 102-3
  related to national security objectives, 35-36
  standards of success, 37-38
  See also national security objectives
military operations other than war, 300
  preparedness for, 99, 103-4
military policies
  brutality, 89-90, 174-75, 185-86
  conflict termination, 91-93
  erratic U.S. shifts, 86
  force vs. finesse, 85-86
  forward presence, 87
  offense vs. defense, 86-87
  power projection, 87-88
  risk avoidance, 90, 284
  War Powers Resolution, 90
  See also military strategies
military power, 300-301
  elements of, 23-25
  importance of will, 25
  in national interest, 15
  supports foreign policies, 52-53
military preparedness
  active/reserve relationships, 101
  elements of, 99
  future requirements for, 102, 106
  geographic influences on, 100
  materiel issues, 105-6

military operations other than war, 99, 103-4
  objectives influence, 102-3
  personnel issues, 104-5
  Principle of Deterrence, 74
  Principles of Preparedness, 99-102
  roles and functions influence, 99-100
  situations influence, 99
military roles and functions, 39, 40, 155-56, 300, 301
  air power, 156
  counterinsurgency, 188
  influence preparedness, 99-100
  synergistic attributes, 156
  See also military missions
military strategies, 291, 301
  active and reactive, 63
  arms control vs. arms competition, 64
  asymmetrical options, 65
  attrition, 63-64
  building blocks of, 59-61
  creative environments, 257-58
  direct and indirect, 62-63
  extremist strategies, 67
  Flexible Response inconsistencies, 66
  geographical influences, 62, 100
  mismatches, 65-67
  sequential and cumulative, 62
  strategic vs. tactical maneuvers, 88
  types described, 3-5
  See also military policies; strategic trailblazers; strategy
military tactics, 301
  compared with strategy, 4, 5, 88
military technologies, basic requirements, 101. *See also* technological warfare
Milosevic, Slobodan
  capitulates in Kosovo, 280
  disregards Rambouillet peace proposals, 278
  no plan to oust, 284
  objectives in Bosnia, 271
  resists secessions, 268
  revokes Kosovar autonomy, 268, 278

tried for war crimes, 282
  undeterred by bluster, 159
MIRVs, proliferation of, 64, 113
mission creep, in Somalia, 41
missions. *See* military missions
Mitchell, Brig. Gen. William (Billy), strategic trailblazer, 253, 254
Mobutu Sese Seko, impoverishes Congo, 17
Moluccan separatist hijackings, 199
Monroe Doctrine, regional center of gravity, 42-43
morality
  Machiavelli's views, 18, 59, 240
  in national security interest, 18
Moro, Aldo, assassination of, 197
multiple independently-targetable reentry vehicles (MIRVs), 64, 113
Mutual Assured Destruction, 73
  deterrent concept, 139
Mutual Force Reductions in Europe, 110

Napoleon Bonaparte
  on physical vs. moral factors, 84
  strategic trailblazer, 252
Nasser, Gamal Abdel
  Israeli dirty tricks against, 73
  nationalizes Suez Canal, 92
national security commitments, compared with policies, 47
national security interests, 5-6, 13, 301
  in Bosnia, 268, 271
  changeability of, 13-14
  coalitions, 239
  conflicts of interest, 18
  freedom of action, 16, 63-64, 82, 83
  geostrategic position, 17-18
  ideology, 17
  intervention checklist, 285-86
  in Kosovo, 278-79, 283
  morality, 18
  NATO's interest in oil, 159
  peace, 16, 93
  priorities, 13, 14
  prosperity, 17
  public support, 13
  stability, 16-17, 136, 138
  survival, 14-15

national security objectives, 302
arms control, 109, 115
in Bosnia, 271
centers of gravity, 7, 41–43
and conflict termination, 91, 92
contexts constrain, 35, 36
counterinsurgencies, 181
Eisenhower's directive, 37, 84
insurgent aims, 168
intervention checklist, 286
in Korean War, 82
in Kosovo, 278–79
limited war, 160
nonlethal warfare, 219–20
and preparedness, 102–3
Principle of War, 81–82
public opinion, 35
purposes and types, 35–36
standards of success, 37–38
typical examples, 36
victory, 38–39
World War II vs. Vietnam War, 84
national security policies, 47, 302
basic attributes, 60
Brezhnev Doctrine, 86, 173–74
casualty avoidance, 280, 284
civil-military, 49–51
counterterrorism, 206–7
cultural contexts, 48–49
foreign vs. domestic, 51–52
human rights, 18
intervention checklist, 286
limited war, 159–61
stability and change, 47–48
national security strategies. *See* grand strategy
national strategies, 3, 4, 302
National War College, first faculty, 259
national will, 25, 42, 84
NATO. *See* North Atlantic Treaty Organization
negotiations
counterinsurgencies, 190
guidelines, 115–116
Strategic Arms Limitation Talks, 110, 115, 116
Strategic Arms Reduction Talks, 116, 136
about Vietnam, 230

net assessments, 30
best balances defined, 157
purpose and types, 28, 29
second opinions preferable, 30
U.S. and Soviet, 156
New Left, 184
Nicaragua, Contras vs. Sandinistas, 174, 207, 243
Nixon, President Richard M.
1½ war requirement, 103
on burden-sharing, 244
force sufficiency, 139, 158
Vietnam policy, 48
nonlethal warfare, 302
increasing importance, 219
limitations, 220
objectives, 219–20
passive resistance as, 63
See also cybernetic warfare; economic warfare; political warfare; psychological warfare; technological warfare
Normandy invasion
Battle of Britain made possible, 157
pre-invasion deception, 76
North Atlantic Treaty Organization
admits former Warsaw Pact states, 241
air power restraints in Kosovo, 280, 284
burden-sharing, 244
Cold War deterrent policies, 53
Cold War reinforcement requirements, 66–67
Conventional Forces in Europe (CFE) Treaty, 112
defensive policy limitations, 86
exit strategy for Kosovo, 284
Flexible Response inconsistencies, 66
forward defense requirements, 88
inflexible plans for Kosovo, 283–84
interests in Bosnia, 268, 271
interests in oil, 159
nuclear shot across the bow, 75
policy options in Kosovo, 278–79
Rapacki Plan, 111

reliance on nuclear weapons, 157
theater nuclear bargaining chips, 116
treaty review requirements, 244–45
treaty terms, 241
U.S. vs. European interests, 239
North Korea, special operations forces, 25. *See also* Kim Il-Sung; Korean War
nuclear arms control
Anti-Ballistic Missile (ABM) Treaty, 113, 116
Baruch proposal, 111, 135–36
counting problems, 112
MIRVed Soviet ICBMs, 64, 113
nuclear-free zones, 111, 156
Strategic Arms Limitation Talks (SALT), 110, 112, 115, 116
Strategic Arms Reduction Talks (START), 116, 136
testing, 114
theater nuclear weapons, 110, 116
Nuclear Club, members, 123, 125. *See also* proliferation
nuclear deterrence
Cold War lessons, 140
disputed value of defense, 136–38
extended deterrence, 138
force-sizing standards, 139
maximum deterrence, 139
minimum deterrence, 138–39
Mutual Assured Destruction, 73, 139
obligatory objective, 136
retaliatory force composition, 139–40, 141
stability as key objective, 136, 138
See also nuclear warfare
nuclear warfare
bonus effects from bombers, 65
casualties, 133–34
civil defense, 142
collateral casualties and damage, 134
counterforce vs. countervalue targeting, 141
decapitation, 142

nuclear warfare, *continued*
  effects, 133–35
  first-strike policies, 140
  launch-on-warning policies,
    140–41
  Massive Retaliation, 65, 66
  missile gap (1960), 76
  NATO's reliance, 157
  response to biological warfare,
    148
  retaliatory force protection, 142
  second-strike policies, 140–141
  Strategic Defense Initiative, 128
  traditional warfare nexus, 161–62
  war termination, 142
  See also nuclear deterrence; nu-
    clear weapons
nuclear triad, 139–40, 141
nuclear weapons
  Hitler's program crippled, 129
  MIRVs complicate arms control,
    64, 113
  proliferation, 124–25
  research and development indica-
    tors, 126–27
  terrorism, 195
  U.S.-Soviet balance, 17

OAS, opposes Algerian independence, 49
Okamoto, Koso, 194
OODA loops, 230
OPEC oil embargo, 17
open cities, 161
"open skies" counterproliferation
  proposal, 128
Operation *Allied Force*, 279–80
operational tempos, 104
Oppenheimer, J. Robert
  quotation at Alamogordo, 125
  "scorpions in a bottle," 136
Organisation de l'Armée Secrète,
  opposes Algerian independence, 49
Organization of Petroleum Exporting Countries, oil embargo, 17
Osama bin Laden
  declares holy war, 193
  funds frozen, 223
  hideout attacked, 212
  terrorist activities, 22

OSS Detachment 101, in Burma,
  176

pacification, as counterinsurgency
  technique, 189–90
Palestine Liberation Organization,
  hijackings, 198–99, 214
Palmerston, Henry John Temple, on
  permanent interests, 13–14
Panmunjom, negotiations at, 230
Partial Test Ban treaty, 114
Patton, General George S., Jr.
  breakout from Normandy beach-
    head, 84
  deception before Normandy inva-
    sion, 221
peace
  preparedness promotes, 74
  as national security interest, 16
  war termination terms influence,
    92–93
peaceful coexistence, Soviet policy,
  16, 60
peacekeeping, 303
  in Bosnia, 268, 272
  deterrent technique, 75
peacemaking, 303
  in Bosnia, 273
  in Kosovo, 279–80
Pearl Harbor attack, deception in,
  221
personnel. *See* military manpower
Philippines, counterinsurgency in,
  184–85
Phoenix counterinsurgency program, 186
PLO hijackings, 198–99, 214
political warfare
  counterterrorism, 211
  deception, 221
  options, 220–22
  Soviet-German nonaggression
    pact, 220–21
  Soviets lose UN veto, 220
  war termination terms, 91–93
posse comitatus, U.S. legal restraint, 206
Powell, Gen. Colin L., opposes intervention in Bosnia, 53
power. *See* military power; national
  power
power projection, 158–59, 303

preemptive and preventive wars,
  303
  causes, 72
  counterterrorism, 207
  nuclear inadvisability, 140
preparedness. *See* military preparedness
prepositioned stocks, pluses and minuses, 87
presence, deterrent value of, 87,
  158
preventive wars. *See* preemptive
  and preventive wars
Principle of Military Necessity, 212
Principles of Deterrence, 73–75
Principles of Preparedness, 99–102
Principles of War, 81–85
proliferation
  causes, 123–24
  delivery vehicles, 124, 126
  NBCR weapons, 124–26
  status in 2001, 124
  See also counterproliferation
propaganda, black, gray, and white,
  227–28
psychological operations, 227, 304
  audiences, 227, 228
  democratic restrictions on, 230
  in Haiti, 103–4
  information, 229
  See also propaganda; psychologi-
    cal warfare
psychological warfare
  counterterrorism, 211
  disinformation, 76, 83, 229–30
  negotiations, 230
  purposes, 227
  rumor campaigns, 228
  techniques, 228–29
  themes, 228
  See also propaganda; psychologi-
    cal operations
public opinion
  intervention checklist, 286–87
  U.S. during Vietnam War, 35
  underpins objectives, 35
Putin, Vladimir, defers START, 136
Pyrrhic victory, 304
  nuclear war, 14
  Vietnam, 39
  World War I, 81
  See also victory

Qadhafi, Mu'ammar al-, and terrorism, 213
Qiao Liang, Col., on nonlethal warfare, 219
qualitative attributes
difficult to assess, 30
factors, 23–25
value of obsolescent forces, 29

radiological weapons
proliferation, 125
terrorism, 195
Rambouillet peace proposals, for Kosovo, 278
ransoms, for hostages, 197–98, 200
Rapacki, Adam, nuclear-free Europe proposal, 111
rationality of irrationality, deterrent technique, 77
reactive strategies, 63
readiness, 99, 304. See also military preparedness
Reagan, President Ronald
disregards War Powers Resolution, 90
doctrine, 37–38
forbids assassination, 90
Star Wars program, 225
unilateral nuclear reductions, 110
Red Brigades (Italian), rise and fall, 213
Red Square (Moscow), unauthorized aircraft lands in, 235
reforms, counterinsurgency technique, 183–84
refugees, Bosnia and Kosovo, 268, 282
Reinhart, General Klaus, occupation of Kosovo, 284–85
resistance, 174–75
World War II, France, 168
World War II, Yugoslavia, 188
See also insurgencies
resource allocation, 7–8
intervention checklist, 286
related to preparedness, 102
See also ends and means
revolutionary warfare. See insurgencies
risks
calculated risks, 294

proclivities to accept, 7–8, 27
U.S. avoidance policies, 90, 284
Rogers, Gen. Bernard W., on Cold War balance, 157
roles. See military roles and functions
Roosevelt, Franklin D., deters chemical warfare, 77
Rowny, Lt. Gen. Edward L., START negotiator, 116
in Kosovo, 278, 279, 280
and Rambouillet proposal, 278
See also Soviet Union

sabotage, counterproliferation option, 129–30
Saddam Hussein
as example of catalytic conflict, 72
defies UN inspection, 43
Iraqi interests, 14
Iraqi Liberation Act targets, 173
as kingpin, 43
proliferates weapons of mass destruction, 124, 125, 126, 129, 130
under sanctions, 224
undeterred after Desert Storm, 158
Saint-Just, Louis, justifies violence, 193
SALT. See Strategic Arms Limitation Talks
sanctions
Cold War use, 222
as economic warfare tool, 222–24
Sandinistas
defeat Somoza, battle Contras, 174
Soviet-Cuban support for, 243
See also Contras
schools. See strategic education; strategic schools of thought
Schwarzkopf, Gen. H. Norman, coalition commander, 242–43
Scipio Africanus
defeats Hannibal, 82
shifts strategic center of gravity, 42, 89
search and destroy, as counterinsurgency technique, 186–87
sieges, as attrition warfare, 88

sequential strategies, 62
Serbia
capitulates in Kosovo, 280
inherits Tito's armed forces, 272
interests and objectives in Bosnia, 268–71
servicewomen, influence on combat capabilities, 105
SFOR. See Stabilization Force
Shah Mohammed Reza Pahlavi, revolutionaries oust, 172–73
Skorzeny, Capt. Otto, World War II operations, 85–86
SLA. See Symbionese Liberation Army
Somalia, mission creep in, 41
Somoza, Anastasio, Sandinistas oust, 174
South Korea
forces in Vietnam, 499
U.S. restricts offensive weaponry of, 64
U.S. forces as tripwire, 76
Soviet Union
civil control of armed forces, 49–50
loses veto power in UN Security Council, 220
technological espionage, 226
Special Air Service (SAS), hostage rescue, 211
special operations forces, military operations other than war, 103–4
special operations school of thought, 62
Spetsnaz, quality, 25
Sputnik I, 16, 83
stability
national security interest, 16–17
objective of deterrence, 136, 138
Stabilization Force
areas of responsibility, 276
replaces IFOR in Bosnia, 275
Stalin, Joseph
nonaggression pact with Hitler, 220–21
nonlethal warfare successes, 219
on military power, 53
purges senior officers, 49–50
second front as horizontal escalation, 89

Stalin, Joseph, *continued*
  spurns Baruch proposal, 111
  "Uncle Joe" as coalition partner,
    239
START. *See* Strategic Arms Reduction Talks
Star Wars, 225. *See also* Strategic
  Defense Initiative
Strategic Arms Limitation Talks
  allowed force increases, 110
  complex counting rules, 112
  negotiating teams, 115
  Soviets disregard linkage, 116
Strategic Arms Reduction Talks
  prospects, 136
  Soviet views, 116
  successes, 136
strategic centers of gravity, 305
  basic purpose, 7
  cities, 41–42
  coalitions, 43
  continents, 42–43
  disbelievers, 43
  hearts and minds, 42
  in space, 43
  kingpins, 42
  Monroe Doctrine, 42–43
strategic concepts, 59, 61, 305
Strategic Defense Initiative, first-
  strike implications, 87, 128
strategic education
  deficiencies, 258
  National Center for Strategic Studies, 258–59
strategic principles, 60, 305
  See also Principles of Deterrence;
    Principles of Preparedness;
    Principles of War
strategic research, 260–61
  See also strategic trailblazers
strategic schools of thought
  cybernetic warfare, 230–31
  land, sea, air, and space, 61
  special operations, 62
strategic theories, 59, 60, 306
  chaos and complexity, 261
  contributors, 59, 251, 253
strategic trailblazers
  common characteristics, 251
  coveted characteristics, 253–54
  creative environments, 257–58
  role models, 251–53

strategy, 2–3
  assumptions influence, 7, 64–65,
    260, 293
  compared with tactics, 4, 5
  formulation described, 7
  main aim, 9
  six-step process, 5–8
  times, places influence, 7
  See also grand strategy; military
    strategies; national strategies;
    theater strategies; tactics
Sudan, suspected terrorist site attacked, 212
sufficiency, force-sizing standard,
    139
Sultan, Prince Khalid bin
  coalition commander, 243
  limits U.S. base rights, 158
Sun Tzu
  attack enemy's strategy, 65
  avoid urban combat, 141
  on deception, 76, 221
  Mao's mentor, 172
  offense vs. defense, 86
  net assessments, 28
  Principle of Concentration, 83
  strategic trailblazer, 251
  value of initiative, 63
  win without fighting, 38, 85
surprise, Principle of War, 83
surrender, conducive conditions,
    91–92
surrogates
  counterproxy warfare, 242
  value of, 241–42
survival, national security interest,
    14–15
sustainability, 99, 306
Symbionese Liberation Army, 197–
    98, 213

tactics. *See* military tactics
technological warfare
  dangers of overdependence on,
    227
  espionage, 226
  forecasting, 106, 224
  high costs, 226
  how to control, 114
  progress in, 225–26
  purposes, 224

whether, when, what to control,
    113
termination. *See* conflict termination
terrorism, 306
  abductions, 197–98, 200, 213
  agro-terrorism, 196
  assassinations, 42, 90, 197
  atypical terrorists, 193–94
  biological warfare, 195–96
  cellular organizations, 171, 194
  chemical warfare, 196
  demolitions, 199
  hijacking, 198–99
  hostage-taking, 198
  Khobar Towers attack, 199
  nightmare scenarios, 200
  nuclear weapons, 195
  purpose, 88, 193
  preferred weapons, 194–95
  self-restraint, 195
  sponsorship and support, 200
  tactics, 197–99
  targets, 196–97, 208–10
  textbooks for, 195
  at World Trade Center (1993),
    199
  See also counterterrorism
theater nuclear weapons, and traditional warfare, 110, 116, 162
theater strategies, 4–5
theories. *See* strategic theories
threats, 306
  assessments, 30
  intelligence estimates, 6–7
  intervention checklist, 285–286
  key questions, 21
Threshold Test Ban Treaty, 114
Tiananmen Square, failed rebellion,
    169
Time, Principle of War, 85
Tito (Josip Broz)
  caches weapons, 273
  forms modern Yugoslavia, 268
Toffler, Alvin and Heidi, strategic research, 260
Tojo, Hieki, overcommits Japanese
  Armed Forces, 157
Tonkin Gulf Resolution, 35
traditional warfare
  compared with counterinsurgencies, 182

"conventional" a misnomer, 155
deterrence, 156–59
forward presence, 158
insurgents assist, 175–76
limited wars, 159–61
net assessments, 156–57
nuclear nexus, 161–62
power projection, 158–59
roles and functions, 155–56, 162
Treaty of Versailles
    Hitler repudiates, 117, 121
    terminates World War I, 221
tripwires, deterrent technique,
    76–77
Truman, President Harry S
    defends South Korea, 75
    objectives in Korea, 27, 160
    sacks Gen. MacArthur, 39
Twining, Gen. Nathan F.
    decries limited war policies, 159
    nuclear strikes against North Ko-
        rea, 160
    regrets nuclear test moratorium,
        114

U.N. See United Nations
Uncertainty, Principle of, 73
unifying school of strategic
    thought, 62
United Nations
    arms embargo against Yugoslavia,
        272
    arms embargo against Serbia, Ko-
        sovo, 278
    assists war termination, 92
    coalition in Korea, 160, 220
    guarantees humanitarian ship-
        ments in Bosnia, 272
    interests in Bosnia, 268–69
    Kosovo refugees, 282
    no exit strategy for Kosovo, 284
    objectives in Bosnia, 271
    objectives in Kosovo, 278, 280
    peacekeeping a specialty, 75

sanctions against Afghanistan,
    North Korea, and Iraq, 223–24
War Crimes Tribunal, 576
United Nations Protection Force
    established, 268
    safe havens, 273
    vulnerabilities, 272
UNPROFOR. See United Nations
    Protection Force
undergrounds, organizations and
    functions, 170
unity of command, Principle of
    War, 84

Van Riper, Lt. Gen. Paul, on casu-
    alty avoidance, 284
verification, arms control require-
    ment, 116–17
vertical escalation, 89
victory
    Churchill on, 14
    MacArthur's view, 38–39
    Pyrrhic, 39, 81, 304
    values of, 38–39
Vidal, Gen. Emilio Mola, Spanish
    Fifth Columns, 175–76
Vietnam War
    competing objectives, 39
    costly communist strategy, 66
    horizontal escalation, 89
    negotiating techniques, 230
    phoenix program, 186
    strategic center of gravity, 42
    time favored communists, 85
    U.S. policies, 48, 53

Walesa, Lech, 36
Wang Xiansui, on nonlethal war-
    fare, 219
War Crimes Tribunal, U.N. estab-
    lishes, 282
War Powers Resolution, causes and
    effects, 90

war termination. See conflict termi-
    nation
Washington, President George,
    quantity vs. quality, 100
Washington Naval Treaty, 110, 113
weapons of mass destruction
    defined, 123, 307
    program indicators, 126–27
    proliferation, 124–26
Weinberger, Caspar W., interven-
    tion rules, 91, 285
Westmoreland, Gen. William C.
    fuzzy objectives, 84
    on national will, 39
    search and destroy, 186–87
White House, unauthorized landing
    on lawn, 235
Wilson, President Woodrow
    on general disarmament, 64
    League of Nations, 238
WMD. See weapons of mass de-
    struction
women. See servicewomen
World Disarmament Conference,
    failure of, 110
World Trade Center, terrorist attack
    (1993), 199
Wylie, Rear Adm. J. C.
    importance of contingency plans,
        283
    strategic theory, 219

Yugoslavia
    cultural crazy quilts, 267–68
    German vs. insurgent force ra-
        tios, World War II, 188
    secessions from, 268
    successive rulers, 267
    Tito's federation, 268
    See also Bosnia-Herzegovina;
        Kosovo

Zhukov, Marshal Georgy
    insurgents assist, 176
    Khrushchev sacks, 50

About the Author

Colonel Collins, a Distinguished Visiting Research Fellow at National Defense University, began to build a solid foundation for *Military Strategy* in 1942, when he enlisted in the U.S. Army as a private. He prepared contingency plans for the 82d Airborne Division, XVIII Airborne Corps, Special Operations Task Force Europe, and Military Assistance Command Vietnam that focused on the Middle East, Cuba, Soviet-occupied Europe, and Southeast Asia in the 1950s and 1960s. All involved close collaboration with counterparts in the Navy, Air Force, and Marine Corps. Colonel Collins culminated his military career as Director of Military Strategy Studies, then as Chief of a Strategic Research Group at the National War College from 1968 until 1972. He thereafter furnished Congress with wide-ranging politico-military assessments for twenty-four more years as Senior Specialist in National Defense at the Congressional Research Service, with particular attention to the U.S.-Soviet military balance and strategic options. Flag officers in every U.S. military service, foreign counterparts, members of the news media, defense industries, think tanks, and academicians frequently solicited Colonel Collins's opinions throughout his lengthy tenure on Capitol Hill. He continues to analyze and write about military matters in retirement. He lives in Alexandria, Virginia.